T0250705

Lecture Notes in Computer Science 3205

Commenced Publication in 1973
Founding and Former Series Editors:
Gerhard Goos, Juris Hartmanis, and Jan van Leeuwen

Nigel Davies   Elizabeth Mynatt
Itiro Siio (Eds.)

UbiComp 2004: Ubiquitous Computing

6th International Conference
Nottingham, UK, September 7-10, 2004
Proceedings

 Springer

Volume Editors

Nigel Davies
Lancaster University, Computing Department
Lancaster, LA1 4YR, UK
E-mail: nigel@comp.lancs.ac.uk

Elizabeth Mynatt
Georgia Institute of Technology
College of Computing
Atlanta, GA 30332, USA
E-mail: mynatt@cc.gatech.edu

Itiro Siio
Tamagawa University, Faculty of Engineering
6-1-1, Tamagawagakuen, Machidashi, 194-8610 Tokyo, Japan
E-mail: siio@eng.tamagawa.ac.jp

Library of Congress Control Number: 2004111706

CR Subject Classification (1998): C.2, C.3, D.2, D.4, H.4, H.5, K.4

ISSN 0302-9743
ISBN 3-540-22955-8 Springer Berlin Heidelberg New York

Springer is a part of Springer Science+Business Media

springeronline.com

© Springer-Verlag Berlin Heidelberg 2004
Printed in Germany

Typesetting: Camera-ready by author, data conversion by Boller Mediendesign
Printed on acid-free paper   SPIN: 11313861   06/3142   5 4 3 2 1 0

Preface

Welcome to the proceedings of UbiComp 2004.

In recent years the ubiquitous computing community has witnessed a significant growth in the number of conferences in the area, each with its own distinctive characteristics. For UbiComp these characteristics have always included a high-quality technical program and associated demonstrations and posters that cover the full range of research being carried out under the umbrella of ubiquitous computing. Ours is a broad discipline and UbiComp aims to be an inclusive forum that welcomes submissions from researchers with many different backgrounds. This year we received 145 submissions. Of these we accepted 26, an acceptance rate of just under 18%. Of course acceptance rate is simply a measure of selectivity rather than quality and we were particularly pleased this year to note that we had a large number of high-quality submissions from which to assemble the program for 2004.

The broad nature of ubiquitous computing research makes reviewing UbiComp submissions a particular challenge. This year we adopted a new process for review and selection that has, we hope, resulted in all authors obtaining extremely detailed feedback on their submission whether or not it was accepted for publication. We believe the process enabled us to assemble the best possible program for delegates at the conference. If you submitted a paper, we hope that you benefited from the feedback that your peers have provided, and if you attended UbiComp 2004 we hope that you enjoyed the technical program. For those of you interested in this process, it is briefly described at the end of the preface.

Of course, whatever the process adopted for reviewing it will fail without a hard-working technical program committee. We were fortunate to assemble a truly world-class committee that worked exceptionally hard under tight deadlines to produce very high quality reviews. In addition to the core technical Program Committee, we also created a pool of external reviewers who each reviewed approximately four paper submissions. This allowed us to draw on the community to obtain expert reviews for all papers and to add new insights to the reviews created by the Program Committee. We would like to thank all those who took the time to review submissions for UbiComp, whether as a member of the Program Committee or as an external reviewer — your hard work and diligence was much appreciated.

We would like to take this opportunity to thank (in no particular order) the numerous people who helped to make this such an enjoyable job: the General Chair, Tom Rodden, for offering us the opportunity to serve as Program Co-chairs for the conference, the Publicity Chair, Fahd Al-Bin-Ali, for helping to ensure that we received a large number of submissions, Elaine May Huang for, among a host of other jobs, her work in processing all of the information needed to assemble the reviewer pool, Craig Morrall for dealing with the huge number of papers that had printing issues or were not properly anonymized when first submitted, and Hazel Glover for handling the preparation of the camera-ready version of these proceedings. We would also like to thank Henning Schulzrinne and the EDAS team who patiently answered all of our questions whatever the time of day — if only all on-line support systems were as responsive!

Finally, thanks must go to all of the authors who entrusted their work to us and to everyone who attended Ubicomp 2004 and enjoyed the program we helped to assemble. We hope you enjoyed and benefited from your time in Nottingham.

July 2004   Nigel Davies, Beth Mynatt and Itiro Siio

UbiComp 2004 Paper Review Process

The review process for UbiComp 2004 was divided into three phases plus the Program Committee meeting and paper shepherding:

Phase 1: Quick Reject and Reviewer Nomination

All papers submitted were assigned a Lead Program Committee (PC) and second PC reviewer, both selected from the Program Committee (PC). These PC members in turn nominated two additional reviewers from a pool of external reviewers suggested by members of the PC and vetted by the PC chairs. Where the PC members considered that the paper was clearly not going to be accepted to UbiComp or was wildly out of scope the two PC members could nominate the paper as a "Quick Reject". In this case the decision was checked by the PC chairs and then returned to the authors with just two reviews. This feature enabled us to concentrate effort on the papers with the best chances of being accepted.

Phase 2: Reviews

Once Phase I was completed, the PC chairs processed all of the papers, allocating external reviewers based on the selections suggested by the PC members in Phase I and adjusting to ensure load balancing across external reviewers. Thus each paper received four reviews — two from PC members and two from external reviewers.

Phase 3: On-line Discussion

After all of the reviews were received the Lead PC member for each paper coordinated discussion among the reviewers to reach a consensus as to the technical merit of the paper. When necessary, the reviewers could ask for additional reviews to be carried out and some papers ended up with several additional reviews.

PC Meeting

In contrast to previous years, we decided to hold a single PC meeting rather than the split-site format that had been used in previous years. Attendance was usually a condition of acceptance to serve on the PC and almost all of the PC attended the meeting (a very small number had to cancel). At the two-day meeting in Atlanta, GA, the committee examined all papers above a threshold and arrived at the final program.

Shepherding

To help authors interpret their reviews, all of the papers were allocated shepherds who guided the authors through the final revisions of their papers. This process helped considerably in a number of cases and ensured that the papers in these proceedings were revised to reflect the feedback provided to the authors by the PC.

Conference Organization

Organizers

Conference Chair
Tom Rodden — University of Nottingham (UK)

Program Chairs
Nigel Davies — Lancaster University (UK)
University of Arizona (USA)
Elizabeth Mynatt — Georgia Institute of Technology (USA)
Itiro Siio — Tamagawa University (Japan)

Demonstrations Chair
Lars Erik Holmquist — Viktoria Institute (Sweden)

Posters Chair
James Scott — Intel Research, Cambridge (UK)

Videos Chair
Michael Beigl — TecO, University of Karlsruhe (Germany)

Doctoral Colloquium Chair
Gregory Abowd — Georgia Institute of Technology (USA)

Workshops Chair
Mike Fraser — University of Bristol (UK)

Panels Chair
Matthew Chalmers — University of Glasgow (UK)

Student Volunteers Chairs
Elaine May Huang — Georgia Institute of Technology (USA)
Holger Schnädelbach — University of Nottingham (UK)

Treasurer
Hazel Glover — University of Nottingham (UK)

Local Arrangements Chair
Hazel Glover — University of Nottingham (UK)

Publicity
Fahd Al-Bin-Ali — University of Arizona (USA)

Webmaster
James Mathrick — University of Nottingham (UK)

Sponsors

Corporate Benefactors	Intel Corporation
	Nokia Corporation
Corporate Sponsors	Fuji Xerox Palo Alto Laboratory
	Microsoft Research
	Samsung Advanced Institute of Technology
	SMART Technologies

Supporting Organizations

UbiComp 2004 is supported by the Equator Interdisciplinary Research Collaboration together with the Engineering and Physical Sciences Research Council (EPSRC) and also enjoys in-cooperation status with the following special interest groups of the Association for Computing Machinery (ACM):

> SIGCHI (Computer-Human Interaction)
> SIGMOBILE
> SIGSOFT (Software Engineering)
> SIGWEB

Program Committee

Gregory Abowd	Georgia Institute of Technology (USA)
Michael Beigl	TecO, University of Karlsruhe (Germany)
Gaetano Borriello	University of Washington and Intel Research Seattle (USA)
Keith Edwards	Palo Alto Research Center (USA)
Ken Fishkin	Intel Research Seattle (USA)
Armando Fox	Stanford University (USA)
Alois Ferscha	Universität Wien (Austria)
Rebecca Grinter	Palo Alto Research Centre (USA)
Bill Gaver	Royal College of Art (UK)
Hans-Werner Gellersen	Lancaster University (UK)
Beverly Harrison	IBM Almaden Research Centre (USA)
Eric Horvitz	Microsoft Research (USA)
Scott Hudson	Carnegie Mellon University (USA)
Stephen Intille	Massachusetts Institute of Technology (USA)
Marc Langheinrich	ETH Zurich (Switzerland)
Toshiyuki Masui	AIST (Japan)
Chris Schmandt	Massachusetts Institute of Technology (USA)
Albrecht Schmidt	University of Munich (Germany)
Yasuyuki Sumim	Kyoto University (Japan)
Hide Tokuda	Keio University (Japan)

Reviewers

Mark Ackerman	University of Michigan (USA)
Fahd Al-Bin-Ali	University of Arizona (USA)
Yuji Ayatsuka	Sony Computer Science Laboratories (Japan)
Stavros Antifakos	ETH Zurich (Switzerland)
Anand Balachandran	Intel Research Seattle (USA)
Rafael Ballagas	RWTH Aachen University (Germany)
Russell Beale	University of Birmingham (UK)
Christian Becker	University of Stuttgart (Germany)

James "Bo" Begole	Sun Labs, Europe (France)
Alastair R Beresford	University of Cambridge (UK)
Mark Billinghurst	HIT Lab NZ, University of Canterbury (New Zealand)
Juergen Bohn	ETH Zurich (Switzerland)
Michael Boyle	University of Calgary (Canada)
Matthew Chalmers	University of Glasgow (UK)
Keith Cheverst	Lancaster University (UK)
Sunny Consolvo	Intel Research Seattle (USA)
George Coulouris	University of Cambridge (UK)
Andy Crabtree	University of Nottingham (UK)
Anind K Dey	Intel Research Berkeley (USA)
Tom Djajadiningrat	University of Southern Denmark (Denmark) and Eindhoven University of Technology (Netherlands)
Paul Dourish	University of California, Irvine (USA)
Thomas Erickson	IBM T J Watson Research Center (USA)
Morten Fjeld	Chalmers University of Technology (UK)
Christian Floerkemeier	ETH Zurich (Switzerland)
Adrian Friday	Lancaster University (UK)
Masaaki Fukumoto	NTT DoCoMo Multimedia Laboratories (Japan)
Saul Greenberg	University of Calgary (Canada)
Robert Grimm	New York University (USA)
William G Griswold	UC San Diego (USA)
Robert Harle	University of Cambridge (UK)
Paul J M Havinga	University of Twente (Netherlands)
Mike Hazas	Lancaster University (UK)
Jeffrey Hightower	University of Washington (USA)
Lars Erik Holmquist	Viktoria Institute (Sweden)
Brad Johanson	Tidebreak Inc (USA)
Henry Kautz	University of Washington (USA)
Scott Klemmer	UC Berkeley EECS (USA)
Gerd Kortuem	Lancaster University (UK)
Gabriele Kotsis	Johannes Kepler University Linz (Austria)
Antonio Krüger	Saarland University (Germany)
John Krumm	Microsoft Research (USA)
Kristof Van Laerhoven	Lancaster University (UK)
Spyros Lalis	University of Thessaly (Greece)
Seon-Woo Lee	Hallym University (Korea)
Darren Leigh	Mitsubishi Electric Research Laboratories (USA)
Joshua Lifton	MIT Media Lab (USA)
Kenji Mase	Nagoya University/ATR (Japan)
Rene Mayrhofer	Johannes Kepler University Linz (Austria)
Margaret Morris	Intel Research (USA)
Max Mühlhäuser	TU Darmstadt (Germany)
Tatsuo Nakajima	Waseda University (Japan)

Table of Contents

The CareNet Display: Lessons Learned from an In Home Evaluation of an Ambient Display

Sunny Consolvo, Peter Roessler, and Brett E. Shelton

Intel Research Seattle
1100 NE 45th Street, 6th Floor
Seattle, WA 98105, USA
sunny.consolvo@intel.com,{roessler,bshelton}@intel-research.net

Abstract. This paper addresses users' experiences with an ambient display for the home. We present the design and *in situ* evaluation of the CareNet Display, an ambient display that helps the local members of an elder's care network provide her day-to-day care. We describe the CareNet Display's design and discuss results of a series of in home deployments with users. We report how the CareNet Display was used and its impact on elders and their care network members. Based on our findings, we offer lessons about how ambient display technologies could be improved to further benefit this growing user community.

1   Introduction

Though the potential benefits of ambient displays have been discussed [4,7,8,10,11,14], little has been shared about users' experiences with deployments of actual ambient displays in the home environment. Previously, we introduced the area of Computer-Supported Coordinated Care (CSCC) [3] which described the many people involved in the care of an elder and how technology might help them. This paper, however, focuses on the details of our first CSCC prototype, the CareNet Display. The CareNet Display is an interactive digital picture frame that augments a photograph of an elder with information about her daily life and provides mechanisms to help the local members of her care network coordinate care-related activities. We describe the CareNet Display's design and its deployments in the homes of several members of four different care networks for three weeks at a time; in these deployments, the data shown on the CareNet Display was collected from daily interviews with the elders and their caregivers. From our findings of these deployments, we suggest how CSCC tools can help elders and the members of their care networks. We also discuss the lessons we learned about the use of an ambient display in the home that we believe can be of benefit to other designers.

Because caring for an elder is often a secondary, yet important focus for most care network members, the nature of ambient displays appears to offer a good solution. This idea was previously explored by the Digital Family Portrait project [14] from the perspective of offering *peace of mind* to *distant* family members who are concerned for an elder. In our research, we are targeting the *local* members of an elder's care network who are responsible for providing the elder's *day-to-day care*. This change

N. Davies et al. (Eds.): UbiComp 2004, LNCS 3205, pp. 1-17, 2004.

in focus resulted in our design sharing much more detailed and potentially sensitive information about the elder, and in some cases, other network members.

In this paper, we discuss the design and *in situ* evaluation of the CareNet Display. We share many findings, including details of how it was used in the home. We then offer considerations for the design of ambient displays for the home and suggest ways in which ambient displays could be used to further benefit this growing community.

2   Design of the CareNet Display

For readers who are not familiar with Computer-Supported Coordinated Care [3], we offer a brief background. Specifically, we discuss the local members of the care network who provide an elder's day-to-day care; these members are the target users for the CareNet Display prototype. We then describe the CareNet Display's design.

2.1   Background on Care Networks for Elders

Our previous eldercare research [3] explored the many people who provide an elder with the care she needs to remain at home. These people – often family, friends, and neighbors of the elder – comprise her *care network*. Paid help, such as professional caregivers, doctors, nurses, pharmacists, and house cleaners, may also be involved. Care network members – particularly the family, friends, and neighbors – face many challenges. For several of these members, caring for the elder is an important but secondary focus, as they have their own families, careers, and problems to manage.

Care network members generally fall into one of three categories, based on how providing care impacts their lives: drastic life changer, significant contributor, or peripherally involved member. The *drastic life changer* has made major changes to her own life to care for the elder. This often involves sacrificing a career, hobbies, and sometimes family. There is usually one drastic life changer per care network, often the elder's spouse, child, or a professional caregiver. Caring for the elder is typically a primary focus for the drastic life changer. The *significant contributor* provides regular care for the elder; this care has a noticeable impact on the significant contributor's life, but she is still able to maintain her own life as a primary focus. There are usually at least a few significant contributors in a network, often the elder's nearby children and close friends. *Peripherally involved* members provide care that is meaningful for the elder, but is usually sporadic social and home maintenance types of care. For the peripherally involved member, providing care generally has minimal impact on her own life. These members are often children who live at a distance, grandchildren, friends, and neighbors.

Technology can help the various members of an elder's care network. Because caring for an elder is often a secondary focus for so many members, ambient display technologies may offer a solution. The idea of using ambient displays was reinforced by the positive feedback from the Digital Family Portrait project.

2.2   The CareNet Display: Target Users and Design

The CareNet Display's target users are the *local* members of an elder's care network who provide her day-to-day care; the elder does not use the display. Most users are aged 40-65, however some could be teenagers and others in the elder's age group. Comfort and experience with technology vary greatly among users. More than one member of a care network would have a CareNet Display — probably at least the *drastic life changers* and *significant contributors*. Most users will use it at home.

The CareNet Display has two basic modes of use: ambient and interactive. The main screen operates like an ambient display, where the user can get a general idea of the elder's condition in passing. Each of the seven main icon types – meals, medications, outings, activities, mood, falls, and calendar – change to convey high-level status (*e.g.*, everything is okay, something unexpected happened, the system is not working). In many cases, the display shows multiple icons of the same type (*e.g.*, three meal icons are used to represent breakfast, lunch, and dinner). The display's interactive quality allows the user to "dig deeper" by touching icons. When the user touches an icon, the photo of the elder is replaced with details for that event (*e.g.*, the morning medications view shares *when* the elder took morning medications, *what* she took, and *if* anything unexpected happened; it also allows network members to add a note to the event). Five-day trend views for the event types are available (**Figure 1**). The user also has access to events from previous days. We chose to include *seven* types of information largely due to considerations of usefulness and memory capacity. Much fewer than seven and the users would not get enough information; more than seven might result in information overload for some users. This, in addition to "Miller's Magic Number of Seven Plus or Minus Two" [12], resulted in our choosing seven types of information for the first version of the CareNet Display prototype.

The data provided in the CareNet Display would be collected by sensors and people, where "people" is the elder and/or certain network members. For instance, to help coordinate care-related activities, a user-editable calendar is provided that includes the elder's appointments and transportation needs (*e.g.*, users may sign up to provide transportation or add/edit an appointment), while sensors may be used to detect which medications the elder took [6]. Because this was an early deployment and one of the goals was to inform sensor design, we used people, not sensors, to collect the information. However, we spoke with other researchers at our lab who were developing the types of sensors we imagined using to ensure that the type and level of detail we collected were reasonable for sensors in the near future.

The types of information shared through the display were chosen based on roundtable discussions we conducted with 17 care network members in summer 2003 [16]. During the discussions, participants rated 20 types of information that they wanted to know about the elder (see Table 1). These 20 types were identified through interviews conducted at the beginning of our research [15]. Because we would have to collect the information about elders through frequent daily phone calls (further discussed in section 3.2), we chose the top seven types of information we could reliably get from elders and their caregivers. For example, though *disease-specific measurements* ranked #3, many elders do not take these measurements frequently enough for us to have collected accurate data for the deployments.

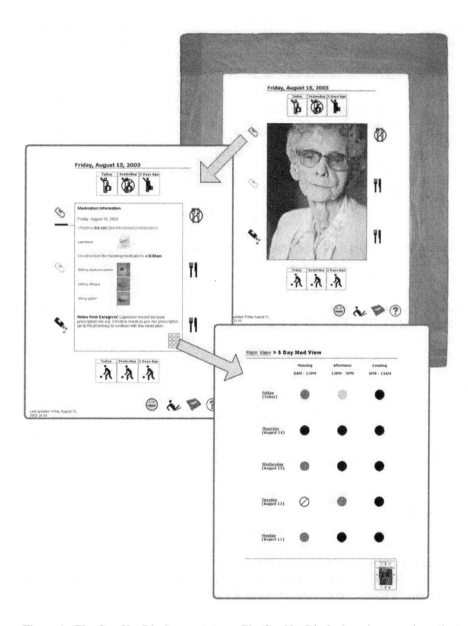

Figure 1. The CareNet Display prototype. The CareNet Display's main screen is on the top right. Users can get an overall picture of the elder's condition while passing by, or interact with the display by touching the icons which represent seven types of events—medications, outings, meals, activities, mood, falls, and calendar. On the left is the "morning medication" detail screen. Users can go from an event detail (such as morning medications) to a 5-day trend view (such as the medications trend shown on the bottom). From the trend view, users can return to individual events or the main screen overviews from previous days

Table 1. Ranking of the types of information care network members want to know about elders, based on results of a card sorting exercise. The information types in bold and followed by a "•" were those used by the CareNet Display. *Distance walked* and *Dressing* tied for #17

1.	**falls •**	11.	visits
2.	**meals •**	12.	weight
3.	disease-specific measurements	13.	water intake
4.	**medications •**	14.	messaging
5.	vitals	15.	bathing
6.	**mood •**	16.	car trips
7.	**calendar •**	17.	distance walked
8.	household needs	17.	dressing
9.	**activities •**	18.	phone calls
10.	**outings •**	19.	toilet use

Because the CareNet Display shares potentially sensitive information about the elder, it is designed to give the elder some control over her information. When the display is set up, the elder chooses which user can see which types of information, for example, it is possible that not all display users would see medications. Once permission has been granted to a user, the elder still has the opportunity to "not share" an event's update. However, if the elder's cognitive abilities are compromised, this control could be given to someone else, for example, her power of attorney.

Once we felt we had a good understanding of the needs of this population and the type of design that might work for them, we conducted a series of *in situ* deployments. This was particularly important, considering the sensitive nature of the types of information we planned to share through the CareNet Display. We also had to investigate how sharing this information among network members would impact the elder's care and the lives of the network members. We built three prototypes of the CareNet Display to deploy in the homes of target users for three weeks at a time to see what impact it would have on elders and the members of their care networks.

3   Details of the *In Situ* Deployments

To test the hypothesis that ambient displays can positively impact the local members of an elder's care network, we conducted a series of three-week long *in situ* deployments of the CareNet Display prototype. The deployments were conducted from September to December 2003 by members of the research team. In this section, we discuss the profiles of the participants and details of the deployments.

3.1   Participant Profiles

Members of four different care networks of elders who live at home and require regular care participated in our CareNet Display deployments. For each care network, the elder and at least two members not living with her (or each other) participated. Participants were recruited by the research team who used a variety of methods:

giving talks at geriatric care networking conferences, placing posters in senior centers, and working with local eldercare experts. Participants were (see Table 2):

- 4 elders, three female, who live at home and receive regular care. All live in the greater Seattle area; the females live alone. Ages ranged from 80-91; and
- 9 members, five female, of 4 different care networks. Participants live in the greater Seattle area and not with the elder or each other. Ages ranged from 51-65.

In most cases, other members of the participants' households – *i.e.*, children and partners/spouses of the participants – who were peripherally involved members of the elders' care networks also provided feedback about the CareNet Display.

Table 2. Participants in the *in situ* CareNet Display deployments. Pseudonyms are used to protect the participants' identities

Elder	Network Member	Relationship to Elder	Role in Care Network
Grace	Vera	Daughter	Drastic Life Changer
	Donna	Daughter	Significant Contributor
Rita	Hannah	Daughter	Drastic Life Changer
	Simon	Son	Significant Contributor
	Zack	Son	Significant Contributor
Minnie	Myra	Daughter	Significant Contributor
	Esther	Daughter	Significant Contributor
Ted	Saul	Son	Significant Contributor
	Cliff	Son	Significant Contributor

3.2   Deployment Details

The three-week long deployments were conducted one network at a time. In each deployment, two or three network members had a CareNet Display in their homes. Members were able to use the display however they liked; they received no special instructions from the evaluators on how or when to use it.

The prototype used a touch-screen tablet PC housed in a custom-built beech wood picture frame (shown in **Figure 2**). The contents of the display were shown through a web browser, though that was not obvious to participants as the "full-screen" mode removed any distinguishing browser characteristics. A wireless GPRS card provided always-on internet access so that the CareNet Display could be updated throughout the day without disturbing the participants' phone lines or requiring them to have broadband internet access.

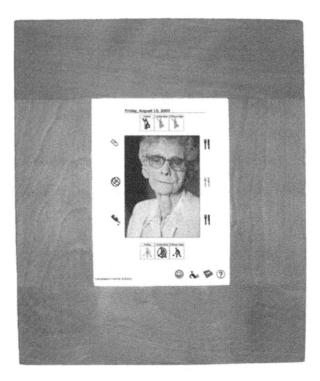

Figure 2. The CareNet Display prototype used in the deployments. The prototype uses a touch-screen tablet PC housed in a custom-built beech wood frame

To collect the data that was shown on the displays, evaluators spoke to the elders and/or their caregivers[1] three to six times per day by phone, including weekends and holidays. At the end of every phone call, the elder was asked if it was okay to share the information with display users. Updates were immediately made by the evaluators using a web-based tool (**Figure 3**). Participants did not receive any notification when updates were made. The substantial level of effort required on the part of the evaluators, elders, and especially the already overburdened caregivers was the main reason for our using a duration of three-weeks; it seemed to be at the limit of the time commitment many of the drastic life changers were willing to make.

All participants, including the elders, were interviewed before and after the three-week deployments. Most interviews lasted 60-90 minutes. Researcher notes, participant-completed questionnaires, audio recordings, and photographs were used to document the deployments. Incentives varied based on level of participation in the deployment. Network members who had the CareNet Display in their homes received $150 US. Incentives for the elder and other data providers varied between $75-300 US based on how often they provided updates.

---

[1] When the elder could provide reliable updates, evaluators spoke directly with her; otherwise the evaluators spoke with the caregiver(s). For Rita's deployment, two of the three caregivers who helped provide data about her were also display users—in this case, different caregivers were responsible for different types of data.

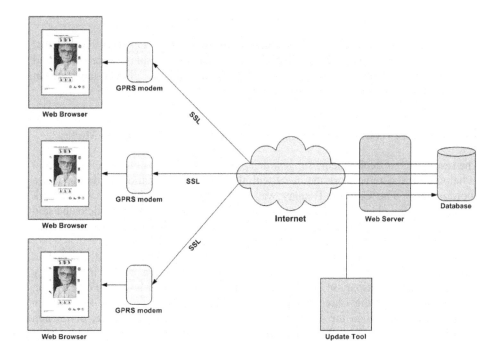

Figure 3. CareNet Display Prototype Architecture. Updates were made by evaluators through a web-based tool. Data was pushed to the displays through an always-on connection from a GPRS modem

The deployment began for care network members with a semi-structured interview and an exercise about the types of information they would like to know about the elder. The CareNet Display was then set up in the participant's home, photographs were taken of his chosen placement, and he was provided with a printed help booklet. Participants were mailed a questionnaire to be filled out half way into the deployment. In most cases, in addition to "official" participants, other network members residing in the same household as the CareNet Display also filled out the questionnaire. The deployment ended with another questionnaire and semi-structured interview. Photos were retaken if the participant had moved the display.

Elders began by answering questions about their schedule (*e.g.,* medication schedule, upcoming appointments), typical activities, fall history, etc. – the information we needed to create their displays. We discussed what information the elder was comfortable sharing with the network members/display users who were participating in the deployments (*i.e.,* the elder chose *who* could receive *which types* of information). We took photos of the elder and her medications. A semi-structured interview was conducted at the end of the three-week deployment.

4   Analysis

In this section, we discuss several findings from the CareNet Display deployments. We share the participants' general feedback on the CareNet Display, where they used it in their homes, and how they interacted with it. We also discuss the CareNet Display's impact on the lives of the care network members and the elders' care.

4.1   General Feedback, Popular Locations, and Typical Interaction Modes

The results of our deployments suggest that ambient displays can be an effective tool in helping local care network members with the tasks of information sharing and care coordination. The CareNet Display was well received both by the care network members and the elders. In all cases, the care network members who participated said that they would use such a display if it were given to them, and in most cases, they would purchase one if it were commercially available and affordable.

Participants thought that the display was aesthetically pleasing and blended in nicely with their décor, though some complained that it was a "little large." They tended to place the display in often used, common areas of their homes. For example, no participant kept the CareNet Display in a bedroom or bathroom. Instead, the displays were placed in the family/TV room, dining area, home office, or kitchen (**Figure 4**). When asked about what the elders thought of these placements, most found them to be acceptable. There was one case where a drastic life changer was uncomfortable with the display being kept in a "publicly accessible" location in her son's home, as she did not trust one of his frequent visitors; this concern was not shared by the elder or that son.

Reports from participants on how they interacted with the CareNet Display varied. As previously mentioned, the CareNet Display was designed to work as an ambient display and an interactive touch-screen device. Because the display's main screen behaves as an ambient display, it was not uncommon for participants to glance at it while passing by, merely to see if any icons were red; red icons signified that an event did not occur as planned, such as a missed, incorrect, or overdosed medication. Other participants often used the display as an interactive device, stopping and digging for details of the events, even when the icons were not red. In general, interaction patterns

Figure 4. The CareNet Display *in situ*. Participants kept the display in places such as (from the left) the kitchen, home office, TV room, and dining area

were dependent on the members' level of participation in the care network. Drastic life changers reported checking the display frequently through casual glancing, supplemented by occasional digging for details; significant contributors and peripherally involved members reported that they tended to interact with the display with higher frequency than drastic life changers – some reported as often as 10 times per day. This difference in behavior may have occurred because drastic life changers were usually already aware of many details about the elder due to their existing care responsibilities. For the significant contributors and those who are peripherally involved, the display offered an opportunity to increase their level of awareness about the elder; the information often gave them something to talk about with the elder (*e.g.,* "How was your ceramics class today, Dad?" "Did you see anything good on TV this afternoon?"). Most participants commented on how nice it was that they could get some information from a casual glance and that they felt comfort in knowing it was always there, but they could chose to ignore it.

4.2   CareNet Display Impact on Care Network Members and the Elder's Care

Participants reported that the CareNet Display had an overall positive effect on their stress levels during the deployment. A majority indicated a reduction in the amount of stress they felt in caring for the elder as a result of having the display in their homes and the homes of other network members; none of the participants reported an increase. As a result of the decreased stress levels, participants such as Myra and Cliff felt that their interactions with their respective elders were "more relaxed."

Getting information through the display, and not directly from the elders, also made network members feel as if they could treat the elder with more respect. For example, Myra enjoyed finding out about Minnie's activities and outings without having to be intrusive. These details are normally not part of their conversations, as Myra "kind of hate[s] to ask her [about them] time and time again." Similarly, Vera feels awkward discussing certain details with Grace, saying she feels she is "treating [Grace] like a child." With the CareNet Display collecting information for her, Vera had the information she needed to provide proper care and was able to have more "meaningful" conversations with Grace.

For all four care networks, the CareNet Display raised network member awareness about the elder's daily life, particularly for the significant contributors and peripherally involved members who lived with those members. In many cases, it also raised awareness of the extent to which other network members contributed to the elder's care. Much of this came from the detailed information the display provided, such as *what* Mom ate for lunch and *when,* or the calendar that showed the elder's various appointments and *who* was providing transportation. This detailed information and the ability to review information from previous days was used to improve the quality of care for some elders. In Rita's case, her son, Simon, and his wife noticed that Rita was eating the same thing, day after day. For a diabetic like Rita with mild dementia, this was not a good sign. Her network was trying to let her remain as independent as possible, but this additional information alerted them to the fact that she needed more care. Until Simon and his wife noticed this, Rita had been doing her own grocery shopping. Now, her care network members help with grocery shopping and make an effort to check the variety in Rita's kitchen when they visit.

These findings suggest that CSCC tools like the CareNet Display can make a meaningful, positive impact on both the care of the elder and the lives of her care network members. In light of these observations and the varied roles of potential users, it seems important for a device of this kind to include both ambient and interactive modalities. We would not be surprised to see the frequency of interactions with the device decrease in a longer term deployment, as it is possible that the high frequencies reported came from the novelty of having a new device. However, the ability to "dig for details" was consistently important to all participants.

5   Considerations for the Design of Ambient Displays

Despite the overall positive feedback the CareNet Display received, we found areas for improvement and challenges for future development. In this section, we discuss several lessons learned, in hopes that ambient display designers can apply our findings to their own designs.

5.1   When an Ambient Display Stops Being Ambient

In addition to the findings mentioned above, there was an additional factor to support the idea of ambient displays being good for local care network members: participants got upset when the CareNet Display stopped being ambient. This is the type of problem that *in situ* deployments are good at uncovering. Like computer screens and the Ceiva picture frame [1], the CareNet Display "glows" in the dark (**Figure 5**). This

Figure 5. The CareNet Display prototype in a dark room. The screen's "glow" can make the display lose its ambient quality

was a problem for participants who put the display either in their TV room or within view of their bedroom. We heard accounts of participants who were disturbed by the display's glow at night from their beds or while trying to watch TV.

This type of display behavior might be a useful way to grab the user's attention if something significant happened, but under normal circumstances, it should be avoided. A solution could come from incorporating a photosensor and/or motion detector in the display to detect when the display could be dimmed.

5.2   Providing Sufficient Information Without Complicating the Display

The CareNet Display's main screen contained icons to represent seven types of information for a number of events, for example, three meal icons were used to represent breakfast, lunch, and dinner. Each icon conveyed the event's state at the time the display was last updated, in an effort to provide the user with complete information and not portray a false sense that "everything is okay" if it may not be. For example, there were icon representations for the following states:

- Event occurred as planned,
- Something unexpected occurred,
- Event has not yet occurred (*e.g.,* it isn't yet time for lunch),
- Event did not occur (*e.g.,* lunchtime has passed, and the elder did not eat),
- The elder has chosen to not share the event, and
- The system cannot report the event

Red icons were used for the "something unexpected" state. Few participants understood the subtle visual differences in icon representation; in all but the "elder has chosen to not share," the states were distinguished only by icon color. Most participants just looked to see if any icons were red. Though the many icon representations did not seem to confuse participants, they may have gotten a false sense that "everything is okay," as most did not notice the difference between, for example, "system is not able to update event" (gray icon) and "event occurred as planned" (black icon). After our end of deployment interviews, it seemed as if "event has not yet occurred" was not an important distinction to make (*i.e.,* care network members know whether or not the time for lunch has passed). However, they seemed to find the other states to be important. Further research should be conducted to investigate how to effectively communicate these distinctions without overly complicating the display or compromising its ambient quality.

5.3   Providing the "Human Touch" from Sensor Data

In the end-of-deployment interviews with both care network members and elders, we talked about the vision of sensors collecting most of the data that the evaluators collected during the deployments. Though there were mixed reactions about sensors in the elder's home, there was a consistent reaction from the significant contributors and peripherally involved members about the type of data that would be provided. Most expressed the importance of the data having a "human touch." They were afraid that sensors would provide impersonal data. In many cases, they wanted to know qualitative details about the events, for example, not just *that* the elder knitted, but *what* she knitted and *for whom*, or *why* the elder was feeling bad, not merely *that* she was feeling bad. A popular suggestion was to incorporate a daily narrative provided by the drastic life changer about how the elder is doing and what her day was like.

When we discussed the idea of adding the "human touch" with the drastic life changers (even before posing the narrative idea), most expressed concern; they immediately suspected that the responsibility would fall to them. An alternative that may be able to satisfy the display users without overburdening drastic life changers could be to use an interactive system that prompts the elder to provide a verbal narrative that could be added to the display. An interesting challenge for future work in this area is how to convey this human quality while using data largely provided by sensors and not adding to the responsibilities of already overburdened members.

5.4   Privacy Considerations

The CareNet Display provides two ways for the elder to control her information: she decides who can see what type of information, and she can choose to not share the update for any event, even after permission for that type of event has been granted. Though no elder in the study took advantage of either of these controls, it was important to both elders and their care network members that the controls were available. For the elders, it gave them an enhanced sense of control and increased their trust in the technology. For care network members, most thought that the controls were important so that the elder could maintain as much of her independence as possible, while a few thought it was important to signify when something was a problem. In one participant's words, "if Mom didn't want to share what she was eating, there'd probably be a reason." Future designs could explore other levels of disclosure, such as only alerting certain network members when something unexpected occurs (*e.g.*, a member who does not normally see medication information, might receive it only if the elder misses or overdoses on a medication).

We also discussed the idea of the CareNet Display being used by more members of the elder's care network (in our deployments, only two or three households per network had displays). Prior to the deployment and in our earlier research, elders claimed to be very comfortable about sharing their information with the local members of their care networks. The only exceptions mentioned were the members who lived at a distance, as the elders saw no reason to share details about events like medications and meals with members who could not immediately come to their assistance if something bad happened. After the experience of the deployments, some elders changed their minds. Though they were still very comfortable sharing their information with the network members who participated in the deployments, they noted special cases – *e.g.,* the alcoholic grandson or the forgetful neighbor – with whom they would not be comfortable regularly sharing information, or at least not all types of information, even though these members are still important to the elder.

Through the CareNet Display deployments, we have shown that ambient displays have the potential to be a powerful tool for local members of elders' care networks. We have also discussed some of the problems with our design, suggested ways to improve these problems, and offered challenges for future work in the area.

6   Related Research

In this section, we discuss research in the areas of ambient displays for care network members and ambient displays that have been evaluated in their intended settings.

As mentioned previously, the CareNet Display builds on research done by Mynatt *et al* on the Digital Family Portrait [5,14], but targets a different audience and uses modified data collection and analysis techniques. The Digital Family Portrait uses an ambient display to provide distant family members of an elder with enough information to give them the peace of mind to allow the elder to age in place, while respecting the elder's privacy. The ambient display's form factor is that of a digital picture frame. However, instead of a static photo of the elder, the border surrounding the static photo of the elder is augmented with daily updates of certain aspects of the elder's life – the sort of information that a neighbor or other member of the elder's household could easily observe. In the first version of the Digital Family Portrait, a photo of the elder was surrounded with 11 days worth of information on one screen, represented by various icon visualizations. The types of information shown were overall measurements of health, relationships, activity, and events (where measurement was based on a scale of 10). A prototype of this first version was evaluated in a field trial (described below). Based on field trial results, the design was revised to be less complicated, the "events" category was dropped, measurements were reduced to a scale of four, the main screen showed 28 days of information, and layers were added for less common needs. They also added representations to the main screen for alarms and system-detected trends. The new visualizations went through usability studies for clarity, but no field trial.

Like the Digital Family Portrait, the CareNet Display uses an augmented digital picture frame to provide information about an elder to members of her care network. However, in the case of the CareNet Display, the target users are the local network members responsible for providing the elder with the day-to-day care she needs to be able to age in place. Even though both projects target members of an elder's care network, the needs of the users are different. Because of this change, the CareNet Display shares information that is potentially much more sensitive and in more detail than what the Digital Family Portrait shares—the types of information the members need to provide the elder with day-to-day care. For example, the CareNet Display not only shows that medications were taken as planned, but includes *which* medications and *when* they were taken. Similarly, the CareNet Display does not show a general measurement of activity per day, but rather *which* activities were performed and *when*. It also provides mechanisms to help the users coordinate care-related activities. Because of the sensitivity of the information on the CareNet Display, it is designed to give the elder some control over what is shared. In addition to sharing information about the elder, it also shares information about other network members (*e.g.,* Mary is taking the elder to the doctor's office on Tuesday; Sam visited the elder last Thursday). Because of the CareNet Display's intended use, updates need to be made throughout the day as events occur, and the level of detail and reliability of the shared information is critical to the CareNet Display's success.

Regarding the evaluation of the Digital Family Portrait, a 9-day *in situ* field trial was conducted of a prototype of the first version of the design with one family—a grandmother and two of her grandchildren. To collect data to update the displays, the evaluators conducted phone interviews once per day with each participant and subsequently updated the displays remotely.   Participants were provided with a laptop, modem, and internet account so they could view the Digital Family Portrait as a web page on the laptop.   At the end of the daily data collection phone call, each participant was asked to view the portrait, then answer a daily questionnaire to provide qualitative feedback.   In this paper, we present a more in-depth study with several care networks validating the general idea of the ambient picture frame form factor and offer specific design lessons for such displays.   Together, the Digital Family Portrait and CareNet Display projects address the needs of most of the members of an elder's care network.

Other research has evaluated ambient displays in the office/academic environment. Mankoff *et al* [11] designed and deployed two ambient display prototypes, the BusMobile and the Daylight Display, in the windowless undergraduate computing laboratories at the University of California, Berkeley.   The BusMobile alerts lab users of how close several commonly used buses are to the nearest bus stop.   The Daylight Display provides information about the level of light that is currently outside.   The results of their *in situ* deployments were used to investigate and propose a new set of heuristics to tailor the discount usability method, *heuristic evaluation,* to ambient displays.   Heuristic evaluation is traditionally used for evaluations of desktop software applications and web sites.

Ho-Ching *et al* [9] designed an ambient display for the deaf that visualizes peripheral sound in the office.   They conducted an in-lab experiment and a one-week *in situ* evaluation of their Spectrograph display with one participant.   Mynatt *et al* [13] deployed the Audio Aura system in their research lab and got feedback from co-workers who experienced the system.   Audio Aura uses sound to keep office inhabitants in touch with events taking place at their desks.   Cheverst *et al* [2] deployed Hermes, a system of interactive office door displays, in the computing department at Lancaster University.   Their system essentially replaces post-it notes by allowing visitors to leave electronic notes for the office occupant when he is out.

Like Mankoff, Ho-Ching, Mynatt, and Cheverst, we evaluated our ambient display prototype with target users in the intended setting.   However, our ambient display was targeted for the home environment, a very different set of users, and included an interactive modality[2].

7   Conclusions and Future Work

We have described the design and in home evaluation of an ambient display prototype, the CareNet Display.   We discussed how the display affected the quality of care and lives of elders and their care network members.   We also shared many of our lessons learned, including successes and areas for improvement.   We hope that this research helps build a body of knowledge about the use of ambient displays in the home environment from which ambient display designers can learn.

Many challenges remain.   An important next step is to explore what happens to the acceptance of technologies like the CareNet Display when sensors are introduced to

---

[2] The Hermes system also included an interactive modality

fill the role of human data collectors. Are elders comfortable living in a home filled with sensors? Do care network members trust the data reported by sensors? How is the network affected by sensor or system failure? A fully working system could also enable longitudinal deployments to uncover other unexplored issues. What happens when the technology gets beyond any novelty effects? How are the privacy controls used, and are they sufficient? What social issues do technologies like the CareNet Display introduce to the care network? Do such technologies contribute to a reduction in communications or visits with the elder overtime?

More work is also needed to investigate mechanisms that elders could reasonably use to control the distribution of their information. In our deployment, the elders controlled their information by talking with human data collectors who controlled the system. Additional design considerations, such as adding audio to the display when a significant or unexpected event is detected and offering form factors other than a picture frame (*e.g.*, handheld computer or computer desktop background), should also be investigated.

Conducting studies of ambient display technologies in their intended environments provides researchers with insight into how new tools are used and what effects they have on the members of the communities who use them. Our explorations indicate that ambient displays can be a key solution for a large and growing community of users who have a significant need for help.

Acknowledgements

We would like to thank the many people who contributed to this work, including: Morgan Ames, Anthony LaMarca, Jeff Towle, Lenny Lim, Jimmi Montgomery, Gaetano Borriello, James Landay, Ken Smith, Cherie Fenner, Michael Ham, Carol Johnston, Asuman Kiyak, Linda Reeder, Sandy Sabersky, Karen Sisson, Jay Lundell, Brad Needham, Margie Morris, Eric Dishman, Batya Friedman, Bill Schilit, Sara Bly, Ken Fishkin, and Miriam Walker.

References

1.   Ceiva Digital Photo Receiver, *http://www.ceiva.com/* (verified June 4, 2004).
2.   Cheverst, K., Dix, A., Fitton, D., Rouncefield, M., "'Out to Lunch': Exploring the Sharing of Personal Context through Office Door Displays," *Proceedings of the 2003 Australasian Computer-Human Conference,* Canberra (2003), pp.74-83.
3.   Consolvo, S., Roessler, P., Shelton, B.E., LaMarca, A., Schilit, B., Bly, S., "Technology for Care Networks of Elders," *IEEE Pervasive Computing Mobile & Ubiquitous Systems: Successful Aging*, Vol. 3, No. 2 (Apr-Jun 2004) pp.22-29.
4.   Dahley, A., Wisneski, C., Ishii, H., "Water Lamp and Pinwheels: Ambient Projection of Digital Information into Architectural Space," *Proceedings of Conference on Human Factors in Computing Systems,* (1998).
5.   Digital Family Portrait Project Website, *http://www.cc.gatech.edu/fce/ecl/projects/dfp/* (verified June 4, 2004).

6. Fishkin, K.P., Wang, M., Borriello, G., "A Ubiquitous System for Medication Monitoring," *Advances in Pervasive Computing: A Collection of Contributions Presented at Pervasive 2004*, (2004), pp.193-198.
7. Gaver, W., Dunne, A., "Projected Realities: conceptual design for cultural effect," *Proceedings of Conference on Human Factors in Computing Systems: CHI '99*, (1999), pp.600-7.
8. Heiner, J.M., Hudson, S.E., Tanaka, K., "The Information Percolator: Ambient Information Display in a Decorative Object," *Proceedings of the 12th Annual ACM Symposium on User Interface Software and Technology*, (1999), pp.141-8.
9. Ho-Ching, F.W., Mankoff, J., Landay, J.A., "Can you see what I hear? The design and evaluation of a peripheral sound display for the deaf," *Proceedings of Conference on Human Factors in Computing Systems*, (2003), pp.161-8.
10. Ishii, H. and Tangible Media Group, *Tangible Bits: Towards Seamless Interface between People, Bits, and Atoms*, NTT Publishing Co., Ltd., Tokyo, (June 2000).
11. Mankoff, J., Dey, A.K., Hsieh, G., Kientz, J., Ames, M., Lederer, S., "Heuristic evaluation of ambient displays," *CHI 2003, Proceedings of the ACM Conference on Human Factors in Computing Systems,* 2003, pp.169-176.
12. Miller, G.A., "The Magical Number of Seven, Plus or Minus Two: Some Limits on Our Capacity for Processing Information," *The Psychological Review*, Vol. 63, (1956), pp.81-97.
13. Mynatt, E.D., Back, M., Want, R., Baer, M., Ellis, J.B., "Designing Audio Aura," *Proceedings of Conference on Human Factors in Computing Systems*, (1998).
14. Mynatt, E.D., Rowan, J., Jacobs, A., Craighill, S. "Digital Family Portraits: Supporting Peace of Mind for Extended Family Members," *Proceedings of Conference on Human Factors in Computing Systems*, (Apr 2001) pp.333-340.
15. Roessler, P., Consolvo, S., Shelton, B., "Phase #1 of Computer-Supported Coordinated Care Project," IRS-TR-04-005, (Jan 2004), *http://www.intel-research.net/Publications/Seattle/022320041335_230.pdf* (verified June 4, 2004).
16. Roessler, P., Consolvo, S., Shelton, B., "Phase #2 of Computer-Supported Coordinated Care Project," IRS-TR-04-006, (Jan 2004), *http://www.intel-research.net/Publications/Seattle/030520041041_233.pdf* (verified June 4, 2004).
17. Weiser, M., Brown, J.S., "Designing Calm Technology," *http://www.ubiq.com/weiser/calmtech/calmtech.htm* (verified June 4, 2004).

Personalized Peripheral Information Awareness Through Information Art

John Stasko, Todd Miller, Zachary Pousman,
Christopher Plaue, and Osman Ullah

College of Computing/GVU Center
Georgia Institute of Technology
Atlanta, GA 30332-0280
stasko@cc.gatech.edu

Abstract. This article describes development of the concept of Information Art, a type of ambient or peripheral display involving user-specified electronic paintings in which resident objects change appearance and position to foster awareness of personally relevant information. Our approach differs from others, however, in emphasizing end-user control and flexibility in monitored information and its resultant representation. The article provides an overview of the system's capabilities and describes an initial pilot study in which displays were given to four people to use for an extended period of time. Reactions were quite favorable and the trial use provided suggestions for system improvements.

1   Introduction

Our lives are filled with information that influences what we do and how we feel. What world events are transpiring? How are my investments doing? Is our project at work nearing completion? What will the weather be like tomorrow? How much traffic will there be on the ride home? What's my child having for lunch at school?

As human beings, we naturally care about such questions as some may have important consequences for our lives while others may simply alter a small facet of our day-to-day experience. Maintaining awareness of such information helps to keep us more informed and presumably assists the multitude of decisions we make every day.

How do people stay aware of such information? Pervasive sources of information such as letters, flyers, newspapers, radio and television programs each have played important roles and they still do. Letters, flyers and newspapers, however, are predetermined and static—the information content is chosen by an author or editor and delivered as such. Conversely, many different radio and television programs exist, thus allowing more choices, but a person must be listening at the right time to acquire the desired information.

The Internet and the WWW now provide a new option for information discovery. Websites on almost any imaginable topic exist and can be opportunistically examined. Accessing a Website, however, frequently takes a few seconds if

N. Davies et al. (Eds.): UbiComp 2004, LNCS 3205, pp. 18–35, 2004.

the site is known or possibly a few minutes if a search must be conducted. While that may not seem like a long time, the simple act of explicitly changing focus and the time it requires can be a significant disruption to a person's previous activity or train of thought.

The use of the periphery of human attention played a key role in Weiser's vision of ubiquitous computing as a calm computing resource—an attempt to mitigate these kinds of cognitive disruptions [24]. As he noted, "A calm technology will move easily from the periphery of our attention, to the center, and back." Furthermore, these types of calm technologies often can become aesthetically pleasing additions to a person's environment.

One form of ubiquitous computing, the ambient display, focuses on conveying low- to medium-priority information to people [25,1]. An ambient display resides in the periphery of a person's attention. The display calmly changes state in some way to reflect changes in the underlying information it is representing. The designers of ambient displays typically stress display aesthetics, providing pleasant, attractive devices usually communicating a piece of information.

In [16], we introduced the InfoCanvas, a concept for a system that maintains some aspects of an ambient display, but provides greater access to more varied information sources. Such a system allows users to create electronic paintings in which objects in the scene represent information sources of interest, and the objects change appearance to reflect state changes in the information source they represent.

That earlier article was primarily an exploration of the concept of user-designed information art. It also described an initial Web-based prototype system that sought to allow users to create their own virtual paintings beginning with a blank canvas upon which to add geometric objects using drawing tools such as pens, paintbrushes, fill markers, etc., or by choosing images from a palette of clip-art style objects. We eventually turned away from that approach, however, as potential users struggled, not knowing where to begin in creating their scenes. Also, potential users expressed that they did not feel artistically talented enough to create scenes that they would be comfortable displaying. Thus, the initial prototype we built was never used outside our research group, and it really only functioned as an exploration of the concept.

This article describes the details of a new, heavily-redesigned version of the InfoCanvas system that is currently being used by many different people now and has been the subject of two evaluation studies. Based upon our earlier experiences, we redesigned the system around the idea of "themes." A theme is a predefined, visually coherent scene that consists of a static background image with nearly all of usual scene objects removed, such as that of a tranquil meadow with only the grass, mountains, and sky shown. A theme also includes optional visual elements such as plants, animals, people, and inanimate objects that represent data of interest. Visual elements fit harmoniously within the background image, creating the illusion of a static piece of art. Elements also utilize a behavior from a set of predefined transformations in order to represent changes in the state of information being monitored.

In the following sections, we describe related research work and then transition to describing the concepts employed in the system and its architecture and operations. The InfoCanvas breaks some existing notions of ambient and peripheral displays, and these differences will be highlighted. We also report on an informal pilot study in which the InfoCanvas was deployed to four people to use for an extended period of time. We describe reactions to the system and facts learned that are influencing its iterative design.

2   Related Work

Recently, a variety of systems have been developed to help communicate information to a person through channels that are not the primary focus of that person. These systems communicate important, but typically not vital, information in a calm manner using output devices ranging from computer monitors to tangible, real-world objects. The systems have been labeled with a variety of terms ranging from ambient displays to peripheral displays to notification systems.

Although no standard, accepted definitions of these terms exist, each has come to refer to slightly differing notions. Ambient displays typically communicate just one, or perhaps a few at the most, pieces of information and the aesthetics and visual appeal of the display is often paramount [25,8,13]. Peripheral displays refer to systems that are out of a person's primary focus of attention and may communicate one or more pieces of information [19,14]. Thus, peripheral displays would likely include ambient displays as a proper subset. Other types of displays such as scrolling tickers or animated news blurbs, however, would also be considered peripheral displays but likely not ambient displays.

Notification systems also deliver information in divided-attention situations in efficient and effective manners, but they more clearly including monitoring as a fundamental user task with the potential for people to react to important stimuli [15]. Ambient and peripheral displays more typically do not communicate critical, urgent information.

In addition to these types of systems, other awareness displays such as Web portals similarly may communicate many different pieces of information, but they typically do so as a person's primary focus of attention.

Examples of ambient displays, the first category described above, include Ambient Orb [2], Busmobile [13], Dangling String [24], Information Percolator[10], Lumitouch [4], Table Fountain [8], and Water Lamp and Pinwheels [5]. These systems often employ physical artifacts to represent information. The InfoCanvas differs from these systems in communicating more information in wider variety of representations.

Many peripheral displays, the second category listed above, use computer monitors to present information. They typically can communicate a greater variety of information in more flexible forms than the ambient display systems listed above, but do so by minimizing aesthetic considerations. Examples include KISS the Tram [12], Notification Collage [9], Scope [23], Sideshow [3], Tickertape [6], and What's Happening [26]. The InfoCanvas stresses aesthetics more than these system and provides a more abstract, symbolic representation of information. Another altogether different peripheral display approach is to use audio rather than visual presentations of information [17].

A few recent systems have used computer displays to convey information in artistic, attractive manners, and thus attempt to bridge the divide between information bandwidth and aesthetic considerations.

The Digital Family Portrait (DFP) [18] uses a computer display to simulate a picture frame and enclosed picture of a loved one. Iconic images in the display (chiefly the frame) represent data about the person's habits and well-being . The InfoCanvas and the DFP share general goals and presentation styles, but the DFP is a much more focused system on one particular domain. The InfoCanvas introduces a more general infrastructure, presumably one that could be used to implement a system just like the DFP.

The Kandinsky system [7] provides an artistic collage of images to represent email notes and news articles. Keywords in the text are used to retrieve particular related pictures that then are made into collages following different artistic styles. Kandinsky focuses on aesthetics as a primary goal, with information conveyance abilities considered almost an added bonus. As a result, information conveyance quality can vary tremendously from collage to collage. InfoCanvas, on the other hand, strongly emphasizes clarity of communication of the information state, even if the representation used is abstract and/or symbolic.

The Informative Artwork project [21,11,22] is the most closely related research effort to ours. It uses LCD displays to produce subtly shifting representations based on well-known modern art pieces by artists such as Mondrian and Warhol. The two projects use the same semiotic approach with pictorial elements representing data, and both have a very similar goal: to facilitate people's peripheral awareness of information through attractive, artistic displays. Their focus is more on the aesthetics, however, and the data represented is usually predetermined and narrow, such as the current time, computer server traffic, or a set of weather forecasts. Each display they have shown has been custom-designed by the researchers themselves for a particular deployment. Our project differs in that we focus on end-user personalization and customization, and we explore the challenges involved in supporting people to design and specify their own information representations. Further, InfoCanvas displays typically consolidate more diverse information into a single display.

The SideShow system [3] is typically used to present very similar information as is done with the InfoCanvas and it supports user-customization as well, but that system uses a much more direct data representation including text and small standard iconic representations. Also, SideShow is primarily a peripheral computer desktop application that resides on one edge of a person's monitor, whereas the InfoCanvas is designed to be deployed in a more ecological location and blend into the surrounding decorations and furniture.

3 The InfoCanvas System

Our objectives in developing the InfoCanvas were different than any of the existing peripheral display systems. We sought to provide an attractive display, one that would fit calmly and comfortably into a person's environment much as many others have, but we also wanted to provide end-users with the power and control to monitor *information of personal relevance*. The system should stress information communication (particularly of a moderate number, e.g., 5 to 15, of different information items), but do so in a way that provides end-users with control and flexibility thus fostering their creative abilities. More specifically, the five objectives below have guided our efforts in building the current implementation of the InfoCanvas:

- **Personalized** - Rather than display some predetermined information source that different people may or may not be interested in, each InfoCanvas should be a highly customized information communicator for the person using it. The individual's particular personal information of interest should be presented.
- **Flexible** - A variety of information sources should be available for display, and should include the types of information that are the focus of peripheral awareness. If the data can be accessed via a Web page or an Internet information service, it should be available for use on an InfoCanvas.
- **Consolidated** - The system should support the presentation of a moderate number (5-15) of information sources and should consolidate their representation in one location, thus saving a person from having to check multiple devices or displays.
- **Accurate** - The system should accurately communicate the current state of monitored information. If for some reason an information source is not functional or not operating properly (which commonly occurs), this fact should be communicated to the user in a clear but non-distracting manner.
- **Appealing** - Simply put, the system should be fun to use and should be an aesthetically pleasing addition to a person's environment.

The basic premise of the InfoCanvas is to allow a user to create a visual scene that serves as an abstract representation of information that is relevant to them. The result is an aesthetically pleasing "picture" that appears to be nothing more than an artistic rendering of a scene, such as a beach or cityscape. The picture is presented on a LCD display and subtly changes to reflect updates in the information being tracked. The InfoCanvas can be displayed in a manner like that of a painting or calendar on a wall, or even a picture on a desk. The goal is to blend into the physical environment of the user, thus providing a type of "virtual painting" or an "electronic illustration." Figure 1 shows an example InfoCanvas mounted on a wall in an office.

As mentioned earlier, an initial prototype InfoCanvas that provided drawing tools (pen, paintbrush, fill, etc.) and a small palette of clip-art icons for display design was developed [16], but creating views was too open-ended and difficult. This experience led us to redesign the system around the idea of *themes*. A

Fig. 1. An example installation of the InfoCanvas mounted on a wall like a picture.

theme consists of a static background image with most of the usual objects removed, such as that of a beach with only the sand, the water, and the sky pictured. A theme also includes many optional visual *elements* that can be placed on it such as seagulls, palm trees, sailboats, crabs, and blankets for the beach theme. Elements are designed to fit both stylistically and thematically with the background image, thus mimicking a static illustration, picture, or painting. Many different visual elements can be in a display, thus promoting our objective of *consolidation* in the awareness display.

An element added to a view represents a specific piece of information being "watched" by the user. A mapping between the state of the information and the visual presentation of the element is constructed. As the information being monitored changes, the visual element representing it also updates its rendering to communicate that change. We call these changes to elements *transformations*. For example, an InfoCanvas could include a flower element that appears whenever a person has received an email from their spouse within the last hour. A bird in an InfoCanvas could represent the daily change of the stock market, with the bird flying higher when the market is up and lower when the market is down. We use the term *scene* to refer to an "active" theme that is representing specific data with various mapping transformations applied to it.

The following set of transformations are included in the InfoCanvas:

- **slider** - An element moves along a straight line to represent different values of an information source. The two endpoints of the line represent minimum and maximum values of the information. *Example*: A crab moves horizontally along the beach to represent the current airfare between two specific cities.
- **swapper** - A set of visual elements is available, and a specific one is displayed depending on the state of the information source. *Example*: The bathing suit color of a person on the beach changes to represent the traffic speed on a particular road (green-fast, yellow-moderate, red-slow).
- **appearance** - A visual element appears when a particular condition is true and is not shown when the condition is false. *Example*: A towel element appears on a chair on the beach when a particular Web page includes a specified keyword.
- **scaler** - An element changes size to represent different values of an information source. *Example*: A sailboat grows and shrinks to represent the forecasted temperature.
- **population** - Repeated copies of an element are displayed to represent a value of an information source. *Example*: A drink glass appears on the beach for each ten unread emails in a user's queue.
- **display** - An image or a text string taken directly from an information source is displayed on an InfoCanvas. *Example*: A lead image from a news Web site is displayed on a billboard in a scene.

Note that the designer of an InfoCanvas has the freedom to specify mappings that are either more concrete/direct or more abstract/symbolic. For instance, the slider element used to represent a best airfare could be an airplane in the sky or it could be a crab on the beach. Similarly, tomorrow's weather forecast may be represented by an image swap putting different weather icons (sun, clouds, lightning, snow) in the sky or it could be an image swap placing different types of cars on a city street. This capability supports the goals of providing mappings that are both *flexible* and *personalized*.

Figure 2 illustrates examples from the wide variety of InfoCanvas themes created by different members of our research group. Themes range from collections of clip-art and hand-drawn objects to photo-realistic scenes as well as artistic Japanese watercolor designs. In the photo-realistic city street theme (at upper right), the trolley car and the bicyclist are sliders; the police car roof lights and a street lamp are image appearance elements (on/off); various cars are image swaps (different car or different color); people on the sidewalk provide a population element; and the awning above a store changes color in an image swap.

Although the freedom to flexibly define a scene exists, we also promote certain conventions to follow in theme design to ensure coherent scenes. For instance, in a *display* transformation, image or text should only be displayed in a context and a manner fitting to the theme, thus ensuring visual continuity. Thus, rather than an image arbitrarily appearing in a scene, it should only appear in locations

Fig. 2. An assortment of different InfoCanvas themes that have been built.

that a picture typically would be seen, such as on a billboard, on a sign, or on a television screen. Similarly, a text string could appear as a banner being pulled by an airplane or on a note lying on a beach.

Calling these scenes "art" may be a bit presumptuous as they reflect more of a clip-art, decorative style. But for a picture to have many different objects that can be moved, altered, or scaled and still look properly integrated, displays likely must take this style. Moving and modifying pieces of great paintings (at least ones other than abstract art) would surely erode their visual appeal.

Internet-based information resources such as Websites may go offline or become temporarily unavailable. As a result, information provided will not be available for presentation on the InfoCanvas. To signify such an event, the data's visual element on the InfoCanvas becomes semi-transparent. This promotes the *accuracy* objective by communicating the data acquisition problem to the viewer, but does so in a more subtle, non-distracting manner that does not destroy the visual continuity of the scene.

The InfoCanvas is written in Java, containing modules to monitor information sources, display scenes, and update visual elements as needed. Accompanying the system is a growing collection of themes, each residing in its own folder and providing a background image and a collection of visual element images. The InfoCanvas takes as input a configuration file specifying the visual theme to be presented, the data to be monitored, and the transformations from data to representation. The configuration file is in XML format and is described in more detail later in this section. Users simply create and modify the configuration file with a text editor. The InfoCanvas then uses the configuration file to construct an initial scene and thereafter refreshes the display at preset intervals. Once the program is started, the no further user intervention is required.

Using a comprehensive "driver" configuration file allows the system to be used in a variety of ways. First, users can take pre-existing scenes with all the elements and transformations specified, but simply substitute in their own personal information sources to drive the transformations. Second, users can modify the transformations in a scene, perhaps even adding new visual elements and information mappings. Finally, the truly ambitious designer can create a theme from scratch beginning with a background image and adding as many visual elements as desired. Presently, a GUI interface is being developed to simplify the transformation specification process and make creating new configuration files easier. Users will interactively position and scale visual elements via menus and control palettes.

Each InfoCanvas scene is stored in the form of an XML file whose format is strictly specified by a Document Type Definition (DTD). The file specifies the theme: name, canvas size, working folder for images, the background image, and a list of visual elements. Visual elements can either be static or active. Static visual elements are images that do not change; they are simply decorations for the scene and are separated from the background to provide more flexibility in scene design. Active visual elements are objects that represent information using one of the six transformations listed earlier (slider, swapper, appearance, scaler, population and display). An active visual element consists of an image or a set of images, the data it represents, and a specification of how the data will transform the image(s).

An example of an active visual element with a slider transformation is shown below. (The XML format uses the term "object" for a visual elements.) This transformation uses a 40-pixel-wide by 22-pixel-high seagull that moves from coordinates (250, 370) to (250, 0) to represent temperature values between 0 and 50 degrees in the geographic area corresponding to postal code 17837.

Note the use of the term *harvester* in the specification. Harvesters are system objects that collect information. Presently, a wide variety of harvester classes exist, gathering data for weather, traffic, email, stock market data, and Web page text strings and images. The *paramname* argument of a harvester identifies the specific aspect of the information class to be queried. For example, the weather harvester includes categories for the current temperature, current conditions, tomorrow's forecasted high and low temperatures, tomorrow's forecasted conditions, etc. Harvesters also use data specific to the harvester type such as the zip code of the geographic region being watched in this example. At a specified interval, a harvester gathers all of its potential data and stores it in a hash table. To prevent harvesters from querying sources more than necessary, each harvester supports a specific harvest interval. For example, a stock harvester will have a shorter harvest interval than a weather harvester.

```
<object type="active">
    <image>gull_small.gif</image>
    <action type="slider">
        <coord type="start"><x>250</x><y>370</y></coord>
        <coord type="end"><x>250</x><y>0</y></coord>
        <dimension><width>40</width><height>22</height></dimension>
        <data classname="infoart.harvesters.WeatherHarvester"
              paramname="curtemp">
            <minval>0</minval>
            <maxval>50</maxval>
            <harvesterdata>zip:17837</harvesterdata>
        </data>
    </action>
</object>
```

Once the InfoCanvas reads the XML configuration file, an internal data structure is created. This data structure consists of images (visual elements), harvesters, and the transformations that link images and harvesters together by specifying the data range for the information as well as how the data from the harvester will modify the image. Once the data structure is built, the InfoCanvas polls each harvester at a regular interval by calling its harvest() method, then extracting the desired information from the updated hash tables. If a harvester is polled before its harvest interval has passed, it will return the same data as the last query. This cycle of polling, harvesting, and updating the display continues until the program is terminated.

4   Evaluation

Evaluating any form of ubiquitous computing application or service is challenging, and that certainly holds true for peripheral displays. Mankoff et al. observe that most ambient displays have not been evaluated at all, and little is known about what makes one display more effective than another [13]. To address this problem, they developed and refined a set of principles for use in guiding a discount heuristic evaluation of an ambient display. This technique is aimed at evaluating a system in its formative stages by analyzing the system with respect to various heuristics. These criteria thus can serve as initial evaluation metrics with which to discuss and consider the InfoCanvas.

First, on heuristics such as "Useful and relevant information," "Peripherality of display," "Aesthetic and pleasing design," and "Match between design of ambient display and environment," the InfoCanvas would, we believe, score well. Each of these is fundamental to the design of the system. The "Sufficient information design" heuristic is about whether too much or too little information is displayed. The InfoCanvas allows users to decide how much and what type of information to convey, therefore it presumably would rate high on that heuristic as well.

Perhaps most interesting are those heuristics on which the InfoCanvas might be rated low. The first stresses the creation of a "Consistent and Intuitive Mapping." The InfoCanvas, however, may use abstract mappings, some of which are not intuitive at all. Another heuristic encourages designers to provide an "Easy transition to more in-depth information." The InfoCanvas intentionally did not allow users to drill down for more information because we wanted to promote a calm, passive interface. (Note that this design decision was questioned and will be discussed later in this section.) Finally, the heuristic "Visibility of State" means that a display should make system states noticeable and state-to-state transitions easily perceptible. The InfoCanvas' use of semi-transparent visual images follows this heuristic as does the general emphasis of clarity in representation state, but we also promote "change-blind" displays in which image updates are relatively difficult to notice and no attention-grabbing visual effects such as animation are employed.

All three of those heuristics would probably not be judged by expert evaluators to be fully realized in the InfoCanvas, but this is not an omission on our part. Rather, these characteristics were consciously designed features of the system. We posit that there are other systems, like ours, that by design reject a heuristic to achieve system goals. In this way, the heuristics can be viewed not just as assisting the evaluation of ambient and peripheral display systems, but also in their design.

Our own to-date evaluations of the InfoCanvas have focused on its objective ability to convey information and the subjective impressions of people with respect to its usefulness and appeal. We also wanted to observe just how people would use the system, the representations they would select, and any problems or unanticipated findings that would arise.

To evaluate its objective information communication capabilities, we conducted an experiment comparing the InfoCanvas to a Web portal-style display and a text display, examining each display's ability to transmit information to people at a glance [20]. We encoded ten different types of information (news, weather, traffic, etc.) together onto each the three different display types respectively, and then we showed instances of each display to experiment participants for eight seconds. Each instance encoded a different set of ten values. The individual then had to recall the value or state of the information sources as presented in the display. Participants in the experiment recalled a statistically significantly higher number of information values per display with the InfoCanvas than with the other two display types. Because the information source-to-visual element mappings were defined by us and not the participants, the result is particularly meaningful in showing that people can learn the types of abstract mappings in an InfoCanvas quickly, and they are able to comprehend, translate, and understand the visual transformations relatively well.

To evaluate the perceived usefulness and aesthetics of InfoCanvas displays, a longitudinal study of actual system use was conducted. Four people were recruited to create their own version of the InfoCanvas and use it in their offices for a period of about two months. We considered this an initial trial evaluation effort and our goals were relatively modest—to gather initial impressions about people's impressions of the system and to gain suggestions for changes or improvements to feed our iterative design process. We were not evaluating their ability to create or configure a display.

A second video card and LCD monitor were purchased to attach to a participant's primary computer. This choice was made for a number of technical, financial, and practical reasons. This decision likely would affect the study in that participants could potentially utilize the second monitor as additional workspace, placing application windows on top of their canvas display. While this could not be easily prevented, participants were instructed that the monitor should be solely for use as an InfoCanvas display.

4.1 Study Methodology

At a first meeting with each participant, we asked them to list information that they currently check semi-regularly, such as email, weather forecasts, or news headlines. The interviewer probed for more details on each item, such as the specific Web site(s) visited, what time(s) throughout the day the information is examined, what information in particular is of the most interest, their motivations for checking, and how they might respond to the information. The interviews lasted approximately thirty minutes.

Within one to two weeks following the initial interview, we performed a more intensive design interview session. At the start of the interview, the information currently monitored by the participant was reviewed, and the person was able to make further clarification or additions.

After the review, we explained to the participant the concept of the InfoCanvas in detail. We summarized how the display will function in their environment and the means by which information can be graphically represented. The study used a set of six themes from which a participant could select their own personal scene. Each theme had at least twenty visual elements that could be used for representing data.

In order to provide a natural, creative process for participants to design their InfoCanvas, we decided to use paper prototyping in the design sessions. This hands-on approach involved giving participants paper cut-outs of images that could be moved around the background image. Participants were told that the size of an element could easily be changed to fit better in the scene.

When a participant selected a theme for use in their canvas, we presented the individual with a paper copy of the theme's background image and the paper cut-outs of visual elements available for use. We would then suggest an item to monitor from the participant's list of information and provide any needed assistance as they created a mapping of that data to a visual element. The mapping was made by placing a cut-out image onto the paper background of their canvas and verbally describing how it would function. This process was repeated for each piece of information to be represented. At the end of the interview, we asked the participant to point out each element and explain what it represented and how it functioned. This action clarified the final mappings as well as tested the participant's ability to remember their design. The entire design interview lasted about an hour.

Within a few days of the design interview, we implemented a functional version of the participant's design and installed it in their office. Participants then were contacted weekly and asked a short series of questions to gauge usage of their InfoCanvas. The questions examined how frequently they looked at their InfoCanvas, what information was most useful, if they had any difficulty remembering or interpreting the visual mappings, and whether any technical difficulties had arisen over the past week.

During the weekly interviews, we encouraged participants to suggest additions or changes to their design, some of which we subsequently implemented depending on the feasibility. This provided the participants added control, allowing them to keep their InfoCanvas useful by updating the representation and adjusting inadequate representations.

After roughly two months had passed, the InfoCanvas was removed from the environment and a final interview was conducted. The participant was asked to comment on their overall experience with the system, including their likes and dislikes, and if the system had any effect on their daily routine.

Our study involved four local people: two faculty members in our own department and two administrators at a nearby university. Two participants chose an aquarium theme, one selected a beach theme, and another selected an office view. (Only the beach theme from the set shown in Figure 2 had been created at the time of the study.) Figure 3 shows where the InfoCanvas was positioned for each person and a sample view of their theme while it was running.

4.2   Study Findings

Utility

All participants stated that they enjoyed having the InfoCanvas display and thought that it was a useful means to portray information. Participant A, before receiving her InfoCanvas, questioned "How is this different from a My Yahoo page? Why would you need a separate screen, a separate application?" She wondered what the advantage would be and thought that a direct, textual representation of information would make more sense. However, after having used the InfoCanvas for an extended period of time she commented, "[The InfoCanvas] has a different feel. It is more private, because the casual observer will not

Participant A

Participant B

Participant C

Participant D

Fig. 3. Shown are the deployment configurations and a sample view from each of the four study participants using the InfoCanvas.

know the meaning of these icons. They won't know you just got email from [your spouse]. In that regard it was unique and different from anything that I have on my computer."

All participants reported that they would look at their InfoCanvas frequently throughout a day. Participant B stated, "I check it when I first come in, in between tasks, and whenever I come back from a meeting. It's situated right where my eyes go when I sit back to think for a second, so I'm always noticing it." In addition, no participant reported their canvas as distracting or felt that it interrupted their normal workflow.

Data Representations

We noted certain trends in the manner that each type of data was represented by the participants. Boolean data, such as whether or not a Web page has been updated, was represented by appearance transformations or by an image swapper with two visual elements. These transformations were apparently the most intuitive mappings, even though others are equally feasible, such as an image slider moving from one side of the display to the other.

Ordinal data was represented by an image swapper or by a population transformation. For example, participant C's coral changed color according to the temperature, using blue for below 50, hot pink for above 80 degrees, and orange for values in between. Traffic was represented by the number of boats sailing on participant B's canvas, with more boats signifying more congestion.

Continuous data was represented by almost every means possible, including sliders, swappers, or direct displays (value shown as digits). The method chosen appeared to correlate with how important the data was to the person and thus it dictated the precision of the representation. For example, participant C's scene utilized an image swap with a happy or sad fish to represent Coca-Cola's daily stock price movement. This mapping conveyed very little about the actual value of the stock, as a gain of half a point would show the same happy fish as a gain of ten points. However, she stated "I really love the happy and sad fish! They're just so cute!" and was satisfied with the level of awareness provided. However, participant D wanted to monitor the three major stock market indices precisely and chose to have the current day's change shown directly as numeric values written on a notepad.

The textual data monitored was mostly limited to news headlines or weather forecasts and was commonly represented in a fairly direct or literal mapping using a swapper or a text display. The natural weather images of the sun, clouds, and rain were used to represent forecasts, and news headlines were always written out textually. One exception was the monitoring for the appearance of stories about evolution on a newspaper Website by participant C, which was represented by a stingray appearing.

Not all themes had elements that lent themselves to intuitive mappings for all of a participant's data. However, participants were innovative in layering elements and creating abstract representations that allowed them to overcome the limitations of the pre-designed themes and paper cut-outs. For example, the stingray used by participant C to represent news stories about evolution does not have a strong visual correlation to evolution, but she had been stung by one in the past and her personal experience helped her to make the connection between the image and the data monitored. Participant A wanted to know the exact high temperature forecast, but was using the aquarium theme. She decided to layer the numerical value on top of a little sign with the forecasted condition dangling in the water from a hook and line. Thus the numerical value was contained within an element and maintained the visual continuity of the theme. It worked so well that when participant C, who worked at the same institution, happened to see it, she immediately requested that we add it to her scene.

Many of the representations chosen by the participants were not intuitive. As mentioned briefly earlier, this finding potentially conflicts with the Mankoff [13] ambient display evaluation heuristic stating that a display should use intuitive representations, because abstract transformations may require too much cognitive processing by the user. Our to-date use of the InfoCanvas has illustrated that people enjoy the highly symbolic mappings it facilitates. The system even generates its own lingo, with expressions such as "The crab's really to the left today—The market is plummeting," becoming commonplace. If one interprets the intuitive heuristic as simply meaning that states of the display are perceptually easy to recognize, then the InfoCanvas matches better.

Ability to Remember and Interpret
No participant reported any difficulty in remembering the mappings that they had created between data and visual elements. Participants also reported that they had no problem understanding the information portrayed on the InfoCanvas. However, two participants did report some difficulty in interpreting the value represented by sliders. Participant A's jellyfish moved horizontally along a path to represent the daily performance of a mutual fund. While she could tell whether the fund was up or down, she found that it was difficult to translate that into a more meaningful number. Participant B had a seagull that represented the current temperature based on the bird's height in the sky. The range was so large (30 to 90 degrees) that it was difficult to tell the difference between small but important differences in temperature. The other movement based mappings employed by these participants were not problematic.

Interaction with the Display
The desire to use the InfoCanvas as an interactive data exploration tool to investigate information was expressed by all participants. This was motivated by a desire to check information that is represented on their canvas, or by noticing that an interesting change in a representation when glancing at their display.

Participants stated that they wanted to be able to mouse over a particular item to receive more information, and furthermore, to be able to click on the item to launch a Web browser or other program that would allow them to quickly get the full details behind the visual element. In response to the first request, we added a mouse-over tool-tip capability to the system. When the mouse cursor moves over a visual element, a tool-tip shows a simple detail, such as the number of new emails or the current temperature. This was one example where feedback from the study has directly influenced system functionality.

We were slightly uneasy about adding this tool-tip capability because it seemed to violate one of our primary goals of making the InfoCanvas be a calm information communication conduit not requiring explicit user interaction. We wondered if this capability was requested because three of the four participants had their monitors on a nearby desk rather than in a more peripheral location such as being mounted on a wall. Interview feedback indicated to us that the participants still thought strongly of the display as a computer monitor, not as a separate stand-alone service.

This initial study provided us with some initial feedback about actual use of the InfoCanvas, but a more careful, comprehensive study is still needed. Presently, we are preparing a more in-depth, longitudinal study that will involve more users and will include both the subjective, qualitative analysis as present in this study and more highly analytical comparisons of people's use and perceptions of the system. In the new study, the InfoCanvas will be hung on a wall or on a shelf more appropriately, and we will see if user views, such as the desire for interaction, still occur.

5   Summary

We have described the concept of Information Art and how it is manifested through the InfoCanvas system. While the system stresses calm, aesthetically pleasing communication of information like other peripheral displays, it differs in providing a user with more control over the information being monitored and the representation of that information. We described the use of themes with visual elements that undergo transformations as a way to assist users to construct attractive and illuminating scenes. We also presented results from an initial study of extended use of the system.

Although current use of the InfoCanvas is primarily as a picture on a wall or desk, one can imagine any number of other possible uses. For instance, an InfoCanvas scene could be shown as a computer's screen-saver or displayed on an extra monitor in a multi-monitor display.[1] Similarly, as televisions and computers become more integrated, an InfoCanvas could be shown on a television when it is turned off. Further, it is possible to imagine simple InfoCanvas themes being used as the "off" displays for small devices such as PDAs and watches.

6   Acknowledgments

This research has been supported in part by a grant from the National Science Foundation, IIS-0118685. Many students have assisted with the project including Julie Hoffman, David Browning, Alex Drake, Nena Hy, Toni Pashley, Shannon Bauman, and Jehan Moghazy.

---

[1] Here, the display should not be a CRT because of the pixel burn-in issue with relatively static scenes such as those in the InfoCanvas.

References

1. Abowd, G., et al.: The Human Experience. Pervasive Computing **1** (2002) 48–57
2. Ambient Orb. Ambient Devices Inc. www.ambientdevices.com
3. Cadiz, J. J., et al.: Designing and deploying an information awareness interface. Proc. CSCW (2002) 314–323
4. Chang, A., et al.: Lumitouch: An emotional communication device. Extended Abstracts of CHI (2001) 371–372
5. Dahley, A., et al.: Water Lamp and Pinwheels: Ambient projection of digital information into architectural space. CHI Extended Abstracts (1998) 269–270
6. Fitzpatrick, G., et al.: Tickertape: Awareness in a Single Line. Proc. CHI (1998) 281–282
7. Fogarty, J., et al.: Aesthetic information collages: generating decorative displays that contain information. Proc. UIST (2001) 141–150
8. Gellersen, H. W., et al.: Ambient display media for peripheral information display. Personal Technologies **3** (1999) 199–208
9. Greenberg, S., Rounding, M.: The Notification Collage: Posting information to public and personal Displays. Proc. CHI (2000) 515–521
10. Heiner, J. M., et al.: The Information Percolator: Ambient information display in a decorative object. Proc. UIST (1999) 141–148
11. Holmquist, L. E., Skog, T.: Informative art: Information visualization in everyday environments. Proc. Graphite (2003) 229–235
12. Lunde, T., Larsen, A.: KISS the Tram: Exploring the PDA as support for everyday activities. Proc. Ubicomp (2001) 232–239
13. Mankoff, J., et al.: Heuristic evaluation of ambient displays. Proc. CHI (2003) 169–176
14. Matthews, T., et al.: A Peripheral Display Toolkit. Intel Research Berkeley Tech. Report IRB-TR-03-018 (2003)
15. McCrickard, D. S., et al.: A Model for Notification Systems Evaluation—Assessing User Goals for Multitasking Activity. ACM Trans. on Computer-Human Interaction **10** (2003) 312–338
16. Miller, T., Stasko, J.: Artistically conveying information with InfoCanvas. Proc. AVI (2002) 43–50
17. Mynatt, E., et al.: Designing audio aura. Proc. CHI (1998) 566–573
18. Mynatt, E., et al.: Digital family portraits: Providing peace of mind for extended family members. Proc. CHI (2001) 333–340
19. Pedersen, E. R., Sokoler, T.: AROMA: abstract representation of presence supporting mutual awareness. Proc. CHI (1997) 51–58
20. Plaue, C., et al.: Is a Picture Worth a Thousand Words? An Evaluation of Information Awareness Displays. Proc. Graphics Interface (2004) 117–126
21. Redstrom, J., et al. Informative Art: Using Amplified Artworks as Information Displays. Proc. DARE (2000) 103–114
22. Skog, T., et al.: Between aesthetics and utility: Designing ambient information visualizations. Proc. Information Visualization (2003) 233–240
23. van Dantzich, M., et al.: Scope: Providing awareness of multiple notifications at a glance. Proc. AVI (2002) 267–281
24. Weiser, M., Brown, J. S.: Designing calm technology. Power Grid Journal **1** (1996)
25. Wisneski, C., et al.: Ambient Displays: Turning Architectural Space into an Interface between People and Digital Information. Proc. CoBuild (1998) 22-32
26. Zhao, Q. A., Stasko, J. T.: What's Happening?: Promoting Community Awareness Through Opportunistic Peripheral Interfaces. Proc. AVI (2002) 69–74

Reminding About Tagged Objects Using Passive RFIDs

Gaetano Borriello[1,2], Waylon Brunette[1],
Matthew Hall[1], Carl Hartung[1], Cameron Tangney[1]

[1] Department of Computer Science and Engineering, University of Washington
{gaetano, wrb, mhall, chartung, cameron}@cs.washington.edu
[2] Intel Research Seattle
Seattle, WA, USA

Abstract. People often misplace objects they care about. We present a system that generates reminders about objects left behind by tagging those objects with passive RFID tags. Readers positioned in the environment frequented by users read tags and broadcast the tags' IDs over a short-range wireless medium. A user's personal server collects the read events in real-time and processes them to determine if a reminder is warranted or not. The reminders are delivered to a wristwatch-sized device through a combination of text messages and audible beeps. We believe this leads to a practical and scalable approach in terms of system architecture and user experience as well as being more amenable to maintaining user privacy than previous approaches. We present results that demonstrate that current RFID tag technology is appropriate for this application when integrated with calendar information.

1   Introduction

One of the promises of ubiquitous computing is that it will make our information systems proactive, that is, information will be made available as we need it, rather than having to request it explicitly. To accomplish this, it is important to have a sense of the user's context which can be defined quite broadly, including such disparate elements as: location, ambient temperature, heart-rate, sound level, other people that may be nearby, the activity the user is engaged in, the task they are trying to complete, etc. [13, 14].

In this paper, we describe our work in implementing a simple proactive application that reminds us of objects we may have mistakenly left behind as we go about our day. It uses a user's location, calendar entries, and the objects they are carrying as their context. The reminding engine takes as input a set of static and dynamic rules and checks that the objects that should be with a person at a given time are, in fact, present. When they are not present the system provides an appropriate alert to the user so that she can retrieve the objects left behind while it is still relatively easy to do so. An example is a lawyer reminded to return a legal brief to their law firm when leaving home in the morning. If the papers are left behind, the alert needs to be delivered to the user before they are too far away from home and it is still efficient for them to go back and retrieve the brief.

Reminding is an application that has wide appeal [18, 19, 20]. Recently, as part of a class on context-aware computing we conducted a short survey of approximately 30

N. Davies et al. (Eds.): UbiComp 2004, LNCS 3205, pp. 36-53, 2004.

members of our department (graduate students and faculty) and found that 75% lose things occasionally [1]. The items most commonly left behind included notebooks, pens, and water bottles with over 50% of respondents saying they forgot to take one or more of the things they needed for a meeting or a class at least once a month. Keys and cell phones were next in line as the most common items left behind. Laptops and PDAs were not as commonly forgotten as the other smaller and less expensive items. Respondents were also concerned about how they would be reminded, as over 75% preferred non-intrusive methods such as e-mail rather than pages or cell phone calls. However, they were not asked if they would want an immediate reminder such as our system provided.

From this and previous work in reminder systems, we find that the following are requirements for a proactive reminder system:

1. it should have the ability to keep track of a large number of small and inexpensive items,
2. reminders should not be too disruptive and must be kept to a minimum,
3. knowing where the user is headed, as opposed to only knowing where they are, is an important element of context needed to keep false reminders to a minimum,
4. it should be relatively straightforward for a user to add reminder rules to their application with minimal programming required for common situations, and
5. the system needs to be incrementally deployable and easy to maintain.

We used these five requirements to formulate the approach we have taken for the design of our system.

To address the first requirement, we use passive RFID tags that are inexpensive (currently on the order of less than $0.50 per tag with the price dropping precipitously as RFID tags are proliferating in supply-chain management) and can be easily affixed to the objects we care about tracking. They do not require batteries; making them virtually free of on-going maintenance costs.

For the second requirement, we use a wristwatch to display two levels of reminders: warnings and alerts. A warning simply adds an item to a list displayed on the screen of the watch. These are intended to be items the user can easily keep in her consciousness by simply glancing down at the wristwatch. Think of these as the equivalent of tying a string around a finger. When a reminder is more certain, an alert is triggered that causes the watch to audibly beep to get the user's attention and display the specific items that appear to be missing. These more forceful reminders are more appropriate when a user is about to leave a location and the cost of leaving something behind is high.

For the third requirement, we provide our reminder system with calendar information to better determine the user's possible destinations when they are leaving a location. In the future, we will rely less on calendar information and integrate our system with a wide-area positioning system that can provide definite information about whether a user is entering or exiting an area rather than just being in the presence of an RFID reader.

To partially fulfill the fourth requirement, we have also developed the concept of an *auto-tag*. This special tag has a predefined home base, and when the tag is taken from this location, it enables a reminder to return the tag to the home base. For example, a user could tag an item at work with a special auto-tag so that if it's taken home, there is a reminder the next morning to bring it back to work. Additionally, auto-tags are registered to a user so that they are not confused with other users' tags. Auto-tags require essentially no day-to-day user configuration but still allow the user to add powerful reminders with minimal effort.

Finally, for the fifth requirement, we have the RFID readers broadcast the tags they read over short-range radio for all nearby users to hear. One important advantage of this feature is it eliminates the need to connect the readers to the networking infrastructure and a central database. Instead, the user's personal server receives the transmissions from nearby readers and maintains its own local database with no need to discover a database service or deal with inter-domain authentication and security issues. Additional readers are easy to deploy as only their location needs to be recorded (we describe later how we plan to make that automatic as well) and the overall system is scalable as there is no central coordination or registration. Because of these properties, it is also a system that can be deployed by a single consumer who can install RFID readers in the places they commonly frequent (e.g., home, work, car, etc.). Although the cost of the RFID readers we used are in the range of PDAs and laptops, these are expected to fall dramatically with coming economies of scale. The proliferation of readers into supply-chain and retail management has the potential to greatly increase the number of reader a user encounters throughout a day.

In summary, our approach has the following combination of features that distinguish it from related work:

- passive RFID tags that require no maintenance,
- broadcasting RFID readers that make the system incrementally deployable,
- an unobtrusive user interface that minimally distracts the user, and
- auto-tags to program common behaviors.

We believe this combination represents important steps toward a practical and usable reminder application.

The remainder of the paper is structured as follows. In the next section, we describe related work in reminder systems and compare them to our approach. In section 3, we present the properties of RFID tags and tag readers and discuss some of their limitations and specifically focus on the issues of broadcasting read events. Section 4 describes our reminder application and its user interface in detail. Section 5 describes our experiments in validating the use of RFID tags as well as a complete reminder scenario. Section 6 provides a discussion of the issues we've uncovered and outlines our future work to resolve these issues and create a truly usable reminder system. Finally, Section 7 summarizes the paper and draws some preliminary conclusions.

2   Related Work

Technology aids for helping people remember what they need to do have been around for quite some time (see [2] for a good survey and [18, 19, 20] for specific applications). In the era of personal computing, most of the work has led to a variety of desktop and palmtop applications that focus on the *when* of a reminder. User interfaces for specifying all forms of recurring events are now standard on PDAs and popular email programs.

More recently, as embedded systems consisting of wireless sensors and wearable devices [17] have become more practical, attention has begun to shift toward reminders for physical objects, or the *what* of a reminder. An early example of this is the CyberMinder system [3]. In CyberMinder, user context (defined in terms of location, username, sound level, or, even, stock price) is used to trigger a reminder message to be delivered to the user. Several delivery methods are supported including wearable user interfaces and printing of paper to-do lists. The CyberMinder system selects the most appropriate method to use. Although CyberMinder added direct context sensing to the desktop reminder applications, it was still a reminder system focusing on information rather than physical objects.

In line with the current work in integrating the physical and virtual worlds, SPECs take reminders a step further by making it possible to remind people about physical objects as well [4]. With SPECs, each object of interest is tagged with a bi-directional infrared sensor package. SPECs beacon their ID over the IR medium to be picked up by other SPECs and SPEC base stations. By collecting this information, reminders can now be based on the presence or absence of particular objects. Discrimination based on location is easy to achieve by simply affixing a SPEC at a particular location. One of the main issues with SPECs is the requirement of line-of-sight between IR transceivers. This makes it impossible to place a tagged object in a bag or pocket and could cause many proximity events to be missed because the IR transceivers on two SPECs do not line up.

Wireless sensor nodes have been used to construct a radio-frequency version of SPECs [5, 20]. As with SPECs, two objects are said to be near each other if they can communicate, not necessarily bi-directionally. Each sensor node records the times at which it hears RF packets from other nodes. This data can then be mined by a base station to generate reminders or study work-flow patterns. Because proximity events are recorded in parallel by all nodes, the clocks of the nodes need to be kept synchronized to an appropriate accuracy for human motion.

The problem with both SPECs [5] and their radio counterparts such as the commercial Dipo [20] is that they are active devices. They have batteries that may last months but will eventually need to be replaced. Their cost consists of a small microcontroller and memory, a radio or IR transceiver, and a battery; although this cost is admittedly small, it is still prohibitive for tagging large numbers of objects. Moreover, if too many are in a small space they may saturate the limited communication bandwidth available.

Another issue with these approaches is the lack of a central repository where the proximity information can be processed to determine if a reminder must be issued. Reminders are issued based on data stored in proximate nodes rather than from a global perspective.

Our approach is distinguished from these in several aspects:

- we use passive RFID tags to tag objects because they are cheap and will soon even be printable onto paper [16],
- RFID tags do not require batteries and are spared associated maintenance issues,
- RFID readers can act as efficient sensors for a large number of tags and broadcast the information to all interested parties in parallel,

- the only devices that require battery power are the user's personal server and user interface that in the future could be combined into a single device such as a cell phone or wristwatch, and
- a single repository, the user's personal server [9], can collect and process all the information relevant to each user.

In addition to these differences with prior work, our approach is likely to be as amenable to privacy protection and can benefit from the same reminder management and user interface.

3   RFID Tags and Readers

Radio-frequency identification tags are a rapidly evolving technology. They were developed to make supply chain management more efficient. In the basic technology, a reader's antenna induces enough power through the tag's antenna to operate the tag's integrated circuit. The tag electronics radiate back to the reader and modulate the signal so as to communicate the identification number of the tag [6].

In recent years, many advances have been made in RFID technology. Among these are: the ability to read multiple tags within range of the reader antenna through a singulation protocol, longer range tags through better antenna design and lower-power tag circuitry, increased storage capacity in the tag to represent other information in addition to ID, and the ability to write the tag memory with new information. Our work leverages all of these advances.

The ability to read multiple tags is essential as we expect users to carry many tagged devices at any one time. Longer read range is important so that readers can be placed in entryways and corridors and read the tags that pass by without requiring a conscious action on the part of the user such as explicitly waving a tag in front of a reader. Large storage capacity in the tag allows us to add more identifiers and, eventually, will allow us to include code for the reminder system within the tag itself. The ability to write all or part of the tag's data allows us to build a more privacy-friendly system with capabilities that can be more easily personalized to each user.

One real-world limitation of RFID readers is that they can occasionally fail to read a tag that is present. This occurs because of interference from other objects, especially human bodies with their high water content that absorbs RF energy. Another reason for missed reads is that the tag reading protocol has trouble with tags that have their antennas very close to each other. Therefore, our system must be designed with false negatives in mind. False positives, where the reader reports a tag as being read when it is not really present, are nearly impossible and we therefore do not consider them.

In our implementation, we use Alien tags and readers [7]. More specifically, we chose the ALL-9250 Alien tag (S1800002-001), also known as the I2-tag and shown in Figure 1 that operates at 915MHz. We found these tags to have a read range of 5-10 feet although they are quite sensitive to proximity to human bodies (read success rates ranged from 68% to 84% for the four types of tags manufactured by Alien – we chose the I2-tag as it was the best performer).

Our RFID readers broadcast the tags they read to anyone in the vicinity (much in the spirit of [15]). We use UC Berkeley sensor motes [8] operating at 433MHz to realize this broadcast. There is a mote attached to each reader and a mote attached to each user's personal server to receive the broadcast. The motes use a low-power connection-less radio protocol that transmits data at only 19.2kbps but does not require the several seconds of discovery time required of such protocols as Bluetooth. However, this is very limiting bandwidth that we will eventually replace with Wi-Fi, but for our purposes, dozens of tags' IDs can be broadcast in less than a second. The range of the radio is an order of magnitude greater than the tag reader's range and consistently reaches 10-15 meters and often much more. This longer range allows ample time to ensure that the user's personal server receives the transmission from the reader.

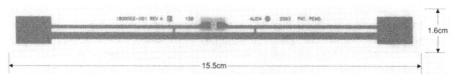

Figure 1. Example of an Alien ALL-9250 915MHz long-range RFID tag (the I2-tag). The tag integrated circuit is at the center of the tag and is connected to an antenna that is approximately 15cm long.

Each tag ID consists of 64 bits. Assuming that the reader reads up to 25 tags at a time, it will take a mote less than 1 second to transmit this data. With human motion usually not exceeding 3m/sec, this translates into the user being no more than 5 meters away from the reader, which is considerably less than the range of the mote radios. Because the data is broadcast, we are not concerned with the number of users that need to receive the data but, rather, only with the total number of tag IDs that need to transmitted. The number of readers required is dependent on the number of locations that need to be instrumented rather than the number of users.

4   The Reminder Application and Its User Interface

We begin the detailed description of our system with a typical reminder scenario. Our example subject is one of the authors, a male with a 9-5 job Monday through Friday. His typical work day follows the pattern of going from home to work, work to lunch, back to work, work to home, and home to the gym and back on most days. We tagged all items he deemed important with appropriate tags and took a day and a half long period from his week as the focus for the experiments we report in the next section. RFID readers are present at each of the locations. Readers for home and car could be purchased as appliances by the user. Readers at work may be purchased by the employer and placed at entrances to the building and/or purchased by employees and installed at their desks. Readers at local restaurants and gyms are likely to be purchased by those businesses to help extend an additional convenience service to their customers. Figure 2 has a schematic for these five locations and lists the items the user has specified they would like to have in their possession at each location.

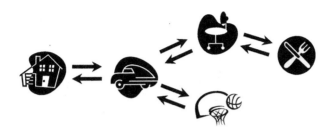

8:00		Leave for work: **keys, wallet, phone, jacket, backpack, keycard**
8:00	- 8:30	In car: **keys, wallet, phone, jacket, backpack, keycard**
8:30		Arrive at work, park car
8:33		Enter building: **keys, wallet, phone, jacket, backpack, keycard**
8:35		Arrive at desk: **keys, wallet, phone, jacket, backpack, keycard**
8:35	- 12:00	At work: **keycard**
12:00	- 13:00	At lunch: **keycard, phone, wallet**
13:00	- 17:00	At work: **keycard**
17:00		Leave work: **keys, wallet, phone, jacket, backpack, keycard**
17:00	- 17:45	In car: **keys, wallet, phone, jacket, backpack, keycard, docs (auto-tag)**
17:45		Arrive home: **keys, wallet, phone, jacket, backpack, keycard, docs (auto-tag)**
19:00		Leave for basketball
19:00	- 19:15	In car: **keys, wallet, phone, gym bag**
19:15		Arrive at gym: **keys, wallet, phone, gym bag**
21:00		Leave for home
21:02		In car: **keys, wallet, phone, gym bag**
21:17		Arrive home: **keys, wallet, phone, gym bag**

Figure 2. Usage scenario for a typical day for our test subject. RFID readers are present at each of the five locations represented by the icons at the top of the figure. Each time interval is detailed with the items carried between the locations and the most likely position of the items on the person.

There are few things to note in this scenario. While at work, the only item needed on the subject at all times is the keycard. Every other item can stay in the office. When leaving a location (for lunch, home, or anywhere) the wallet and phone will always be needed. The subject will likely pass a reader in his office many times throughout the day, so a simple way to tell if he is leaving work is to have a reader at the exits of his building. This need for determining where someone is headed rather than just where they are argues for location tracking to be integrated into the system. We'll revisit this issue in Section 6.

In our scenario, the subject needs to return items to the locations from which they were originally taken. For instance, items taken from home in the morning (like a jacket) should return home at the end of the day. Similarly, items brought home from work will probably need to be brought back the next day. An instance of this concept is captured in our scenario when the subject tags some legal documents with an auto-tag to remind himself to bring them back the following day.

There may, of course, be many variations to the routine presented here. For example, in the morning he may bring his gym bag with him so that he can go straight to the gym after work. In another example, the subject brings his own lunch, so he doesn't have to leave the building for a restaurant. On those days that he brings his lunch, the system should remind him to return his lunch container back home at the end of the day. Figure 3 shows an example of a user arriving at a location.

Figure 3. A user walking through a doorway with several tagged objects. An RFID reader is visible on the left (white box on black stand); tags are visible on the notebooks in his hand; his personal server is in his front left pants pocket; and, our wristwatch UI is on his left wrist (images of the personal server and wristwatch are in Figure 4).

Reminder Specification Language

We wrote a custom language to describe reminders. In the future, we plan to expand our reminder creation system with a graphical UI that enables users to query, sort, and edit their reminders. This graphical UI would be tied to a desktop RFID reader so that users could easily scan tags and manipulate reminder rules without having to type tag IDs, thereby simplifying configuration.

We have developed a very simple, yet powerful, language to help users express reminders (with inspiration from the SPECs' language [4]). The language is built around two basic constructs. The first construct is the keyword 'object' that allows the user to specify symbolic names for objects, rather than having to remember specific ID tags. The syntax is 'object name (tagID)' Where 'name' is a user entered name and 'tagID' is the RFID tag ID of the associated object. Once the user has specified his/her objects he can then begin to specify 'reminders' such as:

```
reminder (day=tuesday, destination=work, location=home, starttime=12:00,
          endtime=1:00, items=[keys, wallet])
```

All of the keywords for the 'reminder' construct are optional except for 'items'. If an option is omitted, it is assumed to mean 'always'. This lets us build a wide variety of expressions with fairly little effort. Since our system uses predictive algorithms, users do not need to enter specific times or even ranges of times, but they can do so if they prefer to be more precise. Leaving out the 'day' keyword indicates every day. By including location but not destination, we indicate 'from location L to anywhere' When we omit location but include destination, we indicate 'from anywhere to destination D'. If we leave out both location and destination we indicate 'anywhere'. Furthermore, if both location and destination are the same it means 'always at the (doubly) specified location'. The relations to time are very similar to destination and location. By leaving out a start time and including an end time we indicate 'before endtime'. Similarly, by leaving out an end time and including a start time we indicate 'after starttime'. The user can combine the above in any way so as to represent all the situations for which our system presents reminders. Below is an example set of reminders for our target scenario.

```
#items to bring to work
reminder (destination=work, items=[phone, keys, wallet, backpack,
          jacket, keycard])

#items I need at lunch
reminder (location=work, starttime=11:00, endtime=2:00, items=[keycard,
          phone, wallet])

#items I always need with me at work
reminder (location=work, destination=work items=[keycard])

#items to bring home from work
reminder (location=work, destination=home, items=[phone, keys, wallet,
          backpack, jacket, keycard])

#items I need any time I go to the gym
reminder (destination=gym, items=[gymbag, wallet, phone, keys])
reminder (location=gym, destination=home, items=[gymbag, wallet, phone,
          keys])

#auto-tag associated reminder
reminder (destination=work, items=[autoTag1])
```

The last reminder in the list above is automatically generated by the presence of the auto-tag. As the auto-tag has been pre-registered by the user to be associated with his work location, it will simply trigger a reminder if the item is not returned to work the next time the user goes there. Auto-tags are pre-registered by a procedure that uses an RFID reader at home or at work to write the reminder into the tag itself and register the tag ID in a database on the user's personal server.

Reminder Application Implementation

Our reminder software runs on the user's personal server [9], shown on the right in Figure 4. The user's personal data such as reminder rules and calendar information is also stored on this personal device. The personal server is a small, embedded server and storage device that runs Linux. It has communication interfaces for Wi-Fi and Bluetooth in addition to the mote radio we use to receive tag IDs broadcast by readers.

The reminding software consists of several concurrent, communicating modules. A reminder control module constantly evaluates the set of reminder rules against the current context. A location module infers the current location from various input sources and maintains a list of possible user destinations. Finally, a radio module listens for beaconing RFID readers and wirelessly communicates warnings and alerts to the wristwatch user interface (see the left half of Figure 4). Each component accesses an SQL database on the personal server to load programmable rules and parameters as well as store persistent state (e.g., past RFID tag read events).

When the radio module receives a packet broadcast from a nearby RFID reader, it parses the packet and sends both the reminder control and location module the list of tags, if any, seen by the reader. While the reminder control component is interested in both which reader was broadcasting and which tags were seen, the location component cares only about which reader. This is why readers periodically broadcast independently of whether they have read any tags or not. This helps the application keep track of locations even in the presence of false negative reads. The radio module also manages outgoing communication to the wristwatch.

Figure 4. Larger views of our wristwatch (showing a reminder alert) and personal server. Note that the personal server has Wi-Fi communication capability in addition to the mote radio.

The location inference component determines the current location of the user from the location corresponding to the RFID reader 'heard' most recently (later we'll explain how we plan to generalize this). The module then cross-references this location with the user's calendar data in order to construct a list of possible future destinations that will be visited before returning to the current location. Together, the destination list and current location are known as the user's 'location context.' Whenever this context changes the location module informs the reminder control unit.

Finally, we come to the core of the reminding software: the control component. Within this module, there are three important tasks to be managed: maintenance of the user's 'item context', which is simply the list of items currently with the user; reminder rule generation and evaluation, which may lead to the generation of warnings or alerts; and personal item tracking.

At this time, the implementation of item context is very simple. If a reader has seen an item, then it is part of the item context. If we pass a reader that does not see the item, the item is removed from the item context list. To better cope with false negatives, deployments with numerous redundant RFID readers would be advantageous. In such situations, more complex implementations might be able to "smooth" changes in the item context over multiple successive reads by accounting for the probability of false negatives. At this time, however, we assume a sparse set of readers, so such smoothing is not included in our prototype.

The control module constantly reevaluates all relevant rules as the user's item and location contexts change. If it is clear that a rule has been violated, the component will trigger a reminder. Depending upon the severity of the consequences of a missed reminder, the reminder either takes the form of an audible alert or a non-intrusive, inaudible warning. Currently, severity is simply a function of whether the location context has changed, and audible alerts are raised when this is the case. Otherwise, the item in question is simply added to the top of the wristwatch's 'consciousness list' interface, an alternate display on the wristwatch.

Finally, the control component tracks the last known location of tagged items. This is done both as an independent service to the user (i.e. "where did I leave my keys?") and as an important input for intelligent decision-making within the rule evaluation system. An example will assist in understanding the importance of the last known location as a rule evaluation variable: our user usually leaves work and heads home where he picks up his gym bag before he leaves for the gym. When the user leaves work, the system checks to see if he has his gym bag (which he does not have) because the gym is in the user's possible destination list. Since the reminding software last saw the gym bag at home, it is able to infer that the user is probably going there to pick up the gym bag preventing an unnecessary alert. Even if this prediction is incorrect the user cannot remedy the situation until he reaches home where his gym bag is located.

We also use the concept of a safe zone to limit the issuance of an alert or warning until the time nears that a user is likely to leave a destination. Basically, users can create personal zones, such as home, car, or office, where any item can be left without warnings being issued.

5   Experiments

We conducted experiments on our underlying RFID technology as well as the reminder application itself.

Initially, we wanted to determine which of the several tags available to us would yield the best results. We configured our reader in a test setup that would minimize the effects of the subject's direction and orientation by placing the antennas on both sides of the likely walking path at slightly different angles as shown in Figure 5. We found this configuration to be the most reliable of those tested. Note that both antennas are connected to a single reader that multiplexes between the two so there is only a small incremental cost to the two-antenna configuration (antennas are much cheaper than readers).

To determine the efficacy of the RFID technology and the rate of false negatives that we could expect, we tagged all the objects in the scenario with the most successful I2-tag and performed many trials under different conditions to see whether the reader would correctly read the tag IDs. All tags were placed directly on the items' surface with the exception of the laptop. Due to the high metallic content of the laptop, we found that the success rate improved dramatically when we placed a 0.125-

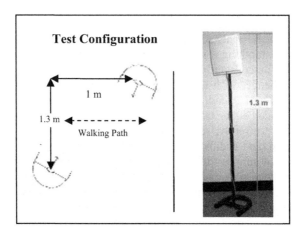

Figure 5. Configuration of the RFID reader antennas. The white box that houses the antenna is approximately 30cm square with a center height of 1.3m. Two antennas are arranged as shown around a walking path to minimize missed tag reads when the user moves in either direction.

inch thick piece of packing foam between the surface of the laptop and the tag (not an unreasonable modification, moreover there are specific tags designed to work on metal objects [10]). Table 1 shows the percentage of the time that each object's tag was successfully recognized by the RFID reader. The different trials included many passes by the reader's antennae (5 times in each direction for a total of 10 trials for each scenario) with the object placed in a plausible carrying position (e.g., notebook in a backpack or cell phone in a pocket). Attempts were made to minimize the effect of item location in this experiment. For instance, no items were placed directly against the subject's skin (for reasons explained later), nor were any items placed within an extremely close proximity to one another. The number of test scenarios in which each item was tested is listed in the 'Number of Scenarios' column.

We also performed experiments to assess tag reliability when items are carried in different positions or arrangements. Table 2 shows the percentages of successful (12-tag) detections for a variety of cases. Items were placed on the subject as dictated by our practical test scenarios. The success rates for each category were calculated using the cumulative averages across all of these scenarios. The number of test scenarios for which each location was tested is included in the 'Number of Scenarios' column. The 'Person' category in Table 2 includes tagged items on a jacket, a gym bag, a cloth bag, and a backpack. It is important to recognize that for 'Person', a substantial amount of material separated the subject's skin from the object's tag. A more indicative reflection of success rates when tags are touching the skin can be found in the 'In Hand' category.

The second set of experiments focused on our reminder software implementation. The first experiment tested our reminding system by using our target scenario as input (see Figure 2 and the reminder code of section 4).

Table 1. Success rates for reading tags affixed to the various items in our example.

Item	Success Rate (cumulative)	Number Of Scenarios	Number Of Trials
Jacket	100%	1	10
Backpack	100%	1	10
Keys	65%	3	30
Cell phone	47%	3	30
Wallet	93%	3	30
Keycard	55%	3	30
Laptop	80%	1	10
Papers	100%	1	10
Gym Bag	100%	1	10
Lunch container	100%	2	20

Table 2. Success rates for tag reads when objects are carried in different locations.

Item Location	Success Rate (Cumulative)	Number Of Scenarios	Number Of Trials
Person	100%	5	50
Jacket Pocket	95%	2	20
Jean Pocket (back)	100%	2	20
Jean Pocket (front)	38%	5	50
Backpack	93%	3	30
In Hand	23%	1	10
Gym Bag	73%	3	30
Cloth Bag	100%	1	10

Figure 6 summarizes our scenario simulation results (we use only a partial trace log due to space limitations). The location transitions are alphabetically labeled by simulation chronology. The ascending number ranges associated with each location correspond to atomic groups of read events (e.g., 1-3 represents 3 reads performed by the reader at the home, each consisting of multiple tag IDs, see the simulation log for details). One can follow the user through the day by starting at home, following transition A to the car, returning home on B, back out on C, to work on D, and so on.

In short, the user leaves home but forgets their cell phone, receives an alert about the missing phone as he reaches the car, and returns home to retrieve the missing item. Now carrying all his important items, he returns to the car and drives to work. While working, he accidentally leaves his keycard behind and receives a prompt alert to that effect at the next reader he passes. The user retrieves the keycard and continues to work until lunch, at which point he intentionally leaves his jacket, keys, and backpack in his office and walks to lunch. When he arrives at lunch, the reminding software does not remind him of the missing jacket, keys, or backpack because it infers that he will return to work before going home without the items.

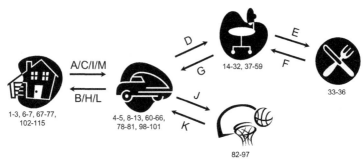

Current location: home – Possible destinations: car
Read #2: keys, wallet, jacket, backpack, and keycard
Current location: car – Possible destinations: work, lunch (transition A)
Alert issued for phone as location was changing.
Current location: home – Possible destinations: work, lunch, car (transition B)
Read #7: phone
Current location: car – Possible destinations: work, lunch (transition C)
Current location: work – Possible destinations: lunch (transition D)
Read #21: no keycard
Alert issued for keycard.
Read #22: keycard
Read #30: no jacket, no keys, no backpack
Current location: lunch – Possible destinations: work, car, home, gym (transition E)
Current location: work – Possible destinations: car, home, gym (transition F)
Read #41: keys, jacket, and backpack
Read #57: auto1-tag
Current location: car – Possible destinations: home (transition G)
Current location: home – Possible destinations: car, gym (transition H)
Read #70: no jacket, no auto1, no keys, no backpack, no keycard, no wallet, no phone
Read #74: keys, wallet, phone, gym bag
Current location: car – Possible destinations: gym (transition I)
Current location: gym – Possible destinations: car, home, work, lunch (transition J)
Read #84: no gym bag
Warning issued for gym bag.
Read #94: gym bag
Current location: car – Possible destinations: home (transition K)
Current location: home – Possible destinations: car, work, lunch (transition L)
Alert issued for auto1 as location was changing.
Read #104: no keys, no gym bag, no wallet, no phone
Read #109: keys, wallet, phone, jacket, backpack, keycard
Current location: car – Possible destinations: work, lunch (transition M)
Alert issued for auto1 as location was changing.

Figure 6. A partial trace log for a typical day of our usage scenario. The numbers under the location icons correspond to the read events recorded at each location. The transitions are labeled in the figure for cross-reference to the log.

After his meal, he returns to work and eventually places a 'Return To Work' auto-tag on a paper that he will revise at home that evening. When he leaves work for home, the auto-tag is recognized and its corresponding auto-tag code is activated in the reminding software. At home he picks up his gym bag and heads to the gym. At the gym, he leaves his gym bag in a locker, causing the reminding software to add a warning about the gym bag to the wristwatch's consciousness list. Afterward, he picks up the gym bag, heads home, and when he arrives, the software recognizes that work will again soon be a valid user destination and reminds him about the papers that must return to work (in the future, we hope to do without this reminder and only issue it on the next day when the user will be heading to work). To further illustrate the auto-tag mechanism, our scenario includes the very start of the following day. The user leaves home in the morning with everything but the tagged papers. As a result, an alert is issued as the user gets into his car, thus concluding our scenario.

To further understand the effect of missed reads, we created a simulation sequence based on our test scenario where all the tags were present at the correct times and locations (unlike our previous example where the user did leave some things behind). Our simulator randomly deleted individual tags from the read events to simulate the effect of false negatives. The averaged results for 100 independent sets of data are show below in Table 3. Notice that there is one warning issued in the 0% drop case. This warning occurs when the subject leaves his gym bag in the locker at the gym (a non-safe zone). According to the reminders that were setup, the user will need to take the gym bag home so the system is issuing a warning in case the user accidentally left it behind.

Table 3. The number of warnings and alerts increase with an increasing number of false negatives, but only moderately so.

Drop Rate	Warnings	Std. Dev	Alarms	Std. Dev
0%	1	0.0	0	0.0
5%	13	3.3	4	2.0
10%	24	3.6	7	2.3
15%	33	4.5	10	2.8
20%	41	4.8	12	2.9
25%	48	5.0	15	2.9
30%	54	4.5	17	2.9
35%	58	4.1	19	3.1
40%	62	4.0	21	3.4

Table 3 shows that our reminder implementation works reasonably well even when 10% of possible tag reads are missed. From our experiments we believe that the most likely value of missed reads will be somewhere between 5% and 10% for the RFID technology we are using. The number of warnings quickly reaches a plateau as the number of false negatives increases. Again, the warnings do not interrupt the user but simply add items to the wristwatch's consciousness list. The number of alerts is more significant and this appears to grow linearly with the drop rate. Even though the system is detecting possible problems, the great majority only cause warnings rather than alerts to be issued. Alerts are only issued when it is important that the user notices the current situation as there may be a larger cost associated with retrieving the item. The results in Table 3 were generated with no smoothing algorithms; however, initial testing with smoothing gives us confidence that we can significantly decrease the number of warnings and alerts that are issued mistakenly.

6   Discussion

In constructing our reminder application, we encountered several important issues that merit further discussion as they can limit the practicality of our system.

Our first set of challenges revolves around the use of location information. Ideally, we would like the system to issue an alert only when the user is about to take an action that will increase the cost to go back and retrieve an item. For the reminder to be issued at the appropriate time, the system needs to know when the user's location is changing. One possible solution is to specify which reader is near a doorway and if detected the system knows the user is at the boundary and is about to change locations. However, detection of a boundary reader does not always accurately indicate a location change because if the user is only walking by the doorway and the reader picks up the user, the system may erroneously assume the user is leaving and issue an unwanted reminder. For example, a user may walk outside to get something off your porch and then walk back inside. To the system, this may look the same as if the user were leaving for work. Ideally, we would want the system to recognize when the user is entering or exiting an area and issue the proper reminders only when it is sure they are changing locations. Currently, due to the system's inability to distinguish entrance from exit, reminder rules must be evaluated in terms of more general location-change events. Furthermore, using location tracking will decrease the need to place a reader at every entrance or exit of a home or workplace as location changes will not require reader sightings.

To address these issues, we plan to integrate Place Lab [11] WiFi-based localization into our system. This will enable us to detect when the user is leaving a location because we can localize the user's personal server to within 30m. We can even apply learning algorithms to automatically discern locations where the user spends considerable time and then allow the user to label them for use with the reminders [12]. Localization to this granularity promises to resolve many of the problems in generating timely alerts and minimizing problems due to false negative reads.

A second set of challenges is presented by the interaction with other users' tags. Of course, a user's own object tags can be registered with their personal server so that any other tag ID is simply ignored (it may simply mean another user was near a reader at the same time). This is why it was necessary to register a user's auto-tags as these would otherwise could be construed to be another user's tags the first time they are seen. Another issue related to this, is the ability to track another user's movements by keeping track of all the tags broadcast by readers. A remedy for this is for a user's home reader to automatically randomize tag IDs every evening. Writable tags with password protection make this feasible [10]. The large space of possible of IDs (64 to 128 bits) makes it unlikely that an ID will collide with another. This ability to re-write tag IDs and having the application run completely on the user's own client, their personal server, make this system much more privacy-friendly than infrastructure-based approaches. Furthermore, it lends itself to incremental deployment as a single user or a group of users can add readers as needed for their needs.

Finally, probabilistic methods and machine learning have much to offer reminding applications. As false negatives are a reality as no tags are likely to ever be perfect, it is imperative that our reminder system be tolerant of possible dropped reads and consider the location of objects probabilistically until it receives incontrovertible evidence. For example, a gym bag might have last been seen at home, but it may have made its way home without being detected by the home reader. The system must maintain a probability that the gym bag is back at the gym or at home. Over time, it may learn what is most likely given past experience. Learning may be extended further to derive reminder rules automatically by observing a user for a period of time after they purchase the application. This may minimize the need for creating reminders explicitly or at least create starting templates that already include parameters such as likely locations, weekend differences, and work hours. Most importantly, learning where the user is likely to go next when they leave a location can greatly mitigate the need for the calendar information that we currently use [12].

7   Conclusion

We have built a working prototype of an RFID-based object reminder system. It uses a novel combination of broadcasting RFID readers, a personal server to run the application, and a wristwatch user interface used to deliver to levels of reminders. Our initial results based on a complete user scenario indicate that the system works well even in the face of a large number of missed RFID tag reads. We are confident that our approach is practical and scalable to a large number of users.

Our next steps are: to integrate our system with a WiFi-based location estimation system that can help us better determine when a user is leaving a location and thereby issue more definitive and timely reminders; create a graphical UI for creating and maintaining reminders; augment the wristwatch interface with the ability to help a user track down a lost object by returning to its last known location and/or retracing steps. A full user study is also planned so that we can better study the interactions between multiple users and their ability to easily adjust their reminders.

Acknowledgements

We would like to thank Mik Lamming and Dennis Bohm for inspiring us to work on this problem and generously providing their time in discussing the issues. Their comments and suggestions, along with those of the reviewers and our paper's sheperd, Michael Beigl, have greatly improved this paper.

References

1. Borriello, G.: CSE590GB: Location-Aware Computing, Department of Computer Science & Engineering, University of Washington, Seattle, WA (www.cs.washington.edu/590gb).
2. Silvermam, B.G.: Computer reminders and alerts. IEEE Computer , Vol. 30 , No. 1 , Jan. 1997, 42 – 49.
3. Dey, A., Abowd, G.: Cybreminder: A context-aware system for supporting reminders. 2nd International Symposium on Handheld and Ubiquitous Computing, Bristol, UK, Sep. 2000, 172-186.

4. Lamming, M., Bohm, D.: SPECs: Another Approach to Human Context and Activity Sensing Research Using Tiny Peer-to-Peer Wireless Computers. 5th International Conference on Ubiquitous Computing, Seattle, WA, Oct. 2003, 191-199.

5. Brunette, W., Hartung, C., Nordstrom, B., Borriello, G.: Proximity Interactions between Wireless Sensors and their Applications. 2nd ACM International Workshop on Wireless Sensor Networks & Applications, San Diego, CA, Sep. 2003, 30-37.

6. Want, R.: RFID: A Key to Automating Everything. Scientific American. Jan. 2004, 56-65.

7. Alien Technology RFID Readers and Tags. http://www.alientechnology.com/

8. Hill, J., et al.: System architecture directions for network sensors. 9th International Conference on Architectural Support for Programming Languages and Operating Systems, Cambridge, MA, Nov. 2000, 93-104.

9. Want, R., Pering, T., Danneels, G., Kumar, M., Sundar, M., Light, J.: The Personal Server: changing the way we think about ubiquitous computing. 4th International Conference on Ubiquitous Computing, Goteborg Sweden, Oct. 2002, 194-209.

10. Intermec Technologies Coporation: Guide to RFID Tag Selection, Sep. 2003 (http://epsfiles.intermec.com/eps_files/eps_brochure/RFIDTagSelectionGuide_brochure_web.pdf)

11. Schilit, B., et. al.: Challenge: Ubiquitous Location-Aware Computing and the Place Lab Initiative. 1st ACM International Workshop on Wireless Mobile Applications and Services on WLAN Hotspots, San Diego, CA, Sep. 2003, 29-35.

12. Ashbrook, D., Starner, T.: Using GPS to learn significant locations and predict movement across multiple users. *Personal and Ubiquitous Computing*, 7(5), 2003, 275–286.

13. P.J. Brown, J.D. Bovey and X. Chen. Context-Aware Applications: from the Laboratory to the Marketplace. IEEE Personal Communications, No. 5, Vol. 4, 1997, pp 58-64.

14. Schilit, B., Adams, N., Want, R.: Context-aware computing applications. IEEE Workshop on Mobile Computing Systems and Applications, Santa Cruz, CA, Oct. 1994, 85- 90.

15. Siegemund, F., Flörkemeier, C.: Interaction in Pervasive Computing Settings using Bluetooth-Enabled Active Tags and Passive RFID Technology together with Mobile Phones. IEEE Conference on Pervasive Computing and Communications, Dallas, TX, Mar. 2003, 378 - 387.

16. Want, R., Fishkin, K., Gujar, A., Harrison, B.: Bridging Physical and Virtual Worlds with Electronic Tags. ACM Conference on Human Factors in Computing Systems, Pittsburgh, PA, May 1999, 370-377.

17. Toney, A., Mulley, B., Thomas, B., Piekarski, W.: Minimal Social Weight User Interactions for Wearable Computers in Business Suits. IEEE 6th International Symposium on Wearable Computing, Seattle, WA, Oct. 2002, 57-64.

18. Lamming, M., Flynn, M.: "Forget-me-not" - Intimate Computing in Support of Human Memory. Invited keynote paper for FRIEND21 Symposium on Next Generation Human Interface, Feb. 1994.

19. Rhodes, B., Starner, T.: The Remembrance Agent: A continuously running automated information retrieval system. 1st International Conference on The Practical Application of Intelligent Agents and Multi Agent Technology, London, UK, Apr. 1996, 487-495.

20. Dipo: Détecteur Individuel de Perte d'Objets. http://www.dipo.fr

Evaluating the Effects of Displaying Uncertainty in Context-Aware Applications

Stavros Antifakos[1], Adrian Schwaninger[2,3], and Bernt Schiele[1,4]

[1] Perceptual Computing and Computer Vision, ETH Zurich
`antifakos@inf.ethz.ch`
[2] Department of Psychology, University of Zurich
[3] Max Planck Institute for Biological Cybernetics, Tübingen
`adrian.schwaninger@tuebingen.mpg.de`
[4] Multimodal Interactive Systems, Darmstadt University of Technology
`schiele@informatik.tu-darmstadt.de`

Abstract. Many context aware systems assume that the context information they use is highly accurate. In reality, however, perfect and reliable context information is hard if not impossible to obtain. Several researchers have therefore argued that proper feedback such as monitor and control mechanisms have to be employed in order to make context aware systems applicable and useable in scenarios of realistic complexity. As of today, those feedback mechanisms are difficult to compare since they are too rarely evaluated. In this paper we propose and evaluate a simple but effective feedback mechanism for context aware systems. The idea is to explicitly display the uncertainty inherent in the context information and to leverage from the human ability to deal well with uncertain information. In order to evaluate the effectiveness of this feedback mechanism the paper describes two user studies which mimic a ubiquitous memory aid. By changing the quality, respectively the uncertainty of context recognition, the experiments show that human performance in a memory task is increased by explicitly displaying uncertainty information. Finally, we discuss implications of these experiments for today's context-aware systems.

1 Introduction

Context awareness is often seen to be a key ingredient for ubiquitous computing. In the literature, several frameworks and architectures for context awareness have been proposed such as the Context Toolkit [1], Context Fabric [2], or the Location Stack [3]. Experience with context-aware systems however shows that often context is not as simple to deal with as it may seem at first glance. This is mainly due to the inherent uncertainty and ambiguity in context information. Greenberg [4] for example argues that external things, such as objects, the environment, and people, might be relatively simple to capture but that internal things such as people's current interests, objectives, and the state of the activity people are pursuing, is extremely difficult to capture. Bellotti and Edwards [5] even argue that there are human aspects of context that cannot be sensed or

N. Davies et al. (Eds.): UbiComp 2004, LNCS 3205, pp. 54–69, 2004.

even inferred by technological means. Such effects have been reported by others in several application domains [6, 7]. So it is important to take into account that context information might be faulty and uncertain because of missing information, unpredictable behavior, ambiguous situations, and differing interpretations.

Even though many of today's context aware systems do not deal with uncertainty of context information they could be extended to do so. Obviously, systems exist which explicitly model and use uncertainty during inference and decision making. Maybe the most advanced systems like the Lumiere [8] project, the Lookout project [9] or the Activity Compass [10] are based on techniques such as Bayesian modelling and inference, utility, and decision theory.

In the context of ubiquitous computing it has been suggested, however, that modelling uncertainties and advanced inference mechanisms might not be enough. Starting from the observation that there are human aspects of context that cannot be sensed or inferred by technological means, Bellotti and Edwards [5] conclude that context systems cannot be designed simply to act on our behalf. Rather they propose that those systems will have to defer to users in an efficient and non-obtrusive fashion. They also present design principles which support intelligibility of system behavior and accountability of human users. Greenberg [4] also states that actions automatically taken by the system should be clearly linked to the respective context through feedback. Chalmers [11] even argues for "seamful rather than seamless design" to reveal the physical nature of the Ubicomp systems in, for example, the uncertainty in sensing and ambiguity in representations. Mankoff et al. [12] developed a toolkit that supports resolution of input ambiguity through mediation by building on various methods of error correction in user interfaces. More recently Newberger and Dey [13] have extended the Context Toolkit by a so-called enactor component that encapsulates application state and manipulation to allow users to monitor and control context-aware applications. Horvitz and Barry [14] extend their framework to also estimate the expected value of revealed information to enhance computer displays to monitor applications for a time-critical application at NASA.

All of the above-mentioned approaches offer solutions to deal with the inherent uncertainty problem of context information. What is common to all of them is to propose the use of different feedback mechanisms and to involve the user in various degrees and forms. While those approaches are well motivated in their respective application context, it is currently difficult to compare and evaluate those approaches and to judge which of those methods are effective and to which degree.

So, the goal of this paper is to propose and explore a particular way of user feedback and involvement in order to deal with uncertain context information. The proposal is based on the fact that users are actually used to and highly successful in dealing with uncertain information throughout their daily lives. So, rather than using uncertainty of context information to try to infer the most sensible action on behalf of the user with mechanisms such as Bayesian inference, we propose to display this uncertainty explicitly and leverage from the user's ability to choose the appropriate action.

In order to explore the display of uncertainty of context information, we use the running example of a context-aware memory aid. As has been noted by Lamming [15] at the Conference on Ubiquitous Computing 2003: "Forgetting is a truly pervasive problem". Humans tend to forget all sorts of things, ranging from objects and appointments to promises made to friends. While everybody is prone to forget something from time to time, this can have more serious consequences for certain professions, such as for airplane pilots, construction workers, or doctors.

Through two experiments we would like to inform the Ubicomp community if displaying uncertainty is indeed useful as a feedback mechanisms in the sense that it improves human performance in a measurable way. The first experiment is a pure desktop-based study in which we analyze the effects of displaying uncertainty in detail. The second experiment replicates the main findings of the first one in a realistic setting using wireless sensor nodes.

In the following Section we give a brief overview over research on memory aids in the ubiquitous and wearable computing community. In Section 3 we introduce the two experiments, which we use to examine specific aspects of displaying uncertainty information. In Sections 4 and 5 we present the details of the experiments. Finally, in Section 6, we set the results into context and give an outlook on the implications of this work.

2   Memory Aids

Our studies on the effects of displaying uncertainty were motivated by the possibility for ubiquitous computing devices to provide context-aware memory aids. As in other context-aware applications it is difficult to reliably extract context information in scenarios of realistic complexity. Even so, in the last decade quite some effort has been put into developing such memory aids. Lamming and Flynn's "Forget-me-not"-project [16] is one such approach. They build upon the idea that humans can remember things better if they know in what context the events occurred. For example, people are better at remembering where and from whom they received a document, than at remembering the document name. By associating such context information over time with file names, the user has the possibility to remember past events by context. Here, wrongly inferred context information would render such associations useless.

CyberMinder, described in [17], is a tool to support users send and receive reminders. These reminders can be associated with context, making their delivery possible in appropriate situations. The Remembrance Agent [18] is a system that exploits the notes people make on a wearable computer. Whenever a word is entered, the system scans previous data for related notes. Here, the notion of context is limited to previously provided information. Context inference is then similar to an information retrieval task in a database system. Again, the relevance of the retrieved information has a direct effect on how useful the system is. Other research efforts towards building context-aware memory aids can be found in [19] and [20].

Besides such prototypes, approaches have been taken to help people remember objects they have in everyday use. Smart-Its friends [21] is such a technique. Users shake two enhanced objects together, thus allowing them to become "friends". These objects then notify their carrier as soon as they loose communication contact between each other. A similar principle has recently even been introduced as a product, see [22] for details. Such systems rely on the explicit action of the user to build associations between objects. If the system should decide automatically which objects are to be associated, then we need some form of context awareness. Lamming [15] describes such a system that consists of simple low-cost sensor nodes which can store information about proximity to other nodes over a whole day. A simple scripting language enables each node to notify its carrier when an object is out of proximity and thus missing (possibly forgotten). Again, the ultimate goal for such a system would be to infer which objects users want with them at which time. Inferring such information from simple sensor readings may work for certain scenarios, but will undoubtedly cause frustration with users, applied to the full complexity of everyday life. Even if the system takes additional schedules and upcoming events into account it will still be missing much personal information that the user may not even be willing to share.

Rather than implementing our own memory aid, we assume a system exists that can infer for what activity a person is packing and which items he would like to have with him. We further assume that this system would infer the correct activity, and thus the correct set of objects, with some known uncertainty.

3 Experiment Overview

In the following, we give a brief introduction into the experiments detailed in Sections 4 and 5. In both experiments we use numbers instead of different sets of real objects. By taking the semantics out of the experiments, we make the experiments repeatable and generalizable across several people. For example, it may be very unfortunate for some people if they forget their mobile phone, whereas others may not care about the fact. Further, associations between real objects can significantly influence the outcomes of memory tasks.

3.1   A Short-Term Memory Task with an Imperfect Memory Aid

The first experiment is a short-term memory task in which volunteers are asked to remember numbers out of a list. The task is designed to be hard enough so that volunteers can only remember approximately half or even less of the numbers. However, before the user is asked to enter the remembered numbers, the system provides a tip on what the numbers might have been. This tip is equivalent to the notification a context-aware memory aid would provide.

While varying the uncertainty of this tip and whether or not the uncertainty is displayed, we measured participants' performance. Often the users reliance on uncertain information is dependent on the stakes at hand. To be able to control this variable, two groups of participants were tested with opposite costs and gains for correctly remembered and wrongly taken objects, respectively.

The experiment was a four-factorial mixed design including the following independent variables:

- **task difficulty** – by varying the stimulus display duration
- **cost** – by varying the number of points gained and lost for hits and false alarms respectively
- **knowledge about uncertainty** – by displaying the uncertainty or not
- **level of uncertainty** – by varying the quality of the tip

3.2   A Short-Term Memory Task with Sensing and Inference Uncertainty

A large number of applications envisioned by the ubiquitous computing community rely on inference based on uncertain sensor values. For some recent examples see [23, 24, 10]. With this second experiment we hope to gain knowledge about the use of displaying uncertainty in such applications.

Experiment 2 uses wireless sensor nodes to simulate a simple packing scenario in which people have to pack objects. Again, participants have to remember as many numbers as possible from a display on a computer screen. Then they have to pack the respective sensor nodes (see Figure 1) into a cardboard box. The sensor nodes, in turn, use light sensors to detect whether they are being packed or not.

To make the task more realistic, we introduced sets of possible numbers that represent objects, which people may want to take with them at the same time. This concept is based on the vision of having a system that infers for what activity a person is packing. Depending on the inferred activity, a different set of objects is proposed for packing. In other words, if the user often goes swimming on Sunday afternoons and he starts packing his bathing suit, the memory aid will infer the *going swimming* activity. It could then notify the user not to forget the shampoo and a bathing towel assuming he might want to take a shower after swimming.

In our experiment we infer which set of objects is being packed by matching the already packed objects with the possible sets. Uncertainty is introduced at the sensing level by artificially discarding objects that have been sensed as packed and accepting objects that were not sensed packed. As the scenario is tested in a laboratory setting, a high reliability in sensing can be achieved. This makes it possible to produce equivalent sensing uncertainty for all participants of the study. By introducing inference and artificially manipulated sensing uncertainty, we hope to come as close as possible to a real-world scenario without making a controlled experiment unfeasible.

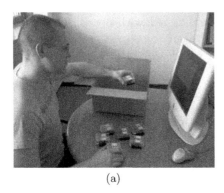

(a)   (b)

Fig. 1. Figure (a) shows a participant during a trial run of Experiment 2 packing the sensor nodes. Figure (b) shows the sensor nodes given to the participants.

4   Experiment 1: A Short-Term Memory Task with an Imperfect Memory Aid

Experiment 1 consists of a short-term memory task aided by an imperfect memory aid. Subjects were asked to remember as many numbers as possible from a list of 10 numbers (chosen from 1–20) that is only displayed a very short time. We call this the *subject's task*. After seeing the numbers the participants can enter what they believed to have seen in an array of checkboxes. To aid the user, the program displays a tip by marking some of the numbers in red. This tip is generated by choosing each object from the subjects task with probability p and the other objects with probability $1 - p$. For an example see Figure 2.

4.1   Method

Subjects: 24 students from either the Computer Science department of ETH Zurich or the Psychology department of the University of Zurich participated in this study. Nine were female and fifteen were male. The median age of the participants was 25. All participants reported normal or corrected-to-normal vision.

Design: This experiment was a mixed design study with four independent variables. The participants were randomly distributed between two equally sized groups. The cost variable was tested between groups. This means that both groups completed the same set of experiments with the only difference being the cost function. The *low-cost* group received two points for each correct answer (hit) and minus one point for each wrongly checked answer (false alarm). The *high-cost* group oppositely received only one point for a hit and minus two points for a false alarm.

Four blocks were carried out with each participant in each group. In all blocks the task display duration was randomized between the three values 200, 800, and

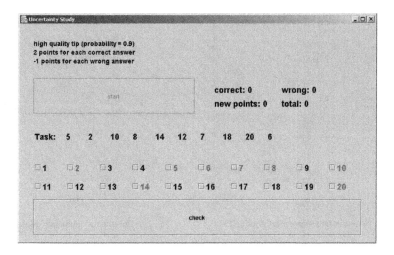

Fig. 2. Screenshot of Experiment 1 with the task field displaying the numbers to be remembered. The task line will disappear as soon as the display duration is elapsed. Information about the tip uncertainty is displayed in the upper left corner. The tip given by the computer consists of the red numbers.

3200 milliseconds. This was approximately perceived as being able to see hardly any objects (two to three), about five, and all of the objects, respectively. Even with the long display time it is hard to remember all ten objects due to the limitations of human memory.

One block did not display any information about uncertainty. Within this block the uncertainty level was randomized between the tip probabilities of 0.6, 0.75, and 0.9. The other three blocks had a fixed tip probability level marked with low (p=0.6), medium (p = 0.75), and high (p = 0.9). It was explained to the subjects that on average, the low quality tip (p = 0.6) would render 6 correct objects, the medium 7.5 and the high would render 9 objects. The order of these blocks was counterbalanced using a Latin Square design.

For each time and probability level, 10 trials were completed, resulting in 90 trials for the blocks with displayed uncertainty and 90 trials for the block with no uncertainty displayed. In total, each participant completed 180 trials.

Equipment: The experiment was conducted using a personal computer running Windows 2000 with the screen resolution set at 1280x1024 on a TFT screen. A program was written to display the memory task and to accept the users answers (see Figure 2).

Procedure: First, the experimental settings were explained to each participant. Next, the graphical user interface elements were described. Each participant was told to try to make as many points as possible in accordance with the actual

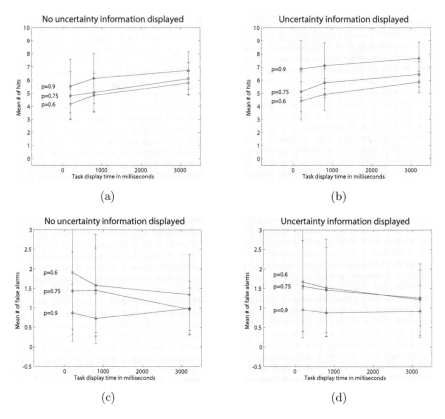

Fig. 3. Results from the low-cost group. The Figures suggest the increase in hit rates when uncertainty information is displayed (compare Figures (a) and (b)). False alarm rates remain similar for both conditions.

cost situation. Prior to the experiment, 20 practice trials were completed using a random order. Each of the four different block settings was represented by 5 trials.

4.2   Results

Figure 3 displays hit and false alarm rates for the low cost condition and Figure 4 for the high cost condition. The plots suggest that displaying uncertainty information results in higher hit rates, especially when tips of high probabilities are shown. This effect seems to be more pronounced in the most difficult condition (short display times). Both effects on hit rates seem to be more pronounced in the high cost condition. The effect of displaying uncertainty is less clear when false alarm rates are concerned, but false alarm rates are substantially reduced in the high cost condition.

The conventional cut-off of $p < .05$ was used for all tests of statistical significance in this study. The performance measures (hit and false alarm rates)

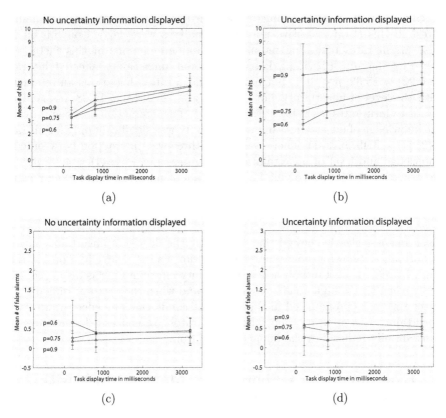

Fig. 4. Results from the high-cost group. The Figures again suggest a large increase in hit rates when uncertainty information is displayed (compare Figures (a) and (b)). False alarm rates remain similar independent of the display of uncertainty information. However, false alarm rates are generally lower than in the low-cost group.

were subjected to a multivariate analysis of variance (MANOVA) with cost (low vs. high) as between-subjects factor and the following within-subject factors: Task difficulty (display times of 200, 800, 3200 milliseconds), knowledge about uncertainty (displayed uncertainty or not), and level of uncertainty (tip probabilities of 0.6, 0.75, 0.9). All main effects were significant. Providing the knowledge about uncertainty affected performance, $F(2, 21) = 8.32$, $p < .01$, as well as costs, $F(2, 21) = 6.27$, $p < .01$, level of uncertainty, $F(4, 19) = 17.50$, $p < .001$, and task difficulty, $F(4, 19) = 65.64$, $p < .001$. There was an interaction between knowledge about uncertainty and the level of uncertainty, $F(4, 19) = 6.52$, $p < .01$. There was also a three-way interaction between task difficulty, knowledge and level of uncertainty, $F(8, 15) = 3.19$, $p < .05$. No other interactions reached statistical significance.

Since the effects of providing the knowledge of uncertainty were of main interest in this study, selective univariate analyses were carried out on hit and false alarm rates regarding main effects and interactions of this factor with the other factors. Providing knowledge about uncertainty affected hit rates, $F(1, 22) = 15.32$, $p < .001$, but not false alarm rates. There was an interaction with the level of uncertainty, both for hit rates, $F(2, 44) = 18.08$, $p < .001$ and for false alarm rates, $F(2, 44) = 7.06$, $p < .01$. The interaction between providing the knowledge of uncertainty and task difficulty was significant only for hit rates, $F(2, 44) = 3.49$, $p < .05$. There was also a three-way interaction between costs, knowledge and level of uncertainty for hit rates only, $F(2, 44) = 4.26$, $p < .05$. No other interactions involving knowledge about uncertainty were significant.

4.3   Discussion

Experiment 1 clearly showed that displaying the degree of uncertainty affected performance. Showing uncertainty information had a clear effect on hit rates. They increased substantially when uncertainty information was displayed, especially when tips of high quality were shown and when the task was difficult. This effect was more pronounced in the high-cost condition. The effect of displaying uncertainty is less clear when false alarm rates are concerned, but they were substantially reduced in the high-cost condition.

5   Experiment 2: A Short-Term Memory Task with Sensing and Inference Uncertainty

As mentioned above, Experiment 1 was designed to test for main effects and interactions between knowledge and level of uncertainty, costs and task difficulty. The aim of Experiment 2 was to replicate the main results of Experiment 1 in a more realistic setting using a less complex experimental design. To this end, a two-factorial design was used in which knowledge and level of uncertainty was manipulated.

The main difference to Experiment 1 is that we introduce real sensing with wireless sensor nodes and inference based upon this uncertain sensing. Smart-Its were used as sensor nodes; for details see [25, 26]. In the Experiment, participants have to remember as many numbers as possible from a list of 7 numbers between 0 and 9. Then they have to physically pack the Smart-Its that represent the numbers into a cardboard box. These detect whether they have been packed or not using a light sensor. Packing objects into a closed cardboard box makes sensing a simple task. To guarantee perfect recognition during all the experiments, an operator constantly checked whether the correct objects were sensed.

To vary the uncertainty in a controllable manner we introduced artificial sensing uncertainty. This was done by only propagating sensing information from packed objects with a certain probability. Similarly, objects that were sensed as not being packed can be regarded as packed by the system. Upon this artificially uncertain packing data, we add inference to determine which objects the user should pack next. This is done by introducing five groups of seven randomly chosen numbers. One of these groups is the actual list of objects the user is trying to pack. The group to be packed by the user is inferred by calculating the matching probability between what has supposedly been packed and all the possible groups.

Figure 5 displays a scenario in which it is most probable to pack the objects 0 and 1 based on an artificial sensing probability of 0.9. Figure 1 displays a person packing the nodes and the wireless sensor nodes in detail.

5.1   Method

Subjects: 10 students from either ETH Zurich or the University of Zurich participated in this study. Two were female and eight were male. The median age of the participants was 28. Two people had participated in the first study. All participants reported normal or corrected-to-normal vision.

Design: A two-way within-subjects design was used. The first independent variable tested the benefit of displaying uncertainty information. The second variable was level of uncertainty. Each participant completed three blocks. In the first block no uncertainty information was displayed. The uncertainty level however, was varied randomly between 0.7 and 0.9. In the second and third block the uncertainty information was displayed. Once it was set to 0.7 and once to 0.9. Block order was counterbalanced using a Latin Square design. For all experiments the task display time was held constant at 400 milliseconds, which let the participants remember 4 numbers on average. Costs were held constant at 1 point for each correct answer and minus 2 points for each wrong answer. Each participant completed 10 trials for the blocks with uncertainty displayed (0.7 and 0.9). In the block with randomized uncertainty and no uncertainty information displayed, 20 trials were completed. This resulted in 40 trials per subject.

Equipment: The experiment was conducted using a personal computer running Windows 2000 with the screen resolution set at 1280x1024 on a TFT screen. A program was written to display the memory task and to display the inferred results (see Figure 5). The program communicated with a sensor node via the serial port of the personal computer. This node acted as a receiver for the data from the other 10 sensor nodes. Finally, we gave the participants 10 Smart-Its sensor nodes and a cardboard box for packing them (see Figure 1). More technical details on the sensor nodes used can be found in [26].

Procedure: The participants were introduced to the experiment by letting them imagine they had a system at home that could help them during packing for different occasions. It was explained that the system would infer which occasion one is packing for and would give hints based on this inference. After the

introductory example, the user interface and the handling of the sensor nodes
was explained. Each user completed at least two trial runs with each of the
three experimental conditions. The order of the three experimental blocks was
counterbalanced using a Latin Square design.

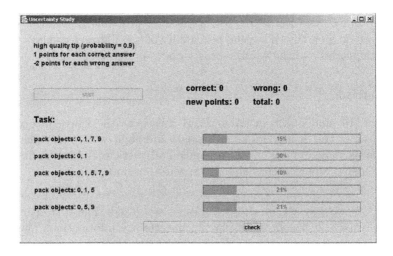

Fig. 5. Screenshot of Experiment 2 after the numbers to be remembered have
been displayed. Information about the tip probability is displayed in the upper
left corner. The lower part of the screen displays the five possible groups of
objects to be packed. Based on the objects that were supposedly packed it is
most probable to continue packing with objects 0 and 1. (second line of "pack
objects:")

5.2   Results

Hit and false alarm rates were subjected to univariate analyses of variance
(ANOVA) with knowledge about uncertainty (displayed uncertainty or not), and
level of uncertainty (tip probabilities of 0.7 and 0.9) as within-subjects factors.

As in Experiment 1, there was a main effect of knowledge about uncertainty
for hit rates, $F(1, 9) = 6.11$, $p < .05$, but not for false alarm rates. The level of
uncertainty also affected hit rates, $F(1, 9) = 9.63$, $p < .05$, while there was no
main effect on false alarm rates. In contrast to the results of Experiment 1, the
interaction between knowledge and level of uncertainty did not reach statistical
significance in Experiment 2, neither for hit rates nor for false alarm rates. [5]

---

[5] It must be noted however, that the smaller sample size and/or the different uncertainty levels used in Experiment 2 could have prevented revealing these interactions.

5.3   Discussion

Experiment 2 provides converging evidence for the view that displaying uncertainty information increases performance in terms of hit rates, whereas false-alarm rates are much less – if at all – affected. Thus the main finding of Experiment 1 was replicated in the more realistic setting used in Experiment 2.

6   General Discussion and Conclusions

For context-aware systems, we often cannot rely on the assumption that context information is highly accurate. Several proposals have been made to deal with those ambiguities and uncertainties through various feedback, monitor, and control mechanisms. However, their respective strength is hardly known since they are rarely evaluated. In this paper, we propose a simple but effective feedback mechanism by displaying the uncertainty of context information. The effectiveness of the feedback mechanism is shown and replicated in two different user studies in the context of a ubiquitous memory aid.

In the first experiment, we analyzed the effects of four factors and their interactions. Displaying uncertainty information resulted in a substantial increase in hit rates when tips of high quality were shown. This benefit was more pronounced for high task difficulty in high-cost situations. False-alarm rates were less affected by displaying uncertainty, whereas a substantial reduction was observed in high-cost situations.

While the first experiment was desktop-based only, experiment 2 was designed in a way as to make the setting as realistic as possible for a Ubicomp scenario. Therefore, we introduced physical objects with sensing, communication and processing capabilities. In order to avoid, however, that humans add too much semantic meaning to the individual objects by having for example objects like keys, towels, pens, or coats, we still used numbered objects. This 'semantic-free' setting allows to compare the results across people by reducing the semantic bias of each individual person. In this more realistic setting, the main results of Experiment 1 were replicated. Both the display of uncertainty and the level of uncertainty showed significant effects on hit rates, whereas the false-alarm rate remained constant.

One issue to be considered in future work is the tradeoff between the cognitive load, which displaying uncertainty information causes, and the added value that it provides. First design guidelines can be gained from the field of signal detection theory in cognitive science. Results presented in [27] show that people perform best in a signal detection task when uncertainty information is encoded as luminance of a display element. This means it is effective to display more-certain information in a brighter mode than less-certain information. However, as feedback presented on a computer screen is only one of many possible modalities in a ubiquitous computing scenario, it remains to be shown how such results can be transferred.

Experiments with similar objectives have also been carried out in domains with very high costs, such as air traffic control and military pilot training [28, 29,

30]. Here the subjects are highly-trained individuals that have practiced dealing with uncertainty information. In our experiments we show that equivalent results can be achieved with untrained individuals.

Another effect mentioned by several participants is that when uncertainty is displayed, it is easier to understand what the system is doing and how well it is doing it. This postulates that displaying uncertainty information as feedback may be a possibility to build intelligible context-aware systems, as desired by Bellotti & Edwards [5].

Last but not least, we'd like to argue that the procedure we adopted in this paper using two user studies has several interesting properties and might be more widely applicable in the context of Ubicomp. In the first experiment, we used a rather idealistic desktop-setting which allowed us to employ a 4-factorial analysis. Looking at four factors simultaneously would be quite hard and time-consuming in a realistic Ubicomp setting. This first experiment then allowed to measure the most significant effects involved and to test those in a different second experiment. We designed the second experiment then to be more realistic in the Ubicomp sense and used a 2-factorial analysis using the two most important factors from the first experiment. In our case, this way of proceeding has four interesting properties. The first is that the experimental design of the second experiment is informed from the first experiment. The second advantage is that the experiment involves only 2 and not 4 factors as in the first experiment and therefore makes it more feasible as a Ubicomp experiment. The third advantage is that the second experiment itself is more realistic. Finally, the fourth advantage is that we were able to replicate the most important findings in two different experiments.

References

[1] Salber, D., Dey, A.K., Abowd, G.D.: The context toolkit: Aiding the development of context-enabled applications. Technical report, Georgia Institute of Technology (2000)

[2] Hong, J.L.: The context fabric: an infrastructure for context-aware computing. In: Conference on Human Factors in Computing Systems (CHI). (2002)

[3] Graumann, D., Lara, W., Hightower, J., Borriello, G.: Real-world implementation of the location stack: The universal location framework. In: Proceedings of the 5th IEEE Workshop on Mobile Computing Systems & Applications (WMCSA 2003), IEEE Computer Society Press (2003) 122–128

[4] Greenberg, S.: Context as a dynamic construct. Human-Computer Interaction Volume 16 (2001) pp.257–268

[5] Bellotti, V., Edwards, K.: Intelligibility and accountability: Human considerations in context-aware systems. Human-Computer Interaction Volume 16 (2001) pp.193–212

[6] Cheverst, K., Davies, N., Mitchell, K., Efstratiou, C.: Using context as a crystal ball: Rewards and pitfalls. Personal Technologies Journal Volume 3 (2001)

[7] Edwards, W.K., Grinter, R.E.: At home with ubiquitous computing: Seven challenges. In: Conference on Ubiquitous and Handheld Computing (UbiComp). (2001)

[8] Horvitz, E., Breese, J., Heckerman, D., Hovel, D., Rommelse, K.: The lumiere project: Bayesian user modeling for inferring the goals and needs of software users. In: Proceedings of the Fourteenth Conference on Uncertainty in Artificial Intelligence. (1998)

[9] Horvitz, E.: Principles of mixed-initiative user interfaces. In: Conference on Human Factors in Computing (CHI). (1999) 159–166

[10] Patterson, D.J., Liao, L., Fox, D., Kautz, H.: Inferring high-level behavior from low-level sensors. In: Proceedings of the Internation Conference on Ubiquitous Computing (UbiComp). (2003)

[11] Chalmers, M., MacColl, I.: Saemful and seamless design in ubiquitous computing. In: Workshop At the Crossroads: The Interaction of HCI and Systems Issues in UbiComp. (2003)

[12] Mankoff, J., Hudson, S., Abowd, G.: Interaction techniques for ambiguity resolution in recognition-based interfaces. In: UIST 2000. (2000)

[13] Newberger, A., Dey, A.: System support for context monitoring and control. In: Workshop At the Crossroads: The Interaction of HCI and Systems Issues in UbiComp. (2003)

[14] Horvitz, E., Barry, M.: Display of information for time-critical decision making. In: Proceedings of the Eleventh Conference on Uncertainty in Artificial Intelligence. (1995)

[15] Lamming, M.: SPECs: Another approach to human context and activity sensing research, using tiny peer-to-peer wireless computers. In: International Conference on Ubiquitous Computing (UbiComp). (2003)

[16] Lamming, M., Flynn, M.: Forget-me-not: Intimate computing in support of human memory. In: FRIEND21, International Symposium on Next Generation Human Interface. (1994)

[17] Dey, A.K., Abowd, G.D.: CybreMinder: A Context-Aware System for Supporting Reminders. In: Handheld and Ubiquitous Computing (HUC'00), Bristol, Uk (2000)

[18] Rhodes, B.: The wearable remembrance agent: A system for augmented memory. In: Proceedings of the International Symposium on Wearable Computing. (1997)

[19] Kern, N., Schiele, B., Junker, H., Lukowicz, P.: Wearable sensing to annotate meeting recordings. In: Proceedings of International Symposium on Wearable Computers (ISWC), Seattle, USA (2002)

[20] Antifakos, S., Holmquist, L.E., Schiele, B.: Grouping mechanisms for smart objects based on implicit interaction and context proximity. In: Adjunct Proceedings of International Conference on Ubiquitous Computing (Ubicomp), Seattle, USA (2003)

[21] Holmquist, L.E., Mattern, F., Schiele, B., Alahuhta, P., Beigl, M., Gellersen, H.W.: Smart-its friends: A technique for users to easily establish connections between smart artefacts. In: Proceeding of the International Conference on Ubiquitous Computing (UbiComp). (2001)

[22] Dipo: Memory Aid. http://www.dipo.fr/ (2004)

[23] Neustaedter, C., Greenberg, S.: The design of a context-aware home media space for balancing privacy and awareness. In: Proceedings of the Internation Conference on Ubiquitous Computing (UbiComp). (2003)

[24] Koile, K., Tollmar, K., Demirdjian, D., Shrobe, H., Darrell, T.: Activity zones for context-aware computing. In: Proceedings of the Internation Conference on Ubiquitous Computing (UbiComp). (2003)

[25] Smart-Its: Project web-page. http://www.smart-its.org/ (2004)

[26] Beigl, M., Zimmer, T., Krohn, A., Decker, C., Robinson, P.: Smart-its - communication and sensing technology for ubicomp environments. Technical Report ISSN 1432-7864 2003/2, TecO Karlsruhe (2003)

[27] Montgomery, D.A., Sorkin, R.D.: Observer sensitivity to element reliability in a multi-element visual display. Human Factors **Volume 38** (1996) 484–494

[28] Nicholls, D., Barsotti, V., Battino, P., Marti, P., Pozzi, S.: Presenting uncertainty to pilots and controllers. In: 5th International seminar on ATM, FAA and Eurocontrol, Budapest (2003)

[29] Gempler, K.S., Wickens, C.D.: Display of predictor reliability on a cockpit display of traffic information. Technical Report ARL-98-6/Rockwell-98-1, Aviation Research Lab, Institute of Aviation, University of Illinois (1998)

[30] Banbury, S., Selcon, S., Endsley, M., Gorton, T., K.Tatlock: Being certain about uncertainty: How the representation of system reliability affects pilot decision making. In: Proceedings of the Human Factors and Ergonomics Society 42nd Annual Meeting. (1998)

The Error of Our Ways: The Experience of Self-Reported Position in a Location-Based Game

Steve Benford[1], Will Seager[1], Martin Flintham[1], Rob Anastasi[1], Duncan Rowland[1], Jan Humble[1], Danaë Stanton[1], John Bowers[1], Nick Tandavanitj[2], Matt Adams[2], Ju Row Farr[2], Amanda Oldroyd[3], Jon Sutton[3]

[1] Mixed Reality Laboratory, The University of Nottingham, Nottingham, NG8 1BB, UK
{sdb, wps, mdf, rma, dar, jch, des}@cs.nott.ac.uk
[2] Blast Theory, Unit 43a, Regent Studios, 8 Andrews Road, London, E8 4QN, UK
{nick, matt, ju}@blasttheory.co.uk
[3] BT Exact, Ross Building PP4, Adastral Park, Martlesham, Ipswich IP5 3RE, UK
{amanda.oldroyd, jon.sutton}@bt.com

Abstract. We present a study of people's use of positional information as part of a collaborative location-based game. The game exploits self-reported positioning in which mobile players manually reveal their positions to remote players by manipulating electronic maps. Analysis of players' movements, position reports and communications, drawing on video data, system logs and player feedback, highlights some of the ways in which humans generate, communicate and interpret position reports. It appears that remote participants are largely untroubled by the relatively high positional error associated with self reports. Our analysis suggests that this may because mobile players declare themselves to be in plausible locations such as at common landmarks, ahead of themselves on their current trajectory (stating their intent) or behind themselves (confirming previously visited locations). These observations raise new requirements for the future development of automated positioning systems and also suggest that self-reported positioning may be a useful fallback when automated systems are unavailable or too unreliable.

Introduction

In recent years there has been a proliferation of interest in systems which exploit positional information to support mobile interactivity. The Xerox PARCTab [14] and Olivetti's Active Badge system [13] provide early examples which have inspired increasing interest in the design of location-aware mobile applications. For many researchers, obtaining reliable positional information for users or devices is seen as an essential aspect of delivering context aware services. For example, Cyberguide [1] employs indoor and outdoor positioning technologies to create a mobile tour guide. Context aware, position-informed approaches have also been proposed in domains as varied as information retrieval [5], workplace activity tracking [9] and network routing and resource discovery [7].

However, there have been relatively few reports of large-scale deployments of these kinds of location-based applications and we do not yet have a detailed under-

N. Davies et al. (Eds.): UbiComp 2004, LNCS 3205, pp. 70–87, 2004.

standing how end users actually use and interpret positional data. The few reports that have been published raise significant challenges for the design of interfaces, applications and the underlying positioning systems. For example, our own previous studies of a location-based artistic game called 'Can You See Me Now?' as it toured several cities, involving several hundred players in each over a period of several days, yielded rich and detailed accounts of how people experienced GPS as a positioning technology [3,6]. 'Can You See Me Now?' was a game of tag in which online players, logged on to the game over the Internet, were chased through a virtual model of a city by street players who, equipped with handheld computers, wireless networking and GPS receivers, had to run through the actual city streets in order to catch them. Online players could also 'tune in' to a real-time audio stream from the street players and could send them text messages in return.

Analysis of the communication between and movements of street and online players revealed that the performance of GPS has a major impact on the game. This stemmed from both the error associated with GPS measurements but – significantly – also its availability; it was often difficult to obtain a good enough GPS fix while running around the city to be able to play the game. Online players experienced these problems in various ways: they were sometimes unaware of them, but at other times they were revealed in a jarring way; and occasionally the players even interpreted them as part of the game or exploited them tactically. Street players on the other hand, were constantly aware of GPS performance. For them, the experience was as much an ongoing battle to obtain a reliable GPS fix as it was about chasing online players. This is not to say that GPS is a poor technology – but rather, that it cannot just be deployed on the streets of a real city and be expected to work continually and seamlessly over the course of several days. Rather than the technology being invisible, street players had to learn to make it work for them, gradually building up a stock of knowledge of its behaviour at particular locations and times.

This paper builds on this previous experience through a study of a further touring artistic game called 'Uncle Roy All Around You'. This has used an alternative 'low-tech' positioning system called self reported positioning in which mobile players declare their own positions to the game server, both explicitly and implicitly, through their use of an electronic map. There are two motivations behind this study.

First, we wish to deepen our understanding of the human issues involved in using positioning systems. The use of self-reported positioning in 'Uncle Roy All Around You' provides a useful vehicle for exploring how end-users collaboratively generate and interpret positional data for themselves as part of a large-scale publicly deployed application. By analysing human behaviour we are able to uncover broader implications for automated positioning systems and beyond this, for the way in which we approach positioning in general. Furthermore, experience with low-tech self-reported positioning can be seen as establishing a baseline of experience against which automated positioning technologies might subsequently be compared.

Second, we are interested in the technique of self-reported positioning in its own right, i.e., as an alternative to, or safety net for, automated positioning systems in situations where they might be unavailable or too unreliable – for example, where there isn't sufficient coverage across an urban environment or where they will be used by users who are unfamiliar with their characteristics.

Method

As with our previous study of 'Can You See Me Now?', our method involves a naturalistic study of a professional-quality application that is publicly deployed and experienced in a realistic setting – the streets of a city – by a large number of people – hundreds of participants – over many days. Our study draws on three sources of data: video-based ethnographic observations of selected participants; direct feedback from participants through questionnaires and subsequent emails and face-to-face discussions; and system logs of all participants' movements and communications. Between them, these sources enable us to build a rich picture of the experience. This approach builds upon a rich tradition of using ethnography to inform system design by studying the use of technologies 'in the wild', i.e., situated in the real-world rather in an artificially controlled settings such as a laboratory, where they are subject to all of the contingencies that this introduces.

Our chosen application is again an artistic game; a touring interactive performance that has been produced in collaboration with professional artists. Our game focuses on collaboration between mobile street players and remote online players and in particular on how the latter can guide the former on a journey through the city. We have chosen this application for two reasons. First, games and artworks provide a good vehicle for engaging the public in large scale experiments. They are engaging, can be deployed in public, can mimic a variety of situations and behaviours; and yet are safe – they involve minimal risk when compared to deploying say, a safety critical system. Second, we anticipate that games will emerge as a major market for ubiquitous technologies, in the same way that conventional games have been a major driving force behind the development of computing technologies, even if this has not always been recognized by the research community. Indeed, several research projects have begun to explore the challenges involved in delivering games on the streets including Pirates! [4], AR Quake [12], Mindwarping [11] and 'Can You See Me Now?' [3].

Positioning systems are an essential but also problematic aspect of such games. Although a variety of systems is available including GPS, cellular positioning, radio pingers, video tracking, inertial systems and others, these vary greatly in terms of cost, availability, coverage, resolution, frequency and accuracy. In particular, there is currently no universal tracking system that can provide reliable, accurate and extensive coverage across a city with the result that game developers and players have to cope with considerable uncertainty with regard to location.

Self-Reported Positioning

With self-reported positioning mobile players declare their own positions to the game rather than having them determined by an automated positioning system such as GPS. Our proposal for self-reported positioning actually consists of two related mechanisms that determine position in different ways. In the first, players explicitly declare their position to the game server by interacting with an electronic map, in effect saying 'I am here', in return for location relevant game content such as clues or messages from other players.

In the second, players interact with the electronic map in the natural course of way-finding. However, their interface, which is delivered on a handheld computer, only allows them to see a limited area of the overall game map at any moment in time, requiring them to pan and zoom their viewpoint. Their current view of the map (a rectangular area) is then taken as an indication of their likely position within the physical world. In short, we assume that where they are looking on the map indicates where they actually are. This second mechanism can be described as *implicitly* self-reported position as it may be transparent to the player who could be unaware that their map manipulations are being interpreted as positions.

This approach is certainly low-cost and also has high availability when compared to systems such as GPS. On the other hand, there is no guarantee that it will produce accurate positional information. Players might be mistaken about where they are or might choose to deliberately lie about their location, and it is far from clear that where you are looking on a map is necessarily a reliable indication of where you are. We have therefore undertaken a study in which we piloted this approach as part of a location-based game that was experienced by members of the public.

An Overview of Uncle Roy All Around You

'Uncle Roy All Around You' is a location-based game that mixes street players who journey through a city in search of an elusive character called Uncle Roy, in interaction with online players who journey through a parallel 3D model of the city, who are able to track the street players, communicate with them and can choose to help or hinder them. The aim of the game is to create an engaging collaborative experience for street and online players based around the theme of trust in strangers.

On arrival at the venue a street player is given a handheld computer, is briefed that their mission is to rendezvous with Uncle Roy and is shown how to use the interface. On entering the city, their first task is to find a red marker on the map, to get to the physical location that this indicates, and then declare their position to Uncle Roy. Once they have achieved this, they move on to the second phase of the game in which 'Uncle Roy' (the game) sends them a series of clues in response to further declarations of position. These clues lead them through the park and into the narrow city streets in search of Uncle Roy's office. During this time, the street player may also receive text messages from online players who are following their progress and who may offer them advice, directions or otherwise. In return, the street player is able to record and upload short (seven second) audio messages for the online players to hear. Eventually they find their way to a physical office and the game switches into its final phase, the details of which are beyond the scope of the present paper.

An online player connected to the game over the Internet journeys through a parallel 3D model of the game space. They move their avatar through this model using the arrow keys on their keyboard, encounter other online players and can send them text messages. They also access a set of on-screen cards that provide details of the current street players, see representations of these players' positions in the model, and can exchange text and audio messages with them as described above. Online players can find additional information in the 3D model, including the location of Uncle Roy's

Figure 1: street player's experience: the park, streets and office

office, which they can use to guide the street players. Finally, online players can 'join' street players in Uncle Roy's office via a live webcam in the final phase of the game.

'Uncle Roy All Around You' was piloted in central London over two weeks in May and June of 2003. During this time it was experienced by 272 street players and over 440 online players. A strong positive reaction from players (through question-naires and email feedback) and press suggests that we created an engaging experi-ence. However, the overall success of the experience is not our concern in this paper. Instead, we are interested in its use of self-reported position.

Implementing Self-Reported Positioning

The street player's interface to 'Uncle Roy All Around You' takes the form of the interactive map shown in figure 2. The overall size of the game map is 1600 by 1000

Figure 2: street player's map, zoomed out and in

meters. The street player views this through a 280 by 320 pixel view area and can swap between two zoom settings: zoomed out, in which one pixel is equivalent to four meters, giving a viewable area of 1120 by 1280 square meters (most of the map); and zoomed in, in which one pixel is equivalent to one meter, giving a viewable area of 280 by 320 square meters. The street player can also rotate the map.

The player pans their view over the map by using a stylus to drag the 'me' icon (a circle of radius of 10 pixels labeled with the word 'me') to a new position. The map then re-centers itself around this position. It is possible to place this icon anywhere on the map, including inside buildings and in the lake, and also to move off of the visible edge of the map in which case the display appears blank. This approach to navigating the map was chosen over other approaches such as using sliders, scrollbars, buttons and thumbwheels, because it allows simultaneous panning in two dimensions with just one simple manipulation, and also because it implies a relationship between the map view and the player's physical location.

Implicit position updates (giving x and y coordinates and rotation and zoom settings) are sent to the game server whenever the player pans, zooms or rotates their view of the map. We refer to these implicit position updates as 'map manipulations'. In order to explicitly declare their position, the player positions the 'me' icon at the appropriate place and then presses the 'I AM HERE' button, sending a 'declaration' event to the game server.

The street player receives a different text clue back from the game server depending on which of 49 regions they declare themselves to be in. These regions vary in size from roughly 150 by 150 meters in the open park area down to roughly 10 by 10 meters in the narrow city streets. A second successive declaration in a region returns a further clue. These clues and also messages from online players pop up over the map and need to be dismissed before further interaction is possible.

Two outer regions bound the game zone and return clues that are intended to guide the player back towards the middle of the map. The innermost of these returns the message: "The policeman was firm but polite, not this way today" followed by (on a second declaration) "You are off track"; while the larger outmost region returns the message "I cannot guide you out here. You have got lost. Go back the way you came" followed by "Retrace your steps, you are too far away and in the wrong place".

The online players interface is shown in figures 3 and 4. The white avatar represents this player, the cards on the right show the current street players and the text boxes at the bottom are for sending text messages to online players or individual street players. Online players can also switch between a first person and bird's-eye view of the model. They see different representations of map manipulations and declarations. The former are represented by the position of a pulsing red sphere, which is labelled with the street player's name (figure 3).

In contrast, declarations are portrayed in a far more dramatic and eye catching manner: over the course of a few seconds a dramatic sound is played, radiating lines emanate from the red sphere, while a much larger translucent sphere appears in the 3D model and gradually shrinks (like a deflating balloon) down to the street player's newly declared position (figure 4). These effects are intended to make declarations highly noticeable and in the case of the shrinking sphere, to give some sense of the street player's location in the 3D model, even when seen from some distance way.

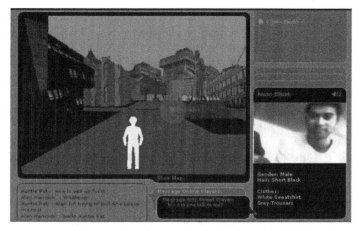

Figure 3: an online player observes a map manipulation

Figure 4: an online player observes a declaration

Performance of Self-Reported Positioning

Our analysis of the use of self-reported positioning draws on three sources of data: system logs of all declarations, map manipulations and text and audio messages from players; feedback from street and online players via email and questionnaires; and video observation of some players.

Our first (rather obvious) observation is that self-reported positioning provided excellent coverage and availability. Street players quickly learned to use it; it was not necessary to wait to get a fix on sensors or satellites; and there were no black spots within the game zone (there were wireless communications problems however, which made it impossible to transmit position updates, although these would have equally affected an on-board positioning system such as GPS). The equally obvious downside is that players had to work to generate position updates themselves (at least the explicit declarations) so that the positioning technology was not invisible. We return to this point later on in the conclusions.

This said, we now continue our analysis by treating self-reported positioning as if it were a technology whose performance (in a narrow technical sense) needs be measured, as this is typical of the way in which automated positioning systems such as GPS are discussed and compared. We focus on three key characteristics of performance: frequency, resolution and accuracy.

To determine frequency and resolution we have analyzed system logs of the 5,309 declarations and 18,610 map manipulations that were generated by all 272 street players. The distributions of duration, distance moved and errors that are discussed below are skewed, with some high outlying values, and so it is most informative to summarize them using the median, and the inter-quartile range. The median duration of declaration events (time between successive declarations by the same player) is 1.14 minutes (inter-quartile range of 1.31=1.98-0.67) whereas the median duration of map manipulations is 0.11 minutes (inter-quartile range of 0.65=0.68-0.03). In other words, declarations occur approximately once every minute whereas map manipulations are roughly ten times more frequent.

The maximum possible spatial resolution of position updates was 1 meter (1 screen pixel equates to 1 meter on the map when zoomed in). However, in practice, updates fall further apart than this. The median distance moved across the map between successive declarations by the same player was 80 meters (inter-quartile range of 82=135-43) and between map manipulations was 40 meters (inter-quartile range of 88=90-2).

Analyzing accuracy involves comparing street players' self-reported positions with their actual positions in the physical world. We followed 10 players and recorded their progress on video. We then manually analyzed the video to transcribe their 174 declarations and 481 map manipulations, estimating the players' actual positions at the times when these events were generated (we believe that our estimates are accurate to within approximately five meters). We derive two measurements of accuracy from these observations. The first is 'distance error', the straight-line distance between reported and observed positions. The median distance error for declarations was 25 meters (inter-quartile range of 36=48-12) and for map manipulations was 39 meters (inter-quartile range of 76=97-21). However, there were a few position updates that were associated with particularly large errors. The maximum distance error for declarations was 240 meters and for map manipulations was 553 meters.

Our second way of expressing accuracy is in terms of 'off map' errors. These are declarations or map manipulations where the error is sufficiently large (greater than 120 pixels East-West or 160 pixels North-South) that the street player's actual physical position would not even appear on their view of the map. This reflects the idea that it is your entire map view, rather than the position of the central 'me' icon, that expresses where you are. 1.7% (3 out of 174) of observed declarations were 'off map', compared to 8.3% (40 out of 481) of map manipulations.

In contrast to these figures, GPS typically produces a reading every second, has a resolution of a meter or so and depending on which kind of GPS is used (e.g., differential or not) and on local conditions, has a typical accuracy of between approximately one and ten meters. For example, two previous experiences of using GPS as

part of location-based games in similarly built up cities reported average errors (estimated by the GPS receivers themselves) of 4 meters (for differential GPS) and 12
meters (for non-differential), although, as with self reported positioning, there were
occasionally very large errors (106 and 384 meters respectively), most likely due to
multi-path reflections at specific locations [3].

At first sight, it seems that self-reported positioning produces less frequent, coarser
and less accurate positional information than GPS and we might be tempted to conclude that it performs less well. However, two issues need to be borne in mind. First
is availability. Reports of previous experiences noted that even GPS knowledgeable
players had to work hard to obtain any GPS readings at all, exploiting knowledge of
good GPS locations that they had built up over several days play, and even then they
often could not obtain a GPS fix [3,6]. A driving motivation behind self-reported
positioning was a concern that poor availability would make GPS too unreliable,
especially in the hands of GPS 'naïve' players. Second, is the underlying nature of the
'errors' involved and their impact on the players, an issue that we now explore in
detail by analyzing street and online players' experience of self-reported positioning.

How Online Players Use Position Reports

In order to understand how self reported positioning is used in the game, we have
examined the way in which online players used position information as part of their
collaboration with street players. Specifically, we have analyzed the private text messages that they sent to street players to see to what extent they were confident in their
knowledge of street player's positions or alternatively, whether they perceived reported positions as suspect or problematic. Of the 3,109 private text messages that
were logged, approximately 1,670 were concerned with location in some way (the
remainder being concerned with other aspects of social interaction). We coded these
location oriented messages into five categories. The first category is messages in
which the online player appears to have a precise enough fix on a street player's location to be able to give directions or tell the street player where they are. There are 735
such messages, such as:

> The big street in front of you
> You are very close now
> And stay on that side of the road
> Literally meters away from you
> U r very close step back 5 feet
> Stop take a right NOW

It is notable how readily and commonly 'deictical' linguistic elements (in front,
close, right, left, there, here – terms which have a sense when one knows the spatial
location of the addressee) are used in these examples. This suggests that on-line players can establish a sense of street players' position and activities using the reported
positions confidently enough to be able to formulate directions and instructions in
such terms.

The second category is messages where the street player appears to have a good
idea of where the online player might be, but is less confident, for example question-

ing whether the street player is at a specific location. There are 112 such messages. Typical examples are:

> Are you near a piece of scaffolding?
> My map shows you near the bridge. Are you?
> Did you just pass some steps?

The third category is messages where the online player gives general directions or makes geographical references that do not necessarily assume precise knowledge of the street player's location (although they also don't raise any doubts about it either). Such messages are broadly neutral with respect to the validity of positional information. There are 569 such messages. Typical examples are:

> Now you need to find the steps
> Go to 12 waterloo place
> Head towards steps by George statue
> Head for the big building with a flag on top
> Waterloo place is near uncle roys office

The fourth category is messages that cast doubt on the usefulness or validity of reported positions or that appear to question the behavior of the positioning system in some way. These messages reflect moments when the operation of the positioning system may have been noticeable or even problematic for the online players. There are only 32 such messages including:

> I can't pin point you
> You are jumping all over the place on my map
> Wow you move fast
> Hi rachel? you keep coming and going
> Your locator shows you standing still in the park is it broken?
> How did you get over there?
> Confirm your location cos this thing is not updating

Our fifth category is requests for location updates. There are 222 messages in which online players are enquiring about the location of a street player. Just over half of these appear to make specific requests for location updates via the map interface. The others are more general queries of the form 'where are you?'. These messages do not appear to cast doubt on the veracity of the position updates, for example questioning their accuracy, plausibility or commenting on jitter or other strange behaviours, although they do imply that online players would like more frequent updates.

What emerges from these observations is that while online players appear to be concerned about the frequency of reported positions (often asking for updates), they hardly appear to notice inaccuracies or other problems, and instead seem to be comfortably working with reported position, often in a very precise way. Of course, the online players experience is not solely based on the positioning system. They also have access to other contextual information including audio messages from the street players. However, it seems that in spite of its apparent inaccuracy, self-reported positioning works well in an integrated way with the online map, audio and within the general context of this particular game. This can be contrasted with previous reports of GPS-based games that mix street players and online players is a similar manner and where apparently smaller errors became noticeable to online players, were commented on and even exploited them as part of the game. To understand why this might be so, we now look at the street players' experience and in particular, how they generated position updates.

How and When Positions Are Reported

It seems that for the practical purposes of playing the game, self-reported positions are adequate to the task. On-line players can develop an adequate sense of where street players are for meaningful, game-related interaction to take place between them. In their turn, it seems that street players commonly report their positions in relation to city features at moments designed to be most useful to on-line players. Our evidence for this derives from our observations of how street players use the map in relation to their unfolding exploration of the streets. Three behaviors stand out.

Declaring at Landmarks and Junctions

Street players would often declare themselves to be at landmarks or junctions even when they were some distance away from them (e.g., half way along a street). We identified six key landmarks that provided focal points for declarations, including the two major entrances to the park, a café in the park, a major crossroads, the Duke of York statue and a crossing over a major road. Of course, the use of landmarks in wayfinding and the development of spatial knowledge of an area is well documented [10]. Beyond this however, our analysis suggests that this strategy of declaring at well defined locations such as landmarks is intended to produce clearer feedback from Uncle Roy and online players and to minimize misunderstandings concerning location.

Looking Ahead and Declaring Prospectively

We observed players naturally position the map so that they could see further ahead than behind. They may do this to prepare themselves for the next leg of the journey, planning ahead and deciding where to go before actually reaching the next major decision point. However, as the 'me' icon is always located at the centre of the map, looking ahead requires them to position it in front of their actual physical position.

We also saw examples of players explicitly declaring themselves to be ahead of their actual position. Sometimes this involved declaring a short distance (up to ten meters) ahead as in the following example:

> While J .is approaching the bridge from the east, he positions the 'me' icon at the centre of the bridge and declares about 5 meters to the east of the north end of the bridge. He then walks to the middle of the bridge and stops to look at the handheld computer.

In this and other similar examples, players appear to be anticipating time delay. Declaring a few seconds ahead of themselves provides time for the system to respond with new information (there was a delay of approximately six seconds between declaring and receiving a clue in return) and maybe even for them to digest it before they reach the next decision point – a strategy that will avoid them waiting around. On other occasions players declared themselves to be a longer distance (up to sixty meters) ahead of their location:

> Having found herself unexpectedly back at the end of Carlton House Terrace where she'd been 10 minutes earlier, J. looks visibly frustrated. After asking directions and receiving more

messages, she decides to head West on Carlton House Terrace. Halfway up, she stops, positions the 'me' icon at the Duke of York statue sixty meters further up the street, declares, and then waits for a response.

Again, our analysis suggests that players were using this strategy to obtain feedback (e.g. clue information and online player messages) in advance of taking a key decision. On several occasions players appeared to be unconfident about their direction and may have been confirming their chosen route (if already walking) or investigating a possible route (if stopped) so that they would know sooner rather than later whether they were heading in the wrong direction. This avoids the wasted time and effort that results from setting off on the wrong route, an important strategy in a game that is played against the clock. It should also be noted that the time delay involved in getting a response from an online player would be of the order of twenty seconds as they would have to compose and enter a text message.

In subsequent email feedback one of the players that we followed confirmed this strategy of declaring in advance of their position so as to obtain clues ahead of time:

"One thing I also remember doing was quite the opposite, that is, reporting my position in advance before I got there to have quicker feedback of whether or not I was on the right track. Maybe through a desire to anticipate and plan ahead ..."

Looking Behind and Declaring Retrospectively

We also see some street players declaring and looking behind their current position. Panning behind would often occur when a player did not manipulate the map for a while and so physically moved ahead of their last reported position. Several map manipulations might then be required to realign their virtual position with their physical position, effectively recreating their recent path on the map. This of course results from not having an automated positioning system. However we also saw cases where players deliberately panned behind from their current map position, revisiting a previous location and then explicitly declaring, as in the following:

C. walks up from the lake to the next junction, then turns right...after about 15 meters, he stops, pans the map to the junction he has just passed and declares there.

In this case the player decides to declare at a landmark that they have already passed. One reason for declaring behind was to retrigger clues from Uncle Roy as these did not remain persistently visible on the interface. Street players also sometimes redeclared a past position for the benefit of online players who had missed it as shown by the following feedback from our previous street player:

"... being pressured by players to report my position, which I probably repeated just to be sure they got the updates."

In summary, street players adopt various strategies for manipulating the map and declaring their position that (in purely numerical terms) generate large positioning errors. However, these strategies make perfect sense in terms of their experience of the game and furthermore, as our previous analysis of text messages suggests, also make sense to online players as part of ongoing collaboration.

Plausibility, Timing, and Communication

These observations of how online and street players experience self reported position-ing raise implications for how we think of self-reported positioning errors.

Plausible Errors

It seems that the positioning errors generated by street players (if it is even appropri-ate to think of them as errors as we discuss later on) are plausible ones that make sense to the online players and that do not 'jar' with their expectations. Further in-sight into this claim is given by figure 5 which plots the positions of all street players' reported declarations on the game map. Visual inspection of this image suggests that a large majority of explicitly declared positions involve plausible locations (defined to be the streets, open squares and parkland) rather than implausible ones (in the middle of buildings or in the lake). This is backed up by statistical analysis. Of the 5,309 declarations plotted there were only 39 (0.7%) where some part of the 'me' icon did not overlap with a plausible location. More surprisingly, the same is broadly true of map manipulations where for the 18,610 that we analyzed there were only 345 (1.8%) where the 'me' icon did not overlap a plausible location. In short, reported positions are credible, even if at first sight they appear to involve a large distance error.

Figure 5: a plot of all explicitly declared positions

Dislocation in Time Not Space

An alternative way to think of discrepancies between reported and actual position is in terms of time rather than space. Rather than reporting themselves to be at a different place, our street players are in fact reporting themselves to be at a different time. The strategies of declaring ahead and behind mean that reported positions tend to fall close to the player's actual physical path, one reason why they appear plausible. As noted previously, strategies such as declaring ahead are useful as they anticipate system delay and human response time. They also help to convey a sense of a player's *trajectory* through the streets. Indeed, a street player who always declared at the exact location they were at might seem sluggish to on-line players and might, in turn, have to stop and wait to receive relevant advice.

We can contrast this attention that people give to ensuring that positions are reported and received in ways which ensure the smooth flow of activity with automated positioning systems such as GPS which, due to the presence of network delays and system response time, effectively report a street player's position as it was several (in this case six or more) seconds ago. We speculate that in this particular game, GPS would fail to anticipate a player's requirement for information in advance of arriving at a decision point and even if available, might deliver information that was essentially out of date.

Reporting Position as a Communicative Act

We suggest that explicitly self-reported positions (declarations) should be interpreted as deliberate acts of communication, the intent of which is not so much to tell Uncle Roy and online players where the street player actually is at that very moment, but rather to solicit useful advice about a course of future action. In this context, declaring one's position is perhaps as much about deixis (pointing at and referencing features of the environment) as it is about telling someone exactly where you are. Put another way, self-reported position updates are not neutral pieces of information, but rather are imbued with meaning by a street player *at the moment that they are generated*. Again, this is something that is not captured by automated positioning systems such as GPS whose reported positions do not reflect any of the higher level semantics of the environment or the task at hand, or at least not at the point of data capture. With such systems, application-related semantics (e.g. what kind of 'context' the data are suggesting the application should be 'aware' of) has to be 'read in' after capture (e.g. by algorithms *operating on* the position data).

This observation reflects other studies of settings in which GPS data, though available, has not been used as anticipated. [8] describes an ambulance control room in which GPS was continually captured from ambulances but where many of the displays routinely used by controllers only updated positions at critical times in the emergency call (when an ambulance arrived at an incident, or at hospital). These junctures were notified by ambulance crews manually pressing keys on a small display in the ambulance cab. While alternative uses of GPS are certainly possible in control and similar domains, findings such as these are eminently understandable from the point of view of our study. Position data becomes relevant when it is timely in its delivery and, as with our players, is understood in terms of the unfolding trajectory of a journey and when communication between remote personnel is required.

Revisiting the Notion of Error

We began our analysis with a strictly numerical view of position error (computed as the difference between actual and reported location) as being typical of the way in which technology developers evaluate the performance of positioning systems. It now appears that a more subtle approach is required. Differences between reported and actual position that at first sight appear to be 'errors' may in fact naturally arise from appropriate strategies in which players communicate intent and accommodate delay while attending to the plausibility of their declared positions. As such, it may be inappropriate to think of them as being errors at all. Indeed, it may even be the case that, at least in these kinds of collaborative situations, automated positioning systems that superficially appear to be more accurate can in fact generate information with a timeliness not appropriate to the trajectory of ongoing user activities or to the specific requirements of communication between users. From this perspective data quality – even at such an apparently 'low' level as raw position data – should be evaluated in terms of its appropriateness to its use-purpose and not just according to an abstract notion of error.

Conclusions and Broader Issues

Through enabling users to self-report their locations, we have presented a low-tech yet adequately reliable alternative to the automated capture of position data for use in the game 'Uncle Roy All Around You'. We have seen that players are able to navigate themselves through a city with help from others who see their location through self-reports. For the practical purposes of collaborative gaming, the declaration and map manipulation system we have designed does not introduce a great overhead – implicit reports fall out naturally from map manipulation and explicit declarations are easy to perform and motivated by the game's 'cover story'. In their turn, online players are able to work with self-reported positioning without greatly noticing inaccuracies.

However, the broader applicability of this approach is an open issue. Two potential limitations of self-reported positioning are that the mobile player has to know where they are and/or where they are heading, and that they may cheat, that is deliberately choose to lie about their position. The former limitation is clear – this is not an approach that will tell you where you are if you are lost. Rather, it is useful for applications where you are trying to inform other remote participants about your activities, especially where you are going. Potential uses are in remote guidance, command and control, arranging to meet or keeping others up to date with a background awareness of your general whereabouts – all activities that can occur outside of games. Cheating is clearly a possibility and self-reported positioning is not appropriate to situations in which users would be motivated to lie about their location and where this would cause a problem. However, in many situations users may not be motivated to lie and in others it may not be a problem (one can imagine games that involve remote users trying to work out where mobile users actually are based upon contextual cues).

As we noted in the introduction, one possible role for self-reported positioning is as a supplement to automated positioning systems, enabling the user to correct erroneous readings, fill in with self-reports while automated systems are unavailable, or possibly even take over from an automated system in order to disguise their position for a while to protect their privacy (another potentially useful reason for 'cheating').

A further issue for self-reported positioning is that it demands the constant engagement of the user in order to maintain an up to date position, and even then remote users may be frustrated at the low frequencies of updates. While this may be acceptable for tasks that are highly fore-grounded – such as playing an absorbing game – it may be less suited to more background tasks, for example where a context aware system spontaneously interrupts the user. We note an interesting tradeoff here between our experience of self-reported positioning and our previous experience with GPS. With the former, players have to continually work the technology to produce position updates, whereas the latter produces them automatically when it is available, but requires players to explicitly work the technology to maintain a fix and is unusable and arguably more visible (as a 'broken' technology) when not available.

Whether ultimately this is a problem however, remains to be seen as it is still an open question as to what extent technologies that are ubiquitous should also fade into the background and become invisible. While this may seem an appealing idea, it raises serious challenges in terms of how users are expected to interact with invisible systems, see for example Bellotti et al's five questions for the designers of sensing based systems [2], and also raises the issue of whether users will ultimately accept technologies that monitor them continuously even when not being explicitly used.

Considering more immediate issues, one approach that we have adopted to try to deal with online players' frustration with infrequent updates is to change the representation of street players in the virtual world. In the most recent versions of 'Uncle Roy All Around You' (staged in Manchester and West Bromwich in the UK in May and June 2004) street players were shown as an avatar that walks an interpolated path between its current position and a newly reported position, giving the impression of continual movement and avoiding sudden jumps in apparent position. Our initial impression is that this refinement offers a much improved online representation.

A final issue concerning the future applicability of this work is whether automated positioning systems will improve to the point where self-reported positioning is no longer required as a low-tech fallback. It seems likely that automated approaches will continue to improve and this paper is not meant to be an argument against using them (we ourselves continue to work with GPS and other sensing systems in a variety of applications).

However, several points need to be borne in mind. First, actual large-scale user experiences reported to date (as opposed to demonstrations or controlled tests) suggest that designers should be careful not to underestimate how difficult it is to deploy technologies such as GPS in the wild and deliver a fluid and seamless experience. Second, improving the performance of sensing technologies may be as much a matter of economics as technical prowess. It may require a very large investment in additional sensors to achieve that last few percent of coverage. After all, why is it that even with a technology as widely used and well developed as GSM, we still routinely encounter communication blackspots when using standard mobile phones? Finally, we reiterate that even when they work, automated systems may not be providing the desired information. Studies of mechanisms such as self-reported positioning can identify new requirements for automated approaches, for example the need to reflect user intent.

Our work, then, opens out a new research challenge: how can we better integrate positioning systems with the natural ways in which humans orient to and communicate their location? Context aware systems need to develop a sense of context that truly is relevant to the activities that their users are performing. When this process is based on position data, exploiting natural features of human activity and communication at the point of data capture may provide solutions which help us to meaningfully measure the error of our ways.

Acknowledgements

We gratefully acknowledge the support of the Engineering and Physical Sciences Research Council (EPSRC) through the Equator project, the Arts and Humanities Research Board (AHRB), the Arts Council of England and Microsoft.

References

1. Abowd, G., Atkeson, C., Hong, J., Long, S., Kooper R., Pinkerton, M., Cyberguide: A mobile context-aware tour guide. *Wireless Networks*, 3, 421-423, 1997.
2. Bellotti, V., Back, M., Edwards, W. K., Grinter, R. E., Henderson, A. and Lopes, C, Making Sense of Sensing Systems: Five Questions for Designers and Researchers, Proc. CHI 2002, CHI Letters, 1 (1), 415-422, Minneapolis, USA, 20-25 April, 2002, ACM.
3. Benford, S., Anastasi, R, Flintham, M., Drozd, A., Crabtree, A., Greenhalgh, C., Tandavanitj, N., Adams, M., Row-Farr, J., Coping with uncertainty in a location-based game, *IEEE Pervasive Computing*, September 2003, 34-41, IEEE.
4. Bjork, S., Falk, J., Hansson, R., Ljungstrand, P. (2001). "Pirates! Using the Physical World as a Game Board", *Proc. Interact 2001,* 2001, IFIP.
5. Brown, P. & Jones, G., Context aware retrieval. *Personal and Ubiquitous Computing*, 5, 253-263, 2001.
6. Flintham, M, Anastasi, R, Benford, S D, Hemmings, T, Crabtree, A, Greenhalgh, C M, Rodden, T A, Tandavanitj, N, Adams, M, Row-Farr, J, Where on-line meets on-the-streets: experiences with mobile mixed reality games, *Proc. CHI 2003,* Fort Lauderdale, Florida, 5-10 April 2003.
7. Imielinski, T., and Navas, J., GPS-based geographic addressing, routing, and resource discovery. *Comm. ACM*, 42 (4), 86-92, 1999.
8. Martin, D., Bowers J., Wastell, D., The interactional affordances of technology: An ethnography of human-computer interaction in an ambulance control centre. *Proc HCI 1997*: 263-281, BCS.
9. Newman, W., Eldridge, M., & Lamming, M., PEPYS: Generating autobiographies by automatic tracking. *Proc. ECSCW 91*, 1991, Kluwer.

10. Siegel, A. W., & White, S. H., The development of spatial representations of large-scale environments. *Advances in Child Development and Behavior*, 10, 9-55, 1975.

11. Starner, T., Leibe, B., Singletary, B., & Pair, J (2000b), "MIND-WARPING: Towards Creating a Compelling Collaborative Augmented Reality Game", *Intelligent User Interfaces 2000*, 256-259.

12. W. Piekarski and B. Thomas, "ARQuake: The Outdoors Augmented Reality System," *Comm. ACM*, vol. 45, no. 1, Jan. 2002, pp.36–38, ACM.

13. Want, R., Hopper, A., Falcao, V, & Gibbons, J., The active badge location system. (1992) *ACM Trans Information Systems*, 10 (1), 91-102.

14. Want, R., Schilit, B., Adams, N., Gold, R., Petersen, K., Ellis, J., Goldberg, D., & Weiser, M., The PARCTab ubiquitous computing experiment. *Tech. report CSL-95-1*, Xerox PARC, 1995.

Particle Filters for Location Estimation in Ubiquitous Computing: A Case Study

Jeffrey Hightower[1,2] and Gaetano Borriello[1,2]

[1] Intel Research Seattle
1100 NE 45th St.
Seattle, WA 98105
[2] University of Washington
Computer Science & Engineering
Box 352350
Seattle, WA 98195

Abstract. Location estimation is an important part of many ubiquitous computing systems. Particle filters are simulation-based probabilistic approximations which the robotics community has shown to be effective for tracking robots' positions. This paper presents a case study of applying particle filters to location estimation for ubiquitous computing. Using trace logs from a deployed multi-sensor location system, we show that particle filters can be as accurate as common deterministic algorithms. We also present performance results showing it is practical to run particle filters on devices ranging from high-end servers to handhelds. Finally, we discuss the general advantages of using probabilistic methods in location systems for ubiquitous computing, including the ability to fuse data from different sensor types and to provide probability distributions to higher-level services and applications. Based on this case study, we conclude that particle filters are a good choice to implement location estimation for ubiquitous computing.

1 Introduction

Location estimation is important in ubiquitous computing because location is an important part of a user's context. Context-aware applications can be proactive in gathering and adapting information for the user if they have location estimates accurate to an appropriate grain-size. By being location-aware, these applications can more seamlessly blend into the user's tasks and minimize distraction. In fact, many applications may act autonomously without explicit user attention. For example, a location-aware to-do list can compare the user's position against to-do items and alert the user when she is near a location where a task can be completed.

Location estimation systems can be based on a wide range of sensing technologies such as GPS [1, 2, 3] , infrared [4, 5], ultrasound [6, 7], WiFi [8, 9], vision [10], and many others (see [11] for a survey). Many of today's deployed systems are stove-piped, that is, an application and sensing technology are coupled so it

N. Davies et al. (Eds.): UbiComp 2004, LNCS 3205, pp. 88–106, 2004.
© Springer-Verlag Berlin Heidelberg 2004

is difficult to change sensors and still be able to use the same application. An example is GPS navigation units in automobiles that would need to be greatly revised if they were instead to use proximity to radio sources and dead reckoning from inertial sensors. In general, the location estimation problem involves:

1. a set of objects whose location must be estimated,
2. a set of potentially heterogeneous location sensors,
3. a timestamped sequence of measurements, each one generated by a sensor about an object,
4. a motion model for the various objects, and
5. an algorithm to update an object's position given a new measurement, the sensor type, and the elapsed time since the last measurement.

There are important issues to resolve for each part of the problem. How many objects can be located and at what granularity? How can heterogeneous sensor measurements be fused? How are measurements collected and where is the location estimation computation performed? Are there a limited set of motion models? How is the result of the positioning algorithm presented to applications (e.g., a single point, a region, a probability distribution)?

This paper presents a case study showing that particle filters are a good algorithmic choice for location estimation for ubiquitous computing. They work well with the sensors, motion models, hardware platforms, and queries relevant to ubiquitous computing. Particle filters are a Bayes filter implementation popularized by the robotics community. They are robust in that they can represent arbitrary probability distributions. Using trace logs from a deployed multi-sensor location system, we show that particle filters can be as accurate as common deterministic location algorithms, they can be run efficiently on a variety of mobile and stationary computing platforms used in ubiquitous computing, and they can fuse heterogeneous sensor data to support useful abstractions for higher-level services and applications.

The sections of this paper are structured to make each point independently. After introducing particle filters in section 2 we begin with accuracy comparisons in section 3, cover performance in section 4, and finally discuss the general advantages of using probabilistic methods in location systems for ubiquitous computing in section 5. Section 6 concludes and describes our current and future work.

2   Particle Filters

A particle filter is a probabilistic approximation algorithm implementing a Bayes filter. Particle filters are a member of the family of sequential Monte Carlo methods [12, 13]. For location estimation, Bayes filters maintain a probability distribution for the location estimate at time t referred to as the belief $Bel(x_t)$. Particle filters represent the belief using a set of weighted samples $Bel(x_t) = \{x_t^i, w_t^i\}, i = 1 \ldots n$. Each x_t^i is a discrete hypothesis about the location of the object. The w_t^i are non-negative weights, called *importance factors* which sum to one. Our previous survey paper [14] provides a tutorial and more in depth discussion of the mathematics of Bayes filters for location estimation and compares particle filters to other Bayesian filtering techniques such as Kalman filters, Multi-Hypothesis Tracking, and grid and topological approaches

Particle filters have proven valuable in the robotics community for state estimation problems such as simultaneous localization and mapping (SLAM) [15, 16]. Our particle filter implementation for this case study is based on a standard approach used in the robotics community for robot localization: each new sensor measurement causes the belief samples to be updated using a procedure called Sequential Importance Sample with Resampling (SISR). In this context, SISR involves predicting each sample's motion using a *motion model*, weighting all samples by the sensor's *likelihood model* for the current measurement, and resampling using importance sampling, that is, choosing a new set of samples according to the weights of the prior samples. The appropriate number of samples is determined at each step using a procedure called *KLD adaptation*. Objects are tracked in three dimensions (x, y, z, pitch, roll, yaw, velocity, weight)[3] for maximum flexibility in locating both people and objects.

Motion Model The motion model implements the Bayes filter prediction step. Unlike in robotics where odometry information provides observations about motion, ubiquitous computing requires a motion model with no explicit input. Some systems can infer motion indirectly through assumptions about the behavior of the underlying sensor technology. For example, Locadio estimates whether a device is moving or still based on the variance of access point sightings and their signal strength values over a sliding window [17]. Our particle filter in this study, however, does not assume the use of any particular sensor technology and therefore employs a general human motion model. Each sample has velocity as part of its belief state along with its location. Each SISR iteration adjusts the velocity of each sample by introducing Gaussian acceleration noise with $\sigma = 0.5$ meters per second per second multiplied by elapsed time. Velocity is clipped to the range 0 to 10.22 meters per second—from stopped to the fastest recorded human running speed. Rotational velocity is modeled similarly. After updating velocities, samples are all moved to new positions according to their adjusted velocities and elapsed time. Sample motion is further constrained by a collision detection algorithm such that no sample may move through walls in the known map of the world.

Sensor Likelihood Model A particle filter can fuse measurements taken by heterogeneous sensor technologies. Adding a sensing technology means creating a new likelihood model characterizing the sensor. Likelihood is the conditional probability $P(z|x)$, the probability of position x of the mobile object relative to the sensor given measurement z taken by the sensor. In this case study, likelihood models are fixed and defined a priori for each sensing technology based on offline experiments to characterize sensor error. For example, our likelihood function for the VersusTech commercial infrared badge

---

[3] Our 3D state vector actually has 9 dimensions instead of 8 because we use a 4-element quaternion to represent the rotational (pitch, roll, and yaw) components.

system is a parametric Gaussian model of infrared range ($\mu = 0, 2\sigma = 15ft$) derived from experiments in which we verified the manufacturer's claims of a 15 foot range. Our ultrasound time-of-flight badge likelihood is a lookup table built from lab experiments characterizing the ultrasound system's measurement error. Visual examples of the infrared and ultrasound likelihood functions are illustrated in Figure 1.

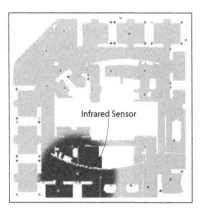
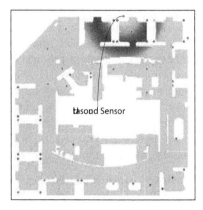

Fig. 1. Example sensor likelihood models for an infrared measurement (left) and a 4.5 meter ultrasound measurement (right) in our 30m x 30m office environment. Darker areas represent higher likelihoods.

KLD Adaptation SISR performance is determined by the number of samples. The minimal number of samples needed to represent the distribution at each iteration is determined using a method called Kullback-Leibler distance (KLD) adaptive sampling. KLD adaptation is the best-known-method in the literature to compute the minimum sample count required to represent a distribution [18]. We use KLD parameters shown by Fox and colleagues to work well with our particular map sizes and motion models: $\epsilon = 0.1$, $\Delta = 0.5m$, $z_{1-\delta} = 0.99$.

Although motion and sensor models used in this case study's particle filters are static and defined a priori, it would be possible to apply machine learning techniques to build the models from training data and even to adjust those models dynamically. Learning represents a tradeoff between accuracy and generality. Learning optimal models for an environment, for example the radio propagation characteristics or motion constraints of a particular building, can greatly increase the algorithm's accuracy in the environment represented in the training data, but naturally decreases the generality of the implementation in environments outside the training data.

3   Accurate Location Estimation

In this section, we present an experiment comparing several position estimation algorithms. We show that a particle filter can do as well as these deterministic algorithms in instantaneous position accuracy and has better dynamic properties.

3.1   Experimental Setup

We have deployed location sensors throughout our building including, among others, a commercial infrared badge system from VersusTech, an ultrasound time-of-flight badge system based on the MIT Cricket boards [6] , and a home-grown WiFi device positioning system. Under normal operation, our distributed location service fuses measurements from all these sensor technologies to track more than 30 lab residents as well as high-value and frequently lost pieces of equipment.

Comparing the accuracies of position estimation algorithms requires knowing ground-truth, which is not available during normal operation. Therefore, for these experiments we gathered measurement logs using a robot programmed to duplicate human-like motion. The robot is not in any way part of the normal configuration or operation of the location system. It is used only to collect sensor traces which also include ground truth for this paper's experimental analyses. The alternative—having a human wearing sensors continually click on a map to indicate their true position as they walk about—is both tedious and error prone in comparison.

The robot is equipped with a scanning laser range finder and can compute its position to a few centimeters and its orientation to one degree. On top of the robot we mounted the "scarecrow," a pole simulating the height and torso of a human. On the scarecrow are sensors consisting of an ultrasound badge, two types of infrared badges, RFID tags, and a WiFi client device. Figure 2 shows a picture of the robot and scarecrow.

We used the robot-plus-scarecrow setup to generate several hours of measurement logs covering our entire $900m^2$ office building. All results presented in this paper are from a 15 minute segment of this larger log. 15 minutes is sufficient length that results are clear yet generalizable. The robot's speed ranged from 0–2 meter per second—reasonable human walking speeds. The robot traveled to waypoints throughout the space on routes generated by a path planner. A collision avoidance algorithm allowed it to avoid people and other transient objects. Indeed, in the interest of realism we made no effort to clear the environment of people and other objects. Finally, to duplicate human-like motion, during data collection we would periodically override the path planner to make the robot accelerate, slow, stop and wait, turn, or "change its mind" by interjecting a new waypoint into the plan.

Sensor measurements were logged at the normal rate for each technology. Infrared badges beacon at approximately 0.5Hz, ultrasound badges at 3Hz. In both cases, packets may be seen by multiple basestations or packets may be dropped

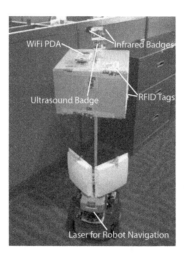

Fig. 2. This robot gathered measurement trace logs which also include ground-truth position information. The robot has a laser range finder to compute its precise position. The "scarecrow" on top simulates the torso height of a human. On the scarecrow is an ultrasonic time-of-flight badge, two types of infrared proximity badges, RFID tags, and a WiFi client device.

if no basestation is visible due to obstructions, packet collisions, or other interference. The ultrasound system is particularly susceptible to packet collisions due to reflections that act to confuse its randomized scheduling algorithm. The infrared system is prone to dropped packets due to its lower beacon rate and sparser basestation infrastructure. In total, the 15 minute log used in this paper has 2932 ultrasound measurements and 537 infrared measurements from the scarecrow-mounted sensors.

3.2   Algorithms We Compared

We compared the accuracy of particle filters described in section 2 and several deterministic position estimation algorithms:

Point The estimate is placed at the same position as the sensor generating the latest measurement. Point is the simplest algorithm for cellular location systems. Point is used by most commercial infrared badge location systems and some cellular telephony location services.

Centroid The estimate is placed at the geometric centroid of the positions of the last c sensors generating measurements. The value c is optimized offline to provide best estimates for a given environment; e.g. $c = 3$ is best for our infrared badge system.

Smooth Centroid Like Centroid, except the latest s estimates are also weighted by their age and positionally averaged to smooth the motion over a sliding window. Smooth Centroid was the algorithm used by the SpotON ad hoc wireless location system [19].

Smooth Weighted Centroid Like Smooth Centroid, except the centroid position computation is weighted by the sensor likelihood models. Using this weighting, SWC can take into account both the error characteristics of the sensors and the parameters of the measurements, e.g. the linear distance measured by an ultrasound badge system or the propagation characteristics of radio beacons. SWC is comparable to the centroid algorithm used by Bulusu and colleagues to implement location estimation in ad hoc wireless mesh networks [20].

3.3   Accuracy Results

The particle filter's instantaneous position accuracy, computed as the weighted mean of its samples, is at least as good as the estimate produced by the deterministic algorithms. Figures 3 and 4 illustrate this result by comparing point-estimate accuracy over the 15 minute trace log for infrared alone and for combined infrared and ultrasound. The trace log and ground truth were the same for all runs and only the choice of algorithm was altered. The particle filter is as accurate as the others and much more so when sensors are combined. Because our ultrasound system is prone to significant timing and multipath errors, the sensor model has a high degree of uncertainty. Particle filtering, being an approximation which also estimates object's motions, is well suited to modeling uncertainty.

The particle filter shows better dynamic motion tracking in Figures 5 and 6. These graphs compare accumulated motion error over time using infrared alone and mixed infrared and ultrasound. The incremental error at each time step is the difference between the estimated distance moved and the actual distance moved. A slower accumulation of error implies that the algorithm better tracks the true motion dynamics of the object. The particle filter excels in cumulative error. The difference most striking in the case of combined infrared and ultrasonic sensors where the accumulated error stays near zero for the entire duration of the test. Note that the y-axis' magnitude in Figure 6 is greater than Figure 5 to capture the greater error in some algorithms when including ultrasonic sensors.

4   Practical Location Estimation

In this section we present performance results. Particle filters, like many probabilistic methods, do require more computation time and memory than simpler deterministic position estimation algorithms like weighted centroids. However, as we show in this section, performance is sufficient to make our particle filter implementation practical on real devices used in ubiquitous computing. Specifically:

– The particle filter is practical on small devices. A modern PDA can position itself using common sensors at a rate of approximately 0.5Hz using 1MB of memory.

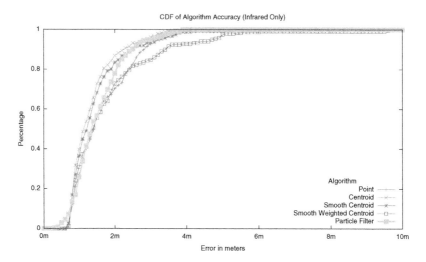

Fig. 3. This cumulative distribution compares the accuracy of several algorithms over a 15 minute log of infrared sensor measurements. The error is the distance between the algorithm's point-estimate of the most likely position and the ground truth.

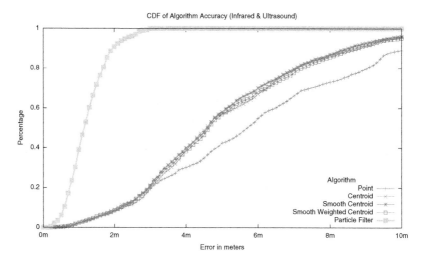

Fig. 4. This cumulative distribution shows the relative accuracy of several algorithms over a 15 minute log of fused infrared and ultrasound sensor measurements. The error is the distance between the algorithm's point-estimate of the most likely position and the ground truth.

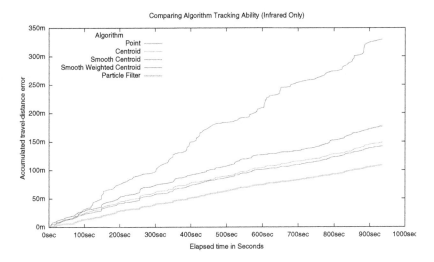

Fig. 5. This time-series shows the cumulative motion distance error of several algorithms over a 15 minute log of infrared measurements. The incremental error at each time step is the absolute value of the difference between the estimated distance moved and the actual distance moved. A slower accumulation of error implies that the algorithm better tracks the true motion dynamics of the object.

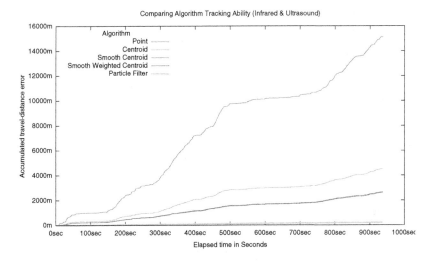

Fig. 6. This time-series shows the cumulative motion distance error several algorithms over a 15 minute trace log of both infrared and ultrasound measurements. The incremental error at each time step is the absolute value of the difference between the estimated distance moved and the actual distance moved. A slower accumulation of error implies that the algorithm better tracks the true motion dynamics of the object.

- Tablet and notebook-class devices can use the particle filter to estimate their position using multiple sensing technologies at a high update rate.
- Particle filters can be used in "enterprise" sensing systems where many tagged objects and people are tracked by central servers. A modern server can track upwards of 18 objects tagged with both infrared and ultrasound badges at a rate of 1 measurement per second per object.

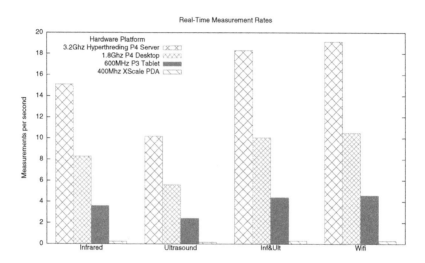

Fig. 7. This graph shows the particle filter's performance on real devices. Bars show the measurement rates that can be maintained in real time for different sensor technologies on four different hardware platforms. This graph combines the average number of samples required under each sensor technology (figure 8) with the time-performance results in figure 10.

Figure 7 summarizes the performance results. In the rest of this section, we deconstruct the respective time and space performance behind Figure 7 to illustrate the particle filter's practicality.

4.1   Memory Usage

Particle filter performance is almost entirely determined by the number of samples needed to accurately represent the probability distribution. Recall from section 2 that each step of SISR uses KLD adaptation to adjust the number of samples to the minimum number needed to represent the belief. Figure 8 shows a cumulative distribution of the KLD-adaptive sample counts and memory usage from our 15-minute trace log. Our space-optimized implementation of particle filters tracking in 3D requires approximately 500 kilobytes of constant memory plus 120 bytes per sample. For comparison to Figure 8, Figure 9 shows the sample count and memory needed to represent several reference distributions with a particle filter. From these graphs we can conclude that on common ubiquitous computing sensor technologies, particle filters can have modest memory requirements of 1-2MB easily met by even PDA-class devices.

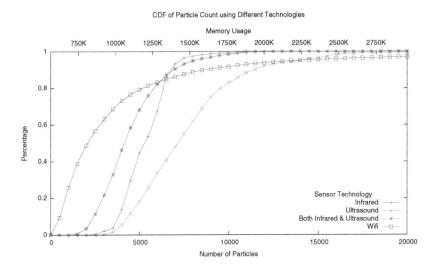

Fig. 8. This cumulative distribution show the KLD-adaptive sample counts (bottom x-axis) and memory requirements (top x-axis) for a 15 minute trace log under different sensor technologies.

4.2   Time Performance

Figure 10 shows the computation time required to perform SISR update on particle filters of different sizes on different platforms. As expected, computational performance scales linearly in the number of particles. Future increases in processor speed will linearly increase the measurement rate or number of trackable objects in a server architecture.

5   Flexible Location Estimation

Beyond the specific accuracy benefits and practical performance shown in the previous sections, in general, probabilistic approaches like particle filters are also more flexible than deterministic methods. Probabilistic methods inherently estimate the actual probability distribution of a location estimate instead of simply a single-point "you-are-here" estimate. This completeness affords low-level sensor fusion, mid-level spatial relationship computations, and high-level value to applications such as traceability and machine learning of context and human activities. These properties make particle filters, as one example of probabilistic

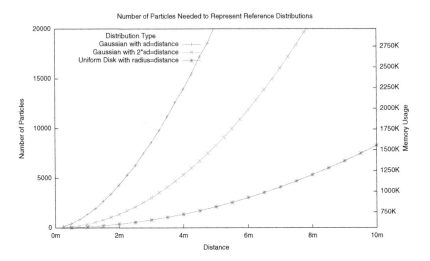

Fig. 9. This plot shows the number of particles (left y-axis) and memory required (right y-axis) to represent several well-known reference distributions.

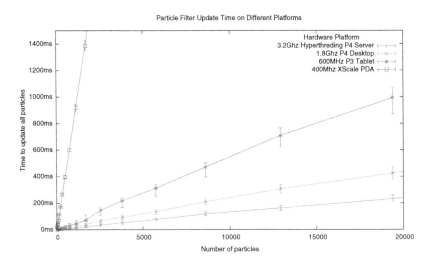

Fig. 10. This graph shows the computation time needed for SISR update on different hardware platforms ranging from a small PDA to a Pentium-4 Hyperthreading server. Particle filters scale computationally linearly in the number of particles.

methods, an ideal tool to implement established location system design abstractions such as Sentient Computing [7] or the Location Stack [21, 22], shown in Figure 11.

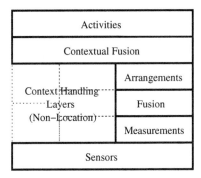

Fig. 11. The Location Stack design abstractions [21, 22] can be implemented flexibly with particle filters. Particle filters readily support multi-sensor location fusion in the Measurements and Location Fusion layers, are easy to use to answer probabilistic Arrangements queries, and are extensible to high-level Context and Activity inference.

5.1   Sensor Fusion

Figure 12 shows the benefits of sensor fusion using particle filters with infrared badges, ultrasound badges, and both. Note that unlike Figures 3 and 4, this figure compares particle filters to particle filters so the error is root-mean-square error instead of simply point error. From this graph we can see that using both sensor technologies preserves the accuracy of the more precise technology and can decrease the standard deviation below the level of either technology alone. Sensor fusion capability gives location system builders the flexibility to deploy heterogeneous sensing hardware in order to minimize cost, increase reliability, or increase coverage. Additional research has increased particle filter's flexibility even further by allowing for the incorporation of anonymous sensors like scanning laser range finders [23].

5.2   Arrangements

Using particle filters for position estimation makes it easy to implement the spatial reasoning abstractions desired by ubiquitous computing systems. A *proximity* engine can compute statistics relating multiple objects by comparing pair-wise distances of the objects' particles. A proximity query returns the estimated distance between two objects along with a confidence value or the probability that two objects are `within()` or `at-least()` a distance d from one another. A *containment* engine can compute the probability that one or more objects are in a

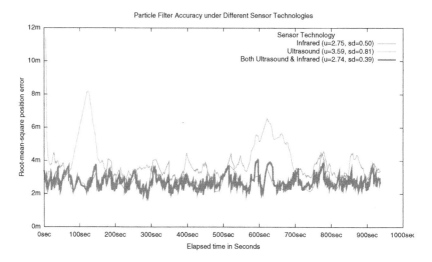

Fig. 12. This 15 minute time-series illustrates sensor fusion: particle filters can combine heterogeneous sensor measurements and achieve the accuracy of the best technology at any given time. The y-axis shows root-mean-square.

room by simply counting the proportion of particles inside the geometric volume of the polygon delineating the room. Containment is illustrated in Figure 13.

Containment and proximity built on particle filters provide a probabilistic implementation of the Arrangements layers seen in many ubiquitous computing location systems such as the "programming with space" metaphor used by location systems such as AT&T's Sentient Computing project [7]. More advanced research into using particle filters for spatial reasoning has shown how to learn and predict motion patterns [24]. In this work, we apply Expectation Maximization to learn typical motion flow of particles along Voronoi graphs of the environment—much like learning "wear lines" in the carpet. The learned motion is then used both to improve the object's motion models and to predict the destination of a moving object based on its learned motion pattern.

5.3   Applications and Activity Inference

Obviously, having probability distributions for location and spatial arrangements provides important information to applications. Application builders can exploit probability information to add understandability to user interfaces. When the system infers that a user is in a particular room, engaged in a certain activity, or existing in a specific context, it can also present traceability information such as: Why did the system make that inference? How sure is the system of the inference it made? What are the alternatives the system considered and with what probability? For example, our handheld mapping interface shows the set

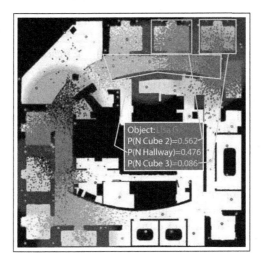

Fig. 13. A *containment* query on a snapshot of 6 people tracked by a multi-sensor location system. The callout shows probabilities for the position of "Lisa G.", the person most likely in the middle upper room. Using particle filters, containment in a room can be computed simply by counting the proportion of particles inside the room's geometric volume.

of rooms in which the user may be located and can use color or opacity cues to indicate the system's belief in each hypothesis.

Probability distributions also enable machine learning of high-level features beyond location. As their input priors, machine learning algorithms usually need to know the true probability distributions of location estimates and spatial relationships. For example, [3] shows how to augment particle filters to estimate mode of transportation in a city (walk, car, bus) based on a stream of GPS positions. Because of these capabilities, we believe particle filters are an enabling technology to ongoing ubiquitous computing work on learning significant locations and motion patterns [2] and inferring situational context other than location [25].

6 Conclusion

In this paper we have presented an in-depth case study demonstrating a particle filter can be an accurate, practical, and flexible location estimation technique for ubiquitous computing.

Accuracy Particle filter's accuracy can be as good as deterministic algorithms plus particle filters can much better estimate dynamic motion.

Practicality Probabilistic methods do require more computation and memory than deterministic algorithms, but our analyses show that particle filter's performance is sufficient for real scenarios on real devices ranging from small handhelds to large servers.

Flexibility Particle filters' affordance for sensor fusion lets developers choose heterogeneous sensing hardware to minimize cost, increase reliability, or increase coverage as needed. Particle filters' support of spatial reasoning such as containment and proximity enables probabilistic versions of established location programming models. Because particle filters inherently represent the probability distributions of estimates, applications developers can enhance user interfaces to indicate the system's confidence in its inference and the viability of alternative hypotheses.

Our implementation of the Location Stack abstractions using the particle filter in this case study has enjoyed significant external adoption including research adoption by the Place Lab project (`www.placelab.org`), commercial adoption in Intel's Universal Location Framework (ULF), and community adoption through our publicly available location estimation library.

Place Lab is illustrative of particle filter's success in a wide-area deployment. It is an emerging global location system with low barrier to entry [26]. Place Lab allows any WiFi client device to estimate its position by listening for WiFi access point beacons and looking up beacons they hear in a local snapshot of a global access point position database. The access point database is built by users who volunteer logs of the access points they encounter. Place Lab uses particle filters to perform both the client's position calculations and the databases' access point position estimation. Particle filters allow Place Lab to provide rich programming interfaces on devices ranging from full-fledged notebook computers to small PDA and cell phone devices. Particle filters' flexibility allows Place Lab to easily explore using additional sensor technologies such as GPS and GSM telephony.

The Universal Location Framework (ULF), Intel's commercial adoption of the approach, focuses on the problem of providing users with a seamless location service and developers with a consistent API as devices move between indoor and outdoor environments. ULF uses GPS receivers when outdoors and WiFi signal-strength triangulation when indoors. Applications are unaware of the shifting reliance on the two sensing technologies. The API provides a position estimate along with a measure of the error. [22] documents the Intel engineers' experiences adopting the Location Stack and estimation library. Figure 14 shows ULF's tablet and multi-radio handset prototypes.

In the future, we seek to further increase particle filters' performance on computationally limited devices by extending the work of Kwok and colleagues on adaptive real-time particle filters [27] to take into account the characteristics of ubiquitous computing environments. More broadly, we plan to blend particle filters with probabilistic techniques such as multi-hypothesis tracking and Rao-Blackwellized particle filters. Many of these variations have characteristics similar to basic particle filters but they are better suited for complex high-level learning problems such as inferring human activities. For example, complex estimation problems often require structured versions of Bayes filters, such as hidden Markov models and dynamic Bayesian networks. Through these efforts

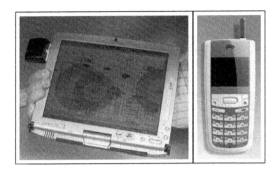

Fig. 14. A tablet (left) and Intel's Universal Communicator (right) are Intel's prototype multi-sensor location devices built with the Location Stack abstractions and particle filter location library.

we hope to bring to location-aware computing the same probabilistic power of representing uncertainty at different levels of abstractions that particle filters have brought to location estimation.

Acknowledgments. We appreciate the comments, advice, and insights of our reviewers and our manuscript shepherd.

References

[1] Misra, P., Burke, B.P., Pratt, M.M.: GPS performance in navigation. Proceedings of the IEEE (Special Issue on GPS) **87** (1999) 65–85

[2] Ashbrook, D., Starner, T.: Using GPS to learn significant locations and predict movement across multiple users. Personal and Ubiquitous Computing **7** (2003) 275–286

[3] Patterson, D.J., Liao, L., Fox, D., Kautz, H.A.: Inferring high-level behavior from low-level sensors. In: Proceedings of the Fifth International Conference on Ubiquitous Computing (Ubicomp 2003), Springer-Verlag (2003) 73–89

[4] Want, R., Hopper, A., Falcao, V., Gibbons, J.: The active badge location system. ACM Transactions on Information Systems **10** (1992) 91–102

[5] Want, R., Schilit, B., Adams, N., Gold, R., Petersen, K., Goldberg, D., Ellis, J., Weiser, M.: The parctab ubiquitous computing experiment. In Imielinski, T., ed.: Mobile Computing. Kluwer Publishing (1997) 45–101 ISBN 0-7923-9697-9.

[6] Priyantha, N.B., Chakraborty, A., Balakrishnan, H.: The cricket location-support system. In: Proceedings of the Sixth Annual ACM International Conference on Mobile Computing and Networking (MOBICOM), Boston, MA, ACM, ACM Press (2000) 32–43

[7] Addlesee, M., Curwen, R., Hodges, S., Newman, J., Steggles, P., Ward, A., Hopper, A.: Implementing a sentient computing system. Computer **34** (2001) 50–56

[8] Bahl, P., Padmanabhan, V.: RADAR: An in-building RF-based user location and tracking system. In: Proceedings of IEEE INFOCOM. Volume 2., Tel-Aviv, Isreal (2000) 775–784

 [9] Bhasker, E.S., Brown, S.W., Griswold, W.G.: Employing user feedback for fast, accurate, low-maintenance geolocationing. Technical Report CS2003-0765, UC San Diego, Computer Science and Engineering (2003)
[10] Brumitt, B., Meyers, B., Krumm, J., Kern, A., Shafer, S.A.: Easyliving: Technologies for intelligent environments. In: 2nd Intl. Symposium on Handheld and Ubiquitous Computing. (2000) 12–27
[11] Hightower, J., Borriello, G.: Location systems for ubiquitous computing. Computer **34** (2001) 57–66 This article is also excerpted in "IT Roadmap to a Geospatial Future," a 2003 report from the Computer Science and Telecommunications Board of the National Research Council.
[12] Doucet, A., Godsill, S., Andrieu, C.: On sequential Monte Carlo sampling methods for Bayesian filtering. Statistics and Computing **10** (2000)
[13] Doucet, A., de Freitas, N., Gordon, N., eds.: Sequential Monte Carlo in Practice. Springer-Verlag, New York (2001)
[14] Fox, D., Hightower, J., Liao, L., Schulz, D., Borriello, G.: Bayesian filtering for location estimation. IEEE Pervasive Computing **2** (2003) 24–33
[15] Fox, D., Burgard, W., Kruppa, H., Thrun, S.: A probabilistic approach to collaborative multi-robot localization. Autonomous Robots **8** (2000) 325–244
[16] Haehnel, D., Burgard, W., Fox, D., Thrun, S.: An efficient FastSLAM algorithm for generating maps of large-scale cyclic environments from raw laser range measurements. In: Proceedings of the IEEE/RSJ International Conference on Intelligent Robots and Systems (IROS), IEEE/RSJ (2003)
[17] Krumm, J., Horvitz, E.: Locadio: Inferring motion and location from wi-fi signal strengths. In: Proceedings of the First Annual International Conference on Mobile and Ubiquitous Systems: Networking and Services, Boston, MA (2004)
[18] Fox, D.: KLD-sampling: Adaptive particle filters. In Dietterich, T.G., Becker, S., Ghahramani, Z., eds.: Advances in Neural Information Processing Systems 14 (NIPS), Cambridge, MA, MIT Press (2002) 713–720
[19] Hightower, J., Want, R., Borriello, G.: SpotON: An indoor 3d location sensing technology based on RF signal strength. UW CSE 00-02-02, University of Washington, Department of Computer Science and Engineering, Seattle, WA (2000)
[20] Bulusu, N., Heidemann, J., Estrin, D.: GPS-less low cost outdoor localization for very small devices. IEEE Personal Communications **7** (2000) 28–34 Special Issue on Smart Spaces and Environments.
[21] Hightower, J., Brumitt, B., Borriello, G.: The location stack: A layered model for location in ubiquitous computing. In: Proceedings of the 4th IEEE Workshop on Mobile Computing Systems & Applications (WMCSA 2002), Callicoon, NY, IEEE Computer Society Press (2002) 22–28
[22] Graumann, D., Lara, W., Hightower, J., Borriello, G.: Real-world implementation of the location stack: The universal location framework. In: Proceedings of the 5th IEEE Workshop on Mobile Computing Systems & Applications (WMCSA 2003), IEEE Computer Society Press (2003) 122–128
[23] Schulz, D., Fox, D., Hightower, J.: People tracking with anonymous and id-sensors using rao-blackwellised particle filters. In: Proceedings of the Eighteenth International Joint Conference on Artificial Intelligence (IJCAI), Morgan Kauffman (2003) 921–926
[24] Liao, L., Fox, D., Hightower, J., Kautz, H., Schulz, D.: Voronoi tracking: Location estimation using sparse and noisy sensor data. In: Proceedings of the IEEE/RSJ International Conference on Intelligent Robots and Systems (IROS), IEEE/RSJ (2003) 723–728

[25] Gellersen, H.W., Schmidt, A., Beigl, M.: Multi-sensor context-awareness in mobile devices and smart artifacts. In: Mobile Networks and Applications. Volume 7., New York, NY, ACM Press (2002) 341–351

[26] Schilit, B., LaMarca, A., Borriello, G., Griswold, W., McDonald, D., Lazowska, E., Balachandran, A., Hong, J., Iverson, V.: Challenge: Ubiquitous location-aware computing and the place lab initiative. In: Proceedings of the First ACM International Workshop on Wireless Mobile Applications and Services on WLAN (WMASH). (2003)

[27] Kwok, C., Fox, D., Meilă, M.: Adaptive real-time particle filters for robot localization. In: Proceedings of the IEEE International Conference on Robotics & Automation (ICRA). Volume 2. (2003) 2836–2841

Some Assembly Required: Supporting End-User Sensor Installation in Domestic Ubiquitous Computing Environments

Chris Beckmann, Sunny Consolvo, and Anthony LaMarca

Intel Research Seattle
1100 NE 45th St, 6th Floor, Seattle, WA 98105, USA
cbeckmann@acm.org, [sunny.consolvo,anthony.lamarca]@intel.com

Abstract. This paper explores end-user sensor installation for domestic ubiquitous computing applications and proposes five design principles to support this task. End-user sensor installation offers several advantages: it can reduce costs, enhance users' sense of control, accommodate diverse deployment environments, and increase users' acceptance of the technology. The five design principles are developed from the design and *in situ* evaluation of the sensor installation kit for the *Home Energy Tutor*, a domestic ubiquitous computing application. To generalize the design principles, factors affecting sensor installation are outlined, and the advantages of end-user sensor installation for three ubiquitous computing application domains are discussed.

1 Introduction

Environmental sensors play an essential role in many types of ubiquitous computing (ubicomp) applications. Fortunately, advances on various technical fronts have made these sensors less expensive and easier to employ. Given the trends in wireless networking, ad-hoc routing and low-power computing, designers of ubicomp applications can reasonably expect that sensors in the near future will be small, cheap, wireless, and last months and often years without needing to be replaced or recharged.

A byproduct of this change is that some factors that were previously second or third-order concerns for researchers now become dominant factors. One such factor is installation. In the past, an automated system with 50 sensors would be prohibitively expensive for consumers, and it was assumed that a professional would do the installation. Recent improvements in technology mean that sensor installation tasks become a relatively simple matter of physical *placement* of the sensor in the environment and making an appropriate semantic *association* to let the application know what object or space the sensor is monitoring. Professional installation will continue to be appropriate for *critical* classes of applications – security systems, life support, dangerous automation or actuation – and for institutions that can afford technicians. However, this approach is not currently feasible for non-critical, everyday applications, especially those in the home. For these applications, the cost of a professional installation may outweigh an application's perceived value.

N. Davies et al. (Eds.): UbiComp 2004, LNCS 3205, pp. 107-124, 2004.
© Springer-Verlag Berlin Heidelberg 2004

This paper focuses on the design considerations for enabling end-user installation of domestic ubiquitous computing applications. Ideally, ubicomp applications should be similar to modular home electronics – cheap, easy to set up, adaptable to a variety of homes, and easily interchangeable when technology advances or users' needs change. To investigate the design issues surrounding end-user sensor installation, we built a mock sensor installation kit using a combination of high and low fidelity sensors. The sensor mock-ups were built in consultation with sensor hardware designers and were chosen to include a variety of sensor types. We conducted an *in situ* evaluation of the mock sensor installation kit in the context of a proposed domestic ubicomp application for home monitoring, the *Home Energy Tutor*. The idea behind the Home Energy Tutor is that a number of environmental sensors would be deployed in the home for one month to track household energy use and provide the homeowner with suggestions on how to reduce energy consumption. The *in situ* evaluation of the installation process was conducted in the homes of 15 homeowners.

From our experiences with the sensor installation study, we developed the following design principles for end-user installation of sensors:

1. Make appropriate use of user conceptual models for familiar technologies
2. Balance installation usability with domestic concerns
3. Avoid use of cameras, microphones, and highly directional sensors if possible
4. Detect incorrect installation of sensors & provide value for partial installations
5. Educate the user about data collection, storage and transmission

We begin by examining the specific advantages of designing for end-user installation. To relate our experience with the sensors used in the mock sensor installation kit to other sensors and applications, we outline the factors involved in a sensor installation task. We then describe the Home Energy Tutor application and the *in situ* evaluation of the sensor installations. We follow with our design principles, including examples from the sensor installation evaluation. We return to the advantages of end-user sensor installation by demonstrating how three domestic ubiquitous computing application domains could benefit. Finally, we conclude by outlining future directions for work in end-user sensor installation.

2   Why Support End-User Installation?

There are several advantages to supporting end-user installation of sensors for domestic ubiquitous computing applications. First, the monetary and time *cost* of professional installation is prohibitive for non-critical applications. Second, end-users who install sensors themselves develop an enhanced sense of *control* over the application: participants in our *in situ* study understood, without instruction, how to disable a given sensor after they had installed it. Third, a complicated or costly installation task inhibits the use of many applications, like the Home Energy Tutor, that offer only moderate *value* for the end-user. Fourth, there is extreme *diversity* of home configurations – the size, layout, type of home, number of residents, and most-used locations are highly variable. Leveraging the fact that an end-user is a domain expert for his own home can lead to an application better tailored to his needs or preferences. Finally, the *rate-of-change* for sensor and computational technology is much higher than that of buildings. Though sensor networks may be built into construction projects now or in the near future, buildings change at a much slower rate than electronics [9]. End-user installation also allows users to change sensor components when more advanced technology is available or as their own needs change. These factors suggest that end-users will be installing their own systems in the future and therefore we as researchers should start to account for this.

3   Domestic Sensor Installation Factors

In order to generalize the types of installation tasks required by the mock sensor installation kit to other sensor types and applications, we characterize the installation of a given sensor along two dimensions: placement and association.

The *placement* constraints of a sensor refer to how carefully a sensor must be positioned for it to accurately measure the desired environmental condition. We further refine placement into two sub-factors: directionality and proximity. *Proximity* refers to how close a sensor is to its ideal deployment position. *Directionality* refers to how sensitive a sensor is to variance from its ideal orientation. A microphone used to detect a dog's bark is an example of a sensor that is not very sensitive to either placement factor. Though installing the sensor in a sound-proof box would render it useless, most any location or orientation would still likely detect the sound of a dog barking in the room. A camera is an example of a sensor that is very sensitive to directionality – it collects substantially different data when aimed at the center of a room than when pointed at the floor. A motion detector with a wide-angle lens is an example of a sensor with a moderate, but less extreme sensitivity to directionality. A thermometer is an example of a sensor that is moderately sensitive to proximity, but not directionality. Placing the thermometer on a window sill or a radiator will not yield temperatures representative of the room in general, but placing it upside down will not change its readings substantially. A moisture sensor is an example of a sensor that is highly sensitive to proximity – a sensor embedded in soil will give very different moisture readings than one laid on the surface. For example, a user might be instructed to: "Place the moisture sensor one inch below the soil surface." If the user did not closely follow instructions, the sensor readings could be very misleading.

Association refers to the semantic connection that must be made between a sensor's data stream and its real-world subject. A sensor's subject can be either a *physical object*, *e.g.,* a light switch to which a piezoelectric sensor is attached, or a *space, e.g.*, the room at which a motion detector is aimed. Certainly, more complicated association models than one-sensor-to-one-subject are possible, but from a human point of view, one-to-one models are the simplest case. While work exists on self-configuring sensors, most applications require a person to make an explicit connection between a sensor and its subject (*e.g.*, RFID tag #42 is on the blender; motion detector #2 is in the master bedroom) [10].

The precision of an association is a function of the sensor's placement requirements and its subject. Generally, association is simpler for proximity-sensitive sensors than directionality-sensitive sensors and for subjects that are physical objects rather than spaces. A proximity-sensitive moisture sensor associated with an object like a potted plant is not likely to collect data about another plant. Unlike objects, the physical extents of domestic spaces are often fuzzy, so a proximity-sensitive thermometer associated with a space like an open kitchen might collect temperature data about both the kitchen and a nearby dining area. Directionality-sensitive sensors such as cameras and motion detectors are challenging to associate because it is difficult to precisely shape or scope a sensor's range. A motion detector associated with an object like a door may collect misleading data when someone walks near it but does not approach the door; similarly, a camera associated with a space like a hallway may inadvertently collect data about activity in a nearby bathroom.

4   Sensor Installation Kit and the Home Energy Tutor

In this section, we describe our mock sensor installation kit and the home monitoring application, the Home Energy Tutor, which provided the context for our evaluation. We also discuss the *in situ* sensor installation evaluation.

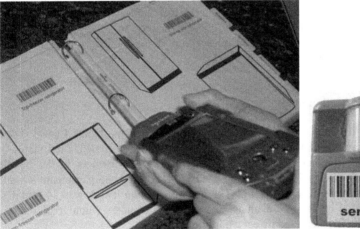

Figure 1. Sensor association in the Home Energy Tutor. At left, a user scans the barcode for a type of appliance from the item catalog using the handheld device; at right is a motion sensor with its barcode

The Home Energy Tutor is the application concept that provided the context for our in situ evaluation of the sensor installation kit. It is intended to help homeowners track their household energy use and learn about ways to reduce it. In our intended deployment plan, a homeowner is shipped a Home Energy Tutor kit, complete with sensors, instructions and supporting computing infrastructure. The homeowner will install and start the system herself and keep it for one month. At the end of the month, she returns it to the energy utility or other sponsoring organization. To install the application, the homeowner places various sensors on appliances and in rooms around his home, creating an association between a specific sensor and a room or appliance by scanning barcodes on the sensor and in a printed catalog (Figure 1). Since the user only has the application for one month, it needs to be easy and safe to deploy and remove; it should not require access to hidden electrical cords and outlets, the electrical mains or breaker box, or other difficult to reach places.

The sensor installation kit for the Home Energy Tutor includes vibration, electrical current, and microphone sensors to detect the use of major appliances, while motion detectors and camera sensors are used to monitor activity and electric lighting. A compact computer, which is included with the kit, is preconfigured to collect data from the wireless sensors. Beyond providing it with power, the users in the home have no interaction with this computer. A handheld scanner and printed instructions guide the homeowner through the sensor installation task. Throughout the deployment, standalone displays provide household members real-time and summary information about household energy usage. Given the energy and activity patterns of the household, the homeowner also receives suggestions about how best to reduce household energy use by changing behavior and upgrading or maintaining appliances.

The Home Energy Tutor is targeted specifically at homeowners, a group particularly concerned with their energy use at home. Homeowners rarely share energy expenses with others, and as they usually have sole control over their property, are better able than renters to take action to reduce energy use. Target users are in their late 20s through their 60s, have technical expertise ranging from none to expert, and have some interest in monitoring or reducing their household's energy use. We believe that homeowners are an especially good population to investigate as they are likely to be the target users for several other future domestic ubicomp applications, including some discussed in Section 6.

4.1   Evaluation Methodology

We investigated the sensor installation kit in the context of the Home Energy Tutor application with an *in situ*, task-based study of 15 homeowners in the United States.

The study was conducted in August 2003 with 15 homeowners in the Seattle metropolitan area. Each of the 15 sessions was conducted in the participant's home by two members of the research team. The average session length was 84 minutes. Data were collected by the two evaluators in the form of notes, photographs, and a written questionnaire completed by each participant.

Participants were recruited by a market research firm, and were screened to be representative of the target user group for the Home Energy Tutor. Participants with technical backgrounds were specifically screened out (though because of a recruiter mistake, one of the participants was a retired programmer). Each participant received $75 USD. Nine participants were female; ages ranged from 28-61. Three of the participants lived alone, while the other households had two to four occupants total; 10 participants had children living at home. 10 of the participants had at least one dog or cat. The sizes of their homes ranged from 900 – 3,000 square feet.

Each session comprised four phases: introduction, exploration, sensor installation, and an interview. The *introduction* phase consisted of personal introductions, a release form, and a questionnaire. During the *exploration* phase, participants were given a high-level description of the Home Energy Tutor application and the sensor installation kit. Participants were asked to do "what they would normally do" when such a package arrived. The kit contained a list of contents, printed instructions, the Item Catalog, a handheld scanner (*i.e.*, a Compaq iPAQ handheld device with an attached barcode reader), a bag of removable adhesives, and 10 sensors—two of each type: vibration, current, motion, sound (microphone), and image (camera) (Figure 2).

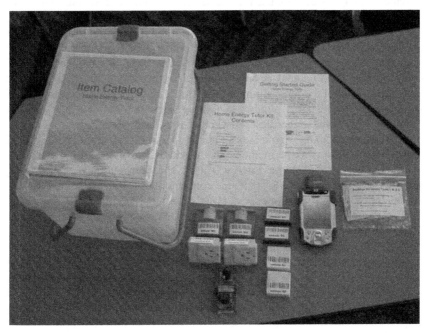

Figure 2. Home Energy Tutor installation kit. It contained a list of contents, printed instructions, Item Catalog, handheld scanner, bag of removable adhesives, and 10 mock sensors

When participants indicated they were ready to move on, the *installation* phase began. The researchers asked participants to install each of the 10 sensors, one at a time, on various appliances or in rooms throughout their homes. Since not all homes have the same appliances or floor plans, participants were given a choice of two appliances or rooms for each task (*e.g.*, install a sensor on the microwave or toaster oven). Though the participants knew the sensors would be taken down at the end of the session, they were asked to imagine that they were installing the sensors for the full month-long deployment. To minimize the effects of their own presence, evaluators did not respond to participants' questions about the process once installation began. Evaluators also took extreme care to offer no hints, coaching, or emotional reactions to the participants' understanding of the installation process or to their sensor placements, even those that were obviously incorrect. Evaluators took photos of each attempted installation. After the installation tasks were completed, the sensors were removed and returned to the kit.

The session ended with a semi-structured *interview*. Questions in the interview were designed to elicit the participants' understanding of the various installation steps and components of the system, any problems they would have leaving the sensors in place for a month, how they would stop a sensor from collecting data, and general feedback on the Home Energy Tutor application concept.

4.2   Design of the Sensor Installation Kit

As aforementioned, the sensors used in the study were not operational. This was a formative study conducted as part of a user-centered design process for the Home Energy Tutor. It took place in parallel with sensor and display development efforts. The sensors included in the installation kit were chosen with the Home Energy Tutor in mind. We chose general sensors over more specific ones. A vibration sensor, for example, can monitor a number of environmental factors: the spinning of a washing machine, the closing of a door, the running of a refrigerator compressor, etc. In a real kit, we would include a large number of these general sensors, and they would be sufficient for most homes regardless of whether they had two refrigerators or more doors than expected. The sound sensor (microphone) was also chosen for its generality. Other sensors were included in the kit due to their ability to measure conditions critical to the Home Energy Tutor. The current sensor, for example measured the current draw of the appliance connected to it. Finally, some overlap in sensor capability was included to expose possible installation difficulties and privacy issues. The motion sensor, for example, was included even though room occupancy could also be measured with the camera sensor.

The five types of mock sensors that were used for this study were designed with the help of team members who were developing the real sensors. Two of the sensors—vibration and sound—were low fidelity prototypes; *i.e.*, pieces of painted medium density fiberboard, cut to approximate the size, shape, and weight of the intended sensors. The other three—motion, current, and image—were higher fidelity prototypes. The current sensor was an off-the-shelf plug-through appliance surge protector, the image sensor was an off-the-shelf camera on a wooden base, and the motion sensor was an off-the-shelf motion sensor. The sensors were color-coded by type: vibration sensors were red, motion sensors were blue, *etc.* While we expect that an application like the Home Energy Tutor would include more than 50 sensors, we included 10, two of each type, in the *in situ* evaluation to allow us to observe multiple installations of the same type of sensor while keeping the session length reasonable.

The sensors could be placed in various ways. All of the sensors had flat sides and afforded placement on horizontal surfaces. The kit also contained a bag of removable adhesives that could be used to attach the sensors to various surfaces (except for the current sensor, which could only be correctly installed by plugging the appliance into the sensor, then plugging the sensor into the outlet). Additionally, the vibration sensors had magnetic strips on one side to afford mounting on ferrous metal surfaces.

To ensure that we were evaluating the concept of homeowners installing sensors in a domestic environment and not just doing a usability study of our documentation, we used three versions of the printed instructions, each of which were pilot tested for clarity prior to the *in situ* study. The three versions contained the same project description and instructions for using the handheld scanner, and varied only in the sensor names and descriptions. Five participants used each version of the documentation. Version A documentation was the most complete: it described how each of the types of sensors worked, how the information they collected was used by the Home Energy Tutor, and how they should be installed. Version B documentation excluded the information about how the Home Energy Tutor used the information provided by the sensors. Version C documentation contained only directive information about how the sensors should be installed, but nothing about how they worked or how the application used the information. Instructions on using the handheld scanner and the installation wizard that ran on the handheld scanner (Figure 3) were written based on feedback from an earlier in-lab study of the same concept.

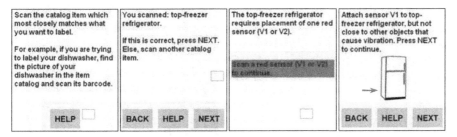

Figure 3.   Installation tool interface. The handheld scanner guides the user through the installation process, from association to placement

The names of the sensor types varied between the documentation versions and were chosen to convey different conceptual models. In versions A and B, the same sensor names were used: current, vibration, motion, image, and sound. Though the image and sound sensors were cameras and microphones, we named them differently, seeking to avoid confusion between their typical use (*e.g.*, video and audio capture) and the sensing tasks they performed for the Home Energy Tutor (*e.g.*, light, activity, and appliance operation detection).   Version C documentation provided no information about sensor operation, and to preserve this distinction, the sensor types were named yellow, red, blue, purple, and white.

The same hardware developers who helped create the sensor prototypes for this study also helped develop criteria as to what a "correct" installation was.   In general, the correctness of an installation task was determined by the placement and association factors presented above.   For the sound and vibration sensors, proximity strongly determined if the sensor was correctly positioned; the sensor had to be placed close to its subject but not within range of interference from other sources of sound or vibration (Figure 4). Proximity was also an important factor for the current sensor: a current sensor was correctly placed only if the subject appliance was plugged into it, and the sensor plugged into an outlet.   For the image and motion sensors, directionality was an important factor: a correctly positioned sensor needed unrestricted line-of-sight to its subject.   All sensors had to be associated with their subject by scanning the sensor and the corresponding subject in the item catalog.

4.3   Evaluation Results

The *in situ* task-based study was largely successful: out of 150 sensor installation tasks, 112 were completed correctly. Five participants completed all installation tasks correctly, while two participants completed no installation tasks correctly.   Correct completion of installation tasks by sensor type is shown in Table 1.

Figure 4. Installing a sensor on the water heater. On the left, a participant *correctly* installed a sound sensor on his water heater. On the right, a different participant *incorrectly* installed a sensor on his water heater. In the incorrect installation, the water heater is on the left side of the room, out of the photograph, and the sensor is closer to the dryer than the water heater. Both participants used Version A documentation

The five participants who successfully completed all ten tasks understood the sensing conceptual model reasonably well. However, the two participants who were completely unsuccessful failed for reasons unrelated to the sensors themselves. Instead, they had difficulty following directions on the handheld scanner's screen (Figure 3). One participant stated *"I was trying to make the computer* [iPAQ] *do something that it didn't want to do."* Meanwhile, the other participant understood the need for associating sensors, even stating that *"...the Palm* [iPAQ] *doesn't know which sensor I'm using,"* but failed to follow the directions onscreen.

As another measure of their understanding of the sensor installation tasks, participants were asked conceptual questions about the sensor types and application as a whole. Of the 15 participants, 13 understood how to correctly disable a sensor they had installed (*e.g.,* simply remove it); similarly, the same 13 understood the purpose of barcodes (to associate a sensor with a room or appliance). The two participants who did not understand these concepts were the same two who were completely unsuccessful at the installation tasks.

5   Five Design Principles for End-User Sensor Installation

As application designers and developers have the opportunity both to consider user needs and to guide the selection of which sensing hardware to use, providing guidance about sensor installation can improve users' experiences with domestic ubiquitous computing applications. From our experience with the sensor installation study, we propose five principles for end-user installation of sensors. The first two principles parallel traditional HCI design principles, while the last three relate findings specific to our work in the domestic environment.

1. Make appropriate use of user conceptual models for familiar technologies

It may be difficult for everyday users to form conceptual models of ubiquitous computing applications as the applications are often highly distributed and break the familiar paradigm of WIMP (Windows, Icons, Menus & Pointers) human-computer interaction. While the application itself may be novel, using familiar technologies in predictable ways can support end-user installation of the application. By choosing sensor types whose usual capabilities are closely associated with their use in the application, designers can avoid the user confusion generated by re-defining existing conceptual models of real-world systems, (*e.g.,* using simple photosensors rather than cameras to monitor lighting). This principle aligns with observations made by Norman and others about user understanding of everyday objects [7]. However, this principle cuts both ways: familiar component technology used in unusual ways may confuse users' understanding of the application, regardless of re-naming the technology. We illustrate this principle with two examples: the barcode scanner used to associate a sensor with its subject, and the sound and image sensors used to detect appliance operation and human activity.

The Home Energy Tutor's sensor installation tool successfully used a familiar technology, barcodes, in a reasonably familiar way. In the course of a sensor installation task, participants were instructed to scan a barcode from the item catalog indicating a sensor's subject, and then to scan a barcode on the sensor itself. Most participants were familiar with the use of barcodes from their experiences in retail stores – 13 of 15 understood that barcodes link a physical merchandise item with a

sensor type	correct installation	correct association	correct placement
current	26 (87%)	26 (87%)	28 (93%)
motion	23 (77%)	24 (80%)	25 (83%)
vibration	22 (73%)	26 (87%)	23 (77%)
image	21 (70%)	26 (87%)	22 (73%)
sound	20 (67%)	23 (77%)	26 (87%)

Table 1. Correct installations by sensor type. For each sensor type, this table shows the total number of completely correct sensor installations, the number of correct sensor associations, and the number of correct sensor placements. Each number is out of a possible 30. Two participants did not install any sensors correctly

database record indicating its price, and 11 had operated barcode readers with self-checkout at a retail store. Several participants had also operated handheld barcode readers when they registered for their weddings. 13 participants were able to transfer the "linking model" of barcodes to the Home Energy Tutor application, correctly inferring that the purpose of scanning was, in one participant's words, *"to connect the two, so the computer would know which sensor went with which appliance."*

The sound and image sensors – microphones and cameras – had many installation errors, partly because familiar technology was being used in unfamiliar ways. Participants were instructed that *"the sound sensor... detects the particular frequencies of sound created by the appliance...the Home Energy Tutor uses this sound information... to calculate the energy use of the nearby appliance or device."* Similarly, participants were instructed that *"the image sensor detects... the locations where people are active within a room, and the use of electric lighting. The Home Energy Tutor uses this activity information... both to calculate the energy usage of the electric lighting, and to provide recommendations about where in your house you should focus your energy conservation efforts."* Both descriptions are unusual, given the familiar model of microphones and cameras as devices for sound and video recording or transmission. Even for the 10 participants who were provided documentation about *what* the sound sensor detected, only five of those participants were able to explain the sensor's actual use at the end of the session. The sound sensor was also the sensor most likely to be misinstalled (67% correct installation rate). Participant understanding of the image sensor was slightly better: 8 of the 15 participants understood what it was detecting, but it also suffered from frequent installation errors (70% correct installation rate).

This principle can be implemented in practice by appropriately utilizing existing conceptual models of real-world systems (*e.g.,* using barcode readers for associative links). When familiar technology must be used in unusual ways – *e.g.*, a camera as an activity detector – it is important to substantially disguise the underlying sensor, both in name and physical form.

2. Balance installation usability with domestic concerns

Deployment of sensors for a domestic ubiquitous computing application raises practical concerns such as aesthetics of sensors and damage caused by application components. In our study, several participants found the sensors to be unsightly, worried that the sensors might attract the attention of house guests, were convinced that their children and pets would move sensors placed within their reach, and were concerned that adhesives would cause damage. Concerns like these must be balanced with the desire for an easy-to-install system and high-quality data. Supporting an end-user's sense of domestic propriety is critical: a system that violates it is likely to be left in the box, as is a system that is difficult to install. Sensors designed to be easily installed may be obtrusive or ugly, and non-destructive adhesives and fasteners may be easily knocked loose. In this spirit, we discuss two tradeoffs between designers' and end-users' goals. Making sensor types easy to discriminate from one other is a practical concern of designers in conflict with users' concern about aesthetics and "obviousness" of the sensors. Likewise, system requirements about placement must be balanced with the potential damage that sensor fasteners can do to surfaces and concerns about placing sensors within reach of pets and children.

Designing sensors for installation usability may conflict with aesthetic concerns, but both can successfully be addressed. The five types of mock sensors were designed to be easy for an end-user to tell apart during installation: to achieve this, we used different, brightly colored sensors. Four participants, while willing to cooperate with placing sensors for the short duration of the study, said they would be reluctant to leave the sensors in place, even for the Home Energy Tutor's relatively short month-long deployment. Three of these participants regarded the sensors as an eyesore; the fourth thought the sensors would prompt too many questions from houseguests. A potential solution was suggested: sensors could be a neutral color, similar to existing home security motion and smoke detectors, with small colored dots to differentiate sensor types. This would allow recognition by color coding during installation and relative unobtrusiveness when installed.

Users' practical concerns about their homes also influenced sensor installation. In particular, study participants expressed concern both about sensor adhesives causing surface damage, and about sensor placements within reach of children and pets. These concerns conflicted with technical needs: some sensor types used for the Home Energy Tutor required either immobile placement or very specific placement locations. Unfortunately, addressing practical home concerns may restrict the feasibility of certain sensing configurations. For example, placement of a vibration sensor on the lower half of the refrigerator concerned some users because of its vulnerability to children and pets, but the location was technically necessary to detect operation of the compressor. Three participants were concerned about sensor placements that could be reached and removed by their young children or pets. Two participants refused to use any adhesives, even though the well-known commercial adhesive pads included in the kit were advertised as removable. It is important to note that technical issues become irrelevant when users are unwilling to install sensors for pragmatic reasons.

In practice, designers and developers need to consider aesthetic and environmental issues. Aesthetic issues can be addressed by minimizing the visual impact of sensors for residents and guests. Similarly, practical placement issues can be addressed by considering the concerns of the target user group and providing a range of sensor attachment options, as well as providing multiple appropriate sensor types per subject.

3. Avoid use of cameras, microphones, and highly directional sensors if possible

Microphones and cameras are highly attractive to application developers due to the rich data sources they provide. Unfortunately, they are a serious privacy concern due to the sensitive data they can capture. Unlike data from other sensors, audio and video can be interpreted by people without context or an association, making them especially dangerous if the system is compromised. Two of the participants refused to place the image sensors in their homes, and several more expressed grave concern about placement of cameras or microphones: "*I didn't like the [image sensors]. I got so freaked out because of the camera,*" and "*[it is] a little too big-brotherish.*" Our results suggest that microphones and cameras should be avoided if data can be collected in another manner, even if it involves using several other sensors.

Our data also suggest that highly directional sensors are problematic, although for a different reason. Of all the sensor types, the image (camera) sensors were incorrectly installed second most often. The alignment of pitch, yaw and roll require positioning the sensor for 6 degrees of freedom. Given the widely varying layouts of homes and end-user concerns regarding attachment methods, this was a considerable issue. Of the nine incorrect image sensor installations in the study, four were due to participants who did not notice or follow through on the aiming directions (Figure 5).

4. Detect incorrect installation of components & provide value for partial installations

Similar to the Home Energy Tutor, many ubiquitous computing applications require the installation of several sensors, and our data suggests that it is unlikely that end-users will succeed in correctly installing all of them. This implies that applications should be able to detect incorrectly installed sensors and either ignore the data or prompt the user to correct the installation. A special case of incorrect installation is a partial installation in which the user does not correctly install all of the sensors the application expects. This can happen because the user either incorrectly installs or refuses to install certain sensors.

Applications that do not recognize or support partial installation by end-users and provide some value may ostracize a majority of their users. 8 of the 15 participants in the Home Energy Tutor study installed at least one but not all of the sensors correctly. While some of the participants may have corrected their errors if the application recognized misinstalled sensors and coached them to correct the installation, at least three of the 13 participants who installed at least one sensor correctly proactively refused to install some sensors due to concerns with adhesive attachment methods, privacy, or frustration with the installation tool, despite the fact that they saw real value in the Home Energy Tutor. Unlike installation errors due to sensor placement or association of a sensor with its subject, these objections are intrinsic to the application design and cannot be overcome by an installation wizard. This implies that some application value for a partial installation is advantageous no matter how simple the sensor installation process.

For applications to recognize sensor misinstallation, they must take into account the data output produced by different types of misinstallation and potential strategies for recognition. Consider the case of a sensor that reports no data whatsoever, such as a motion sensor that is pointed at the ceiling instead of the center of a room: this condition can be recognized and the application user alerted. This strategy depends upon the expected frequency of change for the sensor output: no motion reported in the foyer of an occupied home over two days may be reason for alert, but a report of no motion in the basement for the same period may be normal. Another type of misinstallation occurs when a sensor reports a coherent signal from another source of the phenomena it detects, such as a vibration sensor associated with a washing machine but placed near both the washing machine and the clothes dryer. This case

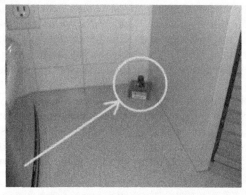

Figure 5. Incorrectly installed image sensor. This image sensor is supposed to be monitoring kitchen use, but is instead monitoring the underside of a cabinet

of misinstallation is difficult to detect without corroborating data from other sensors – for example, noting that reports from the washing machine and dryer sensors are exactly time-correlated with each other. Finally, sensors may report entirely spurious data, a condition to which sensors using a high degree of inference are particularly vulnerable, as the raw data stream doesn't match what the inferencing process expects. For example, this error might occur when a camera intended to monitor the light sources in a room is pointed at the ceiling and captures only the reflections of light sources in the room (Figure 5). This type of error may also occur when a sensor has been moved or removed after a successful installation. This condition can be managed by sanity-checking the input of the inferencing process, ensuring that the sensor output data is consistent with a room interior rather than a ceiling, for example.

Practically, designers should not assume that a sensor has been installed correctly because an association step has been performed or because the sensor is transmitting data. Rather, the application should encode some model of appropriate sensor output and use that capability to detect sensor misinstallation, either to ignore that data stream or to involve the user in correcting a problem. The application should also provide some value for partially installed applications.

5. Educate the user about data collection, storage, and transmission

Domestic ubiquitous computing applications should provide users with clear information about data collection both by individual sensors and the application as a whole. Users who are aware of *what* a sensor senses as well as *how* the application uses the data are better equipped to handle installation difficulties. At the application level, fostering an explicit understanding of what information is collected, where it is stored, and whether it is transmitted outside the home is also critical for acceptance of sensors into a domestic environment. Homes are private spaces, and applications that do not engender the *appearance* of propriety are unlikely to be accepted, regardless of how well the underlying mechanics are designed. We discuss the qualitative effects of providing users with detailed information about the sensors, how the application uses the data, and the need to reinforce the data boundaries of an application.

Though there were no statistically significant differences in installation successes between participants who received different levels of sensor documentation detail, we noted several spontaneous comments from participants about their understanding of the sensors. 3 of the 5 participants in the group who received only installation directions mentioned that they wanted more information about the operation of the sensors. Conversely, a participant who received all of the sensor information noted that it was helpful in installing the sensors. Even merely providing information about what the sensor detects is helpful – a participant who received installation directions and sensor operation noted that: *"you can figure things out when you know what [the sensor] is for,"* referring to how she was able to troubleshoot a sensor installation with her non-standard refrigerator (Figure 6).

Regardless of assurances by application developers, some users are highly skeptical of the privacy supported by a sensing application. For the sensor installation study, we verbally presented a thorough introduction to the application and stated repeatedly that information gathered during the course of the deployment would not be transmitted to any outside parties or used for any purpose other than to provide the homeowner with energy-saving recommendations. Despite our assurances, three participants spontaneously stated that they did not believe that data gathered in the home would not leave the home, and all three noted that it would have altered or prevented their installation of sensors, particularly the image sensors (cameras).

In practice, designers can improve end-users' ability to install sensors and help assuage privacy concerns by providing detailed information about what a sensor detects and how the application uses the data. When designing domestic sensing applications, whether or not data is communicated outside of the home, designers must provide a careful description of what information is collected, how and by whom it is used, where it is stored, and what control the users have over the data.

6   Advantages for Other Ubicomp Application Domains

In this section, we discuss three application domains and how they stand to benefit from the end-user installation of sensors. We also discuss their sensor installation requirements and describe the types of use that end-user installation enables.

6.1   Supporting Health Care and Aging

With increasing healthcare costs and aging populations, it has become a priority to shorten hospital stays and to increase quality of life for elders. Several projects focus on increasing the amount of time an elder or infirm person can remain at home, either directly or by helping monitor her health. Enabling end-user installation of these applications reduces their *cost* which should make them accessible to more people, allows for *diversity* of living situations and user needs, and supports the relatively

Figure 6. Trouble-shooting installation. A participant was able to trouble-shoot installing a sensor on her refrigerator, because she understood what the sensor needed to do and knew that her non-standard refrigerator's compressor was at the top

high *rates-of-change* of the needs of an elder or infirm person. Presently, these applications are installed by researchers [1, 4, 5]. End-user installation of these applications would allow those who provide care – who are sensitive to the individual's condition and needs – to perform the installation.

Several applications have been developed to support aging-in-place for elders. Each requires installation and configuration, ranging from complex tasks where cameras, contact switches, and RFID tag readers are strategically placed throughout a home and associated with semantically meaningful locations, to simple tasks where RFID tags are associated with a person, pill bottle, or everyday object. Morris *et al* have developed prototypes that track an elder's movement and activities in her house to facilitate exercise, support everyday routines, and warn caregivers about dangerous situations [5]. The prototypes gather location and activity information using RFID tags, infrared beacons, and pressure sensors. Fishkin *et al*'s Monitoring Pad helps elders and their caregivers monitor medication usage and reduce missed doses; the system uses RFID tags and a high-precision scale to detect which bottle is lifted from and returned to the MedPad and the number of pills removed [1]. Mihailidis *et al* developed an application to help elders maintain their sense of independence by using a camera and faucet-mounted contact switches to monitor hand-washing [4].

6.2   Home Automation and Monitoring

Many ubiquitous computing applications have focused on automating and monitoring the home. While the vision of these projects is often compelling to researchers or hobbyists, home automation technologies like X10 have not been embraced by casual users. Partially, this is a problem of *value* – the benefits of automation are not worth the hassle of installation. Improving the ease of end-user sensor installation should increase the market penetration of many of these low- to medium-value home-automation applications.

Mozer's neural network house is one of many research systems in this space. Mozer used information gathered from motion detectors, microphones, contact switches, and photosensors to optimally balance comfort with energy cost [6]. While the house also included many hard-wired controls for appliances, sensor installation for the application requires proper placement and association with a particular location. The PlantCare system developed by LaMarca *et al* automated the task of watering houseplants by measuring local light, temperature, and soil moisture for each plant and using this information to actuate a mobile robot which waters the plants [3]. Installation of the system required placing a sensor in the soil of each houseplant and associating that sensor with the type of plant it was sensing.

6.3   Application Evaluation

The evaluation of ubiquitous computing applications is a particularly difficult problem because of the emphasis on implicit interactions and blending into a user's everyday routine. Sensory instrumentation of a study participant's own home has been one approach to improving study realism, but installation of instrumentation applications requires trained researchers or technicians with intimate knowledge of the sensing technology. Chiefly, end-user sensor installation can enable low-cost, early-stage field research to be conducted without requiring a team of technical experts. End-user installation reduces research *cost* by enabling the self-installed, kit-in-a-box model used by the Home Energy Tutor. End-user installation of sensors also manages a potentially low level of *value* on the part of the study participant and enhances their sense of *control* over what information is being collected.

The ubiquitous environment state-change sensor system, developed by Intille *et al*, gathers information about user activity within an environment by using a large number of reed and piezoelectric switches to sense contact or movement of objects [2]. Installation of this system requires choosing the right type of sensor for a particular subject of interest, placing the sensor, and making an association between the sensor and its subject. Guide, developed by Philipose *et al*, is another application that could be used for evaluation purposes [8]. Guide infers a user's activity with a small, short-range RFID wrist-mounted reader worn by the user that detects when he touches RFID tagged objects. Installation of the system requires attaching RFID tags to objects and making an association between the tag and the object to which it is attached. The value of both of these projects for evaluating ubiquitous computing applications would be increased by easy end-user installation.

7   Conclusion and Future Work

In this paper, we described the design and *in situ* evaluation of the end-user sensor installation kit for the Home Energy Tutor, a domestic ubiquitous computing application. From our experiences, we developed five design principles for enabling end-user sensor installation. We discussed the advantages of end-user sensor installation in terms of cost, control, diversity of environment, value, and human and technological rates of change. We identified placement and association as primary factors of a sensor installation task and used them to generalize our experience with the mock sensor installation kit. Finally, we discussed ubiquitous computing research domains that could strongly benefit from end-user sensor installation.

To make installation of domestic ubiquitous computing applications as simple as modular home electronics, much work remains, both in implementation and evaluation. End-user installation would be improved by techniques for detecting sensor installation errors, helping users correct misinstallations, and providing application functionality in spite of erroneous or missing data. Real-time feedback about a given sensor placement – in effect, allowing a user to "see what the sensor sees," would improve both the user's conceptual model of the sensor and the quality of its installation. A qualitative issue to explore is the reusability of a set of sensor hardware for multiple applications, and how the lack of a specific application model influences users' abilities and willingness to install sensors. Longer term studies with functioning sensors could explore how people and applications co-evolve, how acceptable sensor placements are viewed in the long term, how likely sensors are to be moved, removed, or damaged over time, and the degree to which end-users exert control over the system they installed.

Acknowledgments

We would like to thank Min Wang, Ken Camarata, Ellen Do, Brian Johnson, Mark Gross, Anind Dey, Ken Fishkin, and Ken Smith.

References

1. Fishkin, K.P., Wang, M. and Borriello, G. A Ubiquitous System for Medication Monitoring. *Advances in Pervasive Computing: A Collection of Contributions Presented at Pervasive 2004*, 193-198.
2. Intille, S.S., *et al.* Tools for Studying Behavior and Technology in Natural Settings. *5th International Conference on Ubiquitous Computing: Ubicomp 2003*, Seattle, 2003. 157-174.
3. LaMarca, A., *et al.* PlantCare: an investigation in practical ubiquitous systems. *UbiComp 2002: 4th International Conference on Ubiquitous Computing. 316-32.*
4. Mihailidis, A., Fernie, G. and Cleghorn, W.L. The development of a computerized cueing device to help people with dementia to be more independent. *Technology & Disability, 13.* 23-40.
5. Morris, M., *et al.* New Perspectives on Ubiquitous Computing from Ethnographic Study of Elders with Cognitive Decline. *5th International Conference on Ubiquitous Computing: Ubicomp 2003*, Seattle. 227-241.
6. Mozer, M.C. The neural network house: an environment that adapts to its inhabitants. *Intelligent Environments. Papers from the 1998 AAAI Symposium. 110-14.*
7. Norman, D.A. *The Design of Everyday Things.* Bantam Doubleday Dell, New York, 1988.
8. Philipose, M., *et al.* Guide: Towards Understanding Daily Life via Auto-Identification and Statistical Analysis. *UbiHealth 2003: The 2nd International Workshop on Ubiquitous Computing for Pervasive Healthcare Applications*, (Seattle, 2003).
9. Rodden, T. and Benford, S. The evolution of buildings and implications for the design of ubiquitous domestic environments. *Proceedings of the conference on Human factors in computing systems: CHI '03*, 9-16.
10. Scott, J. and Hazas, M. User-Friendly Surveying Techniques for Location-Aware Systems. *5th International Conference on Ubiquitous Computing: Ubicomp 2003*, Seattle. 44-53.

Rapid Authoring of Mediascapes

Richard Hull[1], Ben Clayton[2] & Tom Melamed[2]

[1]Hewlett-Packard Laboratories, Bristol, UK
richard.hull@hp.com
[2]University of Bristol, UK
{ben | tom}@mobileBristol.com

Abstract. Ubiquitous computing promises to enable new classes of application. In this paper, we present research intended to accelerate the exploration of the space of possible application values by enabling domain specialists to develop, deploy and evaluate experimental applications, even if they do not have programming skills. We present a framework for the *rapid authoring* of mediascapes, a commercially important class of media-oriented, context-sensitive, mobile applications. A case study is described in which two artists without prior experience of ubiquitous computing successfully and quickly deployed experimental mediascapes in an urban square. A discussion of their experience suggests future work aimed at closing the gap between application emulation and reality.

Introduction

The technologies that enable ubiquitous computing – small, cheap, low-power processors, memory, sensors, actuators and wireless connectivity – are maturing to the point where real-world applications can begin to emerge. The promise is of a new generation of mobile, context-sensitive and connected applications that offer novel services to users by linking together the physical and digital. However, we are yet to discover which of the potential benefits of such applications will eventually come to be most valued by end users. The meaning of a technology – what it is for – usually evolves along with the technology itself as it is adopted, explored, subverted and adapted by the user base. Part of our role now as researchers in ubiquitous computing is to initiate and participate in this evolutionary process by introducing, evaluating and modifying as many different kinds of applications as possible with their potential users.

The authors are part of a research programme that is beginning to explore the space of potential applications through experimental deployments and evaluations [1]. Our aim is to engage a wide variety of domain specialists in this process so as to diversify the search for potential value. For example, we have recently been involved in experimental applications developed with and by children, educationalists, artists and television programme makers.

We believe that the emergence of a critical mass of such application explorations can best be achieved by enabling the domain specialists to develop applications appropriate to their domains themselves, whatever their current level of programming expertise. Moreover, we believe that the resulting applications must be released from

N. Davies et al. (Eds.): UbiComp 2004, LNCS 3205, pp. 125-142, 2004.

the constraints of the research laboratory into the wider world where their utility and value can emerge (or otherwise) in the market place of competing offerings.

Our approach to tackling these goals is inspired by the democratization of publishing enabled by the World Wide Web. Almost anyone can make and deploy a web site, even if it consists of only a single page of text. Naturally, the nature of the resulting web sites varies enormously. Some are excellent, while some are less so. Some are complex networks of dynamically generated content and scripted interaction, while others consist of just a few words and images. Some are accessed by a millions and some are hardly ever visited. The point is that the barriers to creating web stuff are low, leading to a massively parallel and decentralized search of the possibilities enabled by web technologies and the emergence of new application genres with real value to their users. Our ambition is to enable the same kind of search within the space of applications of ubiquitous computing technologies.

In the main body of this paper, we will present a framework and associated development tools that are intended to accelerate the search for value in this space by enabling (almost) anyone to create and deploy mobile, context-sensitive applications. We will then review a recent use of the framework and its associated tools by two artists, and attempt to draw lessons from their experiences for future work. We will begin, however, with a brief review of related work.

Related Work

Of course, others have been motivated by similar goals to those just outlined and have produced offerings that ease the task of developing ubiquitous computing applications. In our view, these may be thought of as falling into three broad strands of research.

In the first strand, the emphasis has been on providing middleware that avoids the need to develop bespoke mechanisms for each new application. For example, Cool-Town provides a variety of mechanisms for linking the physical world to web pages and for discovering local services [2], Equip provides a consistent shared dataspace across distributed devices [3], and Elvin [4] provides messaging based on the publish and subscribe model [5]. This is a valuable contribution that facilitates the work of system developers but falls short of enabling domain specialists to develop applications without the assistance of skilled computer programmers. To an extent, the approach reported in this paper can be seen as a means of making such middleware accessible to non-programmers.

The second broad strand of research has focused on architecting systems so as to ease the re-use of modules in related applications, such as in the Cyberguide project [6]. Dey et al [7] provide a useful review of this approach and describe a comprehensive architectural framework based on a variety of "context widgets". Their architecture allows sensor, interpreter and the other widget types to be composed into larger systems through standard messaging interfaces, and for such widgets to be shared between different applications. This provides a rich and coherent toolkit that should ease the implementation of context-sensitive applications, particularly if they are to be distributed among different devices. However, we would argue that this approach continues to be aimed at supporting skilled system developers rather than domain specialists and is unlikely, alone, to liberate a much larger and more varied set of application creators.

Together, these two strands of research facilitate the *rapid prototyping* of ubiquitous computing systems by skilled computing professionals. Again, this is a valuable contribution but falls short of our goal of enabling the *rapid authoring* of such applications by domain specialists, where *authoring* can be understood as an activity that focuses on domain-specific content and behaviour rather than on underlying computational mechanisms. Although there is less research in the ubiquitous computing area with this focus, there are a few interesting examples that form the third strand of related work.

In an early example, the Stick-e system aimed to support non-programmer development of context-triggered applications by adopting a strong but limited application metaphor based on post-it notes [8]. More generally, iCAP is a visual programming system intended to enable end-users to develop context-aware applications modeled as if-then rules [9]. Rules are created by dragging objects representing people, places and things into semantically significant regions on the editing interface and using dropdown menus to select relationships between them. Topiary has similar aims but adopts a programming-by-example approach [10]. Having first defined named users and places on a 2D map of the physical location of the application, the user/programmer defines significant events by dragging, say, an avatar for a user into a particular place. This creates a condition that may be used in a second editing stage to trigger transitions between interface elements. The a Capella system takes the use of programming-by-demonstration a step further by learning the conditions for triggering contextual actions from sensor logs of real-world examples [11]. Moving away from contextual triggers, the Jigsaw editor provides an appealing visual interface enabling end-users to define pipelines of components through which events and data might flow in an automated home [12].

Each of these systems contributes valuable ideas that have been validated through emulation of the resulting applications and in laboratory trials. However, their emphasis seems to be on "programming in the small" and it is unclear whether the systems would scale up to real world applications with large numbers of anonymous users, more complex relationships, dependencies on past events, and the uncertainty introduced by real sensing technologies. One of the contributions of this paper is to carry through the notion of application development by non-programmers all the way to deployment, revealing important difference between emulation in the authoring environment and execution in the real world. In the next section, we introduce the authoring framework developed to support this goal.

A Framework for Rapid Authoring of Context-Sensitive Applications

In this section, we turn to the description of a new framework for application development intended to support the rapid authoring of ubiquitous computing applications. In general, we aim to develop a framework that supports any kind of ubiquitous application in any domain. In practice, we have restricted our initial scope to a smaller set of application types that share some common characteristics. Our choice has been to focus on *mediascapes* – applications that are largely concerned with delivering or capturing digital media in response to contextual cues such as the user's location. An example of a simple mediascape can be found in the Walk in the Wired Woods installation reported in [13] in which a physical photography exhibition was overlaid with a virtual *soundscape* in which digital audio was delivered to visitors via location-sensitive, wearable computers as they viewed the photographs. As we shall see, the framework makes trivially easy the development of a simple soundscape with this "what you hear is where you are" functionality, but also supports a richer set of capabilities such as other media types, state variables, conditional logic, path histories, and messaging.

Naturally, a focus on one class of applications tends to inhibit the exploration of other interesting types of application. However, such a focus is inevitable if we are to provide more than weak, general support for authoring. We believe that there are strong commercial opportunities for *experiential* applications delivered as mediascapes in leisure, education, creative and many other domains. Much of our research work is directed towards exploring this hypothesis [14]. For the purposes of this paper, however, we will take this motivation as read, and focus on the systems that we have developed to enable such applications.

Overview

As has been emphasized in earlier sections, the primary objective for the framework is to enable as many kinds of people as possible, many of whom will be non-programmers, to author novel, context-sensitive, ubiquitous computing applications. Initially, we have focused on a class of applications termed mediascapes. Within this focus, however, we wish to retain as much flexibility for authors as possible. For example, we aim to support a variety of application architectures including standalone, peer-to-peer, and client-server systems, and we want to offer a rich set of media primitives. Moreover, it is vital to our larger ambitions that the authored applications can be deployed, at least experimentally, and evaluated for their value to real users. Given that end-user devices for implementing such applications are still not widely available, this introduces new requirements for prototype devices in trial quantities and for mechanisms for sharing those devices among multiple applications.

Given this background, we have developed an overall architecture for the framework that may be seen in figure 1 below. The purpose of the framework is to enable an application author to specify how an end-user's device should behave in context in that application. The device in question may be carried by the user or situated in the environment, may be personal or shared, autonomous or part of some larger ensemble. In any case, the key issue for the author is to be able to say what the device should do, when it should do it, and how. Normally, of course, we call this activity "programming", but remember that we do not want to *require* authors to have programming skills (though we may wish to provide more powerful authoring capabilities to those who do).

The key architectural idea in the framework is the explicit specification of the intended behaviour of the end-user device delivering an application in an XML-based markup language, MBML (Mobile Bristol Markup Language). This specification, known within the framework as a *script*, defines the behaviour of the device in response to *events* that occur within the user's (and application's) context. Event-based programming appears to provide a natural approach to problem solving for non-programmers [15], and is familiar to those with experience of authoring digital media applications. We generalize this familiar concept by adding contextual events, such as the movement of the user, to the interface events commonly found in such applications.

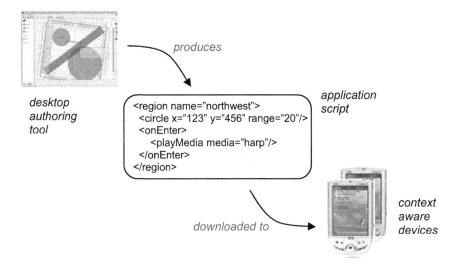

Fig. 1. Overview of Mobile Bristol Application Development Framework

The use of an explicit script specification has several advantages. First, the decoupling of the *specification* of the intended behaviour of a device from the *implementation* of that device makes it much easier to share a limited number of prototype devices between a large number of experimental applications. Furthermore, this separation also facilitates the introduction of new devices with different characteristics, perhaps originating from other sources than our research group. Similarly, the existence of a well-defined and independent specification language allows others who disagree with our designs for authoring tools to offer alternatives

Secondly, the definition of a new specification language (as opposed to the adoption of an existing programming language such as Java) allows us to control the language features that are available to authors. We wish to exert this control for two related reasons; to ensure that the set of features offered to authors exhibits the right balance of expressive power and conceptual simplicity, and to support our ability to import all legal scripts in the language into the graphical editing tools that we believe to be important in enabling non-programmers to access computational mechanisms.

The flow of activity within the framework is probably apparent from figure 1, but is stated here for clarity. An application is created by an author who uses a graphical authoring tool to generate (perhaps unknowingly) an MBML specification of the intended behaviour of a context-sensitive end-user device in that application. After editing, emulation and refinement, the resulting script is published to a convenient web site. Some time later, the user of an appropriate device downloads that script to that device and invokes the application that the script represents.

Of course, this kind of flow will be familiar from the World Wide Web, which provides a similar decoupling of editor, specification and browser for similar motivations to our own. Given our ambition to emulate the open, extensible and democratic nature of the web, this will not perhaps be too surprising.

Once downloaded and invoked, a script controls the behaviour of the device in response to events for the duration of its residency. These events originate from three sources:

- The device's physical context, such as its location
- The user, via interface actions such as pressing buttons.
- Other devices and servers, via messages

The behaviour that the device should undertake in response to such events is specified through a set of built-in primitive actions provided by the device, extension functions defined by the author, and language constructs supporting, for example, conditional logic. The nature of these actions and constructs will be reviewed shortly but we will begin a more detailed exploration of the framework where an author begins, with the authoring environment.

Authoring Environment

The authoring environment in Mobile Bristol has been developed to offer one convenient way of generating application specifications in MBML. As previously stated, we aim to enable a wide variety of application developers with a wide range of technical expertise to author applications, including non-programmers. Consequently, we have adopted an approach to authoring that supports both a point&click interface for the creation of certain kinds of application, and a programmers' editor for power users who wish to go beyond the limited capabilities exposed via this interface. In this, we follow popular web editors such as Microsoft FrontPage and Macromedia Dreamweaver that enable a certain (large) set of web pages to be created using graphical tools but also allow the user to pull away the curtain, as it were, and directly edit the underlying HTML.

The authoring environment consists of a set of specialized tools clustered around a shared representation of the evolving script (see figure 2):

- A media manager that enables the various pieces of digital media to be used in the application to be gathered into the application project workspace.
- A layout editor that simplifies the definition of spatial events though a graphical interface, reflecting a particular initial focus on location-sensitive applications.
- A point&click behaviour editor that allows event handlers to be defined by selecting actions and constructs from a palette.
- A programmer's editor that enables the palette of built-in actions to be extended with new functions defined in a general purpose scripting language.
- An emulator that enables the author to get a feel for what a user's experience of the device might be like once deployed

- A publisher that packages the various elements of the application and posts them to a nominated web site.

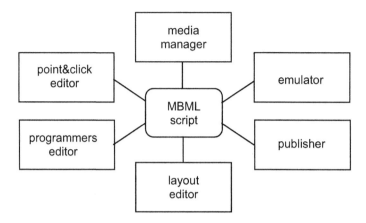

Fig. 2. The tools that make up the authoring environment

An author coming to the environment with the intention of creating a mediascape must essentially perform four tasks (though not necessarily in this order):

- Define *what* digital content is to be encountered by the user, for example, what audio, images, video, text, game moves …
- Define *where* that content is to be encountered, for example in one place or several, inside or outside …
- Define *how* those interactions are to be triggered, for example by the user's movements, or at a certain time, or when a button is pressed …
- Define *how* the interactions are presented to the user, for example via audio, or the user device's HTML or Flash interfaces…

Starting with broad answers to these questions, the author might begin development by using the media manager to collect together the various bits of media involved in the application. This will be a familiar activity for many digital media developers. Next, the author might decide to use the layout editor to create a few spatial regions to trigger media interactions. Using a graphical interface familiar from many drawing packages, the author creates regions on a background representing the street map of the area of interest, as shown in figure 3.

A specification of the regions in MBML is automatically added to the underlying script. Each region is associated with two events that are raised whenever the user enters or leaves the region respectively. By double-clicking on the regions in the layout editor, the author is able to invoke the action dialogue editor and define appropriate handlers for those events by selecting actions from a list (see figure 4).

Note that this description implies some choices about the way in which interactions are triggered in this application, in particular that at least some interactions are to be triggered by the user's movements. Alternatively, the author might attach handlers to other types of events, or combine interaction modes by causing a movement event to display a choice for the user and then triggering further activity on their response.

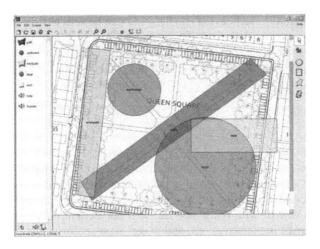

Fig. 3. Screenshot of layout editor showing spatial regions

This last approach in turn implies that the device has a visual interface, which some authors may prefer not to have. Assuming that one *is* wanted in this application, then the author is able to build connections to either an HTML renderer or a Flash movie. And so it goes on, with the author turning to the various tools as needed to create the device behaviour that is desired. At some part in this process, most authors will begin to use the emulator, for example by clicking on the map in the layout editor to simulate the user's movements. Finally, the author becomes satisfied (for now) and uses the publishing tool to distribute the application package to a hosting web site.

Fig. 4. Partial screenshot of handler editor showing palette of media actions

For many application authors, the process just outlined is sufficient to generate an application with the intended characteristics. However, other developers could find that some aspect of application behaviour is difficult to specify in this way. For example, they may wish to include a complicated piece of logic that operates over a history of previous movements together with a random element. In this case, the developer is able to open the programmers' editor in the authoring environment and write (or ask someone else to write) an appropriate function implementing this logic in a C-like scripting language. Once complete, the new function(s) now appear in the palette of actions available for use in event handlers and can be selected via the point&click behaviour editor already described. This structure thus enables a partitioning of responsibility in which a programmer might be used to extend the set of actions available in an application, and the (non-programming) author retains the ability to include this extended functionality when constructing event handlers.

MBML

In this section, we will look briefly at MBML - the script language at the heart of the framework. MBML is an XML-based language intended to specify the behaviour of an end-user's device in response to contextual cues in a given application. The use of XML provides MBML with independence from our current authoring environment and end-user device implementations, and makes it easier for others to offer alternative tools. In addition, it enables validation of MBML scripts against a formal language definition in a DTD (or schema), so making it less likely that a particular script will cause problems during interpretation.

Various other XML-based languages address aspects of the capabilities that we need to define in MBML. For example, GML provides an extensive representation of spatial features [16]. SMIL defines how multimedia objects are to be presented [17], and SOAP and XML-RPC both specify action invocations [18, 19]. However, no other language combines all of these elements with an appropriate emphasis on handling contextual events.

Given the event-driven model of application behaviour underlying the framework, the main function of MBML is to define handlers for the events expected to arise in a particular application context. A simple example is shown in figure 5 .

```
<script>
  <media>
    <audio name="harp" url="http://myserver.com/harp.mp3" />
  </media>
  <layout>
    <region name="r1">
      <circle x="358543.00" y="172523.00" radius="20.00" />
      <onEnter>
        <playMedia media="media$harp" volume="100" loop="true"/>
      </onEnter>
      <onExit>
        <stopMedia media="media$harp"/>
      </onExit>
    </region>
  </layout>
</script>
```

Fig. 5. A simple soundscape script in MBML

Leaving aside syntactic detail, it may be seen that this script defines a simple example of the soundscape behaviour described earlier. In particular, it states that an audio file containing harp music should be played by an end-user device whenever its user enters a circular region of radius 20m centred at the specified grid coordinate, and that the audio should stop playing when the user moves out of that region. The definition of handlers for other events, and the invocation of other actions, should be clear by analogy.

This example hints at the language concepts embodied in MBML. More generally, these are:

- *Event:*   A change in system state or context that is used to trigger activity
- *Handler:*   A set of actions undertaken when an associated event is detected
- *Action:*   An invocation of a built-in or scripted function
- *Resource:*   One of variety of objects used in handling events
- *Script:*   A collection of event handlers and resources
- *Project:*   A collection of scripts and media files defining the application

The main resource types of interest include:
- *Variable:*   As usually understood and scoped globally within a script
- *Region:*   A spatial zone with associated entry and exit events
- *Media:*   A description and address of a media object
- *Notification:*   A message used to carry events between devices and third parties
- *Defined action:*   An extension action written in a scripting language

MBML contains constructs for conditional logic and various state variables and functions. In figure 6, these capabilities are combined to enrich the last example. Now the harp music is only played when the user first enters the specified region, with a second audio file being played at other times.

```
...
<onEnter>
  <if cond="enteredCount('regions$r1')=1") >
    <then>
      <playMedia media="media$harp" volume="100" loop="true"/>
    </then>
    <else>
      <playMedia media="media$drums" volume="100" loop="true"/>
    </else>
  </if>
</onEnter>
...
```

Fig. 6. Using conditional logic to enrich an event handler

The underlying state variable exposed via the built-in *enteredCount/1* function is maintained transparently by the interpreter running on the end-user device. Other, similar state variables (and functions) are also available. However, the author may wish to retain some state that is not so maintained. In this case, MBML allows script-level variables to be defined, initialized, assigned values, and used in expressions in the obvious way.

An author may also want to extend the palette of available actions, for example to achieve some complicated piece of logic, or to avoid having to define the same fragment of script in multiple places. MBML allows the author (or a skilled programmer accomplice) to define new actions, either in MBML itself or in a more traditional programming language. For example, figure 7 shows the functionality of the script fragment from the previous figure re-defined in the simple Simkin scripting language [20]. Once defined, such functions appear may be invoked within event handlers in the same way as built-in actions.

```
<function name = "myPlay"  params = "region,media1,media2"  language = "Simkin"  >
   if (enteredCount(region) == 1) {
      playMedia(media1, 100, true);
   }
   else {
      playMedia(media2, 100, true);
   }
</function>
```

Fig. 7. Extending MBML by defining a new action in a scripting language

MBML also provides a range of other capabilities that have been important in particular applications but which are beyond the scope of this brief introduction, e.g.:

- *Messaging*: MBML provides mechanisms for defining messages, for sending messages to other devices or third parties, and for handling the arrival of incoming messages.
- *Hyperlinks*: MBML allows scripts to be linked such that an end-user device may switch from one to another in a manner analogous to following a hyperlink in HTML.
- *System information*: MBML provides functions and events that allow scripts to respond to changes in system states such as the strength of the device's current wireless network connection, or the level of battery charge.

End-User Device Prototype

MBML scripts may be downloaded and interpreted by any end-user device that conforms to the language semantics. To pursue our wider research aims, we need to have trial quantities of at least one such device. For ease of prototyping, we have adopted a hardware platform consisting of an iPAQ handheld computer with embedded 802.11b wireless networking and an I2C sensor bus to which a GPS unit and other sensors can be attached.

The (somewhat simplified) architecture of the run-time environment developed for this platform is shown in figure 9. The principal components in the architecture are:

- An *event interpreter* that repeatedly takes events from a queue, searches for corresponding handlers in the currently loaded application script, and executes the actions associated with those handlers.
- A *script loader* that is responsible for discovering and downloading application scripts from remote web sites.
- *Sensors* and their associated drivers which monitor the devices physical environment and raise appropriate events.

- A *user interface* with embedded *HTML* and *media engines* that capture and render user inputs and media streams downloaded on demand over the wireless network or cached in local storage.
- A *messaging* subsystem that publishes and receives messages using Elvin.

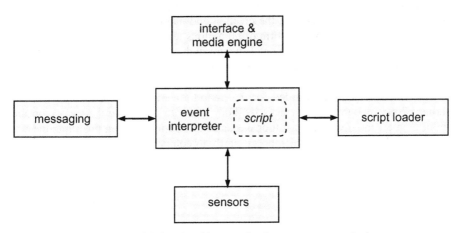

Fig. 8. High-level architecture for the prototype user device

In addition, the run-time system includes the ability to log all aspects of the user's activity, such as their movements and media consumption. The code for this run-time system has been implemented in C++. We have tried to ensure portability by defining a hardware abstraction layer (HAL) that isolates the bulk of the code from the details of the underlying operating system. At present, we have implementations of the HAL for Windows32 and PocketPc 2002/3 (Windows CE), and a port to Symbian is underway.

Arnolfini Case Study

The various generations of the components that we have developed within the framework have been used in a range of applications in addition to the Walk in the Wired Woods installation mentioned earlier. In particular, we have run workshops in which schoolchildren authored soundscapes for a piece of open ground adjacent to their school [21], and a mystery play for the atrium of our building [22]; we have participated in the development of an immersive, educational game simulating the African Savannah [23], trialed a social game in the bar of the Watershed digital arts centre [24], and enabled the development of a location-sensitive heritage guide for the Bristol Ferry Boat Company [25].

In the main, these applications have involved the original research team as co-developers or in a close support role. In this section, however, we report a recent case study in which two artists were commissioned to explore the independent use of the framework with only modest support from our team. The purpose of the exercise was twofold: to discover whether the artists would be able to successfully adopt and apply the new medium enabled by the framework, and to understand how the framework (tools) could be refined to better support similar authors.

The commissions were provided under the auspices of the Arnolfini art gallery in Bristol and awarded to two artists selected from a long list of applicants. The artists, Zoë Irvine and Dan Belasco Rogers, came to the commissions with differing backgrounds and experience of technology. Zoë Irvine [26] is an established sound artist with much experience and skill in the creation and manipulation of audio but no experience of programming or any form of ubiquitous technology. Dan Belasco Rogers [27] has a background in experimental theatre and individual performance but also has some programming experience (in Flash) and an existing interest in and experience of GPS tracking.

The commissions were awarded for the period covering December 2003 to mid-February 2004 though circumstances led both artists to undertake their work on the commission essentially in the last four weeks of this period. During this time, the artists received 5 days of technical support, partly to compensate for the lack of written documentation and partly to provide accelerated fixing of bugs that would have seriously impeded their progress.

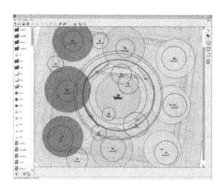   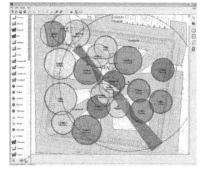

9a. Zoë's layout   9b. Dan's layout

Fig. 9. The layouts used by the two artists

Both Zoë and Dan successfully managed to develop and demonstrate mediascapes in a nearby urban square using the framework and tools described in this paper. Zoë produced a soundscape, *Moulinex*, which blended dialogue and scores from two films, Moulin Rouge and The Matrix, that had recently been shown on outdoor screens in the square. She chose not to have any visual interface. The layout of the regions triggering audio playback in the square is shown in figure 9a. Zoë chose to make the particular audio triggered by movement around the square conditional on the path history of the user. For example, certain audios were only played on first entry into a region, while others were played backwards on re-entry. A bed of background audio was used to create a feeling of continuous immersion. The overall effect was (to this author) very evocative and engaging, though it was quite difficult to develop a mental map relating audio to location, partly as a result of GPS jitter. Of course, this is not necessarily a criticism, as the construction of such a map may not have been a goal of the artist.

Dan's piece, *A description of this place as if you were someone else* [28], is a collection of situated stories relating to the square contributed and spoken by local residents. The audios containing the stories are positioned close to the source of the story as shown in the layout in figure 9b. Dan chose not to use any conditional logic but to create a simple mapping between place and content. To focus the user's attention further on specific locations in the square, Dan used a HTML interface on the device to show images of artifacts at those locations. Again (to this author), the resulting work was very engaging and strongly suggestive of the interest provided by the everyday stories of others.

Fig. 10. Scenes from the artists' installations

Both pieces should be considered as first sketches in a new medium rather than finished artworks. Nonetheless, the private showing of the works in progress drew much interest and comment and both artists have expressed a strong desire to work further on their ideas.

Discussion

The pieces produced by the artists in this case study were surprisingly convincing given the short period in which they were able to work and the relative balance of time spent on different aspects of the projects. Zoë, for example, spent over 75% of her time preparing audio files and less than a week authoring the soundscape. Similarly, Dan spent a significant proportion of his four weeks interviewing subjects and editing their stories. Nonetheless, the artists managed to exercise a significant part of the framework's coverage (see Table 1). Apart from messaging, which fell outside the brief of the commissions, the non-use of a particular feature tended to reflect aesthetic concerns rather than the lack of time or ability.

	Zoë	Dan
user's location triggers device activity	✓	✓
audio playback on the device	✓	✓
display of images on the device	✗	✓
use of logic to condition device behaviour	✓	✗
user input (other than movement around the space)	✗	✗
messaging	–	–

Table 1. Use of framework capabilities by the artists

The artists' success in developing credible pieces so quickly suggests that we too have been at least partly successful in achieving our objective of enabling non-specialist programmers to develop and deploy context-sensitive mobile applications. However, this headline success conceals some interesting detail that is worth elaborating in the following brief sections:

Authoring in the Small – Instructing the Machine

At base, the artists were engaged in supplying instructions to the end-user devices employed in their installations. This involved the use of programming concepts even if not conventional programming languages and tools. It was interesting to discover which concepts came easily, and which were more of a struggle to grasp.

From the point of view of ubiquitous computing, it was satisfying to note that the fundamental notions of context-sensitivity and event-driven behaviour were both simply and immediately assimilated by the artists. For example, the notion of triggering an action when the user entered a particular region was understood (and eagerly anticipated) from the outset. What proved harder, for Zoë at least, was the introduction of conditional logic and (especially) the concept of variables. Both artists also struggled a little with the unforgiving nature of scripting languages that require a complete adherence to a particular syntax. Note that these difficulties cannot be explained in terms of the basic abilities of the subjects. Both Zoë and Dan are intelligent, articulate and skilled practitioners in their own fields. Nor should we understand their difficulties as insurmountable – after all, within a week Zoë had incorporated a quite sophisticated use of conditionals and variables in her script. Nonetheless, it is interesting to consider whether such concepts are fundamentally difficult to grasp [15] or whether the difficulty relates to the fact that is in these areas that the authoring environment most feels like a traditional programming editor and least like a visual end-user editor. The specification of simple conditionals through a graphical editor as in iCAP [9] or a programming-by-example approach as demonstrated by Topiary may have something to contribute here [10].

Authoring in the Large – Working in the Real World

Stepping up a level, the larger difficulty faced by the artists concerned the realization of their ambitions in the real world. In part, this may simply reflect the unfamiliarity of any new medium. Neither artist had any previous experience of ubiquitous computing, and both worked to an imagined concept of what it would be like in practice until quite late in their projects. As it turned out, the real world turned out to be rather different than expected. For example, the effect of positioning errors introduced by the GPS units attached to end-user devices surprised the application authors even though they had been intellectually aware of their existence throughout. As a result, explorations of their early designs soon led to a coarsening of the granularity with which they laid out spatial triggers in the square.

Other examples of difference appeared more benign to the artists. For example, overlapping audios seemed easier to disambiguate in the real setting than in the laboratory, and users tended to traverse the physical space more slowly than anticipated. However, the main issue is not whether such differences are negative – after all, even

GPS errors have been used creatively to enhance applications [29] – but that they are surprising to new authors without prior experience of the technology.

We have attempted to overcome this gap between expectation and reality by providing an emulator within the authoring environment. This allows an author to explicitly raise events expected in the real setting and see how the run-time environment on the device will respond. For example, it is possible to emulate the movements of a end-user around the physical space hosting the application by moving a curser around the 2D map used in the layout editor to represent that space. In practice, it turns out that the emulator is useful for debugging the logical differences between the author's intentions and implementations, and for getting an overall "feel" for the nature of the likely end-user experience. However, the problem is that this emulation, like those found in the other rapid authoring tools mentioned earlier, does not really emulate the real world so much as an idealized representation of that world. For example, positioning in the emulator is precise and stable, the layout of the virtual representation of the physical space is flat rather than contoured, network connectivity is uninterrupted, and the surrounding room is usually warm, dry and quiet.

In fact, we have really always expected this to be the case and have a number of ideas for making emulation more realistic, for example by applying jitter and uncertainty to the emulated position, introducing network outage, and using 3D models of the target space. However, the case study made it clear that these measures, though helpful, would never be a substitute for the authors' authentic experience of their emerging application "in the wild", in the space for which the applications are intended. Consequently, we intend to place a greater emphasis on editing in situ. We have already provided tools that help authors to specify spatial triggers while moving around the physical space. Our intention is to extend these to incorporate other coarse-grained editing actions while retaining a richer authoring environment back at the desktop for filling in the details. For example, one possibility might be to extend the programming-by-example approach of Topiary to allow authors to begin to develop event handlers by manually triggering actions as they move around the physical space.

Conclusions and Future Work

In this paper, we have presented a framework for the rapid authoring, deployment and evaluation of mediascapes – a commercially important class of context-sensitive, media-oriented and mobile applications. The framework consists of three elements:

- A new XML-based language, MBML, that combines spatial, multimedia and invocation elements to provide a event-driven representation of the desired behaviour of a user's device in response to contextual cues, interface events and incoming messages.
- A rapid authoring tool that enables non-programmers to generate application scripts in MBML through a combination of graphical, selection, and textual editors, and that provides media management, emulation and publishing tools to ease application deployment.

- A run-time environment implemented on handheld computers augmented with sensors that can download and invoke particular application scripts from the web.

However, the main contribution of the paper is in the combination of these elements to provide non-programmers with the ability to define, test and deploy context-sensitive ubiquitous applications of realistic scale and ambition. This contribution is validated by a case study described in the paper in which two artists with no prior experience of ubiquitous computing quickly produced and deployed mediascape installations in an urban square. As a result of this case study, we are able to say more about which aspects of application development come easily to the authors and which aspects caused difficulties. In particular, we discuss the important issues raised by the differences between the emulation of an application and its deployed reality.

From this analysis, we have identified two key directions for future work on enabling the rapid authoring of mediascapes:

- The development of an application emulator that more closely reflects the behaviour of devices in the real world, for example by introducing jitter into the position of an emulated end-user.
- The exploration of ways of combining authoring in situ and desktop editing, for example by allowing authors to define simple handlers for spatial triggers as they move around a physical space before adding conditional logic back at the desktop.

Acknowledgements

The authors would like acknowledge the creative and generous collaboration of the artists Zoë Irvine and Dan Belasco Rogers. We would also like to thank the Arnolfini gallery for establishing and hosting the artist commissions, and our colleagues in Mobile Bristol for their help and advice, especially Constance Fleuriot whose championing, support and project management made the commissions possible.

References

1. *Mobile Bristol.* http://www.mobilebristol.com
2. T. Kindberg, J. Barton, J. Morgan, G. Becker, D. Caswell, P. Debaty, G. Gopal, M. Frid, V. Krishnan, H. Morris, J. Schettino, B. Serra, M. Spasojevic. *People, places, things: Web presence for the real world.* in *Proceedings Third IEEE Workshop on Mobile Computing Systems and Applications.* 2000: IEEE Comput. Soc.
3. C. Greenhalgh, *EQUIP: a Software Platform for Distributed Interactive Systems.* 2002, Technical Report Equator-02-002.
4. B. Segall, D. Arnold. *Elvin has left the building: A publish/subscribe notification service with quenching.* in *AUUG97.* 1997. Brisbane, Australia.
5. P.T. Eugster, P.A. Felber, R. Guerraoui, A.-M. Kermarrec, *The many faces of publish/subscribe.* ACM Computing Surveys, 2003. **35**(2): p. 114--131.

6. S. Long, R. Kooper, G.D. Abowd, C.G. Atkeson, *Rapid Prototyping of Mobile Context-Aware Applications: The Cyberguide Case Study*, in *Mobile Computing and Networking*. 1996. p. 97-107.
7. A.K. Dey, D. Salber, G.D. Abowd, *A Conceptual Framework and a Toolkit for Supporting the Rapid Prototyping of Context-Aware Applications*. Human-Computer Interaction (HCI) Journal, 2001. **16**(2-4): p. 97-166.
8. J. Pascoe. *The stick-e note architecture: extending the interface beyond the user*. in *2nd International Conference on Intelligent User Interfaces*. 1997. Orlando, Florida, United States.
9. T. Sohn, A. Dey. *iCAP: Rapid Prototyping of Context-Aware Applications*. in *To appear in CHI 2004 ACM Conference on Human Factors in Computing Systems*. 2004. Vienna, Austria.
10. Y. Li, J. Hong, J. Landay, *Topiary: A Tool for Prototyping Location-Enhanced Applications*. http://guir.berkeley.edu/projects/topiary
11. A. Dey, R. Hamid, C. Beckmann, I. Li, D. Hsu. *a CAPpella: Programming by Demonstration of Context-Aware Applications*. CHI 2004, Human Factors in Computing Systems. 2004. Vienna, Austria.
12. J. Humble, A. Crabtree, T. Hemmings, K.-P. Åkesson, B. Koleva, T. Rodden, P. Hansson. *Playing with the Bits - User-configuration of Ubiquitous Domestic Environments*. Fifth Annual Conference on Ubiquitous Computing, UbiComp2003. 2003. Seattle, Washington, USA.
13. R. Hull, J. Reid, E.N. Geelhoed, *Delivering Compelling Experiences through Wearable Computing*. IEEE Pervasive Computing, 2002. **1**(4): p. 56-61.
14. R. Hull, J. Reid, *Experience Design for Pervasive Computing*. Appliance Design, 2002. **1**(2).
15. J.F. Pane, C.A. Ratanamahatana, B.A. Myers, *Studying the Language and Structure in Non-Programmers' Solutions to Programming Problems*. International Journal of Human-Computer Studies, 2001. **54**(2): p. 237-264.
16. S. Cox, P. Daisey, R. Lake, C. Portele, A. Whiteside, *OpenGIS® Geography Markup Language (GML) Implementation Specification*. 2003.
17. D. Bulterman, *SMIL 2.0 Part 1: Overview, Concepts and Structures*. IEEE MultiMedia, 2001. **8**(4): p. 82-89.
18. *SOAP*. http://www.w3.org/TR/soap/
19. *XML-RPC*. http://www.xmlrpc.com/
20. S. Whiteside, *Simkin: the embeddable scripting language*. http://www.simkin.co.uk
21. C. Fleuriot, M. Williams, L. Wood, O. Jones, *A New Sense of Place?* 2004, Mobile Bristol.
22. R. Hull, J. Reid, *Designing Engaging Experiences with Children and Artists*, in *Funology: From Usability to Enjoyment*, M.A. Blythe, et al., Editors. 2003, Kluwer.
23. S. Benford, D. Rowland, M. Flintham, R. Hull, J. Reid, J. Morrison, K. Facer, B. Clayton. *"Savannah": Designing a Location-Based Game Simulating Lion Behaviour*. International Conference on Advances in Computer Entertainment Technology, ACE 2004. 2004. Singapore.
24. J. Reid, R. Hull, T. Melamad, D. Speakman. *Schminky: The design of a café based digital experience*. in *1AD: First International Conference on Appliance Design*. 2003. Bristol: Springboard.
25. *Bristol Ferry Boat Company*. http://www.bristolferryboat.co.uk/
26. *Zoë Irvine*. http://www.imaging.dundee.ac.uk/people/zoe/Text/Index.htm
27. *Daniel Belasco Rogers*. http://www.planbperformance.net/dan/index.htm
28. D.B. Rogers, *A descripton of this place as if you were someone else*. http://www.planbperformance.net/dan/description.htm
29. S. Benford, R. Anastasi, M. Flintham, A. Drozd, A. Crabtree, C. Greenhalgh, N. Tandavanitj, M. Adams, J. Row-Farr, *Coping with Uncertainty in a Location-Based Game*. IEEE Pervasive Computing, 2003. **2**(3): p. 34-47.

CAMP: A Magnetic Poetry Interface for End-User Programming of Capture Applications for the Home

Khai N. Truong, Elaine M. Huang, and Gregory D. Abowd

College of Computing & GVU Center
Georgia Institute of Technology
Atlanta, GA 30332-0280 USA
{khai, elaine, abowd}@cc.gatech.edu

Abstract. As the trend towards technology-enriched home environments progresses, the need to enable users to create applications to suit their own lives increases. While several recent projects focus on lowering barriers for application creation by using simplified input mechanisms and languages, these projects often approach application creation from a developer's perspective, focusing on devices and their interactions, rather than users' goals or tasks. In this paper, we present a study that examines how users conceptualize applications involving automated capture and playback of home activities and reveals a breadth of home applications that people desire. We introduce CAMP, a system that enables end-user programming for smart home environments based on a magnetic poetry metaphor. We describe how CAMP's simple interface for creating applications supports users' natural conceptual models of capture applications. Finally, we present a preliminary evaluation of CAMP and assess its ability to support a breadth of desired home applications as well as the user's conceptual model.

1 Introduction

Ubiquitous computing technology for domestic environments is becoming an increasingly prominent theme of research to support the needs of families and individuals in their homes. With the growing popularity of technologies like home networking, mobile devices, and information appliances, research on ubiquitous computing for the home illustrates the natural trajectory of the integration between the home and technology. While much of this research has been geared towards developing systems to support specific types of home tasks [13, 19], there has been much recent focus on allowing end-users of the technology to create and configure ubicomp applications to suit their own unique needs [1, 5, 10, 11, 15]. The aim of these projects is not to prescribe technology for home needs and tasks, but rather to empower users living in technology-enriched home environments to appropriate and use the technologies flexibly to suit their lives and practices.

Many of the existing systems focus on the use of simple input languages or metaphor-based GUI interfaces to ease the process of development for end-users who have little or no programming experience. These projects recognize that users need a simple way of specifying applications that does not require specialized technical

N. Davies et al. (Eds.): UbiComp 2004, LNCS 3205, pp. 143-160, 2004.

knowledge in order to extend the power of building customized applications to potential everyday users of such technologies. Despite their use of simplified input languages and mechanisms, these systems tend to be device-centric rather than user-centric, task-centric, or goal-centric. They require that users approach the configuration of ubicomp applications from the perspective of a developer, by treating application development as the configuration and integration of devices and sensors rather than a domestic goal or task that a user is trying to achieve. For example, work by Humble *et al.* [11] uses a "jigsaw puzzle" GUI metaphor in which individual devices and sensors are represented by puzzle piece-shaped icons that the user "snaps" together to build an application. While the metaphor is comprehensible and the interactions are simple, the interface treats application creation as the configuration of devices. Our intuition in approaching this research was that we needed to understand users' natural conceptualizations of ubicomp technologies in order to design interfaces that allow end-users to build ubicomp applications that truly suit their needs.

Although we are interested in the larger arena of allowing end-users to build general ubicomp applications, we decided to focus our research specifically on the domain of context-aware capture applications for the home. We chose to scope the research as such for the purposes of tractability and because of our experience and expertise in the domain. We recognize that there exist potential privacy pitfalls regarding capture services for the home and our studies bear out the fact that some people are not comfortable with the idea of capture devices. While we do not intend that our study results and design be interpreted as a prescription for capture technologies in the home; we believe that they illustrate the potential value for such technologies for the portion of the population who desire them, as well as emphasizing the great need for user customizability of such technologies so that they are useful in ways that suit users' individual privacy needs and comfort level.

We conducted a formative study of how users think about context-aware capture applications to inform our eventual interface design. The purpose of this study was twofold; through it we aimed to understand the ways that users expressed ideas for ubiquitous computing applications as well as the breadth and types of applications that the users desired for a technology-enriched home. As we had hypothesized, the results of our study showed that people who had no experience developing ubiquitous computing applications tended to frame the descriptions of their desired applications in terms of their domestic goals and needs rather than in terms of device behaviors.

Based on the results of the study, we developed CAMP (Capture and Access Magnetic Poetry), an end-user programming environment that allows users to create context-aware capture applications for the home. CAMP has a GUI that is based on a magnetic poetry metaphor; it allows users to create applications in a way that takes advantage of the flexibility of natural language. CAMP enables users to create programs that reflect the way they conceive of the desired application, rather than requiring that users specify applications in terms of devices. From users' magnetic poetry-based application descriptions, CAMP generates a specification of a valid capture application that can be executed in a capture-enabled home environment. In this paper, we present the design and results of the formative study, the CAMP system that we designed and built based on those results, and the results of a preliminary evaluation of the interface.

2 Related Research

Many toolkits and infrastructures have been constructed for the purposes of supporting ubicomp development. Infrastructures have been built to support the development of physical [2, 9], tangible [12] and smart devices/applications [8], context-aware [6] and capture-based applications [17], and collaboration between heterogeneous devices [16]. While such infrastructure toolkits and middleware lower barriers for developers, they are not intended for use by end-users who have little knowledge of programming and devices.

Several current projects and systems are geared towards simplifying the development of ubicomp applications for the purposes of allowing end-users to build and customize technologies. These systems have greatly lowered the barriers to development by offering input mechanisms and languages that require little or no programming knowledge. In addition to the aforementioned work by Humble *et al.* using the jigsaw puzzle metaphor to configure applications, several other systems have been developed using metaphors or simple languages. X10 clients provide form interfaces that allow users to specify the behavior of various devices or objects in the home based on events or conditions [14, 20]. The Speakeasy system [7] supports the *ad hoc*, end-user configuration of devices and applications. Data exchange, user control, discovery of new services and devices, and context-awareness are supported through a set of common interaction patterns defined in mobile code. The HYP system [1] allows users to create applications for context-aware homes on a mobile phone, specifying actions and conditions by navigating through screens of choices such as "tailored alert on cell phone" and "motion detection in room." Media Cubes [10] offers a tangible interface for programming an environment; individual faces of an augmented cube represent different programmatic structures, and the user can assign these structures to different devices or objects in the environment by turning the appropriate face of the cube towards the device. The iCAP system [15] allows users to prototype context-aware applications rapidly using a pen-based interface to specify input and output devices, as well as behavioral rules through drag and drop interactions and pie menus. In SiteView [3], Beckmann and Dey incorporated tangible techniques for programming active environments with predictive visualizations. Dey *et al.* later extended this work to support the ability to program context-aware applications by allowing users to demonstrate the desired context-aware behavior using the "a CAPpella" system [5]. Their system supports the creation of context-aware applications without requiring end-users to write any code.

While the above systems offer users alternatives to extensive programming for building ubicomp applications, they often do so by taking a developer's task and simplifying the input interaction. CAMP attempts to further bridge the needs-technology gap by offering users not only simple input mechanisms but also the ability to specify applications based on their own conceptualization of an application, rather than the more device-oriented perspective of a developer. CAMP builds upon the work above and the INCA toolkit for capture applications [17] by exploring how to allow end-users to realize capture and access applications in their homes.

3   Study Description

We conducted a study in which we introduced participants to the notion of capture and access and presented them with scenarios depicted as comics illustrating uses of this technology. The survey asked participants to explain the applications in the scenarios in their own words and design a capture and access service of their own. The goal of this study was to understand how users naturally conceptualize ubiquitous capture and access applications in a home environment. This required that we be careful to avoid biasing participants' perceptions of how such applications function when introducing the concepts behind capture and access. It was also necessary to recruit a diverse population of participants to address a broad spectrum of needs and skills. To obtain data from a large, diverse subject group, we used a Web-based survey, propagated through email.

We aimed to gather at least forty responses to ensure a breadth of viewpoints. Because participation was voluntary and we could not assume that all recipients would complete it, we needed a method of disseminating the survey to a population larger than our target number of responses. We created an email that included instructions requesting that the readers take the Web survey and then forward the email to ten acquaintances. To prevent over-propagation, the email contained a value that indicated the number of times it had been forwarded. Readers were asked to increment this number before forwarding the email. Recipients who received an email that had been propagated five times were asked not to forward it any further. We initiated the circulation of this email by sending it to friends and family; the email propagation helped to ensure a diverse subject population outside of the researchers' circles of acquaintance.

3.1   Presenting Concepts and Scenarios Through Comics

After reading a brief and simple introduction to ubiquitous capture and access environments, users were shown a pair of "comic strip scenarios"—situations presented in the graphical style of comics (Figure 1). These scenarios depicted a family of three—father Jim, mother Jane, and son Billy—using and creating capture and access applications in a technology-enriched home environment. We opted to present the sample scenarios through pictures and dialogue between characters rather than as text narratives or description in order to avoid biasing how participants described the applications in text later. The scenarios depict the applications in action pictorially to avoid using specific language that would bias the participants' conceptualizations and descriptions of how the applications function. The characters were based on those from Calvin & Hobbes cartoon strip (http://calvinandhobbes.com), but the scenarios are depicted were novel and all frames were individually hand drawn. We opted to use characters based on those from Calvin & Hobbes because that particular strip is family and home-oriented as well as familiar to many. Using this method, we aimed to avoid biasing participants with language while leading them to focus on home-oriented applications.

The following two scenarios are paraphrasings of the comic strip scenarios given to the participants. We present text versions rather than comics here for the purposes of clarity and space; the text versions did not appear in the Web survey.

Scenario 1: Buffering Dinner Time Conversations. Jim and Jane have much to talk about during dinner. Too often, however, little Billy interrupts their conversation with a dinner disaster causing them to forget what they were talking about. To address this problem, Jim creates an application that records conversation and allows the family to review it on demand. The next night it comes into action during dinner when again Billy interrupts them. This time, Jim is able to play back the audio from right before the interruption occurred, allowing Jane and Jim to resume conversation. The application deletes recorded audio when dinner is over.

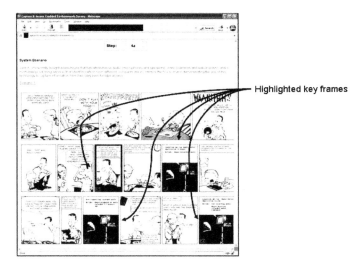

Figure 1. A comic strip scenario presented in the survey, with highlighted key frames.

Scenario 2: Capturing Precious Spontaneous Moments. Jim and Jane often struggle just to take a nice picture of their mischievous Billy. One night, Jane brings Billy to kiss Jim goodnight. It is moments like these that are the hardest to anticipate and photograph. That night, Jim decides to take advantage of the existing cameras in the house and create an application to capture such moments. Very late one night, Billy awakens everyone by getting out of bed and dancing to loud music. After putting him back into bed, Jim tells Jane what transpired. Eager to see for herself, Jane uses the application to review captured photos of Billy dancing. From this collection, Jane saves a few particularly adorable shots. The application automatically deletes the other photos after 15 minutes.

For each comic strip scenario in the survey, we highlighted four key frames in each comic strip and asked participants to describe what is happening in those frames in their own words to assess their understanding of the situation. The scenes in which characters create applications are intentionally ambiguous, with no detail as to how the character actually specifies the application. We then ask our participants to describe what they believe the character did to create the application to understand their intuitive notions of how the system should work.

After presenting the two scenarios, the survey asked participants to describe in their own words a capture and access application that they would like for their home. We asked subjects to provide as much detail as possible to help us understand what the applications would do and how they would work. Participants were given an empty text box in which to describe their application. We chose this free-form format to allow them to express ideas naturally and to avoid imposing any structure that might bias their responses.

3.2 The Study Results

We collected survey data over the course of a three-week period from a total of 45 participants who completed the survey in its entirety. Our study drew responses from diverse participants with a wide variety of professions including attorneys, librarians, bankers, managers, entrepreneurs, homemakers, graphic designers, educators, anthropologists, students, engineers, and analysts. While over ninety-five percent of the subjects use computers daily, only one third actually had hobby or professional programming experience.

Sixty percent of the respondents were female and forty percent were male. Participants ranged from 22 to 64 years of age. We found that the age, marital status, and living situations of the participants influenced their responses regarding the technology. In general, married respondents had family focused responses while single people living alone had individual task-oriented applications, such as a "ubiquitous note-taker". Younger adults who are primary care providers often wanted applications for monitoring their children while middle-aged adults desired the ability to check on the well-being of their elderly parents remotely.

Although seven subjects expressed no use or general desire for the ability to define custom capture services, the majority of the participants described potential applications for capture and access; some even offered multiple different applications. There was significant overlap among the applications suggested, with multiple participants offering variants of the same general idea. Overall we obtained more than a dozen general application ideas that we grouped into three categories:

- providing peace of mind,
- collecting records of everyday tasks or objects, or
- preserving sentimental memories from experiences.

Providing Peace of Mind. The first category consists of applications intended to *provide peace of mind* for the user. These applications help users feel secure by allowing them to monitor their home or children. The most popular application idea provided by participants in our study was a home security system that automatically begins recording when the user leaves the home and allows her to easily review the captured content remotely or when she returns home. Some application ideas suggest monitoring people instead of spaces. For example, many parents of very young children or expectant parents described an application that would allow them to monitor the well being of their children. One participant expressed this idea as follows:

"These technologies could potentially take the place of more traditional baby monitors, allowing caregivers to monitor the activities of young children remotely from other rooms. It would allow greater flexibility, as the technology would not have to be moved into different spaces as the child or the caregiver did."

A related idea was to allow adults to check on the well-being of their elderly parents remotely.

Collecting Records of Everyday Tasks or Objects. The ideas in the second category consisted of applications to help the user collect and keep records of everyday tasks or objects. In these applications, the desired information is not captured for sentimental value or any overarching peace of mind. Instead they provide a record of activity *for convenience.* Participants suggested the use of capture in the home to allow users to help them keep track of objects (such as car keys) and track when and where they were moved. Many people also suggested a simple on-demand audio recording application to allow them to easily record quick notes as needed, possibly for keeping track of to-do items or creative ideas:

"I come up with the best ideas when I'm in the strangest places and at the strangest times (bed, bathtub, etc). A ubiquitous memo pad would be really cool. This tracking of information could extend to a to-do list. Then I could vocalize the to-do list and it would be stored electronically for easy retrieval. The power would be the consolidation of all this important information. Right now I have post-its and papers everywhere. Yuk."

Preserving Memories of Experiences. Many participants suggested applications in which the house captures memories of people during special events, similar to that presented in the scenario. Variations among the applications mainly involved the length of time the captured information should persist. The application would help users record moments they might miss while otherwise engaged during the event. Participants emphasized the importance of being able to partake in and enjoy events in their homes, rather than having to worry about manually capturing them. One user shared with us this possible use of the technology for preserving memories:

"We have an annual pumpkin carving party with about 30 to 50 people at our house every October. It is very difficult to get pictures of everybody at the event, and because we host the event, we don't always know everything that 'happened'. I like the feature of getting pictures of special moments when there is no [handheld] camera around."

Participants expressed a broad range of other application ideas for preserving memories as well, including video to capture baby's first steps or recording fun conversations to share with others later.

3.3 How People Think About Applications

In analyzing the data from our survey, we found several interesting patterns that influenced our formalization of the three conceptual models. We observed two phenomena in particular that influence our understanding of how people comfortably describe capture applications. The first pattern we noticed was the general lack of reference to devices of any kind. Participants rarely mentioned cameras, microphones, digital displays, sensors, or any other type of device in their responses. Though technologists often think first of the devices involved in an application, devices are not at the forefront of users' minds. The following description illustrates how respondents tended to downplay the devices involved in capture:

"I am not very experienced in cooking, so I would want to record friends or relatives cooking [in my kitchen]. I would not have to take notes and I would be able to see and hear, step by step, how to make a particular dish. I would want the house to start recording when I told it to, and to stop when I told it to. Then I could review it and literally SEE [what to do while cooking]."

Our findings suggest that a more natural way for users to describe a service is not to focus on the devices but rather on the function. People are comfortable describing situations when these services are of interest in terms of time, people, locations, and the activity being performed.

Another pattern we found was that most participants described the sensed situation in such a way that the data types for capture are *implied*. Participants were more likely to use statements like, "record a dinner conversation" than to specify the capture of "audio." Words like "record," "remember," or "hear" are synonymous with "capture" but are more natural for users. The remainder of an application description (*e.g.*, "dinner conversation," "party," "reunion") often implies what type of data should be captured—audio, video or both—without specifying it explicitly.

3.4 Deriving Conceptual Models

We observed that in general, users' application descriptions follow three patterns or models. A commonality between all three models is the importance of the "sensed situation" as the object of capture; a sensed situation is a situation that the participant defines using one or more of the "W dimensions" for capture and access applications (who, what, where, when) [18]. In all of the models, participants specified a sensed situation (*e.g.*, "the nanny," "dinner conversation" or "after 7PM") for capture.

Model 1: System as Effector. People who perceive the technology as an *effector* view it as a system that carries out the commands of the user. Taking the first survey scenario as an example, people who subscribe to this model perceive Jim as a user who tells his house to carry out the task of recording the dinner conversation. After being thus programmed, the system acts independently to record dinner conversations as they occur. The respondents who perceived the scenario in this way described application behavior in *command-style*:

"Record all dinner conversations"

In this model, the user commands the system to carry out a task. The task then belongs to the system; the system is the operator whose job is to act upon a sensed situation.

Model 2: System as Assistant. Another perception of the scenarios indicated that some people regard the technology as an assistant or agent that helps the user with a task. In the case of the first scenario, Jim has a task or responsibility and instructs the system to support him in that responsibility. Users who treat the system as an agent used statements phrased as requests for help:

> *"Never let him forget another dinner conversation"*
> *"Help him to remember what they talked about"*

In this model, the task belongs to the user and the system is called upon to provide functionality to help the user in that task. The user is acting upon the situation and the system is supplementing the user's actions.

Model 3: System as Effector-Assistant Hybrid. The third way people perceive the technology is as a hybrid of the first two. In this model, the role of the system is perceived as shifting between effector and assistant, acting independently on user instruction but doing so for the purpose of assisting with the user's task. This model is the least common in our data. Participants who subscribed to this model generally framed their responses in terms of a user's task, but qualified them with system-centric instructions:

> *"Help me to remember dinner conversations by recording audio when there are people in the room."*

Although the users specify a sensed situation, they also express a human-centered task or responsibility.

The lessons we learned from this study and the models we derived from the results led to the design of the CAMP interface for configuring context-aware capture applications. We aimed to design an interface that would support the various models of expression and offer users a simple and flexible way to specify the types of applications they desired.

4   CAMP (Capture and Access Magnetic Poetry)

The CAMP (Capture and Access Magnetic Poetry) system offers users a flexible way to specify desired context-aware capture applications through the use of a "magnetic poetry" metaphor. Users are neither subjected to the rigid rules of conventional programming, nor bound to specify their application in terms of the devices involved. Users are free to construct sentences that can focus on a task or goal as they choose using a subset of natural language. The system still needs to make sense of the user's application description in terms of the devices involved, because these applications must be manifested as the behavior and interaction of devices. Because CAMP makes use of a restricted and domain-specific vocabulary, it avoids many of the difficulties involved in parsing natural language. CAMP serves as an interface to INCA [17], an infrastructure that provides abstractions for the development of capture and access applications. The interface is designed to allow people to use an input language with which they are comfortable and that lets them express their ideas flexibly; CAMP automatically generates the technology-oriented application specifications necessary for realizing the applications.

4.1   The Magnetic Poetry Metaphor

In designing an interface that would be both easy to use and powerful for creating ubiquitous computing applications for the home, we chose to use a "magnetic poetry" metaphor. Conventional magnetic poetry sets consist of small, flexible individual magnets, each of which has a word printed on it. Users can combine the words into "poems" or statements to a variety of effects ranging from profound to humorous, see Figure 2. Magnetic poetry sets often have a theme or topic, such as "love" or "computers" and contain words related to that theme; the resulting poems are geared towards that topic.

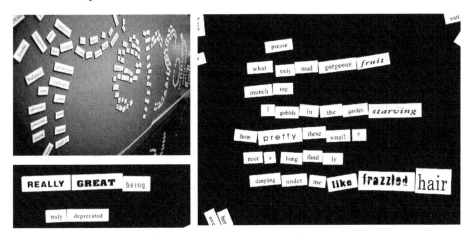

Figure 2. Examples of different magnetic poetry arrangements.

The whimsical, playful nature of magnetic poetry makes it an appealing metaphor to employ in our interface; it offers potential for a fun, non-intimidating way to build applications. As a metaphor, it is easy-to-learn and understand for new users, and already familiar to many. Magnetic poetry requires little or no instruction or specialized prior knowledge to use because it takes advantage of natural language.

Magnetic poetry allows people who might not be naturally "poetic" to create something poetic by virtue of the options available to them. They are not creating anything they could not have created using their own vocabulary, but the choices of words that are available to them make it such that nearly any combination of words they create has "poetic feel" to it. In designing the interface, we leverage the two important properties of magnetic poetry to allow users to specify ubicomp applications: 1) the flexibility of expression allowed by its use of natural language and 2) the constrained vocabulary that restricts users to words that are most meaningful for their context. By doing so, CAMP allows non-developers to create programs that are valid ubicomp applications without having specialized programming knowledge. The constrained vocabulary makes clear to users what their choices are, and what aspects of the system they can play with or configure. The words in the magnetic poetry "set" restrict users to words that have valid meanings in the realm of the technology-enriched home environment, thus alleviating many of the difficulties that arise from migrating from natural language application descriptions to valid ubicomp application specifications. In addition to being an input mechanism by which end-users can potentially create ubicomp applications for their homes, the CAMP interface also serves as a research tool for exploring the design space and vocabulary through which users express their desired applications.

4.2   User Interaction with CAMP

CAMP offers users the ability to create ubicomp applications using a GUI interface that mimics magnetic poetry. Each word of the input vocabulary is on a separate home or capture-themed magnetic poetry "piece"; the pieces are located in the upper frame of the interface and all words in the vocabulary are available and visible to the user. We selected the words in the initial vocabulary primarily because they appeared in the descriptions that participants generated in the initial study. Because visually searching for a desired word in a jumble of pieces can be a time-consuming task for the user, the pieces are color-coded by category. Additionally, the interface clusters words in a single category spatially by default. The results of our initial study showed the prominence of the four w's of capture and access (*who, what, where, when*) in describing applications. We used these w's to form word categories to ease the search process and added a general category for additional useful words. Some examples of each are:

- *who:* I, me, everyone, no one, family, stranger, baby, wife, Billy, *etc.*
- *what:* picture, audio, video, conversation, *etc.*
- *where:* kitchen, living room, home, everywhere, *etc.*
- *when:* always, later, never, a.m., morning, day, week, month, before, hour, minute, Sunday, January, once, now, every time, *etc.*
- *general:* 1, 2, a, the, record, remember, view, save, keep, microphone, speaker, *etc.*

The system employs a third feature to assist users in searching for a word among the pieces; typing the first letter of the word causes the interface to highlight all words that begin with that letter by inverting the text and background color of the piece.

Users select words by clicking on them and dragging them down to the poem authoring area on the interface. They can move and re-order words as desired; the system does not place any restrictions on structure or word order.

CAMP provides an easy way for users to extend the vocabulary of the input language. Using the New Magnet creation feature, users can create new words and define them by using the existing magnetic poetry pieces. For example, a user who wishes to use the word "dinner" could create it by specifying "dinner happens between 7 and 9 PM in the dining room" using existing magnets. The poetry interface allows users to express concepts flexibly, but requiring users to define words in terms of existing pieces offers a restricted vocabulary that allows for easier translation by the system.

4.3   CAMP as a Translator Between User and Technology

After creating a poem for the desired application, the user clicks the "run" button, which prompts the interface to read the poem and generate a text-based parsing that is displayed in the bottom frame of interface as feedback to the user. CAMP, by design, investigates a specific application domain. This restriction allows us to avoid the need to use complex natural language processing techniques to parse application descriptions.

To translate the user's description of an application into instructions and parameters for devices, CAMP uses a custom dictionary to reword the user's description into a format that can be parsed. This dictionary resolves the many different synonymous words (such as "capture" and "record") into a single word; similarly, all the foreseeable ways a phrase can be expressed are also restructured, such as, "*starting at 3 until 5 P.M.*", "*from 3 P.M. to 5*", or "*beginning at 3 P.M. for 2 hours*", into a more succinct phrase: "*between 3:00 P.M. and 5:00 P.M.*"

CAMP recursively decomposes users' descriptions into a collection of sub-clauses. For example, "*Jim in the kitchen or after 6 P.M.*" is treated as "*[Jim in the kitchen] or [after 6 P.M.].*" In some instances the original logic is preserved by replicating information across the sub-clauses. For example, "*Jim or Jane in the kitchen*" becomes "*[Jim in the kitchen] or [Jane in the kitchen].*"

Descriptions can contain redundant information, conflicts, as well as ambiguity. For example, Dinner can be defined to happen "*in the dining room between 7 P.M. and 9 P.M.*" When the user describes her desire for the house "*capture dinner time conversations in the dining room,*" after CAMP restructures the description, the phrase, "*in the dining room*" occurs twice. The parser automatically removes this redundant information. If the user's description was "*capture dinner time conversations in the home*", "*in the home*" conflicts with the "*in the dining room*"

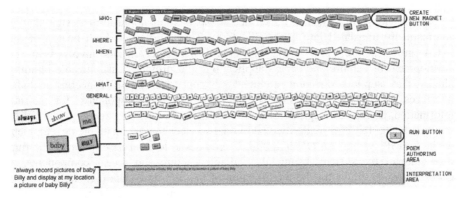

Figure 3. The Capture & Access Magnetic Poetry interface.

portion of the word dinner's definition. The information specified in the user's description overrides the predefined/default parameters obtained from the custom dictionary's definition.

Finally, ambiguity and missing parameters in the rephrased description are flagged or set to predefined/default values. For example, when the user's description is simply "*capture dinner*", CAMP assumes that the user wants pictures stored. If the user's description included words such as audio, conversations, "*what we said*", "*what I talked about*", etc. (*i.e.*, all words or phrases that are defined to imply audio), CAMP would discard this assumption and recognize that the user actually wants audio recorded.

Dimensions such as the time, the duration and frequency, the location, and the people to capture must all be present in the description or are flagged as missing. Dimensions marked as missing in the specification can be indicated to the user, providing her with the opportunity to refine the description. Missing information in the final description is replaced by default predefined values. For example, "*record baby*" implies always taking pictures of anywhere the baby is present. As a result, each sub-clause describes the situation for capture and access that can be parsed.

We treat a behavior as an action on some artifact in a specific situation. In the current prototype, we are only supporting a limited number of artifacts or data types (*i.e.*, still-pictures, audio, and video) and actions (*i.e.,* capture, access, and delete). The user's description of an application can thus be translated into a behavior carried out by the devices in the environment. The user's description can be a single capture, access or delete request or combinations of the above. An example of an application description consisting of both capture and access behaviors is "*always show me where baby Billy is*" which would be interpreted as "*always record pictures of baby Bill and display at my location a picture of baby Billy.*" In situations where the user's description is solely of a capture behavior, we assume access will be defined later when needed. If the behavior defined is solely access, the user can only review information that has been previously recorded. When no delete behavior is defined, we assume the captured information should be stored indefinitely.

4.4 The Architecture of CAMP

CAMP provides users with an interface to specify an application design that is automatically translated into executable form. This interface is built on top of the INCA infrastructure [17]. INCA abstracts lower level details involved in the development of capture and access applications and provides customizable building blocks that support different architectural concerns. These concerns include: interfaces for capturing and accessing information, components for storing information, a way to integrate relevant streams of information and the removal of unwanted data. INCA provides two additional services that facilitate the development of the CAMP system. An *ObserveModule* provides a detailed description of the run-time state of the system, listing all available capture and access components. A *ControlModule* allows for the modification of this run-time state (*i.e.*, initiating and ending capture and access of information, as well as the specification of what to capture or what to access). Together, these features allow for the dynamic adaptation of application features.

All input/output devices available in the physical environment are automatically integrated through INCA. CAMP controls the cameras, microphones, speakers and interactive displays in the environment by assigning the capture and access behaviors of these devices using the *ObserveModule* and *ControlModule* described above. CAMP supports the start and stop of capture and access when two specific context conditions occur: time and presence or absence of a person at a location. Time conditions are supported through a clock object that notifies subscribers when a certain time point is reached or some amount of time has expired on a countdown timer. A condition for a person present in a location is supported through a Context Toolkit [4] widget that maintains the indoor positioning of people in a space. The decision to support these two conditions minimizes the potential design possibilities; however, we wanted to support what is realistically achievable through today's context aware computing sensing. Dey discusses the ability to produce more complex context "situations" in his thesis [4].

5 Preliminary Evaluation

We conducted a preliminary evaluation of the CAMP interface to assess whether it fulfilled our expectations for simplifying the specification of ubicomp applications for the home. The main purpose of this evaluation was to get early feedback on the interface and determine whether the system suited and supported the conceptual models held by potential everyday users of home ubicomp technology. The secondary purpose of this exercise was to evaluate the sufficiency of the initial vocabulary set that we had derived based on the participant responses from our previous study. We selected six participants between the ages of 26 and 60 from diverse backgrounds with little or no programming experience, and conducted a scaled-down version of our initial comic strip scenario study, incorporating the CAMP interface. We chose to format our study as a close parallel to our initial study for the purpose of achieving consistency. Reusing materials from the initial study helped to ensure that evaluation participants received a similar introduction to ubiquitous computing and capture and access as the formative study participants. For the purposes of this early evaluation, we focused on assessing three major questions for the interface:

- Does the CAMP interface allow users to specify or describe desired applications in a natural, task-centric/goal-centric fashion?
- Does CAMP support the creation of the breadth and types of applications that users desire for their technology-enriched homes?
- Does the application that CAMP generates accurately match the user's desired application?

Unlike the formative study, the evaluation was done in person rather than over the Web. Participants were presented with the introductory description of ubiquitous computing and capture and access, as well as the same two comic-strip scenarios as were presented in the initial study. We then asked them to think of a capture and access application that they would like to have in their own home. The participants were then given a laptop running the CAMP interface and asked to describe both scenarios and their desired application. In the evaluation, we asked them to describe the scenes using CAMP's magnetic poetry, rather than in freeform text as we had in the initial study. We intentionally asked them to think of their application prior to showing them the interface for the first time so as not to bias their application ideas with the vocabulary available in CAMP. We encouraged participants to "think aloud" while creating their magnetic poem application description to allow us to assess our question about whether CAMP allowed them to build the application that they desired.

Participants generally fared quite well with the available words. They found that the vocabulary enabled them to build the applications that they desired, such as in this specification of an application to capture memories from a party:

"record video everywhere Saturday night"

The applications that people desired correlated closely with the findings of our initial study; people generally desired applications that would allow them to monitor children, help them find recently misplaced objects, and record parties and special events. We did not observe any instances in which the user was unable to specify the desired application with the words available in the default vocabulary. This suggests that selection of words in the vocabulary that we derived from our initial study is sufficient for creating the most commonly desired home capture and access applications.

We also examined the wording of the descriptions of the comic strip scenarios and of their desired applications to assess our question regarding whether users could specify their applications in the manner we predicted they would based on the results of our initial study. Participants did indeed tend to favor task-oriented descriptions of the scenarios and their desired applications:

"when Jim Jane and Billy talk record and remember for 20 minute"
"record picture in Billy s bedroom at night"
"record 1 picture every 4 minute Billy bed room every night until morning stop"

One especially interesting finding of the evaluation that supports the hypotheses we drew from our initial study was that even though we made words like "camera" and "microphone" available in the CAMP interface, evaluation participants did not use them, eschewing them in favor of person and task-oriented descriptions. Participants were especially partial to the "System as Effector" model for describing scenarios and applications. While words such as "Help" were available in the interface, we found that people using the interface generally built applications that sounded more like commands, unlike some participants of the initial study who phrased applications more like requests for assistance. Because of the small number of participants in the evaluation, we did not explore this phenomenon in depth, but we hypothesize that people perceived the interface and computer as a tool that takes commands.

Although participants were able to specify application descriptions quite easily, they did on occasion find themselves looking for a word that did not exist in the magnets. One user looked for the word "keep," for which there was no magnet; he instead used "remember" as a synonym. While it was our goal to allow users to specify applications using the language most intuitive to them, we also recognize that the CAMP interface cannot scale to display and parse an exhaustive vocabulary.

Fortunately, many participants mentioned that not having some words available was not really a problem for them because they were always able to find synonyms or alternate wordings easily.

After participants specified their desired application, we presented them with the description parsing generated by CAMP. Since CAMP's role in creating ubicomp applications is not only to provide the input interface, but also to generate the application description that will be used by the INCA toolkit, this exercise served as a preliminary way of evaluating whether the application generated matched the user's desired application. We asked participants to tell us whether the description generated by CAMP matched their idea of the application. Although participants generally found that the system's parsing matched their own occasionally, there were a few instances in which the system's default translation was incorrect. In these cases, participants were able to recognize the error easily and fix it by changing or adding a word. For example, when the system defaulted to capturing pictures when a user specified "record dinner," the participant simply edited the application to read "record dinner conversations" to indicate that he wanted audio recorded. Often, the language in the system parsing was more awkward than their own description because of the way that the system resolved synonyms. For example, one user specified, *"capture picture every 5 seconds"* using CAMP, and the system translated this to, *"capture picture each 5 seconds."* CAMP generated a valid parsing that matched the user's intended application but presented it in a way that the user found difficult to understand. In future iterations of the interface, we plan to improve the manifestation of the parsing that CAMP presents to the user to make it more easily comprehensible.

Overall, participants described the system as fun to use and easy to learn, especially because of the familiar magnetic poetry interface, which led one user to say, "you know what to do with it right away." They especially liked the ability to highlight words by typing the first letter; some of them began to use this feature by default when they looked for a word; rather than searching for the word first and then using the keyboard when they could not find it, they immediately typed the first letter of a word when they started looking for it.

Although this study presents only a preliminary evaluation of the first design iteration of CAMP, we believe it illustrates how CAMP brings the state-of-the-art of ubicomp application development closer to end-users. One participant, noticing the flexibility of expression that CAMP afforded, reflected aloud about an incident of wanting to take a photograph:

> *"It's like when I wanted to get a picture, in my mind, it was 'I want a picture of [my friend] and [my baby]', you know? It's only when I couldn't find the camera to take the picture that I thought I really needed the **camera**."*

This statement reaffirmed our belief that in order for end-user programming environments to truly allow users to build the applications that they want for their homes, systems must offer users the ability to express their needs in the way that the users themselves think about them.

6 Conclusions and Future Work

Enabling end-users to create and customize applications for their homes remains a difficult problem; the CAMP interface presented in this paper addresses the challenge of developing a programming environment for users that is both simple to use and powerful. CAMP helps to bridge the needs-technology gap by offering interactions that are not only technically simple, but that fit the user's natural concept of ubiquitous computing applications. Our early evaluation indicates that the magnetic poetry interface is simple to learn and use, and allows users to build the types of applications they want in the way that makes the most sense to them.

We plan to continue testing and evaluating as we iterate upon the design. In terms of understanding the design space and social factors affecting capture applications for the home, we hope to conduct further formative studies using alternate forms of pictorial representation, such as Simpsons cartoons, stick figures, or Batman comics, to understand how the representations affect the scope, breadth, and perception of potential applications. Additional future work includes the exploration of tangible and wall (or refrigerator) mountable versions of the CAMP interface. The current version of this system only allows for the description of a single application; issues involved in extending this work to support the realization of multiple applications in the run-time environment at the same time. An interesting socio-technical direction of interest is the possibility of using the "poems" as visible representations of the applications that are running in the environment; we aim to assess whether the magnetic poetry can act not only as an input mechanism for building applications but also as comprehensible information in the environment that reminds or informs people of the capture applications that are running but are not overtly visible.

Finally, although we scoped our studies and design for the purposes of capture applications for domestic environments, we believe that the CAMP interface and end-user programming interactions have potential value for creating other types of ubicomp applications in a variety of domain. By taking advantage of the metaphor of "themed" and extensible magnetic poetry sets, we hope to apply this design to the exploration of many of these other areas.

References

1. Barkhuus, L., Vallgårda, A: Smart Home in Your Pocket. In: Adjunct Proceedings of UbiComp 2003 (2003) 165-166
2. Ballagas, R., Ringel, M., Stone, M., and Borchers, J.: iStuff: A Physical User Interface Toolkit for Ubiquitous Computing Environments. In: Proceedings of ACM Conference on Human Factors in Computing Systems (CHI 2003). ACM Press, New York (2003) 537-544
3. Beckmann, C., Dey, A.: SiteView: Tangibly Programming Active Environments with Predictive Visualization. In: Adjunct Proceedings of UbiComp 2003 (2003) 167-168
4. Dey, A.K.: Providing Architectural Support for Building Context-Aware Applications. In: Ph.D. Thesis. College of Computing, Georgia Institute of Technology (2000)
5. Dey, A.K., Hamid, R., Beckmann, C., Li, I., Hsu, D.: a CAPpella: Programming by Demonstration of Context-Aware Applications. In: Proceedings of ACM Conference on Human Factors in Computing Systems (CHI 2004). ACM Press, New York (2004) 33-40

6. Dey, A.K., Salber, D., Abowd, G.D.: A Conceptual Framework and a Toolkit for Supporting the Rapid Prototyping of Context-Aware Applications. In: Human-Computer Interaction (HCI) Journal. 16(2-4) (2001) 97-166
7. Edwards, W.K., Newman, M.W., Sedivy, J., Smith, T., Izadi, S.: Challenge: Recombinant Computing and the Speakeasy Approach. In: Proceedings of the Eighth Annual International Conference on Mobile Computing and Networking (MobiCom 2002). ACM Press, New York (2002) 279-286
8. Gellersen, H.W., Schmidt, A., Beigl, M.: Multi-Sensor Context-Awareness in Mobile Devices and Smart Artefacts. In: Mobile Networks and Applications (MONET). 7(5) (2002) 341-351
9. Greenberg, S. and Fitchett, C.: Phidgets: Easy Development of Physical Interfaces through Physical Widgets. In: Proceedings of the 14th Annual ACM Symposium on User Interface Software and Technology (UIST 2001). ACM Press, New York (2001) 209-218
10. Hague, R., Robinson, P., Blackwell, A.: Towards Ubiquitous End-User Programming. In: Adjunct Proceedings of UbiComp 2003 (2003) 169-170
11. Humble, J., Crabtree, A., Hemmings, T., Åkesson, K., Koleva, B., Rodden, T., Hansson, P.: "Playing with the Bits" User-Configuration of Ubiquitous Domestic Environments. In: Proceedings of UBICOMP 2003. Springer-Verlag, Berlin Heidelberg New York (2003) 256-263
12. Klemmer, S.R., Li, J., Lin, J., Landay, J.A.: Papier-Mâché: Toolkit Support for Tangible Input. In: Proceedings of ACM Conference on Human Factors in Computing Systems (CHI 2004). ACM Press, New York (2004) 399-406
13. Nagel, K., Kidd, C.D., O'Connell, T., Dey, A.K., Abowd, G.D.: The Family Intercom: Developing a Context-Aware Audio Communication System. In: Proceedings of Ubicomp 2001: Ubiquitous Computing. Springer-Verlag, Berlin Heidelberg New York (2001) 176-183
14. Smarthome X10 Kit. http://www.smarthome.com
15. Sohn, T., Dey, A. K.: iCAP: An Informal Tool for Interactive Prototyping of Context-Aware Applications. In: Extended Abstracts of ACM Conference on Human Factors in Computing Systems (CHI 2003). ACM Press, New York (2003) 974-975
16. Tandler, P.: Software Infrastructure for Ubiquitous Computing Environments: Supporting Synchronous Collaboration with Heterogeneous Devices. In: Proceedings of Ubicomp 2001: Ubiquitous Computing. Springer-Verlag, Berlin Heidelberg New York (2001) 96-115
17. Truong, K.N., Abowd, G.D.: INCA: A Software Infrastructure to Facilitate the Construction and Evolution of Ubiquitous Capture & Access Applications. In: Proceedings of Second International Conference on Pervasive Computing (Pervasive 2004). Springer-Verlag, Berlin Heidelberg New York (2004) 140-157
18. Truong, K.N., Abowd, G.D., Brotherton, J.A.: Who, What, When, Where, How: Design issues of capture and access applications. In: Proceedings of Ubicomp 2001: Ubiquitous Computing. Springer-Verlag, Berlin Heidelberg New York (2001) 209-224
19. Wan, D.: Magic Medicine Cabinet: A Situated Portal for Consumer Healthcare. In: Proceedings of the First International Symposium on Handheld and Ubiquitous Computing (HUC 1999). Springer-Verlag, Berlin Heidelberg New York (1999) 352-355
20. X10 Client. http://x10controller.sourceforge.net/X10Controller/X10Client/

Designing Capture Applications to Support the Education of Children with Autism

Gillian R. Hayes[1], Julie A. Kientz[1], Khai N. Truong[1], David R. White[1],
Gregory D. Abowd[1], Trevor Pering[2]

[1] GVU Center and College of Computing, Georgia Institute of Technology
Atlanta, GA, USA
{gillian, julie, khai, drwhite, abowd}@cc.gatech.edu
[2] Intel Research
Santa Clara, CA, USA
trevor.pering@intel.com

Abstract. We explore the social and technical design issues involved in tracking the effectiveness of educational and therapeutic interventions for children with autism (CWA). Automated capture can be applied in a variety of settings to provide a means of keeping valuable records of interventions. We present the findings from qualitative studies and the designs of capture prototypes. These experiences lead to conclusions about specific considerations for building technologies to assist in the treatment of CWA, as well as other fragile demographics. Our work also reflects back on the automated capture problem itself, informing us as computer scientists how that class of applications must be reconsidered when the analysis of data in the access phase continually influences the capture needs and when social and practical constraints conflict with data collection needs.

1 Introduction

Parents and teachers of children with autism (CWA) often use several therapeutic interventions, keeping vast records to assess improvement in behavior and learning. Automated capture technologies and the associated access interfaces for exploring past experiences are particularly promising for monitoring the effectiveness of these interventions for behavioral and learning disabilities in children. Behavioral and learning data can be captured, analyzed, and mined over time to provide valuable evidence to track the progress of any intervention. Prototypes developed for this problem must address both technical and social factors to be successful. These factors include providing for all elements of the care cycle, understanding the need for qualitative richness of collected data, minimizing the effort required to use capture technology, addressing privacy concerns, and considering financial constraints. Technically, designers must account for integration of manually and automatically captured data, appropriate distribution in the system architecture and tools for data analysis and visualization that allow for flexible adaptation of capture.

Four researchers conducted two ethnomethodological studies to uncover areas of need in the work practices of caregivers for CWA. The most often reported need

N. Davies et al. (Eds.): UbiComp 2004, LNCS 3205, pp. 161-178, 2004.

involved the recording, storing, and analyzing of data about CWA. We developed three prototypes designed for activities involved in treating CWA and in keeping records about this treatment. Although initial feedback on these prototypes indicated they would be useful in meeting many caregiver needs, no individual prototype meets all of the constraints and characteristics uncovered in our qualitative studies. What we learned as ubiquitous computing researchers is a lesson about the design of automated capture applications. Specifically, in this domain and other related ones, there exists a reflective relationship between access and capture that requires more dynamic configuration of capture capabilities.

This work offers two major contributions. First, the problem domain of monitoring intervention therapies for CWA is important and shares features with other care giving scenarios. Automated capture and access is well suited to providing a solution to this problem. Second, the in-depth social, practical, and technical exploration of this problem sheds light on automated capture and access itself. We describe the two field studies in Section 2 and resulting prototypes in Section 3. The important considerations and recommendations discovered through this work are discussed in Section 4. We discuss related work in health care, education, and ubiquitous computing in Section 5 before concluding with a summary of contributions and future work in Section 6.

2   Methods for Studying Caregivers

Our initial task was to explore the space of data gathering and record keeping in caring for CWA. We defined *care* as all of the education and therapeutic interventions that CWA experience and *caregivers* as the individuals who administer and monitor these interventions. Our research included two separate field studies: the first of which focused on stakeholder interviews at a specialized school and research center for treating CWA, and the second expanded the scope of research to include other places and intervention techniques and included a series of interviews, field data using participant observation, and artifacts from care providers and families of CWA. Our goal in all of these qualitative studies was to determine who was involved in the care, what types of care were provided, how groups of caregivers communicated with one another, and what kind of records and assessment of progress were involved. We initially concluded that the use of capture and access applications could assist with care of CWA because of the reliance on tabulating commentary on live interactions and the difficulty of doing that accurately.

2.1 Interviews and Participant Observation

For two months, we observed the daily activities of a special school, the Walden School at the Emory Autism Center, providing services for CWA in an inclusive setting (a mixture of CWA and neurotypical children). This school is part of a research center on autism, with an emphasis on understanding the relationship between the particular intervention approach to autism and the progress of CWA. In addition to educational activities intended for all students at the school, teachers and research assistants record data on behavioral interventions designed for CWA. We interviewed representatives of various stakeholder groups associated with this school: teachers, researchers, and parents. Interviews were conducted at the school and lasted 30 to 45 minutes. The data consisted of handwritten notes of the observations and interviews.

To broaden our perspective on approaches to intervention therapies for CWA, we conducted a four-month study consisting of more interviews with families, teachers, and other caregivers for CWA. Although we interviewed one current and one former staff member from Walden, most of these new interview participants were not associated with the school. These individuals employed a variety of care techniques including occupational therapy, sensory integration, and discrete trial Applied Behavior Analysis (ABA) [1]. We used semi-structured interviews and participant observation [20] to identify current practices, needs, and privacy concerns of the stakeholder groups. The data consisted of audio and video recordings and observer notes. Participants included two individuals associated with a local school system, six professional therapists from three different consultancies, three parents of CWA, and two part-time therapists. Interviews lasted one to two hours and were conducted in a variety of locations based on the participants' preferences: our offices, the participant's home or office, or the home of a child for which the participant was caregiver. Researcher observation periods were 30 minutes to three hours at a time.

Our research team also participated in discrete trial as therapists. Certified behavior therapists trained the researchers to conduct sessions that lasted two to three hours and were designed to help a child meet goals in such areas as language and motor development. We also recorded behavioral data at those sessions and attended weekly group meetings to assess progress and plan future sessions. The researchers conducted 27 therapy sessions with CWA and attended 40 meetings and three training sessions, conservatively totaling 144 hours of participant observation.

2.2 Artifact Collection

The caregivers we studied employed a variety of techniques to capture data about children, to analyze this information, and to communicate it amongst themselves. Caregivers collected some or all of three distinct types of data:

- Duration: How long was the child engaged in activity X, where activity X can be appropriate (sitting quietly at table) or inappropriate (screaming loudly)?
- Performance: How often is the child correctly responding to request/question Y, where Y might be "Give me the apple." or "Come sit down."
- Narrative: In this case, the caregiver might simply write a few notes or several pages describing the child's behavior.

Caregivers use forms to collect much of the duration and performance data and notebooks or other informal means to collect narrative data. We examined 33 different forms and 12 different types of data graphs used by caregivers and examined 3 notebooks used by care networks to share narrative data among members of the team. We reviewed standardized tests in the special education literature used by schools for diagnosis and monitoring of progress for special needs children [16, 17, 19].

3   Prototypes

After completing the initial study at the specialized school for CWA, we developed a prototype system. Based on the subsequent studies in different locations of a variety of intervention therapies, we developed two other prototype capture and access applications. All prototypes were demonstrated to target user groups, and user comments contributed to the constraints and recommendations discussed in Section 4.

3.1 Walden Monitor: Wearable Prototype for Recording Observation Data

Walden Monitor (WM) is a combination wearable and Tablet PC based system that combines two existing paper-based data-collection instruments: the Child Behavior Observation System (CBOS) and the Pla-Chek (pronounced PLAY-check). CBOS and the Pla-Chek are used to record largely the same data in two different ways. The Pla-Chek is a paper spreadsheet used to record behavioral variables in the inclusive classrooms at the special school we studied. Each calendar quarter, research assistants enter the classroom for ten consecutive days and observe a particular CWA. The research assistant mentally counts a ten-second interval, then records positive or negative results for twelve variables such as proximity to an adult (within 3 feet) or an adult interacting with the target CWA. The research assistant repeats this process twenty times. These data are also gathered using CBOS, in which a research assistant enters the classroom with a handheld video camera and records the child for five minutes. Another researcher watches the video and codes the variables on a spreadsheet similar to Pla-Chek. The teacher tabulates the data and includes it in written reports. Parents may see the videos upon request, but they are not routinely shown.

WM was designed for use by an individual whose primary task is recording data. While we initially considered a distributed solution in which cameras mounted in the room collected video and the researcher carried a TabletPC to record observations, we quickly determined that a localized wearable solution was the most practical and effective approach. WM is based on a TabletPC with a head-mounted bullet camera (see Figure 1a). The research assistant observes the child for a ten-second interval and is then prompted by a beep in the earpiece for optimal user awareness and minimal classroom distraction to record behavioral variables by tapping buttons on the Tablet PC display. As with Pla-Chek, this process is repeated for twenty intervals. The data are synchronized to the appropriate intervals in the video, meaning all observations about a ten-second interval are linked to the beginning of that interval.

The video and handwritten annotations captured — with metadata describing when, what, and for which child information is captured — are stored in a relational database. Two levels of detail are available for access (see Figure 1b). A single session (the twenty recorded intervals) can be viewed, and a timeline interface is provided to replay each ten-second video observation next to the observations made for that interval. Observation columns can be selected to provide more random access through the video observations. Summary statistics for a session are automatically calculated, and a second view visualizes this summary data across many sessions.

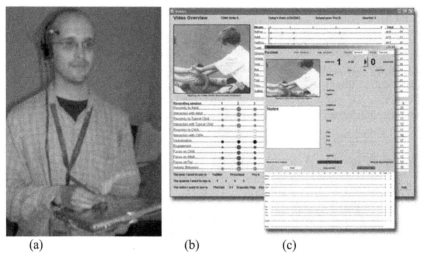

(a)   (b)   (c)

Figure 1: (a) researcher using WM (b) access interface shows video and a timeline (c) capture interface shows video and provides space for recording data.

3.2 Abaris: Environmental Prototype for Recording Discrete Trial Data

Discrete trial ABA therapy consists of one or two therapists requesting a child to perform a predefined set of instructional programs multiple times and recording of data on the child's success in performing each task. For example, in one observed scenario, Katie[1] leads a team of several therapists hired by the parents of Sam, a CWA. Before starting the therapy, Katie, with Sam's teachers and family, evaluated him to find areas of deficiency and designed a tailored education program. The team of therapists takes turns working with Sam for 2-3 hours every day, often completing over a hundred trials in a session. At the end of a session, the therapist sums the data, calculates percentages of trials completed successfully, manually completes graphs that track progress, and writes narrative notes for Katie and the other therapists. This is a tedious and expensive manual process that is prone to error.   When Katie conducts therapy, she also examines the discrete data and narrative notes left by therapists the previous week to monitor Sam's progress. Without video, she often discerns that she is missing information and cannot diagnose problems or plan lessons without spending time observing therapy sessions, and she cannot guarantee that the manually recorded data is accurate and complete.

The Abaris prototype[2] automates some of this process and equips teams of therapists in monitoring the progress of a therapy regime. Abaris was designed for a single user in a confined setting to capture and integrate therapist data with video of the

---

[1] All names of care givers and children have been changed to protect their anonymity.
[2] Abaris was a figure in Greek mythology who was the priest of Apollo and who possessed a golden arrow that, among other things, helped to cure diseases.

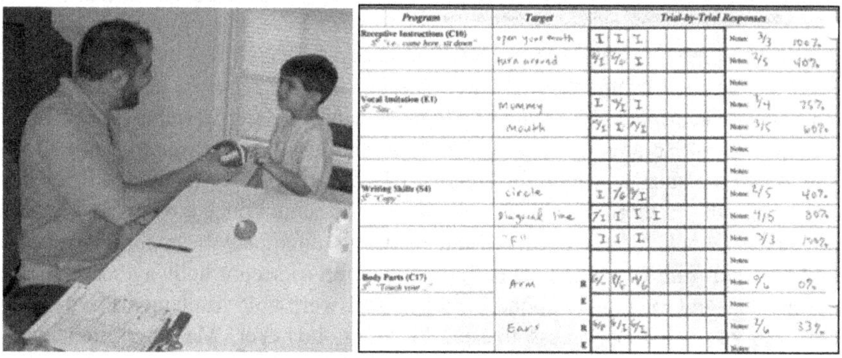

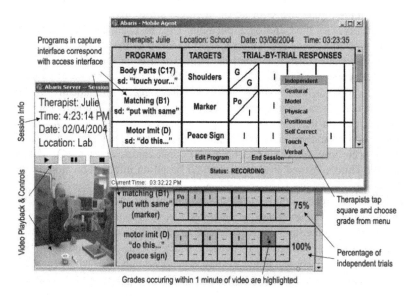

Figure 2: (a) A therapist interacts with a child and records data on a nearby clipboard. (b) Example of ABA paper form.

therapy session. Therapists use the tablet application to customize the child's daily therapy and record data. The therapist records performance data in a form interface on a Tablet PC (see Figure 3, right) while a separate system records audio and video, from a fixed environmental camera and microphone, synchronized to the form data. Because of the variability of routines between therapists, perfect synchronization between grades on the form and capture video is not yet possible, but some simple temporal heuristics associate a grade for a given trial to a segment of video. There are opportunities to use activity recognition during the therapy, but we did not pursue this challenge in initial prototypes. The access interface (see Figure 3, left) allows changes to grades, because therapist error is possible. Summary statistics are calculated automatically and available for graphing.

Figure 3: Users score performance data by choosing a value for each trial. They can replay the entire video of a session or go to salient points using discrete data.

3.3 CareLog: A Distributed Prototype for Recording Semi-structured Data

Diagnosing and treating behavior can be particularly difficult when those behaviors are not seen all the time or are very situation specific. In one reported instance, a school autism consultant, Mark, was trying to diagnose a particularly irregular behavior of a child named Sam. He attempted to escape from the group of classmates and teachers walking down the halls at seemingly irregular times. Sam typically exhibited this behavior once a month. Furthermore, Mark only visited the school once a week, and the likelihood that he would be there when Sam made his attempt was small. The teachers worked together with Mark and school administration to secure hallway security tapes of the incident and eventually found a pattern and were able to change the behavior. Without the serendipitous access to security tapes, however, Mark reported that he would not have solved the mystery.

Because of these difficulties and the impracticality of ubiquitous capture devices (*e.g.,* security cameras) in the life of a child, automatic collection of rich data is nearly impossible. Instead, caregivers are asked to record informal data about incidents in everyday life. These data are usually discrete but can include narratives. CareLog is a mobile system using a confederation of capture and access devices designed to collect this information.

Of all the applications discussed, CareLog has the greatest variety of users. Families and teachers not trained in special education in addition to specialists all keep these types of informal records. Therefore, CareLog requires a distributed architecture allowing the caregiver to use any available wirelessly enabled device (*e.g.,* classroom PC, PDA, home PC, etc.) to record observational data. We wanted to centralize the collected data in order to ease later access. Because the child is the one consistent player in all of these observations, we decided to tie storage to the child, through a pocket-sized device, approximately the size and weight of a deck of cards. This device, a Personal Server [23] (PS), holds a database with all of the child's information and acts as a wireless application server for the CareLog application. The child can leave the PS in a pocket or backpack. Assuming they are within a short distance of the PS, members of the caregiver network can record behavioral data about that child through any nearby device with wireless connection to the PS. When a caregiver makes notation of an incident, the date, time, caregiver, and note-taking device are logged automatically to the child's device. The caregivers can also enter discrete data by checking a box by each characteristic of the incident that applies (e.g. the child was *kicking* in the *kitchen* after a *loud noise*) and add a handwritten or typed note to the record. Users can access data through a standard web browser. The CareLog applet communicates with a SQL database running on the child's PS and loads a custom UI based on information stored in the database and properties of the accessing device.

Based on caregivers' expressed needs, a summary screen supports a detailed visualization of captured data on a large-screen interface, such as a desktop PC. Because these visualizations are quite large, initial attempts to scale them down to a pocket-sized version were met with apprehension from users. Caregivers also reported doing this type of analysis in situations where a larger display is readily available, such as an office. Quantitative records of each incident are available as temporal graphs for any range of dates chosen by the therapist. CareLog provides the facilities to plot any combination of behaviors concurrently on the same graph (see Figure 4) or the user can open multiple

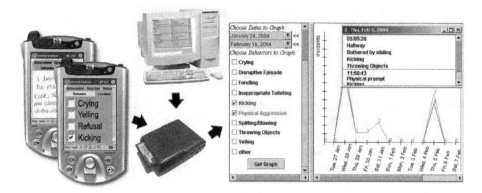

Figure 4: Input is sent to the child's PS, providing views of the data through any PC. Users select a range of dates to view and "drill down" by choosing a day.

CareLog windows to examine these graphs side by side. Users can "drill down" into the details of an individual day by clicking on that day, which displays a new *DayDetails* window with all of the characteristics and context captured about incidents during that day. By clicking on a record, the user can toggle the display of narrative data about that incident on and off. Users might want to examine multiple days concurrently to compare the records of those dates. To accomplish this, CareLog allows users to display multiple *DayDetails* at once. Thus, caregivers can quickly get a sense of how a child is doing or gather more data in an attempt to solve a particular problem or track a particular event.

4   Social, Practical, and Technical Considerations for Capture Applications for Supporting CWA

The formative studies and experience with the three prototypes highlighted a cyclic *care cycle* surrounding the caregiver workload. This cycle imposes particular human constraints on design: the need for rich data, the balance of effort involved, privacy and control considerations, and financial burdens. We further explored certain technical considerations of importance to these applications: the integration of manually and automatically captured data, the level of distribution of the system architecture, and data analysis and visualization techniques.

Although these domain specific constraints and the tensions inherent between them can be identified up front, only end users can appropriately assess how they should be satisfied at any one time. End users must be allowed to evolve the system themselves through iterations on the services available in the environment and the application interface. Evolutionary capture and access applications can better address the social and technical issues identified by capturing minimal data initially in convenient locations and allowing users to hypothesize about the data and test these hypotheses by iterating on the system. For each consideration, we examine how an iterative approach in which caregivers use information accessed from the application to influence what and how they will capture in the future can affect these issues.

4.1 Social and Practical Considerations

For the successful deployment and adoption of working ubiquitous computing systems, designers must consider domain specific human concerns. These issues may be social in nature, focusing on how users work and interact with one another and computing systems. They may also be practical in nature, focusing on the possibility that users can afford new systems and are willing and able to use them effectively.

4.1.1 The Care Cycle

Interventions for CWA emphasize a cycle of care that revolves around recording data about the patient and providing care based on that data. This cycle existed in some form across all of the interventions we studied. The basic steps that therapists perform are:

- Diagnosis based on observation and/or interview data collection.
- Goal setting with various parts of the caregiver network. These goals can sometimes amount to a "contract" with the family or with other caregivers.
- Intervention based on learning and behavior modification particular to the child.
- Evaluation of goals being met or not based on data collection from observation and/or interviews. All of the interventions include some notion of accomplishing pre-determined goals whether by "mastering" a skill or by reducing inappropriate behavior. Although criteria for mastery differ slightly (e.g. 80% vs. 100% success accomplishing a task), they are similar across therapies.
- Based on this evaluation, the cycle begins again with a new diagnosis.

This cycle of care is extremely important to the way therapy is conducted in all of the interventions we studied. The caregivers we interviewed who regularly interacted directly with the child reported commonly setting and assessing goals. Caregivers who interacted with the child less frequently also reported this cyclical behavior. However, they expressed some frustration with occasionally being unable to assess progress towards these goals. In these cases, the hurdle to success was primarily in the data recording capabilities of those individuals directly interacting with the child. The desire to improve data collection techniques motivated all of our prototypes.

WM was designed to support one portion of the care cycle, gathering observational information of certain behaviors. It does not allow users to change the kind of observations they are making based on data gathered previously, but the access interface does allow users to view aggregate data over time and then analyze details. Abaris provides summary views of individual therapy sessions, but users pointed out missed opportunities for seeing trends across a single program over time and across therapists. These additional views of the captured data would better support the iteration on future programs to track. CareLog was designed with the strongest influence from the iterative nature of the care cycle, allowing users to capture data and analyze it at multiple levels through graphs and specific details. Information from this analysis can then be used to configure the capture interface for later use.

4.1.2 Need for Rich Data

Most of the caregivers studied who were responsible for gathering data during teaching sessions expressed some preference for rich, narrative commentary. Those individuals responsible for analyzing that data also recognized this preference but reported being "bogged down in narrative data" and having difficulty in parsing the information contained therein. To avoid this phenomenon, these analysts have developed forms for recording this data. The forms also build in a "prompt" to the caregiver recording the data about what information needs to be gathered. Use of these forms often resulted in caregivers recording data more often, but without the corresponding narrative, the information could be incomplete.

All caregivers we observed were involved in recording data about a child, analyzing that data, or both. Furthermore, all caregivers we interviewed expressed concern about the tension between the need for richer data, including video, and the effort of retrieving and analyzing that data. By using the natural actions of the caregiver to provide effective indexes into rich data, like video or audio, automated capture and access applications can help the users navigate this potentially enormous sea of data.

WM supports capture of rich data through video captured from a head mounted camera and narrative notations captured through the Tablet interface. Abaris automatically captures video associated with a particular therapy session through an environmental service focused on the location of therapy. CareLog limits the richness of the data that can be captured, allowing only for discrete data and occasional short notes. There may be an opportunity in the future to link audio, video or other sensor data to the discrete data, but this may come at a cost to other considerations.

By examining minimal captured data users can estimate when, where, and how they need to gather richer data. They can then add sensors and multimedia capture services to gather the most appropriate data at the most appropriate time. The capture of rich data is a user desire naturally in conflict with many of the other constraints mentioned. An iterative approach allows users to balance dynamically these constraints more effectively as detailed in the following paragraphs.

4.1.3 Reducing the Effort Required to Use the System

When considering healthcare and education, particularly the care networks for CWA, the need to lessen the caregiver's burden becomes magnified. Often in these cases, the user benefiting from the data collection is not the individual directly interacting with the child. Instead, the individual analyzing data and developing therapies benefits from its collection. End users must see an appropriate balance between their required efforts to use the technology and the benefits they will accrue. This is very reminiscent of lessons from the design of groupware systems [13].

Furthermore, it is particularly important that the task of keeping records fades into the background and does not distract from the primary task of educating the child.

Much of the resistance to using technology or to manual recording was due to this secondary task taking away from caring for typical children and for CWA. Capture and access applications will be successful only if relevant information is recorded without undue distraction to caregivers, primarily providing support to CWA [21].

WM reduces user effort by collapsing the video recording activity with the data tabulation, but some users expressed apprehension about wearing a head mounted display, and carrying a Tablet PC that is much heavier and more difficult to use than a clipboard with paper forms. Abaris minimizes user effort by automating several of the activities involved in care that were previously manual, such as tabulating and graphing discrete data. We were pleasantly surprised to see that the Tablet PC interface was not much different to use in this less mobile setting than the original paper forms. CareLog was designed to require minimal effort to record an incident, but all data captured requires some user action. Users can employ handheld devices, a similar form factor to notepads in use by some caregivers, or larger tablet or laptop devices. We also considered other wearable form factors for data collection, aimed at reducing the time between observation and recording. We have yet to determine whether this model of using a variety of devices reduces the hurdles to capture in real life.

By avoiding premature fully automated continual capture and employing an iterative approach, users view many fewer irrelevant data points directly answering the concern of being "bogged down in narrative data." After initial information is accessed and analyzed, users can choose to capture richer data when they believe that it is relevant. This reduces the amount of effort required and can also make users more willing to expend effort, because they have visibility into how the information they are gathering is relevant and useful.

4.1.4 Privacy and Control of Data

The automatic or even semi-automatic capture of very rich and sensitive data, such as video, continues to raise concern about privacy in the ubiquitous computing literature, legislation and the popular press [4, 9, 14]. In the home, where many therapies occur, this concern is arguably somewhat less pressing. At school, however, parents of other children as well as teachers must consent to the capture of any data that might identify themselves, their children or their teachers. The collected information is both personally identifiable and could be considered sensitive. Teachers and school administrators reported that the benefits of continuous capture would not outweigh the invasion of privacy at their schools, which casts doubt on whether a proportionality test (such as those described in [4]) for balancing services against privacy would succeed. Schools also raised concerns about liability, noting that they would not want persistent video data that could be used in a lawsuit between parents and the school or parents and each other. Therapists who worked with teachers voiced concerns about the "closed door policy" common to classrooms, wherein teachers locally negotiate the activity in their classrooms daily and will prevent any interference with or visibility into that process. Parents of typical children might perceive no benefit of this kind of capture, because their children do not need the records for their education and care, so they are less likely to consent to recording.

Incidental to the privacy discussion is one over control of data and responsibility. The individuals providing the care were sometimes not the ones designing it; those who were recording the data were often not the same as those who would analyze it. In designing systems to support these disparate groups of caregivers, we must consider who determines what needs to be captured. Individuals we observed tended to resist those activities in which they had little input or control. As context changes over time and greater benefits of use can be realized, they may then be willing to adapt the application in ways suggested by their supervisors and analysts.

One reaction to this problem of privacy and control in schools would be to track progress only in the home or to use special self-contained classrooms away from neurotypical children for the education of CWA. However, current thinking in the educational and therapeutic communities endorses the approach to including CWA and other special needs children in "regular education" classroom settings. These trends are also encoded in legislation in most industrialized countries, such as the Individuals with Disabilities Education Act (IDEA) in the United States, guaranteeing children with disabilities a "free appropriate public education" in the least restrictive environment [5], often "regular education" classroom settings. Furthermore, the No Child Left Behind Act, which requires that schools track progress of all students and report on that progress regularly [8], provides incentive to school systems to record data about the progress of CWA that cannot be gleaned from standardized tests used to track the progress of typical children.

The WM system only captures what is in the view of the researcher recording data, which can be focused on a particular child. It also operates in a research environment where specific human subject consent is gathered for all children. Because it is wearable, the user can remove the camera or pause recording. Abaris was initially designed for a home environment, and its deployment in schools would likely be confined to special purpose locations tailored to prevent inappropriate recording. It also allows users to change the potential tasks to be performed and for which data will be recorded, thereby controlling what is captured. CareLog allows end users to configure the discrete data that can be collected giving them control over the capture interface. CareLog does not allow for the capture of discrete data about unrelated individuals, but its potential to capture rich data about unrelated individuals incidental to the discrete data is a risk. All of a particular child's data is stored on that child's personal device, simultaneously reducing privacy concerns by keeping the data owned by its subject and increasing security concerns with a single point of failure for data loss.

Using an approach in which end users iterate on the capture services, users of the system are added only as necessary and data is captured only when appropriate to the tasks being addressed, whether changing a behavior or teaching a new skill. Many fewer people can possibly be identified with an iterative approach because rich video data is being captured in fewer locations at fewer times. This reduction in the possibility of identification inherently reduces privacy concerns as well as the need for consent from individuals who might not be relevant to the problem. Interviews suggested that caregivers would be more willing to sacrifice their own privacy and to participate in the recording of the data for the good of the child's care if they reasonably believe that what is being captured is relevant to the care.

We are aware that complying with responsible data protection principles in such a special application also requires addressing the related issues of retention time, system administration and security, and informed consent. For the sake of space, however, we do not address these issues in this paper.

4.1.5 Financial Constraints

Traditional capture and access systems typically have not been built with financial considerations as a primary design constraint. However, the numbers of CWA worldwide are growing at incredible rates. For every two children registered through Individuals with Disabilities Education Act (IDEA) with autism in 1992-93, there were almost eleven by 1999-2000 [22]. Changes in the way CWA are diagnosed and awareness of autism may contribute to some of this increase, but do not account for the entire change. Caring for CWA is a costly endeavor, one that is shouldered by families and school systems that are often already greatly impoverished. Thus, caregivers repeatedly noted that the adoption of any system into their care routine would have to demonstrate significant benefit for the cost incurred.

When designing systems to be truly ubiquitous, researchers must consider not just the cost of a single research installation but also the cost of instrumentation in every environment. Although most classrooms have a PC, many families have a PC in the home, and some of the caregivers interviewed carry a PDA, a wireless network is rarely available in these environments, and the cost is too high to expect caregivers to invest in them. In schools, CWA often change classes throughout the day, both with the other students and to attend special care. They also tend to spend a lot of time in facilities belonging to a disparate group of caregivers, friends, and family members. Capturing rich data in all of these environments can be an enormous undertaking.

All of the prototype solutions we have developed would show significant cost savings over time, because they eliminate much of the paid human work to collect and graph data manually. System acceptance was affected not only by cost over time but initial cost to families and school systems already very low on expendable funds. By these metrics, WM is not a particularly cost effective solution, requiring a dedicated caregiver to record data and each classroom to invest in a Tablet PC and head mounted camera display or to purchase and share some group of them at the school. The cost of the initial implementation of Abaris in a single environment is quickly recovered by the savings of not paying individuals to tabulate data manually. In a single environment, ad hoc networking can be used, and only a few devices need to be added, the most expensive of which is a Tablet PC. This distributed solution, however, would require an expensive implementation in every environment in which therapy takes place and a network between them, making cost an issue as the location numbers rise. CareLog addresses the financial considerations of users by requiring only the purchase of one additional device, the child's device, leveraging the already existing desktop machines and PDAs in the classroom. These systems would need to be augmented with wireless connectivity, but this represents a small incremental cost.

As opposed to instrumenting every person and every location for automatic capture all the time, an iterative approach allows users to capture data only when really needed. As relevant locations change, new equipment can be added or old equipment can be moved. For families and school systems already burdened with heavy costs of education and care, the ability to add or reuse equipment after initial deployment may make adoption possible when high upfront costs might make use of new applications impossible.

4.2 Technical Considerations

Domain-specific human considerations influence and are influenced by technical factors, like available services and architecture of capture and access applications.

4.2.1 Integration of Manually and Automatically Captured Data

One value of an automated capture and access system comes from the integration and synchronization of different streams of captured activity. Because human users sometimes need rich data and systems must remain easy to use, capture applications must relate the streams of data to each other as closely as possible. As designers, we needed to make decisions about how to relate observational data, provided by a human, to the situation being observed. In some cases this is made easy by the routine behavior of the observation. For example, the WM prototype took advantage of the strict protocol for observing and recording data. In other situations, the protocol for recording observations is not as rigid, and the timing between incident and record-keeping can vary between caregivers and from situation to situation. There is an opportunity to use activity recognition to link observational data to recorded incidents, a promising alternative for semi-structured activities like ABA, and we will investigate this for Abaris. For less structured activities that are the subject of CareLog, the challenge of integration remains.

Caregivers accessing and analyzing information about a child would ideally like as much rich data as possible. However, end user decisions made at the point of capture based on the social factors described previously will inevitably determine whether or not this data is available. For example, in deciding how much privacy to preserve, users determine which data streams are captured. A difficulty that arises when allowing users to dynamically evolve the capture application is that different streams of information might or might not be available for a particular event. Allowing end users to iterate on the capture requires support for end-users to iterate on the integration algorithms, using the heuristics known to them near the point of capture. One analyst reported "Families know when they can record data…They'll know they are going to take a few minutes dealing with what happened to write down what happened…And this can take longer sometimes, like during dinner."

4.2.2 Level of Distribution of System Architecture

A capture and access system can vary in the level of distribution of its constituent parts, and these differences may have impact or be impacted by the human concerns discussed. For example, we previously discussed the importance of where data resides for providing user control and answering privacy concerns. In any capture and access application, storage is a key component that can be overlooked. There are many architectural options for its placement as seen through the different prototypes. For Care-Log, distribution is important, because we want to maximize the opportunities for different individuals in the same and different settings to be able to record observations. A standalone solution might be easier to implement, but it would require effort to move that system with the child throughout the course of the day. Our decision to separate video capture from observation data in the Abaris prototype makes video capture easier to implement but requires a replicated system for every environment, a costly decision for a school system. WM began as a distributed system but was quickly changed to a standalone wearable solution due to both cost considerations and a desire to give greater control of data capture to the researcher doing the observation.

In general, the need for rich data, particularly if that need changes often, necessitates the availability of modular capture services. A distributed architecture allows users to add new capture services physically into the environment. Common to software engineering practice, a separation between components (*i.e.,* a separated architecture) enables capture devices to be added easily. Different devices provide different levels of computational power as well as different user affordances. It might be easier for a user to take a note on a PDA, but it would be impractical to use a PDA to capture video. The applications should support dynamic changes to the physical environment by robustly accessing services as available and supporting manual record keeping even if a user has chosen to remove all automatic capture.

4.2.3 Data Analysis and Visualization

Caregivers use the captured data to inform decisions about structuring future therapies as well as to provide evidence to concerned parties about the effectiveness of interventions. They often look for trends in the data as a part of the analysis but also require the ability to examine data points at a more in-depth level. Access interfaces must support both high-level visualizations and querying as well as detailed "drill down" views of the data, while maintaining the link between related streams of information. The WM system provides two levels of visualization, one for a single session of twenty 10-second interval observations and one for viewing aggregate data across these sessions. Abaris provides a query interface to assemble views based on therapist or program. However, it does not provide the ability to view multiple therapist behavior side-by-side, a feature users indicated as important. It also exports data out of the system for generating graphs of performance over time. This feature supports an overview but misses opportunities to link those views to other recorded data. CareLog better integrates the visualization of data over time.

Continued discussions with users reveal that there is also a need to support "what if" exploration of this data. When caregivers first access the data, they begin to formulate hypotheses about it. They must configure their own graphs and charts dynamically depending on these initial assumptions and use custom built visualizations to more easily uncover potential trends. This analysis helps them to determine when and where they need to focus data collection in the future. This narrowing of contexts for data collection helps them to balance many of the social issues discussed previously. With an iterative approach, they can feed back the analysis into the design of capture services, essentially allowing them to test the hypotheses they have just made, while respecting the concerns of the other stakeholders.

4.3 Balancing Considerations

The human constraints imposed by the care cycle of caring for CWA influence and are influenced by the technical considerations inherent to ubiquitous computing and capture and access applications. Applications must balance needs such as ease of use with an architectural separation of concerns. Although designers can identify these needs and the tensions between them, only end users can appropriately assess how they should be satisfied at any time. We recommend an approach in which end users can iterate on the available services and evolve their own applications to dynamically balance these issues and satisfy the constraints specific to that situations. For each factor, we examined how such an iterative approach affects these issues and concluded that the appropriate solution is to allow end users to evolve their applications.

5   Related Work

Both research and commercial software have targeted the tracking of health and education data. The CareView system "utilizes a set of visualization techniques to increase the visibility of temporal trends in clinical narratives" from home healthcare nurses [15]. The Intelligent Dosing System (IDS) uses a custom decision support protocol for doctors managing and treating patients with diabetes [12]. The software provides tools for analysis of an individual's progress with a set of medications over time. The LifeLines project provides a visualization environment for personal medical histories in which the initial screen and visualization act as menus for direct access into the data [18]. Although similar in some ways to application areas we have explored, CareView, IDS, and LifeLines differ from our proposed solution in that caregivers were not able to configure the systems to capture different data based on previously captured information.

Specifically geared towards the treatment of CWA, commercial products like Discrete Trial Trainer [2], CompuThera [11], Labeling_Tutor [6], and Earobics [3] focus on teaching skills such as labeling familiar objects and developing auditory processing skills. They provide interactive activities and games and often adapt to the child based on their responses. Another commercial product, mTrials [7] supports electronic capture of discrete trial data. These products do not, however, provide the level of information access and analysis that capture and access applications can provide.

Capture and access applications offer the type of data collection, mining and analysis capabilities needed by CWA caregivers. Traditional capture applications in classrooms, meeting spaces, and other fixed locations have been designed to provide users with the capabilities to record, view, and analyze important information about human experiences [21]. In an educational environment, the Smart Kindergarten provides parents and teachers with the abilities to investigate young students' learning processes [10]. Although we are similarly motivated to track educational progress, the Smart

Kindergarten project concentrates on the collection, management, and fusion of sensor information. Traditional capture and access applications, such as those discussed in [20], lack the configurability, mobility, and real time interaction required by caregivers. Our approach, on the other hand, concentrates on the iterative inclusion of capture services, both multimedia and sensor, to an inherently human controlled application, compensating for the unfulfilled need to balance user concerns in any context.

6   Conclusions and Future Work

While investigating how technology might address problems in the specific domain of caring for CWA, we have found that automated capture can be successfully applied in a variety of settings to assist with the education and giving of care to CWA, while also providing a means of keeping records of those activities. We built three distinct prototype systems to address the constraints most important for particular tasks. However, predetermined capture and access applications are not malleable enough to support the cyclical activities involved in caring for CWA, and we hypothesize in education and medicine more generally. We have concluded that end users must instead be able to iterate on the capture and access applications, services, and data integration processes available to them through distributed modular systems. When end users can modify their applications in these ways, they are better able to balance their own considerations and satisfy constraints appropriate to the context of their environment. We are currently in the process of developing capture and access applications that can be evolved by the end user and will deploy and evaluate these applications in the future.

Acknowledgements

This work is sponsored in part by the National Science Foundation (ITR grant 0121661) and by the Aware Home Research Initiative at Georgia Tech. The authors would like to thank the various Atlanta-based therapists and educators who provided great insights into the challenges of caring for CWA. We are particularly grateful to the Emory Autism Center and Interactive Behavioral Solutions, Inc. for their continued collaboration with this research. The human subjects research reported here is covered under IRB protocols H03220 and H02136, on file at Georgia Tech.

References

1. Association for Applied Behavioral Analysis, Web site for International Association for Applied Behavioral Analysis.
2. The Discrete Trial Trainer (DTT), Columbia, SC, 2004.
3. Earobics, Inclusive TLC, Boonton, NJ, 2003.
4. European Commission Article 29 Working Party: Opinion 4/2004 on the Processing of Personal Data by means of Video Surveillance, 2004.

5. Individuals with Disabilities Education Act *20 U.S.C. 1401*, 1997.
6. Labeling_Tutor, Millenium Software, Torrance, CA, 2004.
7. mTrials, Mobile Thinking, Inc., San Diego, CA, 2002.
8. No Child Left Behind Act of 2001 *20 USC 6301*, 2002.
9. Bellotti, V. and Sellen, A., Design for Privacy in Ubiquitous Computing Environments. in *Third European Conference on Computer Supported Cooperative Work (ECSCW '93)*, (Milan, Italy, 1993), ACM Press.
10. Chen, A., Muntz, R.R., Yuen, S., Locher, I., Park, S.I. and Srivastava, M.B. A Support Infrastructure for the Smart Kindergarten. *IEEE Pervasive Computing, 1* (2). 49-57.
11. computhera. CompuThera: Seven Steps to Reading for Children with Autism and Visual Learners, Bowie, MD, 2000.
12. Deuel, R. Mobile Handhelds: Handhelds Used to Treat Disease *IEEE Pervasive Computing*, 2002, 7.
13. Grudin, J. Groupware and Social Dynamics: Eight Challenges for Developers. *Communications of the ACM, 37* (1). 82-105.
14. Lessig, L., The Architecture of Privacy. in *Taiwan Net '98*, (Taipei, 1998).
15. Mamykina, L., CareView: Analyzing Nursing Narratives for Temporal Trends. in *ACM Human Factors in Computing Systems: CHI 2004*, (Vienna, Austria, 2004), ACM Press.
16. Maurice, C., Green, G. and Luce, S.C. *Behavioral Intervention for Young Children with Autism*. Pro-ed, Austin, TX, 1996.
17. Pierangelo, R. and Giulani, G. *Special Educator's Complete Guide to 109 Diagnostic Tests*. The Center for Applied Research in Education, West Nyack, NY, 1998.
18. Plaisant, C., Mushlin, R., Snyder, A., Li, J., Heller, D. and Shneiderman, B., LifeLines: Using Visualization to Enhance Navigation and Analysis of Patient Records. in *1998 American Medical Informatic Association Annual Fall Symposium*, (Orlando, FL, 1998), AMIA, 76-80.
19. Rimland, B. and Edelson, S.M. Autism Treatment Evaluation Checklist (ATEC), Autism Research Institute, San Diego, CA, 1999.
20. Spradley, J.P. *Participant Observation*. Holt, Rinehart and Winston, New York, NY, 1980.
21. Truong, K.N., Abowd, G.D. and Brotherton, J., Who, What, When, Where, How: Design Issues of Capture and Access Applications. in *Ubicomp 2001*, (Atlanta, GA, USA, 2001), Springer-Verlag, 209-224.
22. U.S. Department of Education, O.o.S.E.P., Data Analysis System (DANS). SAS Output. Act, U.I.W.D.E. ed., 2000, Number of Children Ages 6-21 Served Under IDEA.
23. Want, R., Pering, T., Danneels, G. and Kumar, M., The Personal Server: Changing the Way We Think About Ubiquitous Computing. in *Ubicomp 2002: Ubiquitous Computing*, (Goteberg, Sweden, 2002), Springer-Verlag.

'This All Together, Hon?' Ubicomp in Non-office Work Environments

John Sherry, Scott Mainwaring, Jenna Burrell, Richard Beckwith, Tony Salvador

Intel Corporation
2111 NE 25th Avenue, Hillsboro, Oregon, 97229 USA
John.sherry@intel.com

Abstract. Ubiquitous computing technologies offer the promise of extending the benefits of computing to workers who do not spend their time at a desktop environment. In this paper, we review the results of an extended study of non-office workers across a variety of work domains, noting some key characteristics of their practices and environments, and examining some challenges to delivering on the ubicomp promise. Our research points to three important challenges that must be addressed, these include: (a) variability across work environments; (b) the need to align disparate, sometimes conflicting interests; and (c) the need to deal with what appear to be informal ways of creating and sharing knowledge. As will be discussed, while daunting, these challenges also point to specific areas of focus that might benefit the design and development of future ubicomp systems.

1. Introduction

Within the computing industry there is a longstanding and widely shared belief that computing needs to come "out of the box" and fit into the world more seamlessly [1], [2], [3]. This vision seems particularly appropriate for those many work domains that lie outside the canonical office environment. There are many types of workers who do not spend their days at a desktop, but nonetheless have the need to create, share and access information, and thus could seemingly derive benefits from access to digital technology. From vineyards to construction sites, hospitals, manufacturing and retail, ubicomp technologies seem poised to fill a need currently unaddressed by traditional computing technologies.

Yet for all the interest, the broad-scale deployment of ubiquitous computing has been elusive. Davies and Gellersen [4] lament that, despite the accumulation of over a decade of research, "many aspects of Mark Weiser's vision of ubiquitous computing appear as futuristic today as they did in 1991." The authors point out numerous barriers, from social and legal considerations of privacy to the lack of effective business models, in addition to technological issues, that still face developers.

This paper attempts to build on some of these initial insights, addressing the issue in the context of non-office workplace settings. It is drawn from ethnographic research focused less on ubicomp technologies and more on the kinds of environments into which it might fit. Our concern was with real-world adoption on a broad scale. What are the factors that might enable (or inhibit) truly widespread use of

N. Davies et al. (Eds.): UbiComp 2004, LNCS 3205, pp. 179-195, 2004.

such new technologies as sensor networks, RFID tags, ambient displays, or other technologies – and what will the implications be for ordinary human beings? Our approach derives from the recognition that work organizations are complex systems, requiring an understanding of human practices and embedding processes on a number of levels, from highly personal subjectivities to social, cultural, political and economic systems that interact at the workplace. Any technological deployment must be viable across all such systems to persist and scale.

1.1. Projects Contributing to This Paper

As mentioned, this paper draws on several projects. Following is a brief summary of projects themselves.

Agriculture. In 2002 and 2003 researchers from PaPR conducted a variety of ethnographic interviews and observations with vineyard owners, vineyard workers, vineyard managers, wine makers, and others involved in the viticulture industry in Oregon's Willamette Valley. In late summer 2002 the team deployed a small number of "Berkeley Motes" in an Oregon vineyard. We later deployed 65 networked sensors at a vineyard in the Okanagan Valley, British Columbia, as part of a collaboration with researchers from the Pacific Agribusiness Research Center. These deployments uncovered many technological issues, but more importantly, issues relating to the human labor and associated costs necessary for a successful sensor network deployment [5,6].

Retail Point of Sale. During this same period, a separate team examined ubiquitous computing potential in retail environments, noting that large retailers and consumer products companies had both identified the retail space as a potential point of cost savings and efficiencies. This research ultimately focused on issues of worker agency in the retail transaction [7]. Methods included ethnographic interviews with workers and mangers at nine retail sites, with an effort to maximize differences among the sites in terms of sales volumes, store size, business models, etc.

Construction. A third team investigated issues relating to the construction industry. This research, which took the team to roughly half a dozen construction sites and involved roughly twenty interviews, was primarily ethnographic in nature and did not progress to conceptual prototypes or trial deployments.

Manufacturing. A fourth team examined issues relating to the use of ubiquitous computing technologies in relation to a highly rationalized manufacturing environment – Intel corporations own manufacturing facilities. Intel's microprocessor "fabs" represent environments of heavily centralized command and control, and yet some efforts have recently been made to provide more local resources. This work involved ethnographic interviews and observations on the manufacturing floor. We also explored conceptual prototypes in discussions with various members of the work organization.

Other sites. Finally, in addition to drawing on literature from reach in Computer Supported Cooperative Work (CSCW) and Human Computer Interaction (HCI), we derived additional insights for this paper from our own prior research across a variety of work domains, including salmon fishery in Alaska, rural veterinary medicine in Iowa, medical clinics and hospital settings in Portland, Oregon, television news production, pulp and paper manufacturing, and event planning and production in

Vancouver, British Columbia. In all such cases, workers both created and accessed vital productive information, yet had limited access to computing or desktop environments.

Our point in conducting this research was to look for patterns beyond the particulars of site or even industry. Computing as a tool for knowledge production has thoroughly colonized offices as we know them, but its application is spotty beyond. Why is that? What is it about these other sites that has defied computerization so far, and do new technologies offer the possibility of changing that?

2. The Challenge of Ubicomp

Key to the ubicomp vision is the notion of "computation that inhabits our world, rather than forcing us to inhabit its own." [8]. Weiser suggests that ubicomp systems "may reverse the unhealthy centripetal forces that conventional personal computers have introduced into life in the workplace."[9] As our understanding grew of the domains described above, our appreciation grew for just how challenging the ubicomp call to action really is.

2.1. Eliminating "Unhealthy Centripetal Forces"

Our research suggests that conventional personal computers are neither wholly responsible for the "unhealthy centripetal forces" of personal computing, nor are these forces necessarily counter-productive. They have not only enabled computing to happen, but have allowed organizations to thrive.

Personal computers have emerged in an ecology of social practices and physical arrangements whose origins (for the sake of brevity) can be traced to what Foucault [10] has called the *examination*, a mode of power involving the disciplined ordering of subjects (read: rows and columns) enabling a regimented, documentable surveillance of subjects over time. From the late seventeenth century onwards, the examination has diffused from the military examination into virtually every domain of Western life, from the classroom, to the hospital ward, to its most notorious manifestation in Jeremy Bentham's *Panopticon*.

In the commercial workplace, the role of the examination has been no less important. In the factory, the power of surveillance enabled by the disciplined ordering of bodies, combined with new ways of representing productivity, profitability and liquidity, led to new forms of management and new needs for structured, document-borne representations of information related to productive work. These innovations in management and work practice certainly contributed to the industrial revolution no less than the steam engine.

With the rise of the modern bureaucratic office, document based representations of work and other formalized written communications exploded. Documents became (and continue to be) a vital point of contact between workers [11]. In the latter part of the nineteenth century "a veritable revolution in communication technology took place" in response to this explosion, giving rise to such familiar technologies as vertical file cabinets, carbon paper (for duplication) and typewriters [12]. These artifacts were more than just stubborn metaphors for personal computing, they were inventions that enhanced productivity in offices. A whole constellation of social, economic and practical arrangements thus pre-existed the PC, and enabled its appearance. The PC is not solely to blame for the fact that, "Even today, people holed up in windowless offices before glowing computer screens may not see their fellows for the better part of each day" [13]. Historical forces thus have shaped the organization of work in the office. In many ways the PC has simply taken advantage of that.

Furthermore, the constraints associated with PC use have been productive. The stability of office environments, the reliance on document-based representations of knowledge and the institution of specific forms of literacy have enabled the rise of what Peter Drucker has famously called the "knowledge worker". [14]. Discussions of "computer literacy" often focus on the technical knowledge required to *operate* a PC, but in fact PC use for most people also requires mastery of specific, usually technical, forms of literacy associated with knowledge work. The *examination* has, after all, diffused to that most recognizable of data structures, the array, and its various manifestations in spreadsheets, databases and web forms. This "slender technique" that unites knowledge and power is so pervasive we hardly think of it as an invention. And yet, it is inextricably tied to specific forms of literacy, skills in reading, analyzing and understanding the ordered presentation of subjects often associated with knowledge work.

Dourish has suggested that an important element of embodied interaction is a model of artifacts-in-use "that rejects a traditional separation between representation and object."[15] Historically, however, this separation has been amazingly productive in knowledge work. Science, law, finance and countless technical and commercial professions have benefited enormously from the rise of conventional representations and disciplined abstractions that enable articulation via documents. Document-centric work benefits, in turn, from familiar and stable physical arrangements and environments (that is, offices) that, while not always pleasant, liberate workers from unbounded variability, thereby enabling productive collaboration. One might even go so far as to say that PCs have effectively become "invisible" in much office work – people most often pay attention to the contents of electronic documents, not the technology itself.

The PC is thus neither as singularly responsible for the current state of office work, nor is that state of affairs necessarily "unhealthy" in every respect. This is not an argument for preserving the dominance of the PC, or to advocate imposing the constraints of the modern office on other domains, but rather a call to researchers to consider how constraints enable as well as limit human action. A goal for the design and development of ubicomp systems might be to identify and understand how to capitalize on productive constraints – boundaries within which to profitably operate.

2.2. Sustainable Alignment of Disparate Actors

At least part of the appeal of the ubicomp vision has been an explicit agenda of both empowering end users and alleviating the stresses associated with the use of current technologies. "Machines that fit the human environment instead of forcing humans to enter theirs will making using a computer as refreshing as taking a walk in the woods"

[16]. Creating a "walk in the woods" experience is one thing; it is quite another, however, to create such an experience that also contributes to a productive system, as the technologies and inventions described above all did.

Productive work regimes are complex autocatalytic systems [17]; the activities of any worker must be brought into alignment with other workers in the service of the overall sustainability (usually meaning "profitability") of the system as a whole. This alignment, as Hutchins [18] (drawing in turn on the work of David Marr) points out, has an interesting implication. The behavior of the system as a whole is defined differently than the definition of any constituent parts. The activities of individual participants in the system must be aligned to produce that emergent, system level behavior.

This is complicated by the fact that in many cases, those with financial, managerial and decision-making power in productive work organizations are often more inclined to invest in technologies that enhance the performance of the system as a whole, rather than providing benefits to individual participants within the system. To put it bluntly, management often doesn't care about providing a "walk in the woods." The history of technology investment, in fact, might be traced as a tension between the needs of management to reduce costs and find efficiencies, and the needs of workers for employment, empowerment and decent working conditions. This tension has been well recognized in CSCW research and ethnographic studies of workplaces [19], [20], and in many ways marks the history of political economy [21]. It is particularly acute in many of the domains we studied, where unlike their relatively empowered "knowledge worker" colleagues, many of the workers we observed had little agency in determining their own activities. In fact, as Suchman and others have pointed out, the practices and activities of many workers at lower levels in the organization are often rendered "invisible" in formal accounts [22].

The challenge, then, of Weiser's laudable vision is more than what is stated. Computing must be more than refreshing as a walk in the woods – it must enable creation of knowledge or other products that circulate among constellations of actors. These constellations, in turn, must be productive and sustainable in larger economic and social systems. The following sections examine this dual challenge from a variety of angles. First, there is a question of the economics of managing variability: how will the variability of physical environments outside the office be effectively and economically addressed? Second, from a "political" perspective we ask: what does one do when the desired practices of individual workers seem to stand at odds with the "needs" of the organization as a whole? Finally, we explore the question of how human knowing and meaning-making might co-exist with systems that have no such capability. In each section we present first a general statement of the challenge, followed by a brief suggestion on implications and how to approach it.

3. Addressing the Costs of Variability

The prior section examines some of the reasons for the success of the PC and its relationship to the sustainability of office work. However, as we get out of the office, into environments where workers directly engage not just structured representations but objects themselves, there seems to be both need and potential for a different approach to computing. Central to the pervasive and ubiquitous computing agenda is the idea that computing artifacts such as wirelessly networked sensors will be dispersed and embedded in numerous physical environments, allowing more direct interactions with the world of "atoms". A problem, however, seems to arise with the tremendous variability across such environments. Office computing is characterized by a fairly circumscribed set of applications, that have enabled hundreds of millions of people to do things like share email, calculate spreadsheets or surf the web. Can we expect such "easy" scaling outside the office? We briefly examine this question in terms of a simple economic issue: the labor involved in deploying and extracting value from sensor networks.

3.1. Variability Among Sites

We couch this discussion in a recent study of sensor networks in agriculture – more specifically, viticulture, the raising of wine grapes. Our research took us to a variety of vineyards, and involved both a brief deployment in an Oregon vineyard and a much more extensive deployment in British Columbia. In both these deployments, researchers used Berkeley motes designed to monitor daily temperature fluctuations and aggregated heat units, which are considered important for initiating harvest and making other decisions in the vineyard. In the Oregon setting, climate conditions are more moderate and humid, with more precipitation than in the British Columbia setting. These differences, along with differences in local topology, the distribution of crops, and chance elements such as the presence of a point source of RF interference, meant that the distribution of the motes in each vineyard required considerable local planning and adaptation, including some amount of pure trial-and-error. As the researchers point out, "Site-specific characteristics will have a profound effect on the ability of mathematical models to predict variation. A hillside site with many swales draining the cold air from the hilltop will require more sensors... A flat plain with little variation in topology will require fewer temperature sensors..."[23].

Beyond the question of network density lie other issues, which will vary not only according to climate but according to specific needs. Different data will require different types of sensors (e.g., chemical sensors, temperature sensors, moisture sensors, etc.) as well as sampling rates, form factors and even physical positioning. Sensors for soil chemistry or conditions, for instance, would obviously need to be on the ground, while the sensors for our deployment (designed for accurate temperature readings at the level of the fruit) required being suspended above the ground, on the vines. Even if one accepts the proposition that the material cost of sensor network technology may be on the order of pennies per unit some day, it does not necessarily follow, based on our data, that motes will one day "be deployed like pixie dust." [24] Labor and skill will be required to properly deploy such sensors. The question is: who will provide that labor? In our own deployments we found that the skill required to successfully lay out a network was beyond the level of most agricultural researchers, let alone ordinary farmers.

User interfaces to sensor networks will likewise need to be optimally tuned, in this case within a vast space of possibilities. Raw "data dumps" from sensor networks proved entirely unintelligible to virtually all parties involved in the ordinary production of wine grapes. At the opposite extreme, completely automated systems that take control out of workers' hands (for instance in irrigation or pesticide treatments) were regarded with considerable suspicion by those we interviewed: environmental conditions and appropriate responses are still too poorly explicated to be trusted to logic-based solutions. Thus, skillful UI design providing data interpretation, with clear implications for required actions, would seem to be an element of a successful deployment. While those we interviewed indicated a preference for map-based representations of vineyard, it was not clear that existing GIS databases could be leveraged – at least some custom mapping would be necessary to provide the level of detail routinely used.

From a purely economic point of view, it is difficult to tell whose labor might be enlisted to address all these needs. The diversity of local needs and environments described above seem to require "local knowledge", that is, people with sufficient knowledge of the domain and local environment to make informed decisions. Deploying and harvesting data from networks does not seem to be a task for non-local technicians. Map design would require at least some "ground truthing," and UI's need to be tuned to individual needs and skills. Conversely, it seems unlikely that grape growers will have the desire, ability or resources to become network engineers or custom UI designers. The real economics of sensor networks thus has yet to be worked out. The "total cost of ownership" of such systems is clearly uncalculated as yet.

It is not clear these are simply issues facing an immature technology (which sensor networks remain as of this writing), as if in the future such customizations will take care of themselves. Raising grapes is sufficiently complex that contingencies of network architecture, data types, and modes of representing information may always be highly variable, and require considerable local design and tuning. Nor is this an issue facing only the seemingly exotic world of viticulture. There is considerable variability and local contingency in all of the work environments we studied. Even in Intel's manufacturing facilities, which are explicitly designed to eliminate variability, local knowledge of the particular environment constituted a vital part of the sustainability of systems. In construction, as we were told simply (and on multiple occasions), "every building is different."

3.2. Implications for Design

Just to reiterate: one of the goals of this paper is to begin to get an understanding of the long-term prospects for ubicomp technologies in the economic, social and political systems that constitute non-office work environments. Following are two simple guidelines that might be used in early evaluation of ubicomp development.

Bound development with productive constraints. While smart environments are interesting illustrations of future visions, it may be that they try to tackle too many problems, and do not lead to the development of easily transferable results. It seems that designing for specific, modular tasks provides a more productive constraint, and one that potentially transfers to other domains more easily. This recommendation seems to echo that of other ubicomp researchers (e.g., [25]). Our brief natural history of the office suggests that constraints have played a positive role in the development of computing so far. The trick for future development is to identify, amidst the apparently greater variability in non-office work environments, productive constraints to exploit.

Maintain a consideration for "total cost of ownership" by allowing decentralized creation. It is not enough to suggest that the cost of the technologies may plummet to pennies per unit or less, or even that such new technologies may come complete with their own infrastructure "for free". The total cost of ownership includes the human labor and expertise to put the technology in place and extract value from it. In this regard, it seems vital that the industry strive to enable decentralized creation and design. As discussed, local variability requires that design happen "on the ground." In the environments we studied, not surprisingly, we did not find many individuals with extensive wireless networking or software knowledge. To scale successfully, the deployment, integration and harvesting of data from tags and sensors will have to be accessible to individuals with little or no technical background. As it stands, there is little evidence to suggest that "end user programming" in these messy environments will be any easier than in the world of desktops.

Tagging and sensing systems often seem to be used to eliminate the role of human workers in the creation of digital information. In the best applications of this approach, the technology creates information beyond the limits of human attention or perception, for example with persistent sensors in vineyard applications, or the use of motes to track vibration on equipment in a manufacturing facility (for proactive maintenance). While the labor involved in deployment remains an issue, it may also be that the physical organization of space, coupled with a noting of the time, provide enough structure for some of the lightweight, "unofficial" kinds of worker-to-worker communications that formed an important practice in virtually all the domains we studied. By incorporating tools for simple, *in situ* annotations tagged with both time and location information, such systems might be leveraged tremendously. Workers able to direct their own or their colleagues' attention to important aspects of both their physical environments and digital information will find data much more useful. This must be incredibly simple: for instance, an enologist using such a system should be able to make a note about a particular vine as he walks the vineyard tasting fruit, without even having to stop. Most importantly, such tools seem most likely to succeed as notes for co-workers (or selves), as opposed to "inputs" to more formal systems that rely on heavily structured data.

4. Supporting Informal Articulation Work

The prior section raised the issue of how considerable environmental variability across sites might raise economic challenges for ubicomp technologies. This section addresses a different kind of variability. As mentioned, in sustainable systems, the activities of individual workers are aligned to produce an outcome that is defined at a different level of description. There thus exists a basic tension between the needs of the organization as a whole and the needs and desires of individual participants – the workers who make up that system. The tension is heightened by the fact that, in manufacturing, construction, retail, agriculture and many of the other non-office environments we studied, the workers we observed hold little power in their organizations. Their productive "alignment" is largely the result of an enforced work routine.

4.1. "Formal" and "Informal" Work

Consider an example from Intel's manufacturing environments, the facilities wherein silicon wafers are turned into microprocessors. These are environments where the logic of manufacturing command and control has reached an extreme. The environment is orders of magnitude cleaner than a typical hospital operating room. Workers wear full body outfits, complete with Plexiglas face masks, to protect the environment from human impurities, not the other way around. The entire operation is subjected to intense scrutiny and management via roughly half a dozen centralized computing systems (dozens more among the various production "tools" in the factory) and a global team of technicians, engineers and managers numbering in the tens of thousands.

In an experiment in 2002, local management at one particular facility provided handheld computers to all technicians. The devices and wireless networks enabled a variety of *ad hoc* communications among technicians. Some of these communicative practices stood in stark contrast to "official" systems of knowledge creation in the factory – and in fact raised alarm. Such was the case with process specifications, the explicit, step-by-step instructions for the maintenance and use of sophisticated tools in the manufacturing process.

From the perspective of engineering and management, these specifications are held to be invariable from factory to factory on a global basis. They are created and protected from unauthorized change through a laborious process involving formal on-line submission procedures (by technicians or engineers) and layers of engineering approval at the local, regional and global level. They are, as one engineering manager explained to us, the company's "family jewels."

For factory technicians, the "specs" are a resource for action – they provide instructions on various aspects of production. But as a resource, they are less than optimal. They are mildly onerous to wade through in search of a particular piece of information. They are impossible to change, even when "everyone" knows that there are better ways to do things. In short, they are too rigid and immutable. So, not surprisingly, the techs used their handhelds to "clip" portions of the specs (usually lists or reference numbers, measurements and settings, etc.) they found they needed most but could not remember easily.

In this case "spec clipping" introduced a direct tension between the "system" needs and "individual" needs. Process engineers and managers saw it as threatening to the integrity of the process – techs ran the risk of saving and sharing outdated information. The technicians, conversely, found that wading through virtual pages of written specs to find the right piece of information, or to go through the "hassle" of submitting updates, to be tedious and unproductive. Simple, easy-to-use and largely ubiquitous computing technologies, then, while potentially highly valuable to technicians, were regarded as a threat to the overall system itself. Engineers and managers effectively banned the use of handhelds for accessing process specifications.

4.2. Implications for Design

Think systemically. To say that new technologies should be designed with human needs in mind is no longer enough in ubicomp systems. Which humans do we design for in complex, multi-participant systems? The computing industry has grown accustomed to thinking about "the end user," as if there is only one. Even considering multiple end users, without thinking about how they align to produce sustainable systems, is insufficient. Disciplines such as CSCW have at least paid sustained attended to both individuals and the systems they form [e.g., 26, 27], but the actual trick of designing to please users and align their activities requires a level of engagement that can be both expensive and elusive. New models of design, perhaps closer approximating those evolutionary processes that have created sustainable ecosystems and cultures might have to be emulated. The challenge of satisfying multiple, dynamic constraints will tax not only engineering skills, but interaction design, human factors, evaluation and testing.

Most importantly, designers must remember that power plays a clear role in work organizations. Technicians themselves have little say-so in determining how process specifications are applied or modified. They are not alone in this regard. Agricultural workers, retail clerks, construction laborers and others we studied have little agency in their respective work environments. This statement is not meant as a value judgment, but rather an observation of a condition that will clearly affect the fate of particular technologies, and is unlikely to change in the near future. Almost by definition, successful technologies have always served the needs of *some* people. Most often, this has meant those who are responsible for extracting profitability from work organizations.

Look for key points of articulation. The goal, then, is to be able to demonstrate that amenable computing technologies will enable alignments of work practices that are profitable for the organization as a whole. This is no easy task, particularly with regards to those workers whose contributions are invisible at upper levels of management. One way out of this potential bind may lie at those points where workers perform what Giddens [28] has called "face work." Key to the notion of "face work" is the recognition that it happens at the juncture between those parts of work organizations that have crystallized into formal structures, and the relatively less constrained world of ordinary human interaction. To illustrate, we offer an example from our construction research.

In construction, a strongly adversarial system persists. Contracts are typically awarded through highly competitive bidding systems. Low bidders who manage to land the job inevitably operate on the very cusp of survival. Their natural inclination is to effectively renegotiate contracts by finding fault with plans and specifications after winning the bid, thus enabling a marginally greater return on the job. The resulting situation, according to some, appears "broken." As one architect informed us, "Lawyers and insurance companies play too important of a role in this industry." And yet, the system persists, largely because – however painfully – all the forces align in the successful production of buildings.

In the midst of this apparent chaos are points of possible technological intervention. Specifically, certain individuals – construction supervisors in particular – occupy key roles in the system. They are responsible for on-the-ground management to ensure that work happens and that the needs of the overall system are met, in the form of a building that fulfills code and specifications. They are the ones engaged in working out the on-the-ground meanings of the wrangling over specs and plans. This bit of structure might be leveraged by developers. By making the right tools available as resources at such key points in work organizations the technology may be leveraged for the greatest overall value.

More specifically, consider the case of changes to work plans. At a very large construction site, thousands of so-called RFIs ("requests for information") may be generated, typically when construction workers identify contradictions or irreconcilable differences in plans (for example, when a given design will cause a pipe to intersect a beam or other solid surface). Typically, site supervisors are responsible for authoring RFIs. By automating some aspects of the process – for instance by automatically encoding location information, and providing speech or pen-based user input – the work of supervisors might be made a little easier. By enabling electronic sending and tracking of these, the overall work process would be more efficient. The key to delivering value seems to lie not in wholesale automation, *per se*, but rather in providing a few additional resources, and simplified "authoring", at a point where loosely structured communications seem to require them.

Would ubiquitous computing make the working lives of construction supervisors better? Possibly, if designed well enough to expedite the "paper work" and preserve the ability to "walk the buildings." Could such technologies enhance profitability? It seems so, given their ability to speed up production. It remains to be seen, however, how many analogous situations might be present in non-office settings.

5. Machine "Actions" and Their Effects

The "design implications" of the two prior sections treated computing as a resource for what Dourish [29] has called "embodied interaction"– that is, as a rather passive tool for use by humans in their creation of meaningful action. But it would be naïve to expect all new computing systems to remain so passive. The allure of technology has long followed an obsession with automating human labor in pursuit of financial return. Computing artifacts have long offered the tantalizing possibility to take actions themselves – this is certainly the vision of "proactive computing" [30], activity modeling, and other computing agendas. As long as computing offers this possibility, those charged with lowering costs of production or otherwise increasing returns will inevitably look to computers to take concrete actions in the work environment – and these actions will inevitably have effects on their human counterparts. Rather than identifying promising applications for such technologies, this section examines how successful applications might behave relative to their human counterparts.

5.1. "Embodiment" Is a Human Thing

We start with a rather blunt observation that, no matter how sophisticated they may be, computers will never experience a work setting (or any other setting) as humans do. As much research has begun to demonstrate, human knowledge and understanding are deeply reliant on and structured by the fact that we inhabit physical bodies with certain perceptual and cognitive equipment not found on any computers [31, 32].

Consider a rather trivial example, from trials of a simulated "automatic checkout" experience in our study of retail environments. In one set of trials, a shopper's items (each individually fitted with RFID tags) were automatically scanned, totaled and listed in a single, compressed event - the ultimate "self checkout" experience. Despite the apparent appeal of this concept in the popular imagination, our "shoppers" (participants in the trial) found the experience disconcerting. It lacked the social rituals by which a deceptively intricate and ritual-laden transaction – the transfer of property ownership – is accomplished.   This discomfort was marked in some circumstances. Midway through trials the RFID reader began to register and charge shoppers for items resting squarely in the baskets of other subjects, who were waiting in line.

While one might argue that a better tuning of the RFID reader, or a better positioning of shoppers in the checkout line, might have solved the problem, these beg the deeper issue: due to a severely limited "sense" of the situation, there was no way for the point of sale system to disambiguate what was obvious to the shoppers – some items were in a different shopper's basket. As Suchman [33] demonstrated in a classic study of "smart copiers", the computing system caused tremendous disruptions largely as a result of its inability to access the moment-by-moment contingencies of context and environment.

More obviously than in office settings, perhaps, the innate human ability to collaboratively attune to the environment was evident in virtually all the domains we studied. Workers frequently expressed a preference for direct sensory engagement of the objects and environments themselves – often among multiple modalities. An enologist walked the fields and tasted grapes, "masticated thoroughly," felt the texture of seeds on his teeth and tongue, while maintaining some peripheral awareness of various other factors, such as his own perceptual experience of the climate, the soil and aspects of the physiology of the plants. A plant manager at an Alaskan fishery climbed into his single engine Cessna and flew over fishing sites, to personally view the positioning of tender boats in relation to the driftnet fishing boats. He needs to "see" the fishermen – and to let them see him (or at least his plane). A construction manager told us he preferred to see work "with my own eyes. I need to walk the building." Among other things, this physical presence where work happens provides a means of organizing perception, most directly and obviously through the physical organization and traversal of the site itself – or through the physical manipulation of objects (cf. [34, 35, 36]).

If direct perception of the space were all that's necessary, one might imagine a future wherein highly accurate location sensing might enable a machine to similarly experience a workplace. The problem is, such data does nothing to solve the problem that social means are used to organize perception, often in ways that differ from obvious physical arrangements. In the retail domain, for instance, couples shopping together may be carrying two "separate" baskets that are, in their minds, together. Conversely, as we learned in both trials and ethnographic interviews, individual shoppers may have numerous items in one basket that they nonetheless want to pay for separately, for instance, items purchased for home office versus personal use that need to be separated for tax reasons, or items purchased for a church group that need to be accounted for separately for reimbursement. Both of these situations are cases where the physical organization of the purchase items hardly matches the *social* categorizations being accomplished by shoppers – and, ultimately, clerks.

Thus, even humans can not always know just by looking.

This is perhaps why most workers exhibited a complex and layered approach to knowledge, involving not just direct sensory inputs, but also incorporating the use of formal data (when available), and dialogue with other human beings about what information "counts", and the meanings and implications thereof. By accessing disparate streams of data, workers may find productive new insights about their environments, particularly in situations where expectations of harmony among these streams were violated.

Verbal interchanges were the dominant medium of information sharing in many of the domains we studied. Morning rounds in a teaching hospital, "pass down" between shifts in factory work, and arguments about the routing of a pipe in a construction site, are all primarily accomplished through verbal means, in the midst of ongoing work, in ways that can appear loosely structured and often heavily dependent on the local, physical setting. These verbal interactions accomplish many things. As Goodwin [37] has pointed out, language interacts with the visual field, enabling workers to highlight, code or otherwise fruitfully draw others' attention to relevant aspects. In our observations, we noted that such instruction and knowledge creation was occasioned and organized temporally as well. It was typically by virtue of unfolding contingencies – when problems arose, for example – that workers engaged in explicit discussions of an object or domain that they might not even think to articulate in the abstract (an observation attested in prior research [38]). Such practices, as has been much discussed, are dependent on "context" – which an increasing number of researchers have begun to recognize is not just an objective setting with measurable parameters, but rather a locally negotiated and shared human accomplishment – a contingent understanding of a situation. [39, 40, 41].

While hard for machines, establishing context for a retail worker at the point of sale, is trivial: she just asks. "This all together, hon?" With a simple deictic reference and four-word question, the clerk and customer are able to clearly define which items belong to whom. In fact, there are many things happening at the checkout counter that allow a clear, lightweight contractual arrangement in the transfer of goods – including the courtesy "did you find everything OK?", the display of the cost of items in serial form as they're processed, the lightweight rituals of bagging the items and handing over of a receipt. All of these are scripted social practices designed to provide both clerks and customers with clear indicators that track the progress of transfer of ownership. Each step in this ritual process comes with its own possibilities for recovery from error – for instance, as subjects pointed out to us, they will hesitate when just through the checkout line to check their receipt to make sure there are no violated expectations. "If I wait until I get out the door it's already too late to fix a problem." This "civil but adversarial" encounter, along with all its potential exceptions and errors, is successfully executed countless times each day.

As Davies and Gellersen [42] point out, enabling machines to share such rich contextualized understandings with humans is an unsolved problem "in anything other than extremely limited domains." One might legitimately question whether a shared understanding of context between people and machines in most of the cases described above is not simply unsolved but ultimately *unsolvable*, given the fact that "context" is the product of both embodied and socially constructed understandings.

This is not to say that requiring workers to provide machine-intelligible accounting of their actions is desirable. In fact, among many of the workers we observed, paperwork was seen as a necessary evil, a distraction from the "real work" of being on site, among the fish, the vines, the patients, the tools, the customers. Computing was most often seen as a yet another example "distraction" work. While management may have the power to instigate onerous regimes of self-reporting, workers have always managed to find a way to resist.

5.2. Implications for Design

Given the persistent mismatch in human versus machine "understandings" of context, might there yet be a legitimate role for computing systems to take actions in work systems? In this section we attempt to discern not the exact uses of proactive systems, but rather some general characteristics of how they might interact with humans. Here are a few recommendations based on our data.

Pay attention to human ritual. If we target "face work" (of which point of sale is one example) we must be aware that many of the practices that might appear to be easily automated for the sake of "efficiency" might in fact be very important for constructing a social order. Many human interactions – such as the purchase of groceries – may have associated rituals by which people are able to construct meaning and make sense. A first impulse, from an engineering perspective, is to regard such rituals as "inefficiencies" in the pure logistics of such mundane activities as transferring ownership of goods. And, to some extent, on-line shopping has eliminated some of the familiar rituals of daily life. But beware – these rituals are the means by which humans make sense of their world.

Enable human layering. Section 3.2 (above) examines the notion of incremental value through modular, bounded applications. This section builds on that insight. By combining several modular systems, users may be able to accomplish the kinds of layering and triangulation that prove useful, even unexpected results. Our own evidence suggests that by allowing users to fold in a manageable number of additional sources of information about an environment, rather than transforming their work practices entirely, new technologies might meet with more acceptance. By comparing multiple streams of input, even with regard to the most simple sensing or proactive functions, systems may become both more robust and flexible. This simple layering of multiple physical inputs, known as "sensor fusion" in the world of robotics, is perhaps familiar to many readers – note as well that the "fusion" we are referring to here will be accomplished by humans, not machines.

Create systems that take care of themselves. A final insight that emerged throughout this work must be mentioned as well. Tennenhouse [43] suggests that the future of computing will feature humans "above" rather than "in" the loop. Our comparison of computing inside and outside the office suggests that, while there do seem to be opportunities for systems that exhibit a certain proactive ability to serve human needs, perhaps the most successful way to enable humans to (gratefully) exit the computing loop would be to create systems that require less constant human intervention – from finding and downloading drivers to troubleshooting incompatible devices. Perhaps an early opportunity for ubicomp is *inside* the box of PCs and other devices, to create systems that are more "self aware" and mutually compatible. One of the key challenges to the widespread, successful deployment of ubiquitous computing technologies will simply be their ability to take care of themselves, first and foremost. With the potential explosion of complexity introduced by the presence of hundreds or thousands of devices per person, particularly in light of the issues raised above, it seems clear that such systems will have to achieve a level of self-configuration that current computing has not yet approached.

6. Summary

From the above, the challenges seem mildly daunting: much of the work we observed was complexly structured, not easily lent to formal articulation, highly variable, and practiced by workers for whom technology investment and assistance have never been a management priority. Ubicomp systems must align the interests, practices and needs of large, often divergent populations of workers where conflicts, power differences and competing agendas occur, and where communications happen in ways that are difficult to formalize. This alignment must allow a sustainable, productive system to emerge. Because of the considerable variability within and among environments, the design of such ubicomp systems must happen "on the ground", by individuals who have much knowledge about the local environment but little expertise in networking, hardware or software. Yet these non-experts must somehow be enabled to make specific judgments about all these technological aspects for a successful deployment. And, this must all happen in environments where the benefits of several hundred years of "colonization" – in the form of document-centered work practices, typewriters, filing systems and other office artifacts – have not paved the way for the introduction of computing.

And yet, there seem to be opportunities. Taking into consideration the preceding discussions, including the labor required for locally customized deployments, the recognition that new models for design might be needed to satisfy multiple constraints simultaneously, and the fact that humans routinely access multiple, disparate sources of information in the course of work in such environments, it seems interesting to investigate the possibility of pursuing a more evolutionary path to ubicomp deployment. By "layering" modular, well bounded systems with discrete, comprehensible functions, users may find the ability to piece together just those functions they need, such systems might fit the political, economic and social complexities associated with non-office work. Key to the success of such an approach will be the interoperability of such systems. This in itself is no small order; as has been pointed out [44], the issue of integration and interference among components of ubicomp remains a challenge in its own right.

The authors readily admit that none of the ideas in this paper, examined in isolation, appear radically new. The purpose of this study was not to set a radical new agenda for ubicomp, but rather to look at real work environments to imagine how ubicomp technologies might fit. Our hope is that, together, these ideas point to a direction for productive and potentially harmonious ubicomp deployment "in the wild" by pursuing a path that maintains an appreciation for the complexity of systems – the needs of real human beings and the social, economic and institutional processes they create.

References

1. Weiser, Mark. The computer for the twenty-first century, *Scientific American,* (1991) 94-110.
2. Bellotti, V. and S. Bly, Walking away from the Desktop Computer: Distributed Collaboration and Mobility in a Product Design Team. *CSCW 1996:* 209-218.
3. Want, R, B. Schilit, N. Adams, R. Gold, K. Petersen, D. Goldberg, J. R. Ellis, and M. Weiser, An Overview of the ParcTab Ubiquitous Computing Experiment. *IEEE Personal Communications*, (December 1995) 28-43.
4. Davies, Nigel and Hans-Werner Gellersen. Beyond Prototypes: Challenges in Deploying Ubiquitous Systems. *IEEE Pervasive Computing* 1:1 (2002): 26-35.
5. Burrell, J. T. Brooke, and R. Beckwith. Vineyard Computing: Sensor networks in agricultural production. *IEEE Pervasive Computing* 3:1 (2004) 38-45.
6. Beckwith, R., D. Teibel and P. Bowen Pervasive Computing and Proactive Agriculture. *Proceedings of Second International Conference of Pervasive Computing*, Vienna Austria (2004).
7. Salvador, T., and K. Anderson. Supporting the re-emergence of human agency in the workplace. *IFIP 8.6*, Leixlip, Ireland (May, 2004).
8. Dourish, P., *Where the action is: The foundations of embodied interaction.* MIT Press (2001):17.
9. Weiser, Mark. (1991): 98.
10. Foucault, M., *Discipline and Punish: The birth of the prison.* Vintage Press (1979)
11. Brown, J.S. and P. Duguid (1996) The social life of documents. *First Monday* (1996) http://www.firstmonday.dk/issues/issue1/documents/
12. Yates, J. *Control Through Communication: The Rise of System in American Management,* Johns Hopkins University Press, (1989).
13. Weiser (1991): 102.
14. Drucker, P. *The Age of Discontinuity: Guidelines to Our Changing Society.* Transactions Pub. (1992 [1969]).
15. Dourish (2001): 177
16. Weiser (1999): 102
17. Kauffman, S., *At Home in the Universe: The search for laws of self-organization and complexity.* Oxford Press (1994).
18. Hutchins, E. *Cognition in the Wild.* MIT Press (1995).
19. Schmidt, K. and L. Bannon, Taking CSCW seriously: supporting articulation work. *Computer Supported Cooperative Work* 1(1-2): (1992) 7-40.
20. Orr, J. *Talking about machines: An ethnography of a modern job.* ILR press (1994)
21. Heilbroner, R., *The Worldly Philosophers: The lives, times and ideas of the great economic thinkers.* Touchstone Books (1999).
22. Suchman, L. Making work visible. *Communications of the ACM* 38:9 (1995), 56-64.
23. Beckwith, Teibel and Bowen (2004)
24. Koerner, B. Intel's tiny hope for the future. *WIRED* 11(12), December 2003.
25. Abowd, G. E. Mynatt and T. Rodden, The human experience. IEEE Pervasive Computing 1:1 (2002), 48-57.
26. Hughes, J., V. King, T. Rodden, H. Andersen, Moving out from the control room: ethnography in system design. *Proceedings of the 1994 ACM Conference on Computer Supported Cooperative Work* ACM (1994): 429-439
27. Schmidt, K. and L Bannon, (1994)
28. Giddens, A. *The consequences of modernity.* Palo Alto: Polity Press / Stanford University Press, (1990).
29. Dourish (2001): 12.
30. Tennenhouse, D. Proactive Computing. *Communications of the ACM* 43(5) (May, 2000)

31. Lakoff, G. and M. Johnson, *Metaphors we Live By*. University of Chicago Press (1980).
32. Damasio, A. *The feeling of what happens: Body, emotion and the making of consciousness.* William Heinneman, Random House (1999).
33. Suchman, L. *Plans and Situated Actions*. MIT Press (1987)
34. Hutchins, E. The technology of team navigation. In Galagher, Kraut and Egido, C (eds) *Intellectual Teamwork: Social and Technological Foundations of Cooperative Work.* Erlbaum. (1990)
35. Bellotti and Bly (1996): 210
36. Luff, P. and C. Heath, Mobility in Collaboration, Proceedings of 1998 *ACM Conference on Computer Supported Cooperative Work,* ACM (1998): 305-314.
37. Goodwin, C., Professional vision, *American Anthropologist* 96:3 (1994): 606-33
38. Forsythe, D. and B.G. Buchanan. 1989. "*Knowledge Acquisition for Expert Systems.*" IEEE *Transactions on Systems Management and Cybernetics* 19(3), 435-442.
39. Suchman, L. *Plans and situated actions*. MIT Press, 1987.
40. Koile, K., K. Tollmar, D. Demirdjian, H. Shrobe and T. Darrell, Activity zones for context aware computing. *Ubicomp 2003*: 90-106.
41. Agre, P. Changing places: contexts of awareness in computing. *Human-computer interaction* 16(2-4) (2001): 177-192.
42. Davies and Gellersen, (2002): 29.
43. Tennenhouse (2000): 48.
44. Davies and Gellersen, (2002): 34.

Security and Trust in Mobile Interactions:
A Study of Users' Perceptions and Reasoning

Tim Kindberg, Abigail Sellen[1], and Erik Geelhoed

Hewlett-Packard Laboratories, Bristol BS34 8QZ, UK
{tim.kindberg, erik.geelhoed}@hp.com, asellen@microsoft.com

Abstract. This paper describes an investigation into the trust and security concerns of users who carry out interactions in ubiquitous and mobile computing
environments. The study involved demonstrating an "electronic wallet" to pay
for a meal in a simulated restaurant, and analyzing subjects' responses based on
structured interviews. We asked the users to rank-order five payment methods
including three choices for the payment target, and both wired and wireless
connections. The analysis led us to classify the users into trust-, social- and
convenience-oriented clusters. We provide a detailed analysis of the users' reasoning about trust-related issues, and draw conclusions about the design of secure interaction technologies for ubiquitous computing.

1 Introduction

It is envisioned that, in the future, people will be able to spontaneously make their
personal, mobile devices interact with other devices in a range of different environments, both public and private, many of which may be new and unfamiliar [4]. For
example, in restaurants and other semi-public places, customers may be able to use
mobile devices and services to carry out electronic transactions where they may have
never visited before. For example, one view of the future is that people will carry a
device that acts essentially as an "electronic wallet" (or "e-wallet"). The e-wallet can
interact with some other device in a restaurant that accepts payment for a meal. Although the devices have never been associated before, it should be possible for users
to make their payments with little time and effort. Moreover, users should be satisfied
that they are exchanging payment reasonably securely, given what they regard as the
trustworthiness or untrustworthiness of the devices and people in the environment.

The potential security threats in such environments are well known from a technical standpoint, and various ideas have been put forward (e.g. [1,5]) for securing interactions between devices. But that work begs several questions about how users perceive and reason about such systems: First, to what extent does concern about security really determine the desirability or usability of such systems? Second, if they are
concerned, what are the particular points of vulnerability they perceive as most salient
in such an environment, and how do they reason about the threats they present?

---

[1] Abigail Sellen is now at Microsoft Research, Cambridge, UK.

N. Davies et al. (Eds.): UbiComp 2004, LNCS 3205, pp. 196-213, 2004.
© Springer-Verlag Berlin Heidelberg 2004

Third, to what extent are the answers to the foregoing questions a function of the configuration of the target device and the method of connection between the devices (for example, whether or not such a connection is wireless)?

We report on a study aimed at exploring the ways in which people reason about such systems, with a particular focus on the extent to which concerns about security impact their perception. Eventually, by understanding people's reasoning processes, we hope to be able to design systems that are not only *technically* more trustworthy and secure, but which users *perceive* to be more trustworthy and secure. The contribution in this first step is to describe the types of perceptions and reasoning found in our subject group and to draw implications for further research from these observations.

2 Related Research

The word 'trust' features in several well-known senses in the technical security literature, but typically where designers and implementers of secure systems refer to legal entities or system components rather than users. A 'trusted third party' is one upon which each of a set of principals depends to make reliable assertions about the others. A 'trusted computing base' is a collection of hardware, software and other types of component whose failure could cause a breach of a security policy. A 'trusted computing platform', by contrast, is one that is more trustworthy than simply trusted, in that certain types of tampering and disclosure of information are impossible by construction. None of those definitions relate necessarily to trust on the part of users, with consequent questions about the usability and acceptability of systems designed without attention to users' perceptions.

The increasing amount of research on constructing and designing secure *ubiquitous* systems has been encountering difficulties with the standard notions of trust and trustworthiness, even from a technical point of view. The difficulties arise because of the volatile nature of ubiquitous systems [4], which means that the 'trusted computing base' cannot be straightforwardly identified; and typically no trusted third parties exist. Cahill et al [2] describe a system for dynamically assessing risk and trustworthiness based on various types of evidence, some of which is assumed to be gathered from previous experience.

Other work [1,5, 9] has focused on spontaneous situations such as the restaurant we described, where little if anything may be known *a priori* about the other parties in the interaction, let alone their former behaviour. That work assumes that users nonetheless make dynamic decisions about the trustworthiness of other users and devices, and it enables them to construct secure communication channels to devices in the control of trusted users. It does so with, it is asserted, little overhead despite the lack of *a priori* data. Those designs beg questions about when, where, and in what users will in fact place their trust. Moreover, while the techniques to achieve secure communication have desirable technical properties, it is not known how trustworthy users will perceive them to be; or how the techniques – involving considerable human attention – play within the user's social circumstances and other considerations.

There is little help with regard to these issues in the social science literature. The considerable literature stemming from psychology and sociology, for example, makes little or no connection with technology. Work that does explore users' perceptions of trust in relation to technology, such as research within Human-Computer Interaction, tends to focus on the internet, and people's willingness and concerns about using Web-related services mainly for internet banking or shopping. As such, most of the work has focused on aspects such as users' previous experience or familiarity with a particular site or vendor, various aspects of the design and layout of a Website, the quality of the content on a site, and the way in which technical aspects of a site or a network manifest themselves (such as speed of connection, feedback, reliability and so on) e.g. [3, 6] and see [8] for an overview. Recently, the topic of mobile e-commerce and users' perceptions of trust in this context has begun to emerge in the literature. Unfortunately, such studies seek to carry over to the mobile context lessons about trust by appealing to research on the use of the internet e.g. [7,11]. There is little or no investigation of how mobile e-commerce transactions may be different, including the physical configurations of mobile devices, the fact that wireless connections are made, or the fact that there may be no history or experience of use built up in such circumstances. The study we report here, therefore, begins to explore this new territory both from a user's perspective, and with an eye to what this means for the design of new ubiquitous computing technologies.

3   Method

In all, 24 subjects were recruited from a variety of non-technical people inside and (to a small extent) outside HP, with a roughly equal mix of the sexes (11 men and 13 women), ranging in age from 16 to about 60. By "non-technical" we mean that we deliberately selected people whose job roles did not involve building, designing, or programming computer systems technology. While all subjects used computers at work and occasionally at home, their jobs ranged from administration, to legal work, to architectural practice.

3.1 Scenario and Set-Up

In choosing the concept of an "e-wallet" and the example of visiting and paying for a restaurant meal with it, we were selecting a scenario which we thought would have many familiar elements, but which also might trigger thoughts and concerns about security issues without the need for prompting.

Each subject was invited to our laboratory in which we set-up "Luigi's": a reasonably restaurant-like environment consisting of an area with tables, crockery and pictures on the wall. Each subject was then told that we wanted to introduce them to the notion of an "e-wallet" and to demonstrate several different ways in which they might use their e-wallet to pay for their meal in a restaurant situation. Since we were interested in the extent to which they might spontaneously raise issues about trust and security (as opposed to being prompted), we begin by stating that our investigation was into their reactions to the different payment methods, and to comment on which things they liked and disliked about each. An e-wallet was described as a device that provides an alternative to cash and credit/debit cards; our only mention of security was to say that the prototype e-wallet (an adapted iPAQ) would have a means of authentication such as PIN entry or thumbprint-detection that we had not yet implemented. They were also informed that the prototype e-wallet was bigger than an actual e-wallet should be. Otherwise, it and the other devices to be demonstrated operated realistically, but without exchanging actual funds.

Fig. 1. Paying by barcode at "Luigi's".

3.2 Payment Methods

Five different payment methods were demonstrated involving variations in (1) whether the connection to the payment-accepting device was wireless or wired (docked with an iPAQ cradle visibly connected to the target device); and (2) whether the target that accepted their payment was either (a) a device that the waiter carried (another iPAQ), (b) an unstaffed "payment kiosk" somewhere in the restaurant (a monitor on a table by the wall with a visible connection to a machine below), or (c) a service accessed by using the e-wallet to read a "pay by wireless" barcode printed on the menu at their table (Fig. 1). These five configurations were chosen so that we could vary both the type of connection, and the nature of the target with respect to the presence and visibility of both the device itself and a human who (apparently) has control over it. Thus, the resulting five configurations consisted of:

- two kiosk systems (kiosk/docked or kiosk/wireless);

- two conditions in which a waiter carried a handheld device (waiter/docked or waiter/wireless); and

- the barcode condition (wireless, of course).

In the wireless configurations, payment involved choosing the Luigi's payment service from a randomly-ordered list of local services that the e-wallet "discovers", including services apparently from adjacent places. In contrast, when the e-wallet was docked or when the barcode was read, the Luigi's payment service appeared directly on the e-wallet. The service first presented a list of unpaid table numbers, from which the (anonymous) user selected their own to see their bill. On affirming and confirming payment of their bill, the e-wallet presented a "receipt" page. The kiosk presented minimal, anonymous feedback during the payment process. The menu and all pages on the kiosk and e-wallet from the payment service bore Luigi's logo.

3.3 Interview

After these five different payment methods were demonstrated (in counterbalanced order across subjects), we carried out a structured interview and questionnaire as follows:

- ❑ **Ranking exercise.** Part 1 of the interview consisted of a ranking exercise in which each subject was presented with five different photographs illustrating the different payment methods. They were then asked to rank-order these five methods in order of general preference using the photographs as reminders. We then asked each subject to explain the basis for their ranking, asking for as much detail as possible about their reasons. No mention or prompting of security issues was made during this part of the interview.

- ❑ **Focussed questions.** Part 2 consisted of four more specific questions asking subjects to compare and contrast: an electronic wallet with a "normal" wallet, docked connections with wireless connections, interacting with a device in the waiter's hand versus a kiosk, and using the barcode method (where there is no obvious device receiving payment) with other methods in which there was a physical receiving device (kiosk or waiter's handheld device). Subjects were prompted to consider security issues only if they did not mention any. These prompts were open and general; no specific issues were raised by us.

- ❑ **Questionnaire.** Part 3 consisted of a questionnaire in which 12 potential security issues in non-technical language (see Table 1) were read out such as "My e-wallet might send my data or money to the wrong person or device." For each of these issues, subjects were asked to fill out a series of rating scales indicating their degree of concern. For ten of the issues there were separate rating scales for each of the five payment methods.

- ❑ **Final ranking and questions.** In the fourth and final part, we asked each subject whether or not they wished to change their ranking (in light of our discussion of security issues) and if so, to explain why.

3.4 Data Analysis

The data analysis consisted of statistical analysis of the rating scales in Part 3 (using SPSS), plus qualitative analysis and coding of subjects' comments and rationale throughout. In the case of the rating scales, scores were calculated by measuring where on a 50 mm line each subject had freely made a mark indicating their level of concern, to a 1 mm accuracy [10].

For Part 1, both positive and negative points subjects mentioned for each of the five payment methods were documented in a table. In Part 2, preferences and points of contrast were noted for each of the four issues, again in a table, both before and after prompting about security. For Part 4, whether or not there had been a change in ranking and, if so, the reasons why were documented. Throughout, interesting or representative quotations were transcribed for each subject.

In the process of documenting the issues and comments, it became clear that there were very different kinds of comments that arose when people described their rationale about the five payment methods. In order to abstract from the data, each of these comments or issues was coded as belonging to one of three categories:

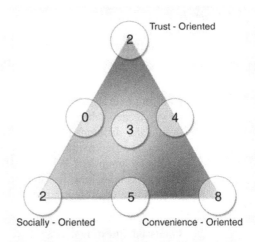

Fig. 2. Numbers of subjects in clusters.

❑ Trust-oriented: These were issues or comments that related to concerns about the risk associated with using a system either because of malicious intent on the part of another person or persons, or because of failure or unreliability of some part of the system. Such comments usually expressed either uncertainty or anxiety.

❑ Convenience-oriented: These were issues that had to do with the ease with which a system could be used, its convenience (or lack thereof), or how its design affected the usability of the system.

❑ Socially-oriented: These were issues that related to the social interaction with others such as the waiter, the accountability of one's actions to others in a restaurant, social protocols, and the value of human interaction.

The few comments that did not fall into the above categories were left uncoded.

4 Results and Discussion

We will begin by describing how subjects ranked the five different payment methods, and the different types of rationale that subjects used to explain their ranking. As we shall see, sometimes trust issues played a role in these rationales, and sometimes they did not. We will then go on to describe the trust issues that arose for different subjects, and the degree to which subjects seemed aware of these potential issues. The relationship between awareness and rationale will then be discussed.

After that, we will look more closely at how subjects reasoned about trust and security, and the range of factors that impacted subjects' perception of different kinds of mobile systems.

4.1 Subjects' Ranking and Rationale

Part 1 of the interview, in which subjects were asked to rank-order the five payment methods and explain their rationale for doing so, gave us a number of insights into the ways in which people perceive, reason about and envision their use of technology. For example, it was clear that, purely on the basis of this first part of the interview, across the 24 subjects, there were very different kinds of rationale that people were using to justify their preferences amongst the five methods. For the most part, such rationales were not heavily based on trust and security issues: almost 2/3 (15) of the subjects gave explanations in which trust and security played no identifiable role at all.

To clarify and characterize the kinds of reasoning processes people *did* use, we looked for a way of meaningfully clustering the 24 subjects. To do this, we began by studying the coded reasons given for each ranking. In drawing on these three classes of explanation, each subject could be seen to be using some combination of these dimensions to explain their choices. As such, we found that they could be broadly placed within a triangular landscape in which each of the vertices represented a rationale entirely based on reasons belonging to that category (see Fig 2). This allowed us to see at a glance clusters of subjects with common kinds of rationale, as well as the ways in which those rationales diverged from others. For example, if a subject gave reasons that were entirely convenience-oriented, that subject was placed in the lower right vertex of the triangle. If the reasons were entirely socially-oriented or trust-oriented, they were placed in the corresponding vertices. Likewise, rationales which contained a mix of issues were placed in the appropriate place in the triangle.

Looking at each cluster in turn gives us insights into the relationship between a subject's rationale and their ranking. It further shows how subjects in the same cluster can sometimes end up with rankings similar to others in the same cluster, and sometimes can use the same *class* of explanation to arrive at a different set of preferences. Let us examine these more closely:

Convenience–oriented: One third of all subjects gave entirely convenience-related reasons for their rankings. Of these eight people, six of them ranked the two waiter conditions lowest because having to call the waiter over was very much seen as detracting from the ease and convenience with which one could pay one's bill. In addition, the step of having to physically dock with the waiter's device was an extra negative factor resulting in the waiter/dock condition finding its place at the bottom of the ranking for seven of these eight subjects.

In terms of positive comments, the barcode condition was the overall favourite for six of the eight people, mainly because it was seen to be about being more "in control" of the process: not having to call a waiter and not having to get up from the table. The kiosk/wireless condition generally was ranked as the next favourite, again for reasons of not being dependent on anyone else to pay, plus the added possibility of being able to connect from one's table. Two people in this cluster, however, were more strongly "pro-wireless" in ranking both the wireless connection with a kiosk as well as a wireless connection with a waiter as amongst their top three configurations. Both of these subjects believed that they would be able to wirelessly connect with the waiter without necessarily getting them to come over to the table. Finally, the kiosk with dock generally was somewhere in the middle of the ranking: on the positive side, not having the waiter involved was seen to speed up the process, but on the negative side, the need to dock raised the possibility of queues, especially in busy times in the restaurant.

Socially-oriented: Only two subjects gave entirely socially-oriented rationales for their ranking. The reasons they gave all related to social interaction and the ways in which different methods of payment supported or interfered with ongoing social protocol within the restaurant setting. Both of these people could be called "waiter-friendly" in that, in contrast to the convenience-oriented people who viewed waiter involvement as negative, interaction with the waiter was seen as a valuable aspect of the experience of being in a restaurant. Both ranked the two waiter conditions as their top preferences, with the docked interaction rated as better than the wireless one. Interaction with the waiter was seen not only as a positive social experience, but someone with whom one could talk in case of problems, to let them know they enjoyed the meal, and so on.

With regard to the two kiosk conditions and the barcode condition, the main issue was how they would affect how one would be viewed by others. In other words, the concern here was one's accountability to others in terms of being seen to have paid, and being seen to be valuing the interaction with others. One of the subjects viewed interacting with a kiosk (and especially docking with it) as removing oneself more and more from the social situation. These methods were the least preferred conditions. For the other, paying by barcode was the least preferred condition because, she reasoned, it would be less obvious to others in the restaurant that she was engaged in paying than if she was seen interacting (and especially docking) with a kiosk.

Trust-oriented: Only two subjects were entirely oriented to trust and security issues as the basis for their ranking. Interestingly, both gave different sets of trust-oriented reasons resulting in different rankings.

One subject based her ranking on a mistrust of both wireless connections and involvement of the waiter. Mistrust of wireless connections appeared to come from a lack of experience with this type of connection, the idea that the information might go somewhere she wouldn't know about, or that something might come "in between" her device and the receiving device. Mistrust of the waiter revolved around fears that someone might impersonate the waiter, or that the waiter might be inherently untrustworthy. For these reasons, this person ranked the kiosk/dock condition as favourite, followed by the barcode condition. The waiter/dock was ranked third, followed by kiosk/wireless, with waiter/wireless the least preferred.

The other subject's rationale appeared to be based entirely on a mistrust of other people, whether that meant the waiter or other people in the restaurant. For this reason, the barcode condition was the favourite in that people were taken entirely out of the loop. The waiter conditions were ranked next on the basis that even if the waiter was untrustworthy, at least one could identify the person with whom one was dealing. Finally, the kiosk conditions were ranked last because other people in the restaurant might be able to see the screen and therefore (he thought) view private information.

Mixed rationales: For the remaining 12 subjects, their rationales and resultant rankings could be seen to be some mixture of concerns spanning two or even three of the themes of trust, social or convenience. In these mixed rationales, the strength of one kind of factor over any other was idiosyncratic. For example, within the cluster of people who gave trust and convenience-oriented rationales for their rankings, for some subjects it was clear that convenience factors were more important, and others that trust issues were more important. Likewise, those people using all three classes of explanation each derived their own patterns of explanation and own resulting ranking.

4.2 Awareness and Trust

In the previous section we looked at the extent to which different subjects were *predisposed* to express and use trust and security issues as a basis on which to make choices about the five payment methods. That raises the question of whether this predisposition is related to a person's general level of awareness: it may be that the more awareness one has of potential risks, the more likely one uses that knowledge to reason about different systems.

We measured awareness of trust-related issues by counting the number of distinct points each subject raised throughout Parts 1, 2 and 4 of the interview. (We did not include the trust-related concerns we ourselves had raised in Part 3.) This analysis included both negative and positive comments made in relation to different points, since both were taken to indicate awareness of potential vulnerability or risk. Further, it included points that subjects spontaneously raised, as well as those that they made when we prompted them to comment on trust and security. Note that when we prompted them, it was by asking generally for "security and trustworthiness issues" in comparing payment methods, and not by mentioning specific issues. Thus it was up to the subjects to generate these issues themselves.

We identified 22 different kinds of trust-related points overall. Individuals mentioned as few as one and as many as nine different ones throughout the course of the interview, with a mean across subjects of 4.8. The points that the subjects raised, together with the number of subjects who mentioned them, are discussed in more detail in the next section (Section 4.3). However, in Figure 3, we show a breakdown of their mean frequency organized by subject and cluster. Because the clustering depended on issues raised in Part 1 (including trust-related ones) we separate out the number raised in total (including Part 1) from the number of distinct points raised in the rest of the interview (shown in brackets).

Because of the small sample sizes for some of the clusters, statistical difference tests would be inappropriate. However, the means do indicate some interesting relationships between a subject's orientation or predisposition, and awareness of trust issues. Figure 3 shows, first, that the difference between the two means (total points minus additional points) for each cluster increases as we move away from the social-convenience axis towards the trust-oriented vertex. While we would expect no difference in means along the social-convenience axis (because no trust-related points are raised in Part 1), it is interesting that people who do raise trust-related points in the initial ranking exercise continue to do so throughout the rest of the interview. Another way of putting this is that such people not only appear to have an initial predisposition to think of trust-related issues, but will find more given more opportunity to do so.

A second perhaps more important point is that subjects who are convenience-oriented show themselves to be, on average, nonetheless quite highly aware of trust-

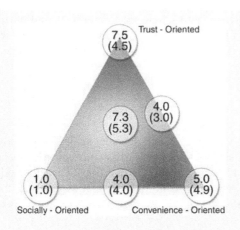

Related issues. For example, if we look at the mean number of trust-related points raised after the initial ranking exercise (when discussion of trust and security was prompted), the convenience-oriented people raised as many points on average as the trust-oriented people. In other words, it appears that subjects who used a convenience-oriented rationale were in fact quite aware of potential security risks, but chose not to take into account such issues in their ranking. By contrast, the two socially-oriented subjects started out their interviews without raising such issues and continued to demonstrate very little awareness of points of vulnerability throughout, even when prompted.

Fig. 3. "Awareness scores". By cluster, the mean number of trust-related points across subjects in the whole interview; and (in brackets) the mean number of additional points raised after the ranking exercise in Part 1.

So far, then, the data suggest that there is no simple relationship between a predisposition to using trust issues as a rationale, and awareness of those issues. Another way of exploring this relationship is to ask whether deliberately raising subjects' awareness of potential issues might cause people to alter or rethink their original choices. Here, we can look at the final section of the questionnaire. At this point, we had prompted discussion on a number of trust and security topics, and had asked subjects to consider 12 potential security issues in detail. Subjects were then asked whether they wanted to change their general preferences for the 5 methods we had presented them with.

In all, only seven of the 24 subjects said that, when all was said and done, they would change their rankings. Interestingly, however, only four of these people expressed reasons to do with increased awareness or concern about security issues. The remaining three people who changed their rankings did so because they had changed their opinions about which conditions would be the most efficient and convenient.

4.3   Reasoning About Trust-Related Issues

In this section we examine the subjects' reasoning about trust-related issues in more detail by looking both at the points the subjects themselves raised in the interviews, and then by examining the degree of concern they indicated for the issues we raised in the rating scale questionnaire. We then examine their reasoning when comparing technologies.

The 22 trust-related points that the subjects raised throughout the interview, grouped by category and ordered by the total frequency of occurrence, were as follows:

- **Attacks on the E-Wallet:** The most frequent references were to attacks on the e-wallet, where subjects identified four vulnerabilities. Five felt the e-wallet was particularly attractive to thieves; four remarked on the total amount that might be lost if the e-wallet was acquired by a thief; fourteen referred to the relative protection of an e-wallet which, unlike a conventional wallet, presented a challenge to the user's authenticity; and three thought the e-wallet could be hacked over the network.
- **Human Agent:** The subjects made a total of eighteen references to who might be a safeguard or attacker and, in some cases, where they would make an attack: a waiter either in or out of sight; another member of staff; another customer; or someone outside the restaurant.
- **Attack on Communications Link:** The communication link scored next in the frequency of references, with a total of fourteen. Ten referred to insecurities of the wireless link, four explicitly to eavesdropping. Interestingly, two mentioned direct connection by dock as a point of vulnerability: they thought malicious access to their e-wallet would be easier than with wireless. Two were generally concerned about whether communications were encrypted.
- **Authenticity of Receiving Device:** Thirteen subjects referred to the authenticity or otherwise of the device their e-wallet communicated with (the "receiving device"). Some users referred to the possibility that their wireless communications might end up at a device that either presented itself spuriously by name as a device belonging to Luigi's, or which they chose by mistake from the list of discovered devices. Others were concerned that, while they could identify the device they were communicating with, it itself might turn out to be untrustworthy – for example, the waiter's own device could be used to steal payments.
- **Attack on Device:** A total of eight references concerned the possibility that either the kiosk or the waiter's device could be hacked into, by staff or by a third party.
- **Doubt about Payment:** There were five trust-related references related to doubts about whether payment had been correctly made: it might not be taken at all; more might be taken than was warranted; the user might mistakenly pay the wrong bill.
- **Context:** There were five references to security afforded by the context of the restaurant: two references to branding as a sign of authenticity, and three to what was "close" or "local" as being more trustworthy. E.g., one subject thought that wireless transmissions were trustworthy as long as they were local to the restaurant.
- **Other:** Finally, two subjects thought that another customer might cheat and pay the subject's cheaper bill; three were concerned about what happened to their payment or their personal information after they had apparently successfully paid the restaurant; one considered that any unfamiliar technology (such as those we demonstrated) was not deserving of his trust; and a sixth thought that people might exploit the feedback from his transaction on the kiosk (even though it was anonymous).

When we compare the points of vulnerability that the subjects generated themselves with the twelve potential trust issues we raised in Part 3 of the interview, (on the basis of our technical knowledge of attacks and failures), it is interesting to note that the subjects collectively showed some awareness of almost all of our issues. (See Table 1 for a list of these issues.) Only one issue we had posed had no counterpart among the subjects' points: no-one raised the possibility that, to paraphrase, "People could intercept and change my transmission".

For the rest of the issues we asked about in Part 3, the degree of correspondence in ranking between the subjects' ratings of concern and the awareness they showed is mixed – and thus, as the previous section suggests, "awareness" is not always to be equated with concern. In particular, there is good correspondence between the subjects' most frequently mentioned point, about an "attacker (who) acquires and breaks into the e-wallet", and the Part 3 issue rated topmost in degree of concern – to paraphrase, that "someone might get hold of my e-wallet and hack into it". However, the second- and third-ranked Part 3 issue, that "the system might be unreliable and take the wrong payment" and that "someone could hack into my e-wallet while I carry it", correspond with points ranked rather lower down in frequency of mention.

There are several points of awareness without counterpart in the Part 3 issues. Those issues deliberately do not mention the identity of the attacker; so there is no 1-1 correlation with the users' points about which "human agent" might be a point of vulnerability or security. The dock as a point of insecurity, and the contextual issues of branding and locality, are interesting points that the subjects raised but which do not themselves have any bearing on *de facto* (from a technical point of view) security. The other uncorrelated points are either refinements of Part 3 or are too vague to correlate exactly (e.g. "wireless net is insecure").

Wireless versus docked connections

One of the key issues that subjects both spontaneously raised and were asked about was the difference between docked and wireless connections with regard to trust and security. When subjects were explicitly asked in the interview to tell us which they thought was more secure, eight of the subjects said they thought docked connections were more secure, three people said wireless connections were more secure, and the remaining 13 people either had no opinion, or thought they were equal.

Of the people who felt a docked connection was more secure, for three of them, it was clear that the anxiety they felt about a wireless connection had to do with the fact that the wireless method meant they had to choose from a range of services, and that they, or the system might inadvertently choose the wrong service to pay. Two people felt that a docked connection protected them from possible malicious intervention of the signal by person or persons unknown. E.g.,

> "I feel safer docking it because you do connect with something so you know where you are and what you're doing but with wireless you never know if there's someone who can log in on it."

This latter quote also indicates the more general sense of unease about wireless. For the remaining three people, knowing where the information is going when the connection is not perceptible was a problem. E.g.,

> "Unless you physically walk up to the station and dock and have a look I wouldn't know where it's gone – it [the information] just disappears into oblivion."

Interestingly, however, three people expressed the opposite view when comparing docked versus wireless connections. One person could not tell us why, but simply

Table 1. Potential security issues raised in part 3 of the interview, and results of significance tests comparing amount of concern for wireless (W) versus docked (D) conditions. The first two issues did not have separate rating scales for the W and D conditions.

Issue (paraphrased from questionnaire)	P values[1]	Result[2]
I might lose my e-wallet, leaving it open to hackers if in the wrong hands.	N/A	N/A
People could wirelessly access my e-wallet even while I carry it.	N/A	N/A
People could eavesdrop on the connection.	$p < .006$	W > D
People could intercept and change my transmission.	$p < .007$	W > D
My e-wallet might send data or money to the wrong person or device.	$p < .001$	W > D
Restaurant / service provider could capture info about me I don't want them to have.	n.s.	–
Receiving devices such as kiosks or handhelds might be subject to hackers.	n.s.	–
Other people could pretend to be me and access my bill.	$p < .019$	W > D.
The system might be unreliable & take my payment incorrectly.	$p < .028$	W > D.
I might not get clear or timely feedback.	$p < .037$	W > D
I might make a mistake entering data into my e-wallet.	$p < .019$	W > D
I would not have a receipt in a long-lasting form.	n.s.	–

[1] Results of ANalysis Of VAriance (ANOVA). P values less than .05 are significant; "n.s." means not significant.
[2] "W>D" means significantly more concern for wireless than docked conditions.

said that it was her hunch wireless was more secure. Another reasoned that "it would be easier to take information off it if it was physically connected to another device." The third person was uncomfortable with the idea of physically handing over his e-wallet in order to dock it:

> "You don't really want to part with it, do you? You e-wallet is yours. You don't know what the other guy is doing."

It was clear that in this case, the potential risk here referred to the waiter having it within his control, and could do something nefarious when out of its owner's hands.

Finally, most people refused to commit themselves to a point of view in our discussions of docked versus wireless connections. For five of these, there were no comments made to the effect that they distinguished between the two types of connection on the basis of trust and security at all. For another three, the reason they made no distinction was that they commented to the effect that they trusted the technologists to ensure that all aspects of the system were secure. E.g.,

> "I'm willing to put my faith that people are doing enough to make these things as secure as possible."

The remaining people in this group (5) did indeed express a range of concerns about wireless connections being insecure or unreliable. Nonetheless, none of them was willing to state that they thought wireless connections would be less secure than docked ones.

It appears, then, that people do express more of an inherent mistrust of wireless versus physical connections when we look at the results of the interviews, but very few people were willing to commit to this view or clearly explain why they felt that way. By contrast, when we examine the results of the rating scales, the results were much more clear-cut. Here we found that for seven of these issues, the wireless conditions gave rise to significantly more concern than the docked conditions, as shown in Table 1. There were no statistical interactions here: this result did not depend on whether the conditions involved a waiter or a kiosk.

This analysis shows that once different potential security concerns are raised, people indicate more concern about wireless methods of payment than with docked methods. However, left to their own reasoning, they may overlook these concerns, have only vaguely formed rationales for a preference for physical over wireless connections, or indeed may rationalise in favour of wireless connections over docked ones.

Kiosk versus handheld interactions

We next turn to the issue of interacting with different kinds of physical receiving devices: a stationary kiosk in the restaurant versus a handheld device in the waiter's hand. Here again we have the subjects' comments in the interviews, including those they made when we asked them to compare interactions with a kiosk versus a handheld device; and we have the rating scale data in which subjects expressed their concern for 10 different issues as a function of method of payment.

Seven subjects said they thought a kiosk was more trustworthy and secure than interacting with a handheld device. All of these judgments were made on the basis that essentially machines are more trustworthy than people. If a device is portable, then people can take them and do things with bad intent. By contrast, a fixed device like a kiosk would not be subject to the same risks:

"There isn't a person there, there's a machine. When you go to a hole in the wall, you think: a machine isn't going to do anything untoward to you. Machines are not programmed to do that, machines are just programmed to do a certain thing."

"I prefer something stationary [the kiosk]. I feel it's more trustworthy than a handheld but I don't know why I feel that. Maybe because it's a large piece of machinery. You know that's stationary whereas an individual – something that's portable, you may wonder where that's going."

Only one person adopted the opposite point of view. In this subject's opinion, a handheld device is more secure precisely because it is in someone's hand. As he said:

"It's a psychological thing. It's the fact that somebody's there so you're paying this person as opposed to something you don't know."

The majority of people, however, were unwilling to commit or make broad generalisations about whether one kind of receiving device would be less secure than another. Nine of this group expressed no opinion or recognized no difference with respect to interacting with a kiosk versus a handheld device in terms of trust and security. Two people said positive things about having a human in the loop, and thus seemed to lean toward trusting the handheld more as a receiving device, but were unwilling to commit on this point. The remaining five people expressed more mistrust in relation to the handheld device but this was also said to be a function not of the device itself, but on the trustworthiness of the waiter.

Looking at the rating scales, unlike the issue of docked versus wireless connections, there were, in general no statistical differences in level of concern between the two kiosk conditions and the two handheld device conditions. (Further, there were no interaction effects here. In other words, the differences between kiosk and handheld conditions did not depend on whether the connection was wireless or not.) One exception to this was in response to the issue of the "devices or network being unreliable". Here, we found that people expressed significantly more concern in the kiosk conditions than the handheld conditions: ANOVA (see Table 1) gave $p < .013$; no significant interaction.

Barcode method versus other methods

In the barcode method the subjects were exposed to an aspect of ubiquitous computing rather than simply mobile computing: the users dealt with a physical token of the restaurant's payment service (a menu with a barcode) rather than any obvious device.

While the subjects tended to be decided about the barcode method in terms of convenience and social factors (many ranked it high because of its convenience, or low because it had poor social connotations), they were less clear about its trust-related properties. When asked whether they had a preference in terms of "security and trustworthiness" between the barcode and the other four methods, only five subjects felt able to express a definite preference: three thought the barcode method was more secure or trustworthy than the other methods, and two thought it less.

Two of those who thought the barcode method was more secure reasoned that this was because of the absence of anyone else involved. E.g.:

"No-one else is there and it's all done in front of you."

No-one else is present during wireless access to the kiosk either, but the quote suggests an absence of remote vulnerabilities that two other subjects echoed E.g.:

"I always feel if you're closer to something you're safer to do it."

However, another subject lowered the barcode method in his final ranking because it cut out the human; yet another wondered whether someone else might find it easier to leave without paying.

The third subject who preferred the barcode method did so because the branding of the menu – and the physicality of the menu – served to reassure him. This thinking seemed to be based on the idea of something's being visibly owned or controlled by the restaurant – which is similar to another's reference to the kiosk as an "electrical representative" of the restaurant.

Of the two subjects who thought the barcode method less trustworthy or secure than the others, one was concerned about not being able to identify the receiving device: "The unknown where the information is going to flow." The other realized that the branding of the menu was not in fact a guarantee of security:

"Someone could put a different barcode on the table which could make the payment go somewhere else."

On the other hand, one subject thought barcodes reduced risk: "Reading the barcode means (it) won't connect to wrong service." Another put this more ambiguously:

> "I can't read barcodes but a machine can ... so I'm going to put my trust into that machine."

In declaring trust, that second quote illustrates a sense of venturing into the unknown with the barcode method, which several other subjects echoed.

Turning to the rating scale data, perhaps the most remarkable result was that the concern ratings for the barcode method lay mid-way between the two docked methods and significantly below the two wireless methods for the two communications-related issues of eavesdropping and message interception. In other words, a method which in fact involves only wireless communication was rated as though it involved something with the distinctive protection of docked communication. This raises the question of whether, in some users' minds, they were "docking" with the menu in a sense – and hence the remarks quoted above that, for example, "it's all done in front of you."

5 Implications

These results raise several important implications for the design of technology for ubiquitous computing environments.

First, it shows that people bring to bear very different kinds of reasons when making judgments about technologies. Trust and security issues may play a role, but other kinds of issue may be equally or even more important, like ease of use and convenience, or social ones. These other kinds of issue may be deliberately traded off or discounted in making decisions and reasoning about technology. As we saw, people who oriented themselves toward convenience as a major determinant of their preferences actually showed themselves to be quite aware of potential risks when prompted. Furthermore, even after deliberately raising discussions about trust and security, most subjects still clung to their original decisions, indicating the extent to which these other kinds of factors may hold sway despite raising awareness of potential risks.

One important implication of all of this is that, when designing technology, features which may impact ease of use or which can be seen to enforce social protocols may be at least as important to "get right" as features that assure people about their trust and security. So, for example, in designing an e-wallet device, it may be as important to build in a way of signaling to others in a restaurant that a person has paid as to deliver feedback ensuring a transaction has taken place with the right device. In other words, enforcing the social protocol may be as important as reassuring the user about the security of their transaction. Designers and technologists need to take these larger issues on board, and they may well be faced with trade-offs in doing so.

Second, the subjects in our study revealed a range of concerns to do with potential vulnerability or risk in relation to the technologies we presented them with, and in the circumstances we described. People varied not only in the extent to which they seemed aware of different risks, but also in the extent to which they could articulate them. Interestingly, most of the perceived risks that subjects generated as a group did in fact reflect the set of real technical risks that might exist in such systems.

However, in fact there was only a loose mapping between the actual technical risks inherent in such systems and subjects' perception of them. More specifically, most of the people in our study could articulate only a handful of the potential risks these systems present, even when prompted. Often, if they did raise a concern, it may only have been vaguely articulated (e.g. "wireless is insecure"). In addition, some potential threats were either never mentioned, or only mentioned very infrequently, such as the risk of interception of a transmission, or of possible abuse of the customer's information. On the other hand, other kinds of risks were much more salient, such as the risk of an e-wallet being lost, stolen or broken into. The potential risks that human agents presented were also highly salient.

A design dilemma that stems from these findings is how to trade actual security against users' perceptions of trust-related issues. An obvious approach is to look at the issues people showed relatively high awareness of and concern about, such as the possibility of paying the wrong device or service, and to design techniques that not only provide actual security but which allay concerns that otherwise might be barriers to acceptance. Conversely, designers also need to look at the threats that the subjects showed little awareness of, and consider designing techniques that enable users to negotiate them securely but without inconvenience. For example, there was little awareness of how a "physical hyperlink" such as a barcoded menu may be inauthentic. Taken generally across ubiquitous environments, this could become a significant threat and there is a need to protect users from potential problems without detracting from the ease of access to the hyperlinked services.

Third, the results point to the ways in which different technology configurations can cause people to radically alter their perception and opinions of the risks inherent in a technology. Subjects in this study expressed much more mistrust about wireless connections than they did about physical ones. To some extent this had to do with unfamiliarity, but the overriding issue seemed to be that of tangibility and the reassurance of having things within one's sight and grasp. While subjects were not clearly able to articulate their specific concerns at first, when presented with the possibilities, the configurations that made use of wireless connections were cause for far greater concerns than those that did not.

Likewise, introducing the human element through the use of a handheld receiving device presented problems for many of the subjects. Human intervention introduced uncertainty into the system, which a kiosk did not. Such views also implied that subjects were more willing to be trusting of the technologists designing the system than the people who might use them. In addition, the fact that a person could take a device "out of sight" raised concerns that visible, stationary devices did not. This was also reflected in subjects' perception of the barcode configuration. Both removing the potentially untrustworthy human from the process, as well as having things "within sight" were seen as positive aspects. The implication here is that some factors, such as the visibility and tangibility of a system, and the role of human agents, need careful consideration in the design of these technologies from the standpoint of users' reasoning about trust and security. These findings are a first step toward understanding those factors.

6 Conclusion

We have presented the results of a study of users' perceptions of and reasoning about trust and security for five payment methods in a simulated restaurant. The study has highlighted the different ways in which trust, convenience and social factors figure in the users' rankings of the payment methods. It also showed how users' awareness of and concern about points of vulnerability varies, and how they reason about them. We noted variations in the users' responses between wireless and docked connections, and between the waiter's handheld device, a kiosk and a barcoded menu as the 'target' for payment. We drew several conclusions about the issues we face in designing systems for secure interaction in ubiquitous systems.

All of this must be considered as a first exploratory step. After all, users' reactions within a simulated environment may bear a tenuous relation to how people might actually act and reason in real situations. As a next step, we are considering how to carry over this study into a working public environment with greater realism in the threats it may present, and with more realistic potential costs for the user.

References

1. Balfanz, D., Smetters, D.K., Stewart, P., and Wong, H.C. Talking to strangers: authentication in ad-hoc wireless networks. *Proc. Network and Distributed System Security Symposium*, February 2002.
2. Cahill, V., Gray, E., Seigneur, J.-M., Jensen, C.D., Chen, Y., Shand, B., Dimmock, N., Twigg, A., Bacon, J., English, C., Wagealla, W., Terzis, S., Nixon, P., di Marzo Serugendo, G., Bryce, C., Carbone, M., Krukow, K., and Nielsen, M. Using Trust for Secure Collaboration in Uncertain Environments, *IEEE Pervasive Computing*, Vol. 2(3), July-September 2003, pp.52-61.
3. Hoffman, D., Novak, T., and Peralta, M. Building consumer trust online. *Communications of the ACM,* Vol. 42(4), 1999, pp. 80-85.
4. Kindberg, T., and Fox, A. System Software for Ubiquitous Computing. *IEEE Pervasive Computing*, Vol. 1(1), 2002, 70-81.
5. Kindberg, T., and Zhang, K. Validating and Securing Spontaneous Associations between Wireless Devices. *Proc. 6th Information Security Conference (ISC'03)*, October 2003.
6. Neilsen, J. *Designing Web Usability*, 1999, New Riders.
7. Siau, K., and Shen, Z. Building customer trust in mobile commerce. *Communications of the ACM,* Vol. 46(4), 2003, pp. 91-94.
8. Siau, K., Sheng, H. and Nah, F. Development of a framework for trust in mobile commerce. *Proceedings of the Second Annual Workshop on HCI Research in MIS*, Seattle, WA, 2003, pp 85-89.
9. Stajano, F., and Anderson, R. The Resurrecting Duckling: Security Issues for Ad-hoc Wireless Networks. In B. Christianson, B. Crispo and M. Roe (Eds.) *Proc. 7th International Workshop on Security Protocols*, LNCS, Springer-Verlag, 1999.
10. Stone, H., Sidel, J., Oliver, S., Woolsey, A. and Singleton, R.C. Sensory Evaluation by Quantitative Descriptive Analysis, *Food Technology*, Nov 1974, pp. 24-34.
11. Ventakesh, V. Ramesh, V., and Massey, A. P. Understanding usability in mobile commerce. *Communications of the ACM,* Vol. 46(12), 2003, pp. 53-56.

WatchMe: Communication and Awareness Between Members of a Closely-Knit Group

Natalia Marmasse, Chris Schmandt, and David Spectre

MIT Media Laboratory
20 Ames Street, Cambridge MA02142, USA
{nmarmas, geek, spectre}@media.mit.edu

Abstract. *WatchMe* is a personal communicator with context awareness in a wristwatch form; it is meant to keep intimate friends and family always connected via awareness cues and text, voice instant message, or synchronous voice connectivity. Sensors worn with the watch track location (via GPS), acceleration, and speech activity; this is classified and conveyed to the other party, where it appears in iconic form on the watch face. When a remote person with whom this information is shared examines it, their face appears on the watch of the person being checked on. The working prototype was used as the focus of interviews to gauge the desirability of such a device.

WatchMe is a watch-based personal communicator that draws upon features of both mobile telephony and context-aware ubiquitous computing and integrates them in a user interface that is novel to both these domains. *WatchMe* extracts information from sensors to provide awareness and availability information to one's closest friends. It supports multiple modes of verbal communication (text messaging, voice messaging, and synchronous voice communication) enabling the recipients of the awareness information to choose the best communication modality. Photographs serve as emotional references to our loved ones, appearing on the watch when one of them is thinking of us.

1 Motivation

Everyone has a small group of people with whom they are emotionally close, a set of people who are very important in their lives. These are typically family members and/or intimate friends; people from our "inner circle" whom we call *insiders*. Nothing can replace the richness of face-to-face communication with these people; however, with our ever mobile and hectic lives, that is not always possible. Our aim is to use mobile communication ubiquitous computing to enable these people to keep in contact with each other. We would like to increase and facilitate communication, in a variety of modalities, among these small sets of intimate people. It is our hypothesis that people would want communication with this very select group of dear people everywhere and all-the-time, as long as it were not too intrusive and they felt in control. We built a working prototype to demonstrate its feasibility and provide a

N. Davies et al. (Eds.): UbiComp 2004, LNCS 3205, pp. 214-231, 2004.
© Springer-Verlag Berlin Heidelberg 2004

focus for evaluation of and discourse about the technology. Our system has different layers of information that afford different degrees of communication.

awareness: Awareness is based on sending some basic information about ones activities. This information must require very low bandwidth since the system is always on, and hence constantly sending a trickle of data. We find that for awareness data to be meaningful at a glance, it must be abstracted; it requires more effort to interpret raw sensor data, so we don't display it. The person receiving our context data is not a stranger, but rather someone who knows us well and therefore can help interpret properly abstracted sensor data. The awareness data must be both collected and abstracted automatically; we simply do not believe that people will update it manually. This awareness data is the background information layer. A person is going about his way, sending out this awareness data to his intimates, having no idea if anyone is paying attention to it.

"thinking of you": This is the second layer of information, and the next layer up in terms of (tele)communication intimacy. The information being sent from one side causes changes to the display on the other side, i.e. person B is made aware that person A is thinking of him. At this stage there has not yet been any formal communication or exchange of verbal messages. This information transfer must require low bandwidth and have a low level of intrusiveness.

message exchange: After checking availability, or in response to "thinking of you", one party sends a message. There are three levels of messages.
- asynchronous text (e.g. text instant messaging)
- asynchronous voice (e.g. voice instant messaging)
- synchronous voice (e.g. full-duplex phone call)

These different modes of messages are increasingly intrusive. The system should enable a person to make an informed decision regarding the mutually preferable mode of communication. Escalation of the mode can occur during the flow of the communication. For example, if a person sees that another is thinking about them, they might respond by sending a message saying "want to talk?", or alternatively "I'm really busy!".

We find that such a system has four basic requirements. First, it should be always with you and always on. Second, the awareness data must be automatically gathered. Third, the system must be able to alert the user in subtle ways –the user needs to be aware of the awareness information if paying attention or not focused on some other task. Finally, it must be able to support communication modalities with multiple degrees of intimacy –i.e. different media.

After considering many alternatives, we selected a combination of a mobile phone and sensors built into a watch (Fig. 1). We strongly believe in the importance of a working prototype both as proof of concept, and to understand the technical difficulties and feasibility of the system. We have found the prototype to be invaluable for evaluation and to engage dialog about the different aspects of the project, both amongst ourselves and with other colleagues or test subjects. We consider evaluation to be a multi-phase process: there is an evolution (of form and function) based on internal critique; we are influenced from our own and other people's investigation of user requirements for such technology [18, 14]; and evaluation continues through user studies and small focus groups.

In this paper we describe *WatchMe*, a mobile communication and awareness platform embodied in a watch. We describe the system hardware, functionality and user interface, including evolution of the design, and situate it in related work. We recount feedback received in a user interface evaluation and a pilot survey we conducted to assess peoples' acceptance of such a technology. Finally, we discuss privacy issues for such a device.

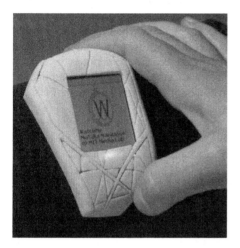 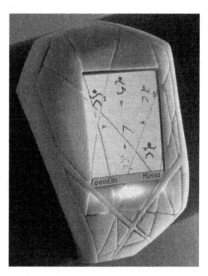

Fig. 1. *WatchMe* prototype displaying the main screen (right). Left image shows size of the current version.

1.1   Why a Watch?

A watch is an artifact very assimilated into our lives. It is something most people wear, something we glance at numerous times a day. It is always accessible, always on, and in the periphery of our attention. Watches are very noticeable, but in a non-intrusive manner.

The device had to include mobile phone capabilities since one can hardly imagine a system for intimate telecommunication that doesn't include duplex synchronous voice. From a telephone network point of view text messaging, asynchronous voice and synchronous voice may be handled in very different ways. However from the user's point of view, they are all just different ways of reaching the same person, with different levels of intimacy.

Building such a system into a watch is a challenge, due to its physical size. A key requirement of the user interface is that it must convey a lot of information in a relatively small amount of space, and in an aesthetically pleasing manner. An additional requirement was a device that could comfortably support switching between the modalities. A watch is in a location that is easily manipulated –albeit with one hand.

2   Hardware

The hardware comprises three components: the display and user input, the communication radio unit, and the sensing and classification unit. Our initial design rationale required that the user interface be easily accessible and frequently visible, which lead to a watch-based design. But to date appropriately sized hardware is not available, nor could we build such tiny phones. Although we see a rapid evolution of phones (display, processing power, size) such that a watch is a reasonable hardware target, we were forced to build our prototype with separate components. This is actually consistent with an alternative hardware architecture with several components, in different locations on or near the body, that communicate via a low power Personal Area Network, such as Bluetooth.

We would like to emphasize the three components of our prototype themselves, since the interconnections between them, although adequate for proof of concept, would have to be refined in a commercialized version.

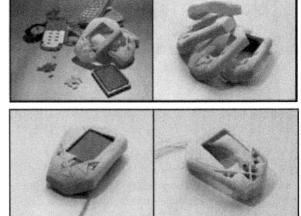

Fig. 2. Hardware at different stages of building.

display and user input: The display was removed from a Motorola iDEN mobile phone and encased in a shell built using a rapid prototyping 3D printer. This same shell includes the buttons for the user input, and is generally (together with the UI) what we refer to as "the watch". At this point the internals of the phone aren't in the watch. The display and buttons are tethered to the base of the phone, i.e. the communication component, via a flat flex cable and thin wires (Fig. 2). The watch shell also contains a speaker and microphone.

wireless communication: The radio component is the base portion of an iDEN phone, i.e. with the display part of the clamshell removed. It is connected to the watch component via a flat flex cable and wires. iDEN is a specialized mobile radio network technology that combines two-way radio, telephone, text messaging and data transmission in one network. It supports an end-to-end TCP/IP connection, the only platform that did so when we initiated this work. Other networks, such as GSM/GPRS, could also support our watch, with a different radio unit. The *WatchMe* system supports text messaging as well as voice messaging, using TCP/IP sockets. It also supports synchronous voice communication, using the ordinary mobile phone telephony functions. In this prototype the phone can be up to 35cms from the watch, limited by the length of the flex cable, so it could be strapped to the user's forearm.

sensing and classification: This component is made up of sensors, connected to or embedded in, an iPaq PDA. The iPaq reads the sensors, does data collection, and classifies the input. The current prototype includes three sensors: a Global Positioning Sensor to classify locations, an accelerometer to classify user activity, and a microphone for speech detection. The iPaq is clipped to the user's belt. The GPS unit can be embedded in the phone or connected to the PDA.

3   Functionality

The system can be divided into three different functional components: the watch, which comprises the user interface and display; the radio, through which the wireless communication is established; and the sensors and classification component, from which the personal context data is abstracted. There is also a server, which simply relays messages and context data from one user to another.

3.1   Watch User Interface

A watch is a personal device, but it is also very public. We often look at other people's watches to know the time when it would be socially awkward to look at our own. Watches are also often a fashion statement, meant to be looked at by others. Since it is at the seam of the personal and the public, the interface has tiers of different levels of information, with different levels of privacy.

The face of the watch is visible to all and conveys information accessible to all, i.e. time. People glance at their watch more often than they perceive. By embedding this high-level information in the watch's default mode, we can keep track of our loved-ones subconsciously and continually throughout our day. The top level, the default screen, also embodies other information meaningful only the owner. The owner of the watch chooses a unique icon and position around the watch face for each insider; although this is visible to others, they do not know the mapping from icons to names. Research has shown [18] that with text messaging clients, users interact recurrently with 5-7 people on a general basis. To play it safe, we chose to display icons for up to eight insiders. At this top level the colour of the icon indicates availability, fading to the background colour in 3 steps: the most faded colour indicates that this insider does not have cellular coverage, the midway colour indicates that the person is in a conversation and hence probably less available. Speech is indicative of social engagement, and it has been found to be the most significant factor in predicting availability [17], therefore it was coded into the top level screen.

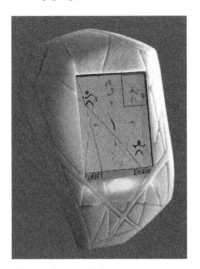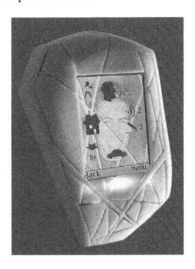

Fig. 3. Screen (left) showing cursor positioned on icon of insider. Pressing the Down navigational button will bring up the more detailed context information screen (right).

From a full-colour icon it is not possible to infer availability without going down a level in the interface and seeing more detail (Fig. 3). This is done by selecting the corresponding icon, via the Left/Right navigational buttons, and then pressing the Down button. On this screen a pre-selected image of the insider appears lightly underplayed in the background, as do the continuous lines of the design.

The more detailed information that can be viewed here (described clockwise from the top left) is the specific person's assigned icon, whether that person is engaged in a conversation, how many voice and text messages this person has left, and the person's mode of transport (walking, vehicle, biking, etc). Also displayed is his current location or next predicted one and expected time of arrival, or his last known location and time elapsed since departure. For example, in Figure 3, we see that Joe left home 10 minutes ago, that he is driving and in a conversation, and that he has sent 2 voice messages and 3 text messages; the top level shows that he has left 5 messages total. Although it is necessary to navigate to this screen for the detailed information, the top level provides an overview of all insiders, displaying salient information regarding their availability, and the number of new messages they have sent.

Since Joe is driving and also talking, this is probably not a good time to phone him. For an insider, this little information can go a long way. With a combination of prior knowledge and a form of telepresence provided by the watch, it is possible to quickly form a meaningful interpretation. For example, knowing Joe and judging by the time and that he is driving and talking, it is possible to presume that he has already picked up his buddy and is heading to the gym. If "gym" is a location Joe has revealed, once the system has enough information to predict he is heading there, the icons will change to reflect that (gym icon, direction arrow, and ETA).

The watch supports text messaging, voice messaging, and phone calls. The content of the text and voice messages, as well as the ability to compose messages or place a phone call to the insider, is accessed through yet a deeper layer.

A fundamental part of communication is its reciprocal characteristic. When an insider lingers viewing another's detailed information (in this case, that she is biking to work and expected to arrive in 18 minutes), her image appears on the reciprocal wristwatch (Fig. 4). In this way one can have a notion of when a specific insider is thinking of the other, and this information may subsequently stimulate an urge to contact that person. This conviction is supported by [18] where a significant fraction of the communication happened immediately after a party appeared online.

Knowing that someone is thinking of you creates opportunity for communication, but not obligation. When the picture appears on the "viewed" insider's watch, one of the following could occur:

- The picture popping up may go unnoticed, especially since it disappears after a couple of minutes, so the "viewing" insider is not interfering with the "viewed" insider in any way.
- The "viewed" insider notices the picture but decides not to reply or divert attention from his current action.
- The "viewed" insider notices the picture and responds by querying the availability of the other user, which causes his or her picture to appear on the other's watch, similar to an exchange of glances without words.
- The "viewed" insider decides to phone the "viewer" or engage in another form of verbal communication, i.e. text or voice messaging.

Fig. 4. When an insider thinks about another and views her detailed context data (left), the "viewer's" photograph will appear on the "viewed" insiders watch (right).

There are a number of alerting modes on the watch. For example, when your picture appears on my watch, indicating that you are thinking about me, the backlight turns on to draw a little attention. The watch can also vibrate or emit sounds and these could be used as well if the wearer wants the watch to be more intrusive. These same features can also be used for non-verbal communication. When a picture appears, the user can send back a photograph from a stored repository, or alternatively manipulate the other individual's watch backlight or vibration actuator enabling them to develop their own non-verbal codes.

The user interface design has been a continual process. It is important that there be harmony between the graphics on the screen and the physical form of the watch itself. Figure 5 shows some previous designs of the interface and drawings of other forms considered for the watch.

 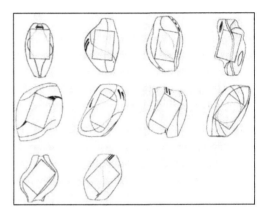

Fig. 5. Left: the first UI design. Right: hand sketches exploring preliminary variations of shape and screen rotation.

3.2   Radio

The radio component (an iDEN phone without the screen or buttons) is connected to the display and buttons in the watch. This unit performs the processing required for the user interface, manages the socket connection to the server (which relays the messages between users), and performs the telephony functions required for the synchronous voice communication.

All mobile phones have microphones, many already have embedded GPS chips (at least in the U.S. due to the FCC E-911 wireless location mandate), and soon some will have embedded accelerometers –these can also be connected via the phone's serial port. So although this unit could encompass all the required sensors, the limiting factor is its computing power. Therefore the classification is performed on an iPaq, and the classifier outcome is communicated to the phone unit.

3.3   Sensors and Classification

Cues from the physical world often help us infer whether a person is interruptible or not. An office with a closed door, for example, may indicate that the person is not around, or does not want to be disturbed. However from prior knowledge we may be aware that this particular person is easily distracted from outside noise and therefore keeps the door shut, but that it is perfectly acceptable to simply knock. If a door is ajar and voices can be heard, then perhaps the person is unavailable –that could depend on the nature of the relationship and the urgency of the topic. Throughout our lives we have acquired a whole protocol of what is appropriate in different (co-located) social contexts. How do we do this at a distance? What is the subset of cues necessary to convey to people (who know us well) that will help them infer our availability?

Locations are classified based on latitude/longitude, founded on an extension to the software from our comMotion system [20]. The original version detected frequented indoor locations, based on loss of the GPS signal. We have enhanced this model to also detect locations where the receiver is stationary with signal. When the system identifies a previously unnamed frequented location, it prompts the user to label it. In this way the system learns from and adapts to the user over time, only prompting him when an unknown location is encountered. The string associated to the labeled locations is what is reported to the other phones. A basic set of strings is associated with default icons, such as "home" and "work". A location will only be sent if it is named, and if the recipient hasn't associated an icon with that name, a text string appears instead. We also enhanced the comMotion model which analyses patterns of mobility to determine routes, positions along those routes, and an estimated time to arrival; a preliminary version of the algorithm was described in [21]. This is used to indicate, for example, that the user left home 10 mins ago, or will arrive at the office in 15 minutes.

GPS data over time allows velocity to be computed with enough resolution to differentiate between walking and driving (as long as not in urban gridlock). Although it is difficult to detect the difference between highway driving and riding a train, for example, the route classifier differentiates these two travel paths and the user has the ability to label them. For higher resolution classification, such as differentiating between walking, running, and bicycling, we rely on two orthogonal 2-axis accelerometers giving 3 axes of acceleration [23]; it is based on hardware developed jointly and a classifier similar to [3] which analyses the mean, energy, frequency-domain entropy and correlation between two different acceleration axes. With 5 sensors it is possible to correctly classify 20 activities such as walking, running, brushing teeth, folding laundry, and climbing stairs; *WatchMe* uses fewer degrees of classification.

The third sensor used is a microphone. Audio data, from the PDA's microphone, is collected and examined in near real-time to detect whether it is speech. The analysis involves taking 10 seconds of audio, looking at the pattern of the voiced segments in the pitch track, and determining whether it corresponds to speech. This is a binary speech discriminator, it is not necessary to know whether the speech is generated by the user himself or someone he is talking to; as he is probably in a conversation in either case. Likewise, we do not try to distinguish whether the conversation is over the phone or with someone physically present, though this could easily be determined. None of the audio is stored, nor do we try to perform any speech recognition.

Others have shown the value of sensors in identifying a person's context [7, 15], especially the determination of speech as a significant factor [17].

4   Privacy

In any awareness system some of the information that is revealed is sensitive to some of the participants at least part of the time. In the course of developing *WatchMe* we encountered a number of privacy issues.

sensitive information: *WatchMe* reveals a lot of information about a user, but only the locations that he has chosen to name; raw geographic coordinates are never revealed. A user might see that another is at the bookstore, but where the particular bookstore is physically located is not displayed. Additionally, *WatchMe* has been designed from the beginning to be a system used by people who are intimate friends. Since they already share much personal information, using technology to do so is less intrusive. People whom we are really close to know much more sensitive information about us than, for example, how long ago we left our house.

photographs: Photographs are very personal and a watch face is semi-public. People may be more sensitive in other cultures, but in ours we often display pictures of family, especially children, in offices and homes. We often carry them in wallets or purses, both to look at ourselves and to show to others. We now have them on phones as well, so displaying pictures of our loved ones on a watch is not that different. The detailed context information would not be readily understood by someone looking at our watch from a distance. It is also invoked only by specific user action.

reciprocity: *WatchMe* enforces reciprocity of data. A user cannot receive context data from another unless he is also sending his. There is also reciprocity of interaction: when user A views B's context data, A's photograph appears on B's watch. So a person can't "spy" on another without them knowing they are doing so, regardless of whether it carries a positive or negative connotation.

peer-to-peer vs. server: The current implementation depends on a server to relay the messages between the users. Now that there is better support of server sockets on the phones, the architecture could be modified to be peer-to-peer, over a secure socket, adding another layer of security. Even in this version, no data is stored on the server.

plausible deniability: The user has control over the locations he decides to share with his insiders, and at any given time he can manually make it seem that his watch is "out of service" (out of cellular range), or that he is in a conversation. We have thought about randomly invoking the "out of service" mode to provide the users with plausible deniability and prevent them from having to explain why suddenly they were disconnected. In this way it can be attributed to a supposed bug in the system, when in fact it is a privacy feature. The user's location is only transmitted to others when he is somewhere he has previously chosen to name, however the hardware that he is wearing is keeping a history of where he has been, to detect these patterns and perform calculations of ETA. In addition to giving the user the option of not sharing the location, he should also have the option of not logging it at all or the ability to delete certain sections from it. No acceleration data or audio is saved.

5   Related Work

A good deal of research has addressed how the awareness of presence, availability and location can improve coordination and communication. Much of it has focused on how to improve collaboration between work teams. Several systems require cameras and microphones set up in the workspace, as well as broadband connections, to support transmission of video and/or audio. Other systems require either infrared or radio frequency sensors, or heavy data processing. Recently there has been a focus on more lightweight systems for mobile devices –lightweight installation as well as easy to use. We will describe only a subset of all of these systems.

awareness through video and audio: The Montage [30] system provided lightweight audio and video "glances" to support a sense of cohesion and proximity between distributed collaborators. It used a hallway metaphor where one can simply glance into someone's office to see if it is a good time to interact. A similar metaphor was used in Cruiser [28, 11] which enabled a user to take a cruise around each office. The purpose of the system was to generate unplanned social interactions. In Portholes [8] non co-located workers were periodically presented with updated digitized images of the activities occurring in public areas and offices. Some systems have focused on awareness solely through audio. Thunderwire [1] was an audio-only shared space for a distributed group. It was essentially a continuously open conference call in which anything said by anyone could be heard by all. ListenIN [32] uses audio to provide awareness of domestic environments to a remote user. In order to add a layer of privacy, the audio is classified and a representative audio icon is presented instead of the raw data; if the audio is classified as speech it is garbled to reduce intelligibility.

location awareness: Groupware calendars have been useful tools to locate and track colleagues. Ambush [24] looked at calendar data to infer location and availability. It used a Bayesian model to predict the likelihood that a user would actually attend an event entered in his calendar. Calendars and Bayesian models have also been used to predict a user's state of attention [16]. Location-aware systems have used infrared or radio frequency sensors to keep track of electronic badges worn by people [33], or GPS [20]. The Work Rhythms project [4] looks at location of computer activity to create a user's temporal patterns. Awareness of these patterns helps co-workers plan work activities and communication. When a user is "away", the system can predict when he will be back.

context and mobile telephony: The so-called context-awareness of computer systems falls very short of what humans can assess. As Erickson [10] puts it: the ability to recognize the context and determine the appropriate action requires considerable intelligence. Several systems keep the human "in the loop" by enabling the potential recipient to select a profile appropriate for the context. In the Live Addressbook [22] users manually updated their availability status and the location where they could be reached. This information was displayed to anyone trying to contact them. Although the updates were manual, the system prompted the user when he appeared to be somewhere other than the location stated. Quiet Calls [26] enabled users to send callers pre-recorded audio snippets, hence attending a call quietly. The user could listen to what the caller was saying and send a sequence of standard answers. Another system that shares the burden of the decision between caller and callee is Context-Call [29]. As with most profile options, the user must remember to update the stated context.

lightweight text communication: ICQ started as a lightweight text message web application in 1996. It has since grown into a multimedia communication tool with over 180 million usernames, and 30 million users accessing per month [2]. A user's availability is automatically set based on computer activity, however it can manually be overridden. Babble [9] aimed to support communication and collaboration among large groups of people. It presented a graphical representation of user's availability, based on their computer interaction. Nardi et. al. [25] studied the extensive use and affordances of instant messaging in the workplace. Desktop tools for managing communication, coordination and awareness become irrelevant when a user is not near their computer. Awarenex [31] extends instant messaging and awareness information to handheld devices. It has the concept of a "peek", an icon that appears in the buddy list indicating a communication request. Hubbub [18] is a mobile instant messenger that supports different sound IDs; the location data is updated manually.

non-verbal communication systems: There are also some systems that have looked at ways to enhance interpersonal communication by adding physical feedback via actuators. ComTouch [6] augments remote voice communication with touch. It translates in real-time the hand pressure of one user into vibrational intensity on the device of the remote user. The Kiss Communicator [5] enabled couples to send each other kisses. One person would blow a kiss into one side of the device and the remote piece would start to blink. The other person could respond by squeezing the communicator causing the lights to blink on the side of the original sender. The Heart2Heart [13] wearable vests conveyed wireless "hugs" by simulating the pressure, warmth and sender's heart-beat as would be felt in a real embrace. Paulos [27] suggests a system with sensors (accelerometer, force sensing resistors, temperature, microphone for ambient audio) and actuators (Peltiers, bright LEDs, vibrator, "muscle wire", speaker for low level ambient audio) to enhance non-verbal telepresence. This system will use Intel's Motes and will include a watch interface.

watches: Whisper [12] is a prototype wrist-worn handset used by sticking the index fingertip into the ear canal. The receiver signal is conveyed from the wrist-mounted actuator (electric to vibration converter) to the ear canal via the hand and finger by bone conduction. The user's voice is captured by a microphone mounted on the inside of the wrist. Commercial handsets built into wristwatches are also starting to appear, such as NTT DoCoMo's wrist phone or RightSpot [19].

6   Evaluation

We conducted both a pilot survey to assess peoples' acceptance of such a technology and a user study of the implemented user interface; we discuss those here. In this section we also discuss the next steps of the project.

6.1   Survey

The pilot survey, besides helping us understand which features are essential, has helped us put together a more comprehensive survey that is being conducted on a much larger scale. It was carried out on a group of 26 people spanning the ages from teens to sixty five, from four different countries (USA, Mexico, Israel and Sweden). The subjects were recruited by email, by people who worked on the project, and asked to answer an email questionnaire. The respondents were encouraged to forward the questionnaire to their friends. The vast majority of the subjects did not know about the project, but they were family or friends of friends of the researchers. The survey included two different scenarios and questions about them.

communication modalities and awareness: The first scenario asked the person to imagine s/he had a device, such as a keychain or mobile phone, which would enable their friends and family to know their whereabouts. The location information would be automatically available without any effort by either party, it would be reciprocal preventing one from "spying" on another, and a person would always have the option of switching the device off. It was pointed out that such a device would, for example, "enable a working mom to know that her husband had already left the office, that her son was still at guitar practice" (probably waiting to be picked up by dad), and that her daughter was already at home".

In this population, when face-to-face communication with family and friends is not possible, the most common alternatives are communication by phone or email, followed by text messaging (IM, SMS). The large majority would be willing to share information on their whereabouts only with immediate family, that is, spouse and children. A few would also share with close friends and siblings. Not surprisingly, some teens seemed much less enthusiastic about giving this information to their family, although an opportunity whereby the parents would be aware of inopportune moments to call was valued. People indicated that they would be willing to disclose locations such as: home, work, school, gym, supermarket, etc., but few would keep the device turned on all of the time.

feature set: New features people want included are: the ability to know who was watching you; the ability to talk to the person observing you; a "busy scale" which could either be set manually or "smartly" by the system; the ability to provide a false location if necessary; the option to leave messages; a "general" vs. "detailed" mode indicating for example "shopping" instead of the name of a particular store; the option to request a person to turn their device on; and preventing children from turning their devices off or overriding the system with a false location.

People definitely did not want the system to include: hidden cameras; the option for people to track you without your knowledge; the possibility of hearing everything said; the option to permanently store the information on a person's movements; and for unauthorized people to get a hold of this information. People were willing to give some location information to a few chosen people they trust, but were very concerned of being monitored without their consent and knowledge. Almost everyone said they would take into consideration a person's location before communicating with them, and would want this courtesy to be reciprocal. We asked what other information, besides location, people would be willing to reveal. The responses received were very bimodal. Many people seem reluctant to provide more of their specific context information and prefer a more abstract "busy" or "do not disturb" label, whereas others want family trying to contact them to know that they are driving, or in a meeting, or on vacation, etc.

"thinking of you": The second scenario asked people to imagine a device that displayed a picture of whoever happened to be thinking about them. We wanted to know who people would be willing to share their thoughts with, so to speak, and how they would respond when the device displayed a picture of someone thinking about them. About 2/3 would share this experience with a combination of immediate family, close friends and siblings. One person said it would be nice to be able to let friends and family know that he was thinking of them without having to take time out to call or write a message, and that he could list at least 30 people he'd like to regularly let know he was thinking about them. About 1/3 found this idea "creepy" and did not like it. Of the group who liked the concept of the device, they would react to receiving a picture by: phoning the person if they were not too busy; have a "warm feeling", send them back a picture and maybe phone depending on who they were; would just be happy but not do anything about it; would respond only to spouse; or would email or call them to get together.

6.2   User Interface Evaluation

We conducted a small evaluation of our watch prototype, focusing on usability, choice of communication modes, and the appeal of such a watch. The 15 subjects (8 female, 7 male) were aged 25 to 48, including students and administrative staff and outsiders. The one-on-one sessions lasted from 20 minutes to 1.5 hours. First, we explained and demonstrated the user interface. Next subjects were given as much time as they wanted to explore the interface display and buttons; no subject spent more than two minutes doing so. Each subject was asked to perform 3 specific communication tasks using the device. The device logged the whole interaction and the subjects were observed while performing the tasks by one of the authors. At the end of the third task, each subject filled out a questionnaire. After completion of the questionnaire most of the subjects felt compelled to talk about the system in general and the prototype in particular, get more detail, and offer comments. Some of these unforeseen conversations over the prototype lasted close to an hour.

The first task was to send a text message to a specific person, the second task was to send a voice instant message to someone else, and the third task was to communicate in any modality to a third person. The first two tasks were directed at the usability of the watch, while in the third we wanted to see the utility of the context information of the remote person, and whether having that information affected the communication mode chosen.

usability: Subjects were asked on a 1-7 scale (1-very hard, 7-very easy) how easy the system was to use, and how well they thought they had performed. The mean and standard deviation for ease of use were $\mu = 5.67$ and $\sigma = 0.9$. For the self-reported performance $\mu = 5.6$ and $\sigma = 0.91$, although the observer considered that all had managed to perform the task and everyone in 6-7 minutes total. Almost all the complaints related to the button interface, rather than system features or functionality. People found the buttons too small, making it hard to navigate. Some found it hard to distinguish the buttons and remember what they did, though this could be due to the novelty of the device. The robustness of the buttons was an issue, requiring us to re-glue them often. Some people liked that it wasn't clear which buttons were functional, making the watch look "more like jewelry, less nerdy". One way to reveal the buttons to the user only is to give them a slightly different texture. Clearly we will have to rethink and redesign the button interface.

A few subjects disliked the "texting". Text messges are composed by choosing characters from a soft keyboard, via the navigation buttons. Each chosen character is appended to the message string. Some users added more than one space character since they had no visual feedback that it had been appended. Once composed, the message is sent by pressing a different button. These two buttons were intentionally placed next to each other to facilitate quick texting with one thumb. Several users confused the buttons, sending incomplete messages. Although most didn't bother to send another message with the remainder of what they had intended to write, this could obviously be done. Perhaps only few mentioned these issues because texting on a small device is known to be problematic and hence their expectations were low.

choice of communication mode: In the third task, the person they were to communicate with had left them 2 text messages and 1 voice message; the context data indicated that she was driving and expected to be home in 35 minutes. 60% chose to give her a call with explanations such as: "she is driving so text is not a good option but she seems available"; "I called because her voice message said *give me a call*"; "it seemed urgent and this was the quickest way to reach her". Three people left a voice message and explained that the recipient was driving and therefore a phone call was not recommended, and three left a text message since it was the easiest for them. Seven said they considered the recipient's convenience, four considered only their own, one person considered both, and three considered neither.

The voice message the subjects listened to indeed said "give me a call when you get a chance", however this was said in a casual tone. Since the messages are from a fictitious person, and not from an insider as the system is envisioned to be used, the subjects' interpretation of the context varied. Those who thought it was urgent to get in touch with her did not believe convenience to be a relevant factor. One person misinterpreted the context data –he thought she had been home for the last 35 minutes, and not that her ETA was 35 minutes– he afterwards said that in that case he would have just waited until he saw that she had arrived home and only then phoned.

We also asked about general preferences of communication channels. Text messaging was the least preferred for sending but, significantly, what people said they preferred for receiving. Composing a text message on a small device with few buttons can indeed be tedious. The asynchronous text mode for reception is generally preferred since it can be accessed at any time and there are no privacy concerns with others listening in. It is also faster to read than to sequentially listen to audio.

appeal: Subjects were asked how much they liked the system (1-not at all, 7-very much), what they specifically liked and disliked about it, and who they would share this type of information with. People seemed to really like the system ($\mu = 6.07$, $\sigma = 0.96$); 2/3 would share this information with their spouse or boy/girl-friend, 7 would share with other family members such as siblings or parents, and 9 would share with some close friends. As to whether they would use such a system, 2/3 said "yes", 3 were undecided, and 2 said they probably would. However 6 said they would not wear it on their wrist (even assuming it was much smaller), and 2 were undecided.

As noted before, the predominant thing said against the system was the button interface. Many liked the icons and especially the information they convey: "this is the perfect device for me, often I call just to get the information that I can just see here". Someone noted that he would like the context data to feel more in touch with his girlfriend and other friends who are all on the other side of the Atlantic.

Comments regarding the different communication modalities were very positive: "I really like the features in this watch. In general I hate all-in-one devices, but this one is great. It groups together things that make sense, they all have to do with communication, and in a simple way"; "it let's me communicate more politely"; "I like the blurring of the boundaries between message types". Overall, subjects enjoyed the trial, found the technology stimulating, and wanted to talk about it at length afterwards. We find this very encouraging.

One surprising result was that seven of our subjects no longer wear watches. For some this is due to the physical constraints (heavy, make you sweaty, etc.), while many noted that the time is readily available, e.g. on their mobile phones, computers, or clocks in the environment. Clearly people who don't wear watches are less inclined to a technology that you wear on your wrist, but if the phone and the watch become the same gadget, this new trend may be reversed. In any case, a surprising number of people liked the technology; those who don't want it on their wrist would like to have a device you could clip to the belt or put in a pocket, or simply on a conventional mobile phone. Not having the device located in the periphery of visual attention would require rethinking the design of the interaction, perhaps relying more on auditory or tactile cues.

6.3   Future Steps

Except for completing the sensor integration, we have a fully functional prototype, in the shape of a wristwatch, built using a real phone. The watch is about 1.5 times the size we would eventually like it to be; new generation phones with their smaller screens will help reduce the size. We have identified a few problems with the current user interface; these will be addressed in the next version. While we don't claim *WatchMe* is suitable for everyone, a significant number of people who used it were very positive. More evaluation would be needed before it were made into a product.

Our previous work successfully evaluated both the GPS, location and route finders, and accelerometer-based classifiers. We do not yet have quantitative data as to the performance of the three classes of sensors (GPS, accelerometer, microphone) operating jointly, but since they are mutually independent we don't anticipate difficulties with fusion of these sensors. Nonetheless we will certainly evaluate the classification component in the field. More importantly, we would like to evaluate how friends or couples would actually use *WatchMe* in real life. This requires robust enough engineering so that they can be taken out of the lab for periods of several months. We're especially concerned with issues of trust and confidence in security of the data between users who are intimate friends.

Our work is predicated in the belief of the importance of having a working prototype to properly evaluate people's response to the underlying concepts. For example, a person who in the survey had expressed some reservations about such a technology, was very enthusiast when she used the prototype in the user study. Each iteration of *WatchMe* has required new hardware and some engineering help from Motorola. We would like to express our sincere gratitude for their extensive support during the course of this project.

References

1. Ackerman, M., Hindus, D., Mainwaring, S., and Starr, B. (1997) Hanging on the 'Wire: A Field Study of an Audio-Only Media Space. *Transactions on Computer-Human Interaction* (TOCHI), vol. 4, no.1, pp.39-66.
2. AIM, Oct 2002. http://news.com.com/2100-1023-963699.html
3. Bao, L. (2003) Physical Activity Recognition from Acceleration Data under Semi-Naturalistic Conditions. M.Eng. Thesis Electrical Engineering and Computer Science, Massachusetts Institute of Technology, Sept.'03.
4. Begole, J., Tang, J., Smith, R., and Yankelovich, N. (2002) Work Rhythms: Analyzing Visualizations of Awareness Histories of Distributed Groups. *Proceedings of the CSCW 2002 Conference on Computer Supported Cooperative Work*, pp. 334-343.
5. Buchenau, M. and, Fulton, J. (2000) Experience Prototyping. *DIS '00 Symposium on Designing Interactive Systems*, pp. 424-433.
6. Chang, A., O'Modhrain, S., Jacob, R., Gunther, E. and Ishii, H. (2002) ComTouch: Design of a Vibrotactile Communication Device. *DIS '02 Symposium on Designing Interactive Systems,* pp. 312-320.
7. Clarkson, B., Mase, K., and Pentland, A. (2000) Recognizing user context via wearable sensors. *Proceedings Fourth International Symposium on Wearable Computers*, pp. 69–76.
8. Dourish, P. and Bly, S. (1992) Portholes: Supporting Awareness in a Distributed Work Group. *Proceedings of the CHI '92 Conference on Human Factors in Computing Systems*, pp.541-547.
9. Erickson, T., Smith, D.N., Kellogg, W.A., Laff, M., Richards, J.T. and Bradner, E. (1999) Socially Translucent Systems: Social Proxies, Persistent Conversation and the Design of "Babble". *Proceedings of the CHI '99 Conference on Human Factors in Computing Systems,* pp. 72-79.
10. Erickson, T. (2002) Ask not for Whom the Cell Phone Tolls: Some Problems with the Notion of Context-Aware Computing. *Communications of the ACM.* Vol. 45, No. 2, pp.102-104.
11. Fish, R., Kraut, R., Root, R., and Rice, R. (1992) Evaluating Video as a Technology for Informal Communication. *Proceedings of the CHI '92 Conference on Human Factors in Computing Systems,* pp.37-48.
12. Fukumoto, M., Tonomura, Y. (1999) Whisper: A Wristwatch Style Wearable Handset. *Pro ceedings of the CHI '99 Conference on Human Factors in Computing Systems*, pp.112-119.
13. Grimmer, N., (2001) Heart2Heart. *Winner of Intel Student Design Competition 2001.* http://www.baychi.org/calendar/20010508/#1
14. Grinter, R. E. and M. Eldridge. (2001) 'y do tngrs luv 2 txt msg?', in W. Prinz, M. Jarke, Y. Rogers, K. Schmidt and V. Wulf (eds.): *Proceedings of the Seventh European Conference on Computer- Supported Cooperative Work ECSCW '01*, pp. 219-238.
15. Hinckley K., Pierce, J., Sinclair, M., and Horvitz, E. (2000) Sensing techniques for mobile interaction. *ACM User Interface Software and Technology*, CHI Letters 2: 91–100.
16. Horvitz, E., Jacobs, A. and Hovel, D. (1999) Attention-sensitive alerting. *Proceedings of UAI '99 Conference on Uncertainty in Artificial Intelligence,* pp.305-313.

17. Hudson, S., Fogarty, J., Atkeson, C., Forlizzi, J., Kiesler, S., Lee, J. and Yang, J. (2003) Predicting Human Interruptibility with Sensors: A Wizard of Oz Feasibility Study, *Proceedings of CHI '03 Conference on Human Factors in Computing Systems,* pp. 257-264.

18. Isaacs, E., Walendowski, A., Ranganthan, D. (2002) Hubbub: A sound-enhanced mobile instant messenger that supports awareness and opportunistic interactions. *Proceedings of the CHI '02 Conference on Human Factors in Computing Systems,* pp. 179-186.

19. Krumm, J., Cermak, G., and Horvitz, E. (2003) RightSPOT: A Novel Sense of Location for a Smart Personal Object. *Proceedings of Ubicomp 2003: Ubiquitous Computing,* pp. 36-43.

20. Marmasse, N., and Schmandt, C. (2000) Location-aware information delivery with comMotion. *Proceedings of HUC2000 International Symposium on Handheld and Ubiquitous Computing,* pp. 157-171.

21. Marmasse, N., and Schmandt, C. (2002) A User-Centered Location Model. Personal and Ubiquitous Computing, vol 6, no. 5-6, pp. 318-321.

22. Milewski, A. and Smith T. (2000) Providing Presence Cues to Telephone Users. *Proceedings of the CSCW 2000 Conference on Computer Supported Cooperative Work,* pp. 89-96.

23. MunguiaTapia, E. and Marmasse, N. (2003) Wireless Sensors for Real-time Activity Recognition, http://web.media.mit.edu/~emunguia/portfolio/html/wsensors.htm

24. Mynatt, E. and Tullio, J. (2001) Inferring calendar event attendance. *Proceedings of the IUI 2001 Conference on Intelligent User Interfaces,* pp. 121-128.

25. Nardi, B., Whittaker, S, and Bradner, E. (2000) Interaction and Outeraction: Instant Messaging in Action. *Proceedings of the CSCW 2000 Conference on Computer Supported Cooperative Work,* pp. 79-88.

26. Nelson, L., Bly, S., and Sokoler, T. (2001) Quiet Calls: Talking Silently on Mobile Phones. *Proceedings of SIGCHI conference on Human Factors in Computing Systems,* pp. 174-181.

27. Paulos E. (2003) Connexus: A Communal Interface. http://www.intelresearch.net/Publications/Berkeley/070220031047_135.pdf

28. Root, R. (1988) Design of a Multi-Media Vehicle for Social Browsing. *Proceedings of the CSCW '88 Conference on Computer Supported Cooperative Work,* pp.25-38.

29. Schmidt, A., Takaluoma, A., and Mäntyjärvi, J. (2000) Context-Aware Telephony Over WAP. *Personal and Ubiquitous Computing,* vol. 4, no. 4, pp. 225-229.

30. Tang, J. and Rua, M. (1994) Montage: Providing Teleproximity for Distributed Groups. *Proceedings of CHI '94 Conference on Human Factors in Computing Systems,* pp. 37-43.

31. Tang, J., Yankelovich, N., Begole, J., VanKleek, M., Li, F., and Bhalodia, J. (2001) ConNexus to Awarenex: Extending awareness to mobile users. *Proceedings of the CHI '01 Conference on Human Factors in Computing Systems,* pp.221-228.

32. Vallejo G. (2003) ListenIN: Ambient Auditory Awareness at Remote Places, M.S. Thesis, Program in Media Arts and Sciences, MIT Media Lab.

33. Want R., Hopper A., Falcao V., and Gibbons J. (1992) The Active Badge Location System. *ACM Transactions on Information Systems,* vol. 10, pp. 99-102.

Everyday Encounters with Context-Aware Computing in a Campus Environment

Louise Barkhuus[1] and Paul Dourish[2]

[1] Department of Design and Use of IT,
The IT University of Copenhagen,
Rued Langgaards Vej 7, Copenhagen 2300
Denmark
barkhuus@it.edu
[2] Laboratory for Ubiquitous Computing and Interaction,
Donald Bren School of Information and Computer Sciences,
University of California, Irvine,
Irvine, CA 92697-3425, USA
jpd@ics.uci.edu

Abstract. As ubiquitous computing technologies mature, they must move out of laboratory settings and into the everyday world. In the process, they will increasingly be used by heterogeneous groups, made up of individuals with different attitudes and social roles. We have been studying an example of this in a campus setting. Our field work highlights the complex relationships between technology use and institutional arrangements – the roles, relationships, and responsibilities that characterize social settings. In heterogeneous groups, concerns such as location, infrastructure, access, and mobility can take on quite different forms, with very different implications for technology design and use.

1 Introduction

Since its origins, a fundamental motivation for Ubiquitous Computing research has been to extend the computational experience beyond its traditional desktop confines. Advances in the processing power and networking capacity of computational devices, along with progress in power management, size and cost reduction, etc., allow us to envision a world in which the experience of computation can be extended throughout the everyday environment, available where and when it is needed.

Shifting the context of computation from the restrictive but well-understood confines of the desktop to the broader and messier environs of the everyday world brings both problems and opportunities. Amongst the problems are the difficulties of managing power [32], locating people, devices and activities [20, 33], and managing interactions between mobile devices [4, 26]. Amongst the opportunities is the ability to adapt to the environment. Recognizing that different places and settings have different properties and are associated with different activities, researchers have become interested in how computational devices can respond

N. Davies et al. (Eds.): UbiComp 2004, LNCS 3205, pp. 232–249, 2004.

to aspects of the settings within which they are used, customizing the interfaces, services, and capabilities that they offer in response to the different settings of use. Context-aware computing attempts to make the context in which technologies are deployed and used into a configuration parameter for those technologies.

A range of context-aware computing technologies have been developed and explored. Perhaps the most common context-aware systems are those that respond to aspects of their location (and, by inference, the social activities being conducted in those settings), e.g. [2, 15, 31]. Context-aware computing presents a number of challenges on technical, analytic and conceptual grounds; not only are there difficulties in inferring context from noisy information, but the very notion of context as a stable feature of social settings has been challenged and is an active area of research consideration, e.g. [18, 23, 30]. However, in this paper, we want to consider context of a rather different sort – the social, organizational, and institutional contexts into which context-aware and ubiquitous computing technologies are deployed.

This broader form of context has, of course, long been an important concern for interactive system developers of all sorts. Research and development experiences over the past thirty years have repeatedly taught us that the success or failure of technologies depend at least as much on the appropriateness of those technologies for specific settings of use as they do on the features of the technologies themselves. Accordingly, as Grudin has noted [25], the focus of attention in interactive system development has gradually moved outwards, from the technology itself to the setting within which that technology will be employed. However, despite ubiquitous computing's interest in understanding how technologies might respond to 'context', this broader context and its impacts on the adoption and use of ubiquitous computing systems has been largely neglected.

In this paper, we report on an empirical investigation of the use of a ubiquitous computing system blending mobile and location-based technologies to create augmented experiences for university students. In particular, we focus on how the technology fits into broader social contexts of student life and the classroom experience. Our study highlights a number of features of student living – from broad concerns such as the temporal structure of everyday life to mundane concerns such as infrastructure access – that can significantly influence the effectiveness and uptake of novel technologies, and in turn suggests that studies of the social organization of everyday activity can provide a strong foundation for computer system design.

2   Institutional Analysis

Our goal in this paper is not to present an evaluation of specific technologies, but rather to use one particular technological setting to reflect upon some broader patterns of technology use, with implications for future designs. Analytically, we take an institutional approach.

2.1   Institutions

Institutional analysis is a 'meso-level' approach to understanding social settings. It falls between the fine-grained analysis of particular settings, such as ethnomethodology, and the broad accounts of social action captured by more 'classical' sociological approaches, such as Marxist or structuralist analysis.

'Institutions' are recurrent social patterns that structure and provide settings for action; they define roles, responsibilities, and expectations that shape and give meaning to encounters between people [10]. Institutions, then, are not specific social entities, but common social forms. Examples of institutions include the family, organized religion, professional sports, education, the law, and traditional medicine. What is of particular interest is the *enactment* of institutions; that is, the way in which they are produced and reproduced in everyday conduct. Institutions give shape and meaning to social interactions, but are also produced and sustained through those interactions.

Given that many ubiquitous computing technologies are developed, deployed, and evaluated in university settings, our particular institutional concern is with student life on a university campus and how these institutional arrangements manifest themselves for students day-to-day. Institutional arrangements – the role of students in the university, their relationships to each other and to other social groups, the expectations placed upon them – are things that students routinely encounter and navigate. They do so in their formal interaction with the university bureaucracy, such as when registering for classes, graduating, or facing disciplinary proceedings; more importantly, though, they also do so casually in the course of every day, as they deal with each other and even with the physical fabric of the campus.

2.2   Institutional Perspectives on Student Life

We are interested in the institutional character of student life. A number of studies have examined aspects of this.

Eckert's [19] study of high school student life identifies the central significance (to the students) of social polarization, around participation not just in the school's formal program, but in its *agenda*. In her studies, 'jocks' and 'burnouts' are social categories that pervade every aspect of life – from what to wear, who to talk with, and where to have lunch, to participation in class, forms of socializing, and expectations of life after graduation. Competition between these social groups, and the process of moving between peripheral and central positions within them, is a dominating theme in the everyday life of the students.

Becker and colleagues [5] studied specifically academic elements of students' college experiences. In other domains (personal, political, social, etc.) students are able to negotiate with university authorities or claim some autonomy from them, but within the academic arena (classes, course requirements, curricula, etc.) they are subject to the dominance of the university. Like others in positions of subjection, they respond by creating an 'oppositional culture' to protect themselves from the whims and vageries of faculty and administration. Becker and colleagues describe an essentially economic model in which work is 'traded' for a good grade point average (GPA); intellectual interests are, to a large extent, subjugated to an overriding concern with a 'good' GPA (where 'good' is, clearly, a relative term), which in turn affects everything from parental approval and financial support to social standing and dating opportunities. Here, students model their relations with faculty and the university as an exchange system, and the various aspects of college life are refracted through the GPA lens.

In addition to illustrating aspects of the structure of student life, these studies also illustrate what it means to take an institutional perspective; they focus on relationship between students' mundane experiences and the patterns of roles, relationships and responsibilities that make up the domain. These structures provide the interpretive resources that everyday experience is meaningful to people within social settings. Here, we take a similar approach, focusing especially on the place of technology in students' everyday engagement in campus life. In analysing our field data, we are interested in how technology is encountered, used, and applied in institutional settings.

3   Ubiquitous Computing in a Campus Setting

The motivation for our study was to look at ubiquitous computing technologies 'in practice.' Our interests were two-fold. First, we wanted to examine the factors that influence adoption and use of ubiquitous computing technologies, and to analyze the factors that contribute to success and failure. Second, we wanted to study the *emergent practices* of ubiquitous computing – aspects of collective practice that emerge when a technology is put into the hands of an active user community.

There are many reasons to expect that campus environments are ideal for the development, deployment, and testing of ubiquitous computing technologies. Clearly, many technologies are developed in university research, and campus environments are therefore convenient. They are highly networked, with strong infrastructure support services. They are populated by large numbers of potential (and cheap) test subjects, who are adept with computers and eager to explore new technologies and opportunities.

Many ideas for ubiquitous technology have been proposed to facilitate campus environments. Weiser for example, made several suggestions for context-aware and ubiquitous computing technologies for campus environments; some have been deployed in the Active Campus (buddy and TA locator), others are related to the general student life (diet monitor) [36]. Several similar functions have also been implemented in the 'Aware Campus' tour guide at Cornell University [12]. It provides visiting students with a social map, illustrating where other students have visited and how much. The Aware Campus guide also lets users attach virtual text notes to a specific location; the Aware Campus refer to this as 'annotated space', where Active Campus calls it virtual graffiti.

Using computing technologies for university teaching is not only widely applied but also well researched. Research generally focuses on improving the lecturing situation [22] and the class atmosphere [35]. Other research focuses on augmented note taking such as NotePals that gives a group of users, for example as a class, access to each other's notes [16]. NotePals is a PDA based system that supports note and document sharing; in its use it is similar to Active Class which is presented in the next section. An example of a larger project is Classroom 2000 (now called eClass) at Georgia Tech [1]. The goal of Classroom 2000 was two-fold: to facilitate the classroom with a way of capturing the lecture for later access to the students and to provide the students with an efficient method for note-taking [3]. Through evaluation the Classroom 2000 team found that although students claim they changed their note-taking habits, they didn't feel strongly that their performance in the class had improved. The students in our study had similar comments that even though the technology can change habits and study structures, their overall performance has not changed.

Another relevant piece of research investigates the increasing use of laptops in the university classroom in general [13]. The authors draw out the advantages such as instant feedback (not unlike the polls and rating sections of Active Class) and online quizzes. Although they point to negative effects such as cheating on tests by surfing for answers when this is not allowed, the overall problems of inattentive students that we find are not mentioned. Moreover, the authors focus on lectures where all students have laptops, meaning classes where this is obligatory. Although requiring all students to have laptops would surely increase the use level of Active Class, it is not likely that such an initiative would happen at public universities any time soon. We have in our study looked at more realistic factors, considering the present state of technology to find what premises exist for context-aware technology in a campus environment.

3.1 Research Setting

Our empirical data focused on the elements of the Active Campus system, developed and deployed at UC San Diego [9, 24]. Active Campus is a pioneering effort in wide-scale ubiquitous computing design. To date, most 'ubiquitous' computing experiments have been far from ubiquitous, generally restricted to specific laboratories and buildings or to specific research groups. Consequently, it has been hard to develop an understanding of what it means for ubiquitous computing to be used ubiquitously – over a wide area, with an expectation that it is available to others, and so on. In contrast, then, Active Campus is designed to explore the broader challenges and effects of introducing ubiquitous computing technologies on a larger scale, both in terms of infrastructure and use. It aims to support students, teachers, researchers and visitors across the UC San Diego campus, and it has attempted to introduce these technologies on a fairly broad scale, encompassing hundreds of users.

Active Campus is an umbrella project which draws together many technologies, functions, applications and services. The core Active Campus infrastructure provides a range of location-based services available through mobile and handheld 802.11b clients, on a densely available network across the campus.

Access point triangulation allows 802.11b-based devices to identify their own locations, and some facilities support integration with other mobile devices such as advanced mobile phones. Services including navigation mechanisms, providing maps showing users' presence as well as landmarks, and graffiti that the users can 'tag'. Further, Active Campus provides a collective instant messaging client, so users can message each other through the system, and a 'conversation locater', where open conversations are placed at certain locations. This way, other people can see where the conversation actually took place for both/all people in the discussion.

Active Class is part of Active Campus [28]. Unlike the core Active Campus functionality, which is designed for general use, Active Class is designed specifically to support classroom teaching. Specifically, it uses mobile devices to provide a further channel of communication between teacher and students in lecture settings. It is built around three primary functions – questions, polls, and ratings. The question section makes it possible for students to ask questions anonymously over the internet and to vote on which questions they think are important to answer. Anyone can answer the questions as well and do this anonymously, but most of the time, it is meant to be raised in class and answered by the teacher. The poll section enables the administrator (usually a teaching assistant) to post a question, for example in regards to which new material should be given extra attention, and the students can then indicate their preference real time; polls allow students to vote on responses. Finally, the rating section lets students rate the speed of the lecture as 'too slow', 'just about right' and 'too fast'. The students can also rate the quality of the lecture on a scale from one to six. The intent of Active Class, then, is to provide further channels of communication between teacher and students, and to broaden participation in class by lowering barriers to interaction.

3.2   Method

Since our research goals were to look at influences of adoption and analyze the emergent practices from an institutional view point, we found primarily qualitative research methods to be appropriate. Rather than simply counting instances of activities, our goal was to understand the technological setting from the perspective of the participants.

Our study took place over a period of 4 weeks, from a point almost half-way into the academic quarter until the last class. We tracked two sets of users. The first consisted of upper-division undergraduate students enrolled in a large (141 students) computer science class on the subject of advanced compiler theory. The second set consisted of freshman students enrolled in a small (4 students), discussion-oriented 4-week seminar class in new media arts (in fact, the topic of the class was the impact of ubiquitous computing classes on future campus life).

We gathered data in three different ways: first, through in-class and out-of-class observations; second, through questionnaires administered to class members; and third, through more focussed interviews with a smaller number of students.

The questionnaire for the freshman seminar aimed at retrieving basic knowledge of the student's experience with ubiquitous technologies and the questionnaire for the larger class focused on their use of Active Class and general class behavior. Observations were made throughout the 4-week period in all the seminar classes and all of the bi-weekly computer science classes. Observational notes were made constantly in regards to the students overall behavior and the activities on the Active Campus technology real-time. The observation was conducted as participant observation but although the observer blended fairly well into the large class, the teacher made the class aware that they were being 'observed' and thereby created an awareness about the observation. The advantage of this was that the students who were interviewed afterwards had thought more about their use of Active Campus and it was not the observer's impression that the awareness of observation had changed their behavior. The seminar, on the other hand, was such a small class that the observer became very noticeable. At first this seemed to create shyness among the students, but after the first half hour, the excitement of the technology and the focus of the class took over their attention.

Interviews were conducted one-on-one in order to gain closer insight into the factors of use in relation to both parts of the system. The interviews with the seminar students were both one-on-one and in groups during class time. Since the seminar was much less structured and often took place outside on campus, the interviews naturally became less structured and sometimes mixed with the observation. All interviews were semi-structured, focusing on common issues but encouraging the respondents to discuss other things that they might find relevant for the system or just general campus behavior.

3.3   Participants

The participant selection was limited by the general use of Active Campus and Active Class. At the time of this study, only one class (as well as the seminar) used Active Class and a limited number of students used Active Campus itself. 35 students participated by answering questionnaires, where four of them were the participants of the freshman seminar and 31 were students in the advanced compiler systems class where Active Class was used. The four freshman seminar students were interviewed as well as 8 of the computer science class students. The Freshman seminar consisted of three females and one male, three of them being 18 and one girl being 19 years old. The eight computer science students were all seniors, between 22 and 26. Six were male and two were female. Table 1 shows general demographics of the participants from the Active Class questionnaire and observational study.

4   Campus Experiences of Ubiquitous Computing

One reason that students (especially computer science students) are often selected as a target population for trials of novel technologies is that young people are often early adopters of digital technologies. Certainly, we found that our

Table 1. Participants of the Active Campus study.

	Active Class Data		Seminar Data	Collective Data
	Questionnaire	Observation	Observation & questionnaire	Interviews
N	31	98–130	4	12
Average age	22.5	N/A	18.25	21.8
Females	23 percent	7–14 percent	75 percent	42 percent
Level of study	4th–6th year undergrad	N/A	Freshman	Freshman–6th year undergrad

participants fit this general profile. Only two of our 35 participants did not have a mobile phone and the average ownership was 3.7 years. Over half (55%) had an MP3 player. Many (42%) had a PDA but only two students were seen to use them in class. Several had also owned pagers before but only one person still used his.

However, familiarity with, and adoption of, novel technologies does not necessarily lead to their use across settings. So, for example, while 65% of the respondents to the questionnaire reported owning a laptop, only 31% of these reported always bringing their laptop to class. Further, observation showed that only a few actually *used* those laptops in class; in interviews, many reported that their laptops would remain in their bags, despite the facilities available for them. During the course of the study, 13-17% of the students had laptops up and running on their desk during class. So, although technology penetration is often cited as supporting the adoption of new applications and services, it is clearly a necessary but not sufficient condition.

4.1 Mobility

Mobile access to information and services is a central element of the ubiquitous computing model. Ubiquitous computing technologies are, almost by their nature, mobile ones – they move around with us in the world, and provide us with access to information and resources as we move from place to place. Accordingly, a good deal of attention has been focused on user communities on the move – tourists [11, 15], conference attendees [17], and others. Focusing on those with a high need for mobility has allowed us to explore the sorts of location-based services that might be useful. Students are, on the face of it, another group whose activities are inherently mobile, as they move around a campus setting from class to class. Active Campus incorporates a range of location-based facilities, such as geo-messaging, navigation, and 'buddy finders' as a way to help mobile students.

Looking at how location and mobility manifest itself among undergraduate students (who are the primary target population for Active Campus), we find a different set of factors influencing their behavior. These students are indeed highly mobile, moving around the campus between classes, laboratories and social spaces. However, we would characterize the students' experience not so much as *mobile* but more as *nomadic*.

The critical distinction is the presence of a so-called 'base'. Many of the research studies of mobile work conducted to date focus on *roving* in office work. In this form of mobility, people may move around through a space, but they also have a 'base' of some sort – a desk, in the case of the designers studied by Bellotti and Bly [7], a control room in the case of the waste-water treatment plant described by Bertelsen and Bødker [8], and so on. In the university setting, this is also the experience of faculty, researchers, and graduate students, but it is not the experience of undergraduate students, most of whom have no assigned space. What the students experience is not simply mobility, but nomadism – a continual movement from place to place, none of which is inhabited more than temporarily, none of which can be relied upon, and with no notion of individual ownership. These issues of 'base' and ownership set the case of undergraduate students apart from the simpler case of roving workers.

The students we interviewed talk about how their classes are spread out through the day. For them it means that they have a lot of in-between time where they either study, meet up with friends, eat or even sleep. Not a lot of space is reserved for these breaks and the 'Library Lounge', according to our participants is almost always full of students reading or typing on the few available desk-top computers. One student is lucky enough to have a desk in a shared office because he works on campus as well and describes a typical day:

> These days I am just so busy with school. Basically I wake up to come to a class or I come to work. I work at [local research center] . . . After that I'll generally have a break, my classes are somewhat spaced out. During the break period I either eat food or do school work. . . I tend to like walking around, sometimes I do [school work] in my office, sometimes I do it various places around the Price Center. A lot of of the time I go to the Library Lounge . . . There are always a lot of people sitting around there, working or just hanging out.

This nomadic existence leads to a number of mundane practical concerns which are, nonetheless, extremely significant for technology adoption. One of these concerns the material that must be carried around, and its weight. Those of us with offices and desks may be mobile, but need only take with us what we need for the next meeting, class, or appointment; for the students we studied, though, the daily environment provided few places to leave belongings (and fewer yet that could be reliably returned to between activities). This places a significant barrier to discretionary use of computer equipment. One of the students even reported that he found his PDA too heavy to carry around!

Another significant consideration is access to traditional infrastructure services, and most particularly power. While sources of power are certainly available to students, they tend not to be *reliably* available, and reliability is critically important when one is budgeting a scarce resource. If the students are not sure when they are able to charge their laptop next time, they are likely to be reluctant to use it for anything other than essential tasks. Another influential factor is one of social kind. Five of the eight computer science students we interviewed reported that they preferred to go to the computer science lab to their programming projects and other computer required tasks. They all reported that this was mainly for social reasons, here they could also talk to other students and even sometimes get help with their work. Two of these students felt that lab work contributed significantly to their social life and the community of their class. They preferred this to working by themselves on a laptop. The behavior indicates that the level of mobility fosters a need for some kind of social but work oriented meeting place but since the lab is common and doesn't allow personal space, it does not offer a work base.

4.2   Location

Separately from the problems of mobility, we can also ask, how and when does location manifest itself as a practical problem for students? Location-based services developed in other settings point to a range of ways in which ubiquitous computing technologies can help people resolve location-based problems - the most common being finding resources, navigating in unfamiliar environments, and locating people.

As we have noted, students' experience is primarily nomadic, and since their activities and concerns are driven as much by the demands of social interaction as by their studies, we had anticipated that services such as the people finder would be of value, helping them to locate each other as they moved around a campus environment. However, further examination showed that, in fact, location rarely manifests itself for them, practically. The students' nomadic existence is, nonetheless, strongly structured; the students we studied live highly ordered lives, at least within the confines of a particular academic quarter. Their location at any time in the week is dependent on their schedule of classes, and the locations where those classes are held. One student describes her lunch habits:

> Well, it is set up, like before we go to class. My room mate and I have lunch every Monday, Wednesday, Friday, because we have class that get out at the same time. Tuesdays, Thursday I meet my guy-friends at [a fast food restaurant on campus]. It is a set thing.

Because of the regularity of their schedules, the students, then, tend to find themselves in the same part of the campus at specific times in the week. Similarly, their friends live equally ordered lives, with locations determined by class schedules, and our respondents seemed as familiar with aspects of their friend's schedules as with their own. Mutually-understood schedules, then, provide them with the basis for coordination. For example, students tend to have lunch with the same people, and in the same places, on a weekly basis, those places and people determined primarily by their collective schedules.

Our observations then suggest that, for undergraduate students, location manifests itself as a quite different problem than it does for faculty, researchers, and graduate students. While the experience of the regular employees of a university is of people who are hard to find due to schedule variability, and who might be sought in a 'home location' but found somewhere else, these problems appear quite differently to undergraduates. There being no home base, students have no expectation of being able to find each other in fixed places; instead, class schedules become a primary orienting mechanism around which location is determined and coordination is achieved.

4.3   Using Technology in the Classroom

As we suggested earlier, the Active Class component of Active Campus provides specific support for the classroom experience. In addition to the practical matters concerning the use of technology in campus settings in general, the classroom introduces a number of important considerations all of its own, in terms of both design and activities.

The primary focus for support is the communication channel between students and teachers. Active Class provides a range of mechanisms to increase this communication, through questions, polls, and ratings. One specific feature of the Active Class design is that questions are anonymous. By making questions anonymous, the designers of Active Class hoped to overcome possible pressure on students, encourage question-asking, and narrow the gap between those who participate in class and those who do not. When asking the students if they ever felt that shy about asking questions, three of the eight students interviewed reported that they did not feel comfortable at all asking questions in class. They also reported that they only answered the teacher's question if they knew it was '150% correct'.

We observed the use of Active Class during eight lectures over the course of our study. Participation using the system was lower than might be hoped, due to some of the problems listed earlier; the practical difficulties of making use of laptops and PDA devices, especially in a class held towards the end of the day meant that only a small proportion of the class would make use of the Active Class facilities.

Although students were asked to log into Active Class by the professor in the beginning of each lecture, only few actually did so. Although between 13 and 20 laptops (and 0–2 PDAs) were in use in every lecture, only between two and eight users were logged in to Active Class. Similarly, rather than being related to the number of laptops in use, the number of logins to Active Class generally decreased through the quarter. When asking the students through the questionnaires why they did not log in, they responded that they had no questions and therefore could not see the use of logging in. In fact, according to the questionnaire results, the laptops in class were rarely used for anything other than casual surfing or communication (email or instant messaging). Only a few (7%) of the students who brought their laptops to class used them for note taking.

Interviews suggested that one major factor of not using the laptop in class was its limited options for unstructured note taking. Notes often consist of loose drawings of stacks and queues and memory allocation analogies, and a text editor does not allow these types of notes. Because the auditorium's chairs are limited to flip-up tables with room for just one Letter-sized (A4) notebook, the students had to choose between a paper notebook or a laptop. One student said that when he could afford a tablet PC, he would start using it more in class, because it facilitates pen-based input. Previous user studies of Active Campus arrive at similar findings that the PDA or laptop competes with paper in the sense of 'desk real estate' [24].

Ironically, this small degree of participation through Active Class can end up exacerbating the effects that it was designed to relieve. Since only a small number of people were using the system, their participation was more visible. Like verbal question-asking, it was restricted to a subset of class participants. In our observations, use of the system was actually higher amongst those who were also attending to the class and participating more fully (sitting towards the front, asking verbal questions, etc.) Although designed to broaden participation by incorporating more people more fully into the class activities, Active Campus in this restricted setting seemed instead to heighten the participation of those who were already engaged with the material, providing them with more channels through which they could engage, and new avenues for exploring material and participating in class. Ironically, then, this may broaden rather than narrow the gulf between those who participate more and those who participate less. This is, perhaps, a consequence of some of the other features noted; Active Class might serve its original function if the technology were used more universally, so that using the system were less distinctive and notable.

By exploring how much attention people paid to the lecture we aimed to see if laptops was a disturbing factor and what the level of attention seen from the students point of view actually was. One claimed to pay close attention to the lecture in the questionnaire returns and two admitted that they were not paying attention at all. The latter two were not using laptops during the lecture, which indicated that non-attention is not necessarily due to laptop use! The rest of the students placed themselves in the two middle categories when rating their own level of attention ('followed most of the lecture' or 'tried to follow the lecture but drifted off occasionally'). The attention level was also affected by the students' understanding of the subject. One student admitted in the interview that there was a lot of the material she simply did not understand. When asked if she thinks the lecturer goes too fast and that perhaps Active Class could help her she responded:

> Uhm.... a little bit but for the most case I like, when I am in there I kind of don't understand a lot of the stuff that he is talking about... I just kind of wait 'till the end when he... pauses afterwards when I can look over it and just like talk about it with my friends...

We found a slight correlation between where the student sat in the particular class and how many different tasks the student did on his/her computer. The further up towards the back the student had placed him/herself, the more tasks the student did on the laptop.

Table 2. Observational results from the use of Active Class.

	Number of Students in class	Number of laptops observed up and running	Number of students logged in to Active Class	Number of questions asked through Active Class
Lecture 1	132	16	8	, 4
Lecture 2	97	14	5	1
Lecture 3	130	17	6	0
Lecture 4	98	13	3	0
Lecture 5	105	18	3	1
Lecture 6	140	20	4	0
Lecture 7	98	17	2	2
Lecture 8	138	18	2	0

Of course, it's important to note that Active Class is not the only technology in use in the classroom; it must coexist with existing technologies for lecture presentation, such as Powerpoint, whiteboards, etc. Powerpoint naturally lends a relatively linear structure to the presentation. Once in a while the professor draws on the slides to emphasize a point (or to correct typing mistakes), through his tablet PC. This increases the interaction that the teacher can provide and enables him to illustrate points raised in class that otherwise would need black board space and thereby a shift in medium. However, the classic path of the lecture reinforces the fairly static one-way interaction. Since the introduction of technology for the sake of technology is not desired in a class room, the limitations in technology use are also partly due to the lecturing tradition as it is present at universities today.

5   Discussion

Although we have focused on Active Class and Active Campus in this description, it is not our intention to critique these systems in particular. They provide concrete examples of a set of general phenomena which are of great importance when attempting to design effective ubiquitous computing experiences at a large-scale, as the ubicomp research community must do to be successful. We focus on five concerns here.

The first is that technological designs must be sensitive to the *variability of institutional arrangements*. This does not simply mean that different user groups have different needs; rather, it means that technology use is systematically related to people's roles and relationships towards each other and towards other infrastructures and technologies. The particular relevance of this concern is that design practice frequently crosses institutional boundaries, and it is critical that we are attentive to these boundaries and their implications. So, as we have seen in the case of Active Campus and its provision of location-based services, "location" manifests itself in daily life quite differently for undergraduate students than it does for faculty, staff, graduate students, and researchers in a university setting. Undergraduate students, because of their role in the university and its life, find themselves subject to a quite different set of demands; the notion of location as a problem in the way in which researchers encounter it requires certain institutional opportunities – for discretionary movement, control over one's own time, flexible scheduling, etc. – that simply does not arise for students. This same problem of institutional discontinuities has also affected other ubiquitous computing efforts, most especially those concerning domestic technologies (which are subject to quite different institutional norms than obtain in office settings). As ubiquitous computing technologies move out of the laboratory, the issue of heterogeneous encounters with technology will become increasingly important. Cross-cultural studies of technology use, such as Bell's studies of the home [6] or Ito and Okabe's investigations of mobile telephony [27], are instructive in this regard.

Second, as others such as Edwards and Grinter [21] or Rodden and Benford [29] have noted, *quite different temporal dynamics apply to laboratory settings and real-world settings*. In laboratory settings, novel technologies and spaces are designed around each other; to set up a new experimental system, we can clear other things out of the way, set a new stage, and coordinate the arrival of different technologies. In real-world settings, though, new technologies must live alongside old ones, new work practices must live alongside old ones, and new forms of working space must coexist with those that are already there. An augmented classroom will also be used for traditional teaching; and similarly, new teaching practices may be introduced into settings that are designed for (and must still support) traditional teaching. Technology is *always, inherently* available differentially in real-world environments. Again, this is a consequence of the institutional perspective; it is a consequence of the ways in which ways of working become 'sedimented' in technological and physical settings.

Third, and relatedly, we must be *particularly attentive to infrastructures of all sorts*. As Star and Ruhleder [34] have noted, one property of infrastructures is that they are embedded in settings, and hence often become invisible. This applies not just to technological but also to procedural infrastructures (ways of achieving ends, such as administrative mechanisms and resources) and conceptual infrastructures (ways of making the world organizationally accountable, such as category systems and schematic models.) What is infrastructure to one person – invisible, unnoticed, and unquestioned – is an obstacle or source of major trouble to another. Infrastructures make their presence (or absence) felt largely through the difficulties that render them suddenly noticeable. In the case of the technologies we have discussed here, for example, the availability of power and the design of classroom seating, which are normally unnoticed elements of everyday campus life, become suddenly visible, apparent, and problematic. In retrospect, these may seem obvious, but it is this very taken-for-granted nature of everyday infrastructures that renders them so difficult to account for successfully in design. More importantly, this perspective on infrastructure places an emphasis not simply on the presence of certain kinds of technologies (power, networking, etc.) but on other elements that condition their practical 'availability', including control, ownership, legitimacy, training, etc. These are as much an aspect of 'ubiquity' as the presence of a technology.

Fourth, the institutional perspective we have been developing here suggests an alternative way to assess technology adoption. Our approach has been to look not simply at particular individuals and their use of the system, but rather at *the relationship between technology and local cultural practices*. While traditional usability analysis concerns specific individuals, the impacts of technology come not just from individual but from collective usage patterns. A collective perspective on the setting that we have been examining suggests new ways to think about the impact of technologies. In particular, rather than asking how specific students might use Active Class, we might ask rather how a *class* might adopt and use it. Clearly, the question mechanism in Active Class impacts the class as a whole, since the whole class hears the answers. Particular technical strategies have broader impact. For example, providing a public view of Active Class activity might extend the reach of the system to class members without networked devices; the impact of the system could be felt by the class as a whole.

Finally, our investigations draw particular attention to the fact that technologies of all sorts (digital, electrical, physical, etc.) are *a means by which relationships between social groups are enacted*. Social grouping are often stubbornly persistent, at east in the short term. Castells, for example, has noted that, while people's 'social reach' is amplified by access to the Internet, most people use the Internet to seek out others like them, rendering their immediate social contact group *less*, rather than more, diverse [14]. Similarly, while the instrumental role of information technology may be to promote interaction across social boundaries, it may also symbolically reinforce those boundaries. In the presence of other obstacles to common use, the adoption of a technology takes on a symbolic importance; it demonstrates affiliation in the face of adversity and, in a classroom setting, can reinforce the 'grade economy' described by Becker et al. [5] and the social polarization described by Eckert [19].

6   Conclusions

We set out to find how different structures influence the use and adoption of ubiquitous computing technology as well as to trace emergent practices for students in a campus setting. Where students, on the surface, seem like the perfect probes for new technology, their inherent social structures and high level of nomadicity creates a tension between their desired use and actual possibility for use. From the perspective of research, many settled practices and infrastructures within the campus environment are inhibiting not only the adoption of new technology but also the foundation for testing new technologies. Only by looking beyond the technologies themselves, towards the broader institutional arrangements within which they are embedded, can we begin to understand the premises for deployment of ubiquitous technology. General evaluation of new applications is important for purposes of usability but to generate further knowledge of the deeper use structures, for the purpose of future design, analyses of real implemented technologies are fundamental. These considerations underscore the importance of observational methods, studies of real-world practice, and in situ evaluation; and more broadly, they point towards the importance of analyses that look beyond surface features to the practices through which these empirical features are shaped, shared, and sustained.

Many of our observations involve not simply institutional arrangements, but rather how people playing different roles have quite different experiences of those institutions and settings. The developers of Active Campus may have encountered some of these problems earlier than most because their approach pioneers a broad-based use of ubiquitous computing technologies, one that encompasses many different groups. In many ways, it is only the broad scope of the Active Campus development that allows these observations to be made, and it is clear that, as we continue to move ubiquitous computing technologies out of the laboratory and into the everyday world, the concerns that we have explored here (and others like them) are likely to be encountered more regularly. Our observations here demonstrate how observational and qualitative methods can offer a set of sensitizing concepts to help attune designers to the everyday concerns that arise in the use of advanced technologies. In particular, they illustrate the importance of institutional arrangements in the development, adoption, appropriation, and use of ubiquitous computing technologies.

7   Acknowledgments

We would like to thank all the students of CS 131B and the freshman seminar VIS 87, section A00 for participating. We also thank William Griswold and Adriene Jenik for letting us observe and participate in their classes. This work was partly funded by The Danish National Center for IT Research (CIT#313), under the Location-Based Services project (within the LaCoMoCo research program), by the National Science Foundation under awards IIS-0133749, IIS-0205724 and IIS-0326105, and by Intel Corporation.

References

[1] G. Abowd. Classroom 2000. an experiment with the instrumentation of a living educational environment. *IBM Systems Journal*, 38(4):508–530, 1999.
[2] G. Abowd, C. G. Atkeson, J. Hong, S. Long, R. Kooper, and M. Pinkerton. Cyberguide: A mobile context-aware tour guide. *Wireless Networks*, 3:421–433, 1997.

248   Louise Barkhuus and Paul Dourish

[3] G. D. Abowd, C. G. Atkeson, J. Brotherton, T. Enqvist, P. Gulley, and J. LeMon. Investigating the capture, integration and access problem of ubiquitous computing in an educational setting. In *Proceedings of CHI '98*, pages 440–447, Los Angeles, CA, 1998. ACM Press.

[4] L. Barkhuus and A. K. Dey. Is context-aware computing taking control away from the user? three levels of interactivity examined. In *Proceedings of UbiComp 2003*, Seattle, Washington, 2003. Springer.

[5] H. Becker, B. Geer, and E. Hughes. *Making the Grade: The Academic Side of College Life*. Wiley, New York, US, 1968.

[6] G. Bell. Other homes: Alternative views of culturally situated technologies for the home. *Presented at CHI 2003 Workshop on Designing Culturally Situated Technologies for the Home*, 2003.

[7] V. Bellotti and S. Bly. Walking away from the desktop computer: distributed collaboration and mobility in a product design team. In *Proceedings of CSCW*, pages 209–218. ACM Press, 1996.

[8] O. Bertelsen and S. Bødker. Cooperation in massively distributed information spaces. In *Proceedings of ECSCW 2001*, pages 1–17. Kluwer Academic Publishers, 2001.

[9] E. Bhasker, S. W. Brown, and W. G. Griswold. Employing user feedback for fast, accurate, low-maintenance geolocationing. In *2nd IEEE Conference onPervasive Computing and Communications (PerCom 2004)*, Orlando, FL, 2004.

[10] M. Brinton and V. Nee. *The New Institutionalism in Sociology*. Stanford University Press, Stanford, CA, 2001.

[11] B. Brown and M. Chalmers. Tourism and mobile technology. In *Proceedings of ECSCW 2003*, pages 335–355. Kluwer Academic Press, 2003.

[12] J. Burrell, G. Guy, K. Kubo, and N. Farina. Context-aware computing: A test case. In *Proceedings of UbiComp 2002*, pages 1–15. Springer, 2002.

[13] A. B. Campbell and R. P. Pargas. Laptops in the classroom. In *Proceedings of SIGSCE '03*, pages 98–102. ACM Press, 2003.

[14] M. Castells. *The Rise of the Network Society*. Blackwell, Oxford, England, 2000.

[15] K. Cheverst, N. Davies K., Mitchell, and A. Friday. Experiences of developing and deploying a context-aware tourist guide: The GUIDE project. In *Proceedings of MOBICOM 2000*, pages 20–31, Boston, Massachussetts, 2000. ACM Press.

[16] R. Davis, J. Landay, V. Chen, J. Huang, R. B. Lee, F. C. Li, J. Lin, C. B. Morrey, B. Schleimer, M. N. Price, and B. N. Schilit. Notepals: Lightweight note sharing by the group, for the group. In *Proceedings of CHI 1999*, pages 338–345. ACM Press, 1999.

[17] A. K. Dey, D. Salber, G. D. Abowd, and M. Futakawa. The conference assistant: Combining context-awareness with wearable computing. In *Proceedings of the 3rd International Symposium on Wearable Computers*, pages 21–28, Los Alamitos, CA: IEEE, 1999.

[18] P. Dourish. What we talk about when we talk about context. *Personal and Ubiquitous Computing*, 8(1):19–30, 2004.

[19] P. Eckert. *Jocks and Burnouts; Social Categories and Identity in the High School*. Teachers College Press, New York, US, 1989.

[20] W. K. Edwards, V. Bellotti, A. K. Dey, and M. W. Newman. The challenges of user-centered design and evaluation for infrastructure. In *Proceedings of CHI 2003*, pages 297–304. ACM Press, 2003.

[21] W. K. Edwards and R. E. Grinter. At home with ubiquitous computing: Seven challenges. In *Proceedings of UbiComp 2001*, pages 256–272. ACM Press, 2001.

[22] D. Franklin and K. Hammond. The intelligent classroom: providing competent assistance. In *Proceedings of the fifth international conference on Autonomous agents*, pages 161–168. ACM Press, 2001.

[23] S. Greenberg. Context as a dynamic construct. *Human-Computer Interaction*, 16(2–4):257–269, 2001.

[24] W. G. Griswold, P. Shanahan, S. W. Brown, R. Boyer, M. Ratto, R. B. Shapiro, and T. M. Truong. Activecampus – experiments in community-oriented ubiquitous computing. Paper CS2003-0750, Computer Science and Engineering, UC San Diego, June 2003.

[25] J. Grudin. The computer reaches out: The historical continuity of interface design. In *Proceedings of CHI, 1990*, pages 261–268. ACM Press, 1990.

[26] K. Hinckley, J. Pierce, M. Sinclair, and E. Horvitz. Sensing techniques for mobile interaction. In *Proceedings of UIST 2000*, pages 91–100. ACM Press, 2000.

[27] M. Ito and D. Okabe. Mobile phones, japanese youth, and the re-placement of social contact, 2003.

[28] M. Ratto, R. B. Shapiro, T. M. Truong, and W. G. Griswold. The activeclass project: Experiments in encouraging classroom participation. In *Computer Support for Collaborative Learning 2003*. Kluwer, 2003.

[29] T. Rodden and S. Benford. The evolution of buildings and implications for the design of ubiquitous domestic environments. In *Proceedings of CHI 2003*, pages 9–16. ACM Press, 2003.

[30] T. Salvador and K. Anderson. Practical considerations of context for context based systems: An example from an ethnographic case study of a man diagnosed with early onset alzheimer's disease. In *Proceedings of UbiComp 2003*, pages 243–255. Springer, 2003.

[31] B. Schilit, N. Adams, R. Gold, M. Tso, and R. Want. The PARCTAB mobile computing system. In *Proceedings of the Fourth Workshop on Workstation Operating Systems (WWOS-IV)*, pages 34–39, Napa, California, October, 1993. IEEE Computer Society.

[32] C. Schurgers, V. Raghunathan, and M. Srivastava. Power management for energy aware communication systems. *ACM Transactions on Embedded Computing Systems*, 2(3):431–447, April 2003.

[33] J. Scott and M. Hazas. User-friendly surveying techniques for location-aware systems. In *Proceedings of UbiComp 2003*, pages 44–53. Springer, 2003.

[34] S. L. Star and K. Ruhleder. Steps towards an ecology of infrastructure: complex problems in design and access for large-scale collaborative systems. In *Proceedings of CSCW 1994*, pages 253–264. ACM Press, 1994.

[35] W. M. Waite, M. H. Jackson, and A. Diwan. The conversational classroom. In *Proceedings of the 34th SIGCSE technical symposium on Computer science education*, pages 127–131. ACM Press, 2003.

[36] M. Weiser. The future of ubiquitous computing on campus. *Communications of the ACM*, 41(1):41–42, 1996.

Cooperative Artefacts: Assessing Real World Situations with Embedded Technology

Martin Strohbach, Hans-Werner Gellersen, Gerd Kortuem, and Christian Kray

Computing Department, Lancaster University, Bailrigg,
Lancaster LA1 4YR, UK
{strohbach, hwg, kortuem, kray}@comp.lancs.ac.uk

Abstract. Ubiquitous computing is giving rise to applications that interact very closely with activity in the real world, usually involving instrumentation of environments. In contrast, we propose *Cooperative Artefacts* that are able to cooperatively assess their situation in the world, without need for supporting infrastructure in the environment. The Cooperative Artefact concept is based on embedded domain knowledge, perceptual intelligence, and rule-based inference in movable artefacts. We demonstrate the concept with design and implementation of augmented chemical containers that are able to detect and alert potentially hazardous situations concerning their storage.

1   Introduction

Many ubiquitous computing systems and applications rely on knowledge about activity and changes in their physical environment, which they use as context for adaptation of their behaviour. How systems acquire, maintain, and react to models of their changing environment has become one of the central research challenges in the field. Approaches to address this challenge are generally based on instrumentation of locations, user devices, and physical artefacts. Specifically, instrumentation of otherwise non-computational artefacts has an important role, as many applications are directly concerned with artefacts in the real world (e.g. tracking of valuable goods [8, 18, 27]), or otherwise concerned with activity in the real world that can be inferred from observation of artefacts (e.g. tracking of personal artefacts to infer people's activity [17]).

Typically, artefacts are instrumented to support their identification, tracking, and sensing of internal state [18, 24, 27]. Complementary system intelligence such as perception, reasoning and decision-making is allocated in backend infrastructure [1, 6] or user devices [26, 28]. This means, only those tasks that could not be provided as easily by external devices are embedded with the artefacts (e.g. unambiguous identification), whereas all other tasks are allocated to the environment which can generally be assumed to be more resourceful (in terms of energy, CPU power, memory, etc). However, this makes artefacts reliant on supporting infrastructure, and ties applications to instrumented environments.

N. Davies et al. (Eds.): UbiComp 2004, LNCS 3205, pp. 250–267, 2004.
© Springer-Verlag Berlin Heidelberg 2004

In this paper, we introduce an architecture and system for *Cooperative Artefacts*. The aim is to facilitate applications in which artefacts cooperatively assess their situation in the world, without requirement for supporting infrastructure. Cooperative artefacts model their situation on the basis of domain knowledge, observation of the world, and sharing of knowledge with other artefacts. World knowledge associated with artefacts thus becomes integral with the artefact itself.

We investigate our concept and technological approach in the context of a concrete application domain, chemicals processing, to ensure that it is developed against a real need and under consideration of realistic constraints. We specifically explore how cooperative artefacts can support safety-critical procedures concerning handling and storage of containers with chemical materials. We show that this is an application field in which the ability to detect critical situations irrespective of where these occur is of highest relevance, hence supporting our case for an approach that is not tied to instrumented environments.

Our contribution is twofold. First, preceded by discussion of the application case, we introduce a generic architecture for cooperating artefacts. This architecture defines the structure and behaviour of artefacts in our system model, and serves as model for design of concrete cooperative artefacts. The distinct contribution is that artefacts are enabled to reason about their situation without need for backend services or external databases. Our second contribution, covered in sections 4 to 6, is the development of a prototype system that demonstrates the Cooperative Artefact approach. At the core of this system are chemical containers that are instrumented and configured to cooperatively detect and alert a set of hazardous situations. This addresses a distinct application problem that can not be solved with approaches that rely on instrumented environments.

2   Application Case Study: Handling and Storage of Chemicals

Jointly with the R&D unit of a large petrochemicals company, we have begun to study issues surrounding handling and storage of chemicals in the specific context of a chemicals plant in Hull, UK. Correct handling and storage of chemicals is critical to ensure protection of the environment and safety in the workplace. To guard against potential hazards, manual processes are clearly defined, and staff are trained with the aim to prevent any inappropriate handling or storage of chemicals. However the manual processes are not always foolproof, which can lead to accidents, sometimes of disastrous proportion.

In an initial phase, we have had a number of consultation meetings with domain experts to understand procedures and requirements. Future work will also engage with actual users in the work place, however our initial development work is based on informal problem statements and design proposals that the domain experts formulated for us. We specifically used the following proposal to derive a set of concrete requirements and test scenarios for our technology:

"Alerting against inappropriate materials being stored together or outside of approved storage facilities. *It is not desirable to store materials together with those with which they are particularly reactive. This applies particularly to Peroxides and* *other oxidising agents. Manual processes and training aim to prevent this, but are not always foolproof. It is proposed that materials which are mutually reactive are tagged and that the tags can recognise the close proximity of other "incompatible" materials and hence trigger an alert. The tags should also trigger when the quantity of a material exceeds a limit. A variant of this problem is to alert when dangerous materials e.g. radioactive materials reside outside of approved areas for too long."*

From this proposal we have derived a set of potentially hazardous situations that a system must be able to detect and react to, in order to effectively support existing manual processes:

1. Storage of dangerous materials outside an approved area for longer than a pre-defined period of time.
2. Storage of materials in proximity of 'incompatible' materials, in terms of a pre-defined minimum safety distance.
3. Storage of materials with others, together exceeding critical mass in terms of pre-defined maximum quantities.

There are a number of important observations to be made with respect to the identified hazardous situations:

- The identified situations can occur in different environments: at the Chemicals plant, in external storage (e.g. with distributors or customers), or in transit (e.g. when containers are temporarily stored together during transport). Most notably, the environments in which hazardous situations can occur are not under uniform control but involve diverse ownership (e.g. producer, distributors, consumer, logistics). This makes it unrealistic to consider a solution that would depend on instrumentation of the environment with complete and consistent coverage.
- The hazardous situations are defined by a combination of pre-defined domain knowledge (compatibility of materials, safety distances, etc) and real-time observations (detection of other materials, determination of proximity, etc). A generic sensor data collection approach, e.g with wireless sensor networks [2], would not be sufficient to model such situations. It is required that observations are associated with specific domain knowledge.
- The described situations involve a combination of knowledge of the state of individual artefacts, and knowledge about their spatial, temporal, and semantic relationships. As a consequence, detection of situations requires reasoning across all artefacts present in a particular situation. This level reasoning is typically centralized and provided by backend infrastructure. To overcome dependency on backend services, reasoning about artefacts relationships needs to be allocated with the artefacts in a distributed and decentralized fashion.

3   Cooperating Artefacts: Architecture and Components

Figure 1 depicts the architecture we developed for cooperative artefacts. The architecture is comparable to generic agent architectures [13], and independent of any particular implementation platform. However it is anticipated that implementation of cooperative artefacts will typically be based on low-powered embedded platforms with inherent resource limitations. As shown in figure 1, the architecture comprises the following components:

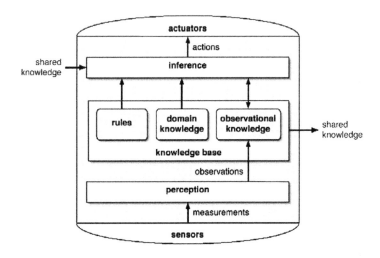

Fig. 1. Architecture of a Cooperative Artefact

- **Sensors.** Cooperative artefacts include sensor devices for observation of phenomena in the physical world. The sensors produce measurements which may be continuous data streams or sensor events.
- **Perception.** The perception component associates sensor data with meaning, producing observations that are meaningful in terms of the application domain.
- **Knowledge base.** The knowledge base contains the domain knowledge of an artefact and dynamic knowledge about its situation in the world. The internal structure of the knowledge base is detailed below.
- **Inference.** The inference component processes the knowledge of an artefact as well as knowledge provided by other artefacts to infer further knowledge, and to infer actions for the artefact to take in the world.
- **Actuators.** Actions that have been inferred are effected by means of actuators attached to the artefact.

3.1   Structure of the Artefact Knowledge Base

It is a defining property of our approach is that world knowledge associated with artefacts is stored and processed within the artefact itself. An artefact's knowledge is structured into facts and into rules. Facts are the foundation for any decision-making and action-taking within the artefact, and rules allow to infer further knowledge based on facts and other rules, ultimately to determine their behaviour in response to their environment. The type of knowledge and rules managed within an artefact are described in tables 1 and 2.

Table 1. Knowledge stored in a cooperative artefact.

Domain knowledge	Domain knowledge built into the artefact, e.g. facts describing the physical nature of the artefact or general world knowledge.
Observational knowledge	Knowledge describing the situation of an artefact in the world. It is based on facts that result from sensor-based observations.
Inferred knowledge	Knowledge inferred from previously established facts, which may be based on domain knowledge, observation, previous inference, and knowledge made available by cooperating artefacts.

Table 2. Rules of a cooperative artefact.

Inference rules	Rules that describe inference of new facts from previously established facts.
Actuator rules	Rules that describe the facts that must be established in order to trigger an action.

3.2 Cooperation of Artefacts

Artefacts need to cooperate to enable cross-artefact reasoning and collaborative inference of knowledge that artefacts would not be able to acquire individually. Reasoning across artefacts is of particular importance in applications that are concerned with artefact relationships rather than individual artefact state, such as the case study discussed in section 2.

Our model for cooperation is that artefacts share knowledge. More specifically, knowledge stored in an artefact's knowledge base is made available to other artefacts where they feed into the inference process. Effectively, the artefact knowledge bases taken together form a distributed knowledge base on which the inference processes in the individual artefacts can operate. This principle is illustrated in figure 2.

For artefact cooperation to be practical and scalable, we require concrete systems to define their scope of cooperation:

- Application scope: artefacts only cooperate with artefacts that operate in the same application or problem domain.
- Spatial scope: artefacts only cooperate with artefacts that are present in the same physical space. The space may be a particular location or defined in relative terms, for example as a range surrounding an artefact.

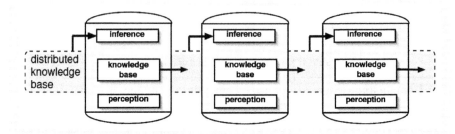

Fig. 2. Cooperation of artefacts is based on sharing of knowledge

4   Modelling Chemical Containers as Cooperative Artefacts

In this section, we return to our case study to illustrate how the Cooperative Artefact approach can be applied to a concrete problem domain. In particular, we describe the knowledge embedded in a chemical container that allows them to detect hazardous situations.

The knowledge base of a chemical container contains facts and rules. As representation formalism we use a subset of the logic-programming language Prolog. Thus, all entries of the knowledge base are formulated in Horn logic [12]. Rules and some facts are specified by the developer. Other facts represent observational knowledge derived from observation events in the perception subsystem: `proximity(<container>,<container>)` indicates that two containers are located close to each other; `location(<container>,<in/out>,<time>)` indicates whether a container has been inside or outside of an approved area for a certain amount of time. The sensor systems that enable the derivation of these facts are described in Section 5. Table 3 lists the facts that can be found in the knowledge base, while Table 4 lists rules. In rules, uppercase arguments are variables, while lowercase arguments are constants. The special constant `me` always refers to the artefact that processes the rule.

Table 3. Fact base of a chemical container.

Domain knowledge	`reactive(<chemical>,<chemical>)`
	`content(me,<chemical>)`
	`mass(me,<number>)`
	`critical_mass(<chemical>,<number>)`
	`critical_time(<chemical>,<time>)`

Observational knowledge	`proximity(<container>,<container>)` `location(<container>,<in/out>,<time>)`

Table 4. Rule base of a chemical container.

Inference rules

```
(R1) hazard_unapproved:-        content(me, CH),
                                critical_time(CH, T1),
                                location(me, out, T2),
                                T1 < T2.

(R2) hazard_incompatible:-      content(me, CH1),
                                proximity(me, C),
                                content(C, CH2),
                                reactive(CH1, CH2).

(R3) hazard_critical_mass:-     content(me, CH),
                                cond_sum(
                                    M1,
                                    (proximity(me,C),
                                     content(C,CH),
                                     mass(C,M1)),
                                    S),
                                mass(me, M2),
                                sum(S, M2, SUM)
                                critical_mass(CH, MASS),
                                MASS < SUM.
```

Actuator rules

```
(R4) alert_hazard:- hazard_unapproved

(R5) alert_hazard:- hazard_incompatible

(R6) alert_hazard:- hazard_critical_mass
```

Rules R1, R2 and R3 define hazards; they are used by the inference engine to evaluate if a hazard can be inferred from the observations.

Rule R1 can be verbalized as follows:

R1: A hazard occurs if a chemical is stored outside an approved area for too long.

This rule is based on three pieces of information: the chemical kept within a container, (modelled by content(<container>,<chemical>)), for how long the container has been inside or outside of an approved area (modelled by location(<container>, <in/out>, <time>)), and how long the chemical is allowed to be stored outside an approved area (modelled by critical_time(<chemical>, <time>). The content and critical_time predicates are built-in knowledge that is defined when a container becomes designated for a particular type of chemical. The location predicate is an observational knowledge and is added to the knowledge base by the perception mechanism.

Rule 2 can be verbalized as follows:

R2: A hazard occurs if 'incompatible' chemicals are stored too close together.

The second rule, in contrast to the first one, uses distributed knowledge. It takes into account the content of the evaluating artefact (`content(me,CH1)`), the content of a nearby artefact (`content(C,CH2)`), and whether the materials they contain are mutually reactive (`reactive(CH1,CH2)`). The `reactive` predicate captures pre-existing domain knowledge built into the artefacts. The `proximity(<c1>,<c2>)` predicate models the fact that container `c2` is in close proximity to `c1` where spatial proximity is defined in relation to an implicitly defined, built-in safety distance. The proximity fact is an observation that is added to the knowledge base by the perception subsystem.

Rule 3 can be verbalized as follows:

R3: A hazard occurs if the total amount of a chemical substance, stored in a collection of neighbouring containers, exceeds a pre-defined critical mass.

This rule uses a special built-in predicate `cond_sum(OPERAND, CONDITION, SUM)` to build a `SUM` over all instances of `OPERAND` (in this case the mass of chemical content) that satisfy `CONDITION` (in this case being the mass of same material content in nearby containers). Note that `CONDITION` refers to a conjunct of predicates, i.e. all predicates that meet the condition. This means, the variable S in Rule 3 is the sum of the masses of chemicals stored in nearby containers. This sum S is then added to the mass of the evaluating artefacts (using the built-in predicate `sum()`) and compared against the critical limit.

Rules 4 to 6 connect the knowledge base to actuators. They are used by the inference engine to determine whether any hazard exists. These rules have procedural side effects and turn LEDs attached to the containers on and off. More details about the inference process can be found further below in Section 5.

5   Implementation

The facts and rules described in Section 4 define on a logical level how chemical containers perceive their environment, and detect and react to hazardous situations. In this section we discuss a prototype implementation of such a container. In particular, we discuss the sensing, perception, inference and actuation mechanisms.

Our container prototype is a plastic barrel to which an embedded computing device is attached (Figure 3). The device consists of two separate boards that are driven by PIC18F252 micro-controllers. The main functional components of the device are as follows:

- **Sensors.** The device contains two sensors: a range sensor for measuring the distance between containers and an infrared light sensor for detecting if the container is located in an approved area. The range sensor is constructed from an ultrasonic sensor board with 4 transducers, and a sensing protocol that synchronizes measurements between artefacts.
- **Actuators.** The device includes an LED to visually alert users of potential safety hazards.

- **Perception.** The perception component mediates between sensors and knowledge base. It translates ultrasonic distance estimates and IR readings into `proximity` and `location` facts, which are added or modified whenever sensor readings change.
- **Inference Engine.** The inference engine is similar to a simple Prolog interpreter and uses backward-chaining with depth-first search as inference algorithm. Compromises in terms of expressiveness and generality were necessary to facilitate implementation on a micro-controller platform (see below).
- **Communication.** Artefacts are designed to cooperate over a spatial range that is determined by the minimum safety distance specified for storage of chemicals. For communication within this range, artefacts are networked over wireless link. In our concrete implementation we assume that sending range exceeds the safety distance.
- **Knowledge sharing.** A query/reply protocol is implemented over the wireless link to give artefacts access to knowledge of other artefacts.

Figure 3 captures the architecture of the embedded device. It is based on two embedded device modules, both driven by a PIC18F252 microcontroller, and connected over serial line (RS232). On one of the modules is used for sensing and perception of proximity which involves synchronization with other artefacts over a wireless channel, using a BIM2 transceiver, and ultrasonic ranging with 4 transducer arranged for omnidirectional coverage. The other module contains the core of the artefact, i.e. its knowledge base and inference engine. It further contains a BIM3 transceiver to establish a separate wireless link for knowledge queries between artefacts, and a LED as output device.

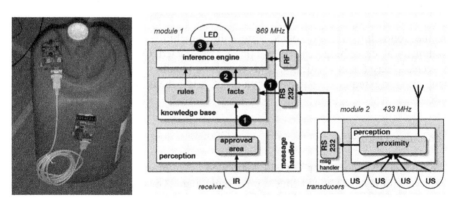

Fig. 3. Physical and architectural view of our augmented chemical container

Inference Process

We have implemented an inference engine with a very small footprint for operation on an embedded device platform with stringent resource limitations. Similar to a Prolog interpreter, the engine operates on rules and facts represented as horn clauses. The inference engine uses a simplified backward-chaining algorithm to prove a goal, i.e. whether a goal (essentially a query to the knowledge base) can be inferred from the facts and rules in the knowledge base.

The process from perception over inference to actuating is as follows:

Step 1. The perception process transforms sensor readings into an observation which is inserted as a fact into the knowledge base.

Step 2. Whenever there is a change to the knowledge base, the inference engine tries to prove a predefined list of goals. In our chemical container example, the predefined goals are the left sides of rules 1 to 3: `hazard_unapproved`, `hazard_incompatible`, and `hazard_critical_mass`.

Step 3. Depending on the outcome of the inferences in Step 2, actuator rules are triggered. These rules are non-logical rules that have procedural side-effects and control the actuators. In our chemical container example, there is only one actuator which is a LED. It is switched on if at least one of the actuator rules can be triggered.

The inference engine is limited in many respects. For example, backtracking is only possible over local predicates and the number of arguments per predicate is limited to 3. The current implementation fully supports our case study, requiring about 30 % of the 4KB ROM and 80% of the 1.5KB RAM of the PIC18F252 microcontroller for a worst case scenario.

6   Scenario-Based Evaluation of Cooperative Chemical Containers

In the following we will demonstrate the capabilities of cooperative chemical containers by describing experiments that we conducted. Our evaluation methodology is scenario-based and involves a testbed and the handling of container prototypes by people. The externally visible behaviour of artefacts is matched against expected outcomes.

Container Testbed

The Cooperative Container Testbed is a scaled-down prototype of a chemical storage facility as it may exist at a chemical processing plant. The testbed is set up in a 16sqm lab space (Figure 4) and consists of

- Cooperative chemical containers as described in Section 5.
- Infrared beacons mounted on cones used for defining approved storage areas
- A set of software tools for remote monitoring of the inference process and communication of augmented containers, and for performance measurement

The purpose of the testbed is to facilitate experimentation with cooperative artefacts in general and chemical containers in particular. Aspects of cooperative artefacts that we are concerned with are correctness, resource consumption, response time, modifiability and scalability. In the following discussion, however, we limit our attention to correctness.

Fig. 4. Container Testbed

Figure 5 shows the spatial layout of the testbed with various container arrangements. The red area indicates an approved storage area. This means that chemical containers may be stored in this area for an indefinite time. The grey area, in contrast, represents an unapproved storage area. Chemical containers may temporarily be located in this area but must be moved to an approved area after a certain amount of time. Technically, approved storage areas are realized by means of IR beacons that illuminate the approved area. Areas not illuminated by an IR beacon are considered to be non-approved areas (perception and reasoning is still exclusively done within artefacts). IR beacons are mounted on cones and can easily be moved around.

The testbed contains three containers a1, a2, and b. The two containers a1 and a2 are assumed to contain a peroxide, while container b is assumed to be filled with an acid. Acids are incompatible with peroxides. The containers are actually empty, but their knowledge bases contain entries defining their respective content. All containers continuously monitor their environment as described in section 5.

Table 5. Initial fact base

Container a1	Container a2	Container b
content(me,"peroxide")	content(me,"peroxide")	content(me,"acid")
mass(me, 20)	Mass(me, 20)	mass(me, 40)
Reactive("peroxide", "acid")	reactive("peroxide", "acid")	reactive("peroxide", "acid")
Critical_mass("peroxide", 30)	critical_mass("peroxide", 30)	-
Critical_time("peroxide", 3600)	critical_time("peroxide", 3600)	critical_time("peroxide", 3600)

The fact bases of the containers holds information about the containers themselves, as well as general domain knowledge. The initial fact base of all the containers, as defined by the application developer, is shown in Table 5. It states, among other things, that container a1 contains 20 kg of zinc peroxide, that the critical mass for this peroxide is 30 kg, that zinc peroxide and acids are reactive (and thus may not be stored at the same location) and that the maximum amount of time container a1 may stored outside an approved storage area is 3600 seconds or 1 hour.

In the following, we will examine a sequence of container arrangements and discuss how the artefacts use the rules in their knowledge to determine whether a safety hazard has occurred.

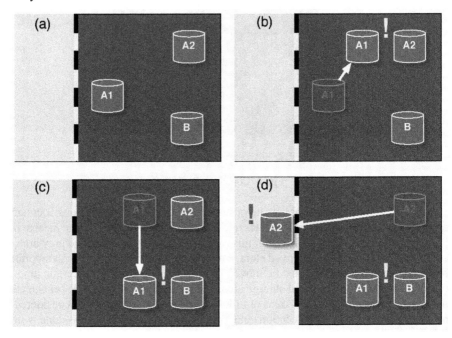

Fig. 5. Example arrangement illustrating different hazards: (a) no hazard, (b) critical mass exceeded, (c) reactive chemicals in proximity, and (d) container stored in a disapproved area too long. The exclamation mark indicates which containers are involved in a hazardous condition.

Scenario 1 (No Hazard)

As soon as the containers are brought into the simulated storage facility, their sensors pick up signals that are translated into facts and added to their knowledge base. Table 6 summarizes the observations of the three containers approximately 1 minute after they are assembled in the arrangement as shown in Figure 5a.

Table 6. Observations in arrangement (a)

Container a1	Container a2	Container b
location(me, in, 35)	location(me, in, 55)	location(me, in, 49)

These observations describe the following situation:

- All containers are currently stored in an approved area. Container a1 has been stored there for at least 35 seconds, container a2 for 55 seconds and container B for 49 seconds..

- The absence of any proximity() fact indicates that containers are not close enough to each other to be detectable by the ultrasound transceivers[1].

In this situation, none of the three hazard conditions can be proven to be true. The goals `hazard_critical_mass` and `hazard_incompatible` fail for all three containers because there is no `proximity` fact in the knowledge base. Goal `hazard_unapproved` fails, because all containers are located in an approved area.

Scenario 2 (Chemical exceeds critical mass)

In Scenario 2 we move container a1 directly next to a2 (Figure 5b.). In this case, both a1 and a2 observe that they are close to one another, and thus `proximity` predicates are added to the knowledge base. Table 7 summarizes the fact bases after the containers have been assembled as shown in arrangement 4b.

Table 7. Observations in arrangement (b)

Container a1	Container a2	Container B
proximity(me, a2)	proximity(me, a1)	-
location(me, in, 70)	location(me, in, 92)	location(me, in, 85)

In this situation, goal `hazard_critical_mass` succeeds. Thus, artefacts a1 and a2 detect – independently of each other – a hazardous situation in which too much of one chemical is stored in one place. In contrast, both `hazard_incompatible` and `hazard_unapproved` fail. During the inference process, a1 and a2 wirelessly send queries to each other to determine each others content and mass.

Scenario 3 (Reactive chemicals stored next to each other)

In Scenario 3, we move container a1 directly next to container b (Figure 5c). As a1 is moved close to b, the proximity facts relating to a1 and a2 are removed and new proximity facts relating to a1 and b are added to the knowledge bases. Table 8 summarizes the fact base of the three containers after they have been assembled in arrangement 4c.

Table 8. Observations in arrangement (c)

Container a1	Container a2	Container B
proximity(me, b)	-	proximity(me, a1)
location(me, in 142)	location(me, in, 154)	location(me, in, 147)

In this situation, goal `hazard_critical_mass` no longer succeeds, thus removing the hazard that previously existed. However, goal `hazard_incompatible` now succeeds, representing a new but different hazard which is detected by simultaneously but independently by containers a1 and b.

---

[1] Intelligent artefacts make use of the closed world assumption: information contained in a knowledge base is assumed to be complete; facts not stored in the knowledge base are thus false.

Scenario 4 (Container stored in unapproved area for too long)

In Scenario 4, we move container a2 out of the approved area and into the unapproved area (Figure 5d). The `location` fact of container a2 is updated accordingly and now indicates that a2 is located outside an approved area. Table 9 summarizes the fact base of the three containers approximately 30 seconds after they have been assembled in arrangement 4d. The proximity facts of containers a1 and b have not changed.

Table 9. Observations in arrangement (d)

Container a1	Container a2	Container B
proximity(me, b)	-	proximity(me, a1)
location(me, in, 210)	location(me, out, 29)	location(me, in, 215)

In this situation, not much has changed as far as hazards are concerned. As in Situation 3, goal `hazard_incompatible` succeeds, but `hazard_critical_mass` and `hazard_unapproved` fail. `hazard_incompatible` succeeds because the proximity facts of containers a1 and b have not changed. `hazard_unapproved` fails because the time a2 has spent in an unapproved area (29 seconds) is still too small to trigger a hazard. However, eventually the time indicator of the location fact of container a2 will exceed the maximum permissible time (which is defined in Table 5 as 3600 seconds). At that point in time, `hazard_unapproved` succeeds and a new hazard is detected by container a2. The observations at this time are summarized in Table 10.

Table 10. Observations in arrangement (d) after 1 hour

Container a1	Container a2	Container B
proximity(me, B)	-	proximity(me, a1)
location(me, in , 3810)	location(me, out, 3629)	location(me, in, 3815)

Scenario 5 (Return to safe situation)

In our final scenario, we move the containers back to the original arrangement (Figure 5a). Immediately, proximity facts are removed from the fact base of containers a1 and b. Similarly, the `location` fact of container a2 is updated to indicate that it is again located within an approved area (Table 11).

Table 11. Observations in arrangement (c)

Container a1	Container a2	Container B
location (me, in, 3920)	location(me, in, 20)	location(me, in 3925)

In this situation, just as in Scenario 1, the goals `hazard_incompatible`, `hazard_critical_mass` and `hazard_unapproved` fail, indicating that this is again a safe situation.

In sum, we have shown how cooperative chemical containers are able to correctly detect hazardous and non-hazardous situations, even if multiple hazards occur at the same time. This highlights an important aspect of the Cooperative Artefact approach:

information gathering and reasoning occur in a decentralized way that enables each artefact to determine the state of the world (i.e. safety) by itself. Consequently, there is no need for an external database or infrastructure.

7   Discussion

The Cooperative Artefacts concept is based on embedding of domain knowledge, perceptual intelligence, and rule-based inference in otherwise non-computational artefacts. The key features of this approach can be summarized as follows: Cooperative artefacts are autonomous entities that actively perceive the world and reason about it; they do no rely on external infrastructure, but are self-sufficient. This enables cooperative artefacts to function across a wide range of (augmented and non-augmented) environments. Collections of co-located artefacts interact to cooperatively assess their situation in the world. Cooperative reasoning enables a system of cooperative artefacts to gain an understanding of the world far beyond the capabilities if each individual artefact. Reasoning occurs in (soft) real-time and is highly context-dependent. This allows cooperative artefacts to be used for time-critical applications. Cooperative artefacts are situated: their ultimate goal is to support human activities in the world. Integration with existing work processes is a key aspect of the design of cooperative artefacts.

Our current implementation of cooperative containers has a number of important shortcomings. Chief among them is the fact that spatial scoping is realized implicitly and that it depends on the capabilities and limitations of the ranging sensors. There is currently no mechanism for explicitly defining the scope of inference rules in a declarative and implementation-independent manner as part of the knowledge base. Furthermore, the complete independence of cooperating artefacts can lead to inconsistent behaviour. For example, it is possible that identical containers interpret the same situation in different ways (for example because of timing issues or slight variations of the sensors readings). Detecting and possibly resolving inconsistencies across a collection of artefacts will become an important issue. Finally, cooperative artefacts have no sense of a global time. This currently prevents to reason about time correlations between observations made by independent artefacts.

A number of questions related to the implementation of cooperative artefacts remain open for future explorations. Among them are: What is the right trade-off between the expressiveness of the representation language and the feasibility of the implementation on an embedded systems platform? Is it necessary to give up completeness of the reasoning algorithms in order to guarantee real-time behaviour (preliminary results indicate that communication is the main limiting factor and not processing)? How can we design the inference engine to minimize energy usage? Although our current implementation provides partial answers, we need to gain a better understanding of requirements and design trade-offs. We thus plan to explore additional application domains and have started further experimentation with the current prototype.

8   Related Work

Our work is generally related to other ubiquitous computing research concerned with instrumentation of the world and with systems that adapt and react to their dynamically changing environment. This includes application-oriented context-aware systems, that make opportunistic use of information on activity in the world as context for system adaptation and user interaction [9, 25], as well as generic sentient computing infrastructures that collect and provide information on dynamic environments [1]. Most of previously reported systems and infrastructures are based on instrumentation of locations (e.g. office [1, 7, 23], home [6, 15, 22]), or of users and their mobile devices (e.g. [19, 26, 28]).

Previous research has also considered the role of artefacts in addition to locations and users. For instance the Cooltown architecture suggests a digital presence for 'things' as well as people and places, to provide information on artefacts and their relations to users and locations as context [16]. A variety of concrete systems have explored artefacts from different perspectives, for example observation of artefacts to infer information on activity. Examples are tracking of lab equipment to create a record of experiments, as investigated in the Labscape project [4], and tagging of personal artefacts with the goal to create rich activity records of an individual for open-ended uses [17]. More closely related to our work are systems directly concerned with artefacts and their situation, for example for tracking of movable assets and innovative business services [10, 18, 27]. Particularly close in spirit is the eSeal system in which artefacts are instrumented with embedded sensing and perception to autonomously monitor their physical integrity [8].

The actual integration of artefacts in ubiquitous computing systems can involve different degrees of instrumentation. For example, artefacts may be augmented at very low cost with visual tags [24] or RFID tags [18, 30] to support their unique identification and tracking in an appropriately instrumented environment. In contrast, our approach foresees instrumentation of artefacts with sensing, computing, and networking, thus facilitating applications that are fully embedded within artefacts and independent of any infrastructure in the environment. A similar approach underlies the SPEC system that enables artefacts to detect each other and to record mutual sightings independent of the environment [17]. Likewise, Smart-Its Friends are collections of artefacts able to autonomously detect when they are manipulated in the same way [11]. Artefact-based collective assessment of situations has also been illustrated in a system that guides furniture assembly, however with cross-artefact reasoning realized in backend infrastructure [2]. In contrast, Mediacup [5] and eSeal [8] are examples in which artefacts autonomously abstract sensor observations to domain-specific context, using specific heuristics. A more generic framework is provided by the Ubiquitous Chip platform, comprised of embedded sensor/actuator devices whose behaviour is described in terms of ECA (Event, Condition, Action) rules for simple I/O control [29].

In terms of our application case study we are not aware of any similar approaches to detection of potentially hazardous situations in handling of chemical materials. However there is related ubiquitous computing research concerned with assessment of critical situations, such as fire fighting [14], avalanche rescue [21], and guidance through dangerous terrain [20].

9   Conclusion

In this paper we have contributed an architecture for cooperative artefacts, as foundation for applications in which artefacts cooperatively assess their situation in the world. We have demonstrated this approach with implementation of a prototype system in which chemical containers are augmented to detect hazardous situations. There are a number of innovative aspects to be noted:

- It is a novel approach to acquire and maintain knowledge on activity and changes in the world, distinct in being entirely embedded in movable artefacts.
- Embedding of generic reasoning capabilities constitutes a new quality of embedded intelligence not previously demonstrated for otherwise non-computational artefacts.
- The proposed instrumentation of chemicals containers is a novel approach to address to a very significant problem space in handling and storage of chemicals.

The main conclusions that we can draw from our investigation are:

- There is an application need for such approaches to assessment of the state the world, that do not assume infrastructure deployed in the application environment
- The Cooperative Artefact approach meets this need, is technically feasible, and can be implemented efficiently on embedded platforms with limited computational resources.
- The Cooperative Artefact approach has been demonstrated to correctly determine the state of the world on the basis of decentralized information gathering and reasoning, without access to external databases or infrastructure.

References

1. Addlesee, M., Curwen, R., Hodges, S., Newman, J., Steggles, P., Ward, A., Hopper, A. Implementing a Sentient Computing System. IEEE Computer 34(5), Aug. 2001, pp. 50-56.
2. Akyildiz, I. F., Su, W., Sankarasubramaniam, Y., Cayirci, E.: Wireless Sensor Networks: A Survey. In Computer Networks, 38(4), March 2002, pp. 393–422.
3. Antifakos, S., Michahelles F., Schiele, B,: Proactive Instructions for Furniture Assembly. Proc. Ubicomp 2002, Gothenburg, Sweden, Sept. 2002.
4. Arnstein, L. F., Grimm, R., Hung, C, Hee, J., LaMarca, A., Sigurdsson, S. B., Su, J., Borriello, G. Systems Support for Ubiquitous Computing: A Case Study of Two Implementations of Labscape, Proc. Pervasive 2002, Zurich, Aug. 2002.
5. Beigl, M., Gellersen H., Schmidt, A. Mediacups: Experience with Design and Use of Computer-Augmented Everyday Artefacts. Computer Networks 35(4), March 2001.
6. Brumitt, B., Meyers, B., Krumm, J., Kern, A. and Shafer, S. EasyLiving: Technologies for Intelligent Environments. Proc. of HUC 2000, Bristol, UK, Sept. 2000.
7. Cooperstock, J.R. Fels, S. S., Buxton, W. and Smith, K.C. Reactive Environments: Throwing Away Your Keyboard and Mouse. Comm of the ACM 40(9), Sept. 1997.

8. Decker, C., Beigl, M., Krohn, A., Robinson, P. and Kubach, U.: eSeal - A System for Enhanced Electronic Assertion of Authenticity and Integrity. In Proc. Of Pervasive 2004, Vienna, Austria, April 2004.

9. Dey, A.K., Salber, D. Abowd, G.D.: A Conceptual Framework and a Toolkit for Supporting the Rapid Prototyping of Context-Aware Applications In Human-Computer Interaction (HCI) Journal, Vol. 16 (2-4), 2001, pp. 97-166.

10. Fano A., and Gershman A.: The Future of Business Services in the Age of Ubiquitous Computing. In Communications of the ACM, Vol. 45 (12), 2002, pp. 83-87

11. Holmquist, L.E., Mattern, F., Schiele, B., Alahuhta, P., Beigl, M., Gellersen, H-W.: Smart-Its Friends: A Technique for Users to Easily Establish Connections between Smart Artefacts. In Proc. Ubicomp 2001, Atlanta, USA, Sept. 2001.

12. Horn, A.: On sentences which are true of direct unions of algebras. Journal of Symbolic Logic, 16, 14-21, 1951.

13. Jennings, N., Sycara, K. and Wooldridge, M. Autonomous Agents and Multi-Agent Systems, Vol. 1, No. 1, July, 1998, pp. 7 - 38.

14. Jiang, X., Chen, N. Y., Wang, K., Takayama, L., Landay, J. A.: Siren: Context-aware Computing for Firefighting. In Proc. of Pervasive 2004, Vienna, Austria 2004.

15. Kidd, C., Orr, R., Abowd, G., Atkeson, C., Essa, I., MacIntyre, B. Mynatt, E., Starner, T and Newstetter, W.: The Aware Home: A Living Laboratory for Ubiquitous Computing Research. In Proc. Cooperative Buildings, CoBuild'99, Pittsburgh, Oct 1999.

16. Kindberg, T., et al.: People, Places, Things: Web Presence for the Real World. In MONET Vol. 7, No. 5, Oct. 2002, Kluwer Publ.

17. Lamming, M., Bohm, D.: SPECs: Another Approach to Human Context and Activity Sensing Research. In Proceedings of Ubicomp 2003. Seattle, WA, USA, October 2003.

18. Lampe M. and Strassner M.: The Potential of RFID for Movable Asset Management. Workshop on Ubiquitous Commerce at Ubicomp 2003, Seattle, October 2003

19. Lukowicz, P. et al.: Recognizing Workshop Activity Using Body Worn Microphones and Accelerometers. Proc. Pervasive 2004, Vienna, Austria 2004.

20. Li, Q., DeRosa, M., Rus, M.: Distributed Algorithms for Guiding Navigation across a Sensor Network. Proc. ACM MobiCom 2003, Sept. 2003, San Diego, CA, USA

21. Michahelles, F. et al.: Applying Wearable Sensors to Avalanche Rescue: First Experiences with a Novel Avalanche Beacon. In Computers & Graphics, Vol. 27, No. 6, 2003.

22. Tapia, E. M., Intille, S. and Larson, K.: Activity Recognition in the Home using Simple and Ubiquitous Sensors. Proc. Pervasive 2004, Vienna, April 2004.

23. Pentland, A.: Smart rooms, *Scientific American*, vol. 274, pp. 54-62, 1996.

24. Rekimoto J. and Ayatsuka, Y.: CyberCode: Designing Augmented Reality Environments with Visual Tags. Proc. Designing Augmented Reality Environments (DARE 2000), 2000.

25. Schilit, B. Adams, N. and Want, R.: Context-aware computing applications. Proc. WMCSA'94.

26. Schmidt, A., Aidoo, K.A., Takaluoma, A., Tuomela, U., Van Laerhoven, K., Van de Velde, W.: Advanced Interaction in Context. In Proc. of HUC99, Karlsruhe, Germany, 1999.

27. Siegemund, F. and Flörkemeier, C.: Interaction in Pervasive Computing Settings using Bluetooth-enabled Active Tags and Passive RFID Technology together with Mobile Phones. Proc. IEEE PerCom 2003, March 2003, Fort Worth, USA.

28. Starner, T., Schiele, B. and Pentland, A.: Visual Context awareness in Wearable Computing. Proc. Intl. Symp. on Wearable Computing (ISWC'98), Pittsburgh, Oct. 1998, pp. 50-57.

29. Terada, T., Tsukamoto, M., Hayakawa, K., Yoshihisa, T., Kishino, Y., Kashitani, A. and Nishio, S.: Ubiquitous Chip: a Rule-based I/O Control Device for Ubiquitous Computing. In Proc. of Pervasive 2004, Vienna, April 2004.

30. Want, R., Fishkin, K.O., Gujar, A. and Harrison, B.L.: Bridging Physical and Virtual Worlds with Electronic Tags. Proc. CHI'99.

I Sense a Disturbance in the Force: Unobtrusive Detection of Interactions with RFID-tagged Objects

Kenneth P. Fishkin[1], Bing Jiang[1, 2], Matthai Philipose[1], Sumit Roy[2]

[1]Intel Research Seattle, 1100 NE 45th St,
Seattle, Washington, 98105 USA
{Kenneth.p.fishkin, Matthai.philipose}@intel.com
[2]Department of Electrical Engineering, University of Washington,
Seattle, Washington, 98195 USA
{bjiang, roy}@ee.washington.edu

Abstract. A novel method to infer interactions with passive RFID tagged objects is described. The method allows unobtrusive detection of human interactions with RFID tagged objects without requiring any modifications to existing communications protocols or RFID hardware. The object motion detection algorithm was integrated into a RFID monitoring system and tested in laboratory and home environments. The paper catalogs the experimental results obtained, provides plausible models and explanations and highlights the promises and future challenges for the role of RFID in ubicomp applications.

1 Introduction

Context inferencing is a cornerstone of ubiquitous computing [1, 2]. A major component of context inferencing is activity inferencing – attempting, via the use of sensor networks, to infer the current activity of a person or group. Recently, several papers have suggested [3, 4, 5, 6, 7] that a fruitful method to infer these activities is by detecting *person-object* interactions: when a person picks up, touches, or otherwise uses an object in their daily home or work domain. We, like other researchers, will focus on the home environment here, as it is particularly rich in objects of many types, but the method is not limited to that domain.

These techniques work by affixing sensors to the objects of interest, but vary in the particular sensors employed. In one approach [3, 4], "stick-on" sensors with an accelerometer, clock, and local memory are placed on the objects. Accelerometers detect touching, and record that to local memory. When the sensors are later removed, the data can be analyzed to reconstruct the set of all object touches and thereafter attempt to infer activity. This approach has the advantage of very high accuracy. False negatives are nearly impossible, and false positives only occur when the object is jostled without being truly used. However, the required stick-on sensors are custom-made, difficult to hide, and do not support *in situ* analysis.

In a second approach [5, 6, 7] the sensors employed are passive RFID (Radio Frequency Identification) tags. Passive RFID tags are an increasingly popular (cf [8, 9]) sensor that consists of a batteryless transponder coupled to an IC chip. An external

N. Davies et al. (Eds.): UbiComp 2004, LNCS 3205, pp. 268-282, 2004.
© Springer-Verlag Berlin Heidelberg 2004

reader emits a low-power radio signal through its antenna to the passive tag. Upon receiving this signal via its own antenna, the IC in the RFID tag extracts the necessary power energize an IC and then reflect back a modulated signal that carries some information, typically a globally unique tag ID (for more detail, see [10]). The reader then provides the list of sensed IDs back to the host application. This list is binary for each ID – it is either sensed, or not. These tags have the advantages of being cheap ($0.30 each and falling rapidly), ubiquitous (forecasted deployments of billions per year), robust (they were originally developed to track livestock), hidable (under surfaces, in clothing, etc.), capable of wireless communication, and batteryless.

However, in this approach, how is the person-object interaction detected? The tag, as constructed, has no way of knowing that it is being moved; even if it did, it can communicate this information only when queried by a distant reader. Accordingly, in this approach the user wears an enhanced "glove", a wearable device that fits over the palm and contains a small RFID reader with an antenna in the palm [6, 5]. The reader is continually polling for nearby tags. The reader range is small (less than a cm), and so detection of an RFID tag can serve as a high-confidence indicator that the tagged object is about to be interacted with. This technique has the advantages of easy and cheap deployment and high accuracy, but has the significant disadvantage of requiring a user to employ a wearable.

In this paper, we attempt to overcome the disadvantages of these two approaches. Our goal is to see if we can unobtrusively detect interactions between an RFID-tagged object and a person without requiring said person to wear any special device at all. By combining the advantage of easy sensor deployment with that of unobtrusive sensor detection, we enable a powerful and attractive inferencing technique.

In the following sections, we explain and report tests of the technique. We first briefly discuss techniques that could potentially detect interactions, and motivate our choice. We then describe that basic technique in more detail, and show how it can be realized on existing unmodified RFID readers. Next, we present a series of experiments characterizing the technique with today's equipment along a number of dimensions, including performance on some representative common use scenarios. We close with a summary and discussion of open areas for future improvement.

2   Constraining the Solution

Given that we wish to detect interactions with RFID-tagged objects without employing a wearable, two general solutions are available:

1) *Enhance a tag.* If we "blended" the two types of sensors described above, we could use the accelerometer from the first to detect interactions and the RF protocol of the second to report them wirelessly. This method has potential, but has the disadvantage of being incompatible with the billions of tags already in existence and those planned for the next few years. We would prefer techniques that can work with existing tags.

2) *Reader energy analysis.* If we wish to use unmodified tags without a handheld reader, we must explore techniques that operate by interacting with long-range

readers. This is the avenue we pursue here. Before we explore it in detail, we must first investigate the nature of the reader-tag communication.

Consider the communication between an RFID reader and a passive tag, as sketched earlier. The RFID reader uses its own antenna to transmit a signal – for the rest of this paper, "reader" refers to the reader coupled with its antenna(e) for simplicity. The tag upon being energized by the impinging signal reflects a modulated version back to the reader. For successful detection by the reader, the tag antenna must capture enough energy from the reader to first energize itself and then send a sufficiently strong modulated signal back to the reader. The amount of energy that makes it back to the originating reader is a function of many parameters, of which the following three are primary: the energy emitted by the reader, the distance between reader and tag (the energy dissipates with distance), and the angle between reader and tag (this affects how much energy is captured by the antennae involved). Our technique relies on the observation that when an object is interacted with, typically *these last two parameters change*: the distance and/or angle of the tags with respect to the reader change. Therefore, when a tagged object is interacted with, the signal strength received by the reader will change.

2.1 Response Rate (α)

Unfortunately, today's RFID readers only report a binary "seen/not-seen" for tags in their range. It is quite possible that a tag may be interacted with while staying "seen" throughout the interaction. Furthermore, today's long-range RFID readers (we examined two of the most popular, those of Alien™ and of Matrics™) do not report or allow direct knowledge of the true back-scattered signal strength at the reader. It is also very difficult to tap in to the signal received by the antenna. For example, most readers use the same antenna to transmit and receive, and the much higher-energy, much noisier transmit signal is very difficult to separate from the received signals. Some readers (like Matrics) do use distinct antennae, but in this case the received signals are so weak as to be very difficult to detect without very expensive hardware.

However, we have found an approximation to this that works well and requires no modifications to current tags or readers, and which we employ in the rest of the paper. Existing readers support a "poll" command, wherein the reader transmits N poll commands per second to tags and reports the number of received responses for each tag. We therefore define a *response rate* α as the ratio of responses to polls. α is thus a scalar on [0...1]. When 0, the tag cannot be seen at all. When 1, the tag is always seen. We will investigate the choice of N later. Fig. 1 (left) shows the response rate of a tag at 4 different distances from a reader: generally, the farther the tag, the lower the response rate. This relationship is analogous to that of received RF signal power with the distance [11]. In other words, the response rate can be used to approximate the RF signal strength and is the basis of our subsequent processing algorithms.

Fig. 1 (left) also demonstrates that α is a noisy signal; some smoothing of the raw response rate is desirable. Thus, in subsequent figures, α denotes a suitably smoothed version of the raw response rates. To disambiguate between signal (a true object interaction) and noise (ambient jitter), the sample set N_s should be large enough to provide a good estimate of the mean signal, while small enough to detect changes quickly. We will amplify on these issues later.

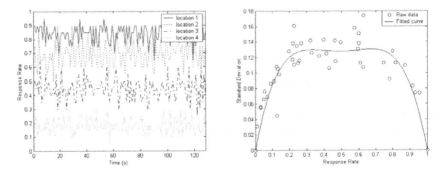

Fig. 1. Left: The response rate at 4 different distances, with N=20. Right: The relationship between mean and standard deviation of response rate (N=10)

To disambiguate between signal and noise, we need to know the standard deviation of an α set. The data shown in Fig. 1 (right) is derived based on $N_s = 256$ consecutive polls at a given location by varying the distance between reader and tag. Three different tag types were used to produce the plot that shows that the standard deviation is lowest when α is at the extreme values (0 or 1).

This affects our noise-signal disambiguation algorithms – a small change in α is more likely to be significant if α was at an extreme. The distances and orientations at which α is 1, 0, and in-between vary depending on the tag, the reader, the environmental conditions, and a host of other lesser factors. As a rough rule of thumb, we have found that with todays Alien™ readers α can detectably change with a motion as small as 3 cm and a rotation as small as 5 degrees.

Fig. 2 (left) illustrates how α changes as a function of the distance between tags and readers, for three different tag types. If the tag is too close (distance less than 150 cm), α is "saturated" at 1 – motions within that range can't be inferred. If the tag is too far (distance greater than about 275 cm in this case), α is saturated at 0. Again, motions within that region can't be inferred. (Fortunately, as we will see below, rotation works much more reliably). We stress that the exact values for the saturation regions are highly dependent on the particular reader, tags, and environmental conditions employed. This makes it vital that an interaction algorithm pay more attention to *changes* in α, rather than its absolute value.

Fig. 2 (right) illustrates how α changes as a function of the angle between the tag and reader antennae. This curve tends to be much smoother than the translation curve, as in this case we are basically reflecting the cosine-wave falloff pattern in how much energy reaches the tag. Inferring interactions from α will accordingly infer interactions which involve a rotation better than those which only involve a translation. Our experiments later will show that in our experience most interactions with an object have a significant rotational component.

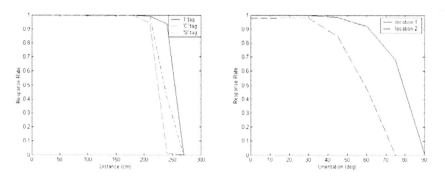

Fig. 2. Response rate as a function of distance from the reader antenna (left), and as a function of angle between the reader and tag antennae (right).

We now discuss two other issues that impact on how we disambiguate true from false signals, namely flooring conditions and the presence of nearby metal.

Fig. 3 has the same axes as Fig. 2(left) (which showed α varying monotonically with distance), but here the relationship is clearly non-monotonic, and much more high-frequency. We have found that this behavior is often obtained in environments with metal floors (such as newly built laboratories). It appears that the metal "slats" in the floor serve as a wave guide, serving to increase the range in which α is non-zero, while making it much more volatile. This volatility actually aids our algorithm, as α becomes more sensitive to small changes in distance. We have found that a similar, coarser effect can be obtained by laying aluminum foil strips down on the floor: one could therefore cheaply modify an existing room for improved reader distance.

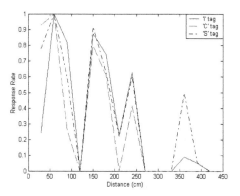

Fig. 3. Response rate as a function of distance from the reader, with a metal floor

A subtler, rarer effect is caused by the proximity of tags to each other or to nearby metal, which we term the "coupling effect". When two tags are placed on top or in front of each other, the top/front tag occludes the return signal from the other. Thus α for a tag could decrease without it being moved (negative coupling). A rarer occurrence is that if two tags are placed at a particular distance and relationship to each other, α for the non-moving tag can actually *increase* if the moving tag helps reflect extra energy onto the second tag (positive coupling). Fig. 4 shows both these cases – note the small increase in response rate at about 8 cm distance in the left example, and at about 32 sec elapsed time in the right example. This can also happen with metal objects other than tags – for example, if a person with a metal belt buckle is at just the right distance, this can cause the α for a nearby tag to increase. Negative coupling is accounted for in our algorithm. In our experience, positive coupling is extremely rare and will henceforth be ignored.

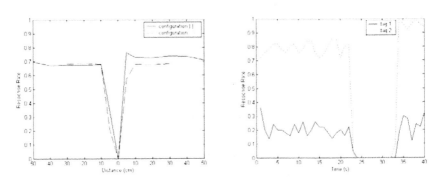

Fig. 4. The coupling effect: the response rate of a fixed tag changes as another tag moves just in front of it. In the left, in case "| |" the tag is moved along the normal direction to the plane of the fixed tag; in case "—" the direction is parallel to that plane. On the right, the direction is again parallel to the plane, and the X axis now shows time as the tag moves

All figures in this section report results obtained by using the commonly available Alien Technology 915 MHz RFID system with the "I", "C", and "S" shaped passive tags, and their 2.45 GHz RFID system with "I" shaped tags. Circularly polarized reader antennae were used.

2.2 Using Multiple Tags/Readers to Increase Accuracy

In the previous section we outlined how the response rate α changes as tags move or are rotated. Unfortunately, this is not that only thing that can cause α to change. RFID signals in this spectrum band are also reflected by metal and blocked by water. If large bags of water such as humans move between a reader and a tag, α will plummet, just as it will when the tag is moved away from the reader – how can we disambiguate between these two cases? This is an inherently unsolvable problem in the base case – there simply is not enough information. We propose a novel method for adding information to help with this problem, namely, by using *multiple* tags on an object and/or *multiple* readers placed with proper topology. By placing multiple tags on the same object at right angles to each other, we can cross-correlate their respective return rates. If α goes up for one tag, but down for another, then we infer that the tag is being rotated but not occluded (occlusion causes *all* alphas to decrease). Similarly, if we use readers located perpendicular to each other, most occlusions will cause only one set of alphas to drop (those obtained at the blocked reader), but those at the un-blocked readers will stay approximately constant. Finally, if a set of tags on disparate objects all have α plummet at the same time, the odds are very good that they are all being occluded. Hence multiply tagged objects along with multiple readers can improve algorithm performance considerably, as shown in section 4.4 and 4.5.

3   Algorithms

Given the broad outlines of our approach, and initial signs that such an approach has the potential to robustly detect interactions with tagged object, we now describe how to turn the approach into a working algorithm. The algorithm must be able to detect interactions *reliably*, and as *quickly* as possible after the event has occurred.

3.1   Selection of N and N_s

The response rate measure α is itself derived from two parameters. From taking N polls per second we derive a sampling of response rate per second. By then taking the mean over N_s seconds we filter out noise and obtain the final value α. A small N means quick sampling, so sudden changes can be detected more quickly. However, the smaller N is, the less the granularity and resolution of α. Accordingly, a time vs. accuracy tradeoff occurs.

Similarly, N_s should be small enough for a quick decision, yet large enough to allow the final α to be a stable and accurate determination. The mean value variation of α decreases exponentially as N_s increases. Generally, the error is less than 5% when N_s is > 10, the value we use hereout.

3.2   Excluding False Positives Due to Mutual Coupling

The negative coupling effect (the change in tag T2's response rate when tag T1 moves near it) can cause a false positive for tag T2. Although there is no fool-proof way to differentiate this effect from a real interaction, it is possible to look at the temporal relationship between the response rates, and use correlation analysis to exclude a false positive when there is a high correlation, as it is extremely unlikely that two tags on two different objects will exhibit the same alpha signatures over time. The correlation coefficient is defined as

$$r_{ce} = \frac{\sum_{i=1}^{N_s}(\alpha_{1i} - \alpha_{1mean})(\alpha_{2i} - \alpha_{2mean})}{(N_s - 1)\sigma_1\sigma_2} \tag{1}$$

where r_{ce} is the correlation coefficient; α_{1i} and α_{2i} are the response rates for tags 1 and 2, and σ_1 and σ_2 are the standard deviations of those rates. Fisher's Z-transformation [12] is used to prove the significance of r_{ce}:

$$\frac{1}{2}\ln\left(\frac{1+\rho}{1-\rho}\right) = \frac{1}{2}\ln\left(\frac{1+r_{ce}}{1-r_{ce}}\right) \pm 1.96\sqrt{\frac{1}{N_s - 3}} \qquad (2)$$

If the two solutions of (2) have the same sign, there is a statistically significant relationship between the two series at the 95% confidence level, giving us a 95% accurate way to detect and exclude negative coupling. Fig. 4 (right) shows an example of a false movement caused by the coupling effect. The statistical test successfully detects this case ($r_{ce} = 0.88$, $\rho_1 = 0.78$, and $\rho_2 = 0.94$).

3.3   The Final Algorithm

Given the considerations outlined earlier, we arrive at the final algorithm which consists of a series of initial checks applied to a new α for rapid detection of obvious motion. If no check is true, more response data is collected for reliable motion detection.   If a check is true, then processing continues with some final screens. The cases checked in order are:

1) *Jump away/to* α = 0/1. α = 0 when the tag is undetectable by the reader, 1 when the tag is quite close to the reader. In either case, if α jumps to or from these extreme values, the check is set. We presently define a "jump" as being a delta of >= 0.1, a threshold that was determined experimentally.
2) *A large change in* α. This check is set if α is greater than 3 standard deviations away from the mean of the preceding set of N_s samples.

If none of these checks has been set, a single α value is insufficient to reach a conclusion. We collect a new *set* of N_s samples, with mean of $α_2$ and apply the following:

3) *Jump away/to* $α_2$= 0/1. Analogous to check #1.
4) *Edge detected.* α2 is essentially a low-pass filter on the N_s most recent samples. This is compared to a low-pass filter on the N_s samples before that: if they differ significantly, then we conclude that a significant change (an edge crossing) has occurred, and the check is set.

If any check is set, we have a reading of interest. Two final screens are then made:

- *Coupling check.* As discussed in section 3.2, we check to see if the data is probably representing a coupling effect, rather than a true interaction. If it does, then no positive is signaled.
- *Occlusion check.* As discussed in section 2.2, if possible we check across multiple tags on the same object, and/or the readings for the same tag across multiple antennae, to see if we can rule out occlusion. If we can, then a positive is signaled.

If neither check has been passed, the algorithm concludes that an interaction has probably occurred, though occlusion is possible. In this case, a positive detect is signaled, with an additional bit raised indicating that occlusion is possible.

4 Experiments and Scenarios

In the previous sections, we have outlined the technique and discussed its many parameters. In this section we characterize the technique and show the effect of these parameters in practice. One difficulty of measuring any RFID technique is that RFID signal strength is impacted by many variables, e.g.:
1) *Flooring.* As mentioned in section 2.1, this has a significant impact.
2) *Distance between tag and reader.* As shown in Fig. 2.
3) *Number of tags on the object and their placement on object*
4) *Number of readers* and their deployment topology
5) *Number of nearby tags*
6) *Number of objects moved simultaneously*
7) *Tag orientation.* As shown in Fig. 2.
8) *Amount and direction of tag rotation*
9) *Tag Type.* Many different tags exist, optimized for different circumstances
10) *Type of Reader.* Different readers, especially those from different manufacturers, have vastly different performance

There are far too many possible combinations of conditions to exhaustively test each. Instead, in this section we rigorously show the performance of the algorithm on a "base condition", and then show the effect of varying each of these 10 parameters independently. To make this more concrete, we then conclude with two parameter "bundles" representing common deployment scenarios.

4.1 The Base Condition

For the base condition, we tagged a single object - a cardboard cube 15 cm on a side that was read by an Alien 915 MHz reader with a circularly polarized antenna. It had a single Alien "I" tag placed on it at the same height as the reader center (100 cm off the ground) at a distance of 50 cm. The object and readers were deployed in a room in one of the authors' houses, with linoleum flooring over concrete.

We then performed 8 experiments, each repeated 10 times. Assume a left-handed (X,Y,Z) coordinate system with the origin in the center of the object, Z pointing towards the ceiling, and Y pointing towards the reader. The "I" tag was placed in two different orientations: once parallel to the Z axis and one parallel to the X axis: 100 events were done for each orientation. The activities can then be described as follows:
1) Rotate 90 degrees about Z
2) Rotate 90 degrees about X
3) Lift up (Z + 20 cm)
4) Pull away (Y − 20 cm)
5) Slide right (X + 20 cm))
6) Wave hand in front of tag
7) Walk in front of tag
8) Do nothing.

The results are graded as either "hits" or "misses". For activities 1-5, a "hit" represents a correctly signaled interaction. For activities 6-8, a "hit" represents a correctly *non*-signaled interaction. The "occlusion is possible" bit from Section 3.3 was not included in the analysis. The results are as follows:

Table 1. Base condition: 1 tag, 1 reader, 50 cm distance

Activity	Hits:Misses	Accuracy
Z rotation	0:10 (Z tag)	0%
	10:0 (X tag)	100%
X rotation	10:0 (Z tag)	100%
	0:10 (X tag)	0%
Lift Up	0:20	0%
Pull away	0:20	0%
Slide Right	0:20	0%
Wave Hand	20:0	100%
Walk	4:6 (Z tag)	40%
	9:1 (X tag)	90%
Nothing	20:0	100%

In the base condition, the algorithm can detect most rotations, and is robust against most false positives, but surprisingly is completely unable to detect translations. In our experience, as the later tables will show, this is largely a function of the particular reader (Matrics readers, which we have not yet exhaustively tested, seem to perform much better than Alien readers) and the environmental conditions, particularly the flooring effect mentioned in Section 2.1. Given this behavior in the base condition, we now show the effects of altering individual parameters of the scenario, to aid in characterization, starting with the just-mentioned floor effect.

4.2 Varying Floor

We repeated the Lift/Pull/Slide activities within a building with a raised metal floor (as is common in many computing environments). The prominent nearby metal acts as a waveguide as discussed above at both 50 and 100 cm distances and significantly improves the accuracy of correct detection.

Table 2. The effect of floor type on accuracy

Activity	Hits:Misses 50 cm	Accuracy	Hits:Misses 100 cm	Accuracy	Hits:Misses 200 cm	Accuracy
Lift Up	10:0	100%	10:0	100%	0:10	0%
Pull away	10:0	100%	10:0	100%	0:10	0%
Slide Right	10:0	100%	10:0	100%	0:10	0%

The metal floor had a huge impact on translations, which now are detected with complete accuracy. We have found this can also be replicated by running a strip of tin foil along a floor.

4.3 Varying Distance

The base condition was performed, but now with 100 cm and 200 cm tag distances from the reader. The 100 cm results were identical to the base condition. At 200 cm, the results were identical except as follows:

Table 3. The effect of 200 cm distance

Activity	Hits:Misses 200 cm Z (X)	Accuracy Z (X)
Wave Hand	6:4 (10:0)	60% (100%)
Walk	4:6 (4:6)	60% (60%)

As the distance increases, the alpha values can get so low that it becomes more difficult to exclude a true positive from a false one when waving a hand.

4.4 Varying Tags per Object

In the first variant, two tags were placed on the object, one parallel to the Z axis, one parallel to the X axis. In the second variant, a third tag was added, parallel to the Y axis. The results were equal to the base condition, except for the rotation activities, which were now detected with 100% accuracy, and the "Walk" activity, which was detected with 50% accuracy with 2 tags and 60% accuracy with 3 tags. So we can see that adding more tags improves accuracy.

4.5 Two Readers

The base condition was repeated, but now employing two readers, located perpendicular to each other. The results were equal to the base condition, except for the rotation activities, which were now detected with 100% accuracy, and the "Walk" activity, which was detected with 90% accuracy. So we can see that adding more readers improves accuracy.

4.6 Multiple Objects in the Field

The base condition was repeated with 3 tagged objects in the field of the antenna, and with 6 tagged objects in the field. The results were equal to that of the base condition, except as shown below:

Table 4. The effect of multiple objects in the field

Activity	Hits:Misses 3 objects	Accuracy	Hits:Misses 6 objects	Accuracy
Walk	21:9	70%	52:8	65%

We see that adding more tagged objects to the field had no significant effect: the algorithm should scale well as the number of tagged objects in the environment increases.

4.7 Multiple Objects Moved Simultaneously

The base condition was repeated, where two objects were moved simultaneously. No difference was detected from the base condition.

4.8 Orientation

The base condition was repeated with the tag original orientation varied to 30, 60, and 90 degrees off the X axis. The results were equal to that of the base condition, for the "Walk" activity, which had 50%, 50%, and 50% accuracy at orientations of 30, 60, and 90 degrees, respectively.

The 90 degree case is the most interesting. In this case, the reader normally does not see the tag, as its antenna is oriented such that it cannot catch and reflect sufficient energy. However, even in this configuration, the algorithm still detected rotation, as this rotation brings the antenna into the view of the reader.

4.9 Magnitude of Rotation

We varied the amount of rotation for the "Z-rotation" and "X-rotation" activities. Instead of being fixed at 90 degrees, 30 degree and 60 degree rotations were also used. These were tested with tags located parallel to the X, Y, and Z axes:

Table 5. Effect of varying magnitude of rotation

Activity	Hits:Misses X-parallel tag	Accu- racy	Hits:Misses Y-parallel tag	Accu- racy	Hits:Misses Z-parallel tag	Accu racy
Z rotation, 30 degrees	0:10	0%	10:0	100%	0:10	0%
Z rotation, 60 degrees	10:0	100%	10:0	100%	10:0	100%
X rotation, 30 degrees	0:10	0%	0:10	0%	10:0	100%
X rotation, 60 degrees	10:0	100%	10:0	100%	10:0	100%

We see that 60 degrees is sufficient to detect rotation. At 30 degrees, it appeared to only work for one of the three possible tag orientations.

4.10 Tag Type

In this condition, we tested two other types of tags, the "S" and "C" tags from Alien. The "S" tag is an older tag which has been largely supplanted by the "I" tag, the "C" tag is a smaller tag optimized for placement near liquid. The results were equal to that of the base condition, except for the "Walk" activity, which was detected with 100% accuracy by the "S" tag and 50% accuracy by the "C" tag. Our conjecture is that the older "S" tags perform better as the newer tags emphasize cost savings over range.

4.11 Living Room Scenario

There are so many variables and parameters that it can be difficult to get a sense for typical real-world performance from the preceding tables. Accordingly, we tested the algorithm on two specific scenarios we felt representative of real-world settings for activity inferencing via tagged objects, namely living rooms and bathrooms in the home [13, 14].

The first scenario represents a typical living-room interaction. Four items were tagged: a hardbound book (2 tags: back cover and spine), a magazine (1 tag: back cover), a deck of cards (1 tag on the box), and a TV remote control (1 tag on the back). The objects were placed in their normal positions on a dresser and magazine rack next to a living room chair. We then performed a sequence of typical interactions with these objects, 30 interactions in total: objects were picked up and/or put down 23 times, an object was motioned with while in the hand 3 times, and a hand was waved in front of each object, for a total of 4 interactions. Two readers were used, both wall-mounted, on perpendicular walls. The algorithm was then left running overnight with no human present in the chair, to guard against false positives.

The results were as follows: all 23 pick up / put down events were detected, all 3 motions with an object were detected, and all 4 hand-waves were correctly labeled as occlusions: 100% accuracy by the algorithm. No false positives occurred.

A second experiment was then performed with the same tagged objects, but this time using only a single wall-mounted reader. This time 9 pick up / put down events were performed and 3 interactions where one object was placed atop another (the book on top of the magazine).

The results were as follows: all 9 pick up / put down events were detected, and one of the 3 placements were detected: the other two were not. No false positives occurred. Overall, 10 of 12 events were detected, for an accuracy of 83%.

4.12 Bathroom Scenario

In this scenario, four tagged items were tagged and placed on a bathroom counter: a canister of hair spray (2 tags: bottom and side), 1 drinking cup (2 tags: bottom and side), a towel (2 tags, placed at right angles to each other on the plane of the towel), and a soap dispenser (1 tag). We used three readers in this scenario, located at right angles to each other – this let us have test conditions with 1, 2, and now 3 readers.

We then performed 6 events where a single object was picked up or put down, and 5 events where a pair of objects were picked up or put down in unison.

Results: all 11 events were correctly detected. However, one false positive occurred. Overall accuracy is therefore 11/12, or 92%

4.13 Experimental Results

The preceding experiments represent a total of 1353 tested events. We can roughly summarize the results with this particular make of RFID reader as follows:

- *Test scenarios.* The system did very well on both "real-world" simple tests, with an overall accuracy of 94%. While the reader placement and the lack of multiple-person movement simplified the situation over a true real-world deployment, we believe that the results are encouraging.
- *Rotation.* The system could nearly always detect rotations, particularly when additional tags and/or readers were employed. As most real-world manipulations involve some degree of rotation, it appears this will be the most common detection mechanism. Another advantage of this emphasis is that the pattern obtained by an occlusion (all response rates dropping) is virtually never seen in a rotation so long as multiple tags are employed – this could greatly reduce false positives.
- *Translation.* The system was nearly unable to detect translation-only movement. This is largely due to the fact that we had to approximate received signal strength by response rate, which is often too insensitive to motion. We believe that this problem is a transient one, as future readers become more sensitive and more open to queries of signal strength.
- *False positives.* This varied the most depending on configuration and setting. In general, with only one tag and only one reader, disambiguation is quite difficult. However, by adding additional tags or especially readers much better performance was obtained.

For a feasible real-world Ubicomp deployment, we would like a system where one or two readers could "strobe" an average-sized room. Present readers and tags don't quite reach this goal due to the energy required to energize the tag, but as RFID tags continue to use Moore's law to reduce their energy requirements, and hence increase their range (for example, in the last 5 years reader range has increased by nearly a factor of 10), we believe that in a year or two room-sized strobing will be feasible.

5 Conclusions

As ubiquitous computing matures, we will need increasingly powerful context inferencing from increasingly unobtrusive sensor networks. In this paper we have described one potentially powerful aid to this goal: using long-range unobtrusive RFID detectors to detect people's interactions with RFID-tagged objects. The algorithm works, albeit in limited circumstances, today. As RFID tags and especially RFID readers continue their exponential rates of improvement in range, size, and cost, we believe the algorithm will become more and more attractive.

There are many areas for future work. On the hardware front, we plan to explore enhanced RFID tags that can detect and report acceleration directly – this would remove the guesswork from the system, albeit at the cost of introducing a new backwards-incompatible sensor. We also plan to explore upcoming RFID readers to see if they can provide more direct measurement of received signal strength than the response rate approximation. On the software front, the algorithm can be improved through improved statistical techniques, for example by analyzing data streams to learn the best values for the "jump" thresholds used in several of the screening tests.

References

1   Dey, A.K., Salber, D., and Abowd, G.D.: "A Conceptual Framework and a Tookit for Supporting the Rapid Prototyping of Context-Aware Applications", HCI Journal 16(2-4), 2001, pp. 97-166.

2   Schilit, B.N., Adams, N.I., and Want, R.: Context-Aware Computing Applications, MCSA '94

3   Munguia, E.T.: "Activity Recognition in the Home Setting Using Simple and Ubiquitous Sensors". MIT M.S. Thesis, 2003

4   Munguia, E.T, Intille, S.S., and Larson, K. "Activity Recognition in the Home Using Simple and Ubiquitous Sensors". Pervasive 2004.

5   Philipose, M., Fishkin, K.P.., Perkowitz, M., Patterson, D., and Haehnel, D.. "The Probabalistic Activity Toolkit: Towards Enabling Activity-Aware Computer Interfaces". Intel Research Seattle Technical Memo IRS-TR-03-013, December 2003

6   Philipose, M., Fishkin, K., Fox, D., Kautz, H.,Patterson, D., and Perkowitz, M. "Guide: Towards Understanding Daily Life via Auto-Identification and Statistical Analysis". Ubi-Health Workshop at Ubicomp 2003

7   Perkowitz, M., Philipose, M., Patterson, D.J., and Fishkin, K.P.: "Mining Models of Human Activities from the Web", WWW 2004.

8   Stanford, V.: "Pervasive computing goes the last hundred feet with RFID systems," *IEEE Pervasive Computing*, vol. 2, no. 2, pp. 9-14, 2003.

9   Want, R.: "RFID: A Key to Automating Everything", Scientific American, January 2004

10 Finkenzeller, K.: Rfid handbook: fundamentals and applications in ccontactless smart cards and identification, Wiley, 2nd ed., 2003

11 Kraus, J.D. : "Antennas", McGraw-Hill, 1988

12 Mode, E. B.: *Elements of probability and statistics*, Prentice-Hall, 1966.

13 Morris, M., Lundell., J, Dishman, E., Needham, B: "New Perspectives on Ubiquitous Computing from Ethnographic Study of Elders with Cognitive Decline". Ubicomp 2003: 227-242

14 Mynatt, E., Essa, I., and Rogers, W.: "Increasing the Opportunities for Aging in Place", Universal Usability, 2000 November 2000

The NearMe Wireless Proximity Server

John Krumm and Ken Hinckley

Microsoft Research
Microsoft Corporation
One Microsoft Way
Redmond, WA, USA
jckrumm@microsoft.com
kenh@microsoft.com

Abstract. NearMe is a server, algorithms, and application programming interfaces (APIs) for clients equipped with 802.11 wireless networking (Wi-Fi) to compute lists of people and things that are physically nearby. NearMe compares clients' lists of Wi-Fi access points and signal strengths to compute the proximity of devices to one another. Traditional location sensing systems compute and compare absolute locations, which requires extensive *a priori* calibration and configuration. Because we base NearMe entirely on proximity information, NearMe works "out of the box" with no calibration and minimal setup. Many "location-aware" applications only require proximity information, and not absolute location: examples include discovering nearby resources, sending an email to other persons who are nearby, or detecting synchronous user operations between mobile devices. As more people use the system, NearMe grows in both the number of places that can be found (*e.g.* printers and conference rooms) and in the physical range over which other people and places can be found. This paper describes our algorithms and infrastructure for proximity sensing, as well as some of the clients we have implemented for various applications.

1 Introduction

One of the goals of ubiquitous computing is to build applications that are sensitive to the user's context. An important part of context is the list of people and places that are close to the user. One common way to determine proximity is to measure absolute locations and compute distances. However, computing absolute location is not necessarily easy (see [1] for a survey), especially indoors, where GPS does not work, and where people spend most of their time. The NearMe wireless proximity server dispenses with the traditional computation of absolute locations, and instead estimates proximity (distance) directly. The advantage of using proximity is that, unlike location sensing techniques, it does not require any *a priori* geometric calibration of the environment where the system is to be used.

NearMe is a server, algorithms, and application programming interfaces (APIs) meant to compute lists of nearby people and places for clients running on various 802.11 Wi-Fi devices. NearMe determines proximity by comparing lists of Wi-Fi

N. Davies et al. (Eds.): UbiComp 2004, LNCS 3205, pp. 283–300, 2004.

access points (APs) and signal strengths from clients. We refer to these lists as "Wi-Fi signatures." By comparing Wi-Fi signatures directly, NearMe skips the intermediate step of computing absolute location, which means it works without calibration for clients equipped with Wi-Fi devices. Our system exploits the growing ubiquity of Wi-Fi access points, using them not necessarily as entry points to the network, but as signatures that distinguish one location from another, much like most Wi-Fi location efforts (*e.g.* RADAR[2] and Place Lab[3]).

NearMe computes proximity as opposed to absolute location. While proximity can be easily computed from absolute location, NearMe demonstrates that computing proximity directly can be much easier. Proximity is useful for polling for nearby people and places and for computing how far away they are. Proximity cannot, in general, answer questions about the absolute location of something nor how to get there. Therefore, our system is not intended to be used to find lost things nor to map routes to destinations. Instead, NearMe is intended to discover what is already nearby and to augment context for ubiquitous computing.

NearMe divides proximity into two types: short range and long range. People and places in short range proximity are defined as those with at least one Wi-Fi access point in common. We have developed a function that estimates the distance between clients in short range proximity based on similarities in their respective Wi-Fi signatures. Short range proximity is primarily intended for finding people and places within the coverage of one access point, which generally ranges from 30-100 meters. Long range proximity means that the two objects of interest are not within range of any one access point, but are connected by a chain of access points with overlapping coverage. The NearMe server maintains a list of overlapping access points that is automatically built from access point data that clients provide during the normal use of the NearMe server. The server periodically scans through all its stored access point data to create a topology of overlapping APs. It also examines time stamps on the data to create travel time estimates between pairs of access points. These travel times and AP "hops" are provided to clients as estimates of the nearness of people and places in long range proximity.

Both short range and long range proximity are computed from Wi-Fi signatures without any explicit calibration, meaning that deployment of NearMe is only a matter of getting people to run the software. People can use NearMe by running one of a few different clients we have written to run on a Wi-Fi-capable device. The client is operated by first registering with the system, sending a Wi-Fi signature to the server, and then querying for people and various types of objects or places nearby. Objects like printers and places like conference rooms and other resources are inserted into the database by a user physically visiting that place, registering as the object or place, and sending in a Wi-Fi signature. Once registered in this way, objects and places can be found by anyone else using the system. Traditional location-based systems use the same sort of registration of meaningful locations, only they also require an intermediate step of calibration to go from sensor measurements to absolute location. For instance, Wi-Fi based positioning systems need a signal strength map generated from either manually measuring signal strengths or from simulating them based on measured access point locations, *e.g.* RADAR[2]. NearMe skips this geometric calibration step in favor of a collaborative process of registering useful locations by multiple users which are then shared with all users. Hence the system can gain acceptance by gradual adaptation without an onerous up-front investment to calibrate a specific environment. This also makes the system potentially more amenable to inevitable changes in Wi-Fi access points: If a Wi-Fi signature is no longer valid, users would be motivated to report a fresh Wi-Fi signature for the places that are important to them.

The next section of this paper describes related work. The NearMe client and server functions are discussed in Sections 3 and 4. Section 5 describes our experimental work to develop a robust function to estimate distance between clients in short range proximity by comparing their Wi-Fi signatures. In Section 6 we describe some of the applications we have implemented using NearMe, and we conclude in Section 7.

2 Related Work

The research described in this paper is related to several other projects and technologies in ubiquitous computing, including location sensing, proximity measurement, and device discovery.

There are many ways to automatically measure location [1], including Wi-Fi signal strengths, GPS, and active badges. Our proximity technique uses Wi-Fi signal strengths. Wi-Fi has been successfully used for computing location, starting with the RADAR system [2] and continuing with Intel Research's growing Place Lab initiative [3], among others. Some location systems require the deployment of specialized hardware in the environment, e.g. satellites for GPS and special receivers and/or transmitters for active badges. All of them require offline setup in the form of calibrating the region of use or mapping of base stations. NearMe is different in two significant ways: (1) it depends only on existing Wi-Fi access points; and (2) for finding nearby Wi-Fi devices, it requires no calibration or mapping. For finding nearby places, it only requires that the place has been registered once with the Wi-Fi signature from that location.

Proximity, as distinct from location, is an important part of a person's context. Schilit et al.[4], in an early paper on context-aware computing, define context as where you are, who you are with, and what resources are nearby. Note that the latter two of these three elements of context depend only on what is in a user's proximity, and do not require absolute location. Hightower et al. [5] describe how location-dependent parts of context can be derived from raw sensor measurements in a "Location Stack". An "Arragements" layer takes location inferences from multiple people and things to arrive at conclusions about proximity, among other things. NearMe jumps directly from sensor measurements (Wi-F signal strengths) to proximity arrangements without the intermediate complexities of computing locations.

Several systems provide wireless "conference devices" that are aimed at assisting conference attendees with proximity information. These are generally small wireless devices that can be easily carried or worn, normally by people in large groups. Examples include nTAG [6], SpotMe [7], IntelliBadge [8], Conference Assistant [9], Proxy Lady[10], and Digital Assistant [11]. Among the features of these devices are their awareness of location and/or who is nearby. Some of them use base stations in the environment to measure location, while others use peer-to-peer communication to find other nearby conference devices. Except for the Conference Assistant, these are specialized hardware devices, whereas NearMe runs on any client that supports network access and Wi-Fi. In addition, NearMe needs no special infrastructure, and it gives proximity information about people and things that can be much farther away than the range of regular peer-to-peer communication by using its knowledge of adjacencies of overlapping access points.

There are well-established protocols for peer-to-peer device discovery using Bluetooth and Infrared Data Association (IrDA) [12]. Bluetooth works in the 2.4GHz RF range and discovers other Bluetooth devices by hopping through a sequence of channels looking for devices of a specified type, like PDAs or printers. NearMe clients may also search for specific types of things, including people, printers, and conference rooms. But unlike NearMe, Bluetooth cannot discover things that are along a chain of devices with overlapping coverage. Thus the discovery range of Bluetooth is limited to about 10 meters. While Bluetooth does not require a clear line of sight between devices, IrDA does, and it only works over a range of about one meter.

Detecting synchronous user operations, or shared context in sensor data, represents another related set of technologies. For example, "Smart-Its Friends" [13], synchronous gestures [14], and "Are You With Me?" [15] detect similar accelerometer readings due to shaking, bumping, or walking. In general, any synchronous user operation can be used to identify devices. For example, SyncTap [16] forms device associations by allowing a user to simultaneously press a button on two separate devices. Stitching [17] is a related technique for pen-operated devices: a user makes a connecting pen stroke that starts on the screen of one device, skips over the bezel, and ends on the screen of another device. This allows the user to perform an operation that spans a specific pair of devices, such as copying a file to another device. NearMe complements this class of techniques, because NearMe allows such systems to narrow the set of potential associations to only those devices that are actually in physical proximity. This helps resolve unintentional coincidences in sensed contexts, and it reduces the number of possible devices that need to be searched for association. Section 6.3 describes how we use NearMe to implement this functionality for the Stitching technique.

NearMe is most closely related to two commercial systems: Trepia [18] and peer-to-peer systems like Apple's "iChat AV" [19]. Trepia lets users communicate with other nearby users that it finds automatically. Users can manually specify their location and Trepia also uses wired and Wi-Fi network commonality to infer proximity. While NearMe also uses Wi-Fi, it makes use of signal strengths to estimate fine-grained proximity, and it also uses an automatically updated table of physically adjacent access points to determine longer range proximity. iChat AV lets users on the same local network find each other for instant messaging or video conferencing. Similar systems for computer games let users on the same network find other nearby gamers. NearMe is more general in that it does not require users to be on the same network in order to find each other, and that it lets users find nearby places as well as other people.

3 The NearMe Client

The client portion of NearMe is a program that users run to interact with the proximity server. The programmatic interface to the server is a web service which presents a simple set of APIs for a client to use, making it is easy to write new clients. We have written seven: four for Windows XP, two for Pocket PC 2003, and one in the form of an active server page (ASP). Each client performs the same three functions:

1. Register with the proximity server.
2. Report Wi-Fi signature.
3. Query for nearby people and places.

We will present a general Windows client as an example as it demonstrates most of the system's functionality. Some of the other application-specific clients are detailed in Section 6. The main work of NearMe is performed by the server, which we discuss in Section 4. The next three subsections explain the above three steps of using the client.

3.1 Register with Proximity Server

The user's first step in using the proximity server is to register with a chosen name, as shown in **Figure 1**-a. New users can type in any name, and they also chose an expiration interval in hours as well as a uniform resource locator (URL) that others can use to look up more information. The expiration interval serves as a trigger for the server to automatically delete old users. More importantly, it allows a user's name to be automatically removed from the server to help preserve privacy after he or she is no longer using the server. One scenario we envision is that a user will register with the server at the beginning of a meeting in order to find the names of other people in the same room. Since this user knows the meeting will end in one hour, he sets the expiration interval to one hour, meaning he will not need to remember to remove his name from the server after the meeting.

Upon registration, the client application receives a globally unique identifier (GUID) from the server. This GUID is used by the server to identify which data to associate with which user. If a user quits the client application and wants to restart later, the registration function gives him or her opportunity to register as a previous user instead of a new one. The server then responds with the GUID of the chosen previous user which is used by the client to tag future transmissions.

A user can register as a person or as any of the possible types below:

person	elevator	kitchen	bathroom
conference room	stairs	mail room	stitchable device
printer	cafeteria	reception desk	demo person

The non-person types are intended to allow a user to tag an object or location with a Wi-Fi signature. Each registered non-person instance is given a name, just like users, but there is no expiration interval. Once tagged, human users can query the server for nearby instances of these types as well as people.

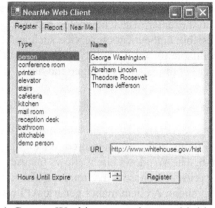

a) George Washington registers with his name and a URL. He could have also registered as one of several different places or things listed in the left column.

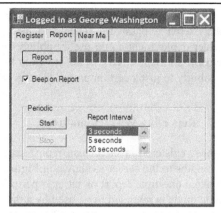

b) He reports his current Wi-Fi signal strengths to the server. He could optionally start a periodic sequence of reports with a chosen time interval.

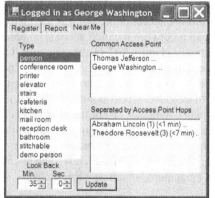

c) George Washington queries for nearby people, finding Thomas Jefferson sharing an access point. Two others are some number of access point hops away, as given in the lower right list. This list gives the distance to the two other both in terms of access point hops and the minimum time it has taken anyone to walk between them.

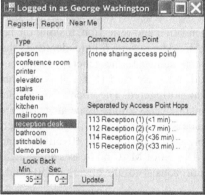

d) He queries for receptionist desks and finds four, but none share an access point. The left list gives the various types of places that can be queried.

Figure 1: These screen shots show a typical series of actions and responses by a user of the NearMe Windows client.

For an enterprise, an alternative, more secure registration method would be to use the username/password scheme in force for the enterprise's computer network. A wider deployment could use a publicly accessible authentication service such as Microsoft's Passport.NET. Also, it would be valuable to add the ability to limit a user's visibility to just a certain group, like his or her list of instant messenger buddies.

3.2 Reporting Wi-Fi Signatures

Once registered, a client can report access points and their measured Wi-Fi signal strengths to the server as shown in **Figure 1**-b. The Windows client allows the user to make a one-time report or set up a periodic series at a chosen time interval. The periodic mode is intended to be used by a moving client. A client makes generic API calls to retrieve a list of access point Media Access Control (MAC) addresses (one for each detectable access point) and the associated *received signal strength indicators* (rssi) from its 802.11 wireless device. This list is the Wi-Fi signature. We only use APs that are in infrastructure mode, not ad hoc, as infrastructure mode APs are normally static. Rssi is normally measured in decibels referred to one milliwatt, or dBm. The usual range is approximately -100 to -20 dBm, and the APIs we use report rssi as an integer. Rssi generally decreases with distance from the access point, but it is affected by attenuation and reflection, making the relationship between location and rssi complex. MAC addresses are 6-byte identifiers that uniquely identify 802.11 access points. Our clients adhere to the general recommendation that one needs to give an 802.11 network interface card (NIC) at least three seconds to scan for access points after the scan is triggered. The clients do no filtering of detected access points, so the list can contain access points associated with any network, whether or not the client has credentials to interact with them. The clients can also detect access points with no network connection that are effectively functioning as only location beacons.

The set of MAC addresses and signal strengths is the Wi-Fi signature. The client's report consists of the client's GUID and Wi-Fi signature, which we represent as

$$\{GUID,(m_1,s_1),(m_2,s_2),\ldots,(m_n,s_n)\} \tag{1}$$

for n detectable access points, were (m_i,s_i) are the MAC address and rssi of the ith detected access point respectively. These ordered pairs are not reported in any particular order.

3.3 Querying for Nearby People and Places

The last client function is to make a query for nearby people or places as shown in **Figure 1**-c and **Figure 1**-d. The user selects a type to query for, either other people or something else from the list of types, *e.g.* printer, conference room, *etc.* The server responds with two (possibly empty) lists of nearby instances of the requested type. The first list, in short range proximity, shows those instances that have at least one detectable access point in common with the querying client, sorted roughly by distance. The second list, in long range proximity, contains instances that can be reached by "hopping" through access points with overlapping coverage, sorted by the number of hops required. Some of the instances found within hopping distance are also reported with an estimate of the amount of time it would take to travel to it. Section 5 explains how we sort the list of short range proximity. Section 4 explains how we compute hops and travel times for long range proximity.

3.4 Other Clients

A web service acts as the API for accessing the NearMe database. This makes it easy to write other clients. We have a PocketPC client that duplicates the functionality of the Windows client described above. We also have an Active Server Pages (ASP) client that runs in a conventional web browser in response to a URL that has the Wi-Fi signature encoded as simple ASCII parameters. Since the web service interface to the server is based on the simple object access protocol (SOAP), any SOAP client could access the service, including those running on Linux and MAC OS.

4 The NearMe Server

The NearMe server is a SQL database that maintains tables of active users, static resources (like printers and conference rooms), and their associated Wi-Fi signatures. It also maintains metric and topological data about the physical layout of access points derived from Wi-Fi signatures. It uses these tables to respond to client requests posed through an API in the form of a web service. The rest of this section describes the major elements of the NearMe server.

4.1 Scan Sources

Scan sources are people or places that can be associated with Wi-Fi signatures. Along with a scan source type, each scan source is represented with a GUID, a friendly name, an optional URL, an optional email address, and an expiration time for people. The NearMe server checks for expired scan sources every hour and deletes their names.

4.2 Wi-Fi Signatures

Wi-Fi signatures are lists of MAC addresses of infrastructure mode access points and their associated signal strengths generated on the client device. On the server, each Wi-Fi signature is tagged with the GUID of its scan source and a sever-generated time stamp. Wi-Fi signatures are never deleted, even if their associated scan source is deleted due to expiration. Because they are only identified with the GUID of the scan source, such orphaned signatures cannot be traced back to their originating scan source. We preserve all the Wi-Fi signatures in order to compute tables describing the layout of access points, described next.

4.3 Access Point Layout

Time-stamped Wi-Fi signatures are a valuable source of information regarding the physical layout of access points. Layout information can in turn be used to aid the computation of long range proximity. The NearMe server processes the Wi-Fi signatures in two ways.

First, the server computes the topology of the access points by examining which pairs of access points have been detected simultaneously by the same client. This indicates that the access points have physically overlapping coverage and are therefore considered adjacent. Note that adjacent access points do not have to be on the same network backbone nor even on any backbone at all. Conceptually, the NearMe server builds an adjacency matrix of access points with overlapping coverage. From this matrix, it computes an undirected graph with access points as nodes and edges between adjacent nodes. In reality, the server computes a table of pairs of access points and the minimum number of edges or hops between them, up to some maximum number of hops (currently eight). Our server is programmed to recompute this table every hour in order to keep up to date with the latest Wi-Fi signatures. In this way, the physical scope of NearMe automatically grows as more users report Wi-Fi signatures from more locations. This table is used to find people or things in long range proximity of a client, where long range indicates that the two share no detectable access points but can be connected by some number of hops between adjacent access points. The number of hops is reported to clients to give the user a rough idea of the distance to a scan source in long range proximity.

This table of adjacent access points is also used as an anti-spoofing guard. Clients can be optionally programmed with a web service call that checks to see if the access points in a Wi-Fi signature have ever before been seen together by any other client. If they have not, this raises the suspicion that the Wi-Fi signature is not valid and that it was created artificially. While this anti-spoofing check helps maintain the integrity of the database, it also prevents any growth in the list of adjacent access points, so it is only used on untrusted clients.

The second piece of layout information concerns the metric relationship between access points, and it comes from the time stamps on the Wi-Fi signatures. These are used to find the minimum transit times between pairs of access points, which can give a user an idea of how long it will take to travel to someone or something that appears on the long range proximity list. Every hour, our server is programmed to create groups of Wi-Fi signatures that share the same GUID, meaning they came from the same scan source (*e.g.* the same person). It constructs all possible unique pairs of access points within each group. For each member of each pair, the server looks up their respective time stamps and assigns the resulting time interval to the pair. All these pairs are recombined, where all but the minimum time interval is kept for duplicate pairs. The result is a list of MAC address pairs and the minimum time any client was able to transition between them. These times are included in the list of scan sources in long range proximity, as shown in **Figure 1** c-d. The times serve as an upper bound on how long it would take to travel directly to that scan source. It is an upper bound because we cannot guarantee that the minimum time observed actually came from a direct traverse between the two access points. A more sophisticated version of this analysis could cluster travel times between access points to account for the different speeds of different possible modes of transportation, like walking, biking, and driving.

Both the topological and metric tables provide valuable proximity information and are computed automatically without any extra calibration work required from either the human clients nor the system maintainer. All the data for these tables is contributed by human users, but their data is anonymized by default after expiration. We envision this type of proximity information to be used to find people and places that might typically be out of range of one access point, like a receptionist desk in a large office building, a cafeteria, a friend on campus, or a custodian. The travel time data would be useful for picking the nearest of the requested items as well as to plan how much time to allow to reach it.

The long range proximity tables are computed based on *all* past data submitted to the server. If access points in the environment are removed or added, long range proximity computations will still be valid. Moving an access point, especially to another part of the topology, would create invalid graph links. One solution we have not implemented is to expire Wi-Fi signatures older than a certain threshold.

As of this writing, our database has 1123 unique access points recorded from around our institution. On average, each access point overlaps with 16.6 other access points. The average number of access points per Wi-Fi signature is 6.1.

Our database of access points is similar in some ways to those used for Intel Research's Place Lab initiative [3] and publicly accessible "war driving" databases like NetStumbler [20] and WiGLE [21]. The main difference is that our database is not dependent on traditional war driving where access point data must include absolute locations. Instead, our database is built up in the normal course of using our clients, with the only ground truth data being the names of locations of interest, like printers and conference rooms. Thus NearMe has a lower barrier to entry, albeit at the expense of not giving absolute locations. The more traditional war driving databases could be easily adapted to work with NearMe. Indeed, one of the NearMe clients allows the database to be updated from a war driving log file. An interesting question is how NearMe could benefit from the addition of some absolute location data.

5   Range Approximation for Short Range Proximity

People and places within short range proximity of a client are defined as those that share at least one access point with the client. In computing the short range list on the server, it is useful to sort the list by distance from the client. Then a user can, for instance, pick the nearest printer or pick the N nearest people. If NearMe were a location-based system, then sorting by distance would be an easy matter of computing Euclidian distances and sorting. However, since we intentionally avoid the computation of absolute location, we must find another way.

Intuitively, the distance between two scan sources should be related to the similarity of their Wi-Fi signatures. If they see several access points in common, and if the signal strengths from those access points are similar, then it is more likely that the two are nearby each other. We designed an experiment to see how accurately we could compute the distance between clients and which features of the Wi-Fi signatures were best to use.

5.1 Similarity Features

Suppose the two Wi-Fi signatures from clients a and b are

$$\left\{\left(m_1^{(a)}, s_1^{(a)}\right), \left(m_2^{(a)}, s_2^{(a)}\right), \dots, \left(m_{n_a}^{(a)}, s_{n_a}^{(a)}\right)\right\} \text{ and } \left\{\left(m_1^{(b)}, s_1^{(b)}\right), \left(m_2^{(b)}, s_2^{(b)}\right), \dots, \left(m_{n_b}^{(b)}, s_{n_b}^{(b)}\right)\right\}.$$

The m's are the AP MAC addresses, and the s's are the associated signal strengths. Client a detected n_a access points and client b detected n_b. In order to define similarity features, we first form the set of access points that were detected by both clients and the associated signal strengths from each client:

$$\left\{\left(m_{\cap,1}, s_{\cap,1}^{(a)}, s_{\cap,1}^{(b)}\right), \left(m_{\cap,2}, s_{\cap,2}^{(a)}, s_{\cap,2}^{(b)}\right), \dots, \left(m_{\cap,n_\cap}, s_{\cap,n_\cap}^{(a)}, s_{\cap,n_\cap}^{(b)}\right)\right\}$$

Here there were $n_\cap$ access points that were detected by both clients, the ith of which was $m_{\cap,i}$, which clients a and b measured at signal strengths $s_{\cap,i}^{(a)}$ and $s_{\cap,i}^{(b)}$, respectively.

Our goal was to find a numerical function of the two Wi-Fi signatures that gives the physical distance separating the two clients. We first had to create numerical features from the two signatures that we thought might be useful for computing distance. The four features we experimented with are:

1. The number of access points in common between the two clients, represented by $n_\cap$. We expect that an increased $n_\cap$ is an indication of shorter range.

2. The Spearman rank-order correlation coefficient [22], denoted by ρ_s. This number represents how closely the two clients ranked their common access points by signal strength. Intuitively, a more similar ranking indicates the clients are closer together. The ranking approach was inspired by the RightSPOT system [23], which uses ranking of FM radio station signal strengths to classify a small device into one of a discrete set of locations. The advantage of ranking is that different radio recievers, such as the Wi-Fi NICs in our clients, may well measure signal strengths in different ways. The ranking of the access points by signal strength will be the same on both clients if they both receive the same signal strengths and they both have a monotonic function relating input and measured signal strengths. While this ignores information contained in the absolute signal strengths, it is robust to inevitable variations in NICs, including differences in design, manufacturing, shielding, and antenna orientation. Mathematically ρ_s is computed by first making two sorted lists of the signal strengths seen in common by both clients. For example, these lists might be $\left(s_{\cap,1}^{(a)}, s_{\cap,2}^{(a)}, s_{\cap,3}^{(a)}\right) = (-70, -50, -80)$ and $\left(s_{\cap,1}^{(b)}, s_{\cap,2}^{(b)}, s_{\cap,3}^{(b)}\right) = (-90, -60, -70)$. In each list, we replace each signal strength with the ascending rank of that signal strength in its own list to make two rank lists, e.g. $\left(r_1^{(a)}, r_2^{(a)}, r_3^{(a)}\right) = (2, 3, 1)$ and $\left(r_1^{(b)}, r_2^{(b)}, r_3^{(b)}\right) = (1, 3, 2)$. The Spearman ρ_s is given by[22]:

$$\rho_s = \frac{\sum_i \left(r_i^{(a)} - \bar{r}^{(a)} \right) \left(r_i^{(b)} - \bar{r}^{(b)} \right)}{\sqrt{\sum_i \left(r_i^{(a)} - \bar{r}^{(a)} \right)^2} \sqrt{\sum_i \left(r_i^{(b)} - \bar{r}^{(b)} \right)^2}} \tag{2}$$

where $\bar{r}^{(a)}$ and $\bar{r}^{(b)}$ are the means of the ranks. In our example, $\rho_s = 0.5$. ρ_s ranges from -1 to 1, indicating poor to exact correlation between rankings, respectively.

3. Sum of squared differences of signal strengths:

$$c = \sum_i \left(r_i^{(a)} - r_i^{(b)} \right)^2 \tag{3}$$

A smaller value of c indicates more similar signal strengths and presumably shorter range. This does not account for the variability in measuring signal strengths that the ranking coefficient ρ_s is intended to ignore.

4. Number of access points unaccounted for in each list. This indicates the number of "left over" access points that are not in the list of common access points, $n_u = n_a + n_b - 2n_\cap$. More unaccounted for access points could indicate that the clients are farther apart.

5.2 Range Experiment

We gathered two sets of Wi-Fi signatures with known distances between scans. One set, used for training, was taken on one floor of a normal office building. The other set, used for testing, was taken in a cafeteria. We walked to various locations in both venues, simultaneously logging Wi-Fi signatures and the device's approximate location by clicking on a building floor plan. In order to test the effect of different Wi-Fi NICs, we gathered data from six different ones:

Dell TrueMobile 1150 Series (built in to laptop)	ORiNOCO (PC Card)	Cisco Aironet 340 Series (PC Card)
Microsoft Wireless (USB Adapter)	Actiontec 802.1b Wireless Adapter (USB Adapter)	Linksys 802.11b Wireless (USB Adapter)

For each of the two venues, we created pairs of Wi-Fi signatures using the location stamps to determine their Euclidian separation distances in meters. We eliminated those pairs that were taken with the same Wi-Fi NIC in order to test the more realistic situation that the two Wi-Fi signatures will come from different NICs. In the office building data set, we gathered a total of 2218 Wi-Fi signatures and created 1,441,739 pairs of Wi-Fi signatures after eliminating those pairs created with the same NIC. For the cafeteria data set, we took 1038 Wi-Fi signatures and created 572,027 pairs.

Our goal was to find a function that takes some or all of the features of a pair of Wi-Fi signatures from Section 5.1 and returns an estimate for the physical distance between them. We chose polynomials as our functions, as there are no well-established physical models that relate our features and distance. For our experiment we varied the order of the polynomials, N_o, from one to four, and we varied the number of features, N_f, from one to four. For each N_f, we tested all $\binom{4}{N_f}$ ("4 choose N_f") possible combinations of features. For example, if $N_o = 2$, $N_f = 3$, and the three features were $n_\cap$, ρ_s, and c, then the polynomial would be

$$\begin{aligned}
d = &\ a_{000} + a_{100}n_\cap + a_{010}\rho_s + a_{001}c + \\
&\ a_{110}n_\cap\rho_s + a_{101}n_\cap c + a_{011}\rho_s c + \\
&\ a_{200}n_\cap^{\ 2} + a_{020}\rho_s^{\ 2} + a_{002}c^2
\end{aligned} \tag{4}$$

where d is the physical distance between the locations at which the two Wi-Fi signatures were taken, and the a's are the coefficients we estimated using least squares. In computing the coefficients, we used weighted least squares to equalize the influence of each possible pair of NICs, because each NIC was not represented exactly equally in the experimental data.

We used the office building data as training data to compute polynomial coefficients. Because of the large number of data points, we performed the actual least squares fitting on 10 subsets each consisting of a random 10% of the data, and we kept the coefficients that gave the minimum rms distance error from each subset. The results are shown in **Table 1**. For the training data, the rms error was in the vicinity of 7 meters, with a minimum of 6.43 meters for the 3rd degree polynomial using all four features. We also evaluated how well the computed polynomials ranked the distances using the Spearman rank correlation coefficient between the actual and computed ranked distances. (Note that we use Spearman twice: once as a way to measure the rank similarity of signal strengths and once as a way to assess how well our various polynomials rank physical distance compared to ground truth.) This is useful since some applications may want to present ranked lists of nearby people rather than their absolute distances. The maximum Spearman correlation for the training set was 0.49, also for the 3rd degree polynomial using all four features.

We used the polynomial coefficients from the office building training set to see how well they worked for the cafeteria data set. This gives us an idea of whether or not we could put forth a broad recommendation for which features and functions to use for any general situation. This will require more testing in the future, but the cafeteria data shows reasonable performance with a minimum rms error of 13.97 meters and a maximum Spearman correlation of 0.43, both using a 1st degree polynomial on $n_\cap$, ρ_s, and c. The number of unaccounted for access points, n_u, was the worst performing single feature in terms of rms error on the test set. Intuitively, the most attractive features are $n_\cap$ (the number of access points in common) and ρ_s (the Spearman correlation of the signal strengths), because they are robust to measurement differences between NICs. The test data indicates that the best performing polynomial for these two features was a 1st degree polynomial, giving an rms error of 14.04 meters and a Spearman correlation of 0.39, both very close to the best performance over all the test cases. The actual polynomial was

Table 1: Results of training and testing polynomials to estimate distance from Wi-Fi signatures.

Number of Features	Feature(s)	Polynomial Degree	RMS Err (m) Train	RMS Err (m) Test	Spearman ρ Train	Spearman ρ Test
1	APs In Common	1	7.13	14.23	-0.36	0.30
		2	7.25	14.22	-0.36	0.30
		3	7.13	14.24	0.32	0.30
	Spearman ρ	1	7.26	14.85	0.19	0.19
		2	7.22	14.67	0.17	0.22
		3	7.20	14.63	0.19	0.19
	RSSI Difference	1	7.58	15.09	-0.27	0.26
		2	7.63	15.08	-0.26	0.26
		3	7.44	15.04	0.33	0.29
	Unaccounted for APs	1	7.23	15.23	0.31	0.30
		2	7.16	15.24	0.31	0.30
		3	7.09	15.13	0.31	0.30
2	APs In Common / Spearman ρ	1	6.83	14.04	0.38	0.39
		2	6.75	14.19	0.41	0.34
		3	6.74	14.26	0.41	0.32
	APs In Common / RSSI Difference	1	7.10	14.31	0.39	0.39
		2	7.12	14.38	0.22	0.39
		3	6.96	14.16	0.40	0.39
	APs In Common / Unaccounted for APs	1	6.87	14.57	0.39	0.35
		2	6.83	14.78	0.40	0.35
		3	6.83	14.80	0.40	0.34
	Spearman ρ / RSSI Difference	1	7.24	14.80	0.15	0.26
		2	7.24	14.68	0.12	0.09
		3	7.07	14.68	0.29	0.37
	Spearman ρ / Unaccounted for APs	1	7.00	15.08	0.33	0.31
		2	6.91	14.91	0.36	0.33
		3	6.83	14.99	0.36	0.33
	RSSI Difference / Unaccounted for APs	1	7.16	15.26	0.28	0.23
		2	7.10	15.22	0.28	0.22
		3	6.91	15.07	0.41	0.34
3	APs In Common / Spearman ρ / RSSI Difference	1	6.81	13.97	0.35	0.43
		2	6.75	14.13	0.37	0.30
		3	6.61	14.10	0.44	0.38
	APs In Common / Spearman ρ / Unaccounted for Aps	1	6.69	14.20	0.43	0.41
		2	6.58	14.42	0.45	0.38
		3	6.52	14.47	0.46	0.35
	APs In Common / RSSI Difference / Unaccounted for Aps	1	6.88	14.39	0.38	0.33
		2	6.88	14.55	0.38	0.30
		3	6.70	14.51	0.44	0.36
	Spearman ρ / RSSI Difference / Unaccounted for Aps	1	7.01	15.00	0.33	0.30
		2	6.91	14.89	0.36	0.29
		3	6.68	14.83	0.42	0.35
4	APs In Common / Spearman ρ / RSSI Difference / Unaccounted for APs	1	6.71	14.30	0.42	0.40
		2	6.64	14.60	0.44	0.35
		3	6.43	14.49	0.49	0.36

Table 1: Results of training and testing polynomials to estimate distance from Wi-Fi signatures. The "Train" column under the "RMS Err (m)" column shows the rms error in meters after the least squares fit to the office building data. The "Train" column under "Spearman ρ" shows how well the computed polynomial ranked the computed distances compared to the actual distances. The two "Test" columns show how well the office building polynomial coefficients worked on the cafeteria data. In general, increasing the number of features and the degree of the polynomial did not significantly improve accuracy.

$$d = -2.53n_\cap - 2.90\rho_s + 22.31 \tag{5}$$

As expected, this equation indicates that the estimated distance in meters (d) decreases when more access points are seen in common ($n_\cap$) and when their relative rankings are more similar (ρ_s). One interesting aspect of this equation is that $\partial d/\partial n_\cap \approx \partial d/\partial \rho_s$, meaning that $n_\cap$ and ρ_s have approximately the same level of influence on the estimated distance. Given this similarity in influence, if the goal is to sort Wi-Fi signature pairs by distance, a reasonable heuristic is to simply sort by the sum $n_\cap + \rho_s$. This is what we do on the server to sort lists of instances in short range proximity.

Although this equation worked reasonably well for our two data sets, the actual coefficients are likely not broadly applicable to other locations where there could be differences in building materials, architecture, access point density, and access point transmission strength. One example of its possible inapplicability is in an area densely populated with access points. In such a case, $n_\cap$ could be large enough that the computed distance is negative. However, this analysis does indicate which features of the Wi-Fi signatures are important, and it leads to the $n_\cap + \rho_s$ heuristic for sorting by distance. No calibration is necessary to apply this heuristic to a new environment, in contrast to Wi-Fi location systems that normally require manually constructed or simulated radio maps. These calibrated systems do provide more accuracy, however, with median absolute location errors of 2.37 meters for RADAR[2], 1.53 meters for LOCADIO[24], and 1 meter for the system of Ladd *et al.*[25]. For proximity, this level of accuracy is not always necessary.

Short range proximity computations are robust to the addition and deletion of access points, because the distance computation is based on only the list of access points that two Wi-Fi signatures have in common. A moved access point could cause large errors. However, for finding nearby people who are updating their Wi-Fi signatures frequently, as our basic client allows (**Figure 1**b), even moved access points are easily tolerated.

6 Applications

The functionality of the NearMe server is exposed as a web service, making it easy to create new clients. This section describes three potentially useful clients.

6.1 Sample Client with URLs

The sample client in **Figure 1** allows people and places to be registered with a URL. For example, people might register with their home pages. For some places, like reception desks, we registered a URL giving a map to help visitors find their way. Instances with a registered URL show up on the proximity lists with a "…" behind their name. The user can click on these names to bring up a web browser showing their URLs. Each registered person and place is essentially tagged with a Wi-Fi signature that serves for filtering based on location. The changing lists of proximal people and places, along with their associated URLs, create a dynamic lookup service of what is available nearby.

6.2 Localized Email

The screen shot in **Figure 2** shows our localized email program. It allows a user to register with NearMe with a name and email address. After updating the database with his or her Wi-Fi signature, a list of nearby registered users appears. The user can select names from this list and send an email to them. This would be useful for nearly immediate requests like going out to lunch or asking for face-to-face help with a problem. Because we sort the list of potential recipients by physical distance, picking the top N in the list is equivalent to picking the N nearest people, up to NearMe's inherent distance approximation errors. Since NearMe's range resolution is in the tens of meters, its errors are likely tolerable for this application. In the future, proximity could be one of a number of filters for email recipients, optionally used in addition to filters on recipient type (*e.g.* friend, colleague, supervisor) and interest area.

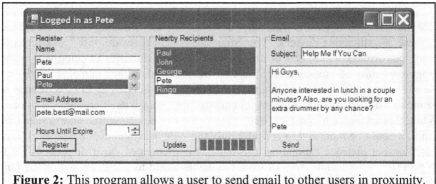

Figure 2: This program allows a user to send email to other users in proximity.

6.3 Detecting Synchronous User Operations

Another client we have implemented uses NearMe to aid in detecting synchronous user operations between mobile devices for co-located collaboration. Stitching [17], synchronous gestures [14], and SyncTap [16] are all examples such techniques. Stitching, for example, must share the screen coordinates, direction, and timing of pen strokes with other nearby devices to establish when a pen stroke spans the displays of two devices. This makes it easy for users to drag a file between two separate pen-operated wireless devices, for example, as shown in **Figure 3**.

A key problem in this class of systems is to determine which devices to consider as candidates for potential synchronous user operations [14]. SyncTap [16] proposes using multicast to share user activity and timing with other devices, but this may needlessly send information to a large number of irrelevant devices that are too far apart to ever be intentionally associated. Restricting communications to devices that are truly nearby reduces the potential for false-positive recognition of synchronous user operations (due to pure chance synchronization of incidental operations on a large number of devices) and also may help to reduce power consumption

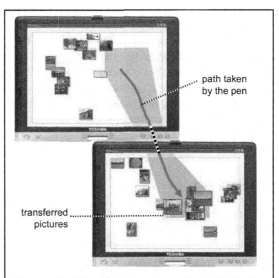

Figure 3: NearMe is used to find which devices are in proximity so they can be associated with a pen gesture spanning both screens.

requirements (by reducing wasted computation and transmission of messages seeking to establish synchronization with non-proximal devices).

NearMe solves these problems by providing a list of nearby devices for every device that seeks associations with other devices. For our Stitching technique, we refer to these as "stitchable devices." Our Stitching system software only looks for correlating pen strokes within sets of devices that NearMe identifies as being within short range proximity of one another. Stitchable devices update their signal strengths with NearMe every 20 seconds so that the set of stitchable devices at any one time is dynamic and discoverable by any new client wishing to make itself eligible for stitching. While this application considers associations for any device within short range proximity, it could be modified to consider only those devices within some physical range based on our distance estimation. But even as implemented, NearMe reduces the list of potentially associable devices from the whole world to just those within the range of one access point.

7 Conclusions

NearMe's main feature is that it gives lists of nearby people and places without computing their absolute locations. This makes it easier to deploy than traditional location-based systems. Even though it is unaware of absolute locations, NearMe can still give absolute and relative distance estimates for short range proximity, and it can give travel time estimates for long range proximity. The database grows as more people use the client, which in turn increases the richness and range of people and places that can be found in proximity. The database helps protect the privacy of users by anonymizing their data after a user specified time period, and it can protect itself against falsified access point signatures by verifying them against what it has already seen.

As this work proceeds, we would like to test the feasibility of using NearMe in a peer-to-peer fashion rather than depending on a central database. For short range proximity, this would be a simple matter of having peers exchange Wi-Fi signatures and then having the clients evaluate our function for estimating separation distance. Another way to expand the scope of NearMe would be to incorporate other types of radio as location signatures, such as Bluetooth, cell towers, and commercial broadcasts of radio and TV.

References

1. Hightower, J. and G. Borriello, *Location Systems for Ubiquitous Computing.* Computer, 2001. **34**(8): p. 57-66.
2. Bahl, P. and V.N. Padmanabhan. *RADAR: An In-Building RF-Based User Location and Tracking System.* in *INFOCOM 2000.* 2000.
3. Schilit, B.N., et al. *Challenge: Ubiquitous Location-Aware Computing and the "Place Lab" Initiative.* in *The First ACM International Workshop on Wireless Mobile Applications and Services on WLAN (WMASH 2003).* 2003. San Diego, California, USA.
4. Schilit, B.N., N. Adams, and R. Want. *Context-Aware Computing Applications.* in *IEEE Workshop on Mobile Computing Systems and Applications.* 1994.
5. Hightower, J., G. Borriello, and D. Fox, *The Location Stack.* 2003, Intel Research Seattle. p. 13.

6. http://www.ntag.com/.
7. http://www.spotme.ch/.
8. Cox, D., V. Kindratenko, and D. Pointer. *IntelliBadge™: Towards Providing Location-Aware Value-Added Services at Academic Conferences.* in *UbiComp 2003: Ubiquitous Computing.* 2003. Seattle, WA, USA.
9. Dey, A.K., et al. *The Conference Assistant: Combining Context-Awareness with Wearable Computing.* in *3rd International Symposium on Wearable Computers.* 1999. San Francisco, California, USA.
10. Dahlberg, P., F. Ljungberg, and J. Sanneblad. *Supporting Opportunistic Communication in Mobile Settings.* in *CHI 2000 Extended Abstracts on Human Factors in Computing Systems.* 2000. The Hague, The Netherlands: ACM Press.
11. Sumi, Y. and K. Mase. *Digital Assistant for Supporting Conference Participants: An Attempt to Combine Mobile, Ubiquitous and Web Computing.* in *Ubicomp 2001: Ubiquitous Computing.* 2001. Atlanta, Georgia, USA: Springer.
12. Woodings, R., et al. *Rapid Heterogeneous Ad Hoc Connection Establishment: Accelerating Bluetooth Inquiry Using IrDA.* in *Third Annual IEEE Wireless Communications and Networking Conference (WCNC '02).* 2002. Orlando, Florida, USA.
13. Holmquist, L.E., et al. *Smart-Its Friends: A Technique for Users to Easily Establish Connections between Smart Artefacts.* in *Ubicomp 2001: Ubiquitous Computing.* 2001. Atlanta, Georgia, USA: Springer.
14. Hinckley, K. *Synchronous Gestures for Multiple Users and Computers.* in *UIST'03 Symposium on User Interface Software & Technology.* 2003.
15. Lester, J., B. Hannaford, and G. Borriello. *"Are You With Me?" – Using Accelerometers to Determine if Two Devices are Carried by the Same Person.* in *Pervasive 2004.* 2004. Linz, Austria.
16. Rekimoto, J., Y. Ayatsuka, and M. Kohno. *SyncTap: An Interaction Technique for Mobile Networking.* in *Mobile HCI.* 2003.
17. Hinckley, K., et al. *Stitching: Pen Gestures that Span Multiple Displays.* in *ACM Advanced Visual Interfaces (AVI 2004).* 2004.
18. http://www.trepia.com/.
19. http://www.apple.com/macosx/features/rendezvous/.
20. http://www.netstumbler.com/.
21. http://www.wigle.net/.
22. Press, W.H., et al., *Numerical Recipes in C.* 1992, Cambridge: Cambridge University Press.
23. Krumm, J., G. Cermak, and E. Horvitz. *RightSPOT: A Novel Sense of Location for a Smart Personal Object.* in *UbiComp 2003: Ubiquitous Computing.* 2003. Seattle, WA: Springer.
24. Krumm, J. and E. Horvitz. *LOCADIO: Inferring Motion and Location from Wi-Fi Signal Strengths.* in *First Annual International Conference on Mobile and Ubiquitous Systems: Networking and Services (Mobiquitous 2004).* 2004. Boston, MA.
25. Ladd, A.M., et al. *Robotics-Based Location Sensing using Wireless Ethernet.* in *International Conference on Mobile Computing and Networking.* 2002. Atlanta, GA: ACM Press.

The ContextCam:
Automated Point of Capture Video Annotation

Shwetak N. Patel and Gregory D. Abowd

College of Computing & GVU Center
Georgia Institute of Technology
801 Atlantic Drive, Atlanta, GA 30332-0280, USA
{shwetak, abowd}@cc.gatech.edu

Abstract: Rich, structured annotations of video recordings enable interesting uses, but existing techniques for manual, and even semi-automated, tagging can be too time-consuming. We present in this paper the ContextCam, a prototype of a consumer video camera that provides point of capture annotation of time, location, person presence and event information associated to recorded video. Both low- and high-level metadata are discovered via a variety of sensing and active tagging techniques, as well as through the application of machine learning techniques that use past annotations to suggest metadata for the current recordings. Furthermore, the ContextCam provides users with a minimally intrusive interface for correcting predicted high-level metadata during video recording.

1 Introduction

An ambition of ubiquitous computing is to create services that perform some of the important yet mundane activities that we would like to do, but do not have the patience or time to perform. One of those tasks is annotation, indicating the salient pieces of information that describe a situation for future reference. A richly annotated family history —pictures, movies, physical artifacts all accompanied by descriptions and narrative that describe their significance— could provide a variety of entertaining and valuable services, but we rarely have the time to do the annotation. There is an opportunity for technology to perform the annotation on behalf of the user.

What would it take to have the ability *today* to record live events and tag them at the point of capture with metadata that can be preserved and aid in review? We present a solution to this problem for live video, called the ContextCam. We developed the ContextCam to solve a problem of simplified annotation of home movies, motivated by a previous mainly manual annotation system we built call the Family Video Archive (FVA) [1], and shown in Figure 1. As we will show, annotation of home movies provides a very meaningful way to share large archives of family history, but only when metadata describing when, where, who and what activity is taking place is added. Although this data can be added manually, as our previous work demonstrated, the real challenge is to automate as much of this tedious task as possible.

N. Davies et al. (Eds.): UbiComp 2004, LNCS 3205, pp. 301–318, 2004.
© Springer-Verlag Berlin Heidelberg 2004

In this paper, we describe how the management of home movies motivated the development of the ContextCam, and discuss related work on automated annotation of digital memories. We then describe the prototype ContextCam device, a digital video recording device with a collection of sensing techniques to annotate video with information concerning when and where the video is being recorded and, more importantly, who is in and around the field of view of the camera. This latter metadata is accomplished through an active tagging technique. We then show how the low level metadata for *who, where* and *when* can be used to infer higher level information with a Bayesian prediction technique that supports a manual technique for assigning higher-level semantic tags to a scene while recording. We also present the user interaction with the ContextCam that integrates the point of capture annotation with the regular use of the augmented video camera. Although the ContextCam was designed specifically to address an opportunity for home movies, its application extends that entertainment motivation.

Figure 1: Manual tagging interface for the Family Video Archive [1].

2 Motivation: A Semi-automated Family Video Annotation System

Historically, families have recorded their history using visual aids such as paintings, photographs or videos. With digital technologies for photography and videography, the storage and manipulation of family history is easier than it has ever been. In addition, families are even beginning to convert old 8mm and VHS films into a digital form. Although tools exist to organize and share digital photographs, the only tools available for digital video are ones for nonlinear editing of video sequences. Despite the increasing relative ease of recording and editing family movies, archiving and retrieving them is not quite as effortless. For instance, consider the overwhelming task of finding and creating a video compilation of a family's Christmas scenes from the past 20 years. This would be a wonderful gift to share with loved ones, but it is often a very time-consuming task to assemble the individually recorded video snippets into a complete presentation. We earlier designed a system, the Family Video Archive, that supports the manual annotation and browsing of a large collection of home movies [1]. Motivated by PhotoMesa's [3] zooming interface for browsing digital photographs, the system provides a flexible semantic zooming interface for browsing and filtering the collection of user-defined scenes. Related scenes can be grouped into albums and exported out of the system, either as input to a nonlinear video-editing suite or as an independent DVD with menus and navigation. These browsing and authoring features will not be described in any further detail in this paper. Instead, we focus on the annotation features of our system, the foundation for any of these browsing and authoring capabilities.

2.1 Annotating Home Video

In our earlier home video annotation system (see Figure 1), users import video files into the system by dragging them into the video files browser in the lower left corner of the interface. Users view video in the video playback panel using a VCR style control interface. A timeline indicates the user-defined scene boundaries within any given video file (there is no assumption that video files contain single scene information). Using a simple frame-by-frame color histogram comparison, the system suggests scene boundaries that the user can accept, modify or remove.

The interface provides a variety of ways to attach metadata to a video scene, and the accumulated metadata is shown in the top middle section of the interface. Date, freeform text, and user-defined metadata tags are possible annotations within this system. Although the metadata categories are completely user-defined and form a potentially complex hierarchical network, we expect that in any home video archive three major categories of interest will emerge: *Who* is in the scene, *Where* that scene is and what *Event* is depicted in the scene. There are a few ways to associate a metadata tag to a video scene, the simplest being to drag the tag from the hierarchy on the right of the interface to the video window.

The freeform text window at the top of the interface is a quick way to associate arbitrary text to video scenes, making it a convenient interface when people are talking aloud about the video during a family gathering. As we describe next, this freeform text can be used to help accelerate assignment of metadata tags to a scene.

2.2 The Need to Improve Annotation Efficiency

Our experience with managing home video motivates the automatic annotation of *who, what, when, where* at the point of capture. Rich and accurate metadata is the key to managing a large video archive. As video content and potential tags grow, it becomes increasingly time consuming to annotate video scenes. Recognizing the trade-off between time and richness of annotation, we designed features available in our original system to speed up annotation without sacrificing correctness. First, the semi-automatic scene detection mentioned earlier can save considerable time by inferring scene changes, but can vary with the quality of the video recording. Second, the application matches the free-form text description against the names of metadata tags, placing suggested tags in a separate part of the annotation interface. The tag suggestion window contains far fewer tags than the tagging hierarchy window making it easier to find appropriate tags. A prioritization function places more likely tag candidates near the top of the list to make things even easier. Third, the same tag can be assigned to multiple scenes. Often, when viewing some scenes, a user suddenly becomes aware of a new piece of information (*e.g.* a new person is identified or the location is clarified) that applies to several of the preceding scenes. Rather than requiring users to load each of those scenes and add the new annotation, users can apply this new tag to all of them simultaneously. Fourth, multiple tags can be assigned to a scene simultaneously by dragging a branch from the tagging hierarchy. For example, dragging the "My Family" category over a scene assigns every person under that category to that scene.

Despite these accelerators for annotation, users still require a large amount of time to do the annotation properly. We observed an expert (both with the video content and the annotation interface) using the annotation interface for one hour. In that time, he was able to annotate 30 minutes of video, using 255 metadata tags (54 unique ones), free form text, and date stamps. We identify the manual annotations in increasing order of occurrence per video scene:

- **Time/Date**: Time information is usually just specified once in a scene.
- **Event**: Scenes typically depict only a small number of events (usually just one) but there may be sub events within a video scene that a user wants to tag.
- **Location**: Location is typically assigned once in a scene but a variety of higher-level location tags may be assigned if the location is hard to determine or unfamiliar.
- **People**: There may be many people in a scene and the user may need to view all of the video to account for everyone.

Much of the tagging overhead is due to the user actually viewing and reviewing various segments of the video to acquire enough context information to make tagging decisions. From our case study, two-thirds (40 minutes) of the whole annotation time consisted of video playback and navigation. The overhead of physically searching and selecting tags accounts for the rest of the annotation time.

Annotation at the point of capture can potentially eliminate time, location and people tagging. The only annotation that remains is event information, which we will show can be inferred based on current time, location, people and past annotations. The problem of losing or forgetting important information because of retrospective manual tagging further motivates the point of capture approach. Manual tagging heavily relies on recalling and recognizing past events that may have faded from memory.

3 Related Work

The proliferation of digital artifacts, such as photographs and videos, has motivated many researchers and companies to address the general problem of collecting, organizing and browsing memories. Much work has been done for digital photographs, including automated methods for organizing based on feature analysis of the images [11, 19, 27], visualization strategies [2, 3, 13, 14, 21, 24, 28] and annotation techniques similar to what we described in the previous section [7, 16]. Other useful research (e.g. CMU's Informedia Project [30]) and commercial (e.g., the VideoLogger from Virage [29]) tools show the promise of tools to browse and search digital video libraries.

However, there is still little work in automatically generating annotations for videos and some of the techniques used in automated photograph annotation do not easily extend to video. We identify four different annotation approaches.

Low-level semantic detection: Automated techniques exist for doing keyframe extraction and scene boundary detection [12], and many of these assume high-quality, structured video and/or textual metadata. These techniques provide little to no higher-level semantic meaning. Although possible with photographs, analyzing content of video is a much more computationally expensive task. Video annotation environments have been developed for detailed analysis of audiovisual data as well [8]. Researchers in linguistics and film studies perform fine-grained analysis of audiovisual data and tools like Anvil and IBM's VideoAnnEx support this kind of analysis [15, 30].

Manual annotation: Systems that provide manual annotation of high-level semantics for home videos are beginning to emerge [1, 4, 7]. These systems typically feature an interface where users can manually enter metadata as they review the video. In addition, television broadcasts are typically manually scripted and often synchronized with closed captioning.

Context acquisition at time of capture: Researchers are also now looking at point of capture tagging of photographs by sensing context information from standalone digital cameras and integrated camera phones [9, 27]. This usually consists of time and location stamping. In addition to spatio-temporal metadata, we are looking to add information about the people in the view of the camera (and nearby but not in the field of view) and to infer event information.

Predictive annotation: The Garage Cinema research group at UC Berkeley has recently produced a prototype point of capture system for camera phones [27]. Time and location information (at a very coarse level) are captured on camera phones and submitted to a network-based prediction algorithm that provides a web interface to select higher level semantic information that is used to feed a prediction system. Our motivation aligns with the work of theirs, which advocates very strongly the need to consider annotation at the point of capture. In addition to working with video as opposed to digital still imagery, we are also distinguished from this previous work because we do not assume a network-based interaction for higher-level semantic annotation in our approach to the ContextCam.

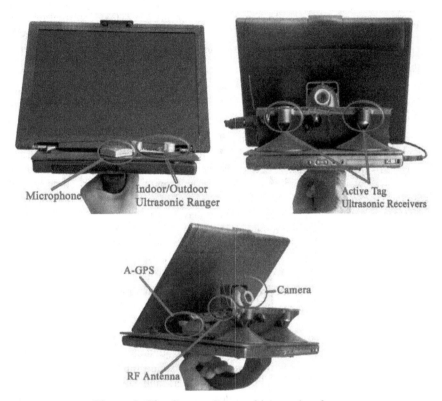

Figure 2: The ContextCam and its sensing features.

4 Low-Level Point of Capture Information for Annotation

Figure 2 shows the ContextCam prototype and some of its context sensing features. This original prototype is a modified Pentium-III laptop with camera and sensors mounted behind a viewing display. The software running on the ContextCam uses the Java Media Framework (JMF) for video capture and access. This prototype was designed as a proof of concept of the underlying technologies. In this section, we describe all of the sensing capabilities of the ContextCam that relate to simple, unambiguous metadata that can be associated to recorded video. In the next section, we demonstrate how this low-level context information, combined with past annotations, helps infer high-level semantic metadata.

4.1 When a Video Scene Is Recorded

The date and time of recording are fundamental and straightforward metadata to associate at the point of capture. Though many camcorders actually record date and time, most capture software does not access or preserve that information. The ContextCam acquires date and time information from an internal clock as well as from GPS satellites. As we will discuss later, this metadata is then encoded in the video itself for later extraction in our annotation/browsing environment.

4.2 Where a Video Is Recorded

To annotate low-level location information, the ContextCam uses a multi-channel assisted-GPS (A-GPS) receiver from a Motorola iDEN i730 handset. The assisted GPS systems provide slightly better accuracy and reliability than standard GPS receivers. We were able to get fixes where a traditional GPS receiver could not, such as some indoor locations and near windows. The GPS provides raw latitude/longitude coordinates and is stored as metadata in the video stream, which is also converted and stored as higher-level semantic tags. However, there are many cases where the ContextCam cannot get a clear fix. We address this limitation by using cached location fixes from the cellular network. Although not as accurate, this still provides at least city level location information.

GPS and cached fixes do not provide information to distinguish between indoor or outdoor shots. Researchers have classified indoor and outdoor locations in photographs using color and texture analysis [19]. Because the ContextCam is present in the environment at the point of capture, it can sense whether it is indoors or outdoors directly. We use the reflection of an ultrasound chirp sent vertically up from the camera to determine if it is indoors. The ultrasound ranger is tuned to about 50 feet, so the lack of a reflection indicates outdoors and any detection indicates an indoor location. Although this solution does not work everywhere, it works for most situations. We considered other approaches such as 60 Hz artificial light detection, but found this ultrasonic solution was better.

4.3 Who Is in or Around the Field of View

One of the most time consuming tasks of manual annotations is tagging all of the people appearing in a scene. From our observation, this accounts for 75% of the annotation process. Retrospective tagging of people in a scene is very slow and does not guarantee that everyone will be recognized. Though the FVA annotation interface provides the ability to indicate exactly when within a scene a particular person was present, it is far too tedious to add this information, so the default setting is individual being "in" the video for the duration of a scene. Because knowing who is in a scene is important, we designed the ContextCam to provide a solution that can quickly and accurately determine this information. As an added bonus, our solution allows us to annotate who is nearby a scene but not in the field of view, something that is difficult to know when annotating retrospectively.

For accuracy and reliability we explore an active tagging approach for detecting people in or around the field of view of the camera. However, we considered passive techniques first. Computer vision would be computationally expensive and unreliable, being further complicated by relatively low quality images and occlusions that are part of home videos. Furthermore, a vision solution would only ever be able to determine people within the field of view of the camera, and we see an opportunity to sense people outside the field of view as well. Sound detection techniques would be even less appropriate for constant tracking of people. Passive tagging techniques, such as some forms of RF ID, would not be practical because of the range limitation for reading tags and the lack of precision for distinguishing tags within and outside the field of view.

We envision people who are part of a captured event wearing or carrying a small active token. The active tag is used to gather information about their position in relation to the camera (in its view or somewhere near it). These tags are low power and small enough to integrate into something that an individual is likely to wear, such as jewelry, or carry, such as a cellphone. Our current prototype tags are bulky and inappropriate for deployment (see Figure 3), but there is no inherent reason why they could not be designed to a more appealing form factor.

Figure 3: An active tag used to determine individuals in the view of the camera. A production tag could be much smaller and aesthetically pleasing.

We explored a variety of active tagging techniques such as Infrared (IR) and radio frequencies (RF). IR is typically limited to short range and is difficult to triangulate at longer ranges. IR is also susceptible to occlusions and is greatly affected by ambient light. RF, on the other hand, is not as completely affected by occlusions and generally provides long-range communication, but RF triangulation is prone to reflections and other conditions which limit its resolution and accuracy. Despite these drawbacks, RF is a good solution to detect people who are near or around the camera.

We chose an ultrasonic time of flight system for our location information. Ultrasound does not provide long-range communication like RF, but it provides very accurate location and position information. Although it also can suffer somewhat from occlusion and multi-path complications, for our needs, we found that it is the best compromise between range and accuracy.

Partly inspired by MIT's Cricket [22, 23] and other location systems in the literature [10, 31], we use ultrasound to triangulate position of active tags around the camera. Each tag periodically chirps an ultrasound sequence and two ultrasound receivers mounted on the camera detect these chirps and calculate the relative distance between the tag and the receivers. The farther apart the receivers on the camera are, the finer the location resolution. For our prototype, we place the ultrasound receivers 6 inches apart, which yields position accuracy within 1 foot.

The ultrasound emitters on the active tags operate at 40 kHz, though less audible higher frequency emitters can be used. They are tuned to operate at ranges up to 50 feet. A higher-powered emitter could also be used for longer-range applications. A 300 MHz TE 99 Ming RF module accompanies the ultrasonic emitter on the tag. A single active tag emit cycle consists of a RF ping, followed by 5 ultrasound chirps. The RF ping, which consists of a 32 bit unique identifier, synchronizes the clock to the time the flight of the ultrasound chirp. Five ultrasound chirps spaced 10 ms apart follow the initial ping. The active tag continuously emits the RF/US sequence and draws at most 50 mA, which lasts about a day on a pair of 1.5-volt lithium ion cell batteries.

We place two ultrasound receivers on a horizontal plane in front of the camera. The cone shaped bases help direct the ultrasound chirp towards the receiver, increasing the likelihood of detection. For our prototype, we only focus on the azimuth angle. We assume people in the view of the camera would likely be on the sample relative plane as the camera, so the elevation angles would be negligible especially as the distance between the tag and the camera increases. Based on the camera's zoom level, we compare the azimuth with the camera view angle to determine if the tag is in the view of the camera.

The ContextCam also captures who is near or around the camera by simply storing the RF pings. This is important for detecting people who are at an event, but not the prime focus of the situation.

The biggest concern with our choice of an active tagging scheme is one of practical deployment. Active tagging enables effortless detailed annotation of people and objects in or around the camera. However, the problem with active tagging is the willingness of someone to actually distribute tags to individuals before capturing an event. Privacy problems also arise from an active tagging scheme. We can imagine that in the future each individual will wear or carry some sort of ubiquitous token. However, there are some motivating reasons why active tagging is a practical option for the ContextCam *today*. Researchers have already been able to successfully deployed large number of tracking or identification tags at events like conferences [5, 20].

Though "spur of the moment" situations would not work well with an active tagging scheme, most home videos depict settings or events that are known in advance, so "active tagging" one's whole family before recording is possible. The willingness to go through the trouble of distributing these tags comes down to the perceived cost-benefit for the user. As we have indicated, annotating the presence of individuals is the most time-consuming task, especially for large events like a family reunion or graduation. Taking 10 minutes to register and distribute the active tags may be a much better option than spending 2 hours to annotate a one-hour video.

Additionally, the active tags can be integrated into existing personal services like a cellphone or a Child Guard (a device that detects when a child wanders too far).

Another concern with active tagging is privacy. The active tags can allow users to opt-out by simply turning the device off or removing it if they do not feel comfortable being tracked on or around the camera. The ContextCam can provide a mechanism for individuals to opt-out of particular scenes, which is not possible with traditional videography. Although the individuals are still resident in the scene, there is an explicit indication in video metadata about their desire to opt-out.

5 Higher-Level Point of Capture Annotation

The metadata produced by the ContextCam at the point of capture is relatively low-level, which implies that some of the information is not directly beneficial to the user. High-level semantic metadata, the information produced manually in our previous annotation system, has more relevant meaning to the user. A tradeoff emerges between these two levels. Automatically captured low-level metadata tends to be very accurate. On the other hand, high-level semantic information is valuable, but introduces potential errors when automatically inferred. With manual annotation, the opposite is true. Whereas humans are good at identifying higher-level meaning and can do it rather quickly, detailed annotation of low-level information (time of day for a scene, when a person comes in and out of a scene) is particularly error prone. We show here how the low-level metadata from the point of capture can be translated and/or used to infer other higher-level semantic metadata. We also explore in the next section a way to help close this semantic gap with minimal human intervention.

5.1 Other Time Information

High-level time and date information is relatively straightforward to produce. Most common time and date semantics can simply be translated without any sophisticated inference scheme. For instance, the ContextCam determines holidays and seasons by simply looking at the timestamp and some calendar information. In this case the high-level semantic metadata is very accurate.

5.2 Inferring More Meaningful Location

The ContextCam produces raw latitude/longitude position coordinates for location information, which is indecipherable by the user. To extract more high-level meaning, we use a publicly available Geographic Information System (GIS) resource to determine the address. From this information, we retrieve street names, city, state, and sometimes landmarks. When used indoors, the ContextCam retrieves city and state information using the cellular network. And if we wanted to expend the effort, the same active tagging scheme could be used to tag indoor locations that could then be recognized automatically by the ContextCam. Cities and states are adequate for many high-level semantic tags, though there are even higher-level tags that may be more appropriate such as "Disney World" or "Grand Canyon." Many of these higher level location tags can be inferred using the same technique we will show for inferring events.

The ContextCam's indoor/outdoor recognizer provides added information to help infer location and event based on other context information and past annotations. Though not directly valuable to the user, this information can play an important role in predicting annotations.

5.3 Inferring Event Information

Event information refers to what a particular video scene is about or *what* is being depicted within the scene, such as a birthday celebration, Christmas party, graduation, family reunion, basketball game, etc. Event information poses the most problems with automated annotation, since it typically consists of purely high-level semantic information that is almost impossible to detect directly with just sensors. However, event information can be inferred from the other context information and higher level semantics such as time, location, and people. For instance, we can infer a child's birthday party from the date, the fact that the child is of prime focus, and the people around, such as friends. All this information can be gathered with the ContextCam. The inference system becomes even more powerful when users validate or confirm the predicted event formation at the time of capture. Although event tags do not completely dominate the video annotation process, inferring and suggesting event tags can help alleviate some of the burden of manually searching and tagging from a large event tag hierarchy.

For the ContextCam we use a naïve Bayesian classifier to help infer higher-level event information based on the low-level context information gathered at the time of capture and verified past annotations. The information used for inferring includes the time, date, location attributes of a scene, and the people in and around the camera. Studies comparing classification algorithms have found the naïve Bayesian classifier to be comparable in performance with classification trees and neural network classifiers [17]. They also have exhibited high accuracy and speed when applied to large databases. The naïve Bayesian classifier is a statistical classifier. Given a scene and its current annotations, it can find the most probable high-level class that is consistent with the relative frequencies of past annotations and context attributes.

The root event node of the classifier represents the "class" of tags that the predictor tries to classify. A user-defined threshold determines the acceptance of inferred tags. Since the classifier determines the probabilities of all classes, there may be multiple tags that are inferred for a particular scene as long as the confidence is over the specified threshold.

The Bayesian classifier starts out with a minimal training set, but every time any scene is automatically annotated and appropriate event tags associated at the time of capture, a new entry is placed in the training set (stored as probability condition matrices on the camera). Thus the training set can grow fairly rapidly with just a few captured events. We tested the predictor using the case study archive mentioned above, which consists of 12 years (approx 12 hours) of video manually annotated with who, what, when, and where metadata. In the experiment, each test case represented one year from our case study archive, and the training set consisted of the one, two, and three years preceding the tested year. We purposely chose one year chunks because most of the events in the archive were yearly (such as birthdays and reunions). Each year roughly included an equivalent number of who, what, when, and where (approximately 50 scenes per year and 400 tags in our case). Table 1 shows the prediction accuracy for the three cases. Our data suggests that one year of annotation data would be sufficient to produce fairly accurate predictions, requiring only three top suggestions to cover 95% of all cases. Taking more years (over 2 years in our case) into consideration actually hurts the accuracies, because family dynamics change over time. For example, family activities may change as a result of the addition of new family members, moving to a new home, and children growing up. However, an inference scheme that takes these potential changes into consideration so that more preceding years can be used in the predictor could be developed.

The accuracies shown in Table 1 do not take into account all the rich metadata that the ContextCam provides. Rather, it provides a baseline performance for simple user specified metadata. We suspect an actual long-term use (1-2 years) of the ContextCam will provide even better results, but we have not validated that claim.

Table 1: Accuracy of a naïve Bayesian classifier used to predict event tags. Each year consisted of approximately 50 user defined scenes with 400 metadata tags.

Number of directly preceding years used for training	Prediction accuracy	Number of event tags representing 95% confidence
1 year	79.6%	3.2
2 years	80.3%	2.8
3 years	80.1%	2.9

6 Storing the Metadata: Embedding Metadata into Video Frames

Storage of both low-level and high-level metadata to video scenes presents some interesting challenges with storage synchronization. MPEG-7 has emerged as a multimedia content description standard. However, MPEG-7 does not specify any standard for automatic AV description extraction or attaching of metadata to actual AV content. Commercial DV tapes allow minimal storage of metadata information like timestamps, but capture software rarely preserves this information and there is no clear standard that DV camera manufacturers follow. More importantly, these metadata storage units typically hold very limited information so they do not have the space to store a lot of metadata. Another approach is to store the information on a separate medium, such as another DV tape or compact flash, but this presents problems with synchronization. Now the user is burdened with two physical artifacts that add more complexity to the system when importing the videos into an archive or video editing tool.

Our solution is to multiplex the metadata directly into the raw uncompressed video captured from a digital video camera. We accomplish this by replacing every 60th frame (every two seconds when capturing at 30 fps) with a binary encoding of the metadata into the frame. So, at the 640 X 480 resolution of the digital camcorder in our prototype, there is 921 KB of space available for two seconds of metadata. When the video is extracted from the camera, the metadata is decoded from the raw video and the metadata frames are replaced with the previous frame. We found that even if the frame is not removed, there is very little perceptible difference between the encoded and non-encoded video. However, a problem arises when the video is compressed. Because the metadata frame is likely to be very different from the rest of the video frames (as a result of the encoded data), the video does not compress well. Replacing the metadata frame with the previous frame before compression alleviates this problem.

We also explored a simple steganographic technique that does not require replacing the metadata frame and encodes the metadata information in the least significant bits (LSBs) of the whole video frame. In other words the data is encoded using the last bits of the RGB values for each pixel. This scheme preserves the content of the video frame and is still visually similar to the original frame. This frame has a negligible impact on video compression and almost no perceptible difference during video playback (see figure 4). The tradeoff with this scheme is that at 640 X 480 the potential storage space decreases to 115 KB for 1 LSB, which is still enough space in our experience. Figure 4 shows the difference in picture quality for the metadata frame using more LSBs for increased storage. The metadata stays resident until compressed to another format. Although not used in the ContextCam, a compression resistant steganographic encoding technique [6] could have also been used to preserve the metadata through compression.

7 Interacting with the ContextCam

Having presented the ContextCam, we now explore the user experience of interacting with a point of capture annotation system. The ContextCam provides automated real-time point of capture annotation. Attributes like time, location, and people are attached to video with no human intervention, freeing the user to capture and enjoy the moment. Similarly, point of capture annotation also frees much of the burden of annotation after capturing the video. Browsing, filtering, and authoring capabilities of our video archive system briefly described in Section 2 are available immediately after recording.

Although our prototype ContextCam is a bulky modified laptop computer, the sensing hardware could be added to a commercial video camcorder with relatively little added bulk. The computational capabilities to support the active tagging triangulation and Bayesian inference engine are not computationally expensive.

Figure 4: An example of metadata encoded in each 8 bit RBG value for each pixel. Top left: Original Picture.   Top right: Metadata encoded in 1 LSB.   Bottom left: Metedata encoded in 2 LSBs. Bottom right: Metadata encoded in 3 LSBs.

What remains to be discovered is how the user would interact with the inference of high-level semantic metadata in order to accept or correct predictions while recording. Many digital video cameras already feature some sort of simple thumb or finger control (jog dial or arrow pad) to navigate a simple menu structure. Figure 5 is a screenshot of the ContextCam's prototype interface. The viewfinder occupies the center of the screen. The top portion of the screen shows the current event inferred by the real-time predictor. A user has two options for the event predictor. One is to set a threshold for an event to automatically associate with a scene. The other is to select the event from a list, ordered by likelihood, displayed near the upper right portion of the screen. After a user selects an event it is placed on the upper left portion of the screen. When the ContextCam suspects an event change, the currently selected event begins to flash. The user can either ignore the cue or select another event from the list. From our experience we found that two levels of event tagging were sufficient: event and sub event. A user can modify the sub event by pulling up the sub event list (same choices as the event list) and selecting the appropriate event. The ContextCam only uses one level when set to automatically assign event tags.

The ContextCam (see Figure 2) is equipped with a short-range, noise-canceling microphone on the back of the camera that is designed to capture audio commentary from the videographer. Although not currently implemented, we can imagine using the voice input and keyword spotting to test against the list of all previously entered events, providing further suggestions to the predictor. A relatively small dictionary of current metadata tags in the family archive makes this a feasible real-time solution with existing speech technology.

Similar in spirit of NaviCam [25, 26], the ContextCam can provide an augmented interaction experience by overlaying context information (who, when, where) on the screen while capturing a scene (see figure 6).

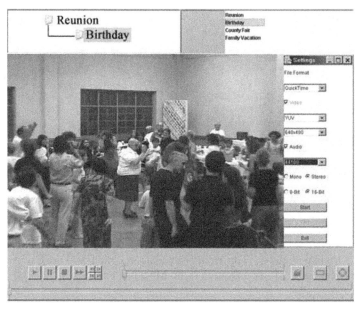

Figure 5: A screenshot of the interface on the ContextCam.

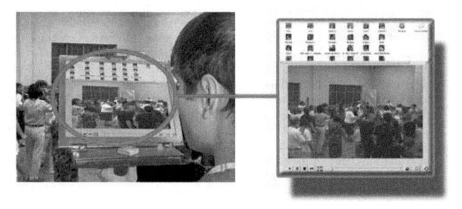

Figure 6: The ContextCam showing some live metadata (who and where) currently in the scene while capturing. The upper portion of the screen shows a thumbnail and name of each person currently in the view of the camera.

8 Conclusions

The ContextCam is a point of capture video annotation system that integrates a variety of sensing techniques to attach metadata of *when*, *where* and *who* directly to recorded video. It also uses simple mappings to infer high-level information of when and where, and a Bayesian predictor that uses point of capture metadata and past annotation history to suggest what event is currently being recorded. We presented the design of the ContextCam in detail and suggested how prediction capabilities and other features of audio annotation might be wrapped seamlessly into the video recording experience.

The original motivation of the ContextCam was to help reduce the arduous and time-consuming task of manual annotation of home videos, further amplifying the capabilities for filtering and sharing a family's recorded history. There may be other uses for point of capture annotation. For example, Su *et al.* suggest that video annotation at the point of capture using networks of wireless sensors might dramatically increase the capabilities for film production [28]. If we increase the accuracy of the ContextCam ultrasonic sensing by placing two more receivers on a vertical axis to determine angle of elevation, we could produce more 3-D tracking information, providing the potential for interesting visualizations of the recorded data. This would even allow for person identification after an event (*e.g.*, "Who is that person standing next to Grandma?") or even during the event (*e.g.*, when you lose a small child while on vacation). Most importantly, except for some issues with deploying tags and associating them to the ContextCam, all of the capabilities discussed in this paper are possible today without tremendous technology. For the visions of ubiquitous computing to become a reality, we need to see more examples of these kinds of capabilities made real in our everyday lives.

Acknowledgments

This work is sponsored in part by National Science Foundation (ITR grant 0121661). The authors thank Motorola, and in particular Joe Dvorak of iDEN Advancing Technologies Group, for the donation of the iDEN handsets used in this research.

References

1. Abowd, G.D., Gauger, M. and Lachenmann, A. The Family Video Archive: An annotation and browsing environment for home movies. *In the Proceedings of MIR*, November, 2003, Berkeley, CA.
2. Adcock, J., Cooper, M.D., Doherty, J., Foote, J., Girgensohn, A., and Wilcox, L. Managing digital memories with the FXPAL photo application. ACM Multimedia 2003: 598-599
3. Bederson, B.B. PhotoMesa: A Zoomable Image Browser using Quantum Treemaps and Bubblemaps. In *Proceedings of the ACM Symposium on User Interface Software and Technology (UIST 2001)*, Orlando, FL, November 2001, pp. 71-80.

4. Casares, J., Myers, B.A, Long, C., Bhatnagar, R., Stevens, S.M, Dabbish, L., Yocum, D., and Corbett, A. Simplifying Video Editing Using Metadata. In *Proceedings of Designing Interactive Systems (DIS 2002)*, London, UK, June 2002. pp. 157-166.

5. Cox, D., Kindratenko, V., and Pointer, D. IntelliBadge: Towards Providing Location-Aware Value-Added Services at Academic Conferences, *UbiComp 2003*, Seattle, WA. Lecture Notes in Computer Science, 2003, vol. 2864, pp. 264-280.

6. Currie III, D.L., Irvine, C.E. Surmounting the Effects of Lossy Compression on Steganography, Proceedings of the 19th National Information System Security Conference, October 1996. 1996. pp. 194-201.

7. Davis, M. Media Streams: An Iconic Visual Language for Video Representation. *In Readings in Human-Computer Interaction: Toward the Year 2000*, eds. Ronald M. Baecker, Jonathan Grudin, William A. S. Buxton, and Saul Greenberg. 854-866. 2nd ed., San Francisco: Morgan Kaufmann Publishers, Inc., 1995.

8. Girgensohn, A., Boreczky, J., Chiu, P., Doherty, J., Foote, J., Golovchinsky, G., Uchihashi, S., and Wilcox, L. A Semiautomatic Approach to Home Video Editing. In *Proceedings of the ACM Symposium on Use rIinterface Software and Technology (UIST 2000)*, San Diego, CA, November 5-8 2000, pp 81-89.

9. Hakansson, M., Ljungblad, S., and Holmquist, L.E. Capturing the Invisible: Designing Context Aware Photography. *Proceedings of DUX 2003, Designing for User Experience*, ACM / AIGA, San Francisco, CA, June 5-7 2003.

10. Hazas, M., and Ward, A. A Novel Broadband Ultrasonic Location System. *In Proceedings of UbiComp 2002: Fourth International Conference on Ubiquitous Computing*, LNCS volume 2498, pages 264-280, Göteborg, Sweden, September 2002.

11. Jeon, J., Lavrenko, V. and Manmatha, R., "Automatic Image Annotation and Retrieval using Cross-Media Relevance Models," in the *Proceedings of SIGIR '03 Conference*, pp. 119-126.

12. Jiang, H., Helal, A., Elmagarmid, A., and Joshi, A. Scene Change Detection Techniques for Video Database Systems. ACM Multimedia Systems, 6:3, May 1998, pp. 186-195.

13. Kang, H. and Shneiderman, B. Visualization Methods for Personal Photo Collections: Browsing and Searching in the PhotoFinder. In *Proceedings of the IEEE International Conference on Multimedia and Expo (ICME 2000)*, New York City, New York, August 2000, pp. 1539-1542.

14. Kender, J.R., and Yeo, B.L. On the Structure and Analysis of Home Videos. *Proceedings of the Asian Conference on Computer Vision*, January 2000.

15. Kipp, M. Anvil video annotation system. http://www.dfki.de/~kipp/anvil/. Page downloaded on August 1, 2003.

16. Kuchinsky, A., Pering, C., Creech, M., Freeze, D., Serra, B., and Gwizdka, J. FotoFile: A Consumer Multimedia Organization and Retrieval System. In Proceedings of the Conference on Human factors in computing systems (CHI 99). Pittsburgh, Pennsylvania, USA, May 15-20 1999, pp. 496-503.

17. Langley, P., Iba, W., and Thompson, K. (1992). An analysis of Bayesian classifiers. Proceedings of the Tenth National Conference on Artificial Intelligence (pp. 223--228). San Jose, CA: AAAI Press.

18. Lavrenko, V., Feng, S.L. and Manmatha, R., "Statistical Models for Automatic Video Annotation and Retrieval," submitted to the *International Conference on Acoustics, Speech and Signal Processing,(ICASSP)*, Montreal, QC, Canada, May 17-21, 2004.

19. Luo, J., and Savakis, A. "Indoor vs. Outdoor Classification of Consumer Photographs," Int. Conf. Image Proc. ICIP'01, Thessaloniki, Greece, Oct. 2001.

20. McCarthy, J.F., Nguyen, D.H., Rashid, A.M., and Soroczak, S. Proactive Displays & The Experience UbiComp Project. UbiComp 2003, Adjunct Proceedings, 12-15 October 2003, Seattle, WA.

21. Platt, J. C., Czerwinskim, M., and Field, B. PhotoTOC: Automatic Clustering for Browsing Personal Photographs. Microsoft Research Technical Report MSR-TR-2002-17, 2002.

22. Priyantha, N, Chakraborty, A., and Balakrishnan, H. The Cricket location-support system. In *Proceedings of the Sixth Annual ACM International Conference on Mobile Computing and Networking*, Boston, MA, August 2000. ACM Press.

23. Priyantha, N, Miu, Balakrishman, H., and Teller, S. The Cricket Compass for Context-Aware Mobile Applications. *In Proceedings of the 7th Annual ACM/IEEE International Conference on Mobile Computing and Networking (MOBICOM 2000)*.

24. Ramos, G. and Balakrishnan, R. Fluid Interaction Techniques for the Control and Annotation of Digital Video. In *Proceedings of the ACM Symposium on User Interface Software and Technology (UIST 2003)*. Vancouver, Canada, November 2-5, 2003.

25. Rekimoto, J and Katashi, N.: The World through the Computer: Computer Augmented Interaction with Real World Environments, *Proceedings of the ACM Symposium on User Interface Software and Technology (UIST '95)*, ACM Press, pp.29-36, Pittsburgh, PA.

26. Rekimoto, J. NaviCam: A Magnifying Glass Approach to Augmented Reality, *Presence: Teleoperator and Virtual Environments*, Vol. 6, No. 4, pp. 399-412, August 1997.

27. Sarvas, R., Herrarte, E., Wilhelm, A., and Davis, M. Metadata Creation System for Mobile Images. *In Proceedings of the Second International Conference on Mobile Systems, Applications, and Services (MobiSys2004)* in Boston, Massachusetts. ACM Press, June 2004.

28. Su, N.M., Park, H., Bostrom, E., Burke, J., Srivastava, M.B, and Estrin, D. Augmenting film and video footage with sensor data. In *Proceedings of the Second IEEE International Conference on Pervasive Computing and Communications (PerCom 2004)*, Orlando, FL, March 2004, pp. 3-12.

29. Virage, Inc.. VideoLogger product.   http://www.virage.com/solutions/details.cfm?sol utionID=5&categoryID=1&products=0. Page downloaded on February 21, 2004.

30. Wactlar, H. D., Christel, M., Gong, Y., and Hauptmann, A. Lessons Learned from the Creation and Deployment of a Terabyte Digital Video Library. IEEE Computer 32(2), 1999, pp. 66-73.

31. Want, R., Hopper, A., Falcao, V., and Gibbons, J. The active badge location system. *ACM Transactions on Information Systems*, 10(1):91-102, Jan 1992.

MouseField: A Simple and Versatile Input Device for Ubiquitous Computing

Toshiyuki Masui[1], Koji Tsukada[2], and Itiro Siio[3]

[1] National Institute of Advanced Industrial Science and Technology
Center Office 18F, Bunkyo Green Court
2-28-8 Honkomagome, Bunkyo, Tokyo 113-659, Japan
masui@acm.org
[2] Graduate School of Media and Governance
Keio University
5322 Endo Fujisawa, Kanagawa 252-8520, Japan
tsuka@sfc.keio.ac.jp
[3] Tamagawa University
6-1-1 Tamgawa Gakuen, Machida, Tokyo 194-8610, Japan
siio@acm.org

Abstract. Although various interaction technologies for handling information in the ubiquitous computing environment have been proposed, some techniques are too simple for performing rich interaction, and others require special expensive equipments to be installed everywhere, and cannot soon be available in our everyday environment. We propose a new simple and versatile input device called the MouseField that enables users to control various information appliances easily without huge amount of cost.

A MouseField consists of an ID recognizer and motion sensors that can detect an object and its movement after the object is placed on it. The system can interpret the user's action as a command to control the flow of information. In this paper, we show how this simple device can be used for handling information easily in ordinary environments like living rooms, kitchens, and toilets, and show the benefits of using it in the ubiquitous computing environment.

1 Introduction

Today, various Internet services are available and many people are using wireless networks at home. We now seem to have all the infrastructure for networked information appliances, but they are not yet available at every corner of the house, because standard computer input devices such as keyboards and mouses are not usable on the walls, on the kitchen table, and in the toilet.

To use computers in the ubiquitous computing environment, various interesting and useful technologies have been proposed. If input and output devices are equipped at many locations in a house, users can control information in a different way than conventional GUI techniques using keyboards and mouses. However, most of such techniques require many expensive and special sensors installed at all the places where interaction is performed.

N. Davies et al. (Eds.): UbiComp 2004, LNCS 3205, pp. 319–328, 2004.

For example, sophisticated interaction between human and a wall or a desk is possible if a precise position sensor and a projector is installed at the place of the interaction[1]. In this case, the user may be able to use his finger as a mouse and control menus and icons displayed on the wall or on the table. This kind of interaction is interesting and possibly useful, but it is unlikely that those devices will be widely used at home in the near future, since they are expensive, heavy, fragile, and difficult to install. Mirrors can be used to reduce the number of projectors[2], but installation and registration of these devices is not easy.

In addition, those devices cannot be used in rugged environments like kitchens and toilets where people may want to handle devices with wet hands. People like to have a computer in the kitchen, but they would not pay a lot of money to construct an IT kitchen just for watching TV programs and reading recipes on the Web. For enjoying real ubiquitous computing at home, robust and inexpensive input/output devices should be used at various corners of a house, and they should also be versatile enough so that they can accept various requirements from users.

RFID tags and printed barcodes have long been the candidate devices for controlling information appliances. Using the tags instead of keyboards and mouses is useful in many cases, since both the tags and readers are robust enough and can be put at almost any place. Also, the system is usually very easy to use, since the only thing a user can do with a tag or a barcode is to put the tag in front of the reader, and there's little chance of suffering from confusion. For example, you may be able to use a "weather forecast card" to check the weather at a nearby display, and you can use a "Yahoo stock tag" to check the stock status instantly without invoking a Web browser.

However, using these systems, a user can tell the system only one thing at a time, and cannot control complex things with one tag. For example, if a user wants to listen to various music using a tag-based music player, he should either use as many number of tags as the number of CDs he has, or use extra tags like "next", "rewind", and "volume up". Using a barcode-based presentation system[3], users have to prepare a number of cards for slide presentation. Tag-based systems are useful for small tasks, but it is difficult to perform complicated tasks with such systems.

2   MouseField

We introduce a robust and versatile input device called the MouseField that can be used at almost any place for controlling information appliances. MouseField is a device which combines an ID reader and motion sensing devices into one package.

Figure 1 shows an implementation of MouseField, which consists of two motion sensors (taken from standard optical mouses) and an RFID reader (Texas Instruments' S2000 Micro Reader) hidden under the surface.

The RFID reader and the two optical mouses are connected to a PC through a USB cable, and they can detect the ID and the motion of the object put on the device. When a user puts an object with an RFID on the MouseField, it first detects what was put on the RFID reader. When the user moves or rotates the object, the motion sensors detects the direction and rotation of the object. The amount of the rotation can be calculated by the difference of the amount of motions in the Y direction.

Front View   Back View

Fig. 1. An Implementation of a MouseField Device.

Table 1. Comparison of using the MouseField and using a mouse for controlling the sound volume.

Using a MouseField	Using a mouse in a computer display
Put an object on the the MouseField	Move the mouse cursor to the knob of a slider
(Wait until the RFID is recognized)	Click the mouse button
Rotate the object on the MouseField	Move the knob of the slider
Remove the object from the MouseField	Release the mouse button

These information are similar to the information we use when we control GUI widgets on PC screens. Just like we can control the sound volume by clicking the knob of a slider widget and move the slider up and down, we can do the same thing by putting a volume control object on a MouseField and moving or rotating the object. In this way, we can perform almost all kinds of GUI operations by putting an object on a Mouse-Field and moving it. For example, a user can put a "TV block" on a MouseField and rotate it to change programs, just like he can select a program using a pulldown menu. We can use a barcode reader instead of an RFID reader, just like our implementation of the FieldMouse[4]. Table 1 shows the comparison between using a MouseField and using a GUI slider for sound volume control.

Table 2. Comparison of using the MouseField and using a mouse for controlling the menu.

Using a MouseField	Using a mouse in a computer display
Put an object on the the MouseField	Move the mouse cursor to the menu title
(Wait until the RFID is recognized)	Click the mouse button
Move the object forward and backward	Drag the mouse cursor up and down
Remove the object from the MouseField	Release the mouse button

Fig. 2. PlayStand++: A Music Player with MouseField.

Similarly, Table 2 shows the comparison between using a MouseField and using a menu for selecting an item from a list. In this way, we can perform various kinds of GUI operations by putting an object on a MouseField and moving it. Nothing happens if the RFID was not recognized by the reader for some reason, just like nothing happens if people do not press the mouse button in standard GUI widgets.

The PlayStand++ system (Figure 2) shows how a user can enjoy music using a MouseField and CD jackets which represent the music in the CD. All the music in the CD are saved in a music server, and an RFID tag is attached to each CD jacket. When a user places a CD jacket on the MouseField, a music player is displayed on the screen, shows the contents of the CD, and starts playing songs. The user can change the sound volume by rotating the CD jacket, and move to the next or previous song by sliding the jacket to the front or to the back (Figure 3). When the user removes the jacket from the MouseField, the sound stops and a screen saver is displayed on the screen. The music player is not only very simple to use, but it allows users to control various parameters without using special controllers.

Just like a mouse can be used for various purposes, a MouseField can be used for whatever purpose you like in the ubiquitous computing applications. It can be used for invoking an application (just like a mouse-click can invoke an application), controlling parameters (just like using sliders and menus), selecting objects (just like dragging a mouse cursor), transferring data (just like mouse-based drag and drop), etc.

If we use multiple MouseField devices, we can utilize them for conveying information between locations. When we perform an operation on one MouseField and perform another operation on another MouseField, those series of operations can be interpreted as cooperative tasks. For example, a person can use one MouseField to tell the system that he wants to retrieve some information at the location, and use another MouseField

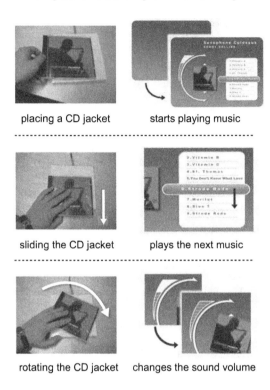

placing a CD jacket   starts playing music

----

sliding the CD jacket   plays the next music

----

rotating the CD jacket   changes the sound volume

Fig. 3. Controlling the Music Player.

to tell that he wants to convey the information to the new location. In this case, virtual Drag and Drop (or sometimes called "Pick and Drop"[5]) can be performed, just like other systems for using objects for carrying information[6][7]. If a person selects a TV program on a MouseField by using a TV block, he can bring the object to a different place with another MouseField and use the object to see the rest of the program there. In this way, MouseField can enable various interaction techniques which were only available with special and fragile input/output devices.

3   A Scenario of Using MouseFields

In this section, we show a scenario of a person's daily life where many MouseField devices are scattered at his house and at other places.

Hiro is a university student living alone in an apartment. In addition to his PC, he has a lot of hidden computers connected to MouseField devices installed in tables, walls, and doors. Those computers are used for various information appliances. Here begins his day:

  – *Hiro gets up in the morning, goes to the living room and wants to awaken his brain by watching today's morning TV news. He puts a "TV block" on the MouseField equipped in the table of the living room. Then the TV is turned on, and a TV program is shown on the display.*

- *Since the channel was not showing a news program, Hiro moves the TV block left and right to select a channel showing the morning news.*
- *He felt that the voice of the newscaster was too low, so he rotates the TV block and makes the sound a little louder.*
- *He then makes up his mind to make a morning coffee, and goes to the kitchen with the TV block. When he puts the block on the kitchen counter, the same TV news is displayed at the kitchen, since there's another MouseField equipped in the kitchen counter.*
- *He puts the TV block on the table and prepares to go to school. At the entrance door of his house, he puts his "Suica" card (a commutation ticket with an RFID) on the door, and check if there's something he has to do on that day. The display at the door tells him that a recycle car is coming to his neighborhood this morning, so he collects liquor bottles from his room and put them into a recycle box at the street corner near his house.*

We do not have to wait long before we can enjoy this kind of ubiquitous computing life. The only equipments required in this scenario are MouseField devices and displays connected via wireless network. There are so many services on the Internet, and wireless LANs and quiet PCs have been available in very low cost.

4   Discussions

4.1   Advantages of MouseField

The biggest advantage of using MouseField is that it can be inexpensive and robust. RFID tags are getting cheaper every day, and it costs less than $1 these days. Printed barcodes are almost priceless, and easily be replicated even when you lose it. Barcode readers, RFID readers, and motion sensors (optical mouses) are not as inexpensive as RFID tags, but they have been around for many years, and the prices are fairly low. You do not have to put MouseField devices everywhere, since people do not have to control information everywhere. In the house shown in the previous scenario, MouseField devices are equipped at only a small number of places including the living room and toilet. These are the locations where people sometimes stay for a while, and the number of those places are limited. If sufficient number of MouseField devices are installed, it would be more convenient than using remote controllers.

In spite of its simplicity, MouseField can be used for various purposes with only a few number of ID tags, owing to the motion sensors. Just like we don't have to use different mouses for different applications, we can use one RFID tag for various purposes. If we can't use the motion sensors, we have to use many RFID tags to do the same things described in the scenario.

4.2   Idioms of UbiComp

Many user interface idioms[8] are now widely accepted in the GUI on current PCs. Sliders and pulldown menus are examples of good GUI idioms. Although sliders and pulldown menus are not found in the real world, people will remember how to use it, once they see it and understand how it works. Idioms like Drag and Drop, Click and Drag, and other operations are now considered to be basic operation for handling computers. On the other hand, good interaction idioms for ubiquitous computing have not been widely accepted yet. Some systems use gestures, and others use special objects like "phicons"[9], but none of the operations are widely accepted to control information in the ubiquitous computing environment.

Since moving something on a MouseField is so easy, we believe that "Place and Move" operation on a MouseField can be one of the basic interaction idioms used in the ubiquitous computing environment, just like Click and Drag is now one of the basic operations used in GUI. It is not clear what is the best mapping between application functions and available operations on the MouseField. Some people may prefer rotation for volume control, and others may prefer sliding operation. We cannot tell which is better at this moment, but one of the mapping would become dominant in the future, and everybody would accept it as a standard idiom.

4.3   Using Feedbacks

In most GUI systems based on direct manipulation, a user can see the effects of his actions as soon as he types the keyboard or moves the mouse. In the PlayStand++ system, users can look at the monitor display to see what happens when they move the CD jacket on the MouseField. Although visual feedback is very important on GUI systems based on direct manipulation, sound feedback or other simpler feedbacks can also be used in systems like PlayStand++. For example, even when a monitor is not present, simple click sound works fine for selecting songs.

4.4   Objects for Controlling MouseField

We can use almost any kind of object for controlling information using MouseField. If we put an RFID tag in an object which represents something, it can be used as a phicon. We can also use existing RFID-based cards like Suica for identifying a user and controlling information. If we use a MouseField with a barcode reader instead of an RFID reader, we can use printed barcode on any product for handling information related to the product. In this way, we can use whatever we like for controlling information, when a MouseField is installed at the place where we need information. We can use a CD/DVD jacket for enjoying a music or a movie. We can use a food package for getting information like its ingredients and the company. In this way, using a Mouse-Field is like using any objects as a standard mouse. In this sense, MouseField is a very universal input device.

5   Related Work

RFID tags have been used in various ubiquitous computing systems and projects[10][11]. For example, in the AwareHome project[11] at Georgia Tech, many RFID readers are placed at the floor and used for identifying people walking in the house. In the real world, RFIDs are now widely used in many warehouses and libraries for identifying the status of packages and books. Many of the ubicomp systems use RFID tags mostly for identifying objects and people, but with MouseField, RFID tags are rather actively used for controlling the flow of information.

Since optical mouses are inexpensive and robust, they are used in various systems for detecting the motion of objects. For example, they are used in Navigational Blocks[12] for detecting the motion of blocks.

FieldMouse[4] is a device which has the same configuration as MouseField: a Field-Mouse consists of a motion sensing device and an ID recognizer. While MouseField is a device installed in tables and walls, FieldMouse is a device carried by people to control various information appliances. Advantages of using a FieldMouse is that people can operate real-world GUI[13] without installing many sensors everywhere. A disadvantage of using a FieldMouse is that a user always has to carry a FieldMouse to control information appliances. Since a FieldMouse consists of an ID recognizer and a motion sensor, it is always heavier than simple RFID tags. Also, it is not suitable to be used in kitchens and toilets.

"Phicons"[9], or physical icons, are sometimes useful for handling information in the ubiquitous computing environment. Using a MouseField, almost anything can be used as a phicon, if an RFID tag is put into it.

MediaBlocks[14] is a system for editing multimedia data like movie clips using multiple blocks. MediaBlocks has a special hardware which can detect the location of blocks, so the user can edit movie clips by changing the layout of the blocks. Mouse-Field can be used as a device to implement MediaBlocks and similar systems in wider range of environment.

DataTiles[15] enables users to perform various interesting operations using transparent square panels equipped with tags. The panels are laid out by the user on a LCD tablet, and the user can move the panel in a variety of way to perform various operations. The "Place and Move" idiom can be used on DataTiles. Since a LCD tablet should be used for DataTiles, it is less robust than the motion sensors used in MouseField.

Various techniques have been proposed for carrying information in the ubiquitous computing environment. In the WebStickers[7] system, users can attach URL bookmarks to barcodes, and carry the barcodes to use the bookmarks at other places. In the i-Land[16] system, a technique called Passage[6] is used for carrying information between different computers. Although people can carry data using a barcode or an RFID, complicated operations cannot be performed on these systems.

A technique called "Pick and Drop"[5] is proposed for picking up data from one computer and placing it to another computer. Using a FieldMouse[4], users can not only pick and drop data between objects, but they can perform arbitrary GUI operations like selecting menus. InfoStick[17] can also get data from one location for transferring it to another location, and PDAs are sometimes used for the same kind of purposes. In these systems, people should carry a special device like PDAs for carrying data.

There are also many ubicomp projects which use video cameras for identifying people and objects[1][18]. Using a camera with a pattern recognition system, we can detect the ID and the motion of the object at the same time, so in some cases using cameras is more appropriate than using RFID tags and readers. The advantage of using

RFID tags is that RFID tags can be hidden in almost any object, and no special pattern should be printed on the surface of the object. The same "Place and Move" idiom can be applied to camera-based systems.

Recently, various toolkits for ubiquitous computing is being proposed[19][20]. Since using a MouseField is almost the same as using a mouse in a GUI environment, adding features for handling MouseField to existing toolkits is easy.

6 Conclusion

We developed a simple, robust and flexible input device called the MouseField for controlling information in the ubiquitous computing environment. Despite its simplicity, MouseField is flexible enough for handling complex information at various places where conventional input devices like keyboards and mouses were not conveniently used. We have shown various possibilities of MouseField used everywhere in the ubiquitous computing environment. We hope MouseField will be one of the standard input devices used in the ubiquitous computing age.

References

[1] Koike, H., Sato, Y., Kobayashi, Y., Tobita, H., Kobayashi, M.: Interctivetextbook and interactivevenndiagram: Natural and intuitive interface on augmented desk system. In: Proceedings of the ACM Conference on Human Factors in Computing Systems (CHI2000), Addison-Wesley (2000) 121–128

[2] Pingali, G., Pinhanez, C., Levas, A., Kjeldsen, R., Podlaseck, M., Chen, H., Sukaviriya, N.: Steerable interfaces for pervasive computing spaces. In: First IEEE International Conference on Pervasive Computing and Communications (PerCom'03). (2003) 315–322

[3] Nelson, L., Ichimura, S., Pedersen, E.R., Adams, L.: A paper interface for giving presentations. In: Proceedings of the ACM Conference on Human Factors in Computing Systems (CHI'99), Addison-Wesley (1999) 354–361

[4] Siio, I., Masui, T., Fukuchi, K.: Real-world interaction using the FieldMouse. In: Proceedings of the ACM Symposium on User Interface Software and Technology (UIST'99), ACM Press (1999) 113–119

[5] Rekimoto, J.: Pick-and-Drop: A direct manipulation technique for multiple computer environments. In: Proceedings of the ACM Symposium on User Interface Software and Technology (UIST'97), ACM Press (1997) 31–39

[6] Konomi, S., Müller-Tomfelde, C., Streitz, N.A.: Passage: Physical transportation of digital information in cooperative buildings. In: Cooperative Buildings – Integrating Information, Organizations, and Architecture. Proceedings of the Second International Workshop (CoBuild'99). LNCS 1670, Heidelberg, Germany, Springer (1999) 45–54

[7] Ljungstrand, P., Redström, J., Holmquist, L.E.: Webstickers: Using physical tokens to access, manage and share bookmarks to the web. In: Designing Augmented Reality Environments (DARE2000) Proceedings. (2000) 23–31

[8] Cooper, A.: About Face – The Essentials of User Interface Design. IDG Books (1995)

[9] Ishii, H., Ullmer, B.: Tangible Bits: Towards seamless interfaces between people, bits and atoms. In: Proceedings of the ACM Conference on Human Factors in Computing Systems (CHI'97), Addison-Wesley (1997) 234–241

[10] Want, R., Fishkin, K.P., Gujar, A., Harrison, B.L.: Bridging physical and virtual worlds with electronic tags. In: Proceedings of the ACM Conference on Human Factors in Computing Systems (CHI'99), Addison-Wesley (1999) 370–377

[11] Abowd, G.D., Atkeson, C.G., Bobick, A.F., Essa, I.A., MacIntyre, B., Mynatt, E.D., Starner, T.E.: Living laboratories: The future computing environments group at the georgia institute of technology. In: Extended Abstracts of the ACM Conference on Human Factors in Computing Systems (CHI2000). (2000)

[12] Camarata, K., Do, E.Y.L., Johnson, B.D., Gross., M.D.: Navigational blocks: Navigating information space with tangible media. In: Proceedings of the International Conference on Intelligent User Interfaces (IUI). (2002) 31–38

[13] Masui, T., Siio, I.: Real-world graphical user interfaces. In Thomas, P., Gellersen, H.W., eds.: Proceedings of the First International Symposium on Handheld and Ubiquitous Computing. Number 1927 in Lecture Notes in Computer Science, Springer-Verlag (2000) 72–84

[14] Ullmer, B., Ishii, H., Glas, D.: mediablocks: Physical containers, transports, and controls for online media. In: SIGGRAPH'98 Proceedings. (1998) 379–386

[15] Rekimoto, J., Ullmer, B., Oba, H.: Datatiles: a modular platform for mixed physical and graphical interactions. In: Proceedings of the ACM Conference on Human Factors in Computing Systems (CHI2001), Addison-Wesley (2001) 269–276

[16] Streitz, N.A., Geissler, J., Holmer, T., Konomi, S., Müller-Tomfelde, C., Reischl, W., Rexroth, P., Seitz, P., Steinmetz, R.: i-LAND: An interactive landscape for creativitiy and innovation. In: Proceedings of the ACM Conference on Human Factors in Computing Systems (CHI'99), Addison-Wesley (1999) 120–127

[17] Kohtake, N., Rekimoto, J., Anzai, Y.: Infostick: An interaction device for inter-appliance computing. In Gellersen, H.W., ed.: Proceedings of the First International Symposium on Handheld and Ubiquitous Computing. Number 1707 in Lecture Notes in Computer Science, Springer-Verlag (1999) 246–258

[18] Wellner, P.: Interacting with paper on the DigitalDesk. Communications of the ACM **36** (1993) 87–96

[19] Klemmer, S.R., Li, J., Lin, J., Landay, J.A.: Papier-mâché: Toolkit support for tangible input. In: Proceedings of the ACM Conference on Human Factors in Computing Systems (CHI2004). (2004) 399–406

[20] Dey, A.K., Salber, D., Abowd, G.D.: A conceptual framework and a toolkit for supporting the rapid prototyping of context-aware applications. Human-Computer Interaction **16** (2001) 97–166

The Iterative Design Process of a Location-Aware Device for Group Use

Holger Schnädelbach[1], Boriana Koleva[1], Mike Twidale[2], Steve Benford[1]

[1]Mixed Reality Laboratory
University of Nottingham
Nottingham NG81BB, UK
{hms, bnk, sdb}@cs.nott.ac.uk
[2]Graduate School of Library and Information Science
University of Illinois
Champaign, IL 61820, USA
twidale@uiuc.edu

Abstract. We present our approach to the design of two generations of outdoors device that enable visitors to view 3D historical reconstructions when exploring present day sites. Reacting to problems revealed through public trials with our first prototype, we describe how we followed a 'physical form inwards' approach for the design of our second prototype – Augurscope II. We began by refining the physical form of the interface through a series of push tests with low-tech wooden prototypes and subsequently added sensors and finally refined the software. Our experience with the Augurscope II highlights the importance of prototyping, early involvement of users within the intended setting and the subtleties involved in matching physical form, sensors and software in the development of ubicomp devices.

1 Introduction

The development of devices that display context sensitive information is a major topic of research for ubiquitous computing. The leisure and tourism industry has been a popular application domain, with context aware devices being used to enhance visitors' experiences. These include tourist guides [6], devices to augment museum visits [4, 19], campus guides [5] and outdoor devices for sites of historical interest [14, 3]. In this paper, we reflect on the process of designing a location-based device for use outdoors at a historical attraction. Our device allows groups of visitors to collaboratively view a 3D model, in this case a historical reconstruction, as they explore a physical site. At each moment, it shows them a view of the 3D model as it would appear from their current physical vantage point, answering the question "what might you have seen if you had been standing on this spot in the past?"

Designing such a device is challenging, as it has to be mobile and suitable for use by small groups of the general public in an outdoors environment. These requirements push the boundaries of current technologies in areas such as lightweight and sharable 3D displays and the integration of sensor technologies. They also require designers to

N. Davies et al. (Eds.): UbiComp 2004, LNCS 3205, pp. 329–346, 2004.
© Springer-Verlag Berlin Heidelberg 2004

achieve an appropriate balance between physical form factor, sensing technologies and software design, which can be a difficult task as we shall see below.

In this paper we present our approach to the design of two generations of device to provide a solution to this problem and the lessons we learned from this process. Both devices were stand-mounted displays that can be shared by groups of visitors and wheeled around to different locations in a relatively flat physical environment. Our first device – the Augurscope I – emerged from a design process that might be characterised as *'software outwards'*. Taking our existing software, which ran on a conventional computer as a starting point, we added sensor technology and finally wrapped this in a physical structure.

Our current device is the product of a redesign that sought to remedy the issues that arose from public trials of the Augurscope I. In contrast to our initial approach for our second prototype – the Augurscope II – we adopted a design approach that can be characterised as *"physical form inwards"*. We began with the physical form factor, carefully considering the ways in which the interface could and should be moved and then integrated sensors and software later on. In turn, this led us to reflect more generally on the issues involved in prototyping ubiquitous computing devices and matching physical form to both sensing technologies and application requirements.

2 The Missing Castle: Design Requirements

The context for the development of our outdoor device focused on visualising a medieval castle as it used to appear in relation to its current, quite different site. Nottingham castle is now a public museum and has provided the backdrop for nearly one thousand years of history. However, although in its heyday it consisted of many buildings and was associated with imposing defences, little of this medieval structure remains at the site today as a result of the civil war of the 17th century. Visitors expect to see a fine example of a medieval castle, but are presented with a 17th century palace in its place. Not only is this disappointing, but it is also difficult to understand how the more complex medieval castle was structured, where its parts would have been in relation to the current site, and how they would have appeared. The museum already employs various mechanisms to give visitors some sense of the relationship between past and present: a physical model, a slideshow, guides, brochures and textbooks are available. In addition, the locations of some of the original walls are marked out on the ground of the current site. However, according to the museum management, not enough is currently being done to explain the history of this site effectively especially as there are remaining medieval structures such as the 'Great Hall' that are entirely missing, having been replaced by areas of open grass.

Our goal then was to design an interface to enable groups of visitors to explore the structure of the medieval Nottingham castle from the site of its modern counterpart and to enjoy this as shared social experience. Our design had to respond to a number of high level requirements.

- **Mobility** – the device should be mobile, enabling visitors to relocate it to various positions around the castle site and from these, to obtain different viewing angles and panoramic views.

- **Outdoors use** – the device must be designed for outdoors use, allowing visitors to explore the castle site. Previous experience with outdoors systems [2] have encountered a number of difficulties that the design needs to address, such as the need for battery power, shielding against adverse weather conditions, poor screen readability in bright sunlight and variable positioning accuracy.
- **Public use** – as our intended application involves directly engaging the public, the device should be usable without significant training or effort. It should be easy to engage with and disengage from without having to strap on significant amounts of equipment (an important issue when there is a regular turnover of visitors, each with a potentially short dwell time). It should also enable new visitors to easily learn how to use it by watching current ones [18].
- **Small group use** – the device should be sharable among small groups of visitors such as families, responding to the growing recognition that people often visit museums with companions and their museums experience is shaped through interaction with others [10, 19].

3 "Software Outwards": The First Augurscope

In the development of the first Augurscope our broad strategy was to rapidly construct a prototype and then evaluate it through public tests at the castle. We considered several general designs that might meet the above requirements including wearable and head-mounted augmented displays [13] or free moving, wireless and tracked handheld displays [6]. However, we eventually opted for a design more closely related to boom-mounted displays [8] and those that are used for public indoor VR experiences (e.g. [7]). Our design is based on a tripod-mounted display that can be wheeled to any accessible outdoors location and then rotated and tilted in order to view a virtual environment, as it would appear from that particular vantage point (figure 1).

Fig. 1. Augurscope I at the castle green

In contrast to wearables or PDAs, a small group can easily share a stand-mounted display, with several users being able to see the screen at once and reach out to point at it or to alter its position. Additionally, users can engage and disengage simply by stepping up to and away from the display. We also felt that a tripod mounting would allow the device to be held in a fixed position for several minutes at a time while visitors discussed the content, and might also support more fine-grained, accurate and stable positioning than a handheld solution. However, there was also a more pragmatic motivation for our choice; we were concerned that a suitably large 3D display combined with the location and movement-sensing technologies would be too heavy and bulky for sustained use.

In order to rapidly construct our first prototype, we used off the shelf technologies. The overall design process can be characterised as augmenting a conventional laptop computer, which ran our existing software to display a 3D model of the medieval castle, and provided the interactive core of the device. We augmented this device by:

- Interfacing a series of movement sensors (a GPS receiver to measure global position and orientation and an accelerometer to measure vertical tilt).
- Mounting the augmented laptop on an existing camera tripod and adding a further sensor (a rotary encoder) to measure the horizontal rotation of the display relative to the tripod.
- Adding wheels to the tripod and a wooden casing around the display to shield it from bright sunlight.

We publicly tested our prototype at the Castle. A detailed account of the design and evaluation of the Augurscope is given in [16]. To summarise, positive findings were that visitors appeared to comprehend the purpose of the interface and responded with enthusiasm. Most could operate it with little training, and rotation and tilting were used frequently. However, several problems also became apparent.

- **Limited mobility** – visitors generally appeared reluctant to move the device because of its weight, physical bulk and the roughness of the grassy surface. When moving the device, one of the tripod legs had to be lifted off the ground making it quite unstable. Consequently visitors seemed to prefer viewing the virtual world from a single location, and movement of the device was limited to short distances.
- **Segmentation of the experience** – the three legs of the tripod appeared to constrain rotation of the display, effectively cutting the space to be explored into three 120° segments. Users, whether individually, or in small or large groups, appeared to treat the legs as cut-off points for standing.
- **Accessibility** – there were also some problems with differences in height, especially for family groups where we saw instances of parents having to lift children to give them a better view. Even when lowered all the way the device was still too high for some visitors.
- **Sunlight readability** – finally, despite our attempts to shield the laptop screen, it was noticeable that users sometimes had difficulty seeing the image, even when directly facing it. This became particularly obvious during sunny spells of weather.

What is of interest here is that many of the root causes of these issues lay not with the interactive software and sensors that provided the core of our initial prototype but rather the eventual physical form that emerged from our approach of augmenting an existing laptop. This form had emerged from a design process that might be characterised as '*software outwards*', meaning that we began with our existing software, which ran on a conventional computer. We then added sensor technology and finally wrapped this in a physical structure. In other words, to generalise somewhat, the order in which we tackled key design issues was: software then hardware/sensors and finally physical form-factor. While this may have been a sensible approach to developing a first prototype, we decided to adopt a different approach to designing the second version of the device and in doing so address the problems noted above – improve the mobility, deal with the barrier introduced by the wide-base tripod legs, provide height adjustability and cope better with bright sunlight.

4 "Physical Form Inwards": The Augurscope II

In response to these issues we decided to concentrate on the physical form of our device, effectively reversing the design process compared to the first Augurscope. Therefore we would begin with the physical design before integrating bespoke rather than off the shelf electronics and then refining the software. The strategy was to drive the design from a consideration of the physical form and to involve users more directly in the prototyping of the physical form. The strategy can be considered in terms of four closely related stages.

- **Phase 1:** The initial physical design proposal that emerged from a series of reflections on the lessons of the initial device and the physical constraints of technology and anticipated use.
- **Phase 2:** Physical prototyping sessions with users through a series of trials of exploring the interactive affordances of the physical form.
- **Phase 3:** Development of the final deployable prototype and the refinement of the interactive software to exploit the new physical affordances.
- **Phase 4:** A series of in-situ evaluations with users to further assess and refine the deployed prototype.

4.1. Phase 1: Developing the Design Proposal

At the outset, we decided to try and reduce the overall weight of the device, but perhaps more importantly, to lower its centre of gravity in order to make it more stable. At the same time, we aimed to improve the wheelbase by using larger bicycle-style wheels in the hope that this would also increase mobility. To improve access to all areas of the experience without segmentation we aimed to reduce the size of the base without affecting its stability or the seemingly comfortable viewing distance (given by the relationship between handle and screen) afforded by the original Augurscope. Finally, we decided to remove the wooden shielding at the top as this added weight and bulk and yet was not very effective at dealing with bright sunlight.

At this point we produced our first general design concept, shown in figure 2. In contrast to the first Augurscope, this had a base unit on two large wheels that housed the main computer that would render the 3D virtual environment. A separate top unit consisted of a sunlight-readable display and tilt and rotation sensors which was to be mounted on a rotating handle, balanced by a counterweight. The entire device would be levelled by rotating its two wheels until horizontal and then using the hinge provided above the base. One of the main features of this proposal was the lightweight top unit that would communicate wirelessly with the computer in the base unit. As well as lowering the centre of gravity of the whole device, this also opened up the possibility that the top unit might be temporarily removed from the stand and used in handheld mode, providing additional flexibility for how the Augurscope II might be deployed.

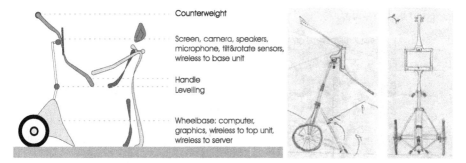

Counterweight

Screen, camera, speakers,
microphone, tilt&rotate sensors,
wireless to base unit

Handle
Levelling

Wheelbase: computer,
graphics, wireless to top unit,
wireless to server

Fig. 2. Design proposal: Version 1 & 2

4.2 Phase 2: From Design Proposal to Physical Prototype

Given this general proposal for the overall form of the device, our next priority was to consider the key issue of how it would be moved. We began by considering two versions as shown in figure 2. To move version 1, shown on the left, the device would have to be tilted forward so the back foot lifts off the ground. Users would walk beside it, balancing the device and would not be able to see the screen while moving. The pencil sketches on the right, drawn at a later stage, show version 2 that included a foldable push handle attached to the base unit. To move it, the handle would need to be picked up and extended to a position that allows walking behind it without treading on the back foot. This would support viewing of the screen during movement, a positive behaviour as we had learned from trials with the first Augurscope.

Comparing these two versions led us to realise that we desired both immediate movement (without having to mess around with extendable handles) as well as the ability to view the screen while moving. It also led us to realise that we needed to base our design on more practical experiences of how people might actually push and move such a device. We therefore embarked on a process of more detailed refinement of our physical design through a series of 'push and rotate' tests with basic wooden structures, initially containing no electronics, but loaded with appropriate weights that matched our estimated targets for the top and base units. From our description of the physical prototyping work below, it will become clear how our approach has led us to implement important changes to our original proposal relatively quickly and at an early stage in the design.

Test 1 – Base unit. The aim of our first test was to establish the basic movement of the platform. We constructed the prototype shown in figure 3 from soft timbers that were easy to cut and shape and whose joints were held together by clamps, so facilitating adjustment during testing. The wheels were two small bicycle wheels. In order to support immediate movement and viewing of the screen during that movement, we changed the original design by moving the foot from the back to the front and by adding a fixed push handle (golf-trolley rather than wheelbarrow style interaction). Simple tests involved colleagues pushing and pulling it around our laboratory. Frequent changes to the clamped joints gave us a better idea of the ideal handle and screen positions. We concluded that the overall design was promising, while the base unit appeared to be too wide.

Fig. 3. Test 1 and 2

Test 2 – Base unit and cantilevered arm. For our second test we added a top unit that could be tilted (but not yet rotated) using a cantilevered arm to achieve an appropriate balance. We also narrowed the base unit and added approximate weights to the structure to represent the electronics that would eventually be integrated. We carried out a series of mobility tests, again with colleagues, but this time on a rough grassy surface. Our aim was to assess general mobility, the tilting action, heights of handles and screen and the distribution of weight. Our tests showed this structure to be fairly mobile and ergonomically more appropriate.

Users could comfortably grasp both handles and tip the prototype onto its two wheels and then move and rotate the whole unit. Critically, the push handle did not hinder interaction with the top unit when the device was stationary. However, the cantilevered arm was heavy and unwieldy and we were also concerned that its protrusion at the back of the device might collide with bystanders when rotated. In addition, with only two wheels, the structure did have to be tipped in order to be moved and in combination with its top-heaviness this made it feel unstable.

Test 3 – Base unit and gimbal. For the third test, a front wheel was added to the base unit. We also replaced the cantilever with a gimbal mechanism, complete with two handles to support both left and right handed users. This also included two fasteners to allow the display (still a wooden frame holding a book) to be removed from and replaced back into the structure. In consultation with local ergonomics experts, a height adjustable central column (with levelling mechanism) and base unit handle were added that would allow use of the device by an adult through to a typical 10 year old child. Our tests suggested that the gimbal was a great improvement and that the additional wheel improved stability and manoeuvrability. Indeed, we were pleasantly surprised so see examples of two handed interaction, where users would be able to grasp the two handles and then move and rotate the whole structure while also rotating the top and occasionally tilting the structure on to its two wheels. The height adjustable joints performed well, however the gimbal and levelling mechanism were far from robust enough and in fact disintegrated completely during testing.

Fig. 4. Test 3 and 4

Test 4 – Covered based unit and final top unit. For test 4 we covered the base unit to make it resistant against adverse weather and added the electronics. A removable tray was attached at the bottom that would hold the main lead acid batteries. The top unit that had been developed and tested in parallel around the electronics hardware (mainly a sunlight readable Corona TFT display and sensors) was added into a new sturdier gimbal. Tests at that point confirmed that the overall design was successful as the device was still very mobile and interaction around the base unit seemed unrestricted. We also consulted with safety experts who suggested further modifications in terms of removing sharp edges, creating a less 'spiky' push handle and adding some safety stops to the base unit to prevent it from falling backwards.

4.3 Phase 3: Realising the Final Deployable Prototype

Our final prototype, shown in figure 5, included two further modifications to the design of the handles. We had experimented with different central handle (tilt and turn) designs. The result shown here provides good access to both left- and right-handed people (slightly favouring the latter) without physically restricting the range of tilt. The push handle was also re-shaped to prevent possible injuries and to allow a good grip from different positions. Finally, the prototype was finished with a coat of paint and a period of technical testing followed, the description of which would go beyond the scope of this paper.

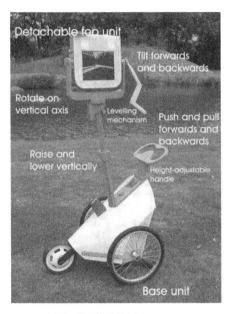

Fig. 5. Final Prototype

4.3.1 Movement Tracking

The sensing technologies for the Augurscope II were chosen to accommodate the new physical form and its interactional affordances. As the top unit is detachable, rotation tracking needs to be independent of tracking the movement of a physical joint. As a result we chose to use a single Honeywell HMR3000 digital compass to measure both global rotation and tilt in place of the accelerometer and rotary encoder from the original Augurscope, enabling the top to be used independently from the base. Similarly a Trimble GPS receiver was used to provide global position as it is lighter and requires less power than the unit used with Augurscope I. In order to take advantage of the increased mobility of the Augurscope II, we used a CSI RTCM receiver for differential GPS corrections, giving us a theoretical accuracy of 1-2 meters for the global position of the device within its environment. Consequently as the device is wheeled around the updates to the virtual environment are more fine grained.

4.3.2 Revisiting the Interactive Software

Once we had integrated the sensing technologies and other electronics (displays, computer, batteries and communications) into our physical design we then revisited the software. We found that we needed to adapt the software to deal with consequences of our design. One obvious alteration was that new software had to be written to communicate the GPS and compass data wirelessly from the top to the base using 802.11b.

Another way that the software had to respond to the physical form was with regard to the relationship between the physical structure and the electronics. Specifically, with the new design the top unit can be tilted through a 180° of movement (in both stand mounted and handheld modes), whereas the HMR3000 digital compass can only sense up to 45° of tilt either way from the horizontal. As a result, a user might tilt the display out of sensor range (beyond 45°) at which point their movement would not be tracked and the display would no longer react. Conversely, it would not be possible for the user to adopt certain viewpoints in the virtual model, for example a bird's eye view or looking directly up into the sky. In response, we refined our 3D software, by exaggerating the effects of tilting of the display on the virtual viewpoint. For every sensed degree of physical tilt of the top unit, two degrees of tilt are applied to the virtual viewpoint. Additionally, between 20° to 45° the virtual viewpoint also pulls upwards. At 45°, the virtual camera has tilted to 90° (i.e., is looking straight down) and has risen several tens of meters into the air to give a bird's eye view. The view remains static beyond 45°. The effect of this mechanism is shown below.

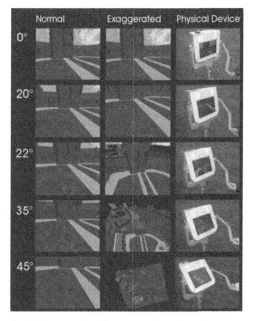

Fig. 6. Normal versus exaggerated tilt

The right hand column of images shows the physical tilt of the top unit. The column on the left shows the virtual viewpoint with no exaggeration applied. The middle column shows the effect of the exaggerated tilting. This mechanism deals with limitations of the chosen sensing hardware, while also enabling users to obtain a useful bird's eye view of the model without having to physically fly up into the air. The completion of the software refinements brought the Augurscope II to a state ready for testing with the public.

4.4 Phase 4: Deployment and Public Testing

Our final stage of the design process was to carry out public testing of our new proto-type at the castle. This was conducted over two consecutive summer days. Just over a 100 visitors experienced the prototype (including people that either directly interacted with the device or who were closely involved in the experience and discussions about the experience when watching others). The age of direct users ranged from 10 to 65 while the age of people merely observing ranged from ~3 to75 years. Most interaction on the device was by groups of people rather than individuals. These groups were couples, parents with children, groups of friends and school groups (7-24 members) from a number of different nationalities. The museum management confirmed that our user profile represented well the visitors to the site during the summer holiday pe-riod. We collected video and audio data, the latter using a wireless microphone that was attached to the Augurscope II, and also logged GPS data in order to establish a trail of movements.

We regard the evaluation as being part of the ongoing design and development process, rather than as a separate assessment of the effects of that prototyping. We consider the implications of that approach later in the paper. The evaluation process itself was developed, or prototyped, over the two days in the light of what was learned, resulting in three distinct phases. Between those phases small adjustments were made to the device, the experience as a whole and our evaluation method, with the aim of maximizing our understanding of the device in use under different circum-stances.

Initial calibration of the device during set-up on day one involved us pushing the Augurscope around the site. This naturally elicited some interest and was in accor-dance with the overall design objectives of encouraging and modelling use as poten-tial users were able to observe and learn something about use from a distance. Subse-quently, when no one was currently engaged with the device, we approached people nearby on the Castle Green, inviting them to try out a device we merely described as developed for a research project, and asking them to tell us if they could work out what it was about. That is, we did not introduce users to the purpose of the device and then set them particular tasks to perform, a common approach in more formal experi-mental evaluations. Rather we presented the device as a puzzle object in order to gain an impression of the degree to which the device supported exploration. We explained to users how they could tip, turn and push the device and then stood back, but accom-panied them in their use. The results were sufficiently promising that we chose to make some minor adjustments for the second phase.

Consequently, for the second part in the morning of day two we added labels to the front of the top unit and the handle of the base unit. The wording for the top was: '(anonymous) Castle in ~1485 / A tour developed by the (anonymous) Lab, Univer-sity of (anonymous)', 'Turn and tilt to rotate your viewpoint'. The wording for the base was: 'Push me to move your viewpoint'. This was intended to replace our expla-nation of how to use the device and to see if these small amounts of labelling were sufficient to enable users to guess how to use the device, supplemented possibly by their observation of earlier users.

Given that initial learning of use seemed very successful, we decided to move to a stronger test of the device in the afternoon. We left the labelled device unattended (al-though observed from a distance) in a strategic position near the entrance to see whether and how people would interact with it then. This was successful, with Augurscope II attracting a great deal of attention from visitors, walking up and trying it out. There were only relatively short periods during which it was not used. In the following sections we consider how our second generation of the device addressed the general shortcomings of the initial version of the augurscope outlined in section 3.

4.4.1 Mobility

In general, mobility was much improved over Augurscope I. Out of 37 distinct groups of users, 29 groups moved the device, compared to 2 out of 30 for Augurscope I. However, visitors were still somewhat reluctant to push the device at first and often had to be encouraged to do so. Especially during phase 3 of the trials when the device was left alone, the distances travelled went down. It seemed that visitors were unsure whether they had permission to move the device. Visitors are used to interactive static museum displays (albeit usually indoors), but public devices that can be moved around are much rarer.

A further issue was that due to our filtering of GPS updates in our software to remove obvious large sudden jumps in reported position and so prevent a jittery display, the virtual viewpoint did not always update if the device was just moved a little way, which may have discouraged some users from pushing it further. Once moving the Augurscope, their journeys ranged from just a few meters to extensive tours of the Castle Green. Data logs showed that between them, users collectively explored the entire Green and use lasted for up to 10 minutes.

An unexpected observation was that users adhered to virtual (apparent) constraints like 3D representations of walls or paths more than we expected (there is no reason why the device can't be pushed straight through them). When we suggested that virtual walls could be 'walked through' many people seemed surprised. In fact, as well as being an amusing activity, it enables a richer sense of the layout of buildings, and is also the only way to see what a building looks like from the inside (the Great Hall, no longer in existence, contained in its virtual representation furniture and wall hangings appropriate for the period).

4.4.2 Segmentation of the Experience

The rotation of the top unit around its base is now unobstructed resulting in an equal, unsegmented access to the whole 360° virtual panorama from any given physical viewpoint. Along with the other improvements this enabled better access to the physical site and the device itself but also as a result to the virtual model, essential for understanding the relationship between the two.

4.4.3 Accessibility

With the re-design we also improved access to groups of users not catered for well with Augurscope I. This did require the occasional adjustment in height of the central column and the push handle by us and users could not have achieved this easily. However, once adjusted we saw a wide range of people interact with the device with for example groups of children from the age of 10 taking it on extensive tours exploring the views of the Great Hall and the Gate House. We found that even when not adjusted correctly Augurscope II remained useable. Users then simply looked up (sometimes also down) on to the screen though this did result in them being unable to use the overview facility. For that the top unit needed to be tilted down far enough requiring an elevated physical viewing position not achievable by some children, and some were lifted up by their parents for a better view.

The handheld mode of the top unit made it accessible to even more people, as for example when parents demonstrated content to their children (see figure 7). The handheld mode was only tested with two people who themselves suggested that this might be an interesting feature. It is clear that this mode proved to be very useful in certain circumstances but generally it makes it less useable for larger groups of people. One person is in control and also very close to the display making it more difficult for others to see what is going on. One user also reported that they considered tilting and turning more difficult compared to when the top is supported by the base. Besides we feel that we could not have expected users to have taken off the top unit on their own initiative and it would certainly have been too heavy for others.

A further observation was that a large proportion of users interacted with one hand while holding something in the other, for example, ice creams, cameras, or a child. Indeed, one parent pushed the Augurscope II with their body while holding their child. This 'encumbered' use made movement more difficult rather than preventing it and yet is to be expected in a public tourist setting. The fact that the Augurscope can be used with one hand was a fortunate effect, but not one that had been planned in its design.

4.4.4 Sunlight Readability

Finally, sunlight readability has improved considerably with the use of the new display. No shading was required, even in very bright conditions, while viewing angle and distance were also very good (see figure 7 (centre) taken from across the Green). When sunlight hit the screen directly, readability was reduced somewhat but the device still remained useable.

As well as highlighting the ways in which our design responded to the shortcomings of the initial device the trials also revealed how minor differences in the physical affordances of a device can considerably affect the user experience. On day one we noticed that when no-one was touching the handle, the default tilt of the Augurscope screen meant that it was in overview mode. Some users seeing this overview mode and rotating the device with the handle but not tipping, did not themselves discover the ground-based virtual view. Furthermore, physical movements of the device only have a small effect in overview mode, leading one user to note that he could see no point in moving the device, as the virtual viewpoint had not changed. Under these circumstances we encouraged people to tilt the top unit, giving them the viewpoint located on the virtual ground, which is the main point of the Augurscope in allowing a comparison between what can be seen here now and what would have been seen here long ago. This need for intervention revealed a design flaw, but observing the problem led to the creation of a simple fix. For the second day we changed the weighting of the handle to provide the ground-based view as the default. Of course such a solution leaves open the risk of some users now failing to tip down and discover the overview, but this seemed a reasonable trade-off. Subsequent design refinements can be envisaged to introduce users to both modes, ranging from yet more labels to encourage tipping the screen (easy to create but cluttering up the artefact), to use of an animated attractor mode showing the different views possible, by analogy with some arcade games.

Fig. 7. Public Trials

5 Implications for the Design of Ubicomp Devices

Through an iterative process of designing, prototyping and testing two generations of the Augurscope, we have managed to create a novel, perhaps even unique, interface in terms of its combination of physical form, sensors and software. We feel that our current prototype demonstrates that this interface has the potential to deliver engaging public experiences that involve exploring an outdoors heritage site. At the same time, we recognise that the current prototype requires considerable further development, especially with regard to weight, bulk, robustness and power, before it can deliver this potential, and that resolving these issues may require us to fabricate an industrial strength prototype.

Beyond the design itself, it is also informative to reflect on the design process, which has drawn upon a number of different design approaches and traditions. Our use of a design proposal as a starting point draws upon techniques common in product design [1]. The involvement of users in the rapid mock up and refinement of the physical form draws upon participative design techniques [9] and our situated formative evaluation [17] of the interactive systems draws upon user centred design [12].

In the following two sections we reflect on the process of prototyping our device. What more general lessons have we learned from our experience and how might these benefit other researchers and designers working on their own quite different novel interfaces?

5. 1 Prototyping of the Physical Form

One important lesson to emerge from this process has been the importance of getting the physical form factor right in detail from an early stage, deciding upon physical size, shape and structure, the movements of key joints and the possibilities for adjustment to suit different users. It was an important step to move from the 'software outwards' process that we followed for the Augurscope I to a 'physical form inwards' process with the Augurscope II. In particular, we feel that iteratively developing a series of low-tech physical prototypes that we then evaluated through 'push and rotate tests' was an essential aspect of evolving the physical design.

When developing ubicomp devices the designer has to consider not just the conventional user experience (just as one would in developing applications for desktop personal computers), but also the constraints of multiple pieces of hardware communicating with each other, and the physical affordances of the artefact as it is used, moved and interacted with in a real setting. With traditional desktop computer applications, this issue of physicality is usually separated off and dealt with by ergonomists who consider seating, screen angle, keyboards etc. The application designer generally can or does ignore the user's body and just deals with the user's mind. Equally ubicomp designers have tended to concentrate on just a subset of these issues, however, we would like to emphasise the importance of considering the ubicomp user experience as a compromise between technological constraints, physical affordances of the artefact and its setting

The issues of physicality do indeed create yet more issues to consider in the design process. However, physicality is not only a problem, it can also be a positive asset. In the case of the Augurscope, the relatively simple and rather large scale body movements and pushing activity that are the means of interacting with the device afford learnability-at-a-distance. Visitors can and did gain a good sense of how to operate the device while observing other users even from 10-30 meters away.

Some issues of stability and failures to fit to human physical constraints can be identified simply by prototyping the physical structure of the device, and the designers trying it themselves or asking colleagues for opinions. This is not to say that authentic user tests are unnecessary, but to note that certain more coarse-grained design problems can be identified quickly, cheaply and easily even in such somewhat unrepresentative contexts. Once these problems have been identified and fixed, it is worthwhile moving to more complex and time consuming evaluations.

5. 2 Prototyping the Evaluation

The prototyping approach to evaluation illustrated in the previous section has various pros and cons compared to traditional, more formal evaluations such as controlled experiments. Just as prototyping a physical device is about producing a version in a short space of time and thereby making compromises over functionality, robustness, or completeness, we would claim that there is a place for a prototyping approach to evaluation. In brief, it trades breadth at the expense for depth [11]. It allows developers to maximize the information that they can obtain from use testing, assuming that gaining access to end users is somewhat complex and time-consuming, so that they can become a bottleneck in a rapid prototyping cycle. The prototyping approach allows for the opportunistic detection and analysis of unexpected kinds of use in relatively authentic settings. An example from our study is our realization of the impact of encumbered use. Once a problematic issue has been identified to the satisfaction of the developers and they have obtained sufficient use information to inform a redesign, it makes sense to move on to investigate a different aspect of use. This can be by adjusting the task to temporarily bypass the problem and look at something else, or even by incorporating the revised version into the evaluation. Examples from this study include initially explaining to users about how to adjust the device to get the ground view, and changing the weighting to make the ground view the default, respectively.

Prototyping is about making something quickly that is not quite real. The designer can choose what to simplify, to omit or to fake. This allows an approximation of the final product to be created quickly in order to assess and revise it. Similarly, for evaluation, the prototype needs to be 'wrapped' in a supportive infrastructure, as by its nature it is not a standalone device. Our prototype for example required continuous support in terms of its initial set-up, ongoing maintenance (failures of batteries, GPS etc.). The design team were at a discreet distance to deal with any problems but also were available to tailor the experience for example adjusting the height of the handles. Equally, the activities of the evaluator are also a form of wrapping such as any initial instructions or suggested tasks or activities to try. Such wrapping or scaffolding [15] allows for evaluation of parts of the interaction experience, but care must be taken to note where and how the scaffolding occurs so as not to attribute success to the device alone.

Ideally, as the prototyping cycle proceeds, various levels of scaffolding are removed so the device is increasingly tested in more authentic standalone situations. In such informal evaluations, negative evidence should be treated as more reliable than positive evidence. Problems with the device, unless easily attributable to a prototyping decision, are more likely to be genuine and in need of analysis to inform a redesign. Successes have to be considered more circumspectly, as they can be artefacts of the scaffolding process, or lack of systematicity in the nature of the users or the activities they do (although in other ways this is an advantage in gaining insights into the diversity of likely actual use).

6 Conclusions

We have presented the process of designing an interface that enables members of the public to explore 3D historical reconstructions from their present day sites. We have briefly introduced our first prototype, Augurscope I, were we started with existing software, chose the sensors and hardware and designed its physical form to accommodate those. This approach to design can be described as *'software outwards'*. In response to our experience with this prototype, we effectively reversed our process and adopted a *'physical form inwards'* design approach as described above, which focuses on first establishing the physical form of the interface before selecting sensors and hardware and finally refining the application software. As a conclusion we would like to emphasise the importance of prototyping for the development of ubicomp devices in general and in particular would like to point at the following key issues that need to be considered.

The early physical prototyping of ubicomp devices, leaving aside hardware and software integration, can reveal issues with a design that are less apparent on a 'paper' proposal. Those can often be identified merely through the process of building the prototype. During the translation of a design proposal into its physical form, problems with its construction and assembly will be revealed, but in addition a designer will also be able to identify problems with its interaction simply through handling the device her/himself.

As a next step, users can and should be involved as early as possible in the process. In house testing (i.e. with the help of colleagues) often reveals the most pressing problems while later stages can benefit more from outside input when more detailed interactional issues with a device can be explored. While this user involvement will be beneficial for smaller, single-user interfaces, it becomes even more important for larger, shared and situated designs. Importantly, in this case not only the interaction of users with the device but that with others and around the device need to be considered. In the case of the Augurscope II we have benefited considerably from this early involvement of users as described above.

Closely related to this is the benefit of deploying a prototype as early as practically possible in its intended setting to be able to consider the situated nature of an experience. In our case, dealing in practice with the very important and well-reported problem of using a device outdoors [2], but also understanding the physical limitations of the actual site and the user profile allowed us to further refine our prototype.

Finally, as the deployment is not that of a finished product, the evaluation can and should be adapted to the requirements of the setting. Some problems with a prototype will only be apparent when deployed and if they can easily be fixed, designers might be able to use the opportunity to test different versions quickly and easily. Furthermore, when the relative success of a design becomes apparent at a certain stage of the evaluation process, successive levels of scaffolding can be removed to be able to test what types of support or set of instructions a design might need as a final product.

Acknowledgements

We thank the EPSRC for their support through the EQUATOR project [GR-N-15986] and the staff at the Nottingham Castle Museum, in particular Denny Plowman.

References

1. Avrahami, D. and Hudson, S.: Forming interactivity: a tool for rapid prototyping of physical interactive products, In Proc. Designing interactive systems (DIS'02), ACM Press, (2002) 141 - 146
2. Azuma, R.T.: The Challenge of Making Augmented Reality Work Outdoors. In Mixed Reality: Merging Real and Virtual Worlds, (Eds. Y. Ohta & H. Tamura), Springer-Verlag, (1999) 379-390.
3. Benford, S., Bowers, J., Chandler, P., Ciolfi, L., Flintham and M., Fraser, M.: Unearthing Virtual History: Using Diverse Interfaces to Reveal Hidden Virtual Worlds, Proc. Ubicmp'01, Springer-Verlag, (2001) 1-6
4. Brown, B., MacColl, I.,Chalmers, M.,Galani, A.,Randell, C.,Steed, A.: Lessons from the Lighthouse: Collaboration in a Shared Mixed Reality System, In Proceedings CHI'03, Ft. Lauderdale, Florida, USA, (2003)
5. Burrell, J., Gay, G., Kubo, K., & Farina, N.: Context-Aware computing: A test case. In Proc. Ubicomp'02, Springer-Verlag, (2002) 1-15
6. Cheverst, K., Davies, N., Mitchell, K. Friday, A. and Efstratiou C.: Developing a Context-Aware Electronic Tourist Guide: Some Issues and Experiences. In Proceedings CHI'00, The Hague, ACM Press, (2000) 17-24

7. Cook J, Pettifer S, Crabtree A. Developing the PlaceWorld environment. In eSCAPE Deliverable 4.1 The Cityscape Demonstrator (Eds. J. Mariani & T. Rodden), Lancaster University, (2000)
8. Fakespace, Verified 10 Dec 2003, http://www.fakespacelabs.com/products/boom3c.html.
9. Greenbaum, J. and Kyng, M.: Design at work,. Hillsdale, NJ: Laurence Erlbaum & Associates, (1991)
10. McManus, P. M.: Good companions: More on the social determination of learning related behavior in a science museum, Journal of Museum Management and Curatorship, Elsevier, 7 (1), (1988) 37-44
11. Nielsen, J.: Usability Engineering, Academic Press, London, (1993)
12. Norman, D.A. and Draper, S.W.: User Centered System Design. Lawrence Erlbaum Associates, Publishers, Hillsdale, NJ. (1986)
13. Piekarski, W., Thomas, B. ARQuake: The Outdoors Augmented Reality System, Communications of the ACM, 45(1), (2002) 36–38.
14. Pletinckx, D., Callebaut, D., Killebrew, A. E. and Silberman N. A.: Virtual-Reality Heritage Presentation at Ename, IEEE Multimedia, IEEE Computer Society, 7 (2), (2000) 45-48
15. Rogoff, B. Apprenticeship in thinking. Oxford University Press, Oxford, (1990)
16. Schnädelbach, H., Koleva, B., Flintham, M., Fraser, M., Izadi, S., Chandler, P., Foster, M., Benford, S., Greenhalgh, C., Rodden, T., The Augurscope: A Mixed Reality Interface for Outdoors. In Proceedings CHI'02, Minneapolis, ACM Press, (2002) 1-9.
17. Twidale, M., Randall, D., Bentley, R.: Situated Evaluation for Cooperative Systems. In Proc. CSCW '94, ACM Press, (1994) 441-452
18. vom Lehn, D., Heath, C. and Hindmarsh, J.: Exhibiting Interaction: Conduct and Collaboration in Museums and Galleries, Journal of Symbolic Interaction, 24 (2), University of California Press, (2001) 189-216
19. Woodruff, A., Aoki, P.M., Hurst, A. and Szymanski, M.H.: Electronic Guidebooks and Visitor Attention, Proc ICHIM 2001, Archives & Museum Informatics, (2001) 437-454

DOLPHIN: A Practical Approach for Implementing a Fully Distributed Indoor Ultrasonic Positioning System

Masateru Minami[1], Yasuhiro Fukuju[2], Kazuki Hirasawa[1], Shigeaki Yokoyama[1],
Moriyuki Mizumachi[1], Hiroyuki Morikawa[2], and Tomonori Aoyama[2]

[1] Shibaura Institute of Technology, 3-9-14 Shibaura, Minato-ku, Tokyo, Japan
[2] The University of Tokyo, 7-3-1 Hongo, Bunkyo-ku, Tokyo, Japan

Abstract. Obtaining indoor location information is one of the essential technologies for enriching various ubiquitous computing applications. Although many indoor location systems have been proposed until now, wide-area deployments in everyday environments are still extremely rare. To deploy indoor locating systems beyond laboratory use, we believe that the initial configuration cost of the system should be reduced. This paper describes a fully distributed ultrasonic positioning system which enables us to locate various indoor objects with lower initial configuration cost.

1 Introduction

Utilizing real-world information, including both low-level sensor data and high-level context, is expected to enhance the potential of future ubiquitous computing applications. So far, many researchers in ubiquitous computing have made concerted efforts to obtain such information, and have tried to utilize it for developing innovative and useful applications. Since real-world information usually depends highly on the movement of people, geographic locations of people and objects are highly relevant to location-aware applications.

Usually, we can easily obtain location information in outdoor environments by using the global positioning system (GPS). Therefore, researchers on location systems for ubiquitous computing applications have focused mainly on indoor environments. To obtain indoor location information, various types of systems have been developed based on the following systems [1]: infrared [2], floor sensors [3], and RF (radio frequency)[4][5][6]. In comparison with these systems, ultrasonic positioning systems [7][8][9] provide the most accurate location information.

There have been two important research efforts on the ultrasonic positioning system: the Active Bat system[7] and the Cricket system[8]. The Active Bat System is the pioneer work in the development of the ultrasonic positioning system. The Active Bat system consists of Active Bat tags, which transmit an ultrasonic pulse, and ultrasonic receivers mounted on the ceiling. The Active Bat system measures the distance between a tag and a receiver based on the time-of-flight

N. Davies et al. (Eds.): UbiComp 2004, LNCS 3205, pp. 347–365, 2004.
© Springer-Verlag Berlin Heidelberg 2004

of the ultrasonic pulse, and computes each tag's position by performing multi-lateration. The Active Bat system also provides direction information, which is useful for implementing many ubiquitous computing applications. However, the Active Bat system employs centralized system architecture, and requires a large number of precisely positioned ultrasonic receivers. Thus, large deployments of the system tend to be prohibitively expensive.

In contrast to the Active Bat system, the Cricket system employs distributed system architecture to avoid the scalability problem. In the Cricket system, ultrasonic transmitters are mounted on the ceiling and a randomized algorithm allows the transmitters to emit ultrasound signals in a distributed manner. Ultrasonic receivers attached on various objects hear these signals and compute their position as well as their orientation. Since the Cricket system has no centralized element and employs a GPS-like positioning model, its privacy protection is advantage. Although both systems are well designed and have the capability of locating indoor objects with high accuracy, there still remains an important problem.

Inherently, a trilateration-based positioning system such as the Active Bat and Cricket systems requires precisely positioned references. In the case of the ultrasonic positioning system, we have to use a lot of references to locate objects in an actual indoor environment since the ultrasonic signal usually can propagate less than five meters and does not penetrate obstacles. For example, in the Active Bat system, ultrasonic receivers are the references, and they are mounted on the ceiling at intervals of around 1.3-1.5 meters. If the room size is a square with 10m sides, we have to use around 70 references and precisely measure their positions. If we apply the system to a larger environment, such as a big conference room or an office building, measuring the positions of all the references becomes more labour-intensive. To avoid this problem, Ward proposed a method for determining the positions of references by using three transmitters [10], but it is not a substantial solution. We believe that reducing the configuration cost is desirable for deploying an indoor location system beyond laboratory use.

On the other hand, there has been interesting work[11] on node localization in wireless sensor networks. In [11], an iterative multilateration technique was proposed to locate huge amounts of sensor nodes by using a small number of precisely positioned references. The idea of iterative multilateration is that a sensor node which can estimate its position using references, becomes a new reference itself. This algorithm proceeds until all sensor nodes are located. Based on this idea, the authors of [11] proposed collaborative multilateration, which can locate a node even if the node cannot receive signals from a sufficient number of references.

The idea of iterative multilateration is applicable to the configuration cost problem, i.e., it can locate many objects using a small number of preconfigured references. In this paper we design and implement a fully distributed indoor ultrasonic positioning system called DOLPHIN (Distributed Object Localization System for Physical-space Internetworking) that locates various indoor objects based on a distributed positioning algorithm similar to iterative multilateration.

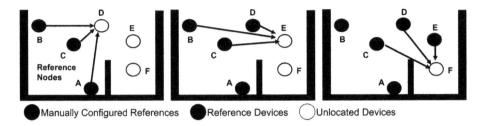

Fig. 1. Iterative Multilateration

The major contribution of [11] is the design of the collaborative multilateration algorithm in a distributed manner and the evaluation of the algorithm via computer simulations; this applies to our interest, which is how to make a workable indoor ultrasonic positioning system which overcomes practical problems, such as the configuration cost, based on the idea of iterative multilateration. Since one important goal of ubiquitous computing is to show the potential of innovative technologies and deploy them beyond laboratory use, we believe that it is important to design and implement a workable system that overcomes the various problems caused in an actual environment. Toward this end, we employed an implementation-based approach to design our indoor ultrasonic positioning system.

This paper is organized as follows. In the next section, we describe our design goals and corresponding approaches in designing the DOLPHIN system. In Section 3, we describe a detailed design of the DOLPHIN system, including the hardware design and positioning algorithm. Then, several techniques for achieving high-accuracy positioning are introduced in Section 4. In Section 5, we evaluate the basic performance of our implemented system in various practical situations. Finally, we summarize our work and discuss our future direction in Section 6.

2   Design Goal

At the start of designing the DOLPHIN system, we listed the following design goals and corresponding solutions:

(1) Easy Configuration
As described in Section 1, one important problem of a conventional triangulation-based indoor positioning system is the configuration cost, because we are forced to measure a huge number of reference positions precisely to achieve high-accuracy positioning. To mitigate this configuration load, we utilize the idea of iterative multilateration.

Figure 1 illustrates the basic idea of the iterative multilateration technique. In the initial state, devices A, B and C have precisely measured positions, and the positions of the other devices are unknown. In the next step, device D, which can directly receive signals from devices A, B and C, can determine its position (here, we assume that one device can compute its position by receiving three or more signals from the references). However, devices E and F cannot yet receive a sufficient number of signals to determine their position due to such physical obstacles as the wall. Here, if the position of device D is determined and device E can receive a signal from device D, device E can compute its position by using signals from devices B, C and D. If the locations of device D and E are determined, device F can compute its position using devices C, D and E. In this way, all devices can be located.

However, iterative multilateration is just an idea to locate huge numbers of objects by using a small number of references. To develop a practical system, we should consider not only how to apply iterative multilateration to our system, but also how to start the system and recover from failures. We introduce such a positioning algorithm in Section 3.

(2) High-Accuracy Positioning
The second goal is achieving high-accuracy positioning in our system for supporting a wide variety of ubiquitous computing applications. Basically, the trilateration-based ultrasonic positioning system shows good accuracy in an indoor environment. However, since ultrasound is seriously degraded by various obstacles, we must design some error mitigation technique to obtain precise distance measurements. And, moreover, because our system is trying to locate many objects using a small number of references in a distributed manner, structural errors such as the accumulation of positioning errors should also be taken into account. To achieve high-accuracy positioning, in Section 4 we introduce several approaches, including reference selection and no-line-of-sight signal rejection techniques.

Usually, existing indoor ultrasonic positioning systems support not only 3D positioning but also additional functions, such as the capability of detecting the orientation of objects. However, much good work [8][10][12] has already been done for such additional functions. From this point of view, we mainly focus on the above basic goals in this paper.

3   Hardware Design and Positioning Algorithm

3.1   Hardware Design

Figure 2(a) illustrates a block diagram of the DOLPHIN device. To implement iterative multilateration, bi-directional ultrasonic transducers (MA40S, MURATA) are used for both sending and receiving ultrasonic signals. As shown in Figure 2(b), we attached five transducers to the cylindrical module to extend the coverage of the ultrasonic signals in every direction. Each transducer is connected to a signal detector circuit, which separately detects the existence of the ultrasonic pulse and received signal strength level. Figure 2(c) shows the sending and receiving patterns of the transducer module. As shown in this figure, the sending pattern has several null points and the receiving pattern is spherical.

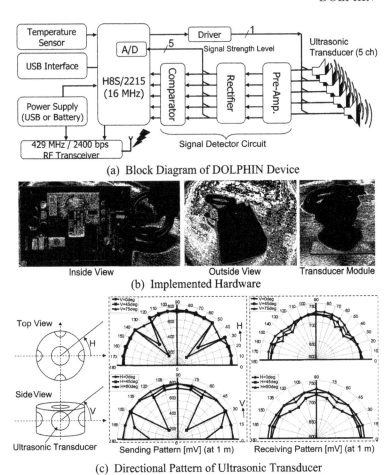

(a) Block Diagram of DOLPHIN Device

Inside View   Outside View   Transducer Module

(b) Implemented Hardware

Top View

Side View

Ultrasonic Transducer   Sending Pattern [mV] (at 1 m)   Receiving Pattern [mV] (at 1 m)

(c) Directional Pattern of Ultrasonic Transducer

Fig. 2. Hardware Design

This is because each ultrasonic transducer has a spherical directional pattern, and the combination of such patterns yields the null point. Moreover, the placement of the ultrasonic transducers is not determined by considering the signal interference among the outputs of the transducers. As a result, there is a little interference among the transmitted ultrasonic signals. Although it is possible to improve the sending pattern by carefully placing the transducers and attaching horns to the cylindrical module, we assume in this paper that the module has an ideal sending pattern.

The DOLPHIN device also has a 2400-bps, 10-channel, 429-MHz RF transceiver (NHM-10185, Nagano JRC) for time synchronization and the exchange of control messages. Because this RF transceiver includes a powerful error collection function, we selected it for the DOLPHIN system so that we do not need to care about errors in the exchange of control messages. However, the transmission speed of this transceiver is relatively slow compared to recent RF transceivers, and so it limits the positioning speed (1-2 times/sec). This is not a substantial problem in the DOLPHIN system, although we are planning to employ a higher-speed transceiver in the next version.

A one-chip microcontroller (H8S/2215 16 MHz, RENESAS) controls both the ultrasonic transducer and the RF transceiver, and calculates a device's position by performing multilateration. The microcontroller detects the received signal strength information of the ultrasonic signal at each transducer via internal A/D converters, and can obtain the temperature from a one-chip temperature sensor (LM35, National Semiconductor) to estimate the ultrasound propagation speed. This CPU has a USB interface, and we can pull location data out through the USB interface as well as supply power to the device by attaching the device to a USB-enabled device such as a laptop or a PDA.

3.2   Distributed Positioning Algorithm

To organize many DOLPHIN devices as a distributed positioning system, we designed a distributed positioning algorithm that implements the idea of iterative multilateration as well as bootstrapping and failure recovery mechanisms. In the positioning algorithm, the nodes in the system play three different roles in a sequence, as shown in Figure 3: there is one master node, one transmitter node, and the rest are receiver nodes. A node which has determined its position can become a master node or a transmitter node. In every positioning cycle, the master node sends a message via the RF transceiver for time synchronization of all nodes. Here we assume that all nodes in the system can hear the RF signal. When a transmitter node receives the message, it sends an ultrasonic pulse. At the same time, each receiver node starts its internal counter, and stops it as the ultrasonic pulse arrives. The receiver nodes that received the ultrasonic pulse then compute the distance to the transmitter node. If a receiver node measures a sufficient number of distances, it computes its position based on multilateration. By using a member list, three RF messages and two internal timer events, as summarized in Figure 4, the distributed positioning algorithm proceeds as follows.

(1) Bootstrapping Sequence

Figure 5 shows an example bootstrapping sequence of the distributed positioning algorithm. In the initial state of the system, the member list in each node is empty. As described later, the distributed positioning algorithm determines both the master and transmitter node based on the member list. Therefore, each node must collect node IDs in the bootstrapping sequence to start positioning. After turning on a manually positioned reference node, it resets its ADVER-TISEMENT_TIMER with an interval of $t_A(t_A = 10 + t_r)$ seconds. Where, t_r is a random initial value in the order of several seconds. In Figure 5, after turning on node A, ADVERTISEMENT_TIMER in the node expires because there is no SYNC_MSG that specifies the node. Then, node A sends ID_NOTIFY_MSG via the RF transceiver. In this example, nothing occurred because there is no node

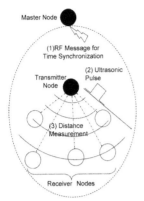

List	MEMBER_LIST	The MEMBER_LIST contains the following information about neighboring nodes that are capable of becoming reference node:	

	Node ID	Node Priority	Node Position	Distance

RF Messages	ID_NOTIFY_MSG	The node which determined its position transmits this message so that the node can be used as a reference. This message contains the node ID of the node.
	SYNC_MSG	This message is used for time synchronization for distance measurement. and contains the ID of the transmitter node selected by the master node.
	LOC_NOTIFY_MSG	This message is used for advertising the latest location of the transmitter node. This message contains the node ID and 3D position of the transmitter node.
Timers	ADVERTISEMENT_TIMER	This timer is set with t_A (t_A=10sec+random initial value) when the node receives SYNC_MSG for the node. It expires when the node capable of becoming reference node does not receive any SYNC_MSG specifying the node from other nodes within t_A.
	RECOVERY_TIMER	This timer is set with t_R (t_R=15sec+random initial value) when the node holds no-empty node list and receives SYNC_MSG. The timer expires if there has been no SYNC_MSG within t_R.

Fig. 3. Positioning Sequence   **Fig. 4.** Definition of List, Messages, and Timers

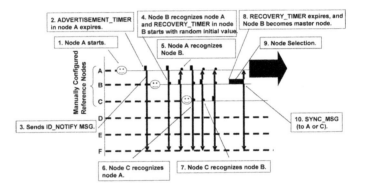

Fig. 5. Example Bootstrapping Sequence

that could hear the message at that time. Therefore, node A simply continues to transmit ID_NOTIFY_MSGs.

After several time periods, node B is turned on next, and starts its AD-VERTISEMENT_TIMER. On receiving ID_NOTIFY_MSG from node A, node B recognizes that there is a node which can act as a master node or transmitter node. Then node B stores the node ID in the received message into its member list. At the same time, node B starts its RECOVERY_TIMER with an interval of t_R($t_R = 15 + t_r$) seconds. When the ADVERTISEMENT_TIMER in node B expires, node B sends an ID_NOTIFY_MSG, then node A recognizes node B and starts its RECOVERY_TIMER. In the same way, every node including node C recognizes each other. Note that each node sets RECOVERY_TIMER when the node recognizes a neighboring node as summarized in Figure 4. However, there is no master node in the system, and the nodes simply exchange ID_NOTIFY_MSG. Once RECOVERY_TIMER in node B expires, node B becomes a master node. Then node B selects one node as a transmitter node based on the member list, and transmits SYNC_MSG to the selected node. In this way, the bootstrapping

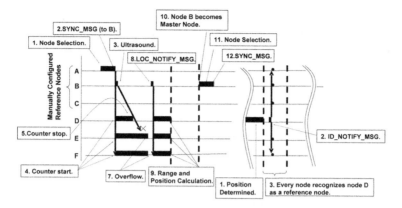

Fig. 6. Example Positioning Sequence

process completes, and the system enters into positioning cycles. Note that our bootstrapping procedure works even if all nodes turned on simultaneously because both ADVERTISEMENT_TIMER and RECOVERY_TIMER are set with random initial values.

(2) Positioning Algorithm

Figure 6 shows an example of the timing sequence in one positioning cycle. In this example, nodes A-C are manually configured references, and nodes D-F are unlocated nodes. Here we assume that nodes A- C have member lists [B, C], [A, C], and [A, B], respectively. Now we consider that node A acts as a master node.

First, node A chooses one node randomly from its node list [B, C]. If node B is chosen, node A transmits SYNC_MSG, including the ID of node B. On receiving the message, node B becomes a transmitter node and generates an ultrasonic pulse. At the same time, nodes D, E, and F become receiver nodes and start their internal counter. If the receiver nodes detect the transmitted ultrasound pulse, they stop their internal counter and calculate the distance from node B.

After several milliseconds (this depends on the time taken by the overflow of the internal counter), node B sends LOC_NOTIFY_MSG to notify the receiver nodes of its position. The receiver nodes that can detect ultrasound store the location of node B and the distance to node B in their member table. After that, all nodes wait and listen for ID_NOTIFY_MSG for a certain period (advertisement period). Any node which can determine the position based on a sufficient number of distances advertises its ID in this phase, and the ID is added to the node list in every node. In the above example, because nodes D, E and F cannot determine their position, no ID_NOTIFY_MSG is sent in this period. The sequence of the above phases is one cycle of the positioning algorithm in the DOLPHIN system. In the next cycle, node B, which acted as a receiver node in the previous cycle, becomes a master node. And, thus, the positioning algorithm proceeds in the same way.

After several cycles of positioning, node D can measure distances from nodes A-C, and position (x_D, y_D, z_D) is obtained by solving the following none-linear simultaneous equations based on a least squares estimation:

$$r_1 = \sqrt{(x_D - x_i)^2 + (y_D - y_i)^2 + (z_D - z_i)^2} \tag{1}$$

where (x_i, y_i, z_i) denotes the position of the i-th reference, and r_i is the measured distance between node D and the reference. At that time, node D sends ID_NOTIFY_MSG in the advertisement period. All of the other nodes that received ID_NOTIFY_MSG from node D add the ID of node D to their member list, and node D is recognized as a candidate for master node or transmitter node.

In our current implementation, a candidate for master or transmitter node sends its average position to achieve high-accuracy positioning. In this way, we can locate all nodes in the DOLPHIN system. Note that we utilize four reference nodes to estimate node position in our current implementation so that we can resolve ambiguity and obtain good estimation, although we considered three reference nodes in this example.

(3) Failure Recovery
In the DOLPHIN system, we have to consider two failures, which are node failure and recognition failure, to continuously execute the abovementioned positioning algorithm. Node failure occurs when a node suddenly stops because of an unpredictable accident, and recognition failure occurs when the ID_NOTIFY_MSG transmitted from a node does not reach the other nodes because of a bad communication channel or message collision.

RECOVERY_TIMER is utilized for recovering from node failure. This timer is set with a random initial value when the nodes receive SYNC_MSG. If any SYNC_MSG is not transmitted for a certain period in the system , the system can be concluded that the positioning algorithm halted because of some node failure. In this case RECOVERY_TIMER in a node expires, and the node becomes a master node. In this way, the positioning algorithm resumes from node failure.

If a node capable of being a master node does not receive SYNC_MSG which specifies the node from other nodes within a certain period, the node conclude that the node is not recognized as a node capable of being a master or transmitter node by neighboring nodes (i.e., recognition failure). In this case, the advertisement timer in the node expires, and the node retransmits ID_NOTIFY_MSG again in the next positioning cycle. Note that, to avoid an ID_NOTIFY_MSG collision, the node sends ID_NOTIFY_MSG at a certain probability similar to the backoff algorithm utilized in 802.11. We have run the above algorithm via 24 DOLPHIN devices for 24 hours, and the algorithm has continued normally.

4   Improving Positioning Accuracy and Scalability

When we utilized the DOLPHIN system in an actual environment, the system suffered from various factors leading to errors. According to our experimentation,

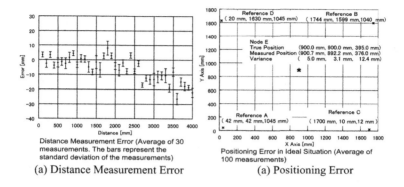

(a) Distance Measurement Error   (a) Positioning Error

Fig. 7. Positioning Performance in Ideal Situation

there are two major factors leading to errors in the DOLPHIN system: error accumulation and a no-line-of-sight signal. The following sections describe how we have tackled these problems.

4.1   Error Accumulation Problem

Basically, our hardware implementation can measure the distance between two nodes with an accuracy within 1-2 cm, if the distance is shorter than 3 m, as shown in Figure 7(a) (based on this measurement, our system determines that a measured distance shorter than 3 m is valid). This accuracy is achieved by using a distance measurement error correction technique. Usually, ultrasound attenuates according to its travel distance, and this change causes variations of the hardware delay in the ultrasound detection circuit (more precisely, combination of the comparator and the rectifier in Figure 2(a) causes this variation). Since the ultrasonic positioning system assumes that the hardware delay is constant, this change causes a distance measurement error. The distance measurement error correction technique corrects this error by using a previously measured hardware delay. By using precisely placed references, the positioning accuracy of the system is less than 2-3 cm as shown in Figure 7(b).

However, the error accumulation problem seriously degrades this accuracy. As shown in Figure 8(a), the error accumulation is caused by the structural characteristic of the distributed positioning algorithm, in which an unlocated node that can estimate its position using references becomes a new reference. Here we assume that nodes A, B, C and D are precisely positioned reference nodes. Node E determines its position based on nodes A, B, C and D, and node F determines its position based on nodes B, C, D and E. Since the measured distances from node E to nodes A, B, C and D contain measurement errors, the accuracy of the position of node F is degraded in comparison with nodes A, B, C, and D. In the example in Figure 8(a), although node F can utilize precise reference nodes A, B, C, and D, the positioning accuracy of node F is lower than that of node D, since node F utilizes node D. This is because node F accumulates

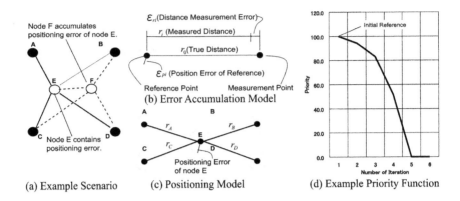

(a) Example Scenario   (b) Error Accumulation Model   (c) Positioning Model   (d) Example Priority Function

Fig. 8. Error Accumulation Problem

the positioning error of node D. This error accumulation becomes larger as the iterative multilateration proceeds. Moreover, there is a possibility that a sharp rising error accumulation occurs between two nodes. For example, there is the case that node D utilizes node F after node F utilizes node D, and vice versa. In this case the positioning error will be exponentially accumulated between nodes E and F.

To avoid the error accumulation problem, we designed a priority-based node selection algorithm. In this algorithm, we assign priority to all candidates of the reference node system based on the position error of the candidates. Let us consider the error accumulation model shown in Figure 8(b). Here we assume that a measurement point obtains a distance from a reference point which contains the position error ϵ_{pi}. In this case the measured distance r_i is described as:

$$r_i = r_0 + \epsilon_{pi} + \epsilon_{ri} \tag{2}$$

where r_0 is the true distance between the two points, ϵ_{ri} is the error in the measurement process. Here we assume that there is no correlation between ϵ_{pi} and ϵ_{ri}. Then, after a sufficient number of trials, the variance of the measured distance σ^2 becomes:

$$\sigma^2 = \sigma_p^2 + \sigma_r^2 \tag{3}$$

where σ_p^2 is the variance of the position error of the reference, and σ_r^2 is the variance of the measurement error. Now we assume the positioning model depicted in Figure 8(c). According to the concept of PDOP (Position Dilution of Precision) in the global positioning system[13], the positioning error E_p in this model is described as:

$$E_p^2 = PDOP^2 \times \sigma_{UERE}^2 \tag{4}$$

where $PDOP$ is a parameter which is determined by the geometry of the references (see [10] and [13] for more detail about PDOP), and σ_{UERE} is a parameter called the User Equivalent Renege Error (UERE)[13]. Using the error propagation rule, the UERE in the positioning model can be computed as:

$$\sigma^2_{UERE} = \sqrt{(\sigma^2_A)^2 + (\sigma^2_B)^2 + (\sigma^2_C)^2 + (\sigma^2_D)^2} \tag{5}$$

where σ^2_A, σ^2_B, σ^2_C, and σ^2_D are variances of the measured distances r_A, r_B, r_C, and r_D, respectively. Assuming $\sigma^2_A = \sigma^2_B = \sigma^2_C = \sigma^2_D = \sigma^2$, we can obtain the positioning error as follows:

$$E_p = \sqrt{PDOP^2 \times \sqrt{4}(\sigma^2_p + \sigma^2_r)} \tag{6}$$

However, in the actual positioning, we cannot simply assume $\sigma^2_A = \sigma^2_B = \sigma^2_C = \sigma^2_D = \sigma^2$, because position error σ^2_p is usually not the same for four reference nodes in the DOLPHIN system. To handle this problem, we utilize the average mean square error for computing σ^2_p as shown in the following equation:

$$\sigma^2_p = \frac{w_A \sigma^2_A + w_B \sigma^2_B + w_C \sigma^2_C + w_D \sigma^2_D}{\sqrt{w_A + w_B + w_C + w_D}} \tag{7}$$

$$(w_A : w_B : w_C : w_D = \frac{1}{\sigma^2_A} : \frac{1}{\sigma^2_B} : \frac{1}{\sigma^2_C} : \frac{1}{\sigma^2_D})$$

Based on equations (6) and (7), we decided on the following formula for assigning priority P to the new reference candidate:

$$\begin{cases} P = 1 - E_p/E_{th} & (E_p < E_{th}) \\ P = 0 & (E_p \geq E_{th}) \end{cases} \tag{8}$$

Here, E_{th} is a design parameter which defines the allowable error in the DOL-PHIN system. Figure 8(d) shows an example of the computed priority function, assuming that the position errors of the manually configured references are 0, the distance measurement error is 1 cm, PDOP is constantly 2.0, and the error threshold is 50 cm. As shown in this figure, the priority function decreases according to the iteration times of positioning. Note that, if there are movable nodes in the system, these nodes are forced to use the lowest priority (i.e., zero).

All nodes in the DOLPHIN system that could be reference candidates broadcast their priority by LOC_NOTFY_MSG, and the received priorities are stored in the member list in each node. When a node computes its position, the node utilizes the priorities of the references to determine which reference should be used for the position computation. Needless to say, utilizing references that have a higher priority yields better positioning accuracy. Although the above algorithm considers that only four references are used for the position calculation, there is the case that a node can measure more than four distances from reference nodes with a good priority. In this case, it is possible to utilize a weighted least squares estimation that can compute the position of the node from more than four references. The priority of the references can be used as a weight parameter in the weighted least squares estimation. Though we do not derive the priority function for more than four references, it is easy to extend equations (6) and (7) to such a situation.

Note that the error accumulation problem is inherently unavoidable problem in iterative multilateration. In other words, though our proposed method can mitigate the error accumulation problem, it cannot completely remove the effect of the error accumulation. This problem becomes serious, if we apply iterative multilateration with minimum number of manually configured references to very large environment. In this case, we have to use sufficient number of manually configured references to obtain acceptable accuracy. Needless to say, there is a tradeoff between accuracy and configuration cost.

4.2 NLOS Reflected Signal Problem

Another error factor in the DOLPHIN system is the no-line-of-sight (NLOS) signal, which is classified into two types: reflected signal and diffracted signal. Basically, our system can correctly locate objects when a receiver node can detect the line-of-sight signal, even if there are reflected or diffracted signals. However, if there are only NLOS signals, such a condition seriously degrades the positioning accuracy of the system. Therefore, we have to detect the NLOS signal and reject it so that the system can provide good positioning accuracy.

According to the physics of acoustic waves, if the size of an obstacle is smaller than the wavelength of the acoustic signal, the diffraction of the acoustic wave is negligible. Since the wavelength of a 40-kHz ultrasonic wave is around 9 mm, we can neglect the effect of the diffracted signal in almost all indoor environments. In addition, generally, reflected signal causes more serious distance measurement erro than diffracted signal. For this reason, we mainly focus on how to reject reflected signals in this section.

Reflected signals arrive at a receiver node in the situation where the direct signal is blocked by an obstacle, and only the reflected signals reach the receiver from the reflector obstacles. Since this reflected signal travels a longer distance than the actual distance between the transmitter and receiver, it seriously degrades the positioning accuracy. To detect and reject the reflected signals, we employed a received-signal-strength-based approach (RSS-based approach). This approach is based on the assumption that the signal strength of a reflected signal is weaker than that of the direct signal because the reflected signal travels a longer distance and is attenuated by the reflector obstacle. That is, we reject the weak signal by comparing the received signal strength to a previously measured reference signal strength.

Figure 9 shows the experimental result of the RSS-based reflected signal rejection technique. As shown in this figure, when the RSSI-based rejection is disabled, the positioning accuracy of the system is seriously degraded with the existence of the reflected signal. On the other hand, the positioning accuracy is dramatically improved when we the reflected signal rejection technique is enabled.

Although this approach is easy to implement, we cannot always reject all reflected signals. As shown in Figure 10, we measured the received signal strength level at various points. The results show that the signal strength level fluctuates largely depending on the geometry of the ultrasonic transmitter and receiver. This is because there are interferences among the reflected signals that form an undulating field of signal strength.

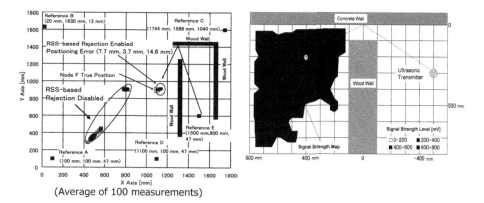

(Average of 100 measurements)

Fig. 9. RSS-based Rejection   **Fig. 10.** Example RSS Map

To handle this problem, we designed a geometry-based reflected signal rejection technique. In this technique we assume that a receiver node can detect the direction of the arrived ultrasonic signal. Now we consider the scenario depicted in Figure 11. In this figure, receiver node R measures the distance to transmitter nodes O and P. However, R can hear only the reflected signal transmitted from P. As a result, the signal from P seems to be transmitted from the virtual node V at receiver R. Since we assumed that R can detect the direction of the arrived signal, R can obtain the angle θ_{ORV}. Then, R can compute the distance between node O and V as:

$$d_{OV} = \sqrt{r_O^2 + r_V^2 - 2r_O r_V \cos\theta_{ORV}} \qquad (9)$$

On the other hand, as we stated in Section 3.2, since the positions of nodes O and P are notified via LOC_NOTIFY_MSG, node R also can compute the distance between O and P, denoted as d_{OP}. Therefore, we recognize that there is a reflected signal by comparing distances d_{OV} and d_{OP}. If node R can hear one more signal from node Q, then we can specify that the transmitted signal from node P is a reflected signal.

Note that the geometry-based technique does not always work well since it is based on the assumption that there is sufficient number of direct paths from neighboring nodes. Moreover, it is necessary to compare all combinations of nodes for detecting reflected signals. However it is possible to improve the algorithm based on the empirical knowledge that an ultrasonic pulse which traveled shorter distance is more reliable. We have implemented the above algorithm in our device. In our implementation, we detect coarse angle of arrival of received signal based on difference of received signal strength among ultrasonic transducers. We also verified that this algorithm could reject reflected signals in some cases. However, the resolution of the detecting angle was too low to reject all reflected signals. We hope to improve the resolution of the angle estimation in our future work.

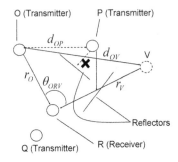

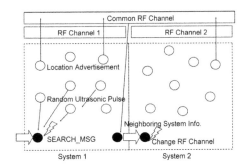

Fig. 11. Geometory-based Approach

Fig. 12. Scalability Problem

4.3 Scalability

Generally, the limitation of scalability in the ultrasonic positioning system is caused by the slow propagation speed of ultrasound. Usually, an ultrasonic positioning system utilizes the RF channel for time synchronization of the system, then measures the propagation time of an ultrasonic pulse to compute the distance between an ultrasonic transmitter and receiver. The propagation time is about 3 milliseconds to travel 1 m. If signal processing is taken into account, the time for one distance measurement would be more than 10 milliseconds. To avoid signal collision and interference, only one ultrasonic transmitter at a time should be permitted to send an ultrasonic pulse, and in that case the maximum positioning speed would be around 50 times per second. If there are 50 transmitters in the same area, the average interval time to transmit an ultrasonic pulse is degraded to 1 second for each transmitter. Since all devices in the DOLPHIN system send and receive an ultrasonic pulse to run iterative multilateration, this limitation causes deployment scalability.

One effective approach to handle this scalability problem is to divide a big group of nodes into multiple small groups based on some dynamic clustering algorithms that have been proposed in various researches on wireless sensor networks. However, utilizing a complicated and dynamic algorithm is not suitable for developing practical system since such an algorithm causes unexpected instability in the system.

From this point of view, we employ a simple approach in which multiple DOLPHIN systems are running in different RF channels that are schematically based on floor plans. Even if we employ such an approach, we must consider how a newly added node joins a running system and how a movable node changes to another RF channel when it enters a different system.

Figure 12 shows the procedure to add a new node to a running system. When a new node is present, it sends a SEARCH_MSG to every channel randomly. On receiving the message, all DOLPHIN devices in the same channel transmit an ultrasonic pulse with random delay. The new node counts the number of received pulses, and selects the channel in which the node could receive the largest number of pulses. Then the node enters the system by following the

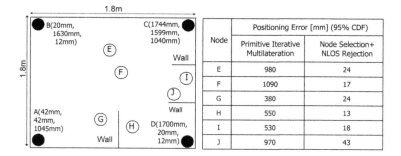

Fig. 13. Experimental Result in Desktop Testbed

bootstrapping algorithm described in Section 3. Each DOLPHIN system shares a common channel to exchange information among systems. This common channel is used for changing RF channels when a movable node enters a new system. As shown in Figure 12, all nodes in all systems are randomly transmitting their location and RF channel via the common channel. The movable node hears this channel and knows what channel is used in the next system. When the node enters the new system, it changes RF channels for that system.

Note that the abovementioned procedure may cause ultrasonic signal collisions at the boundary between two independent systems. However, the time for sending ultrasonic pulses is quite short, and the valid measured distance in our system is limited to 3 m. Therefore, the probability of signal collisions would be negligible. Moreover, we can reject the ultrasonic signal from a neighboring system by using the statistical method and geometry-based reflected signal rejection technique described in the previous section.

5   Performance Evaluation

5.1   Positioning Performance in Ideal Environment

In this experimentation, we placed 4 reference nodes (A-D), 6 unlocated nodes (D-J) and several obstacles in our "desktop testbed" as shown in Figure 13. The size of the testbed is 1.8 meters square, and we placed the 4 reference nodes so that unlocated nodes can obtain good PDOP. When a node is placed inside the boxy area which is constructed from the reference nodes, PDOP becomes around 1.5. In this experimentation, 100 measurements of positioning error are performed with and without techniques for archiving high accuracy positioning. 13 shows the experimental results of positioning error obtained from cumulative distribution function (CDF). Example CDF of node F in this experiment is shown in Figure 14. In our experimentation, we utilized error at 95 % CDF to evaluate accuracy of positioning. Without the techniques, various error factors, such as error accumulation and NLOS signals, seriously degrade positioning accuracy. Estimated location information is no longer acceptable for location-aware

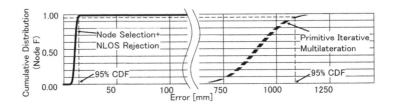

Fig. 14. Example Cumulative Distribution Function (Node F)

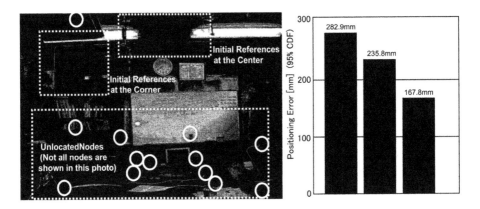

Fig. 15. Experimental Results in Room Environment

applications. On the other hand, positioning accuracy is dramatically improved when we apply all techniques for high accuracy positioning (the worst-case positioning error is less than 5 cm). These result show that designed system can basically provide good positioning accuracy compared to primitive iterative multilateration.

5.2   Effect of Geometry of Initial Reference Nodes

Next, we distributed 24 nodes in a small room (3.6 m x 3.6m x 2.4 m) in our laboratory, as shown in Figure 15. First, we placed 20 unlocated nodes randomly in the room and attached 4 preconfigured references in the corner of the room (Condition (a)). Under this condition, we ran the system with all techniques for high-accuracy positioning. Next, we placed the references at even intervals on the center of the ceiling to improve the PDOP (Condition (b)). The placement of the unlocated nodes was the same as in the above experiment. Finally, we utilize 6 references and 18 unlocated nodes to investigate how the number of references affects positioning accuracy (Condition (c)). In every condition, we performed 100 measurements of positioning error. Figure 15 shows the measurement result. In the case of condition (a), the positioning error was 282.9 mm. The positioning error of the nodes placed around the opposite corner is over 1 m, whereas that of the others is around 10-20 cm. This is mainly because the PDOP of these nodes is quite poor and the accumulated error seriously increased (actually, the PDOP of these nodes was over 10). In the condition (b), the average positioning error of all the nodes was improved compared to condition (a) since this condition yields good PDOP. In the condition (c), the positioning accuracy was improved greatly as compared to previous two conditions. This result shows that utilizing 6 references enhances the chance to obtain good PDOP for each unlocated nodes and the positioning error is reduced as the result.

The above results mean that the geometry of the initial reference nodes seriously affects the positioning error of the system. Therefore, we should carefully place the initial references so that they provide good PDOP for the unlocated nodes. Finding the best way for determining positions of initial references in actual environment is our future work.

6   Summary and Further Work

We implemented and evaluated a fully distributed indoor ultrasonic positioning system in this paper. We designed a distributed positioning algorithm which implements the idea of iterative multilateration to enable us to reduce the configuration cost of the indoor ultrasonic positioning system, and introduced several techniques for achieving high-accuracy positioning. We showed that our system basically works well through various evaluations in an actual indoor environment.

Despite the success of the basic implementation of our system, there still remain several problems we have to tackle. The most important work will be enabling the system to handle movable objects. Basically, we think that it is possible to track movable objects in our system by using high-speed RF transceiver. However, there will be several technical problems in such dynamic environment. For example, current DOLPHIN node can compute its position only if a sufficient number of distances is obtained. If a node is movable, old measurement results contain distance errors that depend on positioning speed, density of neighboring nodes and speed of the movable node. As the result, positioning accuracy of the movable node will be seriously degraded. Therefore we have to analyze positioning error and develop a viable solution. In designing such a solution, we should consider, for example, resource allocation scheme for movable nodes or integration of other sensors and our system [14].

Another important task will be the stabilization of ultrasonic signal reception including the effective rejection of the NLOS signal. Through various kinds of experimentation, we found that stabilizing propagation of ultrasound is quite difficult but important to improve positioning accuracy of ultrasonic positioning systems. However, our current implementation simply utilizes a rectangular pulse for distance measurement, and is unprotected from various kinds of error sources. Therefore, we belive that a more sophisticated signal design and/or new devices such as broadband ultrasonic transducer [15] is necessary to improve the performance of our system.

Acknowledgements

We would like to thank all reviewers for their constructive comments and invaluable help in shaping this work.

References

1. J. Hightower and G. Borriello, Location Systems for Ubiquitous Computing, IEEE Computer, vol. 34, no. 8, Aug. 2001, pp. 57–66.
2. R. Want, A. Hopper, V. Falcao and J. Gibbons, The Active Badge Location System, Trans. on Information Systems, Vol.10, No. 5, Jan. 1992, pp. 42–47.
3. M. Addlesee, A. Jones, F. Livesey, and F. Samaria, The ORL Active Floor, IEEE Personal Communications, Vol.4, No.5, Oct. 1997, pp. 35–41.
4. P. Bahl and V. Padmanabhan, RADAR: An In-Building RF-Based User Location and Tracking System, Proc. IEEE INFOCOMM 2000, Mar. 2000.
5. J. Hightower, C. Vakili, G. Borriello, and R. Want, Design and Calibration of the SpotON Ad-Hoc Location Sensing System, unpublished, August 2001.
6. BlueSoft Inc. Website, http://www.bluesoft-inc.com/.
7. A. Ward, A. Jones and A. Hopper, A New Location Technique for the Active Office. IEEE Personal Communications, Vol. 4, No. 5, Oct. 1997, pp. 42-47.
8. N. Priyantha, A. Miu, H. Balakrishnan and S. Teller, The Cricket Compass for Context-aware Mobile Applications, Proc. ACM MOBICOM 2001, Jul. 2001.
9. Hexamite Website, http://www.hexamite.com/.
10. A. Ward, Sensor-driven Computing, PhD thesis, University of Cambridge, 1998.
11. A. Savvides, C. Han and M. Srivastava, Dynamic Fine-Grained Localization in Ad-Hoc Networks of Sensors, Proc. ACM MOBICOM 2001, Jul. 2001.
12. R. Harle and A. Hopper, Building World Models by Ray-Tracing, Proc. UBICOMP 2003, Oct. 2003.
13. E. Kaplan Eds., UNDERSTANDING GPS: PRINCIPLES AND APPLICATIONS, Artech House, 1996.
14. A. Smith, H. Balakrishnan, M. Goraczko, and N. Priyantha, Tracking Moving Devices with the Cricket Location System, Proc. MOBISYS 2004, June 2004.
15. M. Hazas and A. Ward, A Novel Broadband Ultrasonic Location System, Proc. UBICOMP 2002, Sept. 2002.

The Carrot Approach: Encouraging Use of Location Systems

Kieran Mansley, Alastair R. Beresford, and David Scott

Laboratory for Communication Engineering,
Cambridge University Engineering Department,
William Gates Building, 15 J.J.Thomson Avenue,
Cambridge CB3 0FD. UK
{kjm25,arb33,djs55}@cam.ac.uk

Abstract. The Active Bat system provides the ability to locate users
and equipment with a high degree of accuracy and coverage. Despite
this, participation is low. We are concerned that this is symptomatic of
a fundamental problem in location-aware computing; specifically the lack
of understanding about which applications are useful and what factors
motivate people to use them.

In this paper we provide a retrospective analysis of Bat system usage
grounded in game theory. We have analysed the needs of people within
the coverage area, and used this to motivate a set of highly targeted
location-aware applications which we believe are compelling enough for
individuals to induce a gradual increase in participation. This *carrot*
approach has been successful and has increased the number of people
who wear their Bat.

Finally, this paper provides a critique of our experience with the Active Bat system. We suggest a number of refinements that should be
considered by developers of future location systems.

1   Introduction

1.1   The Active Bat System

The Active Bat [1] system was originally deployed at AT&T Laboratories Cambridge, and later at the Laboratory for Communication Engineering (LCE).
The Bat itself is a small battery-powered device (Figure 1 *left*) with a radio
transceiver, ultrasound transmitter, two push-button switches (which signal their
depressed state over the radio link) and an audible speaker pre-programmed to
play one of twelve different sounds (again, when triggered to do so by radio
communication). The installed infrastructure includes a radio transmitter which
schedules Bats to transmit a pulse of narrow-band ultrasound which is in turn
received by a matrix of time-synchronised ceiling receivers; the time of flight
data to each ceiling receiver is used to multi-laterate the location of the Bat to
within a few centimetres.

In order to write applications which use Bat location data, receive Bat button press events and trigger audio sounds, an extensive software architecture

N. Davies et al. (Eds.): UbiComp 2004, LNCS 3205, pp. 366–383, 2004.

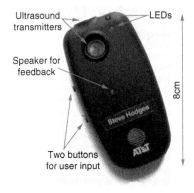

Fig. 1. The features of a Bat (*left*), and a Spatial Poster (*right*)

has been constructed. SPIRIT [2] maintains a world model of the location and state of various Bat-tagged and passive objects (such as people, laptops, computers, desks and chairs) and facilitates *programming with space* via *containers*, which are spatial regions defined by closed polygons and attached to either the floor plan or Bats. Applications can be written in an event-driven style, and receive callbacks whenever containers intersect, subsume or separate from other containers.

One of the innovations at AT&T was the development of *spatial buttons* (Figure 1 *right*) as a means of interacting with the applications. A spatial button is a region of space which has some action associated with it, similar in concept to Want et al's RFID-based augmenting tags [3] but they are completely passive pieces of paper: it is the space they occupy that is important. A user *clicks* on a spatial button by placing their Bat in that space and pressing one of the (physical) buttons located on the side of the Bat. A small poster placed at the same physical location as the spatial button allows the user to discover what the button does (and where it is!). These spatial buttons form an integral part of many of the applications of the Active Bat system: they are a simple, easy to create and use, and offer an intuitive user interface.

1.2 Usage and Applications

Increasing usage of a location system is desirable for a number of reasons: (1) the more people who participate, the more useful some applications become;[1] (2) increased usage affords increased anonymity (this is discussed in Section 3.3); and (3) gathering more data enables more data analysis and research. When the Active Bat system was installed at AT&T, the percentage of employees wearing a Bat was high (around 80%); however its installation at the LCE has resulted in a

---

[1] This is analogous to Metcalfe's Law: *The total value of a network where each node can reach every other node grows with the square of the number of nodes.*

far lower uptake of users (around 20%) in spite of the fact that both installations included very similar applications.

There are three discernible differences between the installations which may explain the lower level of participation in the LCE: (1) the coverage area of the Bat system at AT&T was larger (covering an entire building) leading to a more useful "person-locator" application; (2) participants at AT&T were employees while the LCE is a university lab; and (3) at AT&T, Bats would automatically unlock internal doors between different parts of the building. These differences shall now be considered individually.

First, consider the case of increased location system coverage leading to a more useful "person-locator" application. From a game-theoretic standpoint [4], this application may be modelled by a multi-player prisoners' dilemma. In real-life each person chooses whether to wear their bat or not whereas in the prisoners' dilemma each prisoner chooses whether to co-operate with the authorities or not. Both wearing a Bat and co-operating have an associated (small) cost. If everyone co-operates (i.e. everyone wears their Bats) then the whole group receives a benefit. However, from the point of view of an individual it is always better not to co-operate (i.e. not wear their Bat) while secretly hoping that everyone else does; this is said to be the *dominant strategy*. It does not matter how great the benefit (i.e. the size of the coverage area) is; if all the players are rational then *no-one* co-operates and *no-one* wears their Bats. Therefore coverage area and applications like the "person-locator" cannot explain the difference in uptake between the LCE and AT&T.

The second difference stems from the fact that AT&T was a company whereas the LCE is a university research lab. AT&T was a stable community in which people were encouraged to act selflessly. In contrast the LCE is a University research lab with a high turnover of personnel and not as closely-knit; in fact the LCE has several small social subgroups. These cultural differences could contribute to the difference in uptake between the LCE and AT&T.

The third difference between AT&T and the LCE—the presence of the automatic door opener in AT&T—is noteworthy in that it provides a useful function to an individual even if *no-one* else wears their Bat. In game-theoretic terms, users who wear their Bats always receive a useful payoff irrespective of the actions of others. For this reason we believe the automatic door opener was the first (albeit accidental) "killer app" of the Bat system. It is important to note that at no point in either deployment have any users been mandated to wear Bats: only *carrots* (i.e. positive inducements); no *sticks* (i.e. punishments) have been used.

In order to promote increased Bat usage within the LCE, and provide a mechanism to bootstrap the system from the low-usage state to the high-usage state, we set out to develop a set of location-aware applications with a view to finding similar "killer apps" for the new Bat environment. Unlike in AT&T, in the LCE we assume that everyone acts in their own self-interest or in the interest of a small group and therefore we must make it in the interests of these individuals and groups to participate. We model the utility to an individual of an application by the formula *Utility* $= AU^2 + B$ where U is the number of participating users and A and B are constants. AU^2 is the *Metcalfe-effect* and B the single-user payoff. Applications fall into one of three categories: TYPE I: those useful to isolated individuals (high B); TYPE II: those useful to small subgroups (high A, small set of users U); and TYPE III: those only useful when the whole lab participates (high A, whole lab U). Many traditional applications (e.g. the "person-locator") are TYPE III applications; most of the applications we present here are either TYPE I or TYPE II.

1.3   Relevance to Future Location Systems

The Active Bat system was deliberately designed to be more accurate than is likely to be practical in a commercial location system. As the Active Bat system offers excellent location information across a large indoor area, it constitutes a platform for investigating questions such as "when and where is such accuracy or coverage necessary?" Such analysis should enable a more cost effective location system to be constructed that still supports applications prototyped with the Active Bat system.

A lot of money is currently being spent building large-scale location systems, based on technologies such as GPS positioning, mobile phone triangulation, and RFID. We are concerned that the lack of use of the Bat system is not because of lack of accuracy or coverage (as both are excellent) but is symptomatic of a more fundamental problem in location-aware computing; specifically the lack of genuinely useful applications and a strategy for their deployment. We believe that unless this critical stumbling block is removed it is highly likely that no-one will use the less accurate, expensive, wide-area systems either.

Much of the ubiquitous computing community is currently developing and deploying architectures to record and distribute location information in an efficient and cost effective manner. We hope to provide some insight into what works (and does not work) for both application programmers and end users, and how some simple changes to the technology could make some applications much better. It has been asserted that there is a dearth of useful location-aware applications because with current middleware systems they are too hard to develop [5]; we contend that this is not true in our case (after the initial fixed cost of installation) and that developing applications which concentrate on benefits for the wearer are the key to making ubiquitous computing successful.

The rest of this paper is structured as follows. Section 2 presents a description of some of the applications themselves, while Section 3 discusses the suitability of the programming model and the benefits and limitations of the current implementation of the Bat system from the perspective of both the application writer and user. Section 4 presents some measurements and results of the effect caused by the deployment of these applications. Related work (and in particular previous Bat Applications) are discussed in Section 5; finally Section 6 concludes.

2   The Applications

In this section we begin by developing a classification of the intended users of the location system (in our case, the staff and students within the lab) with the aim of targeting applications at the needs of specific social groups.

2.1   Classifying the Users

The first task in any business is to identify potential customers who have needs which can be addressed by a feasible product. A common mistake (especially for technical people) is to focus mostly on the product itself rather than the needs of the customer—a condition known in business circles as *marketing myopia*. Therefore after a period of consultation, observation and informal chat we divided the population of the lab into the following groups (a process often known as *market segmentation*):

Drinkers : lab members who share the industrial-sized lab coffee machine
Players : a group who play online multi-player games (e.g. Quake III)
Teachers : faculty and students who have teaching responsibilities
Collaborators : those involved in joint projects with other researchers
Socialisers : those who regularly attend lab meetings and talks[2]
Everyone : the whole lab

Note that all lab members fall into at least one group and most people fall into several different groups. Each group was targeted with at least one (TYPE I or TYPE II) application tailored specifically for the needs of that group. It is important to note that each application was designed to be stand-alone and useful for the group concerned even if no other groups wear their Bat; this is the key to how we avoid the bootstrapping problem described earlier. In addition to each application providing users with more of an incentive to wear their Bats, a large number of total applications represents a good way to hedge our bets; in other words the failure of a small number of applications does not endanger the whole project.

The following table lists the applications for each group:

Group	Applications
Drinkers	Fresh Coffee Notification Service
Players	Capture the Flag, Batdar, Bat-Miles
Teachers	Teaching Timer
Collaborators	Visitor Interface, Office-Watcher
Socialisers	Meeting Reminder
Everyone	Daily Diary

---

[2] Even though technically many of these meetings are compulsory many people in practice fail to attend for various reasons.

These applications will now be described in the following sections, grouped together by implementation technique: (1) pager applications where the Bat is used to provide audible reminders of events (which are either explicitly signalled by other users, or inferred from the location data); (2) tracking applications which passively process the location data; and (3) games or other applications where users not only receive information about the virtual world, but also generate updates to virtual objects in the world model.

2.2 Intelligent Paging

The input and output facilities of the Bat are heavily restricted in order to attain long battery life (typically 18-24 months). Pager applications are suited to this restricted environment and allow users to be notified by a short audible sound that an event of interest has occurred. In order to prevent uninterested parties from receiving irrelevant audible alerts, users subscribe (or unsubscribe) to a notification service via spatial buttons (as illustrated in Figure 1 *right*) placed in the environment. A rising or falling trio of tones provides feedback on the status of user subscription whenever a user clicks on a spatial button. The printed paper poster located at the same physical location as the spatial button provides additional visual information about the service to the user.

Many of the pagers discussed below do not rely on high-accuracy location information and therefore could be realised using much simpler technology. Nevertheless we claim that, simple as they are, they are still genuinely useful and will motivate people to wear their Bats. As more people start to wear their Bats, other (TYPE III) applications (like the "person-locator") become increasingly useful. Furthermore, we can use the highly-accurate location information of the user to improve the paging services in a number of ways that would not be possible with simpler technology:

- Notifying only one subscriber per room (reducing the audible distraction resulting from a set of Bats beeping simultaneously).
- Inferring the existence of gatherings or meetings (see Section 2.3) and using this information to delay (or modify in some other way) the notification until the meeting has ended.
- Triggering events automatically from passive location monitoring.

This last point leads us to divide this category of applications into those which require users to actively notify subscribers that an event has taken place by clicking on a spatial button, and those which are able to automatically infer an event.

Active Notification A simple example is the fresh coffee notification service, a TYPE II application. Fresh coffee is generally regarded as superior to coffee that was brewed some time ago and the discerning drinker likes to know when coffee has been made or at least how long the coffee has been brewing.[3] Users

---

[3] The Computer Lab in Cambridge has a long history of using innovative technology to disseminate this information [6].

can subscribe to the service by clicking on a spatial button. When brewing is complete a second spatial button is used to notify coffee fanatics (the **Drinkers**) that fresh coffee is available. Data are retained (and viewable on the intranet) so the age of the latest brew is always available. Similar services exist to support notification of food and nibbles placed in the kitchen, and a notification of the start of group meetings (which has had a noticeable impact on the number of late and missing students).

Another illustrative example is our visitor interface, a TYPE I application (intended to be of use to the **Collaborators**): at the main entrance to our laboratory we have a flat panel touchscreen allowing visitors to specify who they have come to see, and discover where that person is (or if they are out). The service notifies the user that a visitor wishes to meet with them, allowing users to know when visitors arrive, regardless of where in the laboratory they happen to be. It also displays a photo of the visitor on the nearest (to the user) Broadband Phone.[4] Subsequent location information is then displayed to the visitor via the flat panel display, providing feedback on the progress of the notified user toward them.

Context-Aware Paging We are able to use the location information available to infer when events have occurred, without requiring the users to signal them explicitly. To illustrate this, consider the modern equivalent of a knot in a handkerchief for the technologically minded (wo)man-about-town. People frequently need to remember to do a task not at a fixed time, but at the same time as an abstract action. For example: *there is something I want to take out of the fridge when I leave work*, or *there is something I have to do when I go for lunch*. A diary is not always appropriate as the reminder is not based on a fixed time, rather on the context of the user (e.g. *when I am leaving the office*); furthermore a diary needs to be read to be effective, whereas our solution is more proactive.

The simplest application is "remind me when I leave the building": by monitoring the user's movement vector as they approach an exit we can determine when they are leaving the building and provide an audible alert.[5] This TYPE I application has been extended to not only provide audible notification of events, but also execute a configurable task. This extension effectively makes it a context-aware version of the Unix `cron` command scheduler.

A number of graduate students teach small groups of undergraduates for hour-long sessions (the **Teachers**). To prevent sessions over-running and ensure that teaching is not disturbed (or the room double-booked), a spatial button can be used to notify the meeting room management system that a teaching session is about to take place. This TYPE I application marks the meeting room as busy on the lab intranet and provides an audible alert to the teacher's Bat a few moments before the teaching time is up.

---

[4] Broadband Phones are telephones that incorporate a large display that operates as a stateless thin-client running VNC [7], allowing a wide variety of applications to be run on a server and displayed on the phone.

[5] A number of students use this just to remind them to take their Bat off.

The office-watcher (TYPE II) application provides a spatial button for every member of our laboratory next to their own office door. Users who attempt to visit a colleague (the **Collaborators**) and find they are not in can click the office-watch spatial button and receive an audible alert when the person they are interested in next returns to their office. Users can also click their *own* office-watcher button to receive an audible reminder to do something when *they* next return to their office.

2.3   Tracking Applications

This category differs from the Pager Applications in Section 2.2 in that the applications do not notify the user of anything. Instead, they passively gather information for later presentation. Since the user interface of the Bat system is minimal, these applications use the lab intranet to provide a better (visual) display of pertinent data.

Bat-Miles[6] is a TYPE I application. Users subscribe (or unsubscribe) using a spatial button; subscribed users receive details of their distance travelled while standing and sitting, maximum speed and approximate calories consumed.

A personalised daily diary (a TYPE I application) of user events is constructed from the services users subscribe to and includes times at which coffee has been made, supervisions given and photographs of visitors to the front door (taken with a web camera). Details of the times and locations of meetings with other lab members can be automatically inferred [8] and recorded. Figure 2 shows an example screen shot of a daily diary of events.

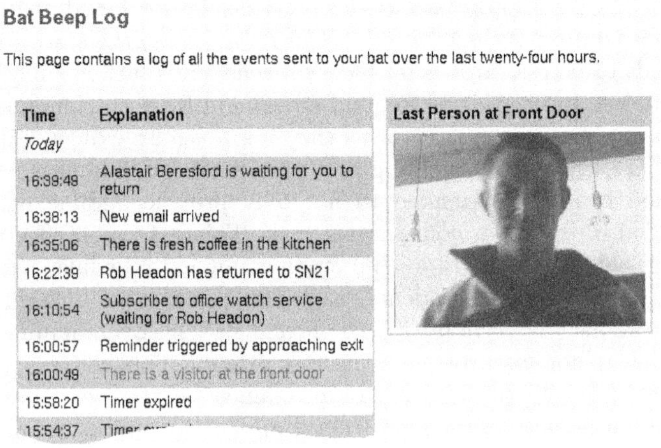

Bat Beep Log

This page contains a log of all the events sent to your bat over the last twenty-four hours.

Time	Explanation	Last Person at Front Door
Today		
16:39:48	Alastair Beresford is waiting for you to return	
16:38:13	New email arrived	
16:35:06	There is fresh coffee in the kitchen	
16:22:39	Rob Headon has returned to SN21	
16:10:54	Subscribe to office watch service (waiting for Rob Headon)	
16:00:57	Reminder triggered by approaching exit	
16:00:49	There is a visitor at the front door	
15:58:20	Timer expired	
15:54:37	Timer	

Fig. 2. The Daily Diary Log.

---

[6] Bat-Miles is named after Air-Miles loyalty schemes.

2.4   Games

Historically games have been a major driving force behind developments in computer technology, and judging by the number of people in the lab who play games regularly (the **Players**) this trend looks likely to continue. We believe that location-aware applications which are fun will both boost participation while pushing the technology to its limits. The games are multi-player and are therefore TYPE II applications.

Counter Strike and Capture the Flag As real-life is, almost by definition, experienced from the first-person, a first-person "shoot-'em-up" is the obvious candidate: traditional games of this type try to *emulate* the first-person perspective whereas the Bats provide *direct access* to this view point, and so provide a natural interface. The game had two design requirements: (1) the experience of playing game by physically moving around the building should be a feature rather than a hindrance; and (2) usage of additional hardware should be minimised so that players only need to carry their Bats. With these requirements in mind we settled on two games which are relatively simple (and similar) in concept:

Counter Strike: The players are divided into two teams: *Terrorists* and *Counter-Terrorists*. The terrorist's aim is to plant a bomb at a pre-defined location, and the counter-terrorists must try to stop them.

Capture the Flag: Two teams each try to retrieve a "flag" from the other team's base, returning with it to their own base. At the same time they must prevent the other team from capturing their own flag.

Traditionally, games of this sort (e.g. Quake III) involve a large amount of weaponry. It was clear that the Active Bat system would struggle to support these sorts of fast moving interactions where choice of weapon, aim (and so orientation) and latency of position information is critical. We therefore opted to support two weapons: land-mines and shotguns.

Players can join either team by going to the relevant base and using a spatial "join" button. This button is also used to rejoin the game if the player dies. The natural overhead of physically returning to your team's base to be reincarnated is sufficient to make death a hindrance.

All of the objects in the game (flags, bombs, shotguns, and land-mines) are entirely virtual. The two weapons are both deployed using the same button on the Bat and the weapon the player intends to use is determined using *gestures*. Land-mines can be placed by bending down and clicking near the floor with the Bat, while the shotgun is fired by clicking twice (to indicate the direction of the shot) at chest level.

Flags and bombs are picked up and put down automatically if the player is in the correct location (i.e. one of the bases). Land-mines are triggered when a user steps within a certain proximity of one once they have been armed, and so cannot be picked up. Each player starts the game with a fixed number of mines, but these are automatically replenished once they have exploded.

All the feedback to the users is done through audible signals. This includes both sounds from the Bat (to acknowledge events that refer to an individual player, such as "you have died" or "you have laid a mine") and from any PCs around the building that are running a special client that listens for game events. Game events are generally things that affect a whole team, such as "your team has won/lost", "your team has the enemy flag", etc. This works well, as the speaker on the Bat is low in volume, localising the sounds about individual players to themselves, while the speaker on the PC is high in volume, broadcasting events of general interest to many players. We found placing one of these PCs in each base led to sufficient feedback to make the game playable. Each PC can also be configured to display a map (Figure 3) of the game area, allowing players in the bases (or just spectators) to see a view of the virtual world. At any point in time a user is able to query their status (alive or dead, and what they are carrying) using the other Bat button, and the result is again conveyed using audible beeps.

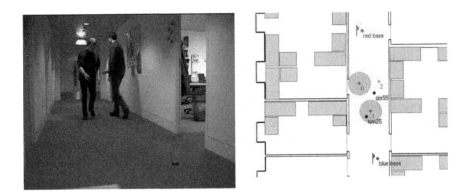

Fig. 3. The Capture the Flag Game

Two players ("djs55" and "kjm25") are playing the game. The
physical world is shown on the left, and a plan view of the
corresponding virtual world on the right. The player "kjm25" has
just triggered the mine labelled "1" (which in turn set off mine "0"),
and has been caught in the blast zone.

These two location-based games demonstrate that it is possible to use a device with very limited feedback capabilities to support games that are genuinely fun to play, and combine elements of the physical world (e.g. moving from one place to another) with those of the virtual world (e.g. weapons) [9]. We believe that its capabilities could easily be extended by providing a richer environment (e.g. augmented reality), or more weapons that are controlled with different gestures.

Batdar While a Bat enables its wearer to be located, Batdar[7] uses the Bat to help the wearer locate other objects. It makes the Bat beep with a period proportional to how close it is to something, in the same way that modern car reversing aids do. It can use a number of metrics to determine the frequency of the beeps: (1) how far away the target is; (2) how much the Bat's orientation differs from the bearing to the target; or (3) how much the Bat's direction of travel (or the direction of a particular gesture) differs from the bearing to the target.

Of these choices the latter seems to be the most effective; the "distance to target" fails when the user is a long way from the target: they have no indication which way to start looking, and the orientation metric fails as orientation accuracy from a single Bat is insufficient. Whilst Batdar can be used to support guiding visitors to a destination, the limitations in user feedback (described in more detail in Section 3) can make this exercise frustrating; a simple map is much more effective at conveying the same information. Batdar is more suitable for "treasure hunt" games where users must seek out a particular target or targets within a certain period of time.

3   Performance of the Active Bat System

The SPIRIT system uses CORBA to connect location-aware applications with live location data and persistent data which is stored in an Oracle database. At the LCE a set of Python language bindings have been implemented to allow rapid application development. The ease with which we developed and deployed the applications described here has encouraged other users of the system to develop their own applications (e.g. using the Bat to notify a user when new email has arrived). In the research environment, having a complete and well-written middleware system for users to take advantage of can be seen as another *carrot*.

Location information available from the Bat system is generally of excellent quality and most aspects of the Active Bat and SPIRIT system have been well thought-out. However a number of compromises had to be made in order to guarantee a long Bat battery life. In this section we discuss our experiences with developing context-aware applications with the Bat system and which areas should be rethought in a future location system design.

3.1   Feedback Issues

The weakness that came to light almost immediately was the limited number of ways that we could provide feedback to the user. The Bats have no means of providing visual cues (other than two LEDs that indicate use of the radio channel) and so feedback relies on the use of a speaker to provide audible tones. This minimal interface stems from the requirement for long battery life (which in turn

---

[7] Batdar is named to allude to SONAR.

was chosen to minimise the cost to the user of wearing the Bat). Future location systems (such as mobile phone networks) whose devices require regular charging anyway (e.g. mobile phones) should be able to have much more sophisticated display facilities.

Each Bat is pre-programmed with twelve tunes which range from simple beeps to more complex sequences similar to mobile phone ring-tones. To achieve a degree of consistency many of these tunes are used universally to signify the same thing. For example, a series of rising tones is used as positive acknowledgement (e.g. "you have turned something on") and a series of falling tones is used as negative acknowledgement (e.g. "you have turned something off").

The remaining tunes are then used to signify a wide range of events. We have experimented with using single pre-programmed tunes that have an obvious association ("Food, Glorious Food"), and combining some simple beeps together to form more significant sequences. In theory messages could be encoded using Morse code or a similar message structure to provide additional meaning.[8]

Combining the existing beeps together to make sequences reveals a second limitation of the Bat system. Triggering a Bat beep requires the use of the radio link to the Bats, consuming considerable battery power; therefore the radio channel is normally turned off whenever it is not required. The interval at which the Bat wakes up (to perform location updates and play audible tones) is highly variable, and so it is difficult to trigger beeps at a high rate. This is illustrated in Figure 4 where (for a stationary or slow moving user) you cannot reliably trigger more than 1 beep per second. If the user moves at a reasonable speed, the achievable update rate increases. Pressing a Bat button also forces an update over the radio channel (and thus removes any latency in user-directed actions). The Bat system provides a partial solution, in that it is possible explicitly request that the Bat be prevented from going to sleep: it forces the Bat into a *high-rate* QoS mode. However, this reduces battery life, and thus should only be used for short periods. Finally, putting too many users into *high-rate* mode overloads the radio channel and reduces the responsiveness of the audio feedback for other users.

With many applications using the speaker on the Bat to convey information, the user can have difficulty attaching meaning to sounds. This difficultly motivated the construction of the user's daily diary application described in Section 2.3 which allows the user to quickly answer the question "why did my Bat just beep?". Web pages were also used for feedback in the tracking applications where the amount of information was too great to feasibly present without a screen. Even a small screen (such as a mobile phone display) may have been able to support these applications (for example, compare the Bat-Miles application with bicycle odometers).

---

[8] Mobile phone users may be familiar with this, as the delivery of a text message is often signalled using the Morse for SMS.

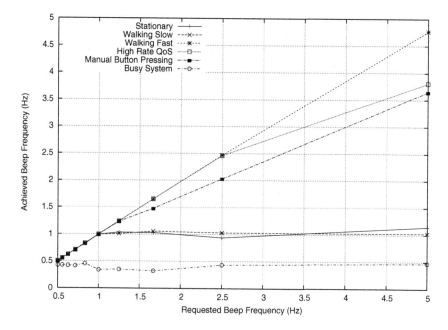

Fig. 4. Audible Feedback Rate of the Bat System.

3.2 Accuracy of Location Data

Many of the applications described in this paper can be implemented using location systems with smaller coverage area or less location accuracy when compared with the Active Bat system. For example spatial buttons could be implemented using visual tag recognition and Bluetooth capabilities of a mobile phone handset [10] or by embedding RFID readers into the spatial button posters or even clothing [11].

The games were the most demanding on coverage area and resolution, and gesture information was used to overcome the inaccuracies in orientation information available from a single Bat. Location systems with greater orientation accuracy would therefore allow a more expressive location-based gaming environment. A high update rate is needed for the games to be playable and fun (if a person is only located every few seconds, interaction with other places and virtual objects, such as mines, becomes intermittent and frustrating). Therefore interactive location-based gaming requires a method of achieving a high quality of service (e.g. the Active Bat system's high-rate mode).

3.3 Privacy

A common difficulty with location-based systems (particularly one as pervasive, centralised and accurate as the Active Bat system) is that they can be very privacy invasive. Some of the applications developed here (e.g. coffee alerts) can be made to work without knowledge of the true user identity, and with some work could be made to function with untraceable pseudonyms (identifiers an attacker cannot associate with any real-world entity). It is possible that anonymising information in this way can prevent an application from determining the true user identity hiding behind the pseudonym [12].

Some applications will always require knowledge of user identity (e.g. the Office-Watcher). Our current solution is to build *reciprocity* into the system—providing feedback via the diary intranet page of requests for location information to the location data owner. This has the effect that frequently watched users can find out who is watching them and take appropriate action if the service is abused. Economists have noticed that adding punishments (as well as rewards) has a positive effect on the outcomes of competitive games [13].

4   Measurements and Results

To quantify the effect of this work we distinguish users who wear their bat from users who do not by performing an off-line analysis of the centralised log of all the location sightings each day. A person is deemed to have worn their Bat if it is sighted in three different rooms and one of the rooms is the central corridor of our laboratory.[9] There are clearly ways in which this could be spoofed (by getting someone to wear more than one bat), and it would not count people who only wear their bat in their office, but, after careful manual observation of user habits, both these outcomes occur very infrequently.

One of our goals for this work was to demonstrate that by providing enough *carrots* in the form of useful applications (and without using any *sticks*) we could encourage users to wear location devices.

By carefully choosing which applications to implement based on an informal lab survey and avoiding the pitfall represented by the Prisoners' Dilemma, this goal has been achieved, as Figure 5 demonstrates. Bat usage is up from an average of 5.2 people (6.8 on weekdays) for the six months prior to the deployment of the new applications to 13.1 (16.3 on weekdays) for the following six weeks. Quantifying the precise level of improvement is difficult since the sample size is small, however, if the difference in occupancy rate of a student lab (like the LCE) and a commercial lab (like AT&T), is taken into account we now have a comparable percentage of users in both deployments.

Despite the increase in usage, a significant minority of people still do not regularly wear their Bat. An informal survey threw up a number of reasons: (1) apathy or forgetfulness—they just do not feel it is worth the effort or forget to put it on; (2) privacy—there are some who are concerned about their privacy, and so do not wear one on principle; and (3) discomfort—some people find wearing a Bat around their neck uncomfortable or annoying.

---

[9] These requirements avoid counting people who just leave their Bat on their desk, and make counting erroneous sightings (due to other sources of ultrasound) unlikely.

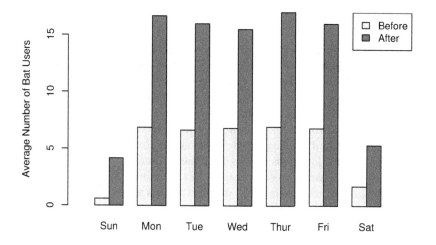

Fig. 5. The Number of People Wearing Bats.

The group represented by (1) could potentially be encouraged by targeted (TYPE I) applications that they would find useful. Other ways of wearing a Bat (such as belt clips or watch straps) are made available to try to resolve the problems of group (3). The group who are concerned about their privacy are unlikely to be persuaded to use the Bat system in its current form, and this group demand a heavily re-designed location system in order meet their privacy concerns.

The popularity of the different applications varied considerably. Given the different usage patterns for each application and their concurrent deployment it is difficult to formally compare them and measure which has had most impact. However, those that have the most subscribers are the fresh coffee (and food) notification pagers, and the Bat-Miles scheme. Perhaps unsurprisingly these are ones for which the users get a tangible benefit with little effort.

Finally, it is clear that novelty value has a large impact on the number of people who wear their Bats. The Active Bat system has now been deployed in two labs, and in each there was a gradual tail off in usage (before stabilising) after an initial high take up. This peak was recovered by the deployment of new applications, but without a continual output of new features[10] it is likely to decline again in the future (although stabilising at a higher level). In an attempt to avoid novelty being the major factor in our measurements, the applications were not hyped or pushed to the users: their presence was announced by email, and by a short presentation at a lab meeting.

---

[10] We have started to observe that the once the system reaches a certain usability, these new features come from applications developed and deployed by the users themselves

5   Related Work

AT&T Labs Cambridge developed a set of location-aware applications as part of their initial deployment of the Active Bat system. Some applications were adapted from the original Active Badge [14] system; for example: locating users, unlocking of internal doors, forwarding phone calls and teleporting desktops using VNC [7]. New applications developed specifically for the Bats included spatial buttons to provide a simple and intuitive interface to control a "sentient" scanner and a method of using the Bat as a mouse pointer on large plasma screens installed at various locations throughout the building.

Presentations given by researchers at AT&T were context-aware—slide shows could be controlled with a Bat, and meeting details were recorded and published on the lab intranet (this system was similar to some of the methods proposed for the Reactive Room [15]). Video conferencing was also context-enabled: the delegates present in a conference room were tracked to select the most useful camera angle automatically.

Other office applications and systems have been proposed, including the stick-e note architecture [16] which allows applications to attach virtual documents to physical spaces. Collaborage [17] used image processing techniques to allow physical notes (e.g. in/out and away boards for employees and "to-do" lists) to be synchronised with their virtual counterparts.

Outside the office environment, GPS systems have been used to build everything from guidance systems for the blind [18] to location-based automated assistance for archaeology fieldworkers [19]. Tourist guide applications are perhaps the most popular with ubiquitous computing researchers; examples include the CyberGuide project at Georgia Tech. [20] and the Lancaster GUIDE project [21].

In the field of ubiquitous computer games a number of projects have been developed [22] to see what existing game functions can be supported with current ubiquitous technology [23], and what new games can be developed to take advantage of possible future advances in ubiquitous technology [24].

6   Conclusions

In this paper we have shown how usage of location systems can be incrementally increased by taking a more business-like, customer-focused approach to application development. We analysed the recent decline in Active Bat usage from a game-theoretic standpoint and argued that many existing location-aware TYPE III applications have fallen into disuse as a consequence of the well-known Prisoners' Dilemma. We described how this trap could be avoided if TYPE I or TYPE II applications are provided which are of immediate use to individuals and small social groups. Furthermore, increased overall participation has an overwhelmingly positive effect as users of the location system receive a community benefit from increased take-up, both from being able to locate colleagues more reliably and from increased privacy. We claim this principle justifies the existence of applications that have no intrinsically useful purpose (such as games).

Due to the limited nature of most location system tags, interaction with the user (rather than location accuracy and coverage) is the current limiting factor in application development. We have shown how best use can be made of a device with limited feedback capabilities, and how alternative channels can be used to provide parallel feedback to the user.

In conclusion we believe that designers of future location systems must urgently consider both the interaction capabilities of their locatable tags and carefully analyse the features required by the applications users actually *want* if they are to have a successful, popular and profitable system.

Acknowledgements

Thanks go to Alastair Tse for building the Python-SPIRIT interface library, Rob Harle for his help with the Active Bat system, Andy Rice for his comments and work on the visitor interface, and Anil Madhavapeddy and Rob Headon for their helpful comments on drafts of this paper. Finally, a big thank you to all those AT&T Labs Cambridge employees who designed and built the Active Bat system and associated SPIRIT middleware.

References

[1] Andy Harter, Andy Hopper, Pete Steggles, Andy Ward, and Paul Webster. The anatomy of a context-aware application. In *5th Annual ACM/IEEE International Conference on Mobile Computing and Networking (Mobicom '99)*, 1999.

[2] Mike Addlesee, Rupert Curwen, Steve Hodges, Joe Newman, Pete Steggles, Andy Ward, and Andy Hopper. Implementing a sentient computing system. *IEEE Computer*, 34(8):50–56, August 2001.

[3] Roy Want, Kenneth P. Fishkin, Anuj Gujar, and Beverly L. Harrison. Bridging physical and virtual worlds with electronic tags. In *SIGCHI conference on Human factors in computing systems*, pages 370–377, 199.

[4] Robert Gibbons. *A primer on Game Theory*. Prentice Hall, 1992.

[5] Anthony Lamarca and Maya Rodrig. Oasis: An architecture for simplified data management and disconnected operation. In *17th International Conference on Architecture of Computing Systems — Organic and Pervasive Computing (ARCS'04)*, March 2004.

[6] Quentin Stafford-Fraser. The life and times of the first web cam. *Communications of the ACM*, 44(7), 2001.

[7] Tristan Richardsonm, Quentin Stafford-Fraser, Kenneth R. Wood, and Andy Hopper. Virtual Network Computing. *IEEE Internet Computing*, 2(1):33–38, January 1998.

[8] William M. Newman, Margery A. Eldridge, and Michael G. Lamming. Pepys: Generating autobiographies by automatic tracking. In *Second European Conference on Computer-Supported Co-operative Work (CSCW)*, pages 175–188, September 1991.

[9] Kieran Mansley, David Scott, Alastair Tse, and Anil Madhavapeddy. Feedback, latency, accuracy: Exploring tradeoffs in location-aware gaming. In *3rd Workshop on Network and System Support for Games (NetGames), part of ACM SIGCOMM 2004*, August 2004.

[10] Anil Madhavapeddy, David Scott, Richard Sharp, and Eben Upton. Using camera-phones in augmented reality applications. Submitted to ISMAR 2004, available from http://www.cl.cam.ac.uk/Research/SRG/netos/uid/spotcode.html.

[11] Robert Headon and George Coulouris. Supporting gestural input for users on the move. In *Proceedings of Eurowearable '03*, pages 107–112, September 2003.

[12] Alastair Beresford and Frank Stajano. Location privacy in pervasive computing. *IEEE Pervasive Computing*, 2(1):46–55, March 2003.

[13] James Andreoni, William Harbaugh, and Lisa Vesterlund. The carrot or the stick: Rewards, punishments, and cooperation. Available from the University of Oregon Economics Department at http://econpapers.hhs.se/paper/oreuoecwp/2002-01.htm.

[14] Roy Want, Andy Hopper, Veronica Falcão, and Jonathan Gibbons. The Active Badge Location System. *ACM Transactions on Information Systems*, 10(1):91–102, January 1992.

[15] Jeremy R. Cooperstock, Signey S. Fels, William Buxton, and Kenneth C. Smith. Reactive environments. *Communications of the ACM*, 40(9):65–73, September 1997.

[16] P. J. Brown. The stick-e document: a framework for creating context-aware applications. In *Proceedings of Electronic Publisher*, number 2 in 8, pages 259–272, January 1996.

[17] Thomas P. Moran, Eric Saund, William Van Melle, Anuj U. Gujar, Kenneth P. Fishkin, and Beverly L. Harrison. Design and technology for Collaborage: collaborative collages of information on physical walls. In *12th annual ACM symposium on user interface software and technology*, pages 197–206, November 1999.

[18] Helen Petrie, Valerie Johnson, Thomas Strothotte, Steffi Fritz, Rainer Michel, and Andreas Raab. Mobic: Designing a travel aid for blind and elderly people. *Journal of Navigation*, 49(1):45–52, 1996.

[19] Nick Ryan, Jason Pascoe, and David Morse. Enhanced reality fieldwork: the context aware archaeological assistant. In *Computer Applications in Archaeology*, 1997.

[20] Sue Long, Rob Kooper, Gregory D. Abowd, and Christopher G. Atkeson. Rapid prototyping of mobile context-aware applications: The cyberguide case study. In *Mobile Computing and Networking*, pages 97–107, 1996.

[21] Keith Cheverst, Nigel Davies, Keith Mitchell, and Adrian Friday. Experiences of developing and deploying a context-aware tourist guide: the guide project. In *International Conference on Mobile Computing and Networking*, pages 20–31, 2000.

[22] Staffan Bjork, Jussi Holopainen, Peter Ljungstrand, and Regan Mandryk (editors). Special issue on ubiquitous games. *Personal and Ubiquitous Computing*, 6:358–458, December 2002.

[23] Robert Headon and Rupert Curwen. Movement awareness for ubiquitous game control. *Personal and Ubiquitous Computing*, 6:407–415, December 2002.

[24] Staffan Bjork, Jussi Holopainen, Peter Ljungstrand, and Karl-Petter Akesson. Designing ubiquitous computing games - a report from a workshop exploring ubiquitous computing entertainment. *Personal and Ubiquitous Computing*, 6:443–458, December 2003.

ActiveBelt: Belt-Type Wearable Tactile Display for Directional Navigation

Koji Tsukada[1] and Michiaki Yasumura[2]

[1] Graduate School of Media and Governance, Keio University, 5322 Endo Fujisawa, Kanagawa 252-8520, Japan,
tsuka@sfc.keio.ac.jp,
http://mobiquitous.com/index-e.html
[2] Faculty of Environmental Information, Keio University,
yasumura@sfc.keio.ac.jp

Abstract. In this paper we propose a novel wearable interface called "ActiveBelt" that enables users to obtain multiple directional information with the tactile sense. Since the information provided by the tactile sense is relatively unobtrusive, it is suited for daily use in mobile environments. However, many existing systems don't transmit complex information via the tactile sense. Most of them send only simple signals, such as vibration in cellular phones. ActiveBelt is a novel belt-type wearable tactile display that can transmit directional information. We have developed prototype systems and applications, evaluated system performance and usability, and demonstrated the possibility of practical use.

1 Introduction

As positioning technologies such as GPS (Global Positioning System) have become popular and widely used, many researchers have developed location-aware information systems in mobile environments using positioning technologies[3][14][24]. Moreover, in Japan, some cell phone companies have provided location-aware information services, such as "eznavigation"[7] by KDDI.

While there are many applications for these location-aware information services, one of the most popular applications is navigation[11]. For example, "eznavigation" provides an application called "GPS Map" that can display a fairly accurate map of the current location in a few seconds using GPS and information of base stations. These navigation systems look useful at first glance. However, users often have difficulty matching geographical information on maps to the real world. For example, people often get lost in a large exhibition even if they have a map of it. Moreover, some people are not good at reading maps.

Since these problems result from a difficulty to match geographical information on 2D maps to the real world, we can address the problems by providing suitable directional information to a destination. For example, when a person gets lost in a large exhibition, it's very helpful for someone to tell her/him what the correct direction to her/his destination is.

N. Davies et al. (Eds.): UbiComp 2004, LNCS 3205, pp. 384–399, 2004.
© Springer-Verlag Berlin Heidelberg 2004

In this paper we propose a novel belt-type wearable interface called "Active-Belt" that enables users to obtain directional information via the tactile sense. First, we describe properties of tactile displays and belt-type devices.

1.1 Types of Display in Mobile Environments

Three types of display used in mobile and wearable computing are: visual displays, auditory displays, and tactile displays. Each of these types of display has advantages and disadvantages. The visual display can transmit vast quantities of information quickly, but it prevents visual attention being directed to other tasks. For example, a user often has difficulty looking at a display of a cell phone while walking. The Auditory display is more easily used with other tasks. However, the auditory display can conflict with other sounds in the surrounding environment. For example, it is difficult for users to use the auditory display in very noisy or silent environments. The tactile display is limited in the amount of information it can transmit. However, it's easiest for users to use the tactile display with other tasks, and so it is suited for daily use in mobile environment.

In this paper we focus on the tactile display as a display type that is well suited to mobile use.

1.2 Types of Forms of Wearable Interfaces

As shown in Table 1, many researchers proposed various forms of wearable interfaces such as glasses, gloves, watches, rings, shoes, vests, pendants, caps, earrings, and so on. We have focused on a belt-type device since the shape of a belt seems suited to transmitting directional information via the tactile sense. Since a belt is worn around the user's torso, it can provide directional information only by activating vibrators. Moreover, since many people usually wear belts, they don't need to wear additional devices. In addition, although many researchers in wearable computing used belts for attaching computers and batteries, the possibility of belts for input/output interfaces has not received much attention. Because of these considerations, we chose a belt-type device.

2 ActiveBelt

2.1 Concepts

In this section we describe the concepts of the ActiveBelt. The main concepts of the ActiveBelt are as follows:

1. Tactile display that enables users to intuitively obtain directional information
2. Belt-type wearable device optimized for mobile use
3. Suited for various applications, especially for location-aware information services.

Table 1. Typical products and research projects of wearable interfaces classified by their forms

Forms	Typical products and research projects
glasses	MicroOptical[13], Poma[17]
gloves	5DTDataGlove[1], CyberGlove[6], Ubi-Finger[25]
watches	Whisper[10]
rings	FingeRing[9], GSR rings[16]
shoes	Expressive Footwear[15], GSR Shoes[16]
vests	Tactual Wearable Display[23]
pendants	GesturePendant[21]
caps	Wearable American Sign Language[22]
earrings	The Blood Volume Pressure earring[16]

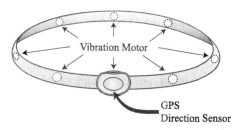

Fig. 1. Basic Concept of ActiveBelt

First, the ActiveBelt can enable users to intuitively obtain directional information in the real world simply by activating vibrators. Since a user can easily match this tactile information to directions in the real world, the ActiveBelt can transmit effective information via the tactile sense.

Second, the ActiveBelt doesn't require the user to wear or carry yet another device, since it attaches vibrators in a typical belt worn by many people in daily life. In addition, since people usually wear belts outside, ActiveBelt is well suited to use in mobile environments.

Third, the ActiveBelt can be used for a variety of applications and especially for location-aware information services like navigation systems.

2.2   Device Architecture

In this section, we describe the device architecture of the ActiveBelt. The ActiveBelt consists of two sensors (a direction sensor and a GPS) to detect a user's location and orientation, multiple vibrators to transmit tactile information, and a microcomputer to control these devices (Fig. 1). The vibrators are attached throughout a belt at regular intervals.

2.3   Sensitivity of the Torso to Vibration

In this section, we discuss the sensitivity of the torso to the vibration. According to van Erp[26], the resolutions of the torso are as follows: In the abdominal area, the resolution has a roughly 0.4 cm jnd(just noticeable difference) interval at the center, and a 1.2 cm interval at the sides. In the back, the resolution is less sensitive about a 1.8 cm interval at the center, and about a 3.0 cm interval at the sides. These results show that the resolutions of a torso are fairly good. Moreover, Yamamoto[30] reported that people can distinguish horizontal direction fairly accurately based on vibration to their torsos.

Thus, the resolutions of a torso are fairly good, and people can tell horizontal direction with vibration. This suggests that the ActiveBelt may help navigation using vibration to indicate the direction to take at each point in time.

2.4   Numbers of Vibrators to Be Used

Human sensitivity allows for the use of a relatively large number of vibrators around the torso. However, too many vibrators may generate problems, such as increases in power consumption, complications of cables, needs for more I/O of microcomputers, and so on.

To avoid these problems, we used eight vibrators. These vibrators and cables can be easily attached inside a belt, and controlled using a microcomputer.

3   Development

3.1   Prototype

We developed a prototype ActiveBelt system based on the above concepts. The prototype system consists of four components: (1)ActiveBelt hardware, (2)a GPS, (3)a directional sensor, and (4) a microcomputer (Fig. 2). Fig. 3 shows the system architecture of the ActiveBelt. Next, we explain each component of the prototype system.

Belt-Type Hardware   We developed the first prototype of the ActiveBelt in the form of a typical belt adjusted using a buckle (Fig. 4). We attached eight vibrators (FM23A by TPC) and LEDs [3] in the belt. The diameter of the FM23A is about 18 mm, and the thickness is about 3 mm. We attached four vibrators in the center of the abdomen, in the center of the back, and the left and right sides close to the hips. We also attached four other vibrators in each midway between two of the first four vibrators.

The frequencies of each vibrator change with voltages, such as 33Hz at 0.3 V, 40Hz at 0.6V, 55Hz at 0.8V, and 77Hz at 1.2V. Thus, we can control the

---

[3] LEDs are turned on and off in sync with vibrators. We used LEDs to check the states of the ActiveBelt.

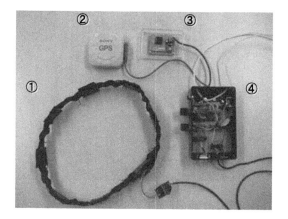

Fig. 2. Prototype system of ActiveBelt (1. ActiveBelt hardware, 2. GPS, 3. directional sensor, 4. microcomputer)

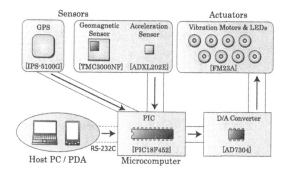

Fig. 3. System architecture of ActiveBelt

strength of vibrators by changing the voltages[4]. For human skin, the most sensitive frequency band is between 200 Hz and 250Hz. We used a less sensitive frequency band between 33Hz and 77Hz in the prototype system. We focused on using cheap and easily obtainable vibrators this time. Other vibrators may be used in later research.

We adjusted the length of the belt to the waist size of one of the authors. The distance between the vibrators was 9.75cm on average (±0.25cm), and the whole length of the belt was about 78.0cm. It was difficult for many users to wear this prototype, since the mapping between vibrators and directions was modified when a user adjusted the length of the belt to her/his waist.

---

[4] Since energies change with frequencies in general, people feel stronger vibration in a high frequency.

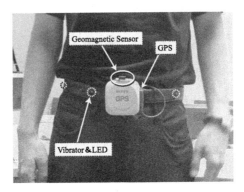

Fig. 4. Hardware of ActiveBelt ver.1

Fig. 5. Hardware of ActiveBelt ver.2 (universal-size)

To solve this problem, we developed a universal-size ActiveBelt ver.2 that consists of leather parts in which vibrators are attached and elastic rubber parts fit to the size of the user's waist (Fig. 5). While the whole length of the belt is about 75.0 cm, a wide range of users with waist circumference less than 98.0 cm can wear the belt without breaking the correspondences between vibrators and directions (Fig. 7j. We have wired each vibrators loosely in consideration of elasticity of rubber parts (Fig. 6).

Directional Sensor and GPS The directional sensor consists of a geomagnetic sensor (TMC3000NF by NEC Tokin) and an acceleration sensor (ADXL202E by Analog Devices)(Fig. 8). We used the geomagnetic sensor to detect the orientation of a user. The output voltages of the geomagnetic sensor are converted to digits with 10 bit A/D converters in a microcomputer. The accuracy of the geomagnetic sensor for detecting directions is about ±1.5 degree. We used the acceleration sensor to detect horizontal angles. We considered using the accel-

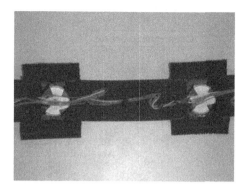

Fig. 6. Wiring inside of universal-size ActiveBelt

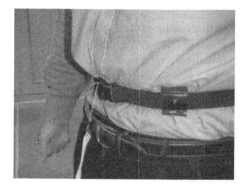

Fig. 7. Example of wearing universal-size ActiveBelt

eration sensor for calibrating the horizontal angles of the geomagnetic sensor, since the geomagnetic sensor must keep its position horizontal to detect precise directions. However, through simple experiment, we found that humans can easily keep the position of their waist horizontal even when they walk on ascents of about 30 degrees. In addition, perfect precision is not needed. Consequently, we don't modify the outputs of the geomagnetic sensor in the current prototype system.

We used the IPS-5100G (by Sony) as a GPS. The IPS-5100G transmits output signals to the microcomputer as serial data, and the microcomputer extracts latitudes and longitudes from the data. We used spherical trigonometry to calculate a relative direction and distance to a destination.

Microcomputer and Surrounding Circuit We used a microcomputer (PIC 18F452 by MicroChip) to control the sensors and vibrators. The functions of the microcomputer are as follows: (1) controlling vibrators and LEDs based on input data from sensors, and (2) communicating with host PC/PDA. For the

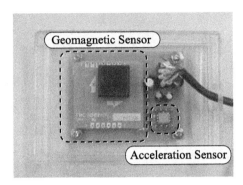

Fig. 8. Circuit board of direction sensor

first function, the microcomputer controls the vibrators and LEDs with a D/A converter (AD7304 by Analog Devices). Since we can easily control output voltages using the D/A converter, we can control the frequencies of the vibrators and the brightness of the LEDs smoothly [5]. For the second function, the microcomputer communicates with the host PC/PDA via RS-232C. Users can register the latitude and longitude of a destination with the host PC/PDA.

3.2   Applications

In this section, we discuss applications of the ActiveBelt. We propose four applications: (1) FeelNavi for human navigation systems, (2) FeelSense for location-aware information services, (3) FeelSeek for search of lost properties, (4)FeelWave for entertainment.

FeelNavi FeelNavi is an application of navigation using tactile information. Users can intuitively reach destinations by walking toward the direction of vibration. In the prototype system, a user registers the latitude and longitude of her/his destination with a host PC/PDA. The ActiveBelt then activates the specified vibrator, based on the current position and orientation of the user (Fig. 9). We express a distance to a destination using pulse intervals of vibration. When a user comes nearer to the destination, the pulse intervals of vibration become shorter.

FeelSense As mentioned before, many researchers and companies have developed location-aware information services. Most of these existing systems used visual displays. Although the visual display has an advantage that it can transmit vast quantities of information quickly, this approach is sometimes unsatisfactory

---

[5] The voltage range we used was between 0V and 1.2V. We could activate vibrators by raising the voltage above 0.3V.

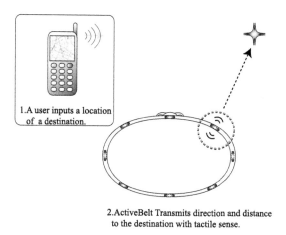

1.A user inputs a location of a destination.

2.ActiveBelt Transmits direction and distance to the destination with tactile sense.

Fig. 9. Basic concept of FeelNavi

for users. Moreover, location-aware information services are expected to extend rapidly in the near future. For these reasons, we should consider new approaches that are more convenient for users.

FeelSense is an always-active tactile display with which users can detect location-aware information while walking around a town. As shown in Fig. 10, users register interesting categories in advance. When they come near to relevant location-aware information, the ActiveBelt activates specified vibrators based on a user's position and orientation, and the location of the target information. For example, they can easily find shops of interest such as boutiques or restaurants.

FeelSeek Recently, RFID (Radio Frequency Identification) tags have become smaller and cheaper, and they are expected to be attached in various commodities[29]. Moreover, a real-world reminder system using proximity information is a useful application in ubiquitous environments[12]. In such a situation, it is useful to attach RFID tags to valuables such as wallets and cell phones, and to tell users immediately if they leave their valuables behind.

FeelSeek is an application to remind users of valuables left behind, and to navigate users toward those valuables. As shown in Fig. 11, when the RFID tagged object moves away from the RFID reader attached on the belt, the ActiveBelt activates all vibrators to remind a user of it. Then, she/he inputs a trigger information if she/he want to search it. Finally, the ActiveBelt calculates a brief position of the item using records of GPS, and navigates the user to it.

FeelWave FeelWave is an application to amuse users with rhythmic vibration in sync with music (Fig. 12). For example, since ActiveBelt can transmit tactile information in all direction, it can be used as a stereophonic tactile display with stereophonic music. In addition, the ActiveBelt may be used as new expressive

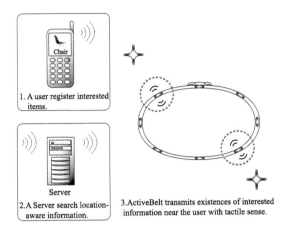

Fig. 10. Basic concept of FeelSense

medium such that it transmits rhythmic vibrations to members of an audience in sync with a turntable played by a DJ.

4   Evaluation

We have evaluated the effectiveness of the ActiveBelt using the universal-size prototype system. As mentioned above, in the application of a human navigation system called FeelNavi, we express the direction to a destination by activating a specific vibrator and express the distance by controlling pulse intervals of vibration. In this evaluation, we examined whether subjects can recognize changes of direction, and pulse intervals of vibration, both in a standing state and in a walking state. We selected six test subjects who had never used the ActiveBelt before. Their ages ranged between 21 and 30.

4.1   Methods

The subjects wore the universal-size ActiveBelt and a wireless RS-232C transceiver. The experimenter controlled the direction and interval of vibration with a PDA and a wireless RS-232C transceiver(Fig. 13). The experimenter activated only one vibrator at a time, and kept the strength of vibration at about 77Hz. The period of each evaluation was about 15 minutes.

There were two postural conditions in the study: standing, and walking. In the standing condition, the experimenter controlled the direction of vibration and asked the subjects to indicate the direction orally or with gestures.We used four pulse intervals of vibration, that is, 250msec (125msec On, 125msec Off), 500msec (250msec On, 250msec Off), 1000msec (500msec On, 500msec Off), and 1680msec (840msec On, 840msec Off). In the walking condition, the experimenter controlled the direction of vibration and asked the subjects to turn to

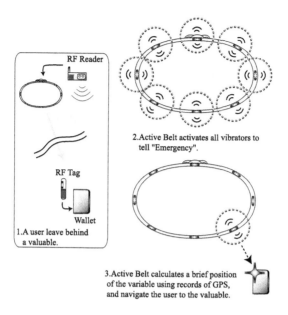

RF Reader

2.Active Belt activates all vibrators to
tell "Emergency".

RF Tag

Wallet

1.A user leave behind
a valuable.

3.Active Belt calculates a brief position
of the variable using records of GPS,
and navigate the user to the valuable.

Fig. 11. Basic concept of FeelSeek

the direction of vibration. We used the same four pulse intervals of vibration as described above.

The experimenter observed the behaviors of subjects during each condition. After each condition, the experimenter asked them questions to obtain their subjective feedbacks about changes in direction and pulse intervals signalled by the vibration. At the end of the evaluation, the experimenter asked each of them about their impressions of the prototype system including what problems they experienced.

4.2   Results

In the standing condition, all subjects were able to recognize all changes in the four pulse intervals. For changes in direction, five subjects were able to tell direction to a fair degree of accuracy within about one second. We asked the subjects "Can you differentiate the eight directions in each pulse interval?". Five subjects said they could easily tell the difference amongst all directions for all intervals. On the other hand, one subject said that he could easily recognize four directions (front, back, left, and right) in all intervals, but could not easily recognize the other four directions. This difficulty may have resulted from his waist being very thin (about 67cm). Since the belt did not fit with his waist, the ActiveBelt was not able to transmit enough tactile information.

In the walking condition, the behaviors of the subjects were quite different for each pulse interval. In the case when the pulse intervals were 1680msec and

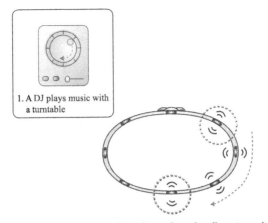

1. A DJ plays music with
a turntable

2. Active Belt worn by each audience transmits
rhythmic vibration in sync with the music.

Fig. 12. Basic concept of FeelWave

1000msec, when the experimenter changed a direction of vibration, all subjects walked for one or two more steps, stopped for a moment, and then turned to the direction of vibration. When questioned, they said that they were able to recognize the changes in vibration while walking, and that they were able to recognize the direction if they stopped for a moment. For the pulse intervals of 500msec, all subjects sometimes failed to recognize the change of vibration. Two subjects said that they were not able to feel vibration in this range. When the pulse intervals were 250msec, all subjects said that they were not able to feel vibration.

Finally, we summarize the impressions that subjects reported about the prototype system.

1. Vibration on the back is perceived to be weaker than vibrations on the abdomen. (5 / 6)
2. For practical use, it is more desirable that the vibrators are activated only when users get lost than that they are always activated. (2 / 6)
3. For practical use, eight vibrators are not necessarily needed, and four vibrators are good enough. (3 / 6)

4.3   Consideration

Based on the above results, we discuss current problems and propose improvements needed for practical use of the ActiveBelt.

Providing Direction When standing, almost all subjects were able to recognize directions within about one second. When walking, and for the pulse

Fig. 13. Prototype system used in the evaluation. left: a subject, upper right: a microcomputer and surrounding circuit, lower right: a controller for the experimenter (1. a directional sensor, 2.a wireless RS-232C transceiver)

intervals of more than 1000msec, all subjects recognized changes of vibration within two steps, stopped only for a moment, and then turned to the direction of vibration. Thus, we confirmed that the ActiveBelt can navigate users to the target direction using vibration both when standing and when walking.

Indicating Distance In FeelNavi, we indicated distance to a destination using pulse intervals of vibration. When standing, all subjects were able to recognize changes in the four pulse intervals. However, when walking, they often failed to recognize vibration with a pulse less than 500msec. We will examine other expressions of distance, along with the pulse intervals.

Navigating In oral interviews, we received interesting feedbacks about navigation. First, some subjects said that it is more desirable that the vibrators are activated only when users get lost than that they are always activated. This approach looks similar to behaviors that people pick up and look at maps only when they get lost.

Some subjects said that they thought four vibrators were good enough for navigation. However, we think it is useful to attach eight or more vibrators, since higher resolutions are useful for versatile applications and for error correction.

5   Discussion

Most existing human navigation systems in mobile environments apply visual displays, that is, they plot users' positions and orientations on 2D displays of PDAs or cell phones. We discuss here the differences between visual navigation systems and the belt-type tactile navigation system described in this paper.

The merits of visual navigation systems are as follows:(1) visual navigation systems can easily transmit complex information such as the layout of buildings near the destination and a detailed route to it, and (2)they usually provide input interfaces, so users can easily use them interactively.

The merits of the belt-type tactile navigation system are as follows: (1)the belt-type tactile navigation system is convenient to use when walking since it doesn't occupy users' visual or auditory senses, (2)users can intuitively recognize directions to their destinations even when the they are not good at reading maps, and (3)it can navigate users to their destinations even in bad conditions such as in heavy fog or deep night, or with no landmarks near locations of users, since it doesn't depend on visual landmarks in the surrounding environment.

Each system, visual and tactile, has its own merits. We will improve our system by combining the merits of visual and tactile navigation systems.

6   Related Work

Other research on human navigation systems and location-aware information services includes Walk Navi[14], Augment-able Reality[19], Touring Machine[8], Cyberguide[3], and Space Tag[24]. Various applications with location-aware information have been proposed, and most of the associated systems used visual displays.

A cell phone equipped with a GPS and a directional sensor[2] can display a map of a user's position, and rotate the map in sync with the orientation of the cell phone. This approach is interesting in helping users to match 2D maps and real world using directional information.

Research has been carried out on wearable tactile interfaces such as Cyber Touch, Tactual Wearable Display and GentleGuide. Cyber Touch[6] can generate tactile feedbacks of objects in virtual world, using six vibrators attached on gloves. Tactual Wearable Display[23] attached a matrix of vibrators to the back of a vest, and tried to transmit directions and other information. It also proposed an interesting tactile system using cognitive characteristics of the tactile sense such as apparent movement [6]. GentleGuide[4] proposed a tactile navigation system via two bracelets. It outputs three commands, left, right, and stop(activate both bracelets). In the meanwhile, our approach used a belt-type tactile display, and can enable users to obtain directional information more intuitively with the tactile sense.

There is research on tactile displays in aircrafts cockpits[18][20][27]. These research projects used vest-type tactile displays to provide pilots with navigation information. Brewster proposed a sophisticated conceptual framework for tactile displays and information presentation[5]. This approach is interesting in discussing many parameters used for designing tactile displays.

---

[6] When a user is stimulated on two point of her/his skin alternatively in a specified interval, she/he feels continuous stimulations as if a small animal is hopping between the two points.

Waist Measure Belt[28] is a unique belt-type wearable device. A user can easily measure her/his waist-size only by wearing it which contains a digital measuring scale. It is interesting in proposing an application of health monitoring using a belt-type device.

7 Conclusion

We have proposed a novel belt-type wearable interface called "ActiveBelt" that enables users to obtain multiple directional information with the tactile sense. We developed prototype systems, and evaluated the possibilities for practical use. When we solve the problems of the current prototype systems, we believe that ActiveBelt will become a useful and intuitive navigation system. We are also examining other applications for entertainment and location-aware information services.

References

[1] 5DT Data Gloves: http://www.5dt.com/hardware.html#glove.

[2] A cell phone equipped with a GPS and a directional sensor: http://www.kyocera.co.jp/prdct/telecom/consumer/a5502k/ez_navi.html (in Japanese).

[3] Abowd, G. D., Atkeson, C. G., Hong, J., Long, S., Kooper, R. and Pinkerton, M.: Cyberguide: a mobile context-aware tour guide, *Wireless Networks*, Vol. 3, No. 5, pp. 421–433 (1997).

[4] Bossman, S., Groenendaal, B., Findlater, J. W., Visser, T., de Graaf, M. and Markopoulos, P.: Gentleguide: An exploration of haptic output for pedestrian guidance, *Proceedings of the Mobile HCI, 8-10-2003*, Springer Publications, pp. 358–362 (2003).

[5] Brewster, S. and Brown, L.: Tactons: Structured Tactile Messages for Non-Visual Information Display, *Proceedings of Australasian User Interface Conference 2004*, pp. 15–23 (2004).

[6] CyberGlove and Cyber Touch: http://www.immersion.com/products/3d/.

[7] Eznavigation: http://www.keitai1bankan.com/phone/ez_navi.html (in Japanese).

[8] Feiner, S., MacIntyre, B., Hollerer, T. and Webster, A.: A Touring Machine: Prototyping 3D Mobile Augmented Reality Systems for Exploring the Urban Environment, *Proceedings of First International Symposium on Wearable Computers(ISWC'97)*, pp. 74–81 (1997).

[9] Fukumoto, M. and Tonomura, Y.: Body coupled FingeRing: Wireless wearable keyboard, *Proceedings of the ACM Conference on Human Factors in Computing Systems(CHI'97)*, Addison-Wesley, pp. 147–154 (1997).

[10] Fukumoto, M. and Tonomura, Y.: Whisper: a wristwatch style wearable handset, *Proceedings of the ACM Conference on Human Factors in Computing Systems (CHI'99)*, pp. 112–119 (1999).

[11] Holland, S., Morse, D. R. and Gedenryd, H.: AudioGPS: Spatial Audio Navigation with a Minimal Attention Interface, *Personal and Ubiquitous Computing*, Vol. 6, No. 4, pp. 253–259 (2002).

[12] Lamming, M. and Bohm, D.: SPECs: Another Approach to Human Context and Activity Sensing Research, Using Tiny Peer-to-Peer Wireless Computers, *Ubicomp 2003*, Springer Publications, pp. 192–199 (2003).

[13] MicroOptical: http://www.microopticalcorp.com/.

[14] Nagao, K. and Rekimoto, J.: Agent Augmented Reality: A Software Agent Meets the Real World, *Proceedings of Second International Conference on Multi-Agent Systems(ICMAS'96)*, pp. 228–235 (1996).

[15] Paradiso, J. and Hu, E.: Expressive Footwear for Computer-Augmented Dance Performance, *Proceedings of First International Symposium on Wearable Computers(ISWC'97)*, pp. 165–166 (1997).

[16] Picard, R. and Healey, J.: Affective Wearables, *Personal Technologies*, Vol. 1, No. 4, pp. 231–240 (1997).

[17] Poma: http://www.xybernaut.com/Solutions/product/poma_product.htm.

[18] Raj, A., Kass, S. and Perry, J.: Vibrotactile displays for improving spatial awareness, *Proceedings of the Human Factors and Ergonomics Society Annual Meeting*, Springer Publications, pp. 181–184 (2000).

[19] Rekimoto, J., Ayatsuka, Y. and Hayashi, K.: Augment-able Reality: Situated Communication through Physical and Digital Spaces, *Proceedings of Second International Symposium on Wearable Computers(ISWC'98)*, pp. 68–75 (1998).

[20] Rupert, A.: Tactile situation awareness system: proprioceptive prostheses for sensory deficiencies, *Space and Environmental Medicine 71*, pp. 92–99 (2000).

[21] Starner, T., Auxier, J., Ashbrook, D. and Gandy, M.: The Gesture Pendant: A Self-illuminating, Wearable, Infrared Computer Vision System for Home Automation Control and Medical Monitoring., *Proceedings of 4th International Symposium on Wearable Computers(ISWC'2000)*, pp. 87–94 (2000).

[22] Starner, T., Weaver, J. and Pentland, A.: A Wearable Computer Based American Sign Language Recognizer, *Proceedings of First International Symposium on Wearable Computers(ISWC'97)*, pp. 130–137 (1997).

[23] Tan, H. and Pentland, A.: Tactual Displays for Wearable Computing, *Personal Technologies*, Vol. 1, pp. 225–230 (1997).

[24] Tarumi, H., Morishita, K., Nakao, M. and Kambayashi, Y.: SpaceTag: An Overlaid Virtual System and its Application, *Proceedings of International Conference on Multimedia Computing and Systems(ICMCS'99), Vol.1*, pp. 207–212 (1999).

[25] Tsukada, K. and Yasumura, M.: Ubi-Finger: Gesture Input Device for Mobile Use, *Proceedings of APCHI 2002, Vol. 1*, pp. 388–400 (2002).

[26] van Erp, J. B. F.: Tactile Navigation Display, *Haptic Human-Computer Interaction, Vol. 2058*, Springer Publications, pp. 165–173 (2001).

[27] van Veen, H. and van Erp, J. B. F.: Tactile information presentation in the cockpit, *Haptic Human-Computer Interaction, Vol. 2058*, Springer Publications, pp. 174–181 (2001).

[28] Waist Measure Belt: http://www.tepia.or.jp/12th/tenji/virtual/photos/mobile/mobMitu.html (in Japanese).

[29] Want, R., Fishkin, K., P., Gujar, A. and Harrison, B., L.: Bridging Physical and Virtual Worlds with Electronic Tags, *Proceedings of the ACM Conference on Human Factors in Computing Systems (CHI'99)*, ACM Press, pp. 370–377 (1999).

[30] Yamamoto, T. et. al: Two-dimensional directional perception using vibro-tactile sense, *Proceedings of Human Interface Symposium 2002*, pp. 21–24 (2002). (in Japanese).

An Audio-Based Personal Memory Aid

Sunil Vemuri, Chris Schmandt, Walter Bender, Stefanie Tellex, Brad Lassey

MIT Media Lab
20 Ames St.
Cambridge, MA 02139 USA
{vemuri,geek,walter,stefie10,lassey}@media.mit.edu

Abstract. We are developing a wearable device that attempts to alleviate some everyday memory problems. The "memory prosthesis" records audio and contextual information from conversations and provides a suite of retrieval tools (on both the wearable and a personal computer) to help users access forgotten memories in a timely fashion. This paper describes the wearable device, the personal-computer-based retrieval tool, and their supporting technologies. Anecdotal observations based on real-world use and quantitative results based on a controlled memory-retrieval task are reported. Finally, some social, legal, and design challenges of ubiquitous recording and remembering via a personal audio archive are discussed.

1 Introduction

The idea of recording everything in one's life is not new. An early proposal, Memex, dates back to 1945 [4]. Just over a decade ago, ubiquitous audio recording systems were built and studied using desktop computers and workstations [12]. Now, improved portability facilitates increased ubiquity and it follows that more and more industry, academic, and government groups are investigating the possibility of recording everything in one's life [8,15,16]. Indeed, computers have reached the point at which continuous, verbatim recording of an individual's life experiences is technologically and economically feasible. The challenges of miniaturization, battery life, storage capacity, and aesthetics are being addressed. A few years ago, palm-sized PDAs with high-speed, wireless networking were choice platforms for these applications; now, miniature units (e.g., iPods) are available with recording ability and capacity to store weeks, if not months, of data. It may be sooner than we think before a commercially-available watch-sized device arrives capable of ubiquitous recording. But recording everything is the easy part.

The outstanding challenge is turning vast repositories of personal recordings into a useful resource while respecting the social, legal, and ethical ramifications of ubiquitous recording. This paper examines amassing data for the purpose of helping people remedy common, everyday memory problems. Previous attempts at building computational, portable memory aids have studied note-taking [22] and passive recording of proximity to people, office devices, and other environmental markers [14]. Memory studies have examined long-term recall in real-world settings [30] and audio recall in

N. Davies et al. (Eds.): UbiComp 2004, LNCS 3205, pp. 400–417, 2004.
© Springer-Verlag Berlin Heidelberg 2004

laboratory settings [33], but the combination of audio and long-term memory in real-world situations is relatively unexplored.

A sampling of related efforts involved in collecting digital audio and video archives include classrooms settings [1], meetings [20], voicemail [32], workplace and telephone discussions [12], informal situations [16], and personal histories [8]. Among these and other similar projects in the domain, indexing techniques such as large-vocabulary speech recognition, speaker identification, face recognition, and audio/video scene analysis are used to mine noisy data for search cues. Whereas much attention has been given to improving the accuracy and robustness of these techniques, less has been done on designing tools to help users make sense of noisy data sources and to understand which analyses prove most useful to specific tasks. For example, differences are expected among the search strategies employed by those trying to remember a previously-witnessed event versus someone trying to find information within an unfamiliar collection; in the former case, retrieving any information that triggers the memory of the event is sufficient; in the later, finding the exact information is necessary.

This paper examines these techniques in light of alleviating memory problems. To this end, we have constructed a wearable "memory prosthesis." The device records audio from conversations (and other sources), applies large-vocabulary speech recognition to it, and provides a suite of retrieval tools to help the user access forgotten memories. Experiences of one of the authors, who has used the device for recording a variety of everyday experiences for two years, are reported. To better understand the utility of such voluminous collections of recordings for memory assistance, and which among a wide range of interaction techniques should be immediately on-hand when a memory problem occurs, an experiment was conducted with an exemplar memory-retrieval task. Before describing the technology and experiment, some relevant background on memory in general is provided. The paper concludes with a discussion of some social and legal implications of ubiquitous recording.

1.1 Memory

Schacter's taxonomy, or the "Seven Deadly Sins of Memory," succinctly describes the most common memory problems [24]. The six involving forgetting and distortion are shown in Table 1. The seventh, "persistence" (i.e., pathological inability to forget), is of less interest to memory-aid designers.

Table 1: Six of the seven "Sins of Memory" [24]

Forgetting	Distortion
Transience (memory fading over time)	Misattribution (right memory, wrong source)
Absent-mindedness (shallow processing, forgetting to do things)	Suggestibility (implanting memories, leading questions)
Blocking (memories temporarily unavailable)	Bias (distortions and unconscious influences)

It is not the goal of the present research nor is it expected that a single memory aid can adequately address all such problems; instead, the focus is to address a subset. Previous studies [6] explore the frequency of some types of forgetting in workplace settings (Table 2). In Schacter's taxonomy, "retrospective memories" are analogous to "transience"; "prospective memory" and "action slips" are both forms of "absent-mindedness."

Table 2: Frequency of some common memory problems in the workplace [6]

Type		Description	Example
Retrospective Memory	47%	Remembering past events or information acquired in the past	Forgetting someone's name, a word, an item on a list, a past event
Prospective Memory	29%	Failure to remember to do something	Forgetting to send a letter, forgetting an appointment
Action Slips	24%	Very short-term memory failures that cause problems for the actions currently being carried out	Forgetting to check the motor oil level in the car before leaving on a trip

The prototype aims to address transience, the most frequent among the memory problems. The approach is to collect, index, and organize data recorded from a variety of sources related to everyday activity, and to provide a computer-based tool to both search and browse the collection. The hope is that some fragment of recorded data can act as a trigger for a forgotten memory.

It is anticipated that blocking problems would also benefit from such an aid. One of the common qualities of both transience and blocking is that the person is aware of the memory problem when it occurs (this is not true for all memory problems). Assuming the person also wishes or needs to remedy the problem, what is needed is a resource to help. This is where the memory prosthesis comes into play.

1.2 Design Goals

The approach to address transience and blocking memory problems is to build capture tools to record daily experiences and retrieval tools to find memory triggers that remedy these problems. Although the current research prototypes do not perfectly achieve all of the ideals described below, they are sufficient to allow sympathetic subjects to start experiencing portable, ubiquitous recording and are proving instructive towards the initial design of memory retrieval tools and validating the approach.

Data Capture

One of the early questions in the design of the memory prosthesis is what data sources should be captured. An ideal data source has maximal memory-triggering value while presenting minimal computational and storage demands. Furthermore, a design goal is to minimize the effort needed by the user to capture daily experiences. This means, when possible, data should be captured with little effort or passively. Finally, to minimize the chance of missing a potentially-valuable memory trigger (at the cost of retaining superfluous ones), nearly-continuous recording of daily activity is desired. To these ends, a wearable recording apparatus was constructed (Section 2).

High on the list of desired data sources was audio, due to the anticipated memory-triggering value of verbatim audio, the desire to capture conversations that occurred in informal settings, the ease of capturing audio using a wearable device, the tractable data-storage requirements, and the readily-available content-analysis tools (e.g., speech recognition). However, for legal and human-subject approval reasons, audio recording requires consent from all participants for each recording. Consequently, collecting these data can neither be completely passive nor continuous. Similar to doppelgänger [21], sources that are captured and archived both continuously and passively include the user's location, calendar, email, commonly-visited web sites, and weather.

Video was considered, but the hardware complexity of a wearable, continuous-video-capture device combined with the data storage requirements and difficulty of analyzing and indexing hundreds of hours of video suggested otherwise. Even so, research on video-retrieval systems has gained momentum with some promising results [26]. Still photography is a common request and is being integrated. Capturing biometrics [9] was also considered and remains an item for future work.

It should be noted that completely passive data capture may in fact hurt memory recollection as evidenced by the disadvantage of no note-taking among students in classroom situations [18]. The choice to prefer passive data capture is to simplify and reduce forgetfulness in the daily data-capture process. Ironically, forgetting to activate the memory prosthesis (i.e., absent-mindedness) is a common problem.

Retrieval

An ideal memory aid would proactively determine when a memory problem occurs and provide just-in-time minimally-intrusive remedies. We are far from this goal and the present approach and technologies still requires active effort.

With enough time and incentive, users could probably remedy most memory problems via a comprehensive archive of past experiences. Since most real-world situations do not provide either such time or incentive, the primary goal for the memory retrieval tools is to remedy problems within the constraints of attention and effort users can and are willing to commit. There is still limited empirical evidence about such willingness: Section 4.1 provides some anecdotal evidence about real-world use. The evaluation described in Section 4.2 offers some insights about memory problem frequencies, how subjects approach memory repair, and what technologies are most useful when given an investigator-invented memory-retrieval task.

Given the present focus on the workplace settings, it is anticipated that users could benefit from retrieval tools on both handheld/wearable devices and desktop/laptop personal computers. Hence, a goal was to design for all of these platforms, taking advantage of the idiosyncrasies of each. This paper describes the wearable capture device (Section 2) and the personal-computer-based retrieval tool (Section 3).

One of the challenges to the design of the prototype is finding ways to manage the large quantity of collected data that is often rife with both noise due to the intrinsic limitations of computational information-extraction from the selected data sources and irrelevance with respect to a specific information need. The former is more typical of a personal memory assistant and will be addressed in more detail throughout the paper. The latter point is addressed in a manner similar to conventional text corpora searches: keyword searches with ranked retrieval results.

2 Memory Prosthesis

The wearable capture device (Figure 1) is implemented on an iPaq PDA coupled with an 802.11b wireless network card. When activated by the user, the device records audio and physical location. It determines location via proximity to numerous stationary 802.11b base stations primarily inside the building. Recorded data are streamed to a server and access is restricted to within our local computer network due to the data-security requests of the users. Previously, the device had been in use outside the local network, including nearby publicly-accessible wireless-networks. The server also passively captures the additional sources mentioned in Section 1.2.

The design reflects a variety of considerations necessary to balance the requirements of obtaining speech-recognition-quality audio while meeting necessary social and legal requirements. Moreover, the investigators tried to satisfy a higher standard by ensuring co-workers felt reasonably comfortable with the presence of potentially privacy-invading technology. The device includes a display with the audio recording status, an audio-level meter, and recordees may request recording deletion via anonymized email.

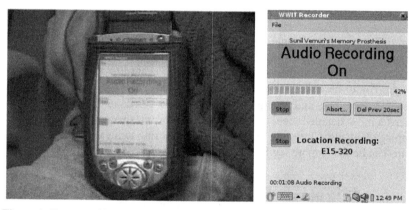

Figure 1: Prototype "Memory Prosthesis" (left) with close-up of screen on the right

When recording, users often move the device from its waist-level belt-clip in favor of chest height. This allows conversation partners a clear view of the screen, the recording status of the device, and serves as a constant reminder that the conversation is being recorded. Chest-height positioning also provides better acoustic conditions for the built-in near-field microphone on the iPaq. An attachable lavalier microphone is also occasionally used. Although speech-recognition-quality recording of all participants in a conversation is desired, this is not always feasible since no cost-effective, portable recording solutions could be found. Placing the iPaq halfway between two speakers results in bad audio for both. Placing the device at chest-height or using the lavalier allows at least one of the speakers, the wearer, to be recorded at adequate quality at the cost of poor quality recordings for all other speakers.

One might question the earlier assertion that "recording is the easy part." Given the forthcoming descriptions of memory-retrieval challenges and the social and legal ramifications, it most certainly remains that "recording is the *easier* part."

3 Memory Retrieval

An anticipated consequence of a daily-worn recording device is the accrual of years of personal interaction and conversation data. To help alleviate transience and blocking memory problems, it is expected that users would want to search such a collection for memory triggers. Given the focus on audio and the state-of-the-art in information retrieval technologies, capabilities such as browsing, skimming, and free-form keyword searches of timeline-organized audio archives were selected for implementation.

We implemented the first memory retrieval tool for use on a personal computer due to the expected desire for retrieval on this platform in workplace settings and the ease of implementing features (some of which are computationally and graphically demanding) compared to a PDA. Little is known about memory retrieval using personal data archives. Hence, one goal of the evaluation described in Section 4.2 is to begin understanding how users approach memory repair and which among the many features prove worthy of inclusion in subsequent iterations and implementation on the PDA.

3.1 Searching Audio Collections

Figure 2 shows the personal-computer-based interface available to search and browse large collections of recordings. Each column along the x-axis corresponds to a single day; time-of-day is on the y-axis. Each calendar event has a corresponding blue rectangle. Audio recordings are represented with a yellow rectangle and an associated icon ◀⟩. Zooming and panning features are provided; double-clicking on an item opens a more detailed view of a recording. Color transparency is used to blend overlapping elements. Cluttering of text from neighboring items is possible and individual items can be made more legible by clicking on them.

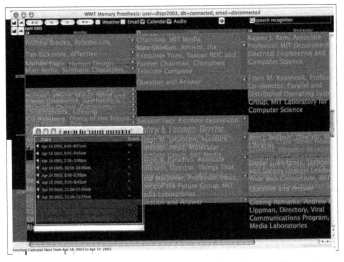

Figure 2: Visual interface for browsing and searching through recordings. A keyword-search feature (upper right) is available with example results shown in lower left.

Error-laden transcripts are generated using IBM's ViaVoice [29] speech-recognition software and users can perform relevance-ranked keyword searches on these transcripts using the Lucene search engine [17]. Issues related to keyword-searching on speech-recognized text are covered in Section 5.3.

The data in Figure 2 reflect the agenda and recordings that took place as part of a three-day conference. This is the same set of conference recordings used in the study described in Section 4.2. For this data set, the calendar entries were copied verbatim from the conference agenda. Word error rate (WER) for speech-recognition systems is defined as the sum of insertion, deletion, and substitution errors divided by the number of words in the perfect transcript. Though not formally computed for the entire set, representative samples show a uniform WER distribution between 30–75%. Variation seemed to depend on speaker clarity, speaking rate, and accent.

3.2 Finding Memory Triggers in a Single Recording

Influenced by ScanMail [32], the interface described in this section addresses the problem of finding memory triggers within a single recording (Figure 3). Listening to long recordings is tedious and browsing error-laden transcripts is challenging [27]. Since recordings may last hours, the interface attempts to: (1) help the user find key-words in error-laden transcripts; (2) bias the user's attention towards higher quality audio; (3) help the user recall the gist of the recording; and (4) provide ways to play audio summaries that may serve as good memory triggers.

Several features are included to improve the utility of the speech-recognizer-generated transcripts. A juncture-pause-detection algorithm is used to separate text into paragraphs. Next, similar to the Intelligent Ear [25], the transcript is rendered with each word's brightness corresponding to its speech-recognizer-reported confidence. A "brightness threshold" slider allows users to dim words whose confidence is below the threshold. This can be used to focus attention on words that are more likely to be recognized correctly. Next, an option to dim all English-language stopwords (i.e., very common words like "a", "an", "the", etc.) allows users to focus only on keywords. A rudimentary speaker-identification algorithm was included and the iden-tifications are reflected as different colored text (seen as red or aqua in Figure 3).

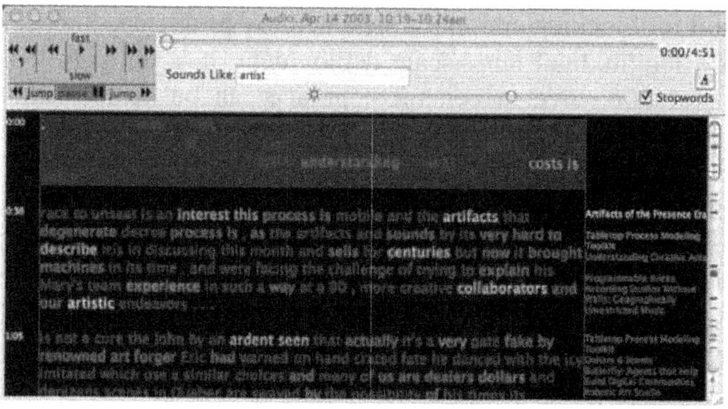

Figure 3: Interface for browsing, searching, and playing an individual recording

A phonetic or "sounds-like" search feature is provided to help users identify mis-recognized, out-of-vocabulary, and morphological-variant words by locating pho-neme-sequence similarity (seen as yellow text and as dark blue marks in the scrollbar in Figure 3). The phonetic search algorithm is similar to [31] and uses CMUDict [5].

A sophisticated audio-playback controller (based on SpeechSkimmer [2]) capable of audio skimming is provided (upper left of Figure 3). Depending on where the user clicks in the controller, audio plays at normal, fast, or slow rates (non-pitch adjusted). The control offers two forms of forward and reverse play: one skips periods of silence and the second plays only the first five seconds of each paragraph.

Finally, annotations to the transcript (seen as white text on the right of Figure 3) show information potentially related to the neighboring transcript text. To generate this, each section of the transcript text is used as a query to a search engine serving a corpus of roughly 800 past and present department-related project abstracts. The top-ranked project names are displayed.

It should be noted that in addition to the features described in this section, the soft-ware currently in use by one of the authors also has the ability to include the other data sources mentioned in Section 1.2 (i.e., email, location, weather, web sites) as part of the memory retrieval process. These tools include additional visualization and search features tuned to these data sources.

Again, it was not clear which, if any, among the retrieval capabilities in either in-terfaces shown in Figures 2 and 3 would prove useful for memory assistance. Among other issues, the study described in Section 4.2 was designed to explore this.

4 Evaluation

The evaluations presented in this section include both anecdotal reports from two subjects (one of whom is an author) who use the memory prosthesis for real-world recording tasks (Section 4.1) and a controlled study of the memory-retrieval tool via artificially-induced memory problems among subjects who are not memory prosthesis users (Section 4.2). The purpose of these evaluations respectively is to (1) identify what tasks people choose to use portable, ubiquitous recording devices; and (2) con-firm the basic assumption that an audio-based information-retrieval tool can serve as a memory aid for blocking and transience memory problems.

Short of a longitudinal large-scale deployment, it is unlikely that an adequately-controlled evaluation over a general populace can be performed. The present ap-proach attempts to approximate the likely requirements of a memory prosthesis user. Examples of more controllable, memory-demanding tasks include students searching through archives of recorded lectures in preparation for a test, or conference attendees wishing to write trip reports. Speech from such presentation-style settings is obvi-ously different from conversations and participants are likely to be less-engaged in a such settings. While neither scenario is ideal, conference talks were chosen, and these studies have helped inform subsequent iterations of the memory retrieval tools.

4.1 Experiences with Ubiquitous Recording

Given the opportunity to record anytime, anywhere, what would one record? Who would one record? Are the recordings useful to a real-world task? In addition to the author (Student P), another student (Student Q) in the department (not directly involved in the research project) is also a frequent audio-recorder of select conversations. Student Q uses a variety of computer-based audio recording tools, including the memory prosthesis. Experiences with the former and interviews with the latter are reported.

Student P has a vested interest in frequent recording and chooses to record at most opportunities (within the bounds of legal, social, and human-subject protocol guidelines). Most of those recorded are within the student's circle of trusted co-workers and have *never* expressed hesitation about recording work-related matters. Others within the circle have been asked and have agreed to be recorded, but Student P felt a sense of recordee-discomfort (either by overt statements, tone of voice, or body language). When among these co-workers, Student P is more cautious about the circumstances and topics when asking permission to record and errs on the side of not recording.

Student Q opts to record only a limited set of experiences: student-advisor conversations. In particular, conversations focused around an impending, time-critical task such as writing a paper: "The things that I record are things that I think ahead of time will be critical and I will need in a short amount of time. I don't record anything or everything…What I do make a point of recording is conversations with my advisor." This recording strategy reflects a desire to minimize absent-mindedness problems in contrast to Student P who wishes to reduce transience.

Similar to Moran et al.'s observations [19], Student Q uses audio recording as a backup to hand-written note-taking: "If I write things down, it's… like pointers into the recording and it organizes the thoughts for me." With regard to recording usage, "I often don't listen to the recording. But, to know that I have it is good. Sometimes I can't read my own writing. If I manage to write enough… that's fine. Sometimes I don't. So then I go and see what I missed, or see what I was trying to write down."

Interestingly, Student P, who has access to a much larger collection of recordings, mainly uses the recordings for the identical real-world task: retrieving student-advisor discussions in preparation for a pending writing deadline. Both students cite common reasons for recording and usage including: limited advisor availability, the anticipated high quality of the conversations, and time-pressure of the task.

Student Q—when using a non-memory-prosthesis recorder—opts not to archive recordings for space-saving reasons, but expresses no objection to keeping them. The recordings are often discarded after the task deadline, and anything important is transcribed before disposal.

4.2 Evaluation of the Memory-Retrieval Aid

To better understand the memory-retrieval tool's value among a larger and broader population, investigators confronted non-memory-prosthesis subjects with artificially-induced memory problems based on past-witnessed events and asked them to resolve these with the tool. Specifically, subjects were presented with a remembering-and-finding task based on information presented in a three-day conference that occurred approximately one month prior to the test. Some subjects were speakers.

Subjects were given a questionnaire with 27 questions. Investigators designed questions with varying difficulty, some with multiple parts, and whose answers could be found and answered unambiguously. For example, a relatively simple question is "What book (title and author) does [Speaker X] cite?" and a more difficult, time-consuming example is "Which projects or people specifically cite the use of a speech recognizer?" Some questions could be answered simply by performing searches using words found in the question, some could not be answered unless the subject remembered the answer or was able to find the answer in the audio.

To maximize audio quality, speakers were recorded using the auditorium's existing recording apparatus and the audio was fed into the memory prosthesis system. This approach, as opposed to using the memory prosthesis device, was in anticipation of ubiquitous-computing-friendly environments that can readily support such data transfers. In total, approximately 14 hours of audio was available from 59 talks. Talk lengths ranged from two to 45 minutes.

No subject attended the entire conference, but all attended at least part of it. The question dispersion was intended to ensure each subject witnessed some of the answers. It was hoped, but not guaranteed, that each subject would find and attempt questions in which they remembered witnessing the answer at the event (as opposed to knowing the answer via another source), and some memory problem occurred such that they required assistance to answer. Hence, the three experimental conditions were:

C1: Unaided: Subjects answered questions without any assistance, either by remembering the answer from the event or from another source.

C2: Aided, Witnessed: Subjects answered a question using both the memory aid and information they remembered from the event.

C3: Aided, Non-witness: Subjects did not witness the event and their answer was based on examination of data during the experiment and possibly using their previous knowledge of the department, its people, and their research in general.

Before the questions were administered, subjects were given a 5–10 minute training session with the memory retrieval software (described in Section 3). After training, subjects were given the full questionnaire. The test was split into two phases. In Phase 1, subjects were asked to answer any questions they already knew, but without the use of any aids (Condition C1). Subjects were instructed to answer as many or as few questions as they wished and were given as much time as needed to answer these questions. In addition to collecting C1 data, this phase allowed subjects to familiarize themselves with all of the questions without any time pressure in preparation for Phase 2. A pilot study indicated that subjects did not read all the questions if under time-pressure. All subjects completed Phase 1 in less than 15 minutes.

After a subject finished unassisted question-answering, Phase 2 began in which the memory-retrieval software tool was provided. However, subjects were now limited to 15 minutes to answer any remaining questions. The reasons for having a time limit included: (1) encouraging subjects to prioritize the questions they wanted to attempt;

and (2) putting a limit on a subject's time commitment. Subjects were allowed to ask user-interface clarification questions without time penalty.

During both phases, subjects were asked to verbalize their thought process as they answered questions. This was audio recorded and an investigator remained in the room taking notes. Upon completion, subjects were informed about the nature of the experiment (i.e. studying search strategies), interviewed about their experience, asked to reflect on their thought process, and elaborate on any details that they might not have mentioned during the task.

Hypotheses are listed below. Time is computed on a per-question basis. Success rate is the number of questions answered correctly or partially-correctly divided by the number of attempts. In addition to these hypotheses, the investigators are also interested in what strategies subjects employed when remedying memory problems and what user interface features subjects found most useful.

Hypotheses

H1a: Unaided question-answering (C1) will take less time than aided (C2 & C3).

H1b: Unaided question-answering (C1) will have a lower success rate compared to Condition C2 (aided, witnessed).

H2a: Aided question-answering of previously-witnessed events (C2) will take less time than aided question-answering of non-witnessed events (C3).

H2b: Aided question-answering of previously-witnessed events (C2) will have a higher success rate compared to aided question-answering of non-witnessed events (C3).

5   Results

Subjects included three women and eight men ranging in age from 18 to 50. Nine were speakers at the conference; two were non-native English speakers. Subjects' prior exposure to the research presented at the conference ranged from one month to many years and in varying capacities (e.g., students, faculty, visitors). No subject attended the entire conference. Among the speakers, most attended only the session in which they spoke. Nine subjects claimed to be fatigued during the conference and all said they were occupied with other activities (email, web browsing, chatting, day-dreaming, preparing for talk, etc.) at least part of the time. Investigators classified six subjects who have prior understanding of how speech-recognition technology works.

5.1 Phase 1 (Unaided Memory)

Answers were labeled as one of "correct," "partially correct," "incorrect," or "no answer." A "correct" answer satisfies all aspects of the question correctly. A "par-tially correct" answer has at least one aspect of the question correct but another part either incorrect, omitted, or includes erroneous extraneous information. This labeling was common for multi-part questions. An "incorrect" answer has no aspects correct. A "no answer" is one in which subjects attempted to answer, verbalizations indicated a memory problem, but no answer was submitted. Among all of these, subjects spent on average 29 seconds to read, verbalize, and answer (or choose to not-answer) a question.

Memory problems that occurred were noted. If investigators either observed or a subject verbalized a memory problem while answering, investigators classified it as one of the six problems listed in Table 1. If it was clear that a memory problem occurred, but there was ambiguity between two types of memory problems, each was assigned 0.5 points. If it was not clear if a memory problem occurred, no points were assigned. In some cases, subjects misread the question, and consequently, answered incorrectly. These were not counted. Aggregate results are summarized in Table 3. Investigators did not observe any of the following memory problems: absent-mindedness, bias, suggestibility, or persistence.

These results correspond to the C1 condition. Without a basis for comparison, it is difficult to say whether the question-answering performances are good or bad. Regardless, the interest with respect to the memory aid designer is the types and frequencies of memory problems. In the present case, both transience and blocking problems were found as expected, but misattribution problems were unexpectedly common. Phase 2 examines how subjects approached the task of remedying some of these.

Table 3: Phase 1 question-answering tallies and memory problem categorization

Answer		Problem	
Correct	47	Transience	22
Partially Correct	27	Blocking	4
Incorrect	20	Misattribution	9
No Answer	12		

5.2 Phase 2 (Aided Memory)

As mentioned previously, the hope in Phase 2 is to observe subjects attempting to remedy memory problems (Condition C2) and understand the strategies they employ under that condition. In Phase 2, all subjects engaged in a series of searches. A search attempt begins with the subject reading the question and ends with them selecting another question (or time runs out). The memory retrieval software recorded logs of what the subject was doing and which question they were answering. This was used in conjunction with the audio recordings of the experimental session to determine time spent on each question. Investigators further classified each question-answering attempt as either Condition C2 (subject witnessed the answer at the original event) or C3 (subject did not witness the answer). Classification was based on subject verbalizations and post-experiment interviews. Finally, attempts were classified as "successful" if the subject correctly or partially-correctly answered a new question, verified a previously-answered question, or improved an answer to a previously-answered question. An attempt was classified as "no answer" if the subject gave up on the search without producing an answer or time ran out. In no instances did a subject provide an incorrect answer during Phase 2. Results are detailed in Table 4 and summarized in Table 5.

The 82% success rate under C2 versus the 70% rate under C1 gives some support for Hypothesis H1b (i.e., higher success rate when aided). While also not conclusive, there is some support for Hypothesis H2b: subjects were able to answer questions more successfully in C2 (82%) compared to C3 (53%). Not surprisingly, in support of Hypothesis H1a, time spent per question under C1 was less than both C2 and C3 ($p<0.0001$). However, with no statistically-significant mean differences between C2 and C3 timing, there is no support for Hypothesis H2a.

Table 4: Phase 2 results. Each subject's (A–K) answering-attempts shown in sequence with time spent in subscript. 𝟡 = subject witnessed answer (no icon=non-witness); ✔=successful attempt (no icon=no answer). Time ran out during the last entry on each row.

A	3:22	✔$_{0:56}$	✔$_{3:40}$	3:30	3:30						
B	𝟡 $_{7:40}$	𝟡✔$_{5:31}$	1:44								
C	𝟡✔$_{2:04}$	0:54	✔$_{1:49}$	✔$_{1:31}$	✔$_{3:12}$	✔$_{1:55}$	✔$_{1:34}$	0:39	1:20	1:10	2:09
D	𝟡✔$_{2:44}$	5:07	3:02	✔$_{4:59}$							
E	𝟡✔$_{1:40}$	1:12	✔$_{3:00}$	1:47	3:02	4:18					
F	✔$_{3:19}$	✔$_{2:23}$	✔$_{2:14}$	2:05	2:33	2:10					
G	𝟡✔$_{2:39}$	✔$_{1:46}$	7:11	3:51							
H	𝟡✔$_{2:32}$	𝟡✔$_{2:40}$	✔$_{3:48}$	✔$_{5:25}$	3:07						
I	1:00	✔$_{4:12}$	𝟡✔$_{1:48}$	1:57	✔$_{1:38}$	✔$_{2:01}$	✔$_{2:48}$				
J	2:57	𝟡✔$_{1:37}$	✔$_{3:52}$	3:03	1:14	2:48	1:06				
K	✔$_{2:01}$	✔$_{1:21}$	3:22	𝟡 $_{4:06}$	✔$_{1:50}$	2:25					

Table 5: Summary of Table 4 question-answering times (in seconds) and question-answering tallies (not counting C3, no answer timouts)

	Witness (C2) 𝟡		Non-Witness (C3)	
	Success ✔	No Ans.	Success ✔	No Ans.
Mean	155	353	160	154
Std. Dev.	71	151	73	94
N	9	2	23	20

The timing data in general has caveats. Some subjects found the interface initially challenging, yet learned how to use it better over time: "I think I'm getting better at figuring out how to search the audio just in terms of thinking about things that might work." Furthermore, question difficulty was not uniform and not all subjects formulated an optimal strategy to maximize the number of answers solved. For example, some subjects intentionally chose questions out of curiosity versus optimizing their overall task-performance. Such confounding factors make it difficult to draw conclusions on timing differences. However, the timing similarity between C2 and C3 might suggest subjects have a condition-independent time threshold (roughly 4 minutes) after which they will move on whether they find an answer or not.

Observations during the experiment revealed what aspects of the interfaces (Figures 2 and 3) were most valuable. Among the nine instances in which subjects were able to remedy failures, seven initiated searches by correctly identifying the talk in the calendar; the remaining two found the correct talk by keyword searching. Once in the recording, in six instances, subjects used phoneme searching to identify potentially-relevant sections and limited audio playback to those. In two instances, subjects played the audio from the beginning until the answer was heard, and in one instance, the subject skipped to various points in the recording, using the transcript as a guide, until finding the answer. In one instance in which a subject was a witness but failed to find an answer, a misattribution memory problem occurred causing the subject to initially open the wrong recording. After four minutes of futile searching within the wrong audio clip, the subject gave up. In the other instance, the subject initially found the right recording, tried listening to audio from various sections (using the transcript as a guide) and phonetic searching, but to no avail.

5.3 Searching Via Speech Recognition

Keyword-searching of audio collections is problematic due to the inherent errors in speech-recognizer-generated transcripts. Not surprisingly, subjects stated that poor-quality speech recognition made the task challenging. Optimistic predictions aside, high-accuracy speech recognition of conversations in poorly-microphoned, heterogeneous environments will not happen anytime soon. Despite this, high-quality transcription—while beneficial—may not be necessary, especially for memory-retrieval tasks.

Witbrock [34] suggests general-purpose audio-information retrieval tasks can still be performed at high WER. Speech recognition has been shown to help in voicemail-retrieval [32] and calendar-scheduling tasks [35]. In previous studies, we found that error-laden speech-recognizer-generated transcripts synchronized with time-compressed audio playback, can improve subject comprehension, especially when word-brightness is rendered proportional to recognizer-reported confidence [28]. Techniques to build and evaluate information-retrieval systems for broadcast-news recorded-speech collections have been studied in detail as part of the TREC Spoken Document Retrieval (SDR) task [7].

In the present study, previous experience with speech recognition seemed to be useful. For example, one subject typed the query "brazil" to find "Breazeal" since the latter was expected to be out-of-vocabulary. Another subject focused on questions that included keywords suspected of being in the recognizer's vocabulary. Other subjects commented that an adjustment period is needed to learn the novel search features and peculiar limitations of searching speech-recognizer-generated transcripts. These subjects added that their adjustment seemed to begin within the 15-minute testing period.

The phonetic "sounds like" searching feature was used often in Phase 2. However, the out-of-vocabulary problem was still observed when subjects attempted queries with domain-specific keywords such as "BeatBugs" and "OMCSNet." The absence of these words from CMUDict [5] prevents a phonetic translation. The overall sense from subject feedback was that this was useful despite the limitation.

6 Discussion

The results give the authors both relief and confidence that the current memory retrieval aid is a good starting point for memory retrieval via audio-based search. Subjects found answers within large collections of audio recordings, typically within a few minutes. In most cases, subjects were able to strategize ways to use the tool along with their remembrance of the past to identify the correct recording and to localize within a recording to the answer. Speech recognition, despite poor-quality transcripts, was useful for both keyword-searching audio collections and for helping subjects localize and select sections of recordings to play back.

Lessons learned from the personal computer study are being applied to our handheld/wearable solution. Searching the calendar and audio playback were common in the witness condition; these capabilities have transferred well to the PDA. Current PDAs lack the computational resources needed for large-vocabulary speech recognition and real-time phonetic searching. Thus, a server-based approach is still required, but this will likely change within a few years. PDA screen-size issues remain as subjects often found the large personal-computer display useful to visually skim large sections of transcripts to help them localize their audio playback choices.

Text-based keyword-searching may not transfer easily to a PDA or wearable device due to text-entry limitations. Query input via speech is an intriguing possibility and speech-recognizer-mediated input for a more-constrained wearable calendaring system has been studied [35]. High WER and out-of-vocabulary problems suggests this approach may not be well suited for exact-match queries. Phonetic searching, with it's looser constraints, may be better suited and might even produce better results. On today's typical PDA, it is possible to generate phonemic transcripts, but text transcripts remain beyond current capabilities.

There is evidence suggesting that people remember better when the original context of the desired memory is reconstructed [10]. A PDA, used *in situ*, could take advantage of such context using, for example, an automatically-input-constrained search based on current location and other contextually-sensed factors.

The results, while emphasizing memory assistance, may have applicability to other audio-search domains. Subjects were able to find answers to questions from events that they did not witness, though not as accurately as in the witness-condition. Since subjects were familiar with the research in general, these results may not generalize to searching unfamiliar collections. But, there may be implications to organizational-memory applications. For example, absentees could have improved ways of quickly finding information within a recorded meeting. This example notwithstanding, memory fades over time and it is anticipated that the search process on events in the distant past will resemble that which is experienced by non-witnesses.

Future Directions

Reported experience in the academic setting suggests one desirable scenario for ubiquitous recording: student-advisor task-based communications. Though a limited application area, it may generalize to other supervisee-supervisor communications, especially when task-based, limited-duration, high-quality, and infrequent. Further examination is needed on this issue and a small-scale deployment of the memory prosthesis with non-investigators is underway.

What is not clear is the necessity for long-term archival for memory assistance. Task completion may be an opportune time for data purge, or at least, extraction of salient parts and deletion of the remainder. This limited- or non-archival strategy has additional benefits. First, a restricted search space may improve search experiences by reducing the time to find answers. Second, an illicit data intrusion would have limited ramifications. Third, if a user were embroiled in legal struggles in which recordings were subpoenaed, an established deletion strategy may avoid allegations of illegal destruction of evidence. Finally, conversation partners might be more willing to be recorded if there is an agreed-upon destruction policy.

7 Social and Legal Issues

Even if memory prostheses and similar ubiquitous recording tools prove significantly valuable, they raise some obvious privacy concerns with respect to what permissions are needed to record, who will have access to the data, what social conventions are needed for such devices, and what legal protections are available. Common use is not expected until these points are adequately addressed.

Most states in the U.S.A. have laws requiring consent before initiating audio recording. There is some state-to-state variation with respect to both the setting (public versus private) and how many people must consent (one or all) [11]. While these standards describe what is legal, social conventions prescribe what is appropriate. The memory-prosthesis-wearing author has observed various reactions to the device. Consent is required and always requested prior to recording. Despite this, when the device is off, some conversation partners ask for verification before speaking freely, some assume the device is off. Also, the social greeting now includes a somewhat awkward request to be recorded (e.g., "Hello. Good to see you. May I record this?"). Others who have used the device found it uncomfortable to request such permission. This is especially true among those in supervisory roles who report more hesitation and discomfort when asking permission of their subordinates as compared to peers. Though people occasionally do decline requests to be recorded, it is not known if there are instances of accepted requests in which the person truly preferred not to be recorded, but agreed simply out of a sense of cooperation for a fellow researcher or other unspecified reasons. Brin posits ubiquitous recording is inevitable [3]. The experiences reported here suggest more studies are needed to understand what social conventions are appropriate for integration of personal recording devices into everyday life.

Assuming such conventions are possible, there is another reason for caution. Once recordings are made, there is very limited protection to prevent legal authorities from searching and seizing recordings via a court-approved warrant. The Fourth and Fifth Amendments to the U.S. Constitution describe protections against self-incrimination, search, and seizure. But, these protections are not expected to extend to memory prostheses. From a legal perspective, a close cousin to a memory prosthesis is a personal diary. US courts have addressed protection of personal diaries, and their current position is diaries can be searched and seized [13]. Hence, it is unlikely that the less-private memory prosthesis would be afforded more protection.

Encrypting is an option. Hiding data is another option and the safest place might be inside one's body. While the courts have not set a limit to what can be seized, the standard for extracting things from one's body is higher than things outside [23].

Conclusion

This paper presented a prototype, wearable memory aid with the goal of helping alleviate some everyday memory problems by creating a searchable, personal archive of everyday experiences. The prototype collects many data sources in support of this and the current focus is on audio.

A personal-computer-based memory retrieval tool allowing browsing, searching, and listening to audio and associated speech-recognizer-generated transcripts was presented. In contrast to traditional information-retrieval evaluations, the present study examines how the tool assists subjects who previously witnessed the recorded events and were familiar with the search collection. Results of a question-answering memory-retrieval task suggest that without assistance, mistakes are primarily attributed to memory problems such as transience, blocking, and misattribution. When their recollection was insufficient, subjects were able to use the retrieval tool in combination with bits they did remember to find answers. Similar to Whittaker et al.'s findings [32], the present observations also found error-laden speech-recognizer generated transcripts useful, especially when accompanied by the revised visualization and phonetic search features. Finally, some social and legal challenges associated with the ubiquitous recordings were presented.

References

1.   Abowd, G.D. Classroom 2000: An Experiment with the Instrumentation of a Living Educational Environment. *IBM Systems Journal*, **38**(4), 508–530, (1999).
2.   Arons, B. SpeechSkimmer: Interactively Skimming Recorded Speech. *Proc. UIST 1993*, 187–196. (1993).
3.   Brin, D. *Transparent Society*. Addison-Wesley (1998).
4.   Bush, V. As We May Think. *Atlantic Monthly* **76**(1), 101–108. (July 1945).
5.   CMU Pronouncing Dictionary. cmudict0.6d. http://www.speech.cs.cmu.edu/cgi-bin/cmudict
6.   Eldridge M., Sellen A., and Bekerian D., Memory Problems at Work: Their Range, Frequency, and Severity. Technical Report EPC-1992-129. Rank Xerox Research Centre. (1992).
7.   Garofolo, J., Auzanne, C., and Voorhees, E. The TREC Spoken Document Retrieval Track: A Success Story. *Proc. TREC 8*. 107–130. (1999).
8.   Gemmell, J., Bell, G., Lueder, R., Drucker, S., and Wong, C., MyLifeBits: Fulfilling the Memex Vision, *Proc. ACM Multimedia '02*, Juan-les-Pins, France, 235–238. (2002).
9.   Gerasimov, V., Selker, T., and Bender, W. Sensing and Effecting Environment with Extremity Computing Devices. *Offspring* **1**(1): 30–41. (2002).
10. Gooden, D., and Baddeley, A.D. When does context influence recognition memory? British Journal of Psychology. **71**, 99–104. (1980).

11. Hidden Cameras, Hidden Microphones: At the Crossroads of Journalism, Ethics, and the Law. http://www.rtnda.org/resources/hiddencamera/allstates.html
12. Hindus, D. and Schmandt, C. Ubiquitous Audio: Capturing Spontaneous Collaboration. *Proc. CSCW '92.* 210–217 (1992)
13. Johnson, C. Privacy Lost: The Supreme Court's Failure to Secure Privacy in That Which is Most Private – Personal Diaries. 33 *McGeorge L. Rev.* 129. (2001).
14. Lamming, M., Brown, P., Carter, P., Eldridge, M., Flynn, M., Louie, P., Robinson, and P., Sellen, A. The Design of a Human Memory Prosthesis. *The Computer Journal.* **37**(3), 153–63 (1994).
15. LifeLog, http://www.darpa.mil/ipto/programs/lifelog/
16. Lin, W. and Hauptmann, A. A Wearable Digital Library of Personal Conversations. *JCDL 2002*: 277–278 (2002).
17. Lucene, http://jakarta.apache.org/lucene/
18. Monty, M.L. *Issues for Supporting Notetaking and Note Using in the Computer Environment*, Ph.D. thesis, Department of Psychology, University of California, San Diego, CA (1990).
19. Moran, T.P., Palen, L., Harrison, S., Chiu, P., Kimber, D., Minneman, S., van Melle, W., and Zellweger, P. "I'll get that off the audio": A case study of salvaging multimediameeting records. *Proc. of CHI'97.* (1997).
20. Morgan, N., Baron, D., Edwards, J., Ellis, D., Gelbart D., Janin, A., Pfau, T., Shriberg, E., and Stolcke, A. The Meeting Project at ICSI. *Human Language Technologies Conference.* (2001).
21. Orwant, J. Heterogenous learning in the doppelgänger user modeling system. *User Modeling and User-Adapted Interaction*, **4**(2), 107–130, (1995).
22. Rhodes, B. *Just-In-Time Information Retrieval.* Ph.D. Dissertation, MIT Media Lab (May 2000).
23. Rogers, M.G., Bodily Intrusion in Search of Evidence: A Study in Fourth Amendment Decisionmaking. 62 *Ind. L.J.* 1181. (1987).
24. Schacter, D.L. The Seven Sins of Memory: Insights from Psychology and Cognitive Neuroscience. *American Psychologist.* **54**(3), 182–203 (1999).
25. Schmandt, C. The Intelligent Ear: An Interface to Digital Audio. *Proc. IEEE International on Cybernetics and Society*, IEEE, Atlanta, GA (1981).
26. Smeaton, A.F., Over, P. The TREC-2002 Video Track Report. *Proc. TREC 11.* (2002).
27. Stark, L., Whittaker, S., and Hirschberg, J. ASR satisficing: the effects of ASR accuracy on speech retrieval. *Proc. ICSLP.* (2000).
28. Vemuri, S., DeCamp, P., Bender, W., and Schmandt, C. Improving Speech Playback Using Time-Compression and Speech Recognition. To appear *Proc. CHI 2004.* (2004)
29. ViaVoice, http://www-3.ibm.com/software/speech/
30. Wagenaar, W.A. My Memory: A study of Autobiographical Memory over Six Years. In *Cognitive Psychology.* **18**, 225–52 (1986).
31. Wechsler, M., Munteanu, E., Schäuble, P.: New Techniques for Open-Vocabulary Spoken Document Retrieval. *Proc. SIGIR 1998.* 20–27. (1998).
32. Whittaker, S., Hirschberg, J., Amento, B., Stark, L., Bacchiani, M., Isenhour, P., Stead, L., Zamchick G., & Rosenberg, A. SCANMail: a voicemail interface that makes speech browsable, readable and searchable. *Proc. CHI 2002*, 275–82 (2002).
33. Wilding, E.L., Rugg, M.D. An event-related potential study of memory for words spoken aloud or heard. *Neuropsychologia.* **35**(9), 1185–95 (1997).
34. Witbrock, M., http://infonortics.com/searchengines/boston1999/witbrock/index.htm, Lycos (1999).
35. Wong, B.A., Starner, T.E., and McGuire, R.M. Towards Conversational Speech Recognition for a Wearable Computer Based Appointment Scheduling Agent. GVU Tech Report GIT-GVU-02-17. (2002).

Infrastructures and Their Discontents: Implications for Ubicomp

Scott D. Mainwaring, Michele F. Chang, and Ken Anderson

Intel Research, 2111 NE 25th Ave. (JF3-377), Hillsboro, OR 97124, USA
{scott.mainwaring,michele.f.chang,ken.anderson}@intel.com

Abstract. Infrastructures (persistent socio-technical systems over which services are delivered) are normally taken for granted by their users, but are powerful forces of constraint and enablement with implications for the design, use, and adoption of ubiquitous computing. To approach the study of infrastructure from an ethnographic perspective, we conducted an exploratory field study of people for whom infrastructure had become visible due to some form of active engagement (rejecting, augmenting, or caretaking). From considering together individuals as disparate as homeschoolers, gated community dwellers, and voluntary simplicity advocates, a number of challenges and opportunities for ubicomp emerged in terms of appropriation, empowerment, and reflection.

1 Introduction

Ubiquitous computing (ubicomp) is a vision of infrastructure. Indeed, it is a vision of multiple infrastructures – some new, some existing; some virtual, some physical; some technical, some social – all coming together in a seamless way [1]. Much attention in the research community has been paid to the plethora of technical and socio-technical challenges set forth by this vision, from techniques for sensing and encoding context, to requirements for new user interfaces and user interaction paradigms, to the need for new kinds of devices, middleware systems, and architectures [2, 3].

In this paper we call attention to the notion of infrastructure itself, particularly the notion of ubiquitous infrastructure, and argue for the utility of an ethnographic approach to the study of infrastructure. By an ethnographic approach, we mean one which seeks to understand how an infrastructure is perceived and conceived, emotionally understood, and interacted with from the first-person perspective of its users. We sketch an initial exploratory study of "infrastructure discontents" by way of illustration, and discuss its potential implications for the design and deployment of ubicomp systems, anticipating new sources of value, concern, and potential backlash.

Merriam-Webster defines infrastructure as the underlying foundation or basic framework of a system. They are often hidden and, to adopt Tolmie et al.'s [4] terminology, unremarkable aspects of daily life, posing obvious challenges for empirical observation and study. The problem of drawing out and making visible for analysis important but taken-for-granted structures of environments and routines is pervasive in qualitative field research. In response, many approaches have been developed, including analysis tools like pause-and-review video [5] or maps that aggregate events over time [6], to call attention to easily overlooked features; filtering schemes that

N. Davies et al. (Eds.): UbiComp 2004, LNCS 3205, pp. 418–432, 2004.

wait for breakdowns or critical incidents [7], abnormal times when hidden phenomena surface, apparent to all; critical readings of "master narratives" latent in the infrastructure itself [8]; or studies of (or by) "outsiders" such as novices (see [9]) or members of different cultures, for whom familiarity has not yet backgrounded the issues of interest.

The approach we took is closest to this last one, of finding special populations for whom one or more infrastructures would be matters of daily effort and engagement instead of hidden forces. But rather than looking at novices or other cultures, we took as a starting point a current stereotype in our own culture: the rugged backcountry individualist living "off the grid." "Grid" here refers most clearly to the public electrical grid, which the off-the-gridder either does without or replaces with self-generation. (It may also reference the typical grid pattern of urban streets imposed by city planners, which the off-the-gridder has escaped by moving beyond the reach of streets, and indeed probably pavement, not to mention zoning regulations.) This schematization of "grid" has an interesting resonance with visions of ubiquitous computing, in which network connectivity becomes just another utility [10, p. 63] (and, in some versions, enforcement of information flow policies becomes integral to the network).

The notion of living off the grid – independently, freely, without being tied to, trusting of, or complicit in the benefits, costs, and responsibilities of mainstream, "modern" life – has a certain subversive appeal. Indeed, that is part of the point, the intentionality behind this lifestyle: to critique the mainstream culture and demonstrate alternatives. There is a surely fascinating and complex reality behind this stereotype, well worthy of research. However, we chose not to narrow our focus at the start to this highly politicized, self-conscious, and perhaps intentionally self-marginalized domain, but to treat it as a provocative jumping off point. We generalized from this initial notion along a number of dimensions. Expanding from the idea of a single "grid," we sought to investigate multiple infrastructures, of various scales and compositions, ranging from public eduction and physical security, to electricity and internet Expanding from a binary, static, all-or-nothing idea of being either "on" or "off," we wanted to consider a range of relationships people might have to infrastructures, how these change over time, and what they are moving *towards* not just what they are reacting *against*. And expanding from a notion of individual radicalism or extremism (and the practical issues it posed in terms of trusting access by a research team representing a major global corporation), we sought people with a range of political orientations and degrees of explicitness in agenda.

In the remainder of this paper, we describe the field study we conducted in the latter half of 2003, introducing some of the people we met and themes that emerged, and finish by revisiting the notion of infrastructure in light of what we learned, and sketching three broad areas for future ubicomp research and design. We see this work as experimental, not as a methodology that compares a treatment to a control group, but as an effort to seek novel perspectives on ubicomp and to give voice to potential users who have not so far been paid much attention to.

2 An Exploratory Study

As an initial ethnographic study of infrastructure, we set out to visit a range of people living in some way beyond the traditional bounds of one or more infrastructures. We conducted a total of 17 interviews. Most (14) were 2-3 hour home visits conducted by a two-person team (a social scientist as lead interviewer, along with an interaction designer as backup interviewer and recorder). Interviews were informal, asking people about their daily routines, neighborhoods, technology and media use, and interactions with people and groups outside the home. Discussion often was structured around a tour of the home, giving interviewers the chance to ask about technologies and other artifacts in the environment. This general discussion guide was amended to focus on particular areas or activities of interest (such as home schooling, living in a gated community, or, as one of our participants was said to be doing, going a year without buying anything) when these were known in advance, and flexible enough to accommodate veering off into such topics were they to come up serendipitously. These home interviews were supplemented by two workplace interviews, a group discussion over dinner, and miscellaneous other observations and collection of artifacts such as promotional materials and specialist magazines. Audio recording and still photography were used extensively, along with some video.

As this was an initial experiment, we limited ourselves to a convenience sample of mostly local participants, many recruited through as friends or friends. 13 of our field visits were in the Pacific Northwest, with the remainder (since gated communities are rare in Seattle and Portland) in the Phoenix, AZ megalopolis. To ensure exposure to a range of infrastructures and non-standard relationships towards them, we organized our sample around four categories: homeschoolers, gated community dwellers, security seekers, and disconnectors. The first two, which correspond to understood social categories, were recruited through friends of friends. Security seekers and disconnectors are artificial categories, with a few exceptions recruited by a marketing research firm screening its database of research volunteers based on a phone questionnaire that asked about events in the last 12 months. Security seekers had joined a group to make their neighborhood safer, created a "safe room," installed a home security system, or some combination of these. Disconnectors had stopped or almost stopped using the internet, TV, credit cards, or some combination. Though in some ways less interesting due to their artificiality, these market research recruiting methods introduced a useful level of randomness and surprise to our sample.

In defining a scope for our study, we faced a complex space of trade-offs, given the large number of parameters of interest within the general topic of infrastructures and their meanings in people's lives. Our choices resulted in sample that was predominantly from the US Pacific Northwest, white, middle-class, suburban, and technologically mainstream (neither early adopters nor laggards). Issues of privacy and security provided a set of unifying themes across all four groups of "off-gridders" we chose to recruit. Our discussions focused on the private and home, as opposed to the professional or work lives of our participants. There were important exceptions to each of these generalizations, cases that opened our eyes to whole sets of questions and contexts we hadn't considered. But insofar as what we found was determined by where and how we chose to look, it is important to acknowledge these trade-offs and resultant biases upfront, and to call for future studies to address areas – such as different conceptions of infrastructures in other cultures – not examined here.

The following sections sketch what we found in our field visits for each of the categories of our sample.

2.1 Homeschoolers

Public education is one kind of ubiquitous infrastructure in the U.S., a complex system of buildings, buses, taxes, laws, standards, labor unions, certification authorities, advocacy groups, elected officials, etc., all of which functions (to a degree dependent on locality) to deliver educational services to children and, indirectly, their parents. More than ubiquitous, it's a mandatory infrastructure, insofar as it sets educational requirements for all children and requires payment through (generally) inescapable taxes. And for much of the population, it's unremarkable: though what goes on in school is certainly a common topic of conversation, but what school *is* is taken for granted. On the face of it, homeschooling challenges this.

The homeschooling movement (which had grown to include 850,000 U.S. children by 1999 [11]) is a complex and controversial topic, of which we obtained only a glimpse. Stevens [12] provides an excellent ethnographic and historical treatment, covering the struggle of both religious and secular homeschoolers to develop an underlying theory/vision, practical resources, and political and legal legitimacy. The homeschoolers we visited, though part of the evangelical Christian branch that dominates (perhaps 90% of) the movement, stressed the practical advantages of keeping their children out of the school system: increased customizability (allowing for differences in temperament, interests, and abilities of their children), control (knowing directly how their children were being taught, filtering out undesirable or dangerous social, intellectual, and physical influences), and convenience (fitting "school" into the family's routine and physical environment, adapting it to them rather than vice versa). They positioned themselves not as theorists or activists, but as good parents, simply taking advantage of an increased set of resources available to them to fulfill their obligations.

Consistent with what Stevens reports, our respondents did not object to the notion of school and authority-based *schooling* (lectures, exercises, memorization, testing, etc.) as the basis for education. They were happy to re-create, quite literally, schoolrooms in their homes and in their church community centers, and to adopt commercially available, pre-packaged workbook-, PC-, and/or DVD-based curricula. They were also willing to use the public schools for specific purposes. One family took advantage of public kindergarten as a means to build the social skills of their children in an open but safe context, before transitioning them to the more closed context of homeschool for subsequent years; another placed their children in one or two classes (foreign languages, which were difficult for the non-speaking mother to teach at home) at the local public school, through its outreach program to homeschoolers. At the end of homeschooling, students are faced with the challenge of gaining admission to college – of moving back onto the grid, so to speak; for this purpose, community college served as a useful transitional zone for establishing a formal transcript.

Given their perhaps surprising degree of agreement with at least the theory behind formal education, why do homeschoolers take on the additional burden of being teacher/grader/school administrator, in addition to all their jobs as parent? First of all, our respondents, even the mothers, who clearly bore the brunt of the workload, all denied that it was in any way a burden. It was how they *wanted* to spend their energy, a way of expressing who they *were*. More surprising, to us, was what their characterization of public schools – for the most part not as ideologically incorrect (though this did come up, particularly around the teaching of evolution, which was seen as dogmatic and closed-minded) – but as *noisy*, chaotic places, full out out-of-control, rude children and a few harried, overburdened teachers/order-enforcers. "Just drop by your local school, you'll see that it's not at all like it was when you and I were that age," we were told repeatedly. Homeschooling was an effort to create a quiet, safe, respectful, orderly environment in which to care to their children's needs.

2.2 Gated Community Dwellers

As a ubiquitous, mandatory infrastructure, public safety has a number of interesting parallels to public education. The same diversity of component types – physical structures, vehicles, taxes, laws, standards, unions, advocacy groups, etc. – comprise both. Both exhibit the same mismatch between an ideals of equal service (and equal protection), and substantial, indeed correlated, geographic variation, be it in drop-out rates or crime rates. And perceived shortcomings have given rise to significant and controversial movements – homeschooling and gated communities – seeking privatization, quiet, and control. Nevertheless, there are important differences between how these infrastructures are perceived by their respective "discontents."

By 2001, 7 million American homes were in gated communities [13, p. 15], with large concentrations in the rapidly growing sunbelt retirement regions of the Southwest and Southeast, such as metropolitan Phoenix, where our field research took place. Gated ("fortress") communities and the closely connected phenomena of quasi-governmental homeowners associations are the subject of a substantial, very critical literature, decrying their implications for diversity, civil society, and public mindedness (see [13, 14, 15]). We found these criticisms echoed to some extent by the people we spoke with, particularly by some former gated community residents in their 20's who were hoping to leave Arizona in search of more diversity, excitement, and less of a "culture of fear." "I don't yet have children, but when I do, I want them to be able to play in the front yard without this making me look like a bad mother," reported one. They saw the gates more as symptoms of fear than as sources of security, and while the residents of gated community we visited were much more positive about their neighborhood, they all agreed that the gate itself was of little real security value, aside from keeping down the level of automobile traffic. Some suggested the gate actually encouraged crime, by keeping police patrols out, while presenting no real barrier to, for example, car thieves who could easily climb the fences, steal their objective, and drive it unchallenged through the checkpoint, which was locked from the outside only. Such views are consistent with general findings of little evidence for gated communities actually preventing crime, even if not inviting it [13]. And the people we visited all kept their doors locked, and either had or were planning to buy, home security systems.

If the gate is not about real nor perceived security, what is its significance? It's possible that it's a marker of community, but we found little evidence for that, either:

not only was there no gathering place for neighbors in the community apart from a collection of mailboxes at the side of the street, but in having residents sketch out and reflect upon their social networks, nearly all the people they felt close to lived beyond the gates. Instead, what emerged in our conversations was a notion of the "nice neighborhood" – predictable, safe, quiet, ready-to-move-in, and actively maintained through inconspicuous, gentle coercion. The gate, like the homeowner's association (which prohibited, for example, parching-prone citrus trees in front yards, a rule enforced by anonymous "narcs" informing on violators), was perhaps a necessary evil, at any rate an almost inescapable part of the lifestyle package Phoenix offered to its exploding population of middle-class immigrants and migrants from elsewhere. We discovered that, in Phoenix, to live "off the grid" as a member of this social class is to go to some lengths *not* to live in a gated community.

2.3 Security Seekers

Unlike homeschoolers or gated community dwellers, "security seekers" is not a natural category its members would recognize, but rather an artifact of our recruiting methodology. Instead of summarizing this group, we sketch a few of its members (names have been changed to protect confidentiality):

Pamela runs a small child-care service out of her split-level home in an inexpensive suburb. Her philosophy is to treat the children in her care as she treats her own, with an attitude of tough love and discipline. She extends this attention out into her neighborhood as well, keeping an eye out for suspicious persons and cars, and generally serving as a nosy neighbor – perhaps not well-liked, but respected, she feels. She once organized a successful neighborhood protest to expel a released sex-offender who had moved in with his parents next door; she would like to keep a camera trained on that property, but it's her understanding that laws prevent that. Compliance with state regulations for her home business is a major concern for her and quite visible in her den/care center, in which hand-drawn emergency exit maps have been posted, warning people not to try to evacuate through the garage, which due to her having walked in on burglars who fled out the garage door, she has now had locked from both sides. Above and beyond this call of duty, her den/care center is also a "safe room," in so far as she has made plywood barricades for the windows and has stockpiled enough supplies to last a week or two, should natural disaster or civil disorder require it. She is proud of her skills of frugality and self-sufficiency ("I know how to cook a *whole* chicken!"), developed over many years of hard economic times, following a crisis in which she and her husband both were laid off.

Tad is the head counselor for a city-run parolee halfway-house (a converted residential hotel) in downtown Portland. He oversees 40 men and women participating in a re-socialization program which aims to help recent drug-offender parolees find work and develop independent living skills for life after prison. Residents can stay at most 90 days according to their contract with the facility, and agree to random drug tests and regular meetings with counselors and parole officers. In addition to these formal requirements, residents are under lightweight, informal surveillance; in fact, Tad relies on their keeping tabs on each other, feeling that the resulting word of mouth keeps him better informed and in contact with his clients than any automated surveillance system could. Tad recently joined a neighborhood association to help make it a safer place – particularly for his clients, who often must face the temptation of drug dealers who congregate just outside the facility's entrance. Tad sees cell phones as similar sources of danger for his clients, though he acknowledges their utility in helping them to find jobs and reintegrate into the community; instead of cell phones, his clients share a single payphone on the wall in the communal kitchen.

Loni's 5-year-old daughter calls their home a "bamboo forest." Though not exactly a forest, and though Loni and her family are not of Asian ancestry, the home does abound with Asian influences, including generous use of bamboo. Huge picture windows look out over a forested landscape in a low-density, semi-rural neighborhood. An atmosphere of calm (and ionicly-cleaned air, thanks to a Sharper Image appliance) permeates the house, at least during our mid-day visit when her husband and teenage boys were absent. (When home, the males are often relegated to a basement den outfitted not with bamboo but video games and home theatre system.) Despite appearances, Loni explains that her rustic neighborhood and peaceful house are not really safe; strange cars sometimes cruise by, and her home has been burgled multiple times, despite a nosy neighbor, her two large Bernese dogs, and an alarm system. She has had an alarm system for years, managed by a small firm whose principals she has come to know personally. Security precautions extend to her shredding any financial documents and maximizing her use of the Internet for financial transactions, which she believes to be more secure and resistant to identity theft.

Space does not permit sketches of the other home visits in this category here, but they were similarly diverse and evocative of the subtleties around the lived meaning and practice of "security." Some important general themes do emerge, however. Pamela, Tad, and Loni all identify themselves a protectors, caregivers, and caretakers for some domain, either a neighborhood, community, or household. They are thus personally invested in supporting a small-scale infrastructure, managing its connections (often threatening) to the outside, and ensuring that it provides a nurturing environment for people for whom they are responsible (professionally or familialy). Each is in some sense concerned with being "off the grid" (Pamela with her safe room, Tad with his halfway-integrated clients, Loni with her deceptively peaceful neighborhood), but in a stronger sense they are all involved in grid-creation, with creating a safe zone, a sanctuary and refuge of some sort in which care can be delivered. These they assemble from a variety of components, including mechanisms of surveillance, though even in Loni's delegation of this authority to an outside service, mechanisms that afford personal engagement.

2.4 Disconnectors

This last category is closest to our original idea of living "off the grid" – people who were disengaged from some pervasive media, information, energy, or financial infrastructure. As with the "security seekers," it's a mixed bag, so we present a couple noteworthy examples.

Margie and Brad live just beyond the reach of the electrical grid, in a remote valley in Oregon's Coast Range, 45 minutes from the nearest paved road, on a historic homestead site. "Out here, you're the power company, the water company, the transportation department, and sheriff and animal control," explained Ben (illustrating this last point by gesturing to a loaded revolver). Working as a freelance writer Margie splits her time between there and Portland, whereas Brad lives there permanently, fighting a never-ending battle against gophers on his putting green and alder saplings springing up every time you turn your back. (One year they were called away for an extended period, returning to find their long driveway impassible due to saplings.) They have a gasoline generator to electrify the house wiring, usually only during Margie's stays, so she can recharge her notebook PC. When Brad is home alone he very rarely uses the generator and prefers to read by the light of a propane-powered floor lamp. Margie and Brad love being directly engaged, for better or for worse, with nature, and the lack of distraction it affords (and requires). In a few years they would like to retire there, though Brad is just recovering from a bad fall he suffered repairing their spring-fed water system and they wonder how long they can hold out.

Katrina lives with her husband and three children in an elegantly remodeled farm house in gentrified former Hippie community. She and her close network of friends live very comfortably, but she feels, wastefully. They have a lot of stuff – books, toys, electronics, clothes; more than they need, yet more kept coming into the house, bringing with it a negative "energy". Rarely did they re-use; it was so much easier to buy a new thing than to look to see if you already have it, she explains. Long interested in voluntary simplicity [16], she decided to conduct an experiment: "going a year without buying anything." What this would mean in practice was designed as a collaborative exercise with her family, including planned house meetings over the course of the year to modify and interpret the self-imposed rules if necessary. For her own part, Katrina was uninterested in drastically modifying her lifestyle and appearance of her home (her "no duct tape" rule headed off cheap-looking repairs), or in encouraging social transactions. So "anything" was defined to exclude comestible or consumable items (food, fuel, services), and "buy" was defined quite strictly, allowing for all matter of bartering, trading, and gift exchange. Between jobs at the start of the experiment, her husband was supported the experiment as means to economize. Children were brought in (or bought in) to the project with a promise of a trip to Hawaii at the year's end. At the time of our visit mid-way through the year, no major changes to the plan had been required (ruling light bulbs to be consumables was the extent of the controversies), and the experiment had become famous among her friends and their friends, facilitating donations and trades for needed items.

Though recruited as "disconnectors," strong desires for connection (with nature, in Margie and Ben's case, with local friends and community in Katrina's) emerged as important themes in these and the other visits placed in this category. Indeed, we found no one who was, or wanted to be, completely disconnected – ubiquitous infrastructures are, is turns out, hard to avoid. Across all our visits, the clearest examples of actual disconnection were involuntary – people who through accidents of economy or health found themselves thrown off the grid, and trying to clamber back on. In contrast, Margie and Ben, and Katrina, are good examples of a desire for selective and reversible disconnection. Rather than the extremist "off the grid" stereotype, they are in fact moderates, seeking to back away from too-easy access, temptation, and distraction the modern infrastructures of communication, transportation, and commerce bring with them, but not too much, and in the service of desires to connect to what is important.

3 Infrastructure, Reconsidered

Typically, when people think of infrastructure they think of the physical installations like public water systems, electrical grids, security systems, or transportation systems. These systems have very tangible points of contact. When a system isn't operating smoothly, like the power going out in the Northeastern U.S. during our study, or a pot-hole in a road, or a security gate that is broken, the results are physically felt. The there are other kinds of infrastructural systems that are less tangible but equally important. Many of our participants were actively engaged with (or against) institutional infrastructures such as school systems, churches, homeowner organizations, and retailers. Here the most visible points of contact (if you can get them to answer the phone) are agents doing "face work" [17] for the organization. (At a still broader level, Star and her colleagues [8, 18, 19] in their insightful analyses of categorizations and information infrastructures underlying communities of practice, take infrastructure as a relational and ecological term. Organizational points of contact, they point out, extend far beyond visible agents and into the very language, materials, and practices that constitute all manner of social arrangements.)

An intermediate level, or aspect, of infrastructure became apparent to us over the course of the study, a social or interpersonal level. People assumed many roles with respect to infrastructures they were developing – they took on roles and responsibilities such as teacher, caregiver, maintainer, nosy neighbor, donor, without necessarily becoming "agents" of a superordinate organization. Assuming these roles, they became a point of contact in a more direct, multivalent, and non-authorized way than an "agent." Contrast school teachers to homeschooling mothers, or Tad's commuting in to his job as parole counselor to Pamela's self-appointment as neighborhood mom. If we regard the institutional infrastructures as "professional," this third layer of infrastructure is at a less formalized and credentialed, more engaged and committed "amateur" level.

One feature of infrastructures is that they envelop people, hence their typical "invisibility." They also tend to envelop each other, becoming entire lifestyle packages [20]. On moves to Phoenix to "upgrade" one's life, buy a larger house, obtain some status, find a good school system for one's kids – and finds oneself living in a gated community, policed by a homeowner's association, unable to let one's kids play in the front yard. One might like to pick and choose which infrastructures to engage with or not, and to what degree, and there is some leeway to do exactly that, but it is heavily constrained. Breaking free of these existing constraints and established ways of living and creating a lifestyle usually takes effort at a larger scale than individual action and choice. For example, the homeschooling movement has done exactly this, creating models and justifications, providing resources, etc. The homeschoolers we visited were reaping the benefits of this past work, and presenting future parents with new questions to be answered about their identities, such as: are *we* homeschoolers?

One overall caveat from this analysis for the prospects for ubicomp is that infrastructure adoption is not likely to be a matter of an individual choosing an app, but of a community buying into a new way of living. Systems need to be designed that not only provide tangible benefits to "users," but which provide multiple symbolic and social values to people who will adopt many different roles and stances towards them. Along these lines, we now call attention to three areas for design.

4 Challenges and Opportunities for Ubicomp

4.1 Appropriable Infrastructures

In many cases, infrastructure is owned by outside authorities, and mediates a relationship between service providers and consumers. Consumers use the infrastructure, but they don't own it – they cannot appropriate it. They must abide by its rules, just as the services provided through the infrastructure conform to its constraints. *Using* the infrastructure can sometimes involve actually *inhabiting* it, as in the case of the gated communities we visited. Their residents had purchased an entire pre-packaged life-style, full of modern amenities, quiet, and "niceness." While they technically own their homes, they accepted (and more or less welcomed) restrictions on how they could modify them and behave around them. These restrictions were welcome in terms of using their home as an investment, ensuring its resale value, in unambiguous terms, without having to rely on messy and unpredictable processes of social negotiation with one's neighbors, for example.

Ubicomp is often understood in terms of habitable infrastructures, be they smart homes [21, 22], or urban districts overlaid by location-based services [23]. Service-provision and regulation-enforcement business models are familiar ones, which may yield great successes for ubicomp technologies, should the economics of provider costs and consumer benefits ever work out. Purveyors of such ubicomp environments would be wise to market them in terms of life-style and identity, leveraging the allure of being able to plug into completely designed system and magically transform one-self, or at least reinforce desired aspects of one's identity. For example, consider the services offered to evangelical homeschoolers, from curricula detailing how each school day is to be "lived," to ISPs that promise a bounded, regulated refuge within the wider, wilder internet in which to live one's online life.

However, there are downsides to merely using or adopting, as opposed to truly owning, through building or appropriating, infrastructure, and it is these we wish to call attention to as a challenge and opportunity for ubicomp systems to address. At a practical level, users are often faced by a mismatch between the standards or requirements of the infrastructure and the circumstances of their needs, desires, and abilities. Sometimes this gap can be addressed by purchasing an additional service or feature (as in supplementing the lack of perceived security by purchasing a home alarm system, or supplementing a homeschool curriculum by "purchasing" outside courses at a public school), but often it requires building (as in the specially constructed rooms we encountered in our home visits, ranging from home classrooms, to daycare safe-zones, to a library in a wilderness cabin; or in Katrina's construction – with buy-in from her family – of an evolving, publicized experiment in non-purchasing). At a more emotional level, users may experience a lack of engagement in or commitment to infrastructures that they have merely adopted, not to mention the emotional conse-quences of mismatches as noted above. Appropriation, in contrast, allows them to express their identities in a more active, self-constructed, gap-less way. In our study, this often surfaced in the form of care-giving and tending. Consider, for example, Brad's pride in taming the wilderness and being the electric company, etc.; Pamela's and Tad's active maintenance of a network of (caring) surveillance; or the homeschooling movement's insistence in creating a new way to educate children.

Gated community residents' reactions to the socially isolating aspects of their neighborhoods through active construction and maintenance of social networks outside their boundaries can also be seen in this light.

Ubicomp is implicated on both sides of this adoption/appropriation fence. In the form of standardized infrastructures deployed (and maintained) by service providers, they could well create gaps, unintended consequences, and emotional detachment due to mismatches between the package of services provided and local needs and desires. On the other hand, ubicomp is often considered in the form of ad hoc networks or do-it-yourself kits of self-assembling components that must function without benefit of a system administrator. Intermediate cases exist, as in the case of grassroots WiFi communities [24] in which networks of hot spots are far from self-assembling, but do only require "amateur" levels of skill to assemble into a form that can serve the community; assembly (and ongoing maintenance) can be seen as a kind of active care-giving and investment in the community. Indeed, there is no clear line between "adoption" and "appropriation," since infrastructures are often layered on top of infra-structures and construction consists of reuse and repurposing of existing commodities. More important, perhaps, than this distinction is ubicomp's potential not only to create gaps and mismatches, but to fill them as well.

4.2 Empowering Infrastructures

Infrastructures are about empowerment, in the sense of providing and controlling access to and facilitating flows of materials and services that in their absence would be far more costly to achieve. Physical infrastructures like electricity and water, and institutional infrastructures like school and legal systems, marshal and direct quite literally (though in infrastructure-specific senses) powerful forces. In exchange for empowerment, these infrastructures demand some element of trust. We entrust them to handle the messy and time-consuming details, to be reliable and accountable should they fail, and indeed often place our own health and security in their hands.

Ubicomp infrastructures have the potential to be similarly powerful, amplifying human capabilities through integrating many mechanisms of sensing, inferencing, and communicating. This harnessed, seamlessly integrated power will be attractive, if their designs can meet the requirements for user trust. More than attractive, it can even be life-saving, as suggested by work our colleagues at Intel are pursuing in pro-active health, seeking to empower the elderly facing the loss of their homes due to cognitive decline [25]. Real or perceived, as a "luxury" or under coercion, needs for empowerment can motivate people to go to considerable lengths to seek out infra-structures that will address them. For example, our homeschoolers were willing to invest their children's time (at some possible spiritual risk) to use secular community colleges to meet needs for accreditation and legitimacy. As the phenomenon of gated communities suggests, even if the systems deliver fewer real benefits (e.g., in increased security) than they are perceived to, they may still succeed in the marketplace. Systems need not be perfect, nor perfectly perceived, nor perfectly trusted.

Reliance on infrastructure, however, creates its own problems and concerns. Our study of discontents illustrates how empowerment in some dimensions can lead to at least perceived disempowerment in others. In many of our interviewees, we encountered concerns about potential side-effects of relying on infrastructures to protect them and cater to their needs. These ranged from homeschoolers wrestling with the line between protectiveness and over-protectiveness of their children, to people looking ahead to easing back in retirement but wanting to keep active and not lose their "edge," to survivors of personal traumas (becoming disabled, losing a home, etc. – being thrown off of the grid, so to speak) who were proud of the skills and self-sufficiency they had had to develop in order to cope. Infrastructure, for all its benefits – indeed, because of all its ready-at-hand benefits – was seen to bring also complacency, stasis, vulnerability.

Disempowering aspects of infrastructure can be addressed, recursively, by more infrastructure. Gaps created by one system can be bridged by others, etc. For example, one might imagine instrumenting homeschooled children to try to measure the "roughness" they are exposed to, and to adjust it over time to some optimum level. But aside from potentially infinite regress, this recursive approach seems to miss the point. The real question seems to be how ubicomp systems can be designed and used in ways that don't invite complacency and de-skilling. This is in fact a clinical question facing projects seeking to alleviate the burdens of aging, which risk creating cures that are worse than (or at least worsen) the syndrome. But it is a design (and ethical) question more broadly, whenever a system helps to alleviate a burden, and by so doing affects the skills that had developed for carrying that burden.

The challenge, then, as we see it, is for ubicomp systems that seek not to automate or even augment/amplify human skills but to exercise and celebrate them, to encourage active engagement, and provide resources to individuals and communities for continuous change and exercise. Such an approach can be seen in existing work on proactive health [25], on technologies to support political struggles of underprivileged communities [26], and promises to reframe the notion of security and safety from a passive commodity to an ongoing, embodied accomplishment [27].

4.3 Reflective Infrastructures

One theme that came up with surprising frequency in our interviews was noise, both literally and figuratively. Disorder and disrespect, conceptualized as loud, unruly behavior, played a central role in homeschoolers criticism of public schools. Our gated community interviewees appreciated the walls around their community for keeping out through traffic, with its noise and potential danger; they also appreciated (grudgingly) the formal rules of the community aimed at enforcing predictability and avoiding visual noise (the eyesore of the dead citrus tree in the front yard, for example). The security seekers were tuned into various sorts of suspicious noise in their neighborhoods, and sought to create in their homes (and in Tad's half-way house) safe zones of quiet and care. The disconnectors were concerned with waste and distraction, and (somewhat like Tad) with removing temptation.

Connecting to an infrastructure often brings with it the risk of noise. This noise may be in the form of nuisance, as when the infrastructure delivers the unwanted along with the wanted as its package of services, or when using the infrastructure requires extra effort or introduces extra complexity (as when the gate in the gated community has to be negotiated via remote control or access code). Or this noise may be in the form of distraction or temptation, as when the infrastructure invites over-consumption or overly-easy access to others.

Noise has also been acknowledged as a risk in ubicomp infrastructures as well. Noise in the form of unwelcome intruders and unpredictable behavior is the concern of research in security, reliability, and transparency of systems. In a humorous informance at the CHI 2002 conference, Bellotti and colleagues [28] enacted a scenario in which Captain Kirk's addressing "Computer: …" was met by a chorus of devices all answering "Yes?" – illustrating the risk of too much helpfulness (without enough deictic restraint) in a smart environment.   And the potential downside of ever-increasing reach of computing and ease of access has been acknowledged from the beginnings of the field, in Weiser and Brown's [29] understanding that to be tenable ubicomp must be "calm" – that it must be attuned to the human perceptual system and its ability to switch attention between center and periphery.

Our study suggests that calm ubicomp – even calm, secure, reliable, univocal ubicomp -- may not be sufficient, at least not in a context of concerns over temptation and self-doubt in one's self-control.   More than calm, many of our interviewees sought a kind of *quiet sanctuary* in terms of freedom from distraction, accessibility, and noise. Calm may not be enough if it is still too easy to re-center on appealing objects from the periphery. What would be enough, and whether people would actually adopt a system more strictly enforcing "allowed" vs. "unallowed" – instead of just wishing they were the kind of person who would/could live quietly – are hard research questions.

One path to "quiet" that arose from our interviews involves the idea of submission to a trusted other as coach, counselor, or mentor. Coincidentally, two of our respondents happened to be active in local Tae Kwon Do groups, and had ongoing relationships with a master teacher who oversaw their physical, mental, and spiritual development. Responsibility for development remained in the individual student, who was nevertheless expected to submit to traditional practices and to a hierarchy of authority. Themes of submission, though more to a system or community than a single person, also arose in our conversations with Tad in the half-way house, and with the homeschoolers pursuing a very demanding practice with the practical and spiritual support of a fellowship of believers. Perhaps ubicomp technologies could offer similar ways for people to put themselves in trusted relationships of nurturing surveillance and critique. Perhaps through technologies of self-monitoring and self-reflection, the trusted other could become, over time, the trusted self.

5 Summary and Future Work

Implicit in the idea of ubiquitous computing is the notion of infrastructure, which has received surprisingly little attention from the ubicomp community outside of purely technical investigations.   Starting with an approach of looking for "trouble" (in Garfinkel's sense [30]) or "discontent" with respect to existing ubiquitous infrastructures, we ventured into the field to uncover practices around, problems with, and meanings of various infrastructures, as they were embedded in alternative and mainstream lifestyles. We consider the experiment was successful insofar as it uncovered a number of interesting themes and novel perspectives, and demonstrated the general viability of this approach for bringing out hidden structure.

As follow-on work, we have begun exploring a design space around intention submission to trusted others, and planning more targeted fieldwork to address in particular questions of temptation and transition surfaced in this work. We also intend to study how these issues play out in other geographies and other cultures, further from home, and in arriving at a more detailed understanding of the practices and materials involved in interfacing with infrastructures, beyond these more abstract concerns of identity and trust.

Acknowledgements

We thank Tim Brooke and Monique Lambert for their help with fieldwork and analysis, and Genevieve Bell for her ongoing interest, critique, and support. We give special thanks to our research participants for all they taught us.

References

1. Weiser, M. The computer for the 21st century. *Scientific American*, 265:3 (1991), 66-75.
2. Davies, N., and Gellersen, H.-W. Beyond prototypes: Challenges in deploying ubiquitous systems. *IEEE Pervasive Computing* 1:1 (2002), 26-35.
3. Satyanarayanan, M. Pervasive computing: Vision and challenges. *IEEE Personal Communications* 8:4 (2001), 10–17.
4. Tolmie, P. Pycock, J., Diggins, T. MacLean, A., and Karsenty, A. Ubiquity: Unremarkable computing. In *Proceedings of the CHI 2002*.
5. Brun-Cottan, F., and Wall, P. Using video to re-present the user. Communications of the ACM 38:5 (1995), 61-71.
6. Crabtree, A., Rodden, T., Hemmings, T, and Benford, S. Finding a place for UbiComp in the home. In *UbiComp 2003* (LNCS 2864), 208-226.
7. Flanagan, J.C. The critical incident technique. *Psychological Bulletin* 51 (1954), 327-358.
8. Star, S.L. The ethnography of infrastructure. *American Behavioral Scientist*, 43:3 (1999), 377-391.
9. Palen, L., Salzman, M., and Youngs, E. Discovery and integration of mobile communications in everyday life. *Personal and Ubiquitous Computing* 5:2 (2001), 109-122.
10. Lally, E. *At home with computers.* Berg, 2002.
11. Bielick, S., Chandler, K., and Broughman, S. *Homeschooling in the United States: 1999.* National Center for Education Statistics, 2001.
12. Stevens, M. Kingdom of children: Culture and controversy in the homeschooling movement. Princeton University Press, 2001.
13. Low, S.M. *Behind the gates: Life, security and the pursuit of happiness in fortress America.* Routledge, 2003.
14. Blakely, E.J., and Snyder, M.G. *Fortress America: Gated communities in the United States.* The Brookings Institution, 1997.
15. McKenzie, E. Privatopia: Homeowner associations and the rise of residential private government. Yale University Press, 1996.
16. Elgin, D. Voluntary simplicity: Toward a way of life that is outwardly simple, inwardly rich. Quill, 1998.
17. Giddens, A. *The consequences of modernity.* Polity Press / Stanford University Press, 1990.

18. Bowker, G.C. and Star, S.L. *Sorting things out: Classification and its consequences.* MIT Press, 1999.
19. Star, S.L. and Ruhleder, K. Steps toward an ecology of infrastructure: Design and access for large information spaces. *Information Systems Research* 7:1 (1996), 111-134.
20. Giddens, A. Modernity and self-identity: Self and society in the late modern age. Stanford University Press, 1991, p. 125.
21. Edwards, W.K. and Grinter, R.E. At home with ubiquitous computing: Seven challenges. In *UbiComp 2001* (LNCS 2201), 256-272.
22. Rodden, T., and Benford, S. Domesticated design: The evolution of buildings and implications for the design of ubiquitous domestic environments. In *Proceedings of CHI 2003.*
23. Schilit, B., LaMarca, A., Borriello, B., Griswold, W., McDonald, D., Lazowska, E., Balachandran, A., Hong, J., and Iverson, V. Challenge: Ubiquitous location-aware computing and the Place Lab initiative. In *Proceedings of The First ACM International Workshop on Wireless Mobile Applications and Services on WLAN (WMASH 2003).*
24. Schmidt, T. and Townsend, A. Why Wi-Fi wants to be free. *CACM* 46:5 (2003), 47-52.
25. Morris, M., Lundell, J., Dishman, E., and Needham, B. New perspectives on ubiquitous computing from ethnographic study of elders with cognitive decline. In *UbiComp 2003* (LNCS 2864), 227-242.
26. Hirsch, T., and Csikszentmihályi, C. Sensible Cities Project. http://www.media.mit.edu/research/ResearchPubWeb.pl?ID=55
27. Palen, L., and Dourish, P. Unpacking "privacy" for a networked world. In *Proceedings of CHI 2003.*
28. Bellotti, V., Back, M., Edwards, W.K., Grinter, R.E., Henderson, A., and Lopes, C. Making sense of sensing systems: Five questions for designers and researchers. In *Proceedings of the CHI 2002.*
29. Weiser, M., and Brown, J.S. The coming age of calm technology. In *Beyond calculation: The next fixty years*, 1997.
30. Garfinkle, H. The conception of, and experiments with, "trust" as a condition of stable and concerted actions. In O.J. Harvey (ed), *Motivation and social interaction.* Ronald Press, 1963.

Opportunity Knocks: A System to Provide Cognitive Assistance with Transportation Services

Donald J. Patterson, Lin Liao, Krzysztof Gajos, Michael Collier, Nik Livic, Katherine Olson, Shiaokai Wang, Dieter Fox, and Henry Kautz

University Of Washington, Seattle WA 98195, USA,
{djp3,liaolin,kgajos,kolson,fox,kautz}@cs.washington.edu
{nlivic,mjc6,shiaokai}@u.washington.edu

Abstract. We present an automated transportation routing system, called "Opportunity Knocks," whose goal is to improve the efficiency, safety and independence of individuals with mild cognitive disabilities. Our system is implemented on a combination of a Bluetooth sensor beacon that broadcasts GPS data, a GPRS-enabled cell-phone, and remote activity inference software. The system uses a novel inference engine that does not require users to explicitly provide information about the start or ending points of their journeys; instead this information is learned from users' past behavior. Futhermore, we demonstrate how route errors can be detected and how the system helps to correct the errors with real-time transit information. In addition we present a novel solution to the problem of labeling positions with place names.

1 Introduction

For many individuals, mobility in the community means using public transportation. It is key to their social life, their employment, and their ability to receive goods and services. Unless they can successfully move through their community they cannot lead an independent life. Public transportation, however, can be daunting for anyone who is born with below average cognitive abilities or whose cognitive abilities have begun to decline, however slightly. There is often no choice but for them to give up their potential future independence and be under direct supervision of their care givers or family members; a healthy individual is needed to detect situations where a mistake made by a cognitively disabled person may cause distress or harm. Thus, the inability to safely use public transportation harms their quality of life as well as that of their formal and informal support network [1, 2, 3]. However, if impaired individuals had effective compensatory cognitive aids to help them use public transportation, their independence and safety would improve, they would have new opportunities for socialization and employment, and stress on their families and care givers would be reduced.

We developed a ubiquitous computing system, called "Opportunity Knocks," (*OK*) to explore the feasibility of just such a cognitive aid. This system targets

N. Davies et al. (Eds.): UbiComp 2004, LNCS 3205, pp. 433–450, 2004.

mentally retarded individuals and individuals with traumatic brain injury, who are generally high functioning but unable to use public transportation due to short-term confusion or memory lapses. These individuals generally show stable levels of cognitive ability over time, are employed, and are either using specialized transportation services or using public transportation with marginal efficacy.

While our system is immediately targeting mentally retarded people and people with traumatic brain injury, it also has promise for other classes of people who exhibit occasional cognitive lapses such as populations with age-related memory loss and even high functioning people who inevitably make mistakes.

The name of our system is derived from the desire to provide our users with a source of computer generated opportunities from which they can learn more efficient transportation routes and correct simple errors before they become dangerous errors. When the system has determined that an especially important opportunity has made itself available, it plays a sound like a door knocking to get the user's attention. Less critical opportunities are simply displayed if the user expresses interest. We desire to support existing cognitive capacities, not replace them, by helping users to remain engaged in their transportation decisions.

The system is implemented on a cell-phone platform and differentiates itself from more familiar web-based route planning or car navigation systems in several ways. First, the system requires no explicit input from the individual: it generates its path planning advice and destination predictions in an unsupervised manner entirely from past observations of the user. Second OK is centered on the individual. As such, it travels with the user and provides value to the user across multiple transportation modalities. Finally, OK can detect novel and explicitly erroneous user behavior.

In this paper we present three main contributions. First we developed a system architecture which could support our goals. This architecture is described in Section 3. Secondly, we present an elegant method of circumventing the onerous task of labeling positions with place names in Section 4. Thirdly, and most importantly, we designed and implemented an inference engine that supports explicitly reasoning about destinations and detecting user errors, as described in Section 5.

Finally, although in this paper we focus on a system which assists cognitively impaired people, the techniques we present can be applied to any user-centric location-based service that would benefit from probabilistically predicted location information (e.g., just-in-time traffic information for specific routes, home climate and appliance control, or reminders for errands-of-convenience).

2   Scenario

In order to ground our system, we present a fictitious running example that will help illustrate the most important features of our system.

Eileen has a physical therapist at a nearby university campus, whom she visits on a bi-weekly basis. After one such visit, Eileen finds herself exiting the building uncertain of which way to proceed. After a few minutes of hesitation, she reaches for her phone and invokes Opportunity Knocks. *OK* offers images of three destinations that she typically travels to after the therapist visit: her home, a grocery store, and the house of her friend Ted. Eileen selects her home and the system suggests her typical route: it provides instructions to find the nearest bus stop and tells her to wait for bus number 372.

Bus number 68 arrives first. Since this is the bus that Eileen normally takes to the *grocery store,* she accidentally boards it instead. Its route initially coincides with that of number 372; while *OK* can identify that she is on *a* bus, it is unable to detect the *identity* of the bus. It remains silent as it observes that Eileen is moving toward home in the expected manner. When the bus suddenly turns west after some time, following the bus route to the grocery store, her phone makes a knocking sound and alerts her that she should get off at the next stop. At that point, it directs her back a few hundred feet to a bus stop where she can board the next 372 bus. This time she gets on a correct bus and arrives home safely.

3 System Architecture

In order to support Eileen in the way we describe in the previous scenario, several technical pieces have to be composed. First, we describe the overall architecture of the system before discussing the individual components in detail.

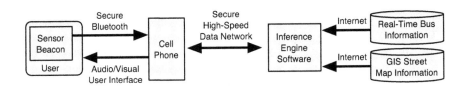

Fig. 1. Architectural Diagram of Opportunity Knocks.

Figure 1 diagrams our overall system architecture. The data flow of our system starts at a sensor beacon which is carried by a user. The sensor samples the environmental context of the user and forwards this information over a secure Bluetooth connection to the cell phone. The cell phone initially acts as a network access point and again forwards the context information to a remote server over the high-speed GPRS data network. The remote server, which is running the *OK* software, uses the sensor information in conjunction with Geographic Information Systems' (GIS) databases to localize the user. When the software has sufficient confidence in the position of the user, it is then able to suggest opportunities about which the user may want to know. These opportunities are sent back to the cell phone for display through the user interface. If an urgent opportunity, such as a plan for recovering from boarding the wrong bus, is recognized, the phone proactively alerts by making a door-knock sound; otherwise the phone remains passive with information available for reference by the user.

If the user selects an opportunity, such as a route to a frequent destination, the cell phone requests supporting information from the server, which may require referencing real-time information about bus schedules.

3.1   Cell Phone

We chose a cell phone as our client hardware because of its role as a defacto standard for a portable computing device. It has inherent value that is related to its primary function as a phone and for many people it is as common to carry as a wallet or a purse. As a result, it is likely to be a familiar, non-stigmatizing method of delivering assistive services. In the cell phone market there is a spectrum of products available, which spans from a traditional phone on one end, to a Personal Digital Assistant (PDA) on the other end. We opted for devices which were more like traditional phones rather than "smart-phones" because of their ubiquity, simple interface, and limited maintenance requirements. Cell phones also offer the promise of a cross-platform development environment which would enable an application written for the J2ME (Java 2 Micro-Edition) platform to work on any compliant phone.

Our system currently uses a Nokia 6600 cell phone. The Nokia 6600 phone is a GSM phone that has a wide-range of features required by our system. First it supports the J2ME Mobile Information Device Profile (MIDP) 2.0 that provides support for secure networking, serial port connection support, and the Application Management System — a push registry that enables authorized applications to be launched remotely. Some model specific features of the phone that we utilize include a high-resolution (176 x 208 pixels), high color (16-bit) screen, a digital camera, Bluetooth support, and high-speed data network capabilities. Under continuous operation our system lasts approximately 4 hours.

3.2   Sensor Beacon

The sensor beacon, which our users are required to carry, is a physically separate unit from the phone. We intend for users to place the sensor beacon in a purse, on their belt, in a backpack or on a wheelchair while transiting. In the future, it appears imminent that at least a simple GPS sensor will be incorporated into the phone itself [4] eliminating the need for a separate sensor beacon.

Currently, however, OK utilizes two different beacon implementations, both of which broadcast exclusively GPS information. One is a commercial package available from Socket Communications Inc. [5], shown at the top of Figure 2. This device measures 50x90x16mm, and contains a rechargeable six-hour battery.

The second is a custom-made device shown at the bottom of Figure 2 that utilizes a Bluetooth serial profile broadcaster and connects to an ATmega 128 processor. The ATmega processor functions as a communication gateway, controlling the multiplexing of several sensors, packaging of the data and sending it to the cell phone via Bluetooth. Our custom system will enable prototyping new sensors (e.g., digital compass, accelerometer, Wi-Fi localizer) in response to new research and our user studies.

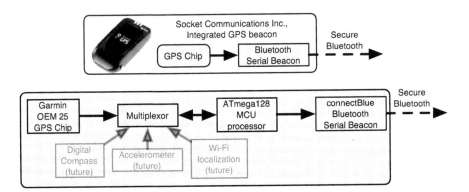

Fig. 2. Top: picture and schematic of off-the-shelf sensor beacon. Bottom: schematic of custom-built sensor beacon.

4   User Interface

4.1   Concept

Based on exploratory interviews with members of our target community, we have focused on a simple user experience. When the user desires transportation assistance, she refers to her phone and observes up to four images of predicted destinations (in Section 5 we describe how this selection is made). If she would like to go to one, she selects it. If the system has observed the user going to this destination in different ways, for example by foot and by bus, it will prompt her for the method she would currently like to take. The previously observed route is then provided in text form.

The system will not present destinations to which the user has not previously traveled, but it will allow the user to select a familiar destination even if it has never observed the user getting there from the current location. In this case *OK* presents a route that is based on a real-time bus route planning service provided by the local transit authority (e.g., [6, 7]).

Notably in the course of this interaction the user did not have to provide any information about where she was and only a very small amount of information about where she wanted to go, yet the system was still able to route her effectively.

4.2   Position to Place

Our system interfaces with the user by suggesting destinations that it has high confidence she is heading toward, and then routing her to that destination. It would be insufficient to present destinations as GPS latitude/longitude positions, and infeasible to require the user to enter a description for every interesting position on a cell-phone keypad.

Ideally, we would like to produce place descriptions automatically. This, however, is recognized as a difficult open problem [8, 9]. When attempting to create a meaningful label for a place, it is clear that the purpose of the labeling and the perspective of the labeler quickly dominate the proposed ontology. Should a description of place focus on demographics, land use, administrative use, functional use, or personal memories of the place? What happens when multiple ontologies define a region in different ways, or don't even separate the region in the same way? And which way is the best way for the current user?

To solve this problem we investigated a novel use of the camera phone. Since our system is monitoring the user's location, it is able to recognize when she has spent a sufficient amount of time in a location to call it significant. When this condition is met, the camera phone alerts the user to take a picture that captures her location. In the future, whenever the system wants to refer to that location, rather than trying to call it something in particular, it simply uses the photo to identify the spot. The advantage of such a system is that the user can decide what is meaningful about their location and can take a picture which reflects that.

5   Inference Engines

In previous sections we have described the desired behavior of our system — a behavior that depends on the system being able to learn and reason about its user's transportation routines. In particular, we require the following:

- the system should learn about its user's transportation routines in an unsupervised and unobtrusive manner;
- the system should be able to predict likely destinations the user may want to go to at any given moment in time;
- the system should be able to recognize anomalous behavior; in particular, if told where the user is going (by the user who requests directions or by a care taker or job coach who specifies the destination), the system should be able to detect, as early as possible, when the user strays from one of the usual paths that lead to that destination.

Because of the inherent uncertainties about human behavior as well as the possible errors from the maps and GPS measurements, we adopt a probabilistic approach that can handle potential errors and uncertainties in a statistically sound way. Two probabilistic models have been proposed in the recent literature for describing outdoor movement routines of a user [10, 11]. We will briefly review them and point out their fundamental inadequacies with respect to the set of requirements laid out above. Then we will discuss a more comprehensive model that subsumes the other two and provides new functionality. In Section 6 we will evaluate the new model with respect to our needs.

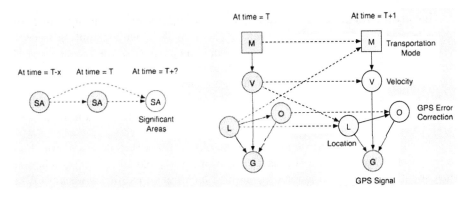

Fig. 3. On the left, a second order Markov Model (2MM) from [10] showing dependencies between observed and hidden variables. Shaded nodes are observed. All links are inter-temporal. On the right, a two-slice Dynamic Bayesian Network (2TBN) from [11] showing dependencies between observed and hidden variables. Shaded nodes are observed. Intra-temporal causal links are solid, inter-temporal links are dashed..

5.1   Previous Models

Ashbrook, et al. have proposed using a second order Markov model (2MM – see Figure 3-left) as a predictive tool for reasoning about likely destinations toward which a user may next be traveling [10]. The system logs continuous GPS signals, extracts places where the user seems to have stopped for a significant amount of time and then clusters them into significant locations. The optimal radius for a significant location is chosen after manual inspection of results for different radii. These results become the basis for training a second order Markov model. The authors have demonstrated that given the last two significant locations visited by the user, the system was able to generate a small and accurate set of the next most likely destinations.

In contrast to our desired behavior, this model is not able to refine estimates of the current goal using GPS information observed when moving from one significant location to another. Since significant locations might be long distances away this causes an unacceptable lag in noticing unusual behavior and significant amounts of GPS information are disregarded. This model also has no timing mechanism, so there is no way to judge when destinations will be reached or to react when too much time has passed. Finally, since the model only considers two previous locations, complex plans involving multiple significant locations cannot easily be reasoned about.

Patterson, et al. have proposed a two slice Dynamic Bayesian Network (2TBN – see Figure 3-right) for inferring a user's transportation mode from continuous GPS signals [11]. A Dynamic Bayesian Network is an extension of Bayesian Networks which allows for time–changing variables (details in [12]). Given a representation of the street maps, the system was able to accurately infer a user's most likely position, compensating for GPS sensor errors. The system was also able to infer locations of parking lots accessed by the user as well as bus routes and bus stop locations, all of which improved its accuracy. Finally, it estimated a user's street to street transition probabilities in an unsupervised manner and was able to use the information to further improve its accuracy.

The 2TBN could easily be adapted to detect when the user strays from a frequently traveled path. But the biggest shortcoming of this model stems from the fact that the system does not explicitly reason about the ultimate goals of a trip. Therefore, the system cannot predict the likely destinations toward which the user may be heading. Moreover, neither model, even if told a user's destination, can reason about the likely paths the user might take and, subsequently, cannot detect when the user strays from a correct path.

5.2   A New Hierarchical Model

To account for the inability of these models to meet our desiderata we have introduced a *hierarchical* Dynamic Bayesian Network model representing transportation routines [13]. The new model subsumes the capabilities of the previous models and bridges the gap between the raw sensor measurements and the abstract goal intentions of a user. A brief discussion of this model follows; refer to [13] for full technical details of the model structure, inference and training.

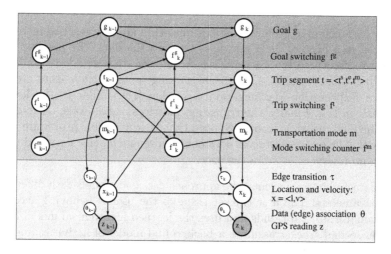

Fig. 4. Hierarchical activity model representing a person's outdoor activities. The top level estimates the current goal, the middle layer represents segments of a trip and mode of transportations and the lowest layer estimates the person's location on the street map.

Figure 4 shows the graphical structure of the new model. At the very highest level of this model, goals g_k (subscript k indicates the discrete time step) are explicitly represented as significant locations. Transitions between goals have specific probability distributions independently of the routes by which they are reached. Each goal destination influences the choice of which *trip segments* the user takes. Trip segments are sequences of motion in which the transportation mode is constant. Each trip segment t includes its start location t_k^s, end location t_k^e, and the mode of transportation, t_k^m, the person uses during the segment. Each trip segment biases the expectation over the mode of transportation and the changes in location. The mode of transportation m, in turn, determines the location and velocity distribution of the user. At the bottom level, we denote by $x_k = <l_k, v_k>$ the location and motion velocity of the person. Edge transition τ_k indicates the next street when passing an intersection and data association θ_k "snaps" a GPS measurement onto some streets around it. The switching nodes f_k^g, f_k^t and f_k^m indicate when changes in a variable's value can happen.

An efficient algorithm based on Rao-Blackwellised particle filters [14, 15, 16] has been developed to perform online inference for this model. At the lowest level, location tracking on the street map is done using graph-based Kalman filtering that is more efficient than the grid-based Bayesian filter and traditional particle filtering [17], used for the 2TBN model. At the highest level, the joint distribution of goals and trip segments is updated analytically using exact inference techniques. As a result, this model makes it possible to reason about high level goals (or significant locations) explicitly. The contribution of this model is that it considers not only previous significant locations visited but also the current location and the path taken so far to reason about likely destinations.

The parameters in the model are estimated in an unsupervised manner. This is a three step process. In a first pass through the data, the possible goals for a user are discovered by observing when the user stays at a location for a long time. Then in a second pass, the usual parking spots and bus stops are inferred using an Expectation-Maximization algorithm [18] similar to the learning of the 2TBN in [11]. Finally, the transition matrices at all levels are re-estimated simultaneously using a second Expectation-Maximization procedure with the full model. The learning process does not require any labeled data and therefore, requires no intervention from the user.

To detect abnormal events, the approach uses two models with different transition parameters. The first tracker assumes the user is behaving according to his personal historical trends and uses the learned hierarchical model for tracking. The second tracker assumes a background model of activities and uses an untrained prior model that accounts for general physical constraints but is not adjusted to the user's past routines. The trackers are run in parallel, and the probability of each model given the observations is calculated. When the user is following his ordinary routine the learned hierarchical model should have a higher probability, but when the user does something unexpected the second model should become more likely.

To compute the probability of each model, we use the concept of *Bayes factors*, which are a standard tool for comparing the quality of dynamic models based on measurements [19]. The Bayes factor H_k is computed recursively as

$$
\begin{aligned}
H_k &\equiv \frac{P(z_{1:k} \mid M_{prior})}{P(z_{1:k} \mid M_{learned})} \\
&= \frac{P(z_k \mid z_{1:k-1}, M_{prior})}{P(z_k \mid z_{1:k-1}, M_{learned})} \cdot \frac{P(z_{1:k-1} \mid M_{prior})}{P(z_{1:k-1} \mid M_{learned})} \\
&= \frac{P(z_k \mid z_{1:k-1}, M_{prior})}{P(z_k \mid z_{1:k-1}, M_{learned})} \cdot H_{k-1},
\end{aligned}
\tag{1}
$$

where $P(z_k \mid z_{1:k-1}, M_{prior})$ and $P(z_k \mid z_{1:k-1}, M_{learned})$ are the likelihoods of the observation z_k given the untrained and the hierarchical model (the likelihoods are extracted as a side-product of tracking). From a Bayes factor, we can compute the probability of abnormal behavior:

$$
\begin{aligned}
P_k(\text{Abnormal}) &\equiv P_k(\text{correct model} = M_{prior}) \\
&= \frac{P(z_{1:k} \mid M_{prior})}{P(z_{1:k} \mid M_{prior}) + P(z_{1:k} \mid M_{learned})} = \frac{H_k}{H_k + 1}
\end{aligned}
\tag{2}
$$

The last step follows directly from (1).

5.3 Errors Versus Novel Behavior

The above approach can detect unexpected events, but cannot distinguish errors from deliberate novel behavior. An important contribution of *OK*, however, is the ability to differentiate these cases using knowledge of the user's destination. This is possible because there are times when the system knows where the user is going, *e.g.*, if the user asks for directions to a destination, if a care-giver or job coach indicates the "correct" destination, or if the system has access to a location enabled date-book. In those situations we can *clamp* the value of the goal node in our model and reinterpret the low level observations. When the observations diverge significantly from the clamped high level predictions, the system is able to signal a possible error. Unlike in the 2TBN model, this model is capable of spotting anomalous behavior even if the user is following a well-trodden path, provided that path does not lead to the specified destination. This is what enabled us, in Section 2, to alert Eileen that she should get off bus number 68 and switch to 372, even though she takes both routes frequently.

Similarly to Equation (2), the probability of erroneous behavior given the user's input g (*i.e.*, the true goal and/or true trip segment) is

$$
P_k(\text{Error} \mid g) = \frac{\hat{H}_k}{\hat{H}_k + 1}
\tag{3}
$$

where the Bayes factor $\hat{H}_k$ is now defined as

$$
\hat{H}_k \equiv \frac{P(z_{1:k} \mid M_{prior})}{P(z_{1:k} \mid M_{learned}, g)}.
\tag{4}
$$

Here, $P(z_{1:k} \mid M_{learned}, g)$ is the likelihood given the clamped model.

In practice, when we track users for a long time, the probability of an error can grow very small and it can take too long for an observed error to cause this probability to cross the recognition threshold. To combat this lag, one could specify a floor that limits the error probability (e.g., 0.01 in our experiments) or compute the Bayes factors using the n most recent measurements.

6   Experiment

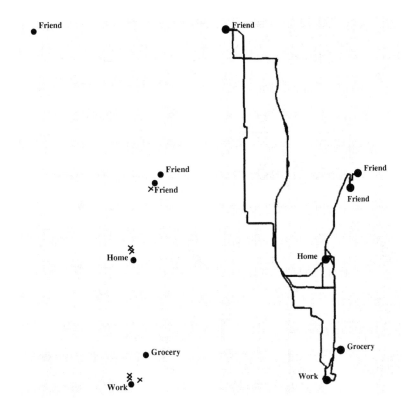

Fig. 5. The left picture shows the street map along with the goals (dots), and usual bus stops and parking lots (cross marks). The right picture shows the most likely trajectories between the goals.

6.1   Experimental Methodology

In order to test our system, we had a user carry a WAAS-enabled GPS logger with him continuously for 24 hours a day for 30 days. We then performed the three stage training on the data without any manual labeling. The learned model correctly identifies six common goals, frequently used bus stops and parking lots, as shown in Figure 5 (left). Furthermore, our system is able to estimate the transition probabilities between goals, trip segments and streets. Using those transition matrices, we calculate the most likely trajectories on the street map between the goals, as shown in Figure 5 (right).

We tested our system using the learned model on a scenario similar to that in Section 2. The results are shown in Figures 6 and 7. These figures present a sequential panel of experimental results. The top of each panel displays a representation of the reasoning process that the inference engine is undertaking. The center portion of each panel displays what the users saw at each stage of the experiment, and the bottom portion holds a text description of the frame.

6.2   Model Clamping for Error Detection

In Figures 6 and 7, we have shown that *OK* is able to detect errors even when the user was on a frequently taken route. The system achieves this by letting the user explicitly select a destination, which we call *model clamping*. Figure 8 shows the impact of model clamping on inference results.

On the left we use the same data as in Section 6.1. In this example for the first 700 seconds both models have approximately equal belief that the user is not making an error, but when the bus took a turn that the user had never taken to get home, the probability of errors in the clamped model instantly and dramatically jumped. In contrast, the unclamped model cannot determine an error occurred because the user had taken that route to get to other destinations.

On the right is the foot experiment in which the user left his office and proceeded to walk in a direction away from the parking lot. When the destination is not specified, the tracker has a fairly steady level of confidence in the user's path (there are lots of previously observed paths from his office), but when the destination is specified, the system initially sees behavior consistent with walking toward the parking lot, and then as the user begins to turn away at time 125, the tracker begins to doubt the success of the user's intentions.

7   Related Work

There is a large body of work centered on localization and location based services, much of which originates with the pioneering work at Xerox PARC and the PARCtab [20, 21, 22] platform. It would be impossible to credit it all, but what follows is a collection that inspired and informed our research.

An important source of localization technology is research on using the known positions of radio frequency beacons to ascertain location. The RADAR system [23] presents results on indoor tracking which was improved by user motion modeling in the SmartMoveX system [24]. There are a number of outdoor wireless localization systems that track and predict movement for the purposes of providing tour guide services. A vision and discussion of this class of applications was titled Cyberguides [25], and several systems of this class have been attempted including Campus-Aware [26] and the GUIDE project [27].

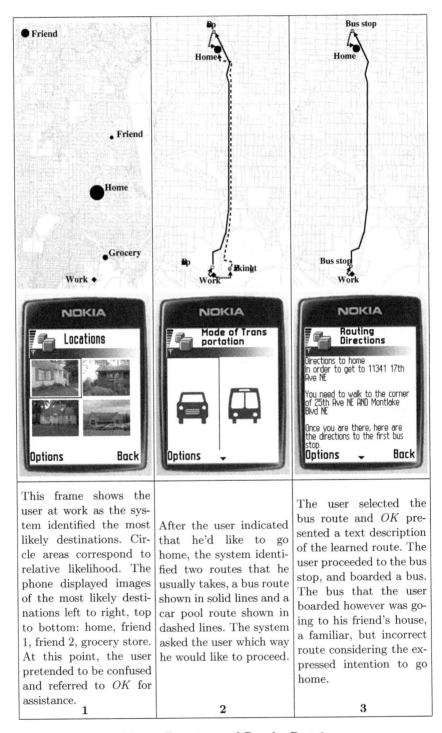

Fig. 6. Experimental Results Part 1

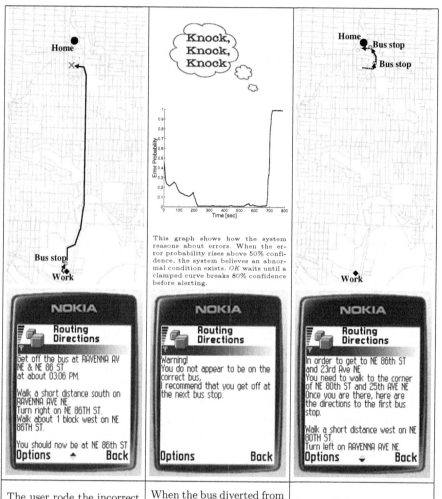

This graph shows how the system reasons about errors. When the error probability rises above 50% confidence, the system believes an abnormal condition exists. *OK* waits until a clamped curve breaks 80% confidence before alerting.

The user rode the incorrect bus and the system monitored his progress. The system was unable to identify that the user was on the wrong bus because the routes coincided for the first portion of the bus ride. Before getting to the correct bus stop for going home, the system observed that the user had departed from the expected trip segment and turned west.

4

When the bus diverted from the correct route, the system identified the behavior condition as an error. This was possible *even though* the user was on a frequently taken route. Because the user has explicitly selected a goal, *OK* identified an actual error (not just a novel behavior) had occurred. In response it proactively made its door knocking alert noise and showed a corresponding message

5

Once off the incorrect bus, the user reselects home as the destination. This time the system has no history of the user ever going home from the current location. As a result *OK* queries a real-time bus planning system for a route home. The user is directed to walk back to the arterial road and catch a different bus that is going the correct way.

6

Fig. 7. Experimental Results Part 2

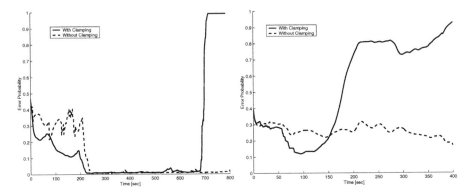

Fig. 8. Impact of Model Clamping on Error Detection. Probability of errors is shown in comparison to time in the presence and absence of a known destination. The dotted line shows the probability of errors when the user's destination is not known. The solid line shows the probability of errors when the destination is known (and clamped). The bus experiment is on the left (error made at time 700) and the foot experiment is on the right (with a gradual error beginning at time 125).

The Place Lab initiative [28] is a recent proposal for making outdoor Wi-Fi localization ubiquitous through mass collaboration so that location services such as those explored by the ActiveCampus project [29, 30] are broadly available.

More generally, outdoor localization on highly resource constrained devices based on radio signals has been proposed and explored in the RightSPOT project [31] and work on abstracting and merging many different sources of localization information is being done in the Location Stack [32, 33].

Another class of related work is probabilistic plan (goal) recognition in the AI community. Bui, et al. [15] introduced the abstract hidden Markov model which uses hierarchical representations to efficiently infer a person's goal in an indoor environment from camera information. Later, Bui [16] extended this model to include memory nodes, which enables the transfer of context information over multiple time steps. Our work goes beyond their work in that we show how to handle a challenging low-level position estimation problem, how to learn the significant transit points, and how to detect errors.

OK itself represents an evolutionary change to an existing system concept [34], which used a graphical "compass" to point a user in the direction he or she should walk on a moment-by-moment basis. Based on preliminary studies and expert feedback, we determined that the compass interface was distracting and required an unavailable resolution of localization. This earlier system did not reason about different modes of transportation, a key feature of *OK*.

Finally, as mentioned in Section 5, our work subsumes related work in user modeling and movement by Ashbrook [10] and Patterson [11].

8 Conclusion

We have presented a system called "Opportunity Knocks" (*OK*) which utilizes a rich model of user motion and behavior based on GPS sensor information to provide transportation assistance to people with mild cognitive disabilities. The primary function of the system is to route an individual from their current location to a chosen destination, but unlike existing route planning systems, it is user-centric, not vehicle-centric and requires very little user input. Instead it relies on observed user history as a basis for predicting likely destinations and identifying novel and erroneous behavior.

Our system utilizes a Bluetooth GPS beacon that talks to a cell-phone, which in turn exchanges information with a remote inference engine. The software on the remote engine runs a new hierarchical dynamic Bayesian network which is able to explicitly reason about how high-level destinations will affect many levels of transportation decisions by the user, down to the street level.

We are able to use the camera function of the phone as a method of labeling places to eliminate the need for a user to manually translate positions to places before the system can communicate about them with the user.

Finally, we have experimentally shown that this system, in conjunction with real-time transit information, has promise for effectively providing transportation assistance in the face of mild confusion, memory lapses, and inattention.

9 Future Work

We are expanding our current system in several ways to address its shortcomings. First we would like to improve power management by lowering duty-cycles, and shutting down power in response to an accelerometer incorporated into the system. Secondly, many of our directions require cardinal compass point orientation which suggest inclusion of a digital compass in the sensor beacon. Thirdly, a Wi-Fi based localizer would help us to handle indoor environments.

We are currently obtaining permission to run a formal user study with mentally retarded individuals. This will be a three stage study. First, we will conduct a user study with normal functioning individuals. Second, we will conduct a user study with mentally retarded people accompanied by a normal functioning safety monitor and, finally, we intend to conduct unassisted user studies. In particular, we will investigate a user interface that employs synthetic speech in addition to, or in place of, graphics.

To support this work we have formed an organization called *Project ACCESS* (Assisted Cognition in Community, Employment and Support Settings) [35] to help address the practical issues of conducting such a study. On the advisory board of this committee are lawyers, care-givers, parents and their children with mental retardation; all of whom are assisting in navigating the social and privacy issues associated with a device like *OK*.

Acknowledgments

This work was funded in part by National Science Foundation grants IIS-0120307, IIS-0307906, and IIS-0093406, National Institute on Disability and Rehabilitation Research grant H133A031739, Office of Naval Research grant N00014-02-1-0932, DARPA's SDR Program (grant number NBCHC020073), and Intel Corporation.

References

[1] Lawton, M.P.: Environment and Other Determinants of Well-Being in Older People. The Gerontologist **23** (1983) 349–357 NLM:0375327;PMID:6352420.

[2] Lawton, M.P.: Aging and Performance of Home Tasks. Human Factors **32** (1990) 527–536 NLM:0374660;PMID:2074107.

[3] Consolvo, S., Roessler, P., Shelton, B., LaMarcha, A., Schilit, B., Bly, S.: Technology for Care Networks of Elders. IEEE Pervasive Computing Mobile and Ubiquitous Systems: Successful Aging **3** (2004) 22–29 http://www.intel-research.net/Publications/Seattle/022320041335_230.pdf.

[4] F.C.C.: U.S. Federal Communication Commission E-911 Website (2004) http://www.fcc.gov/911/enhanced.

[5] Socket Communications Inc.: Socket website (2004) http://www.socketcom.com.

[6] King County Department of Transportation: Trip planner. http://tripplanner.metrokc.gov/ (2004)

[7] Washington Metro Area Transit Authority: The ride guide. http://rideguide.wmata.com (2004)

[8] Crabtree, A., Rodden, T., Hemmings, T., Benford, S.: Finding a Place for Ubi-Comp in the Home. In Dey, A., Schmidt, A., McCarthy, J.F., eds.: Proc. of UBICOMP 2003. Volume LNCS 2864., Springer-Verlag (2003) 208–226

[9] Hightower, J.: From Position to Place. In: Proc. of the 2003 Workshop on Location-Aware Computing. (2003) 10–12 part of the 2003 Ubiquitous Computing Conf.

[10] Ashbrook, D., Starner, T.: Learning Significant Locations and Predicting User Movement with GPS. In: International Symposium on Wearable Computing, Seattle, WA (2002)

[11] Patterson, D.J., Liao, L., Fox, D., Kautz, H.: Inferring High-Level Behavior from Low-Level Sensors. In Dey, A., Schmidt, A., McCarthy, J.F., eds.: Proc. of UBICOMP 2003. Volume LNCS 2864., Springer-Verlag (2003) 73–89

[12] Murphy, K.: Dynamic Bayesian Networks: Representation, Inference and Learning. PhD thesis, UC Berkeley, Computer Science Division (2002)

[13] Liao, L., Fox, D., Kautz, H.: Learning and inferring Transportation Routines. In: Proc. of the 19th National Conf. on Artificial Intelligence (AAAI). (2004)

[14] Doucet, A., de Freitas, J., Murphy, K., Russell, S.: Rao-Blackwellised Particle Filtering for Dynamic Bayesian Networks. In: Proc. of the Conf. on Uncertainty in Artificial Intelligence. (2000)

[15] Bui, H., Venkatesh, S., West, G.: Policy Recognition in the Abstract Hidden Markov Model. In: Journal of Artificial Intelligence Research. (2002)

[16] Bui, H.: A General Model for Online Probabilistic Plan Recognition. In: Proc. of the International Joint Conf. on Artifical Intelligence. (2003)

[17] Doucet, A., de Freitas, N., Gordon, N., eds.: Sequential Monte Carlo in Practice. Springer-Verlag, New York (2001)

[18] Rabiner, L.R.: A Tutorial on Hidden Markov Models and Selected Applications in Speech Recognition. In Waibel, A., Lee, K.F., eds.: Readings in Speech Recognition. Kaufmann, San Mateo, CA (1990) 267–296

[19] West, M., Harrison, J.: Bayesian Forecasting and Dynamic Models. second edn. Springer-Verlag (1999)

[20] Want, R., Schilit, B., Adams, N., Gold, R., Petersen, K., Ellis, J., Goldberg, D., Weiser, M.: The PARCTAB Ubiquitous Computing Experiment. Technical Report CSL-95-1, Xerox Palo Alto Research Center (1995)

[21] Schilit, B.N., Adams, N., Gold, R., Tso, M., Want, R.: The PARCTAB Mobile Computing System. In: Proc. Fourth Workshop on Workstation Operating Systems (WWOS-IV), IEEE (1993) 34–39

[22] Adams, N., Gold, R., Schilit, B.N., Tso, M., Want, R.: An Infrared Network for Mobile Computers. In: Proc. USENIX Symposium on Mobile & Location-independent Computing, USENIX Association (1993) 41–52

[23] Bahl, P., Padmanabhan, V.N.: RADAR: An In-Building RF-Based User Location and Tracking System. In: INFOCOM (2). (2000) 775–784

[24] Krumm, J., Williams, L., Smith, G.: SmartMoveX on a Graph - An Inexpensive Active Badge Tracker. In: Proc. of the 4th international conference on Ubiquitous Computing, Springer-Verlag (2002) 299–307

[25] Abowd, G.D., Atkeson, C.G., Hong, J., Long, S., Kooper, R., Pinkerton, M.: Cyberguide: a Mobile Context-Aware Tour Guide. Wirel. Netw. **3** (1997) 421–433

[26] Burrell, J., Gay, G.K., Kubo, K., Farina, N.: Context-Aware Computing: A Test Case. In: Proc. of the 4th international conference on Ubiquitous Computing, Springer-Verlag (2002) 1–15

[27] Cheverst, K., Davies, N., Mitchell, K., Friday, A., Efstratiou, C.: Developing a Context-Aware Electronic Tourist Guide: Some Issues and Experiences. In: CHI. (2000) 17–24

[28] Schilit, B., LaMarca, A., Borriello, G., Griswold, W., McDonald, D., Lazowska, E., Balachandran, A., Hong, J., Iverson, V.: Challenge: Ubiquitous Location-Aware Computing and the Place Lab Initiative. In: Proc. of WMASH 2003: The First ACM International Workshop on Wireless Mobile Applications and Services on WLAN. (2003)

[29] Griswold, W.G., Boyer, R., Brown, S.W., Truong, T.M.: A Component Architecture for an Extensible, Highly Integrated Context-Aware Computing Infrastructure. In: Proc. of the 25th International Conf. on Software Engineering, IEEE Computer Society (2003) 363–372

[30] Griswold, W.G., Shanahan, P., Brown, S.W., Boyer, R., Ratto, M., Shapiro, R.B., Truong, T.M.: ActiveCampus - Experiments in Community-Oriented Ubiquitous Computing. Technical Report CS2003-0750, UC San Diego (2003)

[31] Krumm, J., Cermak, G., Horvitz, E.: RightSPOT: A Novel Sense of Location for Smart Personal Object. In Dey, A., Schmidt, A., McCarthy, J.F., eds.: Proc. of UBICOMP 2003. Volume LNCS 2864., Springer-Verlag (2003)

[32] Hightower, J., Brumitt, B., Borriello, G.: The Location Stack: A Layered Model for Location in Ubiquitous Computing. In: Proc. of the Fourth IEEE Workshop on Mobile Computing Systems and Applications, IEEE Computer Society (2002)

[33] Hightower, J., Borriello, G.: Accurate, Flexible and Practical Location Estimation for Ubiquitous Computing: A Case Study of Particle Filters. In: Proc. of UBICOMP 2004, Springer-Verlag (2004)

[34] Patterson, D., Etzioni, O., Fox, D., Kautz, H.: The Activity Compass. In: Proc. of UbiCog '02: First International Workshop on Ubiquitous Computing for Cognitive Aids, Gothenberg, Sweden (2002)

[35] Harniss, M.: Project ACCESS website (2004) http://cognitivetech.washington.edu.

Author Index